1992

PUBLISHER'S NOTE

Annual Review of United Nations Affairs is now edited by professional specialists who are part of the staff of the United Nations itself. They are:

Kumiko Matsuura
Programme Planning Officer,
United Nations Industrial Development
Organizations (UNIDO)

Dr. Joachim W. Müller
Programme Planning and Budget Officer,
United Nations Office at Vienna (UNOV)

Dr. Karl P. Sauvant
Acting Assistant Director,
United Nations Centre on Transnational Corporations,
United Nations

We recently issued 1988 in two volumes, developing a totally new format and new focus which brings subscribers in depth coverage of the work of the United Nations.

In an effort quickly to bring the service completly up-to-date, 1989 has been prepared and will be released early in 1992. 1990 will be published sometime in late Spring; and 1991 sometime in late Fall. This will bring the service up-to-date. We are grateful for the patience of our subscribers.

Additionally, we have in the past from time to time published special volumes in ARUNA, such as the periodic *Chronology and Fact Book of the UN*. We here made available a most significant special UN volume *The Reform of the United Nations*, prepared by one of our ARUNA editors, Joachim W. Müller, a participant in the reform process.

The two-volume set will come to subscribers to ARUNA automatically. It is the publisher's conviction that this title is intrinsic to the character and quality of the material now being published as part of the Annual Review. The work is separately offered to purchasers not subscribers to ARUNA.

Dr. Joachim W. Müller is currently Programme Planning Budget Officer, United Nations Office at Vienna (UNOV). He has previously been with the Programme Planning and Budget Division, United Nations, New York, the German Society for Technical Co-operation (GTZ) and Bank of America. Current address: Vienna International Centre, UNOV, E-1485, P.O. Box 600 A-1400 Vienna, Austria.

PREFACE TO VOLUME II

Volume II of *The Reform of the United Nations* brings together the main resolutions, decisions and documents associated with the reform process, issued over a period of five years. They provide the background and reference material for Volume I, in which a detailed report of the reform process is given.

In Part I of Volume II, eleven selected resolutions and decisions adopted by the General Assembly and the Economic and Social Council (ECOSOC) are presented in chronological order. The first is General Assembly resolution 40/237 of 18 December 1985, which mandated the establishment of the Group of High-level Intergovernmental Experts to Review the Efficiency of the Administrative and Financial Functioning of the United Nations (Group of 18), and the last is General Assembly resolution 45/254 of 21 December 1990, which marked the conclusion of the reform process.

In Part II of Volume II, 41 selected documents submitted to the General Assembly or to ECOSOC are presented. They include reports of the Administrative Committee on Co-ordination (ACC), the Advisory Committee on Administrative and Budgetary Questions (ACABQ), the Committee for Programme and Co-ordination (CPC), the Fifth (Administrative and Budgetary) Committee of the General Assembly, the Group of 18, the International Civil Service Commission (ICSC), the Secretary-General and the Special Commission of the Economic and Social Council on the In-depth Study of the United Nations Intergovernmental Structure and Functions in the Economic and Social Fields. The main issues covered by the documents are (i) the progress of the implementation of the reform process, (ii) the implementation of recommendation 15 of the Group of 18 concerning reductions in staff, (iii) the operation of a reserve/contingency fund, (iv) the programme budget outline, (v) the intergovernmental structure and functions in the economic and social fields, and (vi) the problems of priority-setting.

The documents are listed in chronological order, except for those of ACABQ and CPC. Both these committees examined the reports of the Secretary-General and submitted their observations, comments and recommendations to the General Assembly. For ease of reference, the findings of ACABQ and CPC are presented directly after the document on which the committees made their report, starting with ACABQ and followed by CPC

i

where applicable. The first document in this collection is the report of the Group of High-level Intergovernmental Experts to Review the Efficiency of the Administrative and Financial Functioning of the United Nations (A/41/49), issued in 1986. The last document presented is the Secretary-General's analytical report on the implementation of General Assembly resolution 42/213 (A/45/226) of 27 April 1990 and the related reports of ACABQ (A/45/617) of 12 October 1990 and CPC (A/45/16, Part I) of 20 June 1990.

The resolutions and decisions are shown as approved by the legislative body. Documents have been edited, where necessary, by deleting those parts which are of less relevance and by integrating corrigenda wherever possible. No attempt, however, has been made to eliminate inconsistencies within documents. Footnotes denoted by asterisks have been added, as are bracketed texts in the footnotes. Finally, the views expressed in this publication do not necessarily reflect those of the institutions with which the author is affiliated.

Vienna, 1991   Joachim Müller

TABLE OF CONTENTS FOR VOLUME II

Page

Preface to Volume II i
Table of Contents for Volume II iii
List of Abbreviations x

PART I
RESOLUTIONS AND DECISIONS

1.1   Resolution 40/237 2
       Review of the Efficiency of the Administrative and
       Financial Functioning of the United Nations, 18 December
       1985

1.2   Resolution 41/213 4
       Review of the Efficiency of the Administrative and
       Financial Functioning of the United Nations, 19 December
       1986

1.3   Decision 1987/112 12
       In-depth Study of the United Nations Intergovernmental
       Structure and Functions in the Economic and Social Fields,
       6 February 1987

1.4   Resolution 42/170 14
       Implementation of General Assembly Resolution 41/213 in
       the Economic and Social Fields, 11 December 1987

1.5   Resolution 42/211 16
       Implementation of General Assembly Resolution 41/213,
       21 December 1987

1.6   Resolution 1988/77 23
       Revitalization of the Economic and Social Council, 29 July
       1988

1.7   Resolution 43/174 30
       Review of the Efficiency of the Administrative and
       Financial Functioning of the United Nations in the Economic
       and Social Fields, 9 December 1988

1.8   Resolution 43/213 32
       Implementation of General Assembly Resolution 41/213:
       Progress Report and Revised Estimates for the Biennium
       1988-1989, 21 December 1988

1.9   Resolution 43/214   36
       Proposed Programme Budget Outline for the Biennium
       1990-1991 and Use and Operation of the Contingency Fund,
       21 December 1988

1.10   Resolution 44/200   39
       Implementation of General Assembly Resolution 41/213,
       21 December 1989

1.11   Resolution 45/254   45
       Review of the Efficiency of the Administrative and
       Financial Functioning of the United Nations, 21 December
       1990

**PART II
DOCUMENTS**

2.1   Document A/41/49   50
       Report of the Group of High-level Intergovernmental
       Experts to Review the Efficiency of the Administrative and
       Financial Functioning of the United Nations, 1986

2.2   Document A/41/663   94
       Report of the Group of High-level Intergovernmental
       Experts to Review the Efficiency of the Administrative and
       Financial Functioning of the United Nations (A/41/49), Note
       of the Secretary-General, 1 October 1986

2.3   Document A/41/763   98
       Comments of the Administrative Committee on Co-
       ordination on the Report of the Group of the High-level
       Intergovernmental Experts to Review the Efficiency of the
       Administrative and Financial Functioning of the United
       Nations (A/41/49), 24 October 1986

2.4   Document A/41/795   101
       Report of the Group of High-level Intergovernmental
       Experts to Review the Efficiency of the Administrative and
       Financial Functioning of the United Nations (A/41/49),
       Report of the Fifth Committee, 5 November 1986

2.5   Document A/42/225   116
       Questions Relating to the Programme Budget: Inflation
       and Currency Fluctuation, and the Level of the Contingency
       Fund, Report of the Secretary-General, 20 April 1987

2.6   Document A/42/7   129
        Report of the Secretary-General on Inflation, Currency
        Fluctuation, and the Level of the Contingency Fund
        (A/42/225), Report of the Advisory Committee on
        Administrative and Budgetary Questions, 1987

2.7   Document A/42/16   133
        Question of Accommodating all Additional Expenditures
        within the Overall Level of the Budget (A/42/225), Report of
        the Committee for Programme and Co-ordination, 1988

2.8   Document A/42/234 and Corr.1   135
        Reform and Renewal in the United Nations: Progress
        Report of the Secretary-General on the Implementation of
        General Assembly Resolution 41/213, 23 April 1987 and 1
        May 1987

2.9   Document A/42/7   174
        Progress Report of the Secretary-General on the
        Implementation of General Assembly Resolution 41/213
        (A/42/234 and Corr.1), Report of the Advisory Committee
        on Administrative and Budgetary Questions, 1987

2.10   Document A/42/16   180
        Progress Report of the Secretary-General (A/43/234 and
        Corr.1), Report of the Committee for Programme and Co-
        ordination, 1988

2.11   Document A/42/225/Add.1   183
        Questions Relating to the Programme Budget: Inflation
        and Currency Fluctuation, and the Level of the Contingency
        Fund, Report of the Secretary-General, Addendum,
        4 September 1987

2.12   Document A/42/640   190
        Questions Relating to the Programme Budget: Inflation
        and Currency Fluctuation, and the Level of the Contingency
        Fund (A/42/225/Add.1), Report of the Advisory Committee
        on Administrative and Budgetary Questions, 12 October 1987

2.13   Document A/42/16   196
        Question of Accommodating all Additional Expenditures
        within the Overall Level of the Budget (A/42/225/Add.1),
        Report of the Committee for Programme and Co-ordination,
        1988

2.14   Document A/C.5/42/2/Rev.1   201
        Implementation of General Assembly Resolution 41/213:
        Programmatic and Budgetary Aspects - Update of the
        Progress Report of the Secretary-General (A/42/234),
        Report of the Secretary-General, 23 September 1987

2.15   Document A/42/7/Add.1-10   219
        Implementation of General Assembly Resolution 41/213 -
        Programmatic and Budgetary Aspects: Update of the
        Progress Report of the Secretary-General
        (A/C.5/42/2/Rev.1), Report of the Advisory Committee on
        Administrative and Budgetary Questions, 1988

2.16   Document A/42/30   223
        Recommendations of the Group of High-level
        Intergovernmental Experts to Review the Efficiency of the
        Administrative and Financial Functioning of the United
        Nations, Report of the International Civil Service
        Commission, 1987

2.17   Document A/43/286   236
        Reform and Renewal in the United Nations: Second
        Progress Report of the Secretary-General on the
        Implementation of General Assembly Resolution 41/213, 8
        April 1988

2.18   Document A/43/651   261
        Reform and Renewal in the United Nations: Second
        Progress Report of the Secretary-General on the
        Implementation of General Assembly Resolution 41/213
        (A/43/286), Report of the Advisory Committee on
        Administrative and Budgetary Questions, 3 October 1988

2.19   Document A/43/16   263
        Reform and Renewal in the United Nations: Second
        Progress Report of the Secretary-General on the
        Implementation of General Assembly Resolution 41/213
        (A/43/286), Report of the Committee for Programme and
        Co-ordination, 1989

2.20   Document A/43/324   265
        Question Relating to the Programme Budget: Use and
        Operation of the Contingency Fund, Note by the Secretary-
        General, 21 April 1988

2.21   Document A/43/929   269
        Questions Relating to the Programme Budget: Use and
        Operation of the Contingency Fund (A/43/324); Report of
        the Advisory Committee on Administrative and Budgetary
        Questions, 9 December 1988

2.22   Document A/43/16   271
        Questions Relating to the Programme Budget: Use and
        Operation of the Contingency Fund (A/43/324); Report of
        the Committee for Programme and Co-ordination, 13 January
        1989

2.23   Document E/1988/75   272
        Report of the Special Commission of the Economic and
        Social Council on the In-depth Study of the United Nations
        Intergovernmental Structure and Functions in the Economic
        and Social Fields, 1 June 1988

2.24   Document A/C.5/43/1/Rev.1   375
        Plans of the Secretary-General for the Implementation of
        Recommendation 15 on the Reduction of Personnel, as
        requested by the General Assembly in Resolution 41/213 and
        42/211, Report of the Secretary-General, 27 July 1988

2.25   Document A/43/651   391
        Plans of the Secretary-General for the Implementation of
        Recommendation 15 on the Reduction of Personnel, as
        requested by the General Assembly in Resolution 41/213 and
        42/211 (A/C.5/43/1/Rev.1); Report of the Advisory
        Committee on Administrative and Budgetary Questions, 3
        October 1988

2.26   Document A/43/651/Add.1   397
        Plans of the Secretary-General for the Implementation of
        Recommendation 15 on the Reduction of Personnel, as
        Requested by the General Assembly in Resolution 41/213
        and 42/211 (A/C.5/43/1/Rev.1); Addendum to the Report of
        the Advisory Committee on Administrative and Budgetary
        Questions, 19 October 1988

2.27   Document A/43/16   399
        Implementation of Recommendation 15 of the Group of
        High-level Intergovernmental Experts (A/C.5/43/1/Rev.1);
        Report of the Committee for Programme and Co-ordination,
        1989

2.28   Document A/43/524 .... **401**
        Proposed Programme Budget Outline for the Biennium
        1990-1991, Report of the Secretary-General, 16 August 1988

2.29   Document A/43/929 .... **411**
        Proposed Programme Budget Outline for the Biennium
        1990-1991 (A/43/524); Report of the Advisory Committee on
        Administrative and Budgetary Questions, 9 December 1988

2.30   Document A/43/16 .... **420**
        Outline of the Proposed Programme Budget for the
        Biennium 1990-1991 (A/43/524), Report of the Committee
        for Programme and Co-ordination, 1989

2.31   Document A/44/222 and Corr.1 .... **426**
        Final Report of the Secretary-General on the
        Implementation of Resolution 41/213, 26 April 1989 and 11
        July 1989

2.32   Document A/44/7 .... **478**
        Final Report of the Secretary-General on the
        Implementation of General Assembly Resolution 41/213
        (A/44/222 and Corr.1), Report of the Advisory Committee
        on Administrative and Budgetary Questions, 1989

2.33   Document A/44/16 .... **479**
        Review of the Efficiency of the Administrative and
        Financial Functioning of the United Nations (A/44/222 and
        Corr.1), Report of the Committee for Programme and Co-
        ordination, 1990

2.34   Document A/44/272 .... **483**
        All Aspects of Priority-Setting in Future Outlines of the
        Proposed Programme Budget, Report of the Secretary-
        General, 26 July 1989

2.35   Document A/44/7 .... **502**
        All Aspects of Priority-Setting in Future Outlines of the
        Proposed Programme Budget (A/44/272), Report of the
        Advisory Committee on Administrative and Budgetary
        Questions, 1989

2.36   Document A/44/16 .... **504**
        Priority-Setting (A/44/272), Report of the Committee for
        Programme and Co-ordination, 1990

2.37   Document A/44/665   505
        Establishment and Operation of a Reserve Fund, Report
        of the Secretary-General, 20 October 1989

2.38   Document A/44/729   512
        Establishment and Operation of a Reserve Fund
        (A/44/665), Report of the Advisory Committee on
        Administrative and Budgetary Questions, 16 November 1989

2.39   Document A/45/226   514
        Analytical Report of the Secretary-General on the
        Implementation of General Assembly Resolution 41/213,
        27 April 1990

2.40   Document A/45/617   583
        Analytical Report of the Secretary-General on the
        Implementation of General Assembly Resolution 41/213
        (A/45/226), Report of the Advisory Committee on
        Administrative and Budgetary Questions, 12 October 1990

2.41   Document A/45/16 (Part I)   584
        Review of the Efficiency of the Administrative and
        Financial Functioning of the United Nations (A/45/226),
        Report of the Committee for Programme and Co-ordination,
        20 June 1990

LIST OF ABBREVIATIONS

ACABQ	Advisory Committee for Administrative and Budgetary Questions
ACC	Administrative Co-ordinating Committee
CCAQ	Co-ordinating Committee for Administrative Questions
CCISUA	Co-ordinating Committee for Independent Staff Unions and Associations of the United Nations System
CCSQ	Co-ordinating Committee for Substantive Questions
CPC	Committee for Programme and Co-ordination
CSDHA	Centre for Social Development and Humanitarian Affairs
CSTD	Centre for Science and Technology for Development
CTC	Centre on Transnational Corporations
DAM	Department of Administrative and Management
DIEC	Director-General's Office for International Co-operation and Economic Affairs
DIESA	Department of International Economic and Social Affairs
DPI	Department of Public Information
DTCD	Department of Technical Co-operation for Development
ECA	Economic Commission for Africa
ECDC	Economic Co-operation among Developing Countries
ECE	Economic Commission for Europe
ECLAC	Economic Commission for Latin America and the Caribbean
ECOSOC	Economic and Social Council
EEC	European Economic Community
ESCAP	Economic and Social Commission for Asia and the Pacific
ESCWA	Economic and Social Commission for Western Asia
FAO	Food and Agricultural Organization
G77	Group of Seventy-Seven
GATT	General Agreement on Tariffs and Trade
GSTP	Global System of Trade Preferences
HABITAT	United Nations Centre for Human Settlement
IAEA	International Atomic Energy Agency
IBRD	International Bank for Reconstruction and Development (World Bank)
ICAO	International Civil Aviation Organisation
ICJ	International Court of Justice
IDA	International Development Association
IDDA	Industrial Development Decade for Africa
IDS	International Development Strategy
IFAD	International Fund for Agricultural Development
IFC	International Finance Corporation
ILO	International Labour Organisation
IMCO	Intergovernmental Maritime Consultative Organisation
IMF	International Monetary Fund
IMO	International Maritime Organization
INSTRAW	International Research and Training Institute for Advancement of Women
ITC	International Trade Centre
ITU	International Telecommunication Union
JAB	United Nations Joint Appeals Board
JIU	Joint Inspection Unit

LDCs	Least Developed Countries
MULPOC	Multinational Programming and Operational Centre
NAM	Non-Aligned Movement
NGO	Non-Governmental Organisation
NIEO	New International Economic Order
OECD	Organisation for Economic Co-operation and Development
OGS	Office of General Service
OHRM	Office of Human Resource Management
OPPBF	Office of Programme Planning, Budget and Finance
SWAPO	South West African People's Organization
TCDC	Technical Co-operation among Developing Countries
TNC	Transnational Corporation
UK	United Kingdom of Great Britain and Northern Ireland
UN	United Nations
UNCHS	United Nations Centre for Human Settlements (Habitat)
UNCSDHA	United Nations Centre for Social Development and Humanitarian Affairs
UNCSTD	United Nations for Science and Technology for Development
UNCTAD	United Nations Conference on Trade and Development
UNCTC	United Nations Centre on Transnational Corporations
UNDP	United Nations Development Programme
UNDRO	Office of the United Nations Director Relief Co-ordinator
UNEP	United Nations Environment Programme
UNESCO	United Nations Educational, Scientific and Cultural Organisation
UNFDAC	United Nations Fund for Drug Abuse Control
UNFICYP	United Nations Peace-keeping Force in Cyprus
UNFPA	United Nations Fund for Population Activities
UNGOMAP	United Nations Good Offices Mission for Afghanistan and Pakistan
UNHCR	Office of the United Nations High Commissioner for Refugees
UNICEF	United Nations Children's Emergency Fund
UNIDO	United Nations Industrial Development Organisation
UNIFIL	United Nations Interim Force in Lebanon
UNITAR	United Nations Institute for Training and Research
UNJSPB	United Nations Joint Staff Pension Board
UNMOGIP	United Nations Military Observation Group in India and Pakistan
UN-PAAERD	United Nations Programme of Action for African Economic Recovery and Development
UNRISD	United Nations Research Institute for Social Development
UNRWA	United Nations Relief and Works Agency for Palestine Refugees in the Near East
UNTAG	United Nations Transition Group in Namibia
UNIIMOG	United Nations Iran-Iraq Military Observer Group
UNU	United Nations University
UPU	Universal Postal Union
US	United States of America
USSR	Union of Soviet Socialist Republics
WFP	World Food Programme
WHO	World Health Organisation
WIPO	World Intellectual Property Organisation
WMO	World Meteorological Organisation

PART I

RESOLUTIONS AND DECISIONS

1.1 Resolution 40/237*

Review of the Efficiency of the Administrative and Financial Functioning of the United Nations

18 December 1985

The General Assembly,

Recalling the purposes and principles of the Charter of the United Nations,

Recognizing that the Organization is based on the principle of the sovereign equality of all its Members,

Mindful of the vital role of the United Nations in the maintenance of international peace and security and in the promotion of development and international co-operation,

Convinced that the improvement of the efficiency of the administrative and financial functioning of the United Nations could help it to attain the purposes and implement the principles of the Charter,

Considering the unanimous support for the United Nations, expressed by Heads of State or Government or their special envoys and by the representatives of Member States during the commemoration of the fortieth anniversary of the United Nations,

Noting that all participants stressed the need to promote confidence in the United Nations and enhance the political will of Member States to render more positive support to the Organization,

Reaffirming the necessity of securing, in the employment of the Secretarial staff, the highest standards of efficiency, competence and integrity, and the importance of recruiting the staff based on the principle of equitable geographical distribution,

Noting with appreciation the efforts of the Secretary-General, as the chief administrative officer of the Organization, to improve the efficiency and effectiveness of the Secretariat,

Bearing in mind the work of the relevant subsidiary organs of the General Assembly,

---

Official Records of the General Assembly, Fortieth Session, Supplement No. 53 (A/40/53), pp. 60-61.

Taking fully into account the views expressed during the fortieth session,

1. *Expresses its conviction* that an overall increase in efficiency would further enhance the capacity of the United Nations to attain the purposes and implement the principles of the Charter of the United Nations;

2. *Decides* to establish a Group of High-level Intergovernmental Experts to Review the Efficiency of the Administrative and Financial Functioning of the United Nations with a term of one year, to carry out in full accordance with the principles and provisions of the Charter the following tasks:

(a) To conduct a thorough review of the administrative and financial matters of the United Nations, with a view to identifying measures for further improving the efficiency of its administrative and financial functioning, which would contribute to strengthening its effectiveness in dealing with political, economic and social issues;

(b) To submit to the General Assembly, before the opening of its forty-first session, a report containing the observations and recommendations of the Group;

3. *Requests* the President of the General Assembly, in consultation with the regional groups, to appoint as soon as possible the members of the Group of High-level Intergovernmental   Experts with due regard to equitable geographical distribution;

4. *Decides* that the Group will consist of eighteen members, and requests the Secretary-General to convene a meeting of the Group as soon as possible to enable it to elect its officers;

5. *Requests* the Secretary-General to provide the Group with the necessary staff and services;

6. *Also requests* the Secretary General to provide full assistance to the Group, in particular by submitting his views and providing information necessary to conduct the review;

7. *Invites* the relevant subsidiary organs of the General Assembly to submit to the Group, though their chairmen, information and comments on matters pertaining to their work;

8. *Decides* to include in the provisional agenda of its forty-first session an item entitle "Review of the efficiency of the administrative and financial functioning of the United Nations: report of the Group of High-level Intergovernmental Experts to Review of the Administrative and Financial Functioning of the United Nations".

1.2 Resolution 41/213[*]

Review of the Efficiency of the Administrative and Financial Functioning of the United Nations

19 December 1986

The General Assembly,

Recalling its resolution 40/237 of 18 December 1985, by which it decided to establish the Group of High-level Intergovernmental Experts to Review the Efficiency of the Administrative and Financial Functioning of the United Nations,

Having considered the report of the Group[1] and the related report of the Fifth Committee,[2] as well as the comments of the report of the Group made by the Secretary-General[3] and the Administrative Committee on Coordination,[4]

Expressing its appreciation to the Group for its report,

Taking fully into account the views expressed during the consideration of this item at the current session,

Recognizing the need for measures to improve the efficiency of the administrative and financial functioning of the United Nations with a view to strengthening its effectiveness in dealing with political, economic and social issues,

Recognizing the need to improve the planning, programming and budgeting process in the Organization,

Reaffirming the requirement of all Member States to fulfil their financial obligations as set out in the Charter of the United Nations promptly and in full,

Recognizing the detrimental effect of the withholding of assessed contributions on the administrative and financial functioning of the United Nations,

Recognizing further that late payments of assessed contributions adversely affect the short-term financial situation of the Organization,

---

[*]*Official Records of the General Assembly, Forty-first Session, Supplement No. 49* (A/41/49), pp. 57-59.

I

Recommendations of the Group of High-level Intergovernmental Experts to Review the Efficiency of the Administrative and Financial Functioning of the United Nations

1. *Decides* that the recommendations as agreed upon and as contained in the report of the Group of High-level Intergovernmental Experts to Review the Efficiency of the Administrative and Financial Functioning of the United Nations[5] should be implemented by the Secretary-General and the relevant organs and bodies of the United Nations in the light of the findings of the Fifth Committee[6] and subject to the following:

(a) The implementation of recommendation 5 should not prejudice the implementation of projects and programmes already approved by the General Assembly;

(b) The percentages referred to in recommendation 15, which were arrived at in a pragmatic manner, should be regarded as targets in the formulation of the Secretary-General's plans to be submitted to the General Assembly for implementation of the recommendation; further, the Secretary-General is requested to implement this recommendation with flexibility in order to avoid, *inter alia*, negative impact on programmes and on the structure and composition of the Secretariat, bearing in mind the necessity of securing the highest standards of efficiency, competence and integrity of the staff, with due regard to equitable geographical distribution;

(c) The Secretary-General should transmit to the International Civil Service Commission those recommendations having direct impact on the United Nations common systems (recommendations 53 and 61), with the request that it report to the General Assembly at its forty-second session, so as to enable the Assembly to make a final decision; the expertise of the Commission should be availed of in dealing with the other recommendations over which the Commission has a mandate to advise and make recommendations;

(d) The Secretary-General should take into consideration the relevant provisions of General Assembly resolution 35/210 of 17 December 1980, in implementing recommendations 55 and 57, to the extent they are agreed upon;

(e) The Economic and Social Council, assisted as and when required by relevant organs and bodies, in particular the Committee for Programme and Co-ordination, should carry out the study called for in recommendation 8;

(f) The Committee for Programme and Co-ordination, assisted as required by the Joint Inspection Unit and other bodies, shall evaluate the implementation of the recommendations relating to the intergovernmental machinery and its functioning, as indicated in recommendation 70;

(g)   In the implementation of recommendation 24, the provisions of General Assembly resolution 41/201 of 8 December 1986 should be duly taken into account;

2.   *Requests* the Secretary-General and the Committee for Programme and Co-ordination to report to the General Assembly as indicated in recommendations 69, 70 and 71 of the Group;

II
Planning, Programming and Budgeting Process

1.   *Decides* that the planning, programming and budgeting process shall be governed, *inter alia*, by the following principles:

(a)   Strict adherence to the principles and provisions of the Charter of the United Nations, in particular Articles 17 and 18 thereof;

(b)   Full respect for the prerogatives of the principal organs of the Unit ed Nations with respect to the planning, programming and budgeting process;

(c)   Full respect for the authority and the prerogatives of the Secretary-General as the chief administrative officer of the Organization;

(d)   Recognition of the need for Member States to participate in the budgetary preparation from its early stages and throughout the process;

2.   *Reaffirms* the need to improve the planning, programming and budgeting process through, *inter alia*, the following:

(a)   Full implementation of regulation 4.8 of the Regulations Governing Programme Planning, the Programme Aspects of the Budget, the Monitoring of Implementation and the Methods of Evaluation, which governs co-ordination between the Committee for Programme and Co-ordination and the Advisory Committee on Administrative and Budgetary Questions;

(b)   Implementation of the recommendations contained in paragraphs 25 to 54 of the report of the Committee for Programme and Co-ordination on the work of its twenty-sixth session;[7]

(c)   Ensuring follow-up of implementation of the recommendations of the Committee for Programme and Co-ordination;

(d)   Improvement of the representation of Member States in the Committee for Programme and Co-ordination in conformity with the provisions of paragraph 46 of the annex to General Assembly resolution 32/197 of 20 December 1977;

3. *Resolves* to achieve improvement in the consultative process for the formulation of the medium-term plan through:

(a) Full implementation of the Regulations Governing Programme Planning, the Programme Aspects of the Budget, the Monitoring of Implementation and the Methods of Evaluation pertaining to the medium-term plan, as contained in the annex to General Assembly resolution 35/234 of 21 December 1982 and the related Rules;

(b) Submission of the introduction to the medium-term plan, which constitutes and integral element in the planning process, to Member States for wide consultations;

(c) Consultations in a systematic way regarding the major programmes in the plan with sectoral, technical, regional and central bodies in the United Nations;

(d) Drawing up by the Secretary-General, in consultation with the Committee for Programme and Co-ordination and the Advisory Committee on Administrative and Budgetary Questions, of a calendar for such consultations;

4. *Approves* the budget process set forth in annex I to the present resolution;

5. *Reaffirms* that the decision-making process is governed by the provisions of the Charter of the United Nations and the rules of procedure of the General Assembly[8]

6. *Agrees* that, without prejudice to paragraph 5 above, the Committee for Programme and Co-ordination should continue its existing practice of reaching decisions by consensus; explanatory views, if any, shall be presented to the General Assembly;[9]

7. *Considers it desirable* that the Fifth Committee, before submitting its recommendations on the outline of the programme budget to the General Assembly in accordance with the provisions of the Charter and the rules of procedure of the Assembly, should continue to make all possible efforts with a view to establishing the broadest possible agreement;[10]

8. *Requests* the Secretary-General to submit to the General Assembly, through the Committee for Programme and Co-ordination and the Advisory Committee on Administrative and Budgetary Questions, such supplementary rules and regulations as may be deemed necessary for the improvement in the planning, programming and budgeting process;

9. *Also requests* the Secretary-General to submit to the General Assembly at its forty-second session a proposal on the date for submission of the outline

of the programme budget and also on the date for final approval of the outline by the Assembly;

10. *Further requests* the Secretary-General to report to the General Assembly at its forty-second session on the implementation of the present resolution.

Annex I
Budget Process
A. *Off-budget years*

1.   The Secretary-General shall submit an outline of the programme budget for the following biennium, which shall contain an indication of the following:

(a)   Preliminary estimate of resources to accommodate the proposed programme of activities during the biennium;

(b)   Priorities, reflecting general trends of a broad sectoral nature;

(c)   Real growth, positive or negative, compared with the previous budget;

(d)   Size of the contingency fund expressed as a percentage of the overall level of resources.

2.   The Committee for Programme and Co-ordination, acting as a subsidiary organ of the General Assembly, shall consider the outline of the programme budget and submit, though the Fifth Committee, to the Assembly its conclusion and recommendations.

3.   On the basis of a decision by the General Assembly, the Secretary-General shall prepare his proposed programme budget for the following biennium.

4.   Throughout this process, the mandate and functions of the Advisory Committee on Administrative and Budgetary Questions shall be fully respected. The Advisory Committee shall consider the outline of the programme budget in accordance with its terms of reference.

B. *Budget years*

5.   The Secretary-General shall submit his proposed programme budget to the Committee for Programme and Co-ordination and the Advisory Committee on Administrative and Budgetary Questions in accordance with the existing procedures.

6.   The Committee for Programme and Co-ordination and the Advisory Committee on Administrative and Budgetary Questions shall examine the proposed programme budget in accordance with their respective mandates and

shall submit their conclusions and recommendations to the General Assembly, though the Fifth Committee, for the final approval of the programme budget.

C. *Contingency fund and additional expenditures*

7. The programme budget shall include expenditures related to political activities of a "perennial" character whose mandates are renewed annually, together with their related conference costs.

8. The programme budget shall include a contingency fund expressed as a percentage of the overall budget level, to accommodate additional expenditures relating to the biennium derived from legislative mandates not provided for in the proposed programme budget or, subject to the provisions of paragraph 11 below, form revised estimates.

9. If additional expenditures, as defined in paragraph 8 above, are proposed that exceed resources available within the contingency fund, such additional expenditures can only be included in the budget through redeployment of resources form low-priority areas or modifications of existing activities. Otherwise, such additional activities will have to be deferred until a later biennium.

10. A comprehensive solution to the problem of all additional expenditures, including those deriving from inflation and currency fluctuation, is also necessary. It is desirable to accommodated these expenditures, within the overall level of the budget, either as a reserve or as a separate part of the contingency fund set up in paragraph 8 above. The Secretary-General should examine all aspects related to the question and report, through the Advisory Committee on Administrative and Budgetary Questions and the Committee for Programme and Co-ordination, to the General Assembly at its forty-second session.

11. Pending a decision by the General Assembly on the question dealt within paragraph 10 above, the revised estimates arising form the impact of extraordinary expense, including those relating to the maintenance of peace and security, as well as fluctuations in rates of exchange and inflation, shall not be covered by the contingency fun and shall continue to be treated in accordance with established procedure and under the relevant provision of the Financial Regulations and Rules. The Secretary-General should nevertheless make efforts to absorb these expenditures, to the extent possible, through savings from the programme budget, without causing in any way a negative effect on programme delivery and without prejudice to the utilization of the contingency fund.

Annex II
Statement made by the President of the General Assembly
at the 102nd plenary meeting, on 19 December 1989[11]

...I have obtained a legal opinion from the Legal counsel of the United Nations on three paragraphs of the draft resolution. The legal opinion reads as follows:

"You have requested our opinion on the legal consequences of three draft paragraphs which are under consideration for inclusion in a resolution to be adopted by the General Assembly on the United Nations budgetary process. These three paragraphs read as follows:

"'5.   *Reaffirms* that the decision-making process is governed by the provisions of the Charter of the United Nations and the rules of procedure of the General Assembly;

"'6.   *Agrees* that, without prejudice to paragraph 5 above, the Committee for Programme and Co-ordination should continue its existing practice of reaching decisions by consensus; explanatory views, if any, shall be presented to the General Assembly;

"'7.   *Considers it desirable* that the Fifth Committee, before submitting its recommendations on the outline of the programme budget to the General Assembly in accordance with the provisions of the Charter and the rules of procedure, should continue to make all possible efforts with a view to establishing the broadest possible agreement;'.

"It is our opinion that these draft paragraphs read separately or together do not in any way prejudice the provisions of Article 18 of the Charter of the United Nations or of the relevant rules of procedure of the General Assembly giving effect to that Article."

That coincides with the views expressed by all delegations.

I concur with the foregoing, and I take it that the General Assembly also agrees with it.

Notes

1.   *Official Records of the General Assembly, Forty-first Session, Supplement No.49* (A/41/49).
2.   A/41/795.
3.   A/41/663.
4.   A/41/763, annex.
5.   *Official Records of the General Assembly, Forth-first Session, Supplement No. 49* (A/41/49).
6.   A/41/795.

7. *Official Record of the General Assembly, Forty-first Session, Supplement No. 38* (A/41/38 and Corr. 2).
8. See annex II to the present resolution.
9. *Ibid.*
10. *Ibid.*
11. Annexed to the resolution following a decision by the General Assembly.

1.3 Decision 1987/112[*]

In-depth Study of the United Nations Intergovernmental Structure and Functions in the Economic and Social Fields

6 February 1987

At its 4th plenary meeting, on 6 February 1987, the Economic and Social Council, in order to carry out the in-depth study of the United Nations intergovernmental structure and functions in the economic and social fields and its Secretariat support structures, as called for by the General Assembly in its resolution 41/213 of 19 December 1986, decided:

(a)   To establish a Special Commission of the Economic and Social Council on the In-depth Study of the United Nations Intergovernmental Structure and Functions in the Economic and Social Fields, which would be open to the full participation of all States Members of the United Nations on an equal basis and whose proceedings would be governed in all other respects by the relevant rules of procedure of the Economic and Social Council;

(b)   That in undertaking its task, the Special Commission should establish, as appropriate, drafting or working groups;

(c)   To invite Governments to participate at the highest possible level in the work of the Special Commission;

(d)   To request the Special Commission to consider, in the context of the in-depth study, the relevant provisions of recommendation 2 of the Group of High-level Intergovernmental Experts to Review the Efficiency of the Administrative and Financial Functioning of the United Nations;

(e)   That the Bureau of the Special Commission should be composed of five members, one from each regional group, who should serve for the entire duration of the work of the Special Commission;

(f)   To appoint Mr. Abdel Halim Badawi (Egypt) Chairman of the Special Commission and to convene an organizational meeting of the Special Commission on 13 February 1987 for the purpose of electing, following consultations, the other members of the Bureau;

(g)   To convene the first and second sessions of the Special Commission from 2 to 6 and from 18 to 20 March 1987;

---

[*]*Official Records of the Economic and Social Council, Supplement No. 1* (E/1987/87), p. 50.

(h)   That the Special Commission should inform the Economic and Social Council, at its first regular session of 1987 and at subsequent regular sessions, of the progress of its work and should make recommendations to the Council on the future programme of work and calendar of meetings of the Commission;

(i)   To request all subsidiary bodies of the General Assembly in the economic and social sectors and all subsidiary bodies of the Economic and Social Council to submit to the Special Commission, within thirty days of the conclusion of their forthcoming sessions, their views and proposals on achieving the objectives envisaged in recommendation 8 of the Group of High-level Intergovernmental Experts regarding their functioning and that of their subsidiary machinery;

(j)   To request the Secretary-General to submit to the Special Commission:

(i)   Information on the intergovernmental machinery of the United Nations in the economic and social fields and its Secretariat support structures, including information concerning terms of reference, programmes of work, agendas, reporting procedures and periodicity of meetings, that information to be submitted to the Special Commission at its first session;

(ii)   A list of available United Nations studies on the functioning and restructuring of the intergovernmental bodies in the economic and social sectors, as well as legislative decisions taken in that regards;

(iii)   Other studies and analyses as required by the Special Commission;

(k)   Also to request the Secretary-General, to the extent possible within existing resources, to provide conference services, facilities and other necessary support on a preferential basis to the Special Commission to enable it to operate with sufficient frequency as from the first half of 1987 to fulfil its mandate in the limited time available;

(l)   To request the Special Commission to make its final report available in time for consideration by the Economic and Social Council at its second regular session of 1988;

(m)   That the Special Commission should approach its work with a view to strengthening the effectiveness of the United Nations in dealing with economic and social issues, in accordance with the provisions of the Charter of the United Nations and the objectives agreed upon by the General Assembly.

1.4 Resolution 42/170[*]

Implementation of General Assembly Resolution 41/213 in the Economic and Social Fields

11 December 1987

The General Assembly,

Reaffirming the proposes and principles of the Charter of the United Nations,

Recalling its resolutions 32/197 of 20 December 1977 on the restructuring of the economic and social sectors of the United Nations system and 41/213 of 19 December 1986 on the review of the efficiency of the administrative and financial functioning of the United Nations, both of which are elements of a common process,

Taking note of Economic and Social Council decisions 1987/112 of 6 February 1987 on the in-depth study of the United Nations intergovernmental structure and functions in the economic and social fields and 1987/180 of 8 July 1987 on enhancing the co-ordination of the activities of the organizations of the United Nations system,

Bearing in mind the importance of the full implementation of all aspects of its resolution 41/213,

1. *Stresses* the common interest of all countries in the effective and efficient functioning of the United Nations in the economic and social fields which are of particular importance to the developing countries;

2. *Affirms* that its resolution 41/213 should continue to be implemented in the economic and social fields at the intergovernmental and Secretariat levels in a timely, orderly, integrated and well co-ordinated manner in order to enhance the quality and strengthen the implementation of development-oriented programmes and activities of the United Nations in those fields;

3. *Considers* that the implementation of its resolution 41/213 in the economic and social fields should take into account the fact that the in-depth study of the United Nations intergovernmental structure and functions in the economic and social fields, as called for in section I, paragraph 1 (e), of that resolution, is under way;

---

[*]*Official Records of the General Assembly, Forty-second Session, Supplement No. 49* (A/42/49), pp. 129-130.

4. *Recognizes* that adjustments in the structure of the Secretariat in the economic and social fields will be required as a result of ongoing reviews and of the work of the Special Commission of the Economic and Social Council on the In-depth Study of the United Nations Intergovernmental Structure and Functions in the Economic and Social Fields.

1.5 Resolution 42/211[*]

Implementation of General Assembly Resolution 41/213

21 December 1987

The General Assembly,

Recalling its resolution 41/213 of 19 December 1986 on the review of the efficiency of the administrative and financial functioning of the United Nations,

Reaffirming that measures to improve the efficiency of the administrative and financial functioning of the United Nations and to improve the planning, programming and budgeting process should aim at and contribute to strengthening the effectiveness of the Organization in dealing with political, economic and social issues, in order better to achieve the purposes of and respect for the principles set out in the Charter of the United Nations,

Reaffirming also that all Member States must honour, promptly and in full, their financial obligations as set out in the Charter,

Emphasizing that the financial stability of the Organization will facilitate the orderly, balanced and well co-ordinated implementation of resolution 41/213 in all its parts,

Recognizing that the implementation of resolution 41/213 by all concerned - the Secretary-General, Member States and intergovernmental bodies - is a continuing process,

Recalling the relevant parts of its resolutions 37/234 of 21 December 1982 and 38/227 A and B of 20 December 1983,

Taking in account its resolutions 42/170 and 42/207 C of 11 December 1987,

Having considered also the relevant parts of the report of the Committee for Programme and Co-ordination of the work of its twenty-seventh session,[1]

Having considered also the relevant parts of the report of the Committee for Programme and Co-ordination on the work of its twenty-seventh session[2] and of the reports of the Advisory Committee on Administrative and Budgeting Questions,[3]

---

[*]*Official Records of the General Assembly, Forty-second Session, Supplement No. 49* (A/42/49), pp 261-263.

Taking into account the views expressed by Member States during the consideration of this item at the forty-second session,

1. *Calls upon* Member States to demonstrate their commitment to the United Nations by, *inter alia*, meeting their financial obligations in accordance with the Charter of the United Nations;

2. *Stresses* that, in order to carry out successfully the process of reform and restructuring, it is essential that the present financial uncertainties be dispelled;

3. *Reiterates* its support for the Secretary-General in the fulfilment of his responsibilities as chief administrative officer of the Organization;

4. *Reiterates also* that implementation of its resolution 41/213 must not have an adverse effect on mandated activities and programmes;

5. *Stresses* the importance of the timely and successful completion of the in-depth study of the intergovernmental structure and functions in the economic and social fields being undertaken by the Economic and Social Council, as mandated by the General Assembly in section I, paragraph 1 (*e*), of its resolution 41/213, and reaffirms its resolution 42/170, in particular paragraphs 3 and 4 thereof;

6. *Requests* the Secretary-General, in implementing those recommendations contained in its resolution 41/213 for which he has responsibility, to take into account the reviews, studies and decisions entrusted to the intergovernmental bodies and invites him to co-operate with those bodies as required;

7. *Also requests* the Secretary-General, in implementing those recommendations contained in its resolution 41/213 which are within his purview, to seek the approval of the General Assembly for a departure from the approved recommendations;

8. *Stresses* the importance of the revised estimates for the biennium 1988-1989 that the Secretary-General will submit to the General Assembly at its forty-third session, through the Committee for Programme and Co-ordination and the Advisory Committee on Administrative and Budgetary Questions, and requests the Secretary-General, in preparing those revised estimates, to reflect the state of implementation of the relevant provisions of resolution 41/213;

9. *Notes* that the implementation by the Secretary-General of certain recommendations of the Group of High-level Intergovernmental Experts to Review the Efficiency of the Administrative and Financial Functioning of the United Nations,[4] adopted by the General Assembly in its resolution 41/213, is not in accordance with the decisions of the Assembly;

10. *Requests* the Secretary-General, in implementing further recommendations 5, 15, 19, 25, 29 and 37 of the Group, and particularly when preparing revised estimates for the biennium 1988-1989 and proposals for revision of the medium-term plan for the period 1984-1989, to take into account the following guidelines:

(a) Regarding recommendation 5, the General Assembly takes note of the report of the Secretary-General[5] and invites him to proceed as necessary on both already approved projects in accordance with the provision of section I, paragraph 1 (a), of resolution 41/213, on the understanding that no additional appropriation will be required in that regard for the biennium 1988-1989;

(b) Regarding recommendation 15, on the reduction of posts in the United Nations, the Assembly stresses the importance that it attaches to the submission by the Secretary-General to the Assembly of his plans for the implementation of this recommendation in accordance with the provisions of section I, paragraph 1 (b), of resolution 41/213, and reiterates its conclusion that the Secretary-General should implement this recommendation with flexibility in order to avoid, *inter alia*, negative impact on programmes and on the structure and composition of the Secretariat, bearing in mind the necessity of securing the highest standards of efficiency, competence and integrity of the staff, with due regard to equitable geographical distribution;

(c) Regarding the implementation of recommendation 19, on activities relating to Namibia, the Secretary-General is invited to implement this recommendation in consultation with the United Nations Council for Namibia;

(d) The Secretary-General is invited to consider the location of the functions related to liaison with non-governmental organizations in the context of the implementation of recommendation 25; the Secretary-General is further invited to review his decisions on this matter in the context of the decisions to be taken by the Economic and Social Council on the intergovernmental structure and functions in the economic and social fields, as they will pertain to the functioning and servicing of the Committee on Non-Governmental Organizations;

(e) Regarding recommendation 29, the Secretary-General is invited to review his decisions in the light of the debate of the Fifth Committee at the forty-second session and to reflect the results of that review in his revised estimates;

(f) Regarding recommendation 37, the General Assembly takes note of the additional information provided by the Secretary-General with regard to the reform in the Department of Public Information of the Secretariat; stresses that such reform should fully respect the mandated programme of work of the Department as detailed in section 27 of the proposed programme budget for the biennium 1988-1989;[6] takes note of the assurance by the Secretary-General in that respect, including those provided in writing;[7] requests the Secretary-General to complete the thorough review of the functions and activities of the United Nations information centres called for under recommendation 37, as a matter of priority; and further requests the Secretary-General to reflect in his revised estimates the findings of those reviews, the concerns expressed by Member States at the forty-second session and the above-mentioned assurances, when finalizing the reform and work programme of the Department of Public Information;

11. *Further requests* the Secretary-General to submit to the General Assembly at its forty-third session, through the Committee for Programme and Co-ordination and the Advisory Committee on Administrative and Budgetary Questions, a progress report on the state of implementation of resolution 41/213;

12. *Concurs* with the relevant observations and recommendations made by the Advisory Committee on Administrative and Budgetary Questions in its report;[8]

13. *Approves* the guidelines for the contingency fund as annexed to the present resolution;

14. *Requests* the Secretary-General to submit to the General-Assembly at its forty-third session, through the Committee for Programme and Co-ordination and the Advisory Committee on Administrative and Budgetary Questions, proposals for provisional procedures for the use and operation of the contingency fund based on the above-mentioned guidelines;

15. *Decides* to review the procedures for the use and operation of the contingency fund in the light of experience gained, no later than at its forty-seventh session;

16. *Also decides* to consider at its forty-third session the question of a comprehensive solution to the problem of all additional expenditures, including those deriving from inflation and currency fluctuations, on the basis of the reports to be submitted by the Committee for Programme and Co-ordination and the Advisory Committee on Administrative and Budgetary Questions;

17. *Reaffirms* the relevant provisions of resolution 41/213 concerning the role and mandate of the Committee for Programme and Co-ordination;

18. *Decides* that the date for submission of the outline of the programme budget shall be 15 August of he off-budget year.

Annex
Contingency fund

A.   Criteria for use of the contingency fund

The contingency fund should be used for the following:

(a)   Additional resources that may be required as a result of the consideration of statements of programme budget implications;

(b)   Revised estimates in respect of:

(i)   Amounts required over and above the estimates in the proposed programme budget for activities which had been included in the proposed programme budget but which were not acted upon at first reading pending the submission of additional information;

(ii)   Additional requirements for construction related only to changes in the scope of the projects which are so urgent that the matter cannot wait to be considered in the context of the budget outline; additional requirements related to cost increases should be handled under provisions for dealing with inflation and currency fluctuations; similarly, additional requirements related to the effects of natural disasters or unforeseen obstacles should be handled on an *ad hoc* basis and should not be covered by the contingency fund;

(iii)   Additional requirements resulting from legislative mandates, such as those resulting from the decisions of the Economic and Social Council.

B. Period covered and pattern of use of the contingency fund

1.   The fund covers additional expenditures relating to the biennium which are based on decisions taken in the year preceding the biennium and during the biennium.

2.   While prudent use of the fund requires that it should not be exhausted before the end of the period of use, no pre-determined proportion for a given year should be se, pending review of the question, in the light of experience with the actual operation of the fund.

C. Operation of the contingency fund

1.   In the off-budget year, the General Assembly would decide on the size of the fund in accordance with the provisions of annex I to its resolution 41/213.

2.   Starting with the budget year (i.e., the year before the commencement of the biennium) and continuing throughout the biennium, the General Assembly would decide on the actual amounts to be utilized from the fund on the basis

of statements of programme budget implications and proposals for revised estimates.

3. Each statement of programme budget implications and each proposal for revised estimates should contain a precise indication of how the alternative mentioned in paragraph 9 of annex I to General Assembly resolution 41/213 would be applied in case it is not possible to finance all or part of the additional requirements from the fund. It would be understood that each draft resolution accompanied by a statement of programme budget implications would be adopted subject to the provisions of that statement.

4. The statements of programme budget implications and proposals for revised estimates, formulated as indicated in paragraph 3 above, would be considered by the Assembly as in the past. The resolutions could be adopted by the Assembly subject to the understanding described in paragraph 3 above.

5. A deadline should be set for the consideration of statements of programme budget implications and proposals for revised estimates. After that date, the Secretary-General would prepare and submit a consolidated statement of all programme budget implications and revised estimates considered at that session of the General Assembly. The amounts in that statement would correspond to hose previously recommended by the Fifth Committee upon its consideration of individual statements and proposals for revised estimates (see paras. 3 and 4 above). Should the consolidated amount be within the available balance in the contingency fund, the Assembly would proceed to appropriate the required amounts under the relevant sections of the programme budget.

6. Should the consolidated amount exceed the balance available in the fund for that year, the Secretary-General would, in his consolidated statement, make proposals for revising the amount so that it would not exceed the available balance. In so doing, the Secretary-General would be guided by the indications of alternatives included in each statement of programme budget implications and in each proposal for revised estimates. The respective legislative bodies should take action on such alternatives at the time they adopt the decision or resolution in question (see para. 3 above). The Secretary-General would also take into account any indications of relative urgency that each legislative body might wish to make regarding its resolutions and decisions. Upon consideration of the consolidated statement, the General Assembly would proceed to appropriate the funds necessary under the relevant sections of the programme budget.

Notes

1. A/42/225 and Add.1, A/42/234 and Corr.1 and A/C.5/42/2/Rev.1.
2. *Official Records of the General Assembly, Forty-second Session, Supplement No. 16 and addendum* (A/42/16 and Add.1).
3. *Ibid., Supplement No. 7* (A/42/7); *ibid., Supplement No. 7A* (A/42/7/Add.1-10), document A/42/7/Add.2; and A/42/640.
4. *Ibid., Forty-first Session, Supplement No. 49* (A/41/49).

5.   *Ibid., Forty-first Session, Supplement No. 49* (A/41/49).
6.   A/42/6(Sect. 27) and A/42/6/Corr.1.
7.   A/C.5/42/L.22.
8.   A/42/640, paras. 4-14.

1.6 Resolution 1988/77*

Revitalization of the Economic and Social Council

29 July 1988

The Economic and Social Council,

Recalling General Assembly resolutions 41/213 of 19 December 1986, 42/170 of 11 December 1987 and 42/211 of 21 December 1987, concerning the review of the efficiency of the administrative and financial functioning of the United Nations,

Recalling also General Assembly resolution 32/197 of 20 December 1977 on the restructuring of the economic and social sectors of the United Nations system,

Recalling further section IV of the General Assembly resolution 33/202 of 29 January 1979, concerning the role of the Director-General for Development and International Economic Co-operation,

Recalling Economic and Social Council resolutions 1458 (XLVII) of 8 August 1969 and 1982/50 of 28 July 1982,

Recognizing that the process of reforming the economic and social sectors of the United Nations aims at contributing to the full implementation of General Assembly resolution 41/213 and requires continued attention,

Aware that the work of the Economic and Social Council should be enhanced and streamlined in order to make the United Nations system more responsive to the challenges of development, in particular of developing countries, and to the needs of Member State in the coming years,

Fully aware of the urgent need to revitalize the Council in order to enable it, under the authority of the General Assembly, to exercise effectively its functions and powers as set out in the Charter of the United Nations and relevant resolutions of the General Assembly and the Council,

Having heard statements by the President of the Economic and Social Council and by Member State on the revitalization of the Council as the principal organ of the United Nations under the Charter in the economic and social fields,[1]

Official Records of the Economic and Social Council, Supplement No. 1 A (E/1988/88/Add.1).

1. *Affirms* that the Economic and Social Council should make an important contribution to the major issues and concerns facing the international community, in particular, the economic and social development of developing countries;

2. *Decides* to adopt the following measures aimed at revitalizing the Council, improving its functioning and enabling, it to exercise effectively its functions and powers as set out in Charter IX and X of the Charter of the United Nations:

Policy formulation

(a) With a view to formulating and elaborating action-oriented recommendations:

(i) The annual general discussion of "international economic and social policy, including regional and sectoral developments" should take place during the first five working days of the second regular session and should allow enough time for a dialogue and an exchange of views between members and executive heads of the organizations of the United Nations system;

(ii) The Council should undertake annually in-depth discussions of previously identified major policy themes, to be selected on the basis of a multi-year work programme derived, *inter alia*, from the priorities set out in the medium-term plan of the United Nations and the work programmes of other relevant United Nations bodies;

(iii) The Council shall, as and when necessary, address urgent and emerging issues relating to acute international economic and social problems possibly as one of themes identified in accordance with subparagraph (ii) above;

(iv) In the context of the above:

a. The executive needs of the specialized agencies or their senior representatives should participate actively in the deliberations of the Council;

b. The specialized agencies should be invited to resume submission of analytical summaries of their annual reports for the consideration of the Council;

Monitoring

(b) The Council shall monitor the implementation of the overall strategies, policies and priorities established by the General Assembly in the economic, social and related fields as set out in relevant resolution of the

Assembly and the Council; it shall also consider all appropriate modalities for carrying out the recommendations of the Assembly on matters falling within the Council's competence; in this regard:

(i)   The Secretary-General should circulate each year to Member State and all organizations of the United Nations system, as well as to the Council at its organizational session, a consolidated note on the decisions adopted by the General Assembly in the economic, social and related fields, highlighting matters that require action by them;

(ii)   The Council shall obtain information from the specialized agencies on the steps taken to give effect to the recommendations of the General Assembly and the Council on economic, social and related matters that fall within the respective mandates and areas of competence of the agencies; such information is to be included in the analytical summaries of their reports;

(c)   With a view to submitting appropriate recommendations to the General Assembly on the overall and programme priorities of the United Nations in the economy, social and related fields, the Council shall examine in depth the relevant chapters of the proposed medium-term plan and sections of the proposed programme budget of the United Nations in the light of the recommendations of the Committee for Programme and Co-ordination;

Operational activities

(d)   The Council shall recommend to the General Assembly overall priorities and policy guidelines for operational activities for development undertaken by the United Nations system; for that purpose:

(i)   The Council, as part of its co-ordination functions, shall define, as and when necessary, overall priorities and specific activities for the organizations of the United Nations system, within their respective mandates, so that the operational activities for development of the United Nations system are cared out in a coherent and effective manner;

(ii)   The Council shall deal, each year, with a limited number of policy co-ordination issues, including those identified in General Assembly resolutions 42/196 of 11 December 1987; the executive heads of the organizations concerned should be invited to participate actively in such discussions;

(iii)   Once every three years the Council shall conduct a comprehensive policy review of the operational activities for development of the United Nations system, which will be one of its major policy themes and shall be undertaken in connection with the triennial policy review of operational activities carried out by the General Assembly;

(iv)   The Council shall monitor the follow-up to its recommendations; organizations of the United Nations system should report to the Council on progress made in the implementation of those recommendations;

Co-ordination

(e)   The Council shall carry out its functions of co-ordinating the activities of the United Nations system in the economic, social and related fields as an integral part of its work; to this effect:

(i)   Co-ordination instruments, such as cross-organizational reports, the Joint Meetings of the Committee for Programme and Co-ordination and the Administrative Committee on Co-ordination, and reports of the Administrative Committee on Co-ordination and its subsidiary bodies, should be rationalized in order to enable the Council to carry out its co-ordination functions in an effective manner, based on the measures contained in the present resolution; the Committee for Programme and Co-ordination should assist the Council in this regard and submit specific proposals thereon to the Council at its second regular session of 1989;

(ii)   The Administrative committee on Co-ordination, through its Consultative Committee on Substantive Questions (Operational Activities), and the Joint Consultative Group on Policy should prepare suggestions to assist the Council in fulfilling its central co-ordinating role in the field of operational activities for development and should submit them to the Council at its second regular session of 1989;

(iii)   The Council shall consider the activities and programmes of the organs, organizations and bodies of the United Nations system, in order to ensure, through consultation with and recommendations to the agencies, that the activities and programmes of the United Nations and its agencies are compatible and mutually complementary, and shall recommend to the General Assembly relative priorities for the activities of the United Nations system in the economic and social fields; for that purpose, cross-organizational programme analyses shall be discontinued in their present form and be replaced by brief analyses on major issues in the medium-term plan, as referred to in subparagraph (a) (ii) above, to be considered directly by the Council; immediately after the General Assembly adopts the next medium-term plan, the Secretary-General should submit to the Council draft proposals on a multi-year programme for such analyses;

(iv)   In considering the question of regional co-operation, the Council shall concentrate on the policy review and co-ordination of activities, particularly with respect to issues of common interest to all regions and matters relating to interregional co-operation;

Working methods and organization of work

(f)   In formulating its biennial programme of work, the Council shall, to the extent possible, consolidate similar or closely related issues under a single agenda item, in order to consider and take action on them in an integrated manner; the Council shall pay particular attention to bringing the economic and the social activities of the United Nations system close together; to this effect

(i)   In proposing future calendars of conference, the Secretary-General should ensure that meetings of the subsidiary bodies of the Council will end at least eight weeks before the session of the Council at which their reports are to be considered; the Committee on Conferences should be requested to act accordingly;

(ii)   The Council shall further continue to consider the biennialization of the sessions of its subsidiary bodies and items on its own agenda and programme of work, taking into account the need for a balance between economic and social issues;

(iii) The Secretariat shall prepare for the Council, on the basis of report submitted by the relevant organs, organizations and bodies of the United Nations system, issue-oriented consolidated reports on economic, social and related questions that the Council will consider under the consolidated agenda items;

(iv)   All reports submitted to the Council should be prefaced by an analytical executive summary that highlights the main issues addressed and the recommendations made in the report;

(v)   The six-week rule for the circulation of substantive reports of the Secretariat and the eight-week rule for the annotated agenda of the Council should be strictly observed;

(vi)   The Council shall report to the General Assembly on the outcome of its work in a manner that will enable the Assembly, in its Main Committees, to consider the recommendations made by the Council in an integrated manner;

(vii) The Council shall review all relevant documentation prepared for the consideration of questions in the economic, social and related fields;

(g)   The Secretary-General, in the context of the implementation of General Assembly resolution 41/213, should submit to the Council, at its second regular session of 1989, proposals on the structure and composition of a separate and identifiable secretariat support structure for the Council, which would undertake the substantive functions and technical servicing that will be required to implement subparagraphs (b) (i), (b) (ii), (e) (iii) and (f) (iii) above;

(h)   To achieve better and more effective co-ordination of the economic, social and related activities of the United Nations system, including operational activities for development, the Office of the Director-General for Development and International Economic Co-operation should be strengthened; in this context, the relevant provisions of General Assembly resolutions 32/197 and 33/202, including those concerning improved policy planning, should be fully implemented;

(i)   In the recruitment of staff for the United Nations Secretariat in the economic and social fields, due consideration should be given to the principle of equitable geographical representation;

(j)   The Third (Programme and Co-ordination) Committee of the Council shall henceforth focus on:

(i)   Operational activities for development of the United Nations system and system-wide co-ordination of those activities;

(ii)   Programme questions;

(iii)   Co-ordination of the activities of the United Nations and the United Nations system;

(k)   The Council shall elect its President and Bureau early in the calendar year, prior to the organizational session of the Council;

(l)   Prior to the organizational session, the President, with the co-operation of the other members of the Bureau, should arrange for consultations with members of the Council on the draft programme of work and provisional agenda prepared by the Secretary-General and on the allocation of agenda items and make proposals thereon for consideration by the Council; the duration of the organizational session of the Council could consequently be shortened;

3.   *Requests* the Secretary-General to submit a report to the Economic and Social Council at its second regular session of 1989 on the feasibility and comparative costs of holding at the United Nations, with the present in-sessional arrangements, one consolidated or two regular sessions of the Council;

4.   *Decides* to include an item entitled "Revitalization of the Economic and Social Council" in the provisional agenda for its second regular session of 1989 and to consider under that item a report of the Secretary-General on progress in the implementation of the present resolution;

5.   *Requests* the Secretary-General to report to the Economic and Social Council at its second regular session of 1989 on the progress made in the

implementation of the relevant paragraphs of the present resolution and on proposals for incorporating in the biennial programme of work of the Council measures to implement the present resolution;

6. *Also requests* the Secretary-General, in order to enable the Council to continue discussions on how its work can be enhanced so as to make it more responsive to the challenge of development in the coming years, to submit to the Council at its second regular session of 1989 a note on:

(a) The functioning of the Council and its subsidiary bodies in relation to the relevant chapters of the medium-term plan, using the following categories: (i) policy formulation, co-ordination and monitoring; (ii) operations and implementation; (iii) technical support;

(b) The mandates of the bodies established to assist the Council in carrying out its functions, listed according to the same three categories.

Note

1. E/1988/SR.18, 29 and 30.

1.7 Resolution 43/174*

Review of the Efficiency of the Administrative and Financial Functioning of the United Nations in the Economic and Social Fields

9 December 1988

The General Assembly,

Recalling its resolution 32/197 of 20 December 1977 on the restructuring of the economic and social sectors of the United Nations system, 41/213 of 19 December 1986 on the review of the efficiency of the administrative and financial functioning of the United Nations 42/170 of 11 December 1987 on the implementation of General Assembly 41/213 in the economic and social fields, and 42/211 of 21 December 1987 on the implementation of General Assembly 41/213,

Recalling also Economic and Social Councils 1988/77 of 29 July 1988 on the revitalization of the Council,

Emphasizing that the financial stability of the Organization will facilitate the orderly, balanced and well co-ordinated implementation of resolution 41/213 in all its parts,

Emphasizing also that the work of the United Nations should be enhanced and streamlined in order to make the United Nations more effective and responsive to the needs of Member States, particularly developing countries,

Conscious of the fact that the refer of the economic and social sectors of the United Nations is a continuing process aimed at strengthening the effectiveness of the United Nations in dealing wi those issues and requires further attention,

Taking note of the report of the Special Commission of the Economic and Social Council on the In-depth Study of the United Nations Intergovernmental Structure and Functions in the Economic and Social Fields[1] and its Secretariat support structures, and recognizing that, although the Special Commission had conducted the in-depth study entrusted to it, the Special Commission was unable to reach agreed recommendations,

---

Official Records of the General Assembly, Forty-third Session, Supplement No. 49 (A/43/49), p. 60.

1.   *Stresses* the common interest of all countries in the effective functioning of the United Nations in the economic and social fields so that it is more responsive not only to current issues, but also to emerging problems and issues, particularly those related to the development of developing countries;

2.   *Requests* the Secretary-General to consult with all Member States and seek their views on ways and means of achieving a balanced and effective implementation of recommendations 2 and 8 of the Group of High-level Intergovernmental Experts to Review the Efficiency of the Administrative and Financial Functioning of the United Nations,[2] taking into consideration all relevant reports, including the report of the Special Commission of the Economic and Social Council on the In-depth Study of the United Nations Intergovernmental Structure and Functions in the Economic and Social Fields, as well as the outcome of the discussions in 1989 on the revitalization of the Economic and Social Council, and to submit to the General Assembly at its forty-fourth session a detailed report in order to enable Member States to consider and take appropriate action with a view to enhancing the effectiveness of the intergovernmental structure and its Secretariat support structures as well as programme delivery in the economic and social fields;

3.   *Decides* to consider, at its forty-fourth session, the report of the Secretary-General called for in paragraph 2 above, and his final report on the implementation of resolution 41/213, under the item entitled "Review of the efficiency of the administrative and financial functioning of the United Nations".

Notes

1.   E/1988/75.
2.   See *Official Records of the General Assembly, Forty-first Session, Supplement No. 49* (A/41/49).

1.8 Resolution 43/213*

Implementation of General Assembly Resolution 41/213:
Progress Report and Revised Estimates for the Biennium 1988-1989

21 December 1988

The General Assembly,

Recalling its resolution 41/213 of 19 December 1986 on the review of the efficiency of the administrative and financial functioning of the United Nations and its resolution 42/211 of 21 December 1987 on the implementation of General Assembly resolution 41/213,

Reaffirming that measures to improve the efficiency of the administrative and financial functioning of the United Nations and to improve the planning, programming and budgeting process should aim at and contribute to strengthening the effectiveness of the Organization in dealing with political, economic and social issues in order better to achieve the purposes of and respect for the principles set out in the Charter of the United Nations,

Noting from the report of the Secretary-General on the work Organization[1] that the emerging world situation is bound to impose additional responsibilities on the United Nations,

Reaffirming also that all Member States must honour, promptly and in full, their financial obligations as set out in the Charter,

Re-emphasizing that the financial stability of the Organization will facilitate the orderly, balanced and well co-ordinated implementation of resolution 41/213 in all its parts,

Having considered the relevant reports of the Secretary-General,[2]

Having considered also the relevant parts of the report of the Committee for Programme and Co-ordination on the work of its twenty-eighth session[3] and of the reports of the Advisory Committee on Administrative and Budgetary Questions,[4]

Taking into account the views expressed by Member State during the consideration of this item at its forty-third session,

---

Official Records of the General Assembly, Forty-third Session, Supplement No. 49 (A/43/49), pp. 249-251.

1. *Renews its appeal* to Member State to demonstrate their commitment to the United Nations by, *inter alia*, meeting their financial obligations on time and in full, in accordance with the Charter and the Financial Regulations of the United Nations;

2. *Stresses* that, in order to carry out successfully the process of reform and restructuring, it is essential that the present financial uncertainties be dispelled;

3. *Welcomes* the determination of the Secretary-General to continue his efforts to implement fully the recommendations of the Group of High-level Intergovernmental Experts to Review the Efficiency of the Administrative and Financial Functioning of the United Nations[5] which fall within his purview, as adopted in resolution 41/213 and in accordance with paragraph 7 of resolution 41/211;

4. *Reiterates* its support for the Secretary-General in the fulfillment of his responsibilities as chief administrative officer of the Organization;

5. *Stresses* that the implementation of its resolution 41/213 must not have a negative impact on mandated programmes and activities;

6. *Emphasizes* in this respect that, in accordance with the existing regulations and rules, while output revisions in programme budgets may be proposed in order to comply more efficiently with the objectives of those programmes and activities, outputs specifically requested in mandates should be fully delivered;

7. *Requests* the Secretary-General to submit disposed revisions referred to in paragraph 6 above to the General Assembly in the context of proposed programme budgets;

8. *Reiterates* that further implementation of its resolution 41/213 should be carried out in a balanced way and with flexibility so as to improve the structure and composition of the Secretariat;

9. *Endorses* the recommendations of the Committee for Programme and Co-ordination[6] on the Secretary-General's report on the implementation of recommendation 15 of the Group of High-level Intergovernmental Experts, as adjusted by a 10 per cent reduction in the staffing of conference services in New York and Geneva entailing an overall post reduction of 12.1 per cent by the end of the biennium 1988-1989[7] and further endorses the recommendation of the Advisory Committee on Administrative and Budgetary Questions that the adjustment under section 29 of the programme budget should entail the restoration of 100 posts on the understanding that this restoration would not require additional appropriations for the biennium 1988-1989,[8]

10. *Requests* the Secretary-General to submit, in the context of his proposed programme budget for the biennium 1990-1991, concrete recommendations for absorbing the costs of the posts referred to above including, to the maximum extent possible, through the elimination of additional posts, under the criteria set out in paragraphs 5, 8 and 9 above and paragraphs 11 to 13 below.

11. *Endorses* the recommendations of the Committee for Programme and Co-ordination and the Advisory Committee on Administrative and Budgetary Questions pertaining to small offices, regional commissions and other units referred to therein, and also requests the Secretary-General to keep in mind the concerns expressed by Member States in the Fifth Committee on proposed reductions of staff in small units such as the United Nations Environment Programme and the United Nations Centre for Human Settlements (Habitat);

12. *Concurs* with the comments and observations of the Advisory Committee on Administrative and Budgetary Questions in paragraph 33 of its report[9] regarding the organization, functions and staffing of the administrative and common services unit at Nairobi;

13. *Requests* the Secretary-General in further implementing recommendation 15 to continue to take into account the following guidelines:

(a)   This recommendation should be implemented flexibly taking due account of work-load analyses, where applicable;

(b)   Its implementation should have no negative impact on programmes;

(c)   Its implementation should have no adverse effect on the structure and composition of the Secretariat bearing in mind the necessity of securing the highest standards of efficiency, competence and integrity of staff with due regard to equitable geographical distribution;

(d)   It should be implemented in a balanced manner, taking into account recommendations 41, 46, 47 and 54;

14. *Invites* the Secretary-General to continue the implementation of recommendations 41, 46, 47 and 54 and to report thereon to the General Assembly at its forty-fourth session in the context of the report referred to in paragraph 18 below;

15. *Invites* the Secretary-General, as regards recommendation 19, to proceed with the reclassification of the post as indicated in paragraph 7 of his report;[10]

16. *Endorses* the recommendations of the Committee for Programme and Co-ordination and the Advisory Committee on Administrative and Budgetary Questions as regards recommendation 25, relating to the location of the liaison functions with non-governmental organizations, and recommendation 29;

17. *Invites* the Secretary-General to implement recommendation 37 in accordance with the recommendations of the Committee for Programme and Co-ordination as contained in paragraphs 82 to 88 of its report[11] and the comments and observations of the Advisory Committee on Administrative and Budgetary Questions as contained in paragraphs 40 to 60 of its report;[12]

18. *Requesting* the Secretary-General and the Committee for Programme and co-ordination to report to the General Assembly on the implementation of resolution 41/213 in accordance with recommendation 71, taking into account the views expressed in the Fifth Committee;

19. *Also requests* the Secretary-General to submit to the General Assembly at its forty-fifth session an analytical report assessing the effect of the implementation of resolution 41/213 on the Organization and its activities as a whole, and the way in which it has enhanced the efficiency of its administrative and financial functioning.

Notes

1. *Official Records of the General Assembly, Forty-third Session, Supplement No. 1 (A/43/1).*
2. A/43/286 and Corr.1, A/43/324, A/43/524 and A/C.5/43/1/Rev. 1 and Add.1 and 2.
3. See *Official Records of the General Assembly, Forty-third Session, Supplement No. 16 (A/43/16).*
4. A/43/651 and Add.1 and A/43/929.
5. See *Official Records of the General Assembly, Forty-first Session, Supplement No. 49 (A/41/49).*
6. *Ibid., Forty-third Session, Supplement No. 16 (A/43/16),* part one, para. 36.
7. A/C.5/43/1/Rev.1, para. 26.
8. See A/43/651, paras. 15-19.
9. A/43/651.
10. A/C.5/43/1/Rev.1/Add.1.
11. *Official Records of the General Assembly, Forty-third Session, Supplement No. 16 (A/43/16),* part two.
12. *Ibid.*

1.9 Resolution 43/214*

Proposed Programme Budget Outline for the Biennium 1990-1991 and Use and Operation of the Contingency Fund

21 December 1988

The General Assembly,

Recalling its resolution 41/213 of 19 December 1986, by which, *inter alia*, it requested the Secretary-General to submit in off-budget year an outline of the programme budget for the following biennium and to include in the programme budget a contingency fund and recognized the necessity of finding a comprehensive solution to the problem of all additional expenditures, including those deriving from inflation and currency fluctuation,

Recalling also its resolution 42/211 of 21 December 1987 in which it decided to consider at its forty-third session the question of a comprehensive solution to the problem of all additional expenditures, including those deriving from inflation and currency fluctuation,

Having considered the report of the Secretary-General[1] the relevant parts of the report of the Committee for Programme and Co-ordination and the report of the Advisory Committee on Administrative and Budgetary Questions,[2]

Taking into account the views expressed by Member States during the consideration of this item at its forty-second and forty-third sessions,

1. *Emphasizes* that sound programme budgeting, including a greater level of predictability of resources required, is not fully achievable until the current financial crises is fully brought to an end by the full and prompt payment of assessments by Member State;

2. *Recognizes* that the outline of the proposed programme budget is part of the process of improving the efficiency and effectiveness of the Organization;

3. *Affirms* that the outline, being a part of the new budget process defined in its resolution 41/213, is in a developmental period, that its methodology requires further improvement and that the whole exercise should be applied with flexibility, in accordance with resolutions 41/213 and 42/211;

Official Records of the General Assembly, Forty-third Session, Supplement No. 49 (A/43/49), p. 251.

4. *Recognizes also* that the outline should provide a greater level of predictability of resources required for the following biennium, while ensuring that such resources are adequate for the fulfillment of the objectives, programmes and activities of the Organization, as mandated by the relevant legislative bodies of the United Nations, thereby facilitating the widest possible agreement on the programme budget;

5. *Decides* that the Secretary-General should prepare his proposed programme budget for the biennium 1990-1991 on the basis of the total preliminary estimate of 1,767,060,000 United States dollars at 1988 rates (equivalent to 1,982,523,700 dollars at 1990-1991 rates) as shown in paragraph 16 of the report of the Advisory Committee on Administrative and Budgetary Questions;[3]

6. *Decides also* that the contingency fund of the programme budget for the biennium 1990-1991 shall be established at a level of 0.75 per cent of the preliminary estimate at 1990-1991 rates referred to above, i.e. 15 million dollars, shall be appropriated as needed and shall be used according to the purpose and procedures set out in the annexes to its resolutions 41/213 and 42/211 and relevant regulations and rules;

7. *Decides further* to keep under review, during the implementation of the programme budget for the biennium 1990-1991 and in the light of the evolving situation, the appropriateness and adequacy of the level of the contingency fund, as well as its mode of operation;

8. *Reaffirms* the need for a comprehensive and satisfactory solution to the problem of controlling the effects of inflation and currency fluctuation on the budget of the United Nations,

9. *Notes with appreciation* the work undertaken on this issue by the Advisory Committee on Administrative and Budgetary Questions and its observations on the establishment of a reserve that would cover additional requirements due to currency fluctuation, non-staff costs inflation and statutory cost increases for staff;[4]

10. *Agrees* to the concept of a reserve as described in paragraph 9 above, requests the Secretary-General to formulate a set of procedures for the operation of the reserve to be submitted through the Advisory Committee on Administrative and Budgetary Questions to the General Assembly at its forty-fourth session, and agrees to address further at that time the question of setting up such a reserve for the biennium 1990-1991;

11. *Stresses* the importance of indicating in the outline of the proposed programme budget priorities reflecting general trends of a broad sectoral nature, endorses the recommendations of the committee for Programme and Co-ordination in this regard,[5] and requests the Secretary-General to submit a

report on all aspects of priority-setting in future outlines to the General Assembly at its forty-fourth session through the Committee for Programme and Co-ordination;

12. *Requests* the Secretary-General to present his proposed programme budget for the biennium 1990-1991 in accordance with the present resolution and paragraph 10 of resolution 43/213 of 21 December 1988.

Notes

1.   A/43/524.
2.   A/43/929.
3.   *Ibid.*
4.   *Ibid.*, paras. 27-31.
5.   *Official Records of the General Assembly, Forty-third Session, Supplement No. 16* (A/43/16), part two, para. 34.

1.10 Resolution 44/200*

Implementation of General Assembly Resolution 41/213

21 December 1989

A

The General Assembly,

Recalling its resolution 41/213 of 19 December 1986 of the efficiency of the administrative and financial functioning of the United Nations and resolutions 42/211 of 21 December 1987 and 43/213 of 21 December 1988 on the implementation of General Assembly resolution 41/213,

Reaffirming that measures to improve the efficiency of the administrative and financial functioning of the United Nations and to improve the planning, programming and budgeting process should aim at and contribute to strengthening the effectiveness of the Organization in dealing with political, economic and social issues in order better to achieve the purposes of and respect for the principles set out in the Charter of the United Nations,

Emphasizing that this process requires careful monitoring and the continuing support of Member States, including in financial terms, so as to permit its orderly and balanced implementation and to avoid negative impact on programmes,

Recognizing that the process of implementation of its resolution 41/213 has taken place in a situation of persistent financial crisis,

Reaffirming that all Member State must honour, promptly and in full, their financial obligations as set out in the Charter,

Reiterating its support for the Secretary-General in the fulfilment of his responsibilities as Chief Administrative Officer of the Organization,

Noting the process made in the implementation of its resolution 41/213, including the new budgetary process,

Noting also that further efforts are required in implementing, in a balanced manner, the various recommendations approved in its resolution 41/213, including those related to personnel issues,

---

Official Records of the General Assembly, Forty-fourth Session, Supplement No. 49 (A/44/49), pp. 289-291.

Recognizing that the implementation of certain recommendations approved in its resolution 41/213 depends upon further review by intergovernmental bodies,

Recalling its request contained in its resolution 43/213 for the Secretary-General to submit to the General Assembly at its forty-fifth session an analytical report on the implementation of resolution 41/213,

Having considered the relevant reports of the Secretary-General and noting also that the report of the Secretary-General on the implementation of resolution 41/213[1] did not cover the entire three-year period foreseen in recommendation 71 of the Group of High-level Intergovernmental Experts to Review the Efficiency of the Administrative and Financial Functioning of the United Nations,[2]

Having considered also the relevant parts of the report of the Committee for Programme and Co-ordination on the work of its twenty-ninth session,[3] and of the report of the Advisory Committee on Administrative and Budgetary Questions,[4]

Taking into account the views expressed by Member States during the consideration of this item at its forty-fourth session,[5]

1.   *Renews its appeal* to Member State to demonstrate their commitment to the United Nations by, *inter alia*, meeting their financial obligations on time and in full, in accordance with the Charter and the Financial Regulations of the United Nations;

2.   *Stresses* that, in order to carry out successfully the process of reform and restructuring, it is essential that the present financial uncertainties be dispelled;

3.   *Encourages* the Secretary-General and Member States to intensify their efforts with respect to implementation of the provisions of its resolution 41/213 that fall within their respective purviews, particularly those aspects which have not been implemented;

4.   *Stresses* that implementation of its resolution 41/213 must not have a negative impact on mandated programmes and activities;

5.   *Emphasizes* in this respect that, in accordance with the existing regulations and rules, while output revisions in programme budgets may be proposed in order to comply more efficiently with the objectives of those programmes and activities, outputs specifically requested in mandates should be fully delivered;

6. *Reiterates* that further implementation of its resolution 41/213 should be carried out in a balanced way and with flexibility, so as to improve, *inter alia*, the structure and composition of the Secretariat;

7. *Decides*, with regard to recommendation 15 of the Group of High-level Intergovernmental Experts to Review the Efficiency of the Administrative and Financial Functioning of the United Nations:[6]

(a) To recognize the progress achieved to date in the implementation of the overall post reduction mandated by the General Assembly in resolution 43/213;

(b) To acknowledge that the Secretary-General is not in a position at the present stage to propose further post reductions;

(c) To consider, in the light of the analytical report to be submitted to the General Assembly at its forty-fifth session, proposals that may be put forward by the Secretary-General for further implementation of recommendation 15 as approved in resolution 41/213;

8. *Invites* the Secretary-General to implement recommendation 37 in accordance with the recommendations of the Committee for Programme and Co-ordination at its twenty-ninth session, as contained in paragraph 19 of its report;[7]

9. *Concurs* with the observations of the Committee for Programme and Co-ordination, in paragraph 21 of its report,[8] regarding the provision of conference services;

10. *Reiterates its requests* that, in his implementation of recommendation 5, the Secretary-General should ensure close adherence to the schedule outlined in his report to the General Assembly at its forty-third session,[9]

11. *Stresses* the need for greater transparency and coherence in personnel management, especially in the Staff Regulations of the United Nations, as set out in paragraph 18 of the report of the Committee for Programme and Co-ordination;[10]

12. *Also stresses* the need to strengthen the role of the Secretary-General with respect to co-ordination within the United Nations system, as well as the role of Member State through the relevant intergovernmental bodies through out the United Nations system;

13. *Requests* the Secretary-General, in his capacity as Chairman of the Administrative Committee on Co-ordination, to consider appropriate organizational arrangements for the secretariat of the Committee with a view

to ensuring its adequacy in addressing the increasing responsibilities of the Committee;

14. *Requests* the Secretary-General to provide to the General Assembly at its forty-fifth session a compendium of mandates of subsidiary administrative and budgetary bodies of the Assembly, together with information on relevant reviews carried out over the past five years, on the understanding that the decisions of the Assembly relating to those mandates remain valid;

15. *Reaffirms its request* to the Secretary-General to submit to the General Assembly at its forty-fifth session on analytical report assessing the effect of the implementation of its resolution 41/213 on the Organization and its activities, as a whole, and the way in which it has enhanced the efficiency of its administrative and financial functioning;

16. *Reaffirms* that the report should be structured along the following lines:

(a) The first part should be an exhaustive presentation of recommendations fully implemented, partially implemented and not implemented, as well as those which, in the view of the Secretary-General, could not be implemented;

(b) The second par to the report should provide explanations with regard to such implementation and an assessment of its impact on programmes, giving particular emphasis to those programmes which have been terminated or completed;

(c) The final part should provide a general critical assessment of the implementation of its resolution 41/213 in the light of the objectives of that resolution, namely, the enhancement of the administrative and financial functioning of the Organization.

B

The General Assembly,

Recognizing the need for improvement in the format and methodology of the programme budget and its outline, including the question of comparability of estimates in those two instruments,

Mindful of the fact that the operation and use of the contingency fund is still at an experimental stage and that statements of programme budget implications play an important role in the budget process,

Recognizing the need for a comprehensive solution to the problem of all additional expenditures, including those deriving from inflation and currency fluctuation,

Recognizing also the growing level of extrabudgetary resources available to the United Nations and the need to define more precisely their impact on the activities and programmes of the Organization,

1. *Endorses* the relevant conclusions and recommendations of the Committee for Programme and Co-ordination[11] and the relevant observations and recommendations of the Advisory Committee on Administrative and Budgetary Questions;[12]

2. *Requests* the Secretary-General to take into account the relevant comments and recommendations of the Committee for Programme and Co-ordination and the Advisory Committee on Administrative and Budgetary Questions on the format and methodology of the outline and the programme budget, when submitting the outline and the proposed programme budget for the biennium 1992-1993;

3. *Also requests* the Secretary-General to extend progressively, in accordance with paragraph 28 of his report,[13] the provision of statements of programme budget implications to all subsidiary bodies of the General Assembly and the Economic and Social Council, taking into account the feasibility of such extension in order to facilitate their decision-making process, and to keep under review the format and content of statements of programme budget implications in the context of the new budgetary process;

4. *Further requests* the Secretary-General to submit to the General Assembly at its forty-sixth session, through the Advisory Committee on Administrative and Budgetary Questions and the Committee for Programme and Co-ordination, and in the light of the experience gained during the implementation of the programme budget for 1990-1991, a single report on the review of the procedures for the provision of statements of programme budget implications and for the use and operation of the contingency fund;

5. *Decides*, given the shortcomings of the present system, to keep under review the question of a comprehensive solution to the problem of all additional expenditures, including those deriving from inflation and currency fluctuation, and to consider it again at its forty-sixth session;

6. *Requests* the Secretary-General to take fully into account the conclusions, recommendations and observations of the Committee for Programme and Co-ordination and the Advisory Committee on Administrative and Budgetary Questions on the treatment of extrabudgetary resources when preparing and presenting the outline and the proposed programme budget for the biennium 1992-1993.

C

The General Assembly,

Recognizing the importance of technological innovations in relation to the search for efficiency in the Organization,

Requests the Secretary-General to prepare, submission to the General Assembly at its forty-fifth session, a report on the status of the introduction of electronic data-processing and new technologies in the United Nations, which should include:

(a)   A review and assessment of current policies and processes;

(b)   A review and assessment of co-ordinating mechanisms, including those between the Department of Conference Services of the Secretariat and other units within the United Nations system;

(c)   A preliminary assessment of the results obtained with the introduction
of technological innovations, including cost-benefit analyses, utilization capacity and budgeting and accounting practices;

(d)   An outline of future plans and anticipated results for the efficiency of the Organization.

Notes

1.   A/44/222 and Corr.1.
2.   See *Official Records of the General Assembly, Forty-first Session, Supplement No. 49* (A/41/49).
3.   *Ibid., Forty-fourth Session, Supplement No. 16* (A/44/16).
4.   A/44/729.
5.   See A/C.5/44/SR.11-18, 46, 49 and 59.
6.   See *Official Records of the General Assembly, Forty-first Session, Supplement No. 49* (A/41/49).
7.   *Ibid.*
8.   *Ibid., Forty-fourth Session, Supplement No. 16* (A/44/16).
9.   A/C.5/43/16.
10.   *Official Records of the General Assembly, Forty-fourth Session, Supplement No. 16* (A/44/16).
11.   *Ibid.*
12.   A/44/729.
13.   A/44/234.

1.11 Resolution 45/254˙

Review of the Efficiency of the Administrative and Financial Functioning of the United Nations

21 December 1990

A

The General Assembly,

Recalling its resolution 41/213 of 19 December 1986 on the review of the efficiency of the administrative and financial functioning of the United Nations and its resolutions 42/211 of 21 December 1987, 43/213 of 21 December 1988 and 44/200 of 21 December 1989 on the implementation of General Assembly resolution 41/213,

Reaffirming that measures to improve the efficiency of the administrative and financial functioning of the United Nations and to improve the planning, programming and budgeting process should aim at and contribute to strengthening the effectiveness of the Organization in dealing with political, economic and social issues in order better to achieve the purposes of and respect for the principles set out in the Charter of the United Nations,

Having considered the reports of the Secretary-General,[1] the report of the Committee for Programme and Co-ordination[2] and the report of the Advisory Committee on Administrative and Budgetary Questions,[3]

Recognizing that the reform measures undertaken so far in accordance with resolution 41/213 have contributed to improving the efficiency of the Organization in certain areas,

Recognizing also that the involvement of Member States in the new planning, programming and budgeting process has facilitated a broader agreement of Member States on the programme budget of the United Nations,

Noting that, while having somewhat improved, the financial situation of the Organization remains uncertain,

1.   *Takes note* with appreciation of the analytical report of the Secretary-General;[4]

˙*Resolutions and Decisions adopted by the General Assembly during the First Part of its Forty-fifth Session*, Press Release GA/8165 (New York, United Nations, Department of Public Information), 21 January 1991, pp. 642-644.

2.   *Endorses* the relevant conclusions and recommendations of the Committee for Programme and Co-ordination[5] and of the Advisory Committee on Administrative and Budgetary Questions;[6]

3.   *Renews its appeal* to all Member States to demonstrate their commitment to the United Nations by, *inter alia*, meeting their financial obligations on time and in full in accordance with the Charter of the United Nations and the Financial Regulations of the United Nations;

4.   *Emphasizes* that the strengthening of the effectiveness of the Organization is a continuing process requiring the joint efforts of Member States and the Secretariat;

5.   *Stresses* that measures for the improvement of the effectiveness of the Organization should aim at the fulfilment of all its objectives;

6.   *Reiterates* its support for the Secretary-General in the fulfilment of his responsibility as Chief Administrative Officer;

7.   *Recognizes* the importance of the new budget process in order to enhance the effectiveness of the Organization;

8.   *Encourages* the Secretary-General and Member States to pursue the objectives of resolution 41/213, particularly those that have yet to be met, and invites the Secretary-General to consolidate and build upon the results achieved through the reform process and to submit proposals, whenever necessary, for improvements in the administrative and financial functioning of the Organization, in order to enable it to fulfil more effectively its role;

9.   *Also encourages* the Secretary-General to continue to implement provisions of resolution 41/213 and other relevant resolutions on questions of personnel and posts in the Organization, particularly those that have yet to be implemented, and invites Members States and the Secretary-General to exercise maximum restraint in their proposals for the staffing table of the Organization, particularly for high-level posts;

10.   *Stresses* that the relationship between posts and programmes funded from the regular budget and those funded from extrabudgetary resources requires further analysis and consideration;

11.   *Invites* the Secretary-General to ensure a greater transparency in the management and use of the extrabudgetary resources made available to the Organization in order, in particular, to assess more precisely the impact of those resources on the activities, programmes and priorities of the Organization;

12.   *Requests* the Secretary-General to present to the General Assembly at its forty-sixth session a report on all aspects of the role and use of extrabudgetary resources, as outlined by the Advisory Committee on Administrative and Budgetary Questions in its report to the forty-fourth session of the General Assembly;[7]

13.   *Encourages* the intention of the Secretariat to develop management and work-load analysis techniques and invites the Secretary-General to take into account the results of such techniques in the course of the preparation of his proposed programme budgets in order to ensure the full and effective implementation of all programmes and activities of the United Nations;

14.   *Reiterates* the importance of a comprehensive solution to the problem of all additional expenditures, including those deriving from inflation and currency fluctuation;

15.   *Reiterates also* the importance of the review of the procedures for the provisions of statements of programme budget implications and for the use and operation of the contingency fund, and recalls that it will consider a single report on the questions at its forty-sixth session;

16.   *Calls upon* Member States to provide the conditions for the effective functioning of the Organization, in particular through the fulfilment of their financial obligations as set out in the Charter, in order to sustain the desirable effects of the process of reform and renewal;

17.   *Decides* to continue considering annually the administrative, structural and other aspects of the improvement of the efficiency of the Organization, and invites the Secretary-General to report accordingly.

B

The General Assembly,

Reiterating the importance of co-ordination as a policy instrument in improving the performance of the organizations of the United Nations system, ensuring complementarity of efforts and increasing cost-effectiveness,

Stressing again the need to strengthen the role of Member States in the relevant intergovernmental bodies of the United Nations system and of the Secretary-General with respect to system-wide co-ordination,

1.   *Endorses* the relevant conclusions and recommendations of the Committee for Programme and Co-ordination in the field of co-ordination;[8]

2.   *Endorses also* the conclusions and recommendations of the report of the joint meeting of the Administrative Committee on Co-ordination and the Committee for Programme and Co-ordination;[9]

3.   *Requests* the Secretary-General to include in the annual review report of the Administrative Committee on Co-ordination a section on the measures taken or envisaged to implement the conclusions and recommendations of the Committee for Programme and Co-ordination and the Joint Meeting of the Administrative Committee on Co-ordination and the Committee for Programme and Co-ordination;

4.   *Reiterates* its request to the Secretary-General to make available to the General Assembly at its forty-sixth session the annual overview report of the Administrative Committee on Co-ordination, together with the relevant conclusions and recommendations of the Committee for Programme and Co-ordination and of the Economic and Social Council on that report.

C

The General Assembly,

Takes note of the report of the Secretary-General on the status of technological innovations in the United Nations,[10] and requests that an updated version of that report be submitted in the context of the proposed programme budget for 1992-1993.

Notes

1.   A/45/226 and A/45/370.
2.   *Official Records of the General Assembly, Forty-fifth Session, Supplement No. 16* (A/45/16), Part I.
3.   A/45/617.
4.   A/45/226 and A/45/370.
5.   *Official Records of the General Assembly, Forty-fifth Session, Supplement No. 16* (A/45/16), Part I.
6.   A/45/617.
7.   *Official Records of the General Assembly, Forty-fourth Session, Supplement No. 7* (A/44/7 and addenda).
8.   *Official Records of the General Assembly, Forty-fifth Session, Supplement No. 16* (A/45/16), Part I.
9.   A/45/835.
10.   A/45/478.

PART II

DOCUMENTS

2.1 Document A/41/49*

Report of the Group of High-level Intergovernmental Experts to Review the Efficiency of the Administrative and Financial Functioning of the United Nations

1986

CONTENTS

		Para-graphs
I.	Introduction	1-15
II.	The intergovernmental machinery and its functioning	16-27
	A. Specific recommendations (recommendations 1 to 7)	21
	B. Comparative study of the intergovernmental machinery and its functioning (recommendation 8)	22-24
	C. Co-ordination (recommendations 9 to 13)	25-27
III.	Structure of the Secretariat	28-44
	A. General recommendations (recommendations 14 and 15)	35
	B. Political affairs (recommendations 16 to 24)	36-37
	C. Economic and social affairs (recommendations 25 to 29)	38-41
	D. Administration and other fields (recommendations 30 to 40)	42-44
IV.	Measures regarding personnel	45-50
	A. General recommendation (recommendation 41)	50
	B. Recommendations to be reflected in the staff rules and regulations (recommendations 42 to 52)	50
	C. Other recommendations (recommendations 53 to 62)	50
V.	Monitoring, evaluation and inspection (recommendations 63 to 67)	51-56
VI.	Planning and budget procedure	57-69
	A. General considerations	57-61
	B. Setting of priorities (recommendation 68)	62-64
	C. Planning and budget mechanisms	65-69
VII.	Implementation of the Group's recommendations (recommendations 69 to 71)	70-71
Annex.	Organizational matters	

Official Records of the General Assembly, Forty-first Session, Supplement No. 49 (A/41/49).

I. Introduction

1. The basic objectives of the Charter of the United Nations have been reaffirmed and further developed throughout its 40 years of existence. Changing international circumstances and new challenges have led to a gradual but significant expansion in the scope, range and volume of the work of the Organization.

2. As new tasks have emerged and old ones persist, the agenda of the United Nations has shown a sustained growth. This larger, more diversified and complex agenda has led to a parallel growth in the intergovernmental machinery. New organs, committees, commissions and expert groups have been established at different levels in pursuit of the objectives of the Charter. In this process of institutional growth, sufficient attention has not always been given to avoid overlapping of agenda and duplication of work. This is the case for the United Nations itself and its affiliated bodies, as well as for the relationship between the United Nations and the specialized agencies. The United Nations own intergovernmental machinery for dealing with political, economic and social problems, including operational activities, has an overly complex structure which generally suffers from lack of cohesion and which makes co-ordination difficult.

3. The increase in activities and the institutional growth have led to a significant growth in the number of conferences and meetings held annually under United Nations auspices. Such conferences and meetings constitute an integral part of multilateral diplomacy and represent important tools in the search for mutual understanding and for a harmonization of policies and actions with regard to common problems. The number, frequency and duration of conferences and meetings has, however, reached a level which presents difficulties for all Member Sates, in particular smaller States with limited personnel resources, to participate fully. Another problem is that too often the considerable resources allocated to conferences and meetings are not put to maximum productive use. The volume of documentation, both in relation to conferences and meetings as well as in general terms, has increased considerably and has, to some extent, surpassed the limit of what can be studied and constructively used by Member States.

4. The United Nations Secretariat, which services the intergovernmental machinery, has undergone a parallel growth. As an example, the number of posts funded from the regular budget of the United Nations has grown from 1,546 in 1946 to 11,423 in 1986. This growth has, at times, been rapid, particularly at the end of the 1970s. Management capacity, especially with regard to the need to maintain overall administrative efficiency, productivity and cost effectiveness, has lagged behind this pace of growth. The quality of work performed needs to be improved upon. The qualifications of staff, in particular in the higher categories, are inadequate and the working methods are not efficient. Today's structure is too complex, fragmented and top-heavy. The Secretariat is divided into too many departments, offices and divisions.

There are at present nine political departments or offices and some 15 economic and social departments or offices. This is exemplified by the excessive number of Under-Secretaries-General and Assistant Secretaries-General.

5. The larger agenda of the United Nations, which responds to the demands and requirements of the international community, has led to a gradual growth in the regular budget of the Organization. The regular budget appropriation for the present biennium (1986-1987) financed through assessed contributions stands at $1,663 million. However, this portion of the budget covers only a part of the activities of the United Nations. The remainder, amount to roughly $1,200 million per year, is financed through voluntary contributions. Moreover, the budget of the United Nations is only one of many budgets covering the activities of the network made up of the United Nations and its affiliated organizations, whose secretariats fall directly or indirectly under the control of the Secretary-General.

6. Activities financed through assessed contributions under the regular budget fall into several distinct categories: political activities (10.4 per cent), economic and social activities (31.0 per cent), conference-servicing activities (19.5 per cent), technical co-operation activities (4.4 per cent), humanitarian activities (2.9 per cent), activities relating to international law (1.7 per cent), public information activities (5.2 per cent and administrative activities (24.9 per cent). These activities are, as will be seen, extremely varied in nature. The activities financed from voluntary contributions (extrabudgetary resources) are less diverse, comprising humanitarian and operational activities.

7. Over a number of years, there has been disagreement on the content and level of the budget of the Organization. This situation reflects to some extent political disagreement among Member States on parts of the substantive activities included in the programme budget. It also reflects some degree of dissatisfaction with aspects of the management and administrative functioning of the Organization. These problems are compounded by shortcomings in the present planning and budget which wide agreement should evolve on activities to be financed from the budget of the Organization. In practice, it has not fulfilled its purpose. Many of the existing procedures for preparation and approval of the programme budget still correspond to the times when the budget was formulated by object of expenditure and not in terms of programmes. Furthermore, Member States can only give their opinion on the programme budget at a very late stage in the process. There is a need to develop budget procedures which would associate Member States more actively with the preparation of the medium-term plan and the programme budget and which would better facilitate broad agreement among Member States on budgetary matters, while fully preserving the principle of sovereign equality of States enshrined in the Charter.

8. As the Group of High-level Intergovernmental Experts began its work, it acknowledged that was not within the mandate of the Group to address the

immediate and short-term financial problems of the United Nations. The Group had rather been called upon by the General Assembly to identify, within the framework of the Charter, measures for further improving the administrative and financial functioning of the Organization in medium and longer term.

9. The Group furthermore noted that it had been requested to consider only the administrative and financial matters of the United Nations and its subsidiary bodies. The relationship between the Organization, including its subsidiary bodies, and the specialized agencies, as well as system-wide co-ordination and co-operation, thus falls outside the mandate of the Group.

10. On this basis, the Group undertook a review of the intergovernmental machinery of the United Nations and its subsidiary organs, the structure of the United Nations Secretariat, the personnel policy of the Organization, activities related to co-ordination, monitoring, evaluation and inspection and budgetary matters. Throughout this process, the Group did consistently seek to identify measures to improve the administrative and financial functioning of the Organization. The Group noted also that some of the measures it recommended would improve the cost effectiveness of the Organization, thereby increasing the resources available to substantive activities.

11. The time constraints under which the Group had to work did not allow it to make a comprehensive study of some of the extremely complex problems put before it. The Group was established in late February 1986. It had to spread its research, its discussions and the drafting of its report over four sessions, the total meeting time representing only eight weeks.

12. In accordance with paragraph 6 of General Assembly resolution 40/237 of 18 December 1985, the Secretary-General met with the Group on several occasions to give his views on questions before it. The Secretariat of the Organization responded to requests from the Group for information which enabled the Group to have before it a considerable volume of documentation.

13. In these circumstance and in view of the breadth and complexity of the subject considered, the Group felt that a distinction should be drawn between:

(a) Those questions on which it was possible for it to submit precise recommendations that might be taken into consideration by the General Assembly upon the submission of its report;

(b) Those questions that merited and required examination in greater depth and with regard to which it had to be satisfied with defining lines of approach and suggesting methods for subsequent research.

14. The Group has performed its work on the basis of full respect for the principles and provisions of the Charter. The recommendations of the Group are set out below. The Group is convinced that the measures it recommends will contribute to improve further "the efficiency of the administrative and

financial functioning" of the United Nations, "which would contribute to strengthening its effectiveness in dealing with political, economic and social issues".

15. The Group remains convinced that it has only begun a reform process. This process must now be carried further by other intergovernmental bodies and by the Secretary-General of the Organization. The Group considers that it has fully discharged its mandate and concluded its work with the submission of this report. The continued commitment of Member States to the United Nations and the process of multilateral diplomacy that it represents is indispensable if this process is to succeed.

II. The intergovernmental machinery and its functioning

16. As new tasks have emerged without old ones being solved, the agenda of the United Nations has shown sustained growth. This expansion in the agenda has led to a parallel growth in the intergovernmental machinery, which has in some cases resulted in duplication of agenda and work, particularly in the economic and social fields. The efficiency of the Organization has suffered through this process and there is a need for structural reform of the intergovernmental machinery.

17. The Group is convinced that reforms should also be carried out with regard to the frequency and duration of United Nations conferences ad meetings and to the volume of documentation. Many recommendations to this effect have been suggested in the past, to little or no avail. There is ample room for reductions in many areas. In addition to having a positive effect on the substantive work to be done, such reductions would lead to economics in conference and documentation costs.

18. Besides eliminating obvious duplication in the agenda and programmes of work, there is also an urgent need for improved co-ordination of activities undertaken both within the United Nations itself and throughout the United Nations system. This is particularly valid for activities within the economic and social sectors, and encompasses the work of the various secretariats as well as of the intergovernmental machinery. The structure of the present system makes co-ordination of activities a difficult undertaking. The large number of mechanisms established for co-ordination testify to this.

19. The magnitude and complexity of the intergovernmental structure is such, however, that recommendations for more fundamental structural reforms require a comprehensive review of the present situation. On account of the limited time available to it, the Group has not found it possible to undertake such an in-depth review. As suggested below, the Group is of the opinion that such a careful and thorough review should be entrusted to an intergovernmental body.

20. Pending such a comprehensive review of the intergovernmental machinery of the United Nations and its subsidiary organs, the Group considers that there are some specific changes that can and should be implemented without delay.

21. On this basis, the Group submits the following recommendations:

A. *Specific recommendations*

Recommendation 1

The Committee on Conference should be strengthened and be given broader responsibilities:

(a) The highest level of membership on the Committee should be ensured;

(b) The Committee should be entrusted with monitoring the implementation of the recommendations of the General Assembly on all organizational aspects dealing with conferences, meetings and related documentation, and report to it annually. It should also monitor the policy on publications, with the assistance of the Publications Board and taking into account positions adopted by the Committee on Information;

(c) The Committee should also ensure the harmonization of working procedures of conference services among all United Nations offices performing such services;

(d) Within an overall level of resources allocated for conference services by the General Assembly, the Committee should be entrusted with the task of preparing the calendar of conferences and meetings within this level, in close co-operation with the Advisory Committee on Administrative and Budgetary Questions; such calendar should be submitted to the General Assembly for approval;

(e) The Committee should plan and co-ordinate conferences and meetings, in particular by staggering them throughout the year; this would ensure better utilization of conference facilities and established resources, limit the use of temporary personnel and reduce overtime.

Recommendation 2

The number of conferences and meetings can be significantly reduced and their duration shortened without affecting the substantive work of the Organization. To this end:

(a) The Economic and Social Council should be invited to hold an annual session;

(b)   The General Assembly and the Economic and Social Council should request their subsidiary bodies to review urgently their current agenda and schedules of meetings in order to reduce substantially their number, frequency and duration. In this context, the move towards biennialization of conferences and meetings, which has been initiated particularly in the economic and social fields, should be vigorously pursued;

(c)   As there continues to be large differences between planned and actual utilization of available conference resources by numerous United Nations bodies, these bodies should be requested to provide a more realistic assessment of their needs.[1]   The Committee on Conferences should, in co-operation with the bodies concerned, ensure that wastage of conference - service resources is minimized through a reduction in the projections of the length and, where appropriate, the frequency of meetings of those bodies that have consistently utilized a lower level of resources than planned;

(d)   Until 1978, a number of resolutions had requested that only one major conference be scheduled annually.   The decision of the General Assembly that no more than five special conferences should take place in a given year and that no more than one special conference should be convened at the same time should be strictly implemented.

Recommendation 3

The procedures and methods of work of the General Assembly and its subsidiary organs, particularly its Main Committees, should be streamlined and thereby made more effective. Many recommendations have been put forward to this effect.[2] In this connection, the following points should be emphasized:

(a)   The high cost of holding meetings of the principal organs of the United Nations makes it imperative to utilize fully available services.   The responsibility for this rests with the presiding officers of these organs, as well as the representatives of Member States;

(b)   The agenda of the General Assembly should be rationalized by grouping or merging, to the extent possible, related items and by setting an interval of two or more years for the discussion of certain items;

(c)   The possibility of holding the meetings of the Fourth Committee and the Special Political Committee in sequential order should be addressed;

(d)   The distribution of agenda items among the Main Committees of the General Assembly and between those Committees and the plenary meetings of the Assembly should be reviewed, in order to ensure the best possible use of the expertise of the Committees and of the time and resources available;

(e)   As a rule, the General Assembly should not create new subsidiary organs without discontinuing existing ones;

(f) Efforts should be made to reduce the number of resolutions adopted by the General Assembly. Resolutions should request reports of the Secretary-General only in cases where that would be indispensable for facilitating the implementation of these resolutions or the continued examination of the question.

Recommendation 4

The existing principle that United Nations bodies should meet at their respective established headquarters, as provided for in General Assembly resolution 40/243 of 18 December 1985, should be strictly enforced. Whenever the Assembly accepts an invitation from the Government of a Member State to hold a conference or meeting away from established headquarters, the additional cost should be borne in full by that Government. The methods of budgeting these costs should be improved so as to ensure that all additional costs are accounted for.

Recommendation 5

Construction of United Nations conference facilities should only be undertaken when sufficient resources are available, bearing in mind the desirability of decentralizing the activities of the United Nations wherever appropriate.

Recommendation 6

Reimbursement of travel costs for representatives of Member States attending the General Assembly should be limited to the least developed countries.

Recommendation 7

Since the cost of processing and distributing as official documents communications received from Member States is estimated at $2 million per biennium, Member States should co-operate in significantly curtailing this practice. The provisions of General Assembly decision 34/401 should be strictly adhered to.

B. *Comparative study of the intergovernmental machinery and its functioning*

22. As stated in paragraphs 16 to 19, the Group is of the opinion that the magnitude and complexity of the intergovernmental machinery, particularly in the economic and social fields, is such that recommendations for more fundamental structural reforms require a comprehensive review of the present situation. There are, for instance, in these fields more than 150 committees, commissions, sub-committees, sub-commissions and working groups. Within

the time span set for the Group's work by the General Assembly, it has been impossible to address in depth this complex issue and the Group will consequently recommend that this be done by an intergovernmental body.

23. The need to improve the efficiency of the United Nations, the importance of the economic and social activities and the fact that they require a significant proportion of resources of the Organization make it necessary to implement reforms in these areas a matter of priority.

24. The Group therefore submits the following recommendation:

Recommendation 8

(1)   A careful and in-depth study of the intergovernmental structure in the economic and social fields should be undertaken by an intergovernmental body to be designated by the General Assembly. This body should preferably have a limited membership, at the highest possible level of representation and based on the principle of equitable geographical distribution. In discharging its tasks, the body should seek the co-operation of the intergovernmental organs whose functions are being reviewed in the study and draw on the expertise of relevant United Nations bodies, such as the Joint Inspection Unit and the United Nations Institute for Training and Research.

(2)   In general terms, the study should include a comparative analysis of agenda, calendars and programmes of work of the General Assembly, the Economic and Social Council and related subsidiary bodies, in particular the United Nations Conference on Trade and Development, the United Nations Development Programme, the United Nations Fund for Population Activities, the United Nations Children's Fund, the United Nations Environment Programme, the United Nations Centre for Human Settlements (Habitat), the Office of the United Nations High Commissioner for Refugees and the World Food Council. The study should also include their support structure.

(3)   The purpose of the study should be, *inter alia*, to:

(a)   Identify measures to rationalize and simplify the intergovernmental structure, avoid duplication and consider consolidating and co-ordinating overlapping activities and merging existing bodies in order to improve their work and make the structure more responsive to present needs;

(b)   Develop criteria for the establishment and duration of subsidiary bodies, including periodic reviews of their work and mechanisms for implementing their decisions;

(c)   Define in precise terms areas of responsibility for the various bodies. Particular attention should be given to strengthening the coherence and integrity of the structure, to facilitating the formulation of a comprehensive approach to development issues and to the necessity of putting more emphasis on regional and subregional co-operation;

(d) Consider the establishment of a single governing body responsible for the management and control, at the intergovernmental level, of United Nations operational activities for development;

(e) Improve the system of reporting from subsidiary to principal organs, thereby reducing the number of reports and avoiding duplication of documentation;

(f) Strengthen on a continuous basis the co-ordination of activities in the economic and social fields under the leadership of the Secretary-General.

(4) The study should be undertaken as a matter of priority and its findings and recommendations should be presented to the General Assembly not later than at its forty-third session.

C. Co-ordination

25. The United Nations has been entrusted, under Article 58 of the Charter, with the responsibility of making "recommendations for the coordination of the policies and activities of the specialized agencies". The mandate of the Group is to improve the efficiency of the United Nations. The Group realizes that effective co-ordination between organizations in the system is a necessity and took note of General Assembly resolution 32/197 of 20 December 1977, in which the Assembly called upon the Director-General for Development and International Economic Co-operation to provide effective leadership in exercising overall co-ordination within the system and the standing agreements between the United Nations and the specialized agencies, which called upon each agency to co-ordinate its activities with those of the United Nations.

26. A number of attempts to improve co-ordination of the United Nations system have failed. The Group nevertheless believes that efforts have to be pursued and that they should begin by the main agencies of the United Nations system defining a common approach to the possible solutions of the economic and social problems. The executive heads of these main agencies should accordingly exchange views on the policies and programmes they are proposing to Member States, in order to improve the compatibility of these programmes.

27. The Group therefore submits the following recommendations:

Recommendation 9

The machinery for inter-agency co-ordination should be streamlined. Maximum use should be made of flexible *ad hoc* arrangements designed to meet specific requirements.

Recommendation 10

Executive heads of the International Labour Organisation, the United Nations Educational, Scientific and Cultural Organization, the Food and Agriculture Organization of the United Nations, the World Health Organization, the United Nations Industrial Development Organization, the United Nations Conference on Trade and Development, the International Atomic Energy Agency, the General Agreement on Tariffs and Trade, the International Bank for Reconstruction and Development and the International Monetary Fund should be invited to hold an annual one-week session under the chairmanship of the Secretary-General, assisted by the Director General for Development and International Economic Co-operation and the Under-Secretary-General for International Economic and Social Affairs, to discuss major policy questions in the economic and social fields and improve the co-ordination of their programmes. They would report on a biennial basis to their respective governing bodies.

Recommendation 11

In order to strengthen the co-ordination of operational activities at the national level, in conformity with the policies of the Governments concerned, the central co-ordinating role of the United Nations Development Programme (UNDP) in these matters should be reaffirmed and the authority of the resident co-ordinators should, wherever possible, be clarified and confirmed with respect to non-UNDP programmes.

Recommendation 12

The cost effectiveness and efficiency of the field representation of the various programmes should be reviewed by the relevant governing bodies, with a view to merging field offices of the United Nations whenever feasible, thereby achieving better co-ordination and reducing some of the administrative costs.

Recommendation 13

The efforts to harmonize the format of the programme budgets of the organizations of the United Nations system should be vigorously pursued. The administrative budgets of the United Nations affiliates, sh as the United Nations Development Programme, the United Nations Environment Programme, the Office of the United Nations High Commissioner for Refugees, and the United Nations Fund for Population Activities, should, as far as possible, adopt the format of the United Nations budget.

III. Structure of the Secretariat

28. Over the years, there has been a significant growth of the Secretariat. This expansion in the Secretariat structure has, at times, been rapid and has resulted

in duplication of work and reduced productivity and has made it difficult to make maximum use of resources. Co-ordination of activities has been made difficult on account of the extent and complexity of the Organization's structure.

29. The Group has examined the present organizational structure, bearing in mind that the aim should be to enhance the capacity of the Organization to implement the tasks entrusted to it as efficiently and cost-effectively as possible. The Group is convinced that in many areas there is room for changes which can lead to an overall increase in the productivity and efficiency of the Secretariat, and which would make it more responsive to the needs of Member States.

30. Firstly, today's structure is both too top-heavy and too complex. In the regular budget, there are 28 posts at the Under-Secretary-General level and 29 posts at the Assistant Secretary-General level. In addition, there are seven and 23 posts at these levels, respectively, that are financed from extrabudgetary sources. These posts include those of the United Nations-affiliated bodies, such as the United Nations Development Programme and the United Nations Children's Fund. The establishment of this large number of top-echelon posts has inevitably resulted in dispersion of responsibility, as well as diffuse lines of authority, accountability and communication. A substantial reduction in the number of these posts, together with clear and simpler lines of authority and responsibility, will have a positive impact on the Organization's ability to carry out the tasks entrusted to it. The aim must be a Secretariat with an increased capacity and ability to deliver the services required with high quality.

31. Secondly, the present organizational structure is too fragmented. For example, the Secretariat has nine political and 11 economic and social departments, centres or offices, excluding the regional commissions. Such a fragmentation inevitably leads to duplication of work, both within the Secretariat and *vis-à-vis* other organs of the United Nations system. It makes co-ordination more difficult and leads to a reduced quality of performance. To improve and strengthen the Organization, offices, departments and other units dealing with matters of a similar or related character should therefore be consolidated.

32. Thirdly, concerning the size of the Secretariat, even with the present organizational structure, a leaner Secretariat will enhance productivity and improve efficiency. Furthermore, increased efficiency could be achieved in the administrative and related functions of the Secretariat, without affecting the quality of the services provided, through the elimination of duplication, the strengthening of authority by suppressing hierarchical layers and by improving the personnel policies, particularly through the use of objective methods of recruitment.

33. Fourthly, in many countries a variety of United Nations offices are at present established at the same location. In many cases, they may be consolidated, with resulting increased efficiency and financial savings.

34. Emphasizing both the leadership responsibilities and prerogatives of the Secretary-General as chief administrative officers of the Organization in accordance with the provisions of the Charter, and noting with appreciation his efforts to improve the efficiency of the Secretariat, the Group, in accordance with its mandate, submits the recommendations set forth below. The implementation of the recommendations relating to the organizational structure of the Secretariat and the redeployment and reduction of personnel should be guided by the legislative mandates and the relative importance and objectives in the political, economic and social fields as approved by the various legislative bodies. It should also take into account the principles laid down in the Charter relating to the staff of the Organization. The Group suggests that the recommendations set forth below should be implemented over a period of three years.

35. The Group therefore submits the following recommendations:

A. *General recommendations*

Recommendation 14

The organizational structure of the Secretariat should be simplified. In so doing, the following consideration should be borne in mind:

(a)   The present structure is top-heavy and too complex. There is a need for simplification and for developing clearer lines of authority, responsibility, accountability and communication;

(b)   Departments, offices and other units dealing with questions of a similar or related character should be merged when such a consolidation would contribute to improving the efficiency of the Organization;

(c)   There is a need for improved co-ordination on a continuing basis of the work of departments, offices and other units in order to avoid duplication of work;

(d)   United Nations offices are at present established at the same location in many cities and countries. In most cases, they may be consolidated with no loss of efficiency and with resulting economies both in personnel and general costs.

Recommendation 15

(1)   A substantial reduction in the number of staff members at all levels, but particularly in the higher echelons, is desirable. It should be possible to undertake such a reduction in a relatively short period of time without causing any negative impact on the current level of programme activities of the United Nations, as determined by the General Assembly and other legislative organs.

(2)   To this end:

(a)   The overall number of regular budget posts should be reduced by 15 per cent within a period of three years;

(b)   The number of regular budget posts at the level of Under-Secretary-General and Assistant Secretary-General should be reduced by 25 per cent within a period of three years or less, with a comparable reduction in posts at those levels funded from extrabudgetary sources.

(3)   The Secretary-General should submit to the General Assembly his plans for implementing the recommendations in paragraphs (1) and (2) above. When drawing up such plans, the Secretary-General should, *inter alia*, be guided by:

(a)   The necessity of securing the highest standards of efficiency, competence and integrity of the staff, with due regard to equitable geographical distribution;

(b)   An analysis of work-loads in the various departments and offices, taking into account the efficiency that can be gained through the consolidation of functions and the elimination of duplication;

(c)   The need to avoid any negative effects on the implementation of programmes;

(d)   The continuing need to recruit new staff members, especially at the junior Professional levels, to ensure vigorous Secretariat structure. The number of staff members recruited at the P-1, P-2 and P-3 levels should not fall below the average number of those recruited during the years 1982, 1983 and 1984.   Such new recruitment should, however, be balanced with an equivalent reduction in staff, so that the aim of a net reduction of 15 per cent is achieved within a three-year period.

(4)   A further reduction in the overall number of posts could be undertaken as a result of restructuring of the intergovernmental machinery and the Secretariat.

B. *Political affairs*

36. As indicated in paragraph 31, the Secretariat has nine political departments, centre or offices. Such fragmentation inevitably leads to duplication of work, dispersion of responsibility and blurred lines of authority, accountability and communication.

37. The Group therefore submits the following recommendations:

Recommendation 16

A review of the political departments and offices that carry out a wide variety of functions should be undertaken, with a view to consolidating and streamlining the organizational structure in this field in order to strengthen the Organization's capacity to deal with these important matters.

Recommendation 17

The administrative functions of the Office for Field Operational and External Support Activities should be transferred to the Department of Administration and Management. Most of the staff in the field offices should be recruited locally. The number of internationally recruited field service officers should be substantially reduced. The political information functions entrusted to the Office should be reassigned, taking into consideration recommendation 18.

Recommendation 18

There is a duplication efforts with regard to the dissemination of news and political analysis activities in various departments, namely, the Office for Field Operational and External Support Activities, the Department of Political and Security Council Affairs, the Department of Political Affairs, Trusteeship and Decolonization and the Department of Public Information. These activities should be rationalized and co-ordinated with a view to achieving substantial savings and better utilization of resources.

Recommendation 19

Activities relating to Namibia are currently undertaken by several offices in the Secretariat, each of which requires its own administrative structure and specialized substantive staff. In order to enhance the Organization's capacity to deal with this important matter and without in any way limiting the programmes and services in this area, support activities of the United Nations Council for Namibia and of the Office of the United Nations Commission for Namibia should be consolidated and strengthened by providing full support, as recommended by the recent International Conference for the Immediate Independence of Namibia.

Recommendation 20

The Department for Disarmament Affairs should be structured in such a way that it may better assist Member States in following the disarmament negotiations and related disarmament questions.

Recommendation 21

In view of the decrease in the work-load of the Department of Political Affairs, Trusteeship and Decolonization as a result of progress achieved in matters of decolonization and trusteeship, there should be a corresponding reduction in the number of its staff.

Recommendation 22

Special economic assistance programmes currently administered by the Office for Special Political Questions should be transferred to the United Nations Development Programme. Future programmes should be administered by the Programme once they are approved. This measure should in no way affect these programmes or reduce their effectiveness.

Recommendation 23

Several United Nations offices are at present administering emergency, humanitarian and special economic assistance programmes. Wherever feasible, the work of those offices should be co-ordinated and rationalized to minimize duplication and to ensure the most efficient utilization of the United Nations resources in this field.

Recommendation 24

The United Nations Development Programme should be requested to consider the feasibility of taking over the functions currently performed by the Office of the United Nations Disaster Relief Co-ordinator.

C. *Economic and social affairs*

38. The economic and social sectors are of great importance to Member States and entail a very high percentage of allocated resources. They are also without a doubt the most complex and varied area of United Nations activities, which require an extensive and in-depth study that the Group was not in a position to carry out.

39. The problems identified by the Group in the economic and social fields relate not only to the duplication noted in the political area but also to the fact that the offices responsible for the research, analysis and operational activities in economic and social matters are not sufficiently responsive to the changing

realities at the global and regional levels. The multiplicity of offices dealing with economic and social matters and their dispersion create additional problems of co-ordination and communication that are not found in the political field.

40. In many cases it has not been possible for the Group to recommend concrete solutions to the present deficiencies, as such solutions can only emerge as a result of a more in-depth review. The Group has, however, endeavoured to identify and briefly analyse these issues, and to point to possible avenues for solutions, keeping in mind the importance of ensuring that the work of the Secretariat fully meetings the needs of Member States. In this context, it should be borne in mind that the structure of the various offices of the Secretariat and other United Nations entities in this area are intimately linked to the intergovernmental structure, which is dealt with in section II of the present report.

41. The Group submits the following recommendations:

Recommendation 25

(1)   A review of the tasks performed by the Department of International Economic and Social Affairs (DIESA), the Department of Technical Co-operation for Development (DTCD), the secretariats of the United Nations Conference on Trade and Development, the United Nations Environment Programme, the United Nations Centre for Human Settlements (Habitat) and other Secretariat offices and those of other United Nations bodies such as the United Nations Development Programme, the Office of the United Nations High Commissioner for Refugees, the United Nations Children's Fund and the World Food Programme should be undertaken with a view to eliminating duplication and to ensuring that the offices concerned are able to be more responsive to the needs of Member States. The General Agreement on Tariffs and Trade should be invited to participate in this review.

(2)   Any reorganization in the important sector should help to ensure that the Secretariat has the ability to assist Member States. In this context, the activities of the Centre for Science and Technology for Development should be evaluated and the feasibility of integrating the Centre in to DIESA and DTCD should be considered. The purpose should be to achieve a higher level of effectiveness in this sector, which is of particular importance to the economic and social development of Member States.

(3)   In this context, the functions of the Office of the Director-General for Development and International Economic Co-operation should also be reviewed. The authority of the Director-General should be enhanced so that he may fully exercise the functions envisaged by the General Assembly in its resolution 32/197 of 20 December 1977 as regards co-ordination within the system in the field of development and international economic co-operation.

(4)   Consideration should be given to establishing at a single location all departments and offices of the United Nations dealing with economic and social matters.

Recommendation 26

The Department of Technical Co-operation for Development should be made more responsive to the actual needs of the developing countries. Duplication and overlapping of activities between the Department and other United Nations Development Programme, should be avoided. For these purposes, a review of the Department should be undertaken.

Recommendation 27

Some of the activities of the regional commissions are not fully suited to the current needs of Member States in the region concerned.   Greater specialization is needed in areas of importance to Member States while keeping of mind the need to avoid duplication and overlapping with other organizations of the United Nations system. The structures and activities of the commissions should therefore be examined in the context of the study suggested in recommendation 8, with a view to improving their effectiveness in furthering multilateral, subregional and interregional co-operation in the economic and social fields.

Recommendation 28

It is observed that the regular budget allocation for the Economic Commission for Europe (ECE) does not include the cost of administration, conferences and general services. These services are provided by the United Nations Office at Geneva to ECE and were to the tune of $35,281,500 in 1984-1985. This figure was provided by the SecretaryGeneral in his proposed programme budget for the biennium 1984-1985. On account of inflation, the comparative figures for the biennium 1986-1987 could perhaps be increased by 10 per cent, to $38.8 million.   The total amount for conference services, administration and common services in the budget for 1986-1987 for the Economic and Social Commission for Asia and the Pacific is $18.5 million, for the Economic Commission for Latin America and the Caribbean, $21.3 million, for the Economic Commission for Africa, $18.7 million and for the Economic and Social Commission for Western Asia, $13.5 million. These are, however, included within the regular budgets of these commissions, unlike ECE. Therefore, the format for the presentation of resources pertaining to the regional commissions should be harmonized in future programme budgets.

Recommendation 29

Keeping in mind the need to avoid duplication, the functions of the Office of Secretariat Services for Economic and Social Matters should be reassigned to the Department of Conference Services for technical servicing activities (such as the editing of documents) and to the Department of International Economic and Social Affairs for substantive, servicing and co-ordination matters.

D. *Administration and other fields*

42. The administrative and related functions of the Secretariat require a sizeable share of the budget of the Organization. The Group believes that increased efficiency could be accomplished in these fields without affecting the quality of the services provided. This could be achieved through eliminating duplication, strengthening lines of authority and suppressing hierarchical layers. In particular, the process of programme planning and budgeting needs to be brought under a more coherent structure. The Group attaches major importance to bringing about more coherence into the administrative and programme planning procedures and this objective should be reflected in the reorganized structure of the Secretariat.

43. The Group is also of the opinion that administrative and general service costs should be reduced. The share of common service costs in the programme budget should be gradually reduced so that maximum resources would become available to substantive activities. To this end, the present financial and administrative procedures should be simplified. Procurement procedures and practices should be improved to ensure maximum efficiency. Automation and use of modern technical equipment should be further pursued where it results in net savings compared to personnel costs. Such a streamlining will not only improve the Organization's cost effectiveness, but will also increase the resources available to substantive activities.

44. The Group therefore submits the following recommendations:

Recommendation 30

The Department of Administration and Management should be streamlined to increase its efficiency and to achieve cost effectiveness of administrative services. Particular attention should be given to the need to avoid duplication of work, fragmentation of responsibility and diffuse lines of accountability.

Recommendation 31

The Management Advisory Services, which was established to advise on management techniques and to evaluate management structures and weaknesses, is of marginal usefulness and the Service should be abolished.

Recommendation 32

All activities relating to programme planning and budgeting should be brought together under a coherent structure.

Recommendation 33

Support activities for the permanent liaison offices in New York of various Secretariat entities should be consolidated in a single office.

Recommendation 34

The Department of Conference Services should be rationalized with a view to making it more efficient. The current external printing arrangements should be made more cost-effective. The publication programme should be more closely monitored and streamlined with a view to reducing the overall number of publications, improving their quality and maximizing the sale of successful publications.

Recommendation 35

The amount spent on outside consultants exceeds at present $8 million per biennium. Although, for certain tasks and on an *ad hoc*, basis, it might be beneficial to the Organization to use outside consultants on a diversified geographical basis, the amount spent on such services is too high and should be reduced by 30 per cent with immediate effect. Particularly, the practice of hiring retired staff members should be abolished.

Recommendation 36

Concurrent with the reduction in the overall size of the Secretariat, there should be a reduction in the requirements for rented premises. In this connection, optimum utilization of space should be pursued. Member States and other users occupying office space on United Nations premises should pay a rent based on current commercial rates.

Recommendation 37

(1) A thorough review of the functions and working methods as well as of the policies of the Department of Public Information should be conducted, with a view to bringing its role and policies up to date in order to improve the capacity and ability of the Department to provide information on United Nations activities as approved by the intergovernmental bodies. To this end, the working methods of the Department should be rationalized, in order that the funds allocated to that Department should, to a larger extent than hitherto, be used for programme activities.

(2) The Group has noted that information activities are currently conducted by several departments and offices in the Secretariat. Such activities should, to the extent possible, be consolidated in the Department of Public Information.

(3) A review of the functions and activities of the United Nations information centres should be undertaken by the Secretary-General and, to the extent that the quality of public information activities would not be hampered, the consolidation of such centres with other existing United Nations offices should be undertaken as mentioned in recommendation 12.

Recommendation 38

(1) The present level of official travel should be reduced by 20 per cent. There are too many missions and the Secretariat staff assigned to service conferences tends to be excessive, particularly from the Department of Public Information. The number and duration of missions should be reduced, as should the number of staff members attending conferences. Such a reduction can be done without prejudice to the quality of services and public information coverage.

(2) As a rule, first-class travel should be limited to the SecretaryGeneral.

Recommendation 39

The international audit function should be separated administratively and be independent from the function of implementation and disbursement of funds. To this end, the Internal Audit Division, which is now a part of the Department of Administration and Management, should become an independent unit.

Recommendation 40

The functions of the executive office in each department or office should be consolidated into the office of the head of department or office in a compact and streamlined unit.

IV. Measures regarding personnel

45. The efficiency of the United Nations depends to a large extent on the performance of its Secretariat and other organs; the quality and usefulness of the Secretariat are, in turn, dependent upon the quality and dedication of its staff. Article 97 of the Charter, in designating the Secretary-General as the chief administrative offices, confers upon him the responsibility for managing the Organization. In selecting and managing the staff, the Secretary-General is guided by Articles 100 and 101 of the Charter, which state that the staff should not seek or receive instructions from any Government or from any other authority external to the Organization and that the paramount consideration in the employment of staff shall be the necessity of securing the highest standards of efficiency, competence and integrity, with due regard being paid to the importance of recruiting staff on as wide a geographical basis as possible.

46. The Group is aware of the fact that, particularly during the last 10 to 15 years, numerous studies (mostly by the International Civil Service Commission and the Joint Inspection Unit) have been made on the management of human resources in the United Nations. Many of the recommendations resulting from such studies have been reflected in resolutions of the General Assembly. There is therefore now a body of guidelines and mandates on a wide variety of subjects such as recruitment methods, the recruitment of women, the principle of geographical distribution particularly at higher-level posts, the age of appointment, the retirement age, occupational groups and career development. These mandates guide the Secretary-General in the discharge of his important responsibilities.

47. The Group is convinced that efficiency management of the staff should rest upon clear, coherent and transparent rules and regulations. This will enable the Organization to secure and retain the services of staff meeting the highest standards.

48. Clear and coherent rules and regulations are not in themselves, however, sufficient to ensure that the ability and the qualifications of the staff are utilized in the most efficient way or that the staff derive satisfaction and pride from their work. The officials responsible for the management of the staff, that is, not only the office responsible for human resources management, but also every manager who is in charge of au nit, section, division or department, must implement these rules and regulations and create a challenging environment where the staff can and are motivated to give their best efforts to further the goals of the Organization. It is important, indeed fundamental, to develop an institutional spirit in the Organization and to strengthen it as an entity. In this endeavour, staff members at every level have an indispensable role to play. Special responsibility for creating a healthy climate rests with the senior managers. In this respect, the importance of selecting high-level officials with the necessary management skills cannot be over-emphasized.

49. In approaching questions of personnel policy, the Group also believes that it is essential to acknowledge the responsibility and prerogatives of the Secretary-General as chief administrative officer of the United Nations and to emphasize that his authority under the Charter should in no way be prejudiced.

50. With these considerations in mind, the Group submits the following recommendations:

A. *General recommendation*

Recommendation 41

Personnel policy and management in the United Nations has suffered as a result of the considerable political and other pressures that have influenced the selection of staff. The Secretary-General should exercise greater leadership in personnel matters and ensure that the selection of staff is done strictly in accordance with the principles of the Charter. He should improve the management of human resources, protect the authority of the official in charge of personnel and instruct all other senior officials to refrain from influencing the selection of staff. The office responsible should be renamed "Office of Human Resources Management".

B. *Recommendations to be reflected in the staff rules and regulations*

Recommendation 42

The personnel management of the Organization must be based upon clear, coherent and transparent rules. Present inconsistencies and ambiguities should be eliminated. The current staff rules and regulations should be revised to take into account the resolutions and decisions on personnel policy already adopted by the General Assembly and the specific recommendations set forth below. Measures taken to implement these rules and regulations should be clearly set out in a personnel manual which should be widely available and kept up to date. These revised rules and regulations should be applicable to all entities under the authority of the Secretary-General in the Organization, that is, the Secretariat and other subsidiary organs of the Organization. Moreover, while the Group recognizes that its mandate pertains only to a review of the United Nations, it wishes to emphasize its belief that a coherent common system is highly desirable and, in this spirit, the applicability of these new rules and regulations to other organizations in the United Nations systems should be considered.

Recommendation 43

(1)   The Group endorses the principle of recruitment of the staff through national competitive examinations for posts at the P-1 to P-3 levels, in order to ensure that the candidates selected meet the highest standards. Such examinations should be organized without discriminating against any Member State so as to ensure that the principles of selecting staff on the basis of merit and competence and on as wide a geographical basis as possible are respected. The internal and external examinations should be governed by the same standards and criteria.

(2)   Selection of candidates for all posts when competitive examinations are not used should be based on objective methods and clear criteria. For P-4 and P-5 levels, tests or individual examinations designed to determine drafting ability should be part of such methods.

Recommendation 44

The proportion of appointments at various levels in the Professional category should be considered, with a view to having a greater proportion of appointments at the junior Professional levels (P-1 to P-3).

Recommendation 45

Staff members should be eligible for permanent appointments after having served three years in the United Nations. This period should be sufficient to evaluate the performance of a staff member and determine whether or not the staff member meetings the criteria for such appointments.

Recommendation 46

Additional measures hold be taken by the Secretariat to ensure that an increasing proportion of the posts in the Professional category, particularly at the higher levels are filled by women, in accordance with the relevant resolutions of the General Assembly.

Recommendation 47

The Secretary-General should take additional measures to ensure that nationals of developing countries are duly represented at senior levels, in accordance with the relevant resolution of the General Assembly.

Recommendation 48

Staff members who are recruited on a post-by-post basis rather than in the context of an occupational group may be tied too closely to their post and their reassignment to different functions may be difficult. Staff members should therefore be recruited and their careers developed on the basis of occupational groups. This would facilitate mobility and ensure optimum use of their qualifications and experience.

Recommendation 49

A job rotation system among the various duty stations should be developed for staff members in the Professional category as part of the career development plans.

Recommendation 50

The Secretary-General should include in his annual reports to the General Assembly on personnel questions a section related to the ratings of the performance of staff and their promotion. The system of performance evaluation should be improved by introducing an element of comparison in the rating of staff.

Recommendation 51

Strict and clear criteria should be developed for the promotion of staff at all levels. In this context, the functions and the composition of the appointment and promotion bodies should be reviewed, with a view to securing fairness and objectivity in the management of appointments and promotions. Such bodies should be structure on the basis of occupational groups.

Recommendation 52

The mandatory retirement age of 60 should be strictly applied in accordance with General Assembly resolution 35/210 of 17 December 1980.

C. *Other recommendations*

Recommendation 53

The International Civil Service Commission is responsible for establishing standards in matters dealing with personnel management. The mandate of the Commission should be modified so that it can also monitor the implementation of such standards by the United Nations and report thereon to the General Assembly.

Recommendation 54

It would be in the interest of the Organization to renew periodically the leadership of departments and offices. To this effect, the Secretary-General should not, as a rule, extend the service of Under-Secretaries-General and Assistant Secretaries-General for a period exceeding 10 years.

Recommendation 55

The General Assembly, in its resolution 35/210 of 17 December 1980, reaffirmed the principle that "no post should be considered the exclusive preserve of any Member State, or group of States" and it requested the Secretary-General "to ensure that this principle is applied faithfully in accordance with the principle of equitable geographical distribution". In order to facilitate the implementation of this recommendation, no more than 50 per cent of the nationals of any one Member State employed by the United Nations should be appointed on a fixed-term basis.

* * *

Some members of the Group indicated that the second sentence of recommendation 55 violated the provisions of section I, paragraph 4, of General Assembly resolution 35/210 and, therefore, should not be included in the report of the Group.

Recommendation 56

A vacant post should not be filled merely because it becomes vacant. The work-load in the organizational unit in which the post is located should be considered before deciding whether it is necessary to fill that post. Such a measure will ensure an efficient use of the resources of the Organization.

Recommendation 57

In order to secure the necessary flexibility, the ratio between permanent staff members and staff members on fixed-term appointments should be reviewed with the objective of having an adequate range between the two categories. However, in order to ensure that the principle of equitable geographical distribution is faithfully reflected among the Secretariat staff holding permanent appointments, at least 50 per cent of the nationals of any Member State working in the Secretariat should be employed on a permanent basis. The report of the Secretary-General on this question should be submitted to the General Assembly at its forty-third session.

* * *

Some members of the Group indicated that the second sentence of recommendation 57 ran counter to the principle of equitable geographical distribution and violated section I, paragraph 4, of General Assembly resolution 35/210 referred to in recommendation 55 and, therefore, should not be included in the report of the Group.

Recommendation 58

The content of the United Nations training programmes should be strictly geared to the needs of the Organization and their effectiveness carefully monitored to ensure optimum utilization of allocated resources.

Recommendation 59

The efficiency of the Organization would be increased if clear guidelines were established for the role and functions of the staff union, in order to ensure that the union does not infringe upon the managerial responsibilities of the Secretary-General. Staff unions or associations should finance all their activities from their own funds.

Recommendation 60

The system of administration of justice, as constituted at present, is cumbersome. The procedures should therefore be simplified to render the system more efficient and less costly. In its resolution 40/252 of 18 December 1985, the General Assembly endorsed the recommendations of the Advisory Committee on Administrative and Budgetary Questions that the

Secretary-General be requested to prepare an analysis of the problem and indicate which steps he has taken or intends to take simplify the procedures. This recommendation should be implemented without delay and the measures recommended taken as rapidly as possible.

Recommendation 61

The total entitlements (salaries and other conditions of service) of staff members have reached a level which gives reason for serious concern and it should be reduced. In particular, the elimination of the education grant for post-secondary studies and the establishment of a four-week annual leave system for all staff members should be considered for prompt implementation.

Recommendation 62

A serious effort should be made by the Secretary-General to discourage the present practice of transferring extrabudgetary posts to the regular budget.

V. Monitoring, evaluation and inspection

51. Monitoring, evaluation and inspection of the activities of the United Nations are of particular importance in order to secure administrative efficiency and proper use of funds. To safeguard and promote the confidence of Member States and of the international community in the United Nations, it is important that the activities of the Organization are undertaken in the most efficient manner, that resources available are used in an optimum way, and that the relevance, effectiveness and impact of the activities are assessed in the light of established goals and objectives. Monitoring, evaluation and inspection constitute an indispensable tool to achieve these goals.

52. The functions of the Joint Inspection Unit are, among other things, to monitor, inspect and evaluate the activities of the participating organizations, satisfying itself "that the activities undertaken by the organizations are carried out in the most economical manner and that the optimum use is made of resources available for carrying out these activities". Furthermore, the Joint Inspection Unit not only advises organizations on their methods for internal evaluation, but also makes *ad hoc* evaluations of programmes and activities. As to internal evaluation and monitoring, these functions are to varying degrees undertaken by the United Nations and its system of organizations. The Group believes that there is a need to improve further the present system.

53. Firstly, it is necessary to see that the reports of the Joint Inspection Unit are adequately dealt with at the intergovernmental level. Sufficient attention is not always given either to the reports as such or to the implementation of the recommendations contained therein. The competent and relevant bodies and organizations should, therefore, ensure that the reports are adequately dealt with and that the recommendations approved by them are implemented.

54. Secondly, the Group is of the opinion that more emphasis should be put on evaluation in order to increase the awareness of the bodies concerned regarding the status of implementation of the programmes adopted and their relevance, effectiveness and impact in achieving the goals set. It is also important in order to improve the internal evaluation system.

55. Thirdly, the work performed and some of the reports submitted by the inspectors should be improved upon. The quality and standard of the work performed are of course intimately linked to the competence of those entrusted with these tasks, as is true for the Secretariat. To a larger degree than hitherto, it is important to ensure that the inspectors appointed possess the necessary qualifications to undertake the variety of tasks with which they are faced. As laid down in the statute of the Joint Inspection Unit, it is also important to secure that the independence of the inspectors is safeguarded and that they are appointed on the basis of equitable geographical distribution.

56. The Group therefore submits the following recommendations:

Recommendation 63

In order to improve management, secure administrative efficiency and achieve greater co-ordination between organizations and organs, the members of the Joint Inspection Unit (JIU), in discharging their duties, should put more emphasis on the evaluation aspect of their work, a function which is already included in the statute of the Unit. To reflect this added emphasis on the preparation of the evaluation reports to be directed to intergovernmental bodies, JIU should be renamed Joint Inspection and Evaluation Unit and its statute revised accordingly.

Recommendation 65

The General Assembly should give the Joint Inspection Unit greater guidance on its programme of work with respect to the United Nations.

Recommendation 66

The reports of the Joint Inspection Unit, with summaries thereof, should be made available to all Member States. The General Assembly, in its resolution 38/229 of 20 December 1983, invited the United Nations organs, when considering reports of the Unit, to indicate those recommendations which they approved and those which they did not. The organizations of the system should be invited to follow the same procedure.

Recommendation 67

There should be increased co-operation between the Joint Inspection Unit and the External Auditors. The External Auditors should, on their part, put greater emphasis on management audits and other areas of importance as required by the legislative organs concerned. The internal and external audits should continue to be kept as two separate functions.

VI. Planning and budget procedure

A. *General considerations*

57. As a result of changing international circumstances, which give rise to new concerns and problems, and a corresponding change in the needs of Member States and the international community, the United Nations must constantly adjust its tasks within the provisions of the Charter. The medium term plan and the programme budget should have the necessary flexibility so that priorities and resources could be adjusted to the changing international circumstances and to the new challenges and problems that might arise. The procedures for reaching the widest possible agreement on the context and level of the budget, including the criteria for the setting of priorities and the mechanisms for applying them, are therefore particularly important.

58. Over the past 15 years, the General Assembly has established principles, methods and instruments which should have made it possible to reach satisfactory results in this area. The six-year medium-term plan should reflect the consolidated objectives and goals of Member States and should constitute the principal policy directive of the United Nations. It should serve as the basis for transforming these goals and objectives into action by guiding the resource allocation and the setting of priorities in the two-year programme budget.

59. The medium-term plan, the programme budget, the monitoring system and the evaluation system are meant to constitute an integrated process through which wide agreement should evolve on activities that should be financed over the regular budget of the Organization. The criteria for setting priorities among programmes adopted pursuant to General Assembly resolution 37/234 of 21 December 1982 and 38/227 A and B of 20 December 1983 should assist Member States and the Secretary-General in this process.

60. However, in terms of the programme budget, the medium-term plan does not, in reality, serve as the principal policy directive. The regulations and rules pertaining to the setting of priorities have not served the purposes for which they were intended to. The current decision-making procedures with respect to priorities do not correspond to those stipulated in the regulations and rules.

61. In the opinion of the Group, it is therefore important to rectify the present deficiencies and to develop planning and budget procedures, including the setting of priorities, which can facilitate agreement among Member States on the content and level of the budget of the Organization.

B. *Setting of priorities*

62. The criteria for the setting of relative priorities are set out in the Secretary-General's bulletin entitled "Regulations and Rules Governing Programme Planning, the Programme Aspects of the Budget, the Monitoring of Implementation and the Methods of Evaluation" (ST/SGB/204). These Regulations and Rules devote special attention to the application of priorities at all levels. Regulation 3.15, relating to the medium-term plan, states that "the establishment of priorities among both substantive programmes and common services shall form an integral part of the general planning ... process". The determining criteria are defined as being based "on the importance of the objective to Member States, the Organization's capacity to achieve it and the real effectiveness and usefulness of the results". Regulation 3.16 defines the process according to which intergovernmental bodies formulate recommendations on priorities among the subprogrammes in their field of competence. The idea of priority is taken even further in regulation 3.17, which calls for the establishment of priorities by the General Assembly among the subprogrammes, and in regulation 4.6 relating to the programme budget, which requests the Secretary-General to identify "programme elements of high and low priority".

63. These criteria are by and large satisfactory. The problems experienced regarding the setting of priorities are primarily related to the lack of application of these criteria by the intergovernmental machinery and the Secretariat. Under the current rules and regulations, priority setting in the medium-term plan takes place at the subprogramme level, while resource estimates are to be provided at the major programme level. In the programme budget, priority setting takes place at the programme level only, while comprehensive resource requirements are given at the programme level, with summary information given at the subprogramme level. Consequently, there is no clear linkage between priority setting and resource requirements either in the medium-term plan or in the programme budget. This has led to the fact that activities that are considered obsolete, of marginal usefulness or ineffective have not always been excluded from the programme budget.

64. The Group therefore submits the following recommendation:

Recommendation 68

In order to facilitate agreement among Member States on the content and level of the budget, the existing rules and regulations pertaining to the setting of priorities should be strictly applied by the intergovernmental bodies concerned and by the Secretariat. The Committee for Programme and Co-ordination should be requested to monitor their application and report thereon to the General Assembly.

C. *Planning and budget mechanisms*

65. The Group has considered the present procedure for preparing the medium-term plan and the programme budget and the structure and functioning of the intergovernmental machinery responsible for these tasks.

66. The present procedure used in preparing the medium-term plan fails to provide Member States with an opportunity to consider in depth the content of the programme of the Organization. The introduction to the medium-term plan is not conceived in conformity with the definition given in article 3 of the Regulations and Member States have, therefore, not been able to make use of it in order to initiate a constructive dialogue on the policy orientations of the plan. Nor do the description of the major programmes and the programmes contain, in most cases, the analyses necessary for considering the effect of these programmes. Furthermore, the text of the medium-term plan, like the programme budget, is prepared by the Secretariat in a form which is almost final, the Member States have neither the means nor the time to undertake major changes in the draft medium-term plan.

67. Furthermore, the medium-term plan does not in reality serve as "principal policy directive" for the programme budget. In fact, the programme budget is merely the financial compilation of a number of decisions and recommendations taken by a large number of intergovernmental bodies and interpreted in the various departments and divisions of the Secretariat. The establishment of the programme budget may be described in the following manner:

(a) The already existing activities are extended, with some minor modifications, from biennium to biennium. The determination of activities that are obsolete, of marginal usefulness or ineffective, and which consequently shall not be included in the budget, is not being undertaken in an appropriate manner;

(b) Decisions to include new or additional expenditures in the budget are based upon decisions taken by the General Assembly, major conferences, the Economic and Social Council etc., or emanating from the Secretariat. Such decisions are general confirmed by a biennial modification of the medium-term plan, which permits the Committee for Programme and Co-ordination to make useful observations, but no central organ really monitors the overall conception of the plan on such occasions;

(c) The Secretariat prepares the programme budget itself; the Budget Division sends the budgetary directives around June of the year preceding the year in which the General Assembly votes on the budget. Preparation lasts about 11 months; in May of the following year, the Committee for Programme and Co-ordination, on the one hand, and the Advisory Committee on Administrative and Budgetary Questions, on the other, begin reviewing the programme budget: the former examines the programme content while the latter examines the administrative and financial aspects of the programme budget, after which the two committees submit their reports so that the Assembly can begin its consideration of the programme budget in September and complete it by the end of the year. The opportunities which the two above-mentioned committees have for recommending modifications in the content of the programme budget are very slight and relate almost entirely to details, because the Secretariat tends to consider the submission of budget fascicles to be practically definitive.

68. The Group is of the opinion that it is essential to rectify the deficiencies of the present planning and budget mechanisms. It is above all important to secure that Member States take apart in the planning and budget procedure from the very beginning and throughout the process. Today that is not the case, as the procedures instituted to this effect for the medium-term plan are not correctly followed and because the present methodology of preparation of the programme budget does not allow for the participation of Member States in the process of definition of the programme budget. The programme budget is prepared in detail before Member States are being brought into the process. A procedure must therefore be developed which makes it possible for Member States to exercise - at the very beginning of the planning and budget process, as well as throughout the whole process - the necessary intergovernmental leadership, particularly regarding the setting of priorities within the resources likely to be available.

69. The members of the Group had a detailed and intensive discussion on this important and admittedly difficult question relating to the planning and budget mechanism. Notwithstanding the many points of convergence, the Group could not reach a consensus on the different proposals submitted:

(a) *Several members were in favour of a solution along the following lines:*

The intergovernmental decision-making process must be adjusted to take into account the methodological change in programme budgeting. The existing machinery separates the consideration of the financial and administrative aspects of the budget from the review of the content of the programmes, as the first is the responsibility of the Advisory Committee on Administrative and Budgetary Questions and the latter the responsibility of the Committee for Programme and Co-ordination. What is needed is an intergovernmental mechanism which can consider and give recommendations on the medium-term plan as well as the programme budget, particularly with regard to the priorities among programmes, resource allocations which reflect these priorities within the context of the resources that are estimated to be available, and recommend redeployment of resources for increased activity in high-priority areas from areas with lower priorities when the need arises and the resources are limited.

Recommendation A

The terms of reference of the Committee for Programme and Coordination (CPC) should be fully implemented and adjusted to reflect its status as the principal advisory body for the General Assembly on matters relating to the medium-term plan and the programme budget. The latter function should be performed with full respect for the mandate and responsibilities of the Advisory Committee on Administrative and Budgetary Questions (ACABQ) and in conformity with regulation 4.8 of the Regulations Governing Programme Planning, the Programme Aspects of the Budget, the Monitoring of Implementation and the Methods of Evaluation, relating to co-ordination between CPC and ACABQ.[3] Furthermore, the relevant recommendations made by CPC in its report to the General Assembly at its forty-first session[4] should be implemented in order to reinforce its role and improve its performance.

Recommendation B

To reflect its new responsibilities and tasks, the Committee for Programme and Co-ordination should be renamed the Committee for Programme Budget and Co-ordination.

Recommendation C

The revised Committee for Programme and Co-ordination should take part in the planning and budget procedure from the very beginning and throughout the process. Its schedule of meetings should be expanded and adjusted accordingly, and it should discharge its duties in close co-operation with the Secretary-General and the Advisory Committee on Administrative and Budgetary Questions.

Recommendation D

With regard to the medium-term plan:

(a)   The revised Committee for Programme and Co-ordination should consider and make recommendations to the General Assembly on the priorities among the programmes on the basis of decisions adopted by the respective legislative bodies and established criteria. These priorities should be accompanied by resource estimates;

(b)   The regulations and rules adopted pursuant to resolutions of the General Assembly pertaining to the medium-term plan should be fully implemented;

(c)   The introduction to the plan should be subject to wide consultations among Member States;

(d) In formulating the plan, sectoral, technical, regional and central bodies in the United Nations should be consulted in a systematic way regarding the major programmes in the plan;

(e) The Secretary-General should, in co-operation with the revised Committee for Programme and Co-ordination, draw up calendars for the consultations described above.

Recommendation E

With regard to the programme budget:

(a) The revised Committee for Programme and Co-ordination should consider and submit recommendations to the General Assembly on:

(i) Priorities among programmes on the basis of the medium-term plan, decisions adopted by the respective legislative bodies and established criteria;

(ii) Resource allocations which reflect these priorities within the level of resources it expects to be available for the biennium;

(iii) When necessary, the redeployment of resources for increased activity in high-priority areas from areas with lower priority within the budget level adopted by the General Assembly.

(b) The procedure should be as follows:

(i) In the spring of the non-budget year, the revised Committee for Programme and Co-ordination should receive from the Secretary-General an outline of the programme budget for the next biennium, based on the medium-term plan and decisions by the legislative organs of the United Nations, with an indication of resources that the Secretary-General expects to be available. This outline (and the draft programme budget to be prepared later by the Secretary-General) should include expenditures related to the political activities of a "perennial character" and their related conference costs. It should also include a contingency fund (financial envelope) to cover additional expenditures resulting from legislative action in the year in which the budget is being adopted and in the biennium. This contingency fund should not exceed two per cent of the estimated budget;

(ii) The revised Committee for Programme and Co-ordination would consider this outline and make recommendations thereon to the General Assembly through the Fifth Committee. Such recommendations should indicate the level of resources that can be expected to be available for the biennium and the allocation of resources to various programme activities within that level;

(iii) Decisions on these matters by the General Assembly should guide the Secretary-General in preparing the draft programme budget;

(iv) In the budget year, the revised Committee for Programme and Co-ordination would consider the Secretary-General's draft budget and submit its recommendations thereon to the Fifth Committee;

(v) Throughout the process described above, the Advisory Committee on Administrative and Budgetary Questions will, in the same manner as at present, examine and report on the costing of the budget.

Recommendation F

The General Assembly, in order to define the roles to be played regarding the programme budget by the revised Committee for Programme and Co-ordination and the Advisory Committee on Administrative and Budgetary Questions, should consider establishing new rules which would clearly identify the areas of common collaboration and interaction and those of separate responsibilities of the two organs.

Recommendation G

Additional expenditures resulting from legislative decisions, either in the year the budget is being adopted or in the biennium, must be accommodated within the budget level decided upon by the General Assembly (i.e. within the contingency fund for additional expenditures). If additional expenditures are approved that are above the resources available within this fund, such expenditures can only included in the budget through redeployment of resources from low priority areas or modifications of subprogrammes. Otherwise, such additional activities will have to be deferred to a later biennium.

Recommendation H

(1) The members of the revised Committee for Programme and Co-ordination should be elected by the General Assembly, upon the nomination of Member States, for a period of three years, and they may be re-elected. The Committee should continue to be an intergovernmental body, with the same representative composition as at present, but its members should be elected in an expert capacity. In nominating representatives to the Committee, Member States should take into account their technical competence and professional experience. Each expert could have one deputy. The Chairman should be elected for the three-year period. The revised Committee for Programme and Co-ordination should continue to take its decisions by consensus.

(2) The necessary permanent secretariat services should be made available to the revised Committee for Programme and Co-ordination.

(b) *Several other matters were in favour of a solution along the following lines:*

The proposed mechanism set forth above for the consideration of the programme budget lacks clarity as to the respective roles of the Committee for Programme and Co-ordination and the Advisory Committee on Administrative and Budgetary Questions in the consideration of the programme budget. This lack of clarity will inevitably lead to major conflict between the two organs in the performance of their respective roles, thereby worsening rather than improving the existing machinery.

This lack of clarity should be removed and the respective roles of the two organs should be made unambiguously clear. The aim should be to improve the functioning of the Committee for Programme and Co-ordination and at the same time maintain the existing mandate of the Advisory Committee on Administrative and Budgetary Questions on which there is unanimous agreement on the excellent performance of its role. To this end, the following proposals are made:

The intergovernmental decision-making process must be adjusted to take into account the methodological change in programme budgeting. The existing machinery separates the consideration of the financial and administrative aspects of the budget from the review of the content of the programmes, as the first is the responsibility of the Advisory Committee on Administrative and Budgetary Questions and the latter the responsibility of the Committee for Programme and Co-ordination.

Recommendation A

The terms of reference of the Committee for Programme and Coordination should be fully implemented to reflect its status as the principal intergovernmental body for the General Assembly on matters relating to the medium-term plan and the programme aspects of the programme budget. The latter function should be performed with full respect for the mandate and responsibilities of the Advisory Committee on Administrative and Budgetary Questions, and in conformity with regulation 4.8 of the Regulations Governing Programme Planning, the Programme Aspects of the Budget, the Monitoring of Implementation and the Methods of Evaluation.[5] Furthermore, the relevant recommendations made by the Committee for Programme and Co-ordination in its report to the General Assembly at its forty-first session[6] should be implemented.

Recommendation B

The Committee for Programme and Co-ordination should take part in the planning and budget procedure from the very beginning and throughout the process. Its schedule of meetings should be expanded and adjusted accordingly, and its should discharge its duties in close co-operation with the

Secretary-General and the Advisory Committee on Administrative and Budgetary Questions.

Recommendation C

With regard to the medium-term plan:

(a)   The Committee for Programme and Co-ordination should consider and make recommendations to the General Assembly on the priorities among the programmes on the basis of decisions adopted by the respective legislative bodies and established criteria. These priorities should be accompanied by indicative resource estimates;

(b)   The regulations and rules adopted pursuant to resolutions of the General Assembly pertaining to the medium-term plan should be fully implemented;

(c)   The introduction to the plan should be subject to wide consultations among Member States;

(d)   In formulating the plan, sectoral, technical, regional and central bodies in the United Nations should be consulted in a systematic way regarding the major programmes in the plan;

(e)   The Secretary-General should, in co-operation with the Committee for Programme and Co-ordination, draw up calendars for the consultations described above.

Recommendation D

With regard to the programme budget:

(a)   The Committee for Programme and Co-ordination and the Advisory Committee on Administrative and Budgetary Questions, each in accordance with its mandate, should consider and submit recommendations to the General Assembly on:

(i)   Priorities among programmes on the basis of the medium-term plan, decisions adopted by the respective legislative bodies and established criteria;

(ii)   Aggregate resource allocations which reflect these priorities;

(iii)   When necessary, the redeployment of resources for increased activity in high-priority areas from areas with lower priority within the budget level adopted by the General Assembly.

(b)   The procedure should be as follows:

(i)   In the spring of the non-budget year, the Committee for Programme and Co-ordination and the Advisory Committee on Administrative and Budgetary Questions should receive from the Secretary-General an outline of the programme budget for the next biennium, based on the medium-term plan and decisions by the legislative organs of the United Nations, with an indication of resources that the Secretary-General expects to be available. This outline (and the draft programme budget to be prepared later by the Secretary-General) should include expenditures related to the political activities of a "perennial character", their related conference costs and estimates for inflation and exchange rate fluctuations. It should also include a contingency fund (financial envelope) to cover additional expenditures resulting from legislative action in the year in which the budget is being adopted and in the biennium;

(ii)   The Committee for Programme and Co-ordination and the Advisory Committee on Administrative and Budgetary Questions will consider this outline and make recommendations thereon to the General Assembly through the Fifth Committee.   Such recommendations should indicate the level of resources that can be expected to be available for the biennium and the allocation of resources to various programme activities within that level;

(iii)   Decisions on these matters by the General Assembly should guide the Secretary-General in preparing the draft programme budget;

(iv)   In the budget year, the Committee for Programme and Co-ordination and the Advisory Committee on Administrative and Budgetary Questions will consider the Secretary-General's draft budget and submit their recommendations thereon to the Fifth Committee.

Recommendation E

Additional expenditures resulting from legislative decisions, either in the year the budget is being adopted or in the biennium, must be accommodated within the budget level decided upon by the General Assembly (that is, within the contingency fund for additional expenditures). If additional expenditures are approved that are above the resources available within this fund, such expenditures can only be included in the budget through redeployment of resources from low-priority areas or modification of subprogrammes. Otherwise, such additional activities will have to be deferred to a later biennium unless another decision is taken by the General Assembly.

Recommendation F

(1)   The members of the Committee for Programme and Co-ordination should be elected by the General Assembly, upon the nomination of Member States, for a period of three years, and they may be re-elected. The Committee should continue to be an intergovernmental body, with the same representative composition as at present, but its members should be elected in an expert

capacity. In nominating representatives to the Committee, Member States should take into account their technical competence and professional experience. Each expert could have one deputy. The Chairman should be elected for the three-year period.

(2) The necessary permanent secretariat services should be made available to the Committee for Programme and Co-ordination.

(c) *Some other members were in favour of yet another solution along the following lines:*

Recommendation A

The budgeting process and the programme planning process in the United Nations should be merged. These two functions are to be entrusted to a single intergovernmental expert body. This body should work on the basis of consensus.

Recommendation B

Before the Secretary-General starts his work on the budget estimates, the overall limit of the future budget should be determined by the intergovernmental expert body on the basis of the amount of resources that Member States can and are prepared to make available to the Organization.

Recommendation C

After the overall limit of the budget is set, the intergovernmental expert body should proceed with the setting of relative priorities within this limit. This body should also co-operate closely with the Secretary-General in the preparation of the budget estimates.

Recommendation D

It is desirable that decisions of intergovernmental bodies, including the Fifth Committee, on the overall limit of the budget and on the level of remuneration of the United Nations personnel are taken by consensus.

VII. Implementation of the Group's recommendations

70. The Group is fully aware of the fact that, over the years, many recommendations on administrative and financial reforms have been adopted by the General Assembly. A substantial number of these recommendations have, however, remained unimplemented. The reasons for this are partly that the body or organ in question has shown little willingness to implement the recommendations and partly that the General Assembly itself has not taken the steps necessary to ensure such implementation of its recommendations.

71. The Group therefore recommends that the General Assembly should take the following steps to ensure that the recommendations contained in the present report, if approved by the Assembly, are speedily and effectively implemented:

Recommendation 69

The Secretary-General should be requested to implement those recommendations that are within his purview. These recommendations should be implemented as soon as possible and, under all circumstances, within the time-limit set. To this effect, he should submit a progress report to the General Assembly by 1 May 1987, outlining which recommendations have been implemented and his plans for implementing those remaining.

Recommendation 70

The General Assembly should request the Committee for Programme and Co-ordination, assisted, as required, by the Joint Inspection Unit and other bodies, to co-ordinate and monitor the implementation of the recommendations relating to the intergovernmental machinery and its functioning. The Committee for Programme and Co-ordination should report to the General Assembly before the beginning of its forty-second session on which recommendations have been implemented and the plans for implementing those remaining.

Recommendation 71

The Secretary-General and the Committee for Programme and Co-ordination should report to the General Assembly at its forty-fourth session on the implementation of all the recommendations contained in the present report and approved by the Assembly.

ANNEX
Organizational matters

A. *Establishment of the Group*

1.   At its 121st plenary meeting, on 18 December 1985, the General Assembly adopted resolution 40/237, entitled "Review of the efficiency of the administrative and financial functioning of the United Nations", the operative part of which read as follows:

"*The General Assembly,*
"...
"1.   *Expresses its conviction* that an overall increase in efficiency would further enhance the capacity of the United Nations to attain the purposes and implement the principles of the Charter of the United Nations;

"2.   *Decides* to establish a Group of High-level Intergovernmental Experts to Review the Efficiency of the Administrative and Financial Functioning of the United Nations, with a term of one year, to carry out in full accordance with the principles and provisions of the Charter the following tasks:

"(a) To conduct a thorough review of the administrative and financial matters of the United Nations, with a view to identifying measures for further improving the efficiency of its administrative and financial functioning, which would contribute to strengthening its effectiveness in dealing with political, economic and social issues;

"(b) To submit to the General Assembly, before the opening of its forty-first session, a report containing the observations and recommendations of the Group;

"3.   *Requests* the President of the General Assembly, in consultation with the regional groups, to appoint as soon as possible the members of the Group of High-level Intergovernmental Experts with due regard to equitable geographical distribution;

"4.   *Decides* that the Group will consist of 18 members and requests the Secretary-General to convene a meeting of the Group as soon as possible to enable it to elect its officers;

"5.   *Requests* the Secretary-General to provide the Group with the necessary staff and services;

"6.   *Also requests* the Secretary-General to provide full assistance to the Group, in particular by submitting his views and providing information necessary to conduct the review;

"7. *Invites* the relevant subsidiary organs of the General Assembly to submit to the Group, through their chairmen, information and comments on matters pertaining to their work;

"8. *Decides* to include in the provisional agenda of its forty-first session an item entitled 'Review of the efficiency of the administrative and financial functioning of the United Nations: report of the Group of High-level Intergovernmental Experts to Review the Efficiency of the Administrative and Financial Functioning of the United Nations'."

B. *Membership*

2. In compliance with paragraphs 3 and 4 of resolution 40/237, the President of the General Assembly appointed the following persons as members of the Group of High-level Intergovernmental Experts to Review the Efficiency of the Administrative and Financial Functioning of the United Nations:

Mr. Mark ALLEN (United Kingdom of Great Britain and Northern Ireland)
Mr. Maurice BERTRAND (France)
Mr. Bi Jilong (China)
Mr. FAKHREDDINE Mohamed (Sudan)
Mr. Lucio GARCIA DEL SOLAR (Argentina)
Mr. Ignac GOLOB (Yugoslavia)
Mr. Natarajan KRISHNAN (India)
Mr. Kishore MAHBUBANI (Singapore)
Mr. Hugo B. MARGAIN (Mexico)
Mr. Elleck MASHINGAIDZE (Zimbabwe)
Mr. Ndam NJOYA (Cameroon)
Mr. Vasiliy Stepanovich SAFRONCHUK (Union of Soviet Socialist Republics)
Mr. Shizuo SAITO (Japan)
Mr. Edward O. SANU (Nigeria)
Mr. David SILVEIRA DA MOTA (Brazil)
Mr. José S. SORZANO (United States of America)
Mr. Tom VRAALSEN (Norway)
Mr. Layachi YAKER (Algeria)

C. *Officers*

3.   At its 2nd meeting, on 26 February 1986, the Group elected the following officers:

Chairman: Mr. Tom VRAALSEN

Vice-Chairmen: Mr. Ignac GOLOB
                      Mr. Shizuo SAITO
                      Mr. David SILVEIRA DA MOTA
                      Mr. Layachi YAKER

D. *Adoption of the agenda*

4.   At the same meeting, the Group adopted the following agenda:

1.   Opening of the session by the Secretary-General.
2.   Election of the Chairman.
3.   Adoption of the agenda.
4.   Organizational matters:
     (a) Election of the Vice-Chairmen;
     (b) Organization of work.
5.   Thorough review of the administrative and financial matters of the United Nations, with a view to identifying measures for further improving the efficiency of its administrative and financial functioning, which would contribute to strengthening its effectiveness in dealing with political, economic and social issues.
6.   Adoption of the report.

E. *Proceedings of the Group*

5.   At its 1st meeting, on 25 February, the Group decided to hold closed meetings.

6.   The Group held its first session from 25 February to 4 March (1st to 9th meetings), its second session from 1 to 11 April (10th to 26th meetings), its third session from 16 to 27 June (27th to 43rd meetings) and its fourth session from 28 July to 15 August (44th to 67th meetings).

Notes

1.   See A/AC.172/88/Add.4.
2.   See A/40/377, annex, and A/41/437, annex.
3.   Regulation 4.8 reads as follows: "The Committee for Programme and Co-ordination shall prepare a report on the proposed budget, containing its programme recommendations and its general assessment of the related resource proposals. It shall receive a statement by the Secretary-General on the programme budget implications of its recommendations. The report of the Committee for Programme and Co-ordination shall be communicated simultaneously to the Economic and Social Council and to the Advisory Committee on

Administrative and Budgetary Questions. The Advisory Committee shall receive the report of the Committee for Programme and Co-ordination and study the statement by the Secretary-General. The reports of the Committee for Programme and Co-ordination and the Advisory Committee on each section of the proposed programme budget shall be considered simultaneously by the General Assembly."

4. *Official Records of the General Assembly, Forty-first Session, Supplement No. 38* (A/41/38).

5. Regulation 4.8, *op.cit.*

6. *Official Records of the General Assembly, Forty-first Session, Supplement No. 38* (A/41/38).

2.2 Document A/41/663*

Report of the Group of High-level Intergovernmental Experts to Review the Efficiency of the Administrative and Financial Functioning of the United Nations (A/41/49)

Note by the Secretary-General

1 October 1986

1. In addressing the Group of High-level Intergovernmental Experts when it first convened on 25 February 1986, I expressed the belief that it could make a vital contribution to the search for solutions that would ensure the long-term administrative and financial viability of the United Nations. The report that the Group has submitted to the General Assembly constitutes such a contribution, including, as it does, many valuable and constructive proposals. It reflects the commitment of the 18 members, who were drawn from all geographic regions, to a strong United Nations, able to deal more effectively with political, economic and social issues that are all related to the establishment of lasting peace.

2. The Group of Experts, which had less than a year to devote to the very large task given it by the General Assembly, could not realistically be expected to formulate definitive proposals in all the areas to which it gave attention, and it did not. It provides, however, a crucial basis for a process of change that can bring the improvements in the administrative and financial functioning of the Organization needed for its long-term viability. While I would expect, as the Assembly pursues the necessary detailed consideration of the report, to submit comments on individual proposals, I believe it may be useful, at this stage, to make some initial observations of a broader nature.

3. The report of the Group of Experts contains a total of 71 recommendations. All pertain to improvement of the administrative and financial functioning of the Organization, an objective towards which I have worked during my five-year-term as Secretary-General and which, I am firmly convinced, should be vigorously pursued.

4. The efforts must entail, in a manner consistent with the Charter, substantial reform in procedures and structures both in the intergovernmental machinery and the Secretariat. In order to achieve clarity not only on what needs to be done, but also on how and when it can best be accomplished, the significant interrelationship among some of the measures proposed needs to be taken into careful account. There is, for example, a direct relationship between possible changes in the intergovernmental machinery and modifications in the

---

*A/41/663.

size, composition and work of the Secretariat staff. Similarly, changes in the structure and staffing in those areas of the Secretariat where the Group of Experts has recommended a functional review can best be made after these reviews are completed.

5.   I mention this to emphasize the importance of seeing the changes that need to be made as an orderly, sequential process that will permit rational and adequately planned implementation. Moreover, as we proceed, the essential objective of enhancing the effectiveness of the Organization in carrying out its substantive programmes and activities must be borne in mind. There should be, however, no doubt that we must move ahead expeditiously and with a constructive sense of purpose in carrying out, as soon as possible, the reforms that are called for. I have taken steps to ensure that the Secretariat is in a position to start this process as soon as the decisions of the General Assembly are known.

6.   The work done by the Group of Experts on the budgetary process is of major importance to the future of the United Nations. While full agreement was not reached, exploration of the subject was extensive and there is evident agreement on several central points, including the need for an improved intergovernmental machinery that can deal more thoroughly with questions related to the budget; the advisability of earlier participation by Member States in the programme and budget process; the importance of co-ordinated programme planning and programme budgeting; and the need for early establishment of guidance by the General Assembly on the level of resources within which expenditures during a biennium would be accommodated.

7.   This measure of congruence, especially when seen in the context of the vital interests of the organizations that are involved, would suggest that with a further effort by the General Assembly agreement on this subject can yet be reached. The authority of the Assembly to determine the size of the budget, the establishment of priorities and the apportionment of expenses as provided for in the Charter should, of course, be preserved. I believe improved intergovernmental machinery, with adequate time, continuity and expertise to give comprehensive consideration to programmes, priorities and resources, could be of much assistance to the Assembly and its Fifth Committee in reaching timely budgetary decisions - decisions that would enjoy the broad support that the health of the Organization requires. There is need for a practical procedure that can facilitate and encourage broad agreement on the budget notwithstanding political differences on substantive issues that may persist among Member States.

8.   The effectiveness with which the varied and demanding mandates of the United Nations are met depends heavily on the quality and the performance of the Secretariat staff. The management of personnel in all of its aspects must, therefore, be - and is - an intrinsic and essential part of the responsibility of the Secretary-General as Chief Administrative Officer. To the extent that his authority in this field is reduced by resolutions of the General Assembly or by

pressure from Member States, his capacity to assure a well-managed Secretariat is adversely affected. Any reduction in the number of posts will need to be carried out on the basis of principles that will assure humane and fair treatment of staff members and the maintenance of a vigorous and capable Secretariat. I would state, at this point my agreement with the suggestions contained in the Group of Experts' report that the influx of new blood should not be stemmed even during a time of staff reductions. While any formula should allow for flexibility as to precise numbers of percentages, the principle itself is essential to the future of the Organization.

9.   The United Nations requires a staff representing the highest standards of efficiency, competence and integrity, with due regard to the importance of recruiting the staff on as wide a geographical basis as possible, as stated in the Charter. Working conditions, including salaries and entitlements, must be such as to attract and retain such personnel. To seek to solve the Organization's financial difficulties at the expense of staff entitlements would be extremely short-sighted and counter-productive and would have adverse implications for the common system. The possibility of discriminatory and divisive measures relating to working conditions that would apply to the United Nations alone must be avoided. Member States have long and consistently maintained that common personnel standards and conditions of employment are desirable for the United Nations system as a whole. I believe this is highly important and that, therefore, the General Assembly should continue to look to the International Civil Service Commission to play a central role as regards the regulation and co-ordination of the conditions of service of the United Nations common system.

10. The constructive and loyal attitude of the staff that has been evident during this difficult period will be a vital element in the success of the further measures needed to resolve the longer-term financial problems of the Organization. This needs to be taken into account as the General Assembly weighs the decisions to be made and the manner in which they are formulated. In accordance with the relevant staff regulations as approved by the General Assembly, the staff of the Secretariat expects to be consulted with respect to the various actions proposed that could affect their conditions of employment, as I will certainly do.

11. As the General Assembly undertakes its examination of the report of the Group of High-level Intergovernmental Experts, which is rightly directed towards the future of the United Nations, the Organization continues to face a grave and immediate financial crisis. Whether the United Nations will remain solvent in the last months of this year remains even now an open question. It is, in any event, clear that the crisis will not be satisfactorily overcome until we find ways to deal successfully with its root causes, which, as I have observed in the past, are primarily political in nature. I believe that the present time, while difficult in the extreme, may be propitious for doing this. I sense that there is both a renewed awareness of the crucial role of the United Nations in the increasingly interdependent world of the future and a clearer

perception of the jeopardy in which the Organization at present stands. The report of the Group of Experts provides a basis on which Member States can come together and, in accordance with their obligations under the Charter, restore a sound and lasting financial foundation for the Organization. It is now the urgent task of the Assembly to reach decisions that will fulfil the intent of the membership in appointing the High-level Group. This forty-first session has the opportunity to take action that will result in a United Nations that will enjoy the wide confidence and cohesion required by the global needs it was created to meet. This is an opportunity that could make this a session of seminal importance in the history of the United Nations.

2.3 Document A/41/763*

**Comments of the Administrative Committee on Co-ordination on the
Report of the Group of the High-level Intergovernmental Experts to
Review the Efficiency of the Administrative and
Financial Functioning of the United Nations (A/41/49)**

24 October 1986

1. In the past year the United Nations has been subjected to a crisis that has
challenged both its viability and its solvency. Its work has been overshadowed
by financial constraints that stem primarily from the failure of certain Member
States to meet their obligations under the Charter of the United Nations. The
Organization is now confronted with problems of such magnitude as to have
profound implications for its survival and its future ability to further the vital
objectives for which it was established. The Administrative Committee on
Co-ordination (ACC) views these problems, which have been brought to the
attention of Member States by the Secretary-General, with the most serious
concern, in particular as they have direct and indirect implications for the
United Nations system as a whole. While the underlying causes of the growing
budgetary problem are political, the structural and administrative efficiency of
the Organization has also been called into question. In this context, ACC
noted that the report of the Group of High-level Intergovernmental Experts to
Review the Efficiency of the Administrative and Financial Functioning of the
United Nations[1] is currently under consideration by the General Assembly.
ACC is of the view that this report provides a useful contribution to the
process of improving the mechanisms of multilateral co-operation. For their
part, members of ACC, both individually and collectively, will continue their
efforts to contribute to the improvement of the functioning of their organizations and of the United Nations system as a whole. At this stage, ACC
confines its views to three recommendations in the report of the Group of
High-level experts that are of immediate concern to the organizations of the
system as a whole.

2. In recommendation 9,[2] the Group of High-level Experts proposes that the
machinery for inter-agency co-ordination should be streamlined and that
maximum use should be made of flexible *ad hoc* arrangements designed to
meet specific requirements. The system has already responded in a flexible
manner in respect of the critical economic situation in Africa. A review of the
functioning of the main subsidiary bodies of ACC, instituted in 1985, has now
been completed and will result in a concentration of efforts in the standing
consultative committees. In addition, a review of the other subsidiary bodies
has been initiated. The report of the Secretary-General on all aspects of
co-ordination in the United Nations and the United Nations system, called for

---

*A/41/763.

by the General Assembly in its resolution 40/177 of 17 December 1985, will afford an opportunity for a comprehensive response. Furthermore, ACC attaches great importance to the co-ordination of activities at the country level, which could be usefully examined in a number of countries for the purpose of drawing further lessons from the experience acquired.

3. ACC welcomes the emphasis placed by the Group of High-level Experts, in its recommendation 10,[3] on the need for discussion by the executive heads of major policy questions in the economic and social fields and for subsequent reporting to their respective intergovernmental bodies. In the context of its periodic consideration of the item on development and international economic co-operation, such discussion is already being undertaken by ACC in its regular biannual sessions. ACC believes that the objective of this recommendation could be further achieved by convening subject-oriented sessions of ACC and by recourse to functional groups, instead of creating a new mechanism as proposed by the Group of High-level Experts.

4. The efficiency, competence and integrity of international civil servants are universally considered to be of paramount importance. To attract staff with these attributes, it is crucial to maintain appropriate conditions of service and staff entitlements. Recommendation 61[4] mentions that the total entitlements of the staff have reached a level that gives reason for serious concern and should be reduced. ACC fully supports the stand of the Secretary-General that to seek to solve financial difficulties at the expense of staff entitlements would be extremely short-sighted and counter-productive, and would have widespread adverse implications for the United Nations common system case, the conditions of service of staff members are kept under permanent review by the International Civil Service Commission, which has been set up by the General Assembly for that purpose. The elements of conditions of service are interdependent and cannot be dealt with piecemeal, and should be considered in the first instance by the International Civil Service Commission where the views of administrations and staffs can be heard. Indeed, salaries for Professional and higher categories have remained unchanged for the past 11 years, subject to cost-of-living adjustments; cost-of-living adjustments have been frozen for the past two years, while pension entitlements have been the object of successive reductions in the past four years. Moreover, conditions of service and life of international staff in the field have further deteriorated over this period, and in many cases of local staff, compensation is proving to be clearly inadequate. Although executive heads can still, fortunately, count on the sense of duty and professional conscience of their staff, the generally negative attitude towards the international civil service and repeated questioning of conditions of service create feelings of insecurity and discouragement. From the long-term point of view, it is far from assured that the international civil service would attract and retain staff of the required highest calibre. ACC considers that mediocrity will ultimately be the price of further reductions in staff entitlements.

Notes

1. *Official Records of the General Assembly, Forty-first Session, Supplement No. 49 (A/41/49).*
2. *Ibid.*, para. 9.
3. *Ibid.*
4. *Ibid.*, para. 50, sect. C.

2.4 A/41/795[*]

Report of the Group of High-level Intergovernmental Experts to Review the Efficiency of the Administrative and Financial Functioning of the United Nations (A/41/49)

Report of the Fifth Committee

5 November 1986

Findings of the Fifth Committee

1.   At its 3rd plenary meeting, on 20 September 1986, the General Assembly decided to include in the agenda of its forty-first session the item entitled "Review of the efficiency of the administrative and financial functioning of the United Nations: report of the Group of High-level Intergovernmental Experts to Review the Efficiency of the Administrative and Financial Functioning of the United Nations". At the same meeting, the General Assembly also decided that the item would be considered in plenary meetings of the Assembly, and that, during the course of this consideration, the Fifth Committee would, within the scope of its responsibilities, undertaken a factual examination of the report and submit its findings to the plenary.

2.   For the consideration of this question the Fifth Committee had before it the report of the Group of High-level Intergovernmental Expert (A/41/49) as well as a note by the Secretary-General (A/41/663). The Committee also noted the text of a communications from the Chairman of the Committee on Co-ordination (ACC) (A/41/763) and communications from the Chairman of the Committee on the Exercise of the Inalienable Rights of the Palestinian People (A/C.5/41/25) and from the President of the United Nations Council for Namibia (A/41/781).

3.   The Fifth Committee considered this item at its 11th, 13th to 19th and 21st meetings, on 16 and 23 to 30 October and 5 November 1986. In addition, the Committee held 11 informal meetings during the period from 16 to 23 October, in order to conduct a first reading of the report. Further informal consultations were held during the period from 24 October to 5 November 1986 with a view to elaborating a draft of the Committee's submission to Plenary.

4.   During these informal meetings, a number of questions were posed by delegations to which answers were subsequently provided, at formal meetings, by the Chairman of the Group of High-level Intergovernmental Experts, the Chairman of the Advisory Committee on Administrative and Budgetary

---

[*]A/41/795.

Questions, the Chairman of the International Civil Service Commission and the representatives of the Secretary-General.

5.   The Committee also decided, in keeping with the practice it has followed pursuant to General Assembly resolution 35/213 of 17 December 1980, to invite a representative of the staff of the United Nations Secretariat (who spoke also on behalf of the Co-ordinating Committee of Independent Staff Associations and Unions (CCISUA)) and a representative of the Federation of International Civil Servants's Associations (FICSA) to present their views to the Committee.

"*General findings*

The Fifth Committee noted, as stated in paragraph 11 of the report of the Group of High-level Intergovernmental Experts, that:

"The time constraints under which the Group had to work did not allow it to make a comprehensive study of some of the extremely complex problems put before it."

The Committee also noted that not all relevant subsidiary organs of the General Assembly submitted to the Group information and comments on matters pertaining to their work, as envisaged in paragraph 7 of General Assembly resolution 40/237.

The Committee noted that the Group had decided not to make reference in the report to the scale of assessment or to the questions of withholdings and of arrears in payment of assessed contributions. The payment of assessed contributions affects directly the efficiency of the administrative and financial functioning of the United Nations not only in the short, but also in the medium and long term. In reply to questions posed by the Fifth Committee in this regard, the Chairman of the Group of High-level Intergovernmental Experts stated that:

"as part of its deliberations pertaining to the financial functioning of the Organization, the scale of assessments had been discussed, *inter alia*, questions of lowering the ceiling of contributions, raising the floor and criteria for deciding upon the contributions of Member States. These discussions had proved inconclusive. As a result, the Group has unanimously decided not to reflect this discussion in its report."

In submitting its findings to the General Assembly, the Fifth Committee wishes to stress the importance attached to the need for full respect for the relevant provisions of the Charter, its principles and its aims, in the implementation of those recommendations of the Group that the Assembly may approve.

It is recognized that the objective of all such recommendations is to achieve an improvement in the efficiency of the administrative and financial functioning of the United Nations. Accordingly, their implementation should be consistent with that goal. It was stressed that the approved measures should be put into effect in a coherent, orderly and co-ordinated manner.

The findings submitted by the Fifth Committee are aimed at assisting and facilitating the work of the General Assembly in reaching its conclusions. The findings would serve as a point of reference in the implementation of those recommendations that may be approved by the General Assembly.

Findings on specific recommendations

The findings of the Fifth Committee with regard to the recommendations of the Group of High-level Intergovernmental Experts are set out in the following paragraphs.

The Intergovernmental Machinery and its Functioning
(A/41/49, sect. II)

Recommendation 1

The aim of this recommendation is to strengthen the Committee on Conferences and to give it broader responsibilities. The objective is to increase the harmonization of working procedures of conference services and to improve implementation of decisions on all organizational aspects dealing with conferences by legislative bodies, on the understanding that there should be full respect for the mandates and other legislative organs and the responsibilities of the Secretariat and in accordance with the provisions of General Assembly resolution 40/243. The "highest" level of membership referred to in subparagraph (a) of this recommendation should be regarded in terms of expertise.

Recommendation 2

The objective of this recommendation is to reduce the number, frequency and duration of meetings, without affecting negatively the substantive work of the Organization. In view of Article 72 of the Charter, the General Assembly should invite the Economic and Social Council to consider recommendation 2 (a).

Recommendation 3

The sequential order of the Fourth Committee and the Special Political Committee referred to in subparagraph (c) of this recommendation should be during each session of the General Assembly and the number of meetings accorded to each of these Main Committees should be in conformity with their respective programmes of work.

With regard to subparagraph (e), its implementation should be in accordance with the provisions of Article 22 of the Charter. The decision to establish a new subsidiary organ should be taken only after it is determined that the task could not be performed by an existing one with a similar mandate.

In regard to recommendation 3 (f), the Fifth Committee reiterated the right of Member States to present resolutions which they deem necessary.

Recommendation 4

The implementation of this recommendation should be in line with the provisions of General Assembly resolution 40/243.

Recommendation 5

In respect of this recommendation, the Fifth Committee wishes to draw to the attention of the General Assembly that it has approved two projects relating to construction of United Nations conference facilities, which are yet to be completed. The Committee also notes the principle that programmes, once approved by the General Assembly, should be implemented.

Recommendation 8

The Committee found that the study referred to in recommendation 8 (1) could be undertaken by an existing intergovernmental body such as the Economic and Social Council or the Committee for Programme and Co-ordination.

In connection with recommendation 8 (3) (d), the intergovernmental body conducting the study should seek the co-operation and views of the intergovernmental organs concerned with United Nations operational activities for development.

Subsection II.C

The Committee noted that, in paragraph 9 of its report, the Group had indicated that "The relationship between the Organization, including its subsidiary bodies, and the specialized agencies, as well as system-wide co-ordination and co-operation, ... falls outside the mandate of the Group." The recommendations contained in this subsection (recommendation 9 to 13) should be viewed in this context.

Recommendation 9

This recommendation should be viewed in the light of the above observation and addressed to the concerned Charter organs of the United Nations.

Recommendation 10

The Committee was not able to find a clear indication as to whether the intention of this recommendation is the establishment of a new co-ordinating body in addition to or instead of the Administrative Committee on Co-ordination (ACC). The Committee did note, however, the statement of ACC (A/41/763) to the effect that the discussion proposed "is already being undertaken by ACC in its regular biannual sessions. ACC believes that the objective of this recommendation could be further achieved by convening subject-oriented sessions of ACC and by recourse to functional groups, instead of creating a new mechanism as proposed by the Group of High-level Experts."

Structure of the Secretariat
(A/41/49, sect. III)

Recommendation 15

The Fifth Committee noted that the percentages referred to in this recommendation were arrived at in a pragmatic manner. Taking into account the need to avoid any negative effect on the implementation of programmes, the percentages represent targets that should be utilized by the Secretary-General in formulating his plans to be submitted to the General Assembly. In formulating such plans, the Secretary-General should take into account the relationship between the intergovernmental machinery and existing legislative mandates and the need to secure an effective and efficient secretariat structure, bearing in mind the necessity of securing the highest standards of efficiency, competence, and integrity of the staff, with due regard to equitable geographical distribution.

During its examination of this question, the Committee was apprised of the manner in which the Secretary-General would approach the implementation of this recommendation, if approved, notably, that:

"The process of reviewing and reducing posts, including those at the higher level, could begin immediately and not await the completion of all the reviews (recommended by the Group). A reduction could take place but, until such time as the Assembly approves any structural changes in the Secretariat, the Secretary-General would need to have authority to implement reductions in 1987 with flexibility, within the total level of posts for the Secretariat as a whole.

"Post reductions would have to be done initially on a pragmatic basis, designed to match available resources with the least possible disruption to programmes and to the lives and rights of the people involved. Final determination of the reductions in 1988 and 1989 that are feasible and compatible with minimal disruption to programmes and the lives and rights of staff members can only be judiciously made after the full impact of any retrenchments in 1987 has been assessed.

"The Secretary-General, of course, would aim at achieving these reductions to the maximum extent possible through the full utilization of the attrition mechanism. Such a mechanism, however, might not be compatible with minimizing disruption to programmes. If this were to be the case, additional financial costs may be required to achieve the post reductions targeted. Mechanisms such as the redeployment of staff between programmes and between duty stations might also need to be applied and these may entail additional expenditures.

"In summary, if the Assembly accepts the intent of recommendation 15 to reduce posts by the order of magnitude indicated in it, the Secretary-General would aim at the targets given in the manner and under the considerations ... indicated. He would need to proceed with flexibility under the provisions of the Charter and the Staff and Financial Rules and Regulations. Similarly, some flexibility will be needed to defer or modify approved programmes or terminate approved activities considered to be of low priority. The Secretary-General would, of course, consult with the ACABQ and the CPC."

The Fifth Committee understood that these consultations would be conducted in accordance with pertinent rules and regulations.

As to the effect of any reduction in posts on the geographical distribution of the staff, the Committee noted the following statement by the representative of the Secretary-General:

"Any reduction in the overall number of posts will certainly imply a reduction in the number of staff in posts subject to geographical distribution. This will in turn entail a revision of the desirable ranges of representation and the base figure used to calculate them."

The Committee also noted the indication by the representative of the Secretary-General as to the savings that could be gained from the reductions in posts proposed in recommendation 15, namely, that:

"As 15 per cent reduction in the number of posts would result, at current costs, in direct savings of approximately $141 million per biennium; the indirect savings had not been calculated. As regards a 25 per cent reduction in the higher echelon, savings would amount to approximately $3.3 million on salaries and common staff costs."

As to the impact on the United Nations Joint Staff Pension Fund of the recommendation for reduction of posts by 15 per cent over three years, the Committee was informed that the Fund's Consulting Actuary had indicated that:

"... on the assumption that the reduction would be achieved by attrition, it would entail a decrease in the active participant population of the Fund by

1 per cent a year for three years. This would increase the actuarial imbalance by up to 0.17 per cent of pensionable remuneration. To offset this impact, the Fund would need additional contribution income of up to $3 million per year."

As to that part of the recommendation dealing with the recruitment of staff at the P-1, P-2 and P-3 levels, the Committee noted the statement by the representative of the Secretary-General that:

"... assuming approval by the Assembly, it would be the intention of the Secretary-General to recruit, in the course of 1987, staff at the P-1, P-2 and P-3 levels. However, he would not wish to be held to an exact figure at this time, or to those three levels alone. This will, of course, be influenced by the financial situation in 1987."

Furthermore, the representative of the Secretary-General indicated that:

"... although a preliminary review of existing vacancies and projected attrition indicates that it might be possible, at least initially , to maintain the average number of recruitment at P-1, P-2 and P-3 levels at the rate of appointments comparable to those for the period 1982-1984, one cannot be definite as this would depend on the overall reduction of posts and its effect on the reduced career progression of junior and intermediate staff. It might therefore not be possible to maintain the same level of appointments as immediately appear feasible."

The Fifth Committee highlighted the interrelationship between recommendation 15 and other recommendations in the report.

The Committee noted that the General Assembly would consider in more detail the implications of this recommendation, if approved, when the Secretary-General presents the plan of implementation called for in paragraph 3 of the recommendation. In this regard the Committee noted the statement by the Secretary-General (A/41/663, para. 4) that:

"... there is ... a direct relationship between possible changes in the intergovernmental machinery and modifications in the size, composition and work of the Secretariat staff. Similarly, changes in the structure and staffing in those areas of the Secretariat where the Group of Experts has recommended a functional review can best be made after these reviews are completed."

Recommendation 19

The Committee noted that any decision that may be adopted in this respect should be clearly aimed at strengthening the efficiency of all Secretariat activities relating to Namibia, without in any way limiting the programmes and services in this area, in order to enhance the Organization's capacity to deal with this matter of high importance.

Recommendation 21

The Committee noted that there has been a decrease in the work-load of the Department of Political Affairs, Trusteeship and Decolonization as a result of progress achieved in matters of decolonization and trusteeship; on the other hand, the reorientation of tasks assigned to the Department has resulted in an increase in its work-load related to political affairs. This recommendation should be implemented in the light of the findings of the Fifth Committee under recommendations 15 and 19.

Recommendation 22

The Committee noted that special economic assistance programmes are currently approved by the General Assembly, funded by voluntary contributions and administered by the Office for Special Political Questions, which is funded by the regular budget. The Committee noted that this recommendation involves transferring the administration of special economic assistance programmes from the regular budget to the United Nations Development Programme (UNDP). In implementing this recommendation, if approved, the impact of the transfer of the administration of these programmes on the functioning of UNDP should be ascertained. Implementation of this recommendation should neither hinder the approval nor negatively affect the delivery of special economic assistance programmes.

Recommendation 24

The Committee noted the different nature and functions of the Office of the United Nations Disaster Relief Co-ordinator and the United Nations Development Programme, and considered that the Secretary-General should participate in the consideration referred to in this recommendation.

Recommendation 25

In its examination of recommendation 25 (1), the Committee noted that the General Agreement on Tariffs and Trade would be the only organization external to the United Nations that would be invited to participate in an internal United Nations review.

With regard to recommendation 25 (2), the Committee pointed out that, at its last meeting, the Intergovernmental Committee on Science and Technology for Development evaluated and approved the activities of the Centre for Science and Technology for Development. Accordingly, if this recommendation were adopted, that evaluation should be taken into account when considering the feasibility of integrating the Centre into the Department of International Economic and Social Affairs and the Department of Technical Co-operation for Development.

In connection with recommendation 25 (3), the Committee noted that the functions of the Director-General for Development and International Economic Co-operation were specified in General Assembly resolution 32/197 and subsequent resolutions, most recently Economic and Social Council resolution 1986/74. It also noted that, in the Secretary-General's view, no further legislative authority is required.

Should consideration of recommendation 25 (4) be envisaged, it should be done in observance of relevant General Assembly resolutions.

Recommendation 27

The Committee noted that the suitability of the activities of the regional commissions is a matter to be determined primarily by the Member States concerned and that the regional commissions should be consulted on any action to be taken in this regard.

Recommendation 29

The Committee recalled that the General Assembly, at its thirty-ninth session, noted a report of the Joint Inspection Unit commenting favourably upon the Office of Secretariat Services for Economic and Social Matters.

Recommendation 31

The Committee noted the view expressed by the representative of the Secretary-General that the function of the Management Advisory Service would continue to be necessary, precisely at a time when the administrative and financial efficiency of the Organization is being examined.

Recommendation 32

The Committee pointed out that co-ordination between different units of the Secretariat in the areas of planning, programming and budgeting is at present dealt with at the level of the Programme Planning and Budgeting Board, which was created in 1982. The manner in which this recommendation will be implemented, if approved, should be viewed in the light of the decisions that the General Assembly may take regarding section VI of the Group's report.

Recommendation 35

The Committee was informed that the intention of the Group was that the 30 per cent reduction proposed for outside consultants related to the original appropriations approved by the General Assembly for this purpose for the current biennium.

Measures regarding personnel
(A/41/49, sect. IV)

The Committee noted that, in any question regarding the administration of the staff, the responsibilities and prerogatives of the Secretary-General under the Charter as the Chief Administrative Officer of the Organization must be acknowledged and respected. Furthermore, in connection with the consideration of section IV of the report, the Committee emphasized the importance of observing fully the provisions of Article 101, paragraph 3, of the Charter.

The Committee also noted the importance of the preservation of the common system and the need to avail of the expertise of the International Civil Service Commission, in accordance with the provisions of the Commission's statute, in dealing with those recommendations relating to issues over which the Commission has a mandate (recommendations 53 and 61 would have a direct impact on the common system, while recommendations 42, 43, 45, 48, 49, 50, 52, 55, 57, 58 and 60 deal with issues over which ICSC has a mandate under articles 14 and 15 of its statute, to advise and make recommendations to organizations).

The Committee also took note of paragraphs 9 and 10 of the note by the Secretary-General (A/41/663).

Recommendation 41

The Fifth Committee notes the emphasis in recommendation 41 on the need for leadership by the Secretary-General in personnel matters, for management improvement in this area and for protection of the authority of the official in charge of personnel. This emphasis is in line with previous resolutions of the General Assembly. The Fifth Committee notes the intention of the Secretary-General "to review all delegations of authority in the personnel field to determine the possible existence of either conflict or confusion and if found, to correct that situation". The Fifth Committee notes that a report on this subject was requested in General Assembly resolution 40/258 for submission to the Assembly at its forty-first session.

Recommendation 43

The Fifth Committee notes the need to ensure that, in the competitive examination process, procedures should be non-discriminatory (in terms, *inter alia*, of content, methods and languages) and should be based on objective methods and criteria. The Committee further notes that so far competitive examinations at the P-3 level have been proposed only on an experimental basis.

Recommendation 44

The Committee found that the objective of this recommendation is to increase the proportion of appointments at the junior professional levels (P-1, P-2 and P-3). In this process, the paramount consideration shall be the necessity of securing the highest standards of efficiency, competence, and integrity, with due regard being paid to the importance of recruiting staff on as wide a geographical basis as possible.

Recommendation 45

The Committee noted the statement of the Chairman of the International Civil Service Commission that the Group had recommended a three-year eligibility period for permanent appointment, instead of a five-year period established by the General Assembly in resolution 37/126. However, the Committee also noted the indication given by the representative of the Secretary-General that:

"... the current eligibility for a permanent appointment is already three years and, in some cases, even less. A permanent appointment should not depend only on length of service. Therefore, no hard-and-fast rule should be established."

Recommendations 46 and 47

The Committee noted that the expression "relevant resolutions" includes all resolutions on personnel questions. The Committee also noted that the General Assembly will consider these matters in more detail when the Secretary-General presents his progress report on the measures taken to implement these recommendations as called for in recommendation 69.

Recommendation 51

The Committee noted that, in relation to the last sentence of this recommendation, the structuring of the appointment and promotion bodies on the basis of occupational groups is linked with recommendation 48.

Recommendation 53

The Committee noted the statement of the Chairman of the International Civil Service Commission that the role of monitoring the implementation of standards dealing with personnel management is already assigned to the Commission under its statute, and his interpretation of "monitoring" as "regulation and co-ordination" in the context of article 1 and "reporting" in the context of article 17 of the ICSC statute.

Recommendation 55 and 57

The Committee noted that, as stated in the report itself, some members of the Group had indicated that the second sentence of each of these recommendations should not be included in the report of the Group. It further noted the statement by the Chairman of the Group indicating that these recommendations had not enjoyed the necessary support.

Recommendation 58

The Committee noted the necessity for effective training programmes geared to the needs of the Organization and to ensuring the optimum utilization of the human and financial resources to be allocated.

Recommendation 59

The Committee noted the Secretary-General's view that:

"The facilitating of staff representational activities and of the activities of joint staff-management bodies, as provided for int he Staff Regulations and Rules, does not derogate from his managerial prerogatives, nor should it. "Self-financing by the staff unions of all their activities could be a step backward in staff-management relations in the international civil service".

The Committee also noted the Group's recommendation that:

"The efficiency of the Organization would be increased if clear guidelines were established for the role and functions of the Staff Union ..." and that "Staff unions or associations should finance all their activities from their own funds".

Recommendation 61

The Committee noted that the matters dealt with under recommendation 61 are covered under the provisions of the statute of ICSC and that implementing this recommendation without consulting ICSC could be damaging to the common system. The Committee noted also that the Chairman of the Group of High-level Experts envisaged that:

"... this recommendation, if adopted by the General Assembly, will be subject to thorough consideration by the competent organs of this Organization, particularly the ICSC, before the final recommendations are being presented to the General Assembly for approval".

Monitoring, evaluation and inspection
(A/41/49, sect. V)

Recommendations 63-67

The Committee noted that the proposed revision of the statute of the Joint Inspection Unit, if accepted by the General Assembly, would be only for the purpose of changing the name of the Unit.

These recommendations should, if adopted, be implemented in a manner consistent with the provisions of the statute of the Unit and with due regard for the need to avoid duplication of work being done by Secretariat units and offices and technical and expert bodies.

Planning and budget procedures
(A/41/49, sect. VI)

With due regard to the responsibilities of the Secretary-General, the Committee noted that Member States should be involved, in a more structured manner, in the planning, programming and budgeting procedure from the very beginning and throughout the whole process.

The intergovernmental machinery must be improved (and adjusted if necessary).

The Committee recognized that there is a need for early establishment of guidance by the General Assembly on the overall level of resources to accommodate the activities of the Organization during the following biennium and on priorities. The Committee noted in this regard the statements by the representative of the Secretary-General that:

"The Secretary-General would welcome the earlier involvement of Member States in the budgetary process, say in the year of issuance of the budget instructions, at which time they could give their views on the appropriate level of real growth in the forthcoming budget and also on such policy matters as the priorities to govern the distribution of resources in that forthcoming budget."

and that

"Once priorities are set by Member States as part of their review of the next medium-term plan, these priorities would govern the formulation of the three programme budgets to be made up in conformity with this plan."

The Committee notes that, in order to facilitate agreement among Member States on the content and level of the budget, the existing rules and regulations pertaining to the setting of priorities should be strictly applied by the intergovernmental bodies concerned and by the Secretariat.

With regard to the medium-term plan:

(a)   The Regulations and Rules Governing Programme Planning, the Programme Aspects of the Budget, the Monitoring of Implementation and the Methods of Evaluation pertaining to the medium-term plan should be fully implemented;

(b)   The introduction to the plan will constitute a key, integral element in the planning process and should be subject to wide consultations among Member States;

(c)   In formulating the plan, sectoral, technical, regional and central bodies in the United Nations should be consulted in a systematic way regarding the major programmes in the plan;

(d)   The Secretary-General should draw up calendars for the consultations described above.

With regard to the programme budget:

(a)   The formulation and presentation of the proposed programme budget is a responsibility of the Secretary-General. Accordingly, at an appropriate time in the non-budget year, the Secretary-General should present, for consideration and approval by Member States, an outline of the programme budget for the next biennium, based on the medium-term plan and on decisions taken by the legislative organs of the United Nations, with an indication of the overall level of resources to accommodate the activities of the Organization during the following biennium and on priorities;

(b)   This outline should include expenditures related to the political activities of a "perennial character" and their related conference costs;

(c)   The outline should also include a contingency fund covering the same budget period, expressed as a percentage of a the overall level of resources, to accommodate "add-ons";

(d)   If "add-ons" are proposed that exceed resources available within the contingency fund, such "add-ons" can only be included in the budget through redeployment of resources from low-priority areas, or modifications of existing activities. Otherwise, such additional activities will have to be deferred to a later biennium (unless the General Assembly decides otherwise).

An indicative list of points still to be resolved follows:

(a)   The decision-making process;

(b)   The intergovernmental machinery;

(c)   The definition of "add-ons";

(d)   The basis for determining the level of resources (i.e. "available", "necessary" or "amount of resources that Member States can and are prepared to make available").

2.5 Document A/42/225*

Questions Relating to the Programme Budget: Inflation and Currency Fluctuation, and the Level of the Contingency Fund

Report of the Secretary-General

20 April 1987

1. The present report is submitted in pursuance of annex I, paragraph 10, of General Assembly resolution 41/213 of 19 December 1986, which states:

> "A comprehensive solution to the problem of all additional expenditures, including those deriving from inflation and currency fluctuation, is also necessary. It is desirable to accommodate these expenditures, within the overall level of the budget, either as a reserve or as a separate part of the contingency fund set up in paragraph 8 above. The Secretary-General should examine all aspects related to the question and report, through the Advisory Committee on Administrative and Budgetary Questions and the Committee for Programme and Co-ordination, to the General Assembly at its forty-second session."

The report also addresses the question of the contingency fund, which, under the new budget process and in accordance with paragraph 8 of the same annex, will be included in the programme budget to accommodate additional expenditures derived from legislative mandates not provided for in the proposed programme budget or from revised estimates excluding those relating to unforeseen and extraordinary expenses and those relating to fluctuations in the rates of inflation and exchange. In this connection, a procedure that could be followed for the administration of such a fund is outlined, and a level that might be appropriate for the forthcoming biennium is proposed.

2. The circumstances that give rise to adjustments in the level of resources submitted by the Secretary-General in his proposed programme budget - adjustments that usually, but not always, tend to be additions - and the stages at which such adjustments are made are outlined in the following paragraphs.

I. Nature and level of adjustments in current and previous programme budgets

3. The Secretary-General submits his proposed programme budget in April of the year preceding the beginning of a biennial period (e.g., in April 1985 for the biennium 1986-1987). The proposed programme budget lists the activities

---

*A/42/225, pp. 1-12.

that would be covered and the services that would be provided during the biennium, together with estimates of the financial resources required. The proposed programme budget also contains a provision for inflation but makes no provision for currency fluctuations. Provision for inflation is made on the basis of the best assumptions available at the time of the preparation of the proposed programme budget regarding cost increases, where anticipated, in respect of non-salary-related items, and of standard cost parameters, that is, salaries of the General Service and related categories, post adjustments of the Professional and higher categories and the related common staff costs. No provision is made for the effects of movements of rates of exchange in view of the unpredictable nature of currency fluctuations. The rates of exchange used for converting, into United States dollars, anticipated expenditures in other currencies are those that had been approved by the General Assembly on the basis of the first programme budget performance report for the previous biennium.

4. The proposed programme budget is reviewed first by the Committee for Programme and Co-ordination and the Advisory Committee on Administrative and Budgetary Questions and subsequently by the Fifth Committee. Consideration of the proposed programme budget by the Fifth Committee begins with a general debate, during which Member States have an opportunity to express their views on the programme budget as a whole and on such issues as the overall level of resources and the overall policies established by the Secretary-General. The Committee then proceeds to an examination of the budget section by section and, taking into consideration the estimates proposed by the Secretary-General and the related recommendations of the Advisory Committee on Administrative and Budgetary Questions and the Committee for Programme and Co-ordination, approves an amount of resources for each section. This section-by-section review and approval is commonly referred to as the "first reading".

5. The Committee also considers and takes action on a number of reports that require changes in the level of resources approved on first reading. These reports may be broken down into the following categories:

(a) Statements of the programme budget implications of draft resolutions, that is, activities being considered directly by the plenary or on the recommendation of a Main Committee, for which resources were not included in the proposed programme budget and which, if approved, would require additional resources;

(b) Revised estimates submitted by the Secretary-General relating to: (i) items not included in the proposed programme budget owing to the unavailability of information at the time of the preparation of the proposed programme budget; (ii) items that were included in the proposed programme budget but were not acted on at first reading pending submission of further information; and (iii) developments that took place after the preparation of the proposed programme budget;

(c)   The consolidated statement of conference-servicing costs: that is, during the course of a session of the General Assembly, in the consideration of draft resolutions that call for the convening of meetings not provided for in the proposed programme budget, statements of programme budget implications are submitted in which the conference-servicing costs for additional conference activities are provided for on the basis of full costing, that is, on the assumption that no part of the conference-servicing requirements would be met from existing resources; such statements do not, however, contain a request for additional resources in respect of these costs; instead, an indication is provided that towards the close of the session, a consolidated statement would be prepared, outlining the net financial impact of the various additional conference activities requested during the session in the context of the overall conference-servicing work-load for the following year, and the related additional resources would be requested;

(d)   The recosting of the resources approved on first reading and of subsequent adjustments, based on the latest available operational rates of exchange, the latest information regarding rates of inflation and adjustments to standard costs.

6.   Prior to this consideration by the Fifth Committee, the reports enumerated in paragraph 5 above are examined by the Advisory Committee on Administrative and Budgetary Questions, which submits its recommendations to the Fifth Committee.

7.   The amounts approved on first reading, to which are added the adjustments approved under (a), (b), (c) and (d), are approved on second reading and become the initial appropriations that the General Assembly approves for the biennium.

8.   When approving the initial appropriations, the General Assembly also makes provision, by a separate resolution, for unforeseen and extraordinary expenses that may arise at some point in the biennium when the Assembly is not in session. This resolution spells out the conditions under which the Secretary-General may enter into commitments in the biennium to meet unforeseen and extraordinary expenses arising either during or subsequent to that biennium.

9.   The initial appropriations voted by the General Assembly, in the year immediately preceding the biennial budget period, are revised at the end of the first year of the biennial period. At the session falling in the first year of the biennial period, the Fifth Committee considers and takes actions on: (a) statements of programme budget implications; (b) revised estimates; (c) the consolidated statement of conference-servicing costs; and (d) the first performance report.

10. The first performance report outlines the adjustments required to the initial appropriations as a result of: (a) changes in rates of exchange and inflation

and adjustments to standard costs; (b) unforeseen and extraordinary expenses incurred; and (c) other changes (adjustments deemed unavoidable and, to a large extent, of a non-recurrent nature) that, for all intents and purposes, constitute a form of revised estimates. Adjustments (increases or decreases) to standard costing parameters used for calculating salary and common staff costs provisions, consisting of average payroll charges by grade and duty station, turnover rates and common staff costs rates as a percentage of salaries, formerly were included under the heading of inflation. Since the biennium 1984-1985, they have been separately identified in performance reports as part of continuing efforts to refine the elaboration of standard costs and in order to provide greater transparency. Though separately identified, they remain inflationary in nature.

11. Adjustments are also made to the programme budget implications and revised estimates on the basis of changes in rates of exchange and inflation and adjustments to standard costs approved in the context of the first performance report.

12. The initial appropriations approved by the General Assembly, as modified by adjustments approved in respect of the statements of programme budget implications, the revised estimates, the consolidated statement of conference-servicing costs, the first performance report and the recosting, are then approved by the Fifth Committee and become the revised appropriations that are submitted to the General Assembly for approval.

13. Prior to this consideration by the Fifth Committee, the reports enumerated above are examined by the Advisory Committee on Administrative and Budgetary Questions, which submits its recommendations to the Fifth Committee.

14. During the second year of the biennium, the second performance report is submitted and reviewed by the Fifth Committee. The second performance report lists the adjustments proposed in respect of: (a) changes in rates of exchange and inflation and adjustments to standard costs; (b) any unforeseen and extraordinary expenses that may have been incurred; and (c) an assessment of the resources actually required on the basis of expenditure incurred during the first 18 months of the biennium. The adjustments approved by the Fifth Committee are submitted to the General Assembly and become the final appropriations for the biennium.

15. Prior to this consideration by the Fifth Committee, the reports enumerated above are examined by the Advisory Committee on Administrative and Budgetary Questions, which submits its recommendations to the Fifth Committee.

16. Adjustments to the proposed programme budget as submitted by the Secretary-General are therefore made at three points in the biennial cycle: (a) prior to its adoption and the beginning of the biennium; (b) at the end of the

first year of the biennium; and (c) at the end of the second and final year of the biennium. The estimates contained in the proposed programme budget for the biennium, together with the subsequent adjustments resulting from the procedure described in the preceding paragraphs, are outlined in annex I*, covering the bienniums 1980-1981, 1982-1983 and 1984-1985 and up to the first year of the biennium 1986-1987.

17. These adjustments can also be broken down into seven categories: (a) adjustments made at the time of the first reading; (b) those resulting from the statements of programme budget implications; (c) those resulting from the consolidated statement of conference-servicing costs; (d) those resulting from revised estimates; (e) those resulting from unforeseen and extraordinary expenses; (f) those resulting from changes in the rates of inflation and exchange and adjustments to standard costs; and (g) those resulting from a reassessment, towards the end of the biennium, of the level of appropriations required. Annex II* provides a breakdown of the level of resources resulting from such adjustments on a biennial basis, both in dollar terms and as a percentage of the proposed programme budget in respect of the last three bienniums for which complete data are available, namely 1980-1981, 1982-1983 and 1984-1985. Partial information relating to the current biennium is also provided.

Adjustments made at first reading

18. Adjustments made at first reading invariably result in reductions of the proposed programme budget submitted by the Secretary-General. This is due to the fact that the reductions recommended by the Advisory Committee on Administrative and Budgetary Questions following its examination of the proposed programme budget tend to be accepted by the Fifth Committee. These reductions fall into three broad categories:

(a) The resources requested are not sufficiently justified and/or stricter controls and more efficient management could lead to economies; for example, in the consideration of the proposed programme budget for the biennium 1984-1985, the resources requested for the Department of International Economic and Social Affairs in respect of consultants and *ad hoc* expert groups were reduced by $134,900, on the basis of a review of expenditure patterns in previous years - a reduction that had been recommended by the Advisory Committee on Administrative and Budgetary Questions in its report[1] - and those required for utilities at the Vienna International Centre were reduced by $330,800 on the basis of the recommendation of the Advisory Committee on Administrative and Budgetary Questions,[2] as economies were felt possible with strict monitoring of consumption;

---

*Not reprinted here.

(b) The costing parameters on which the estimates were based need to be modified; for example, the estimates in respect of Professional posts at the Economic and Social Commission for Asia and the Pacific (ESCAP) in the proposed programme budget for the biennium 1984-1985 were based on the assumption of a turnover deduction of 5 per cent; in the light of the vacancy rate then prevailing at ESCAP, the Advisory Committee on Administrative and Budgetary Questions recommended that the turnover deduction should be increased from 5 per cent to 8 per cent;[3] acceptance of this recommendation resulted in a reduction of $613,200 in the estimates proposed for ESCAP;

(c) A review of the estimates needs to be deferred pending the submission of further information; for example, in the context of the proposed programme budget for the biennium 1984-1985, the resources requested for the continuation of activities in the field of population at the regional level, $711,400, were not acted on at first reading pending the submission of a report by the Secretary-General on alternative courses of action to enable the continuation of such activities.[4]

19. Reductions effected under (a) above are not normally the subject of further requests in the course of the biennium. Those effected under (b) may be adjusted in the context of the performance reports, should experience in the course of the biennium so warrant. Those effected under (c) are usually temporary in nature and are reconsidered during the biennium on the basis of further reports, and resources subsequently approved are treated as revised estimates. To the extent that these revised estimates do not exceed the level of resources that was initially included in the proposed programme budget but not considered on first reading, they may not be termed additional expenditures.

Programme budget implications

20. Activities that give rise to programme budget implications tend to vary from year to year, except for a core of such activities that have become known as "perennials"; "perennials" are characterized by the fact that they are primarily of a political nature and their mandates are renewed by the General Assembly on an annual basis. Annex III* contains a list of resources added to the programme budget as a result of the consideration of programme budget implications, broken down by biennium, General Assembly session and three main functional categories: (a) perennials; (b) special conferences, international years and anniversaries and decades, including preparatory and follow-up work; and (c) other activities that do not fit into either of the first two categories.

21. On a biennial basis, the overall amount of resources added as a result of the consideration of statements of programme budget implications declined

---

*Not reprinted here.

both in dollar terms and as a percentage of the resources contained in the proposed programme budget. There has, however, been a significant shift among the three categories, with the "perennials" assuming an ever-increasing share of the resources added as a result of the consideration of statements of programme budget implications, as may be seen in annex IV*.

The consolidated statement of conference-servicing costs

22. The amounts added through the consolidated statement are a reflection of the meetings added to the "regular" calendar of conferences through legislative action. There have been sizeable variations in the amounts so added and the tendency has been towards a reduction over the last three bienniums.

Revised estimates

23. The subjects covered through revised estimates and the amount of resources added as a result of consideration of revised estimates are outlined in annex V*. They are so varied that they do not lend themselves to any sort of meaningful classification. The only revised estimates recurring with regularity are those resulting from decisions of the Economic and Social Council.

Unforeseen and extraordinary expenses

24. The amount of resources added as a result of the provisions contained in the resolutions concerning unforeseen and extraordinary expenses has always been modest. Such expenses do not sizeably affect the level of resources, and they constitute a mechanism that has proven its essential value over the years.

Currency, inflation and standard costs adjustments

25. Adjustments falling in this category have the largest impact on the level of the budget, as may be seen in annex II*. Unlike those resulting from programme budget implications, the consolidated statement, revised estimates or unforeseen and extraordinary expenses, they do not have a programmatic basis and do not affect the scope or content of the activities contained in the programme budget. They are technical adjustments reflecting the revised level of resources (be it an increase or a decrease) necessary to maintain the approved level of programmatic activities.

Changes arising from a reassessment, toward the end of the biennium, of the level of appropriations

26. This category consists of the residual amounts contained in the performance report submitted at the end of the biennium, that is, those which

---

*Not reprinted here.

do not result from changes in rates of exchange and inflation or from unforeseen and extraordinary expenses but are due to factors that have turned out to be different from those anticipated in the programme budget. Examples are the reduction of $356,100 in the biennium 1984-1985 because fewer members than anticipated took part in the sessions of the International Law Commission and the reduction of $64,900 in respect of the Trusteeship Council in the same biennium because only one mission was dispatched to the Trust Territory of the Pacific Islands rather than the two missions usually carried out by the Council during a biennium.

II. The new budget process

The contingency fund

27. Paragraph 8 of annex I of General Assembly resolution 41/213 provides that the programme budget shall include a contingency fund expressed as a percentage of the overall budget level, to accommodate additional expenditures relating to the biennium derived from legislative mandates not provided for in the proposed programme budget or from revised estimates, excluding those arising from the impact of extraordinary expenses and from fluctuations in rates of exchange and inflation. Paragraph 9 of the annex provides that if additional expenditures, as defined in paragraph 8, are proposed that exceed resources available within the contingency fund, such additional expenditures can only be included in the budget through redeployment of resources from low-priority areas or modifications of existing activities. Otherwise, they will have to be deferred to a later biennium.

28. In terms of practical application, it is envisaged that the fund would be utilized to provide for additional resources that may be required as a result of the consideration of statements of programme budget implications and revised estimates as defined in paragraph 8 of annex I of General Assembly resolution 41/213, in the year preceding the biennium and in the first year of the biennium. As regards revised estimates dealing with activities that had been included in the proposed programme budget but were not acted on at first reading pending the submission of additional information, it would seem reasonable that only the amount requested over and above that included in the proposed programme budget, if any, should be met from the contingency fund.

29. The fund would not be used to meet unforeseen and extraordinary expenses covered by the resolution on unforeseen and extraordinary expenses adopted each biennium; such expenses would continue to be dealt with as heretofore. It would also not be necessary to appropriate resources for the contingency fund. General Assembly action that would seem to be required in respect of the fund would be as follows:

   (a)   In the off-budget year (i.e., in 1988 for the biennium 1990-1991), the Assembly would decide on the size of the fund in accordance with the provisions of annex I of General Assembly resolution 41/213;

(b)   During the budget year (i.e., in 1989 for the biennium 1990-1991), the Assembly would decide on the actual amounts to be utilized from the fund on the basis of statements of programme budget implications and revised estimates approved during the session and would appropriate such amounts in the context of the initial appropriations under the relevant sections for which they would be required;

(c)   The balance of the fund, that is, the difference between the amount originally approved for the contingency fund under (a) above and the amounts approved in the context of the initial appropriations under (b), would be available to accomodate additional expenditures that might arise during the next session of the General Assembly (i.e., in 1990 for the biennium 1990-1991);

(d)   At that session, the Assembly would decide on the further amounts to be utilized from the fund for the second year of the biennium, subject to the availability of resources remaining in the fund, on the basis of statements of programme budget implications and revised estimates approved during that session and would appropriate such amounts under the relevant sections for which they would be required;

(e)   Should expenditures be proposed that would exceed resources available in the fund, the provisions of annex I, paragraph 9, of General Assembly resolution 41/213 would be applied;

(f)   Any unutilized balance would, following the approval of the revised appropriations, be cancelled.

30. As regards the level of such a fund, a review of additional expenditures that have arisen over the last few bienniums reveals no common factors from biennium to biennium that would permit the establishment of a contingency fund on an historical basis, except that the types of activities that are now to be provided for through the contingency fund have always led to additional expenditures. The inclusion of resources for "perennials" and the introduction of full budgeting for conference-servicing costs in the future proposed programme budget should, to some extent, reduce the need for additional expenditures.

31. As pointed out in paragraph 21 above and as may be seen in annexes III* and IV*, there has been a downward trend in the amount of additional resources obtained through programme budget implications, with a sharp reduction in the current biennium due to the fact that the number of programme budget implications, other than those relating to "perennials", decreased from 23 in respect of the 1984-1985 biennium to four in respect of the current biennium, including none at the forty-first session of the General

---

*Not reprinted here.

Assembly, and the related additional expenditures declined from $12.4 million to $1.9 million.

32. With regard to conference-servicing costs, it should prove possible to obviate the need for an annual consolidated statement and for additional expenditures to be met from the contingency fund by providing in the proposed programme budget an amount of resources sufficient to cover the costs not only of meetings known at the time of budget preparation but also of meetings that would be subsequently authorized. Such a provision has been made in the proposed programme budget for the biennium 1988-1989, and it can reasonably be assumed that the resources would be sufficient to enable the Organization to service a number of meetings and conferences consistent with the pattern of meetings and conferences over the past five years. At the same time, indications of meeting costs at full costs, where applicable, will continue to be provided, for information purposes, in statements of the programme budget implications of draft resolutions submitted to the General Assembly and the Economic and Social Council; information will also continue to be conveyed to the Committee on Conferences when it considers changes in the calendar of conferences.

33. As regards revised estimates, no discernible trends can be identified. While biennial comparisons may point to a downward trend (see annex II*), the amount of additional expenditures arising from revised estimates in 1986-1987, namely $12,389,200, is misleading. This amount includes, as may be seen from annex V*, a reduction of $38,759,200 resulting from the separation of the United Nations Industrial Development Organization; it also includes additional expenditures resulting from revised estimates in respect of the Department of Administration and Management, $23,253,800, of which only $266,600 can be termed additional expenditures, as the balance of $22,987,200 was included in the proposed programme budget but not acted upon at first reading.

34. Past experience in respect of programme budget implications and revised estimates, while useful, cannot be used as the basis for determining the level of the contingency fund. The establishment of such a level cannot be done on a scientific basis and must, in the final analysis, be judgmental. As regards the forthcoming biennium for which preparations are under way, the new budget process will not be followed in its entirety, in view of the date of its adoption. Nevertheless, it would seem desirable to establish a contingency fund. The proposed programme budget for 1988-1989, whose preparation is nearing completion, will amount to $1,681,372,400. It reflects the impact of the recommendations of the Group of High-Level Intergovernmental Experts as adopted by the General Assembly in its resolution 41/213, in terms of reduction in travel and consultant funds and reduced provisions for staff costs in anticipation of the reductions in the number of posts that are required. Such

---

*Not reprinted here.

reductions, together with structural and other changes that are being or will be effected, will be the subject of a report complementary to the proposed programme budget. In this period of far-reaching changes, and while awaiting the outcome of intergovernmental studies, it would not seem unreasonable to anticipate that legislative action requiring new and additional activities will be at a lower level than has heretofore been the case. It is also unlikely that there would be revised estimates involving substantial additional expenditures. In the circumstances, a contingency fund amounting to 0.75 per cent of the budget, or $12,610,300, appears reasonable in order to accommodate, at the forty-second and forty-third sessions of the General Assembly, additional expenditures relating to the biennium 1988-1989 derived from legislative mandates not provided for in the proposed programme budget or from revised estimates excluding those arising from the impact of extraordinary expenses as well as fluctuations in rates of exchange and inflation.

Inflation and currency fluctuations

35. Adjustments resulting from inflation, including adjustments to standard costs, and from currency fluctuations have, at times, led to reductions and at other times to additional expenditures. These adjustments can be and have been substantial.

36. The budgetary impact of these adjustments during the bienniums 1980-1981, 1982-1983 and 1984-1985 in dollar terms and as a percentage of the estimates contained in the proposed programme budget is summarized below.

Increase (decrease) due to changes in the rates of inflation and exchange and standard costs adjustments

Biennium	United States dollars	Percentage of the proposed programme budget
1980-1981	51 680 400	4.3
1982-1983	(122 737 200)	(8.0)
1984-1985	(47 762 100)	(3.0)

As regards the current biennium, such changes have so far resulted in increases totalling $49,993,600. The strengthening of other currencies *vis-à-vis* the United States dollar since early January 1987 will, if it continues, require a further increase of $27 million in the second performance report for the biennium 1986-1987.

37. Paragraph 11 of annex I of General Assembly resolution 41/213 states that the Secretary-General should make efforts to absorb additional expenditures of this nature, to the extent possible, through savings from the programme

budget, without causing in any way a negative effect on programme delivery and without prejudice to the utilization of the contingency fund. It is evident that the impact of these adjustments, caused primarily by the volatility of currencies, can be such as to make any savings that could be effected in the course of the implementation of the budget totally inadequate to meet them. Even if it were to be agreed that additional requirements arising from changes in the rates of inflation, including adjustments to standard costs, and exchange should be met through a reduction of programme activities, the level of savings that might be required (and this could not be known in advance) and the inability of the Organization to effect such savings at short notice would force the adoption, on a continuous basis, of measures such as those that have been taken in response to the current financial crisis.

38. The new budget process approved by the General Assembly in its resolution 41/213, providing as it does for greater participation by Member States from the early stages of the process, legislative decision by the General Assembly to guide the Secretary-General in the preparation of the proposed programme budget, the establishment of priorities and the establishment of a contingency fund, implies a desire on the part of Member States to be in a position to know at the outset of a biennium the likely level of expenditures and the related level of assessments. The magnitude of adjustments due to changes in the rates of inflation and currency exchange and standard adjustments (changes that, on the one hand, are caused by circumstances beyond the control of the Secretary-General, and of the General Assembly for that matter, and, on the other, are impossible to forecast with any degree of accuracy) is such as to make it a virtually impossible task to foresee from the outset the level of expenditures in a biennium.

39. To ensure that the maximum level of expenditures is known at the outset would require a provision for potential changes in the rates of inflation, including standard costs adjustments, and currency exchange of a size sufficient to meet all eventualities. On the basis of experience in the last few bienniums, a provision of $125 million would not appear unreasonable.

40. Such a provision could be made by establishing, at the beginning of a biennium, at the time of the adoption of the proposed programme budget, a reserve that would form part of the appropriations as a separate section and would be assessed. Any increases during the biennium due to changes in the rates of inflation, including standard costs adjustments, and currency exchange, including increases that might arise prior to the approval of the proposed programme budget and the initial appropriations, would be met from the reserve. At the relevant appropriation stage, such additional requirements would be appropriated under all the sections of the budget so affected, and the appropriations for the section relating to the reserve would be reduced commensurately. Where such changes would result in reductions, these reductions would likewise be reflected, at the appropriation stage, in sections so affected, and the appropriations for the section relating to the reserve would

be increased accordingly up to the level of $125 million. Once the reserve had been replenished, further reductions would be credited to Member States.

41. The effect of such a procedure would be that increases during a biennium resulting from changes in the rates of inflation, including standard costs adjustments, and currency exchange, would not result in increases in assessments; they would have been provided for in advance. Should the need arise to replenish the reserve at the beginning of a biennium, however, this could result in sizeable increases in the level of assessment. Additional expenditures that might arise from changes in the rates of inflation, including standard costs adjustments, and currency exchange, would therefore continue to be appropriated and assessed; they would, however, be assessed every two years rather than annually as is presently the case. In the circumstances, it would appear that the current method of dealing with such adjustments, that is, increasing the appropriations and assessments whenever they give rise to additional expenditures and reducing the appropriations and assessments whenever they give rise to reductions, might still be the least inconvenient way of dealing with such changes.

Notes

1. *Official Records of the General Assembly, Thirty-eighth Session, Supplement No. 7* (A/38/7 and Corr. 1), para. 6.6.
2. *Ibid.*, para. 28.186.
3. *Ibid.*, para. 11.4.
4. *Ibid.*, paras. 27 and 28.

2.6 Document A/42/7*

**Report of the Secretary-General on Inflation, Currency Fluctuation
and the Level of the Contingency Fund (A/42/225)**

**Report of the Advisory Committee on Administrative
and Budgetary Questions**

1987

104.   The first part of this report contains a review of the nature and level of adjustments in current and previous programme budgets. A brief chronology of events in the budget cycle, from initial consideration by the Advisory Committee on Administrative and Budgetary Questions and the Committee for Programme and Co-ordination in the year preceding the start of the biennium to consideration of the second performance report during the second year of the biennium, is contained in paragraphs 3 to 15 of the report.

105.   In paragraphs 16 to 26, a description is provided of what the Secretary-General considers to be the seven major categories of adjustments made during the budget cycle: (a) adjustments made at first reading; (b) programme budget implications; (c) consolidated statement of conference-servicing costs; (d) revised estimates; (e) unforeseen and extraordinary expenses; (f) currency, inflation and standard costs adjustments; and (g) changes arising from a reassessment, towards the end of the biennium, of the level of appropriations.

106.   The second section of the report of the Secretary-General concerns the new budget process. As stated in paragraph 27 of the report:

"Paragraph 8 of annex I of General Assembly resolution 41/213 provides that the programme budget shall include a contingency fund expressed as a percentage of the overall budget level, to accommodate additional expenditures relating to the biennium derived from legislative mandates not provided for in the proposed programme budget or from revised estimates, excluding those arising from the impact of extraordinary expenses and from fluctuations in rates of exchange and inflation. Paragraph 9 of the annex provides that if additional expenditures, as defined in paragraph 8, are proposed that exceed resources available within the contingency fund, such additional expenditures can only be included in the budget through redeployment of resources from low-priority areas or modifications of existing activities. Otherwise, they will have to be deferred to a later biennium."

---

*Official Records of the General Assembly, Forty-second Session, Supplement No. 7 (A/42/7), pp. 34-37.

107.   In paragraphs 28 to 34 of his report, the Secretary-General presents a series of considerations and proposals on the question of the contingency fund. In the opinion of the Advisory Committee, they raise a number of additional questions that need to be addressed before further implementation of the provisions of General Assembly resolution 41/213 relating to the fund. The Committee therefore requests the Secretary-General to present to it, not later than 15 September 1987, a further analysis that would deal with the issues set forth in paragraphs 108 to 114 below.

(a)   *Criteria for use*

108.   In paragraph 28 of his report, the Secretary-General states:

"In terms of practical application, it is envisaged that the fund would be utilized to provide for additional resources that may be required as a result of the consideration of statements of programme budget implications and revised estimates as defined in paragraph 8 of annex I of General Assembly resolution 41/213."

In this connection, the Committee believes that it is essential for the Secretary-General to present, for the consideration of the General Assembly, his analysis and views on how the reference in paragraph 8 of annex I to "legislative mandates not provided for in the proposed programme budget" should be interpreted.

109.   Paragraph 28 of the Secretary-General's report also states:

"As regards revised estimates dealing with activities that had been included in the proposed programme budget but were not acted on at first reading pending the submission of additional information, it would seem reasonable that only the amount requested over and above that included in the proposed programme budget, if any, should be met from the contingency fund."

The Committee points out that the amounts involved as a result of the submission of additional information with regard to construction could be quite substantial and may fluctuate. Therefore, the question of how additional requirements related to construction would be dealt with needs to be addressed.

110.   A more general question that arises with regard to criteria for use involves the mechanics of the fund's operation: Will recourse to the fund be had on a "first come, first served" basis, or can procedures be developed to ensure that the General Assembly, at any given session, is aware of all potential needs at that session before a final decision is taken on the allocation of resources?

(b)   *Period covered and pattern of use*

111.   The outline provided by the Secretary-General in paragraph 29 of the report appears not to cover action that might be taken by the Assembly in the second year of a biennium with regard to that year(i.e., at the forty-second session with to activities in 1987); indeed, in paragraph 28, reference is made to use of the fund "in the year preceding the biennium and in the first year of the biennium". In the opinion of the Advisory Committee, the possibility of additional requirements in the second year of the biennium, albeit slight, needs to be taken into account. In this connection, the Advisory Committee recalls the provisions of General Assembly resolution 41/213, annex I, paragraph 8, as quoted in paragraph 106 above.   Another question that needs to be addressed is whether there should be a limit on the proportion of the fund to be used is whether there should be a limit on the proportion of the fund to be used in any given year or whether the pattern of use should be unregulated.

(c)   *Steps to be taken in the event that the fund is fully utilized*

112.   In paragraph 29 (e) of his report, the Secretary-General states that "should expenditures be proposed that would exceed resources available in the fund, the provisions of annex I, paragraph 9, of General Assembly resolution 41/213 would be applied" (see also para. 106 above). The Advisory Committee believes that it is essential for the Secretary-General to analyse the practical implications of this requirement.   For example, exactly how will such redeployments be effected and upon what authority; and how will a new activity be implemented when the balance of the contingency fund falls short of the resources required fully to finance it, but is not yet exhausted. It is also important to address questions relating to the treatment to be accorded to new mandates in the event that there is a shortfall of resources to fund fully all the additional programmes and activities approved for inclusion in the contingency fund.   In particular, consideration should be given to whether the related statement of programme budget implications should include alternative proposals to deal with the possibility that the contingency fund might not cover the related activities; this will also have a bearing on to points raised in paragraph 110 above. In addition, thought will also have to be given to how the format of the proposed programme budget can be refined so as to facilitate decisions on redeployment of resources.

(d)   *Procedures for the fund*

113.   In keeping with what has already been proposed by the Secretary-General in paragraphs 28 and 29 of his report and what may emerge as a result of a study of those questions raised in the paragraphs above, a comprehensive set of procedures governing the establishment, criteria for use, operation and monitoring of the fund should be developed for consideration by the General Assembly.

(c)   *Level of the fund*

114.   The Advisory Committee notes the statement in paragraph 34 of the report that "past experience in respect of programme budget implications and revised estimates, while useful, cannot be used as the basis for determining the level of the contingency fund". While recognizing the difficulties inherent in such an exercise, the Advisory Committee would prefer to see a more complete analysis of past experience and of the circumstances that may give rise to additional requirements in future bienniums than is contained in A/42/225 before reaching any conclusion on what to recommend to the General Assembly.

115.   Inflation and currency fluctuations are discussed in paragraphs 35 to 41 of the report of the Secretary-General. As stated in paragraph 35:

"Adjustments resulting from inflation, including adjustments to standard costs, and from currency fluctuations have, at times, led to reductions and at other times to additional expenditures. These adjustments can be and have been substantial."

116.   In paragraph 37 of his report, the Secretary-General states:

"It is evident that the impact of these adjustments, caused primarily by the volatility of currencies, can be such as to make any savings that could be effected in the course of the implementation of the budget totally inadequate to meet them. Even if it were to be agreed that additional requirements arising from changes in the rates of inflation, including adjustments to standard costs, and exchange should be met through a reduction of programme activities, the level of savings that might be required (and this could not be known in advance) and the inability of the Organization to effect such savings at short notice would force the adoption, on a continuous basis, of measures such as those that have been taken in response to the current financial crisis."

117.   The Advisory Committee is mindful of the requirement to effect "a comprehensive solution to the problem of all additional expenditures, including those deriving from inflation and currency fluctuation" and that "it is desirable to accommodate these expenditures, within the overall level of the budget, either as a reserve or as a separate part of the contingency fund ..." (General Assembly resolution 41/213, annex I, para.10).

118.   The Advisory Committee believes that the question merits further study. The Advisory Committee intends to look into this matter closely with a view to formulating specific recommendations to the General Assembly at its forty-third session. Pending these recommendations, and in view of the particularly volatile situation with regard to currencies experienced during the last year, the Committee recommends that the adjustment system now in place should be maintained.

2.7 Document A/42/16*

Question of Accommodating all Additional Expenditures within the Overall Level of the Budget (A/42/225)

Report of the Committee for Programme and Co-ordination

1988

315. At its 38th and 44th meetings, on 21 and 26 May, the Committee considered the report of the Secretary-General entitled "Questions relating to the programme budget: inflation and currency fluctuation, and the level of the contingency fund" (A/42/225).

Discussion

316. The Committee carefully examined the proposal of the Secretary-General for a contingency fund; varying opinions were expressed about the adequacy of the contingency fund proposed. Questions were raised about the practical aspects of its operation and many delegations emphasized the need to develop suitable guidance and criteria for its use and administration. Some delegations considered that the proposed contingency fund should have been incorporated in the proposed programme budget for the biennium 1988-1989. Others favoured postponing its introduction until the biennium 1990-1991.

317. Other delegations, also recalling the budget process elaborated in annex I of General Assembly resolution 41/213, were of the view that the proposal for the establishment of a contingency fund for the biennium 1988-1989 was premature. Still other delegations suggested that *ad hoc* fund could be introduced in the programme budget for the biennium 1988-1989 on an experimental basis.

318. With regard to the proposal to accomodate expenditures resulting from inflation and currency fluctuation, objections were expressed by some delegations regarding the way this question was addressed in the report of the Secretary-General (A/42/225, para. 39). There was, however, general agreement that the question needed further study.

319. Some delegations were of the opinion that such a study should be prepared by the Advisory Committee on Administrative and Budgetary Questions and submitted to the General Assembly for its consideration at the forty-second session. Some delegations considered that pending further consideration of this matter it would continue to be dealt with in the same way

---

Official Records of the General Assembly, Forty-second Session, Supplement No. 16 (A/42/16), pp. 56-57.

it had been dealt with until the present. Some delegations were of the view that $125 million proposed in the report was inadequate.

Conclusions and recommendations

320.   While acknowledging the need for further consideration of the question of accommodating all additional expenditures within the overall level of the budget, the Committee recommended that the questions of inflation and currency fluctuations should be studied in depth. In that regard, it noted that the Advisory Committee on Administrative and Budgetary Questions was also seized of those questions. The Committee decided to study the matter further in its resumed session with a view to making recommendations to the General Assembly and it decided to request the Secretary-General to present a report to it at its resumed session taking into account, views, questions and points raised in the course of the discussion including the question of a fund, as set out in General Assembly resolution 41/213.

2.8 Document A/42/234 and Corr.1*

**Reform and Renewal in the United Nations:
Progress Report of the Secretary-General on the
Implementation of General Assembly Resolution 41/213**

23 April and 1 May 1987

CONTENTS

		Para-graphs
I.	INTRODUCTION	1 - 3
II.	FOUNDATIONS FOR THE FUTURE	4
III.	THE REFORMS	5 - 65
	A. Planning the reforms	5 - 6
	B. The contents of this report	7 - 11
	C. The structure and functioning of the Secretariat	12 - 49
	1. The political sector	14 - 24
	2. The economic and social sectors	25 - 33
	3. Public information	34 - 38
	4. Conference services	39 - 42
	5. Administration and finance	43 - 49
	D. Matters pertaining to personnel and related to budgetary and administrative questions	50 - 65
IV.	CONCLUDING OBSERVATIONS	66 - 67
Chart on the implementation of reforms		

---

*A/42/234 and Corr.1.

ANNEX

ADMINISTRATION AND MANAGEMENT

			Para- graphs
I.	INTRODUCTION		1
II.	ADMINISTRATION, FINANCE AND PERSONNEL		2 - 55
	A.	Structure of the Department of Administration and Management	2 - 7
	B.	Travel costs	8 - 11
	C.	Budgetary matters	12 - 19
	D.	Rented space	20 - 21
	E.	Consultants	22 - 23
	F.	Meetings and conferences	24
	G.	Conference facilities	25
	H.	Management of human resources and delegation of authority	26 - 28
	I.	Staff regulations, staff rules and personnel manual	29 - 31
	J.	Principles and methods guiding the filling of posts	32 - 38
	K.	Women	39 - 42
	L.	Nationals of developing countries	43
	M.	Occupational groups	44 - 45
	N.	Rotation	46
	O.	Performance evaluation and promotions	47 - 50
	P.	Training	51 - 53
	Q.	Staff union activities	54
	R.	Administration of justice	55
III.	OTHER MATTERS		56 - 57
APPENDIX:	Index of recommendations by the Group of High-level Intergovernmental Experts		

I. INTRODUCTION

1. The fortieth anniversary of the United Nations was marked by a universally expressed desire on the part of Member States to strengthen the world body so that it could better serve the great purposes and principles for which it was established. The forty-first session gave practical form to this intent. Faced with a crisis that threatened the very viability of the Organization, Member States rose above their differences to agree on a series of practical steps to improve its functioning.

2. The resolution of 19 December 1986 to Review the Efficiency of the Administrative and Financial Functioning of the United Nations,[1] adopted by the General Assembly on the report of the Group of High-level Intergovernmental Experts and particularly the consensus reached on the budgetary process, could signify a historic turning point. It will do so if Governments and the Secretariat meet the imperatives of the present juncture. For it is not only the familiar concerns of efficiency and effectiveness, of streamlining and rationalization, and paring away the excessive layers of bureaucratic procedures that have inevitably built up over the years - important as these are - that are at issue. We are grappling with something much more fundamental: how to make the world organization at once more responsive to the increasingly complex and intractable global problems of today and better prepared to face the yet unknown challenges of the coming decades.

3. The process of renewal and reform must recapture the sense and purpose of the Charter of the United Nations in a world that is changing with a rapidity unprecedented in history, where one of the few constants is the ever-closer interweaving of the destinies of all countries and all peoples. This is the wider vision that I believe must guide our endeavours. I have set about the tasks incumbent upon me through General Assembly resolution 41/213 from this perspective. It is thus fortunate that we shall simultaneously be addressing not only the 1988-1989 programme budget, in which the tangible financial benefits of our efforts will begin to be reflected, but, even more significantly, the preparation of the medium-term plan for 1990-1995, which must map out the horizons of the future.

II. FOUNDATIONS FOR THE FUTURE

4. In order to pursue the goal of reform in a manner that will increasingly witness the realization of the ideals that we have accepted under the Charter, certain common points of reference must be established at the outset:

(1) A genuine commitment to the revitalization of the Organization must be shared by all its Members.

(2) There must be an end to the present financial uncertainties. No process of sound, long-term reform or rationalized management can prosper in an atmosphere of daily emergency that consumes energies and

wastes resources in devising short-term, *ad hoc* solutions. An unequivocal budgetary framework with a clearer indication of priorities, accompanied by an equally unequivocal commitment on the part of Member States to honour their obligations under the Charter, is essential to the health of the Organization. Furthermore, it is essential that all arrears be promptly paid.

(3) The essentially political roots of the financial crisis and the call for reform must both be reflected in the solutions. Improving the administrative and financial functioning of the United Nations without addressing the fundamental issue of "efficiency to do what?" will not achieve the desired objective. The implementation of the recommendations of the Group of High-level Intergovernmental Experts is therefore only one dimension of the necessary action. To enable an institution made up of sovereign States of such varying national interests to function more effectively, Member Governments must define with clarity the issues to be collectively addressed in the coming decades.

(4) The Secretariat is a principal organ of the United Nations and the Secretary-General, as its Chief Administrative Officer, has, under the Charter, the responsibility to manage its financial and human resources. This responsibility must not be eroded or divided if the Secretary-General is to organize the internal structures of the house and make the necessary personnel decisions in a manner that enhances the efficiency and the effectiveness of the Organization.

(5) Renewal and reform must be a continuing and dynamic process following an orderly and sequential approach. Rational and adequately planned implementation of the report is assured by the larger framework of the programme planning and budgeting process. The requirement that the draft programme budget for 1988-1989 be submitted at the normal time to the Committee for Programme and Co-ordination (CPC) and the Advisory Committee for Administrative and Budgetary Questions has not permitted me to reflect some of the results emanating thus far from the implementation of the recommendations made by the Group of High-level Intergovernmental Experts. Therefore, for the programme budget for the biennium 1988-1989, I shall be submitting revised estimates which, together with the 1990-1991 programme budget, will reflect the implementation of the various recommendations. At the same time, the elaboration of the medium-term plan for the period 1990-1995 should provide Member States with a unique opportunity to reflect and agree on a new and dynamic agenda for the 1990s. To that end, I shall submit a plan which will embody a vision of the long-term goals and objectives of the Organization and aim to strengthen its relevance to the global issues of peace, security and sound development.

(6) Ideally, the restructuring of the Secretariat should follow that of the intergovernmental machinery, since a direct relationship exists between

possible changes in the latter and the size, composition and work of the Secretariat staff. The Group of High-level Intergovernmental Experts pointed to the magnitude and complexity of the intergovernmental structures and the pressing need for reform. The results of the review now being carried out by Governments will not, however, be available until the three-year period for accomplishing actions within the Secretariat is nearing its close and the preparation of the 1990-1991 programme budget is far advanced. This obliges me to proceed without awaiting the outcome of the review and may therefore entail subsequent adjustments.

(7) The complexities of the reform process, as well as the impact of significant reductions of posts in circumstances of continuing financial stringency, impose a period of transition during which it will not be possible to get all the variables in place. This interim phase must be carefully planned and used to assemble the different parts of the mosaic so that, at the end of the three-year period, the full pattern will be realized. Patience and pragmatic understanding will be needed on the part of Member States and, wherever possible, the reservation of final judgements until the whole exercise has been completed.

(8) While the report of the Group of High-level Intergovernmental Experts spoke of the need to reduce staffing and costs without causing any negative impact on the current level of programme activities, it must be understood that some adjustments will be needed. This is not only on account of limited resources, but much more important, if the Organization is to keep pace with the times, then both Member States and the Secretariat must ensure that all its mandated programmes reflect genuinely priority concerns.

(9) There is also a need for both Member States and the Secretariat to accept the practical consequences of the drive for rationalization and streamlining. This will require an unprecedented degree of restraint on both sides and a willingness to set aside national, sectoral or purely bureaucratic interests.

III. THE REFORMS

A. *Planning the reforms*

5. The reform process is based on General Assembly resolution 41/213, which in turn resulted from the report of the Group of High-level Intergovernmental Experts to Review the Efficiency of the Administrative and Financial Functioning of the United Nations. I have also taken full account of the findings of the Fifth Committee in its report to the General Assembly (A/41/795), as well as of the other indications included in resolution 41/213.

6. I have on numerous occasions reiterated my own strong commitment to economy and administrative efficiency and had taken energetic steps from the

very outset of my first term in office. The ambitious and comprehensive programme of reforms now envisaged clearly requires special impetus and careful preparation. To that end I appointed, in September 1986, a Special Co-ordinator, working out of my office in close co-operation with the Director-General for Development and International Economic Co-operation and the Under-Secretary-General for Administration and Management, and assisted by a small team of officials redeployed from their regular functions. The intention was not to duplicate existing mechanisms or create new structures, but to provide, under my personal direction, the necessary planning and co-ordinating framework and the initial momentum. In short, the role of the Special Co-ordinator's Office has been catalytic rather than operational. Now that the process is well underway, the office is being disbanded, and the follow-up actions will be taken through the normal channels, with the key responsibility assigned to the Under-Secretary-General for Administration and Management.

B. The contents of this report

7. Since the actions prescribed over the three-year period 1987-1989 cover virtually all facets of the Organization's work and structures, only partial results can be chronicled in this first progress report, which is written barely three months after the General Assembly adopted the resolution.

8. One of the complicating factors in this immense task is that many of the required actions are intimately interrelated. Much of this initial period has therefore been necessarily devoted to planning the overall operation, lest we lose sight of the wood for the trees. It is accordingly my aim not only to record here those actions towards reform that have already been taken, together with their implications, but also to map out the strategy for completing the rest of the work over the remainder of the three-year period.

9. There are also problems of presentation. The recommendations that I am called upon to implement vary from injunctions of a broad, sweeping nature to others of close administrative detail, even minutiae. Their impact is similarly diverse: at one extreme, with consequences of a policy, and even political, nature; at the other, of a technical character requiring to be reflected in budget fascicles or administrative instructions. In order to do justice to these widely different aspects and concerns, while still maintaining the concept of the reform process as a composite whole, I am confining the main body of this report to a broad description of the actions taken, and planned, in the context of the general policy and philosophical thrust of the reforms, and attaching as an annex more detailed information on specific administrative, financial and personnel matters.

10. In order to facilitate comprehension of the time-frame and the complex interrelationships between the work of the intergovernmental bodies and that of the Secretariat on the issues relating to the reforms, the medium-term plan

for the period 1990-1995 and the programme budget, a chart of the whole process is provided on page 23 of the present report.*

11. The 71 recommendations contained in the report of the Group of High-level Intergovernmental Experts, in so far as they affect the Secretariat, can be considered as falling into two broad categories: those entailing structural reviews, leading to streamlining and rationalization; and those concerned with personnel and administrative matters, ranging from reduction in the number of posts to specific budgetary and administrative concerns. The two categories are obviously interlinked, but in order to present the overview more clearly I shall deal with them separately.

C. The structure and functioning of the Secretariat

12. The recommendations of the Group of High-level Intergovernmental Experts posit reviews in virtually every aspect of the Secretariat's activities:

(a)   The political sector;

(b)   The economic and social sectors;

(c)   Public information;

(d)   Conference services;

(e)   Administration and finance.

13. Reviews have been launched in all of these areas. Some are virtually completed, others still in progress. In all cases I have instructed that close attention be paid to the general concerns expressed in section III of the report of the Group of High-level Intergovernmental Experts, namely, the need to eliminate duplication and increase productivity and cost-effectiveness, thus enabling the Organization to be more responsive to the needs of Member States; to reduce top-heaviness, fragmentation and undue complexity, in order to arrive at a leaner and more efficient Secretariat; and to consolidate field offices wherever possible.

1. The political sector

14. In the case of the political sector, the Group of High-level Intergovernmental Experts pointed out that no less than nine departments, centres or offices existed and made a number of recommendations for simplifying them.

---

*See *Chart on the implementation of reforms* following para. 67.

15. In consonance with the approach described in the introduction to the present report, I have, in reviewing the political sector, not only taken into account the general and specific issues raised by the Group, but also the equally impelling need to fashion a structure for dealing with political issues that will equip the Organization to serve the goals of the Charter in the decades ahead.

16. One of the main tasks of a forward-looking and dynamic United Nations must surely be to try to guide the often opposing tendencies of interdependence and national interests into courses that may ultimately converge, in the interests of the future security - in the widest sense of the term - of the world community as a whole. What is necessary is understanding of the critically important interests that transcend national ambitions or concerns and constitute a unifying element for all nations and societies.

17. How can we best embark on such a daunting endeavour?   First and foremost, I believe that we must concentrate on seeing problems in the proper light. One of the duties of the United Nations in a crisis, or in anticipation of a crisis, is to be alert to all the nuances and to serve as an ever-available forum for contacts between Governments that can allay the underlying fears and suspicions.   Within the framework of the United Nations, solutions may develop which the adversaries, left to themselves, would never consider. However, this requires conscious support on the part of Member States continuously to strengthen the means available to the United Nations to keep watch over actual and potential points of conflict.

18. Information and communication, properly used, are key instruments here. Yet, the means at the disposal of the United Nations for obtaining up-to-date, publicly available information have been primitive by comparison with those of many Member States - and indeed most transnational corporations. In order to carry out successfully his responsibilities under the Charter and implement the political tasks mandated to him by the Security Council and the General Assembly, the Secretary-General needs to be able to marshal more effectively than at present the available information so as to enable him to institute expeditiously the most appropriate means of preventive diplomacy in particular situations of tension and potential conflict. What is needed, in sum, is a more refined instrument which will increase the Organization's preparedness for emergencies and enable it to act surely and swiftly. Moreover, strengthening the institutional basis of preventive diplomacy would also facilitate the work of the Security Council. Information and sound analysis are essential tools for breaking down the barriers to peace-making.

19. In order to make the fullest use of available resources for this purpose, the changes that I have introduced into the political sector, and announced on 2 March 1987, included the establishment of the Office for Research and the Collection of Information, in which the collection and dissemination of publicly available data previously performed in various offices have been consolidated and a structure created to take full advantage of the Secretariat's capacity to

identify threats to peace at an early stage. The Office will co-ordinate long-range analysis and related research to be provided by the appropriate departments, to which the data resources of the new office will be available, as appropriate. This arrangement responds to the concerns of the Group of High-level Intergovernmental Experts regarding duplication of such efforts and the consequent need to consolidate them, expressed in their recommendation 18.

20. Rationalization has also been the keynote of the other changes made in these structures. As a result, five offices have been consolidated into other entities, namely:

(a)   The work of the Office for Field Operational and External Support Activities (aside from information dissemination) has been integrated into the Department of Administration and Management, in accordance with recommendation 17;

(b)   The political responsibilities of the Office for Special Political Questions have been consolidated into the Department for Special Political Questions, Regional Co-operation, Decolonization and Trusteeship. Secretariat support for the Commissioner for Namibia is also being consolidated in that Department where service is provided for the Council for Namibia. This arrangement responds both to recommendations 19 and 21 of the Group of High-level Intergovernmental Experts;

(c)   The functions of the Office of Secretariat Services for Economic and Social Matters relating to the technical servicing of meetings are being assumed by the Department for Political and General Assembly Affairs and Secretariat Services;

(d)   The functions of the Special Representative of the Secretary-General for Co-ordination of Humanitarian Assistance Programmes to Kampuchea have been assumed by the Executive Secretary of the Economic and Social Commission for Asia and the Pacific, in the field, and by the Under-Secretary-General for International Economic and Social Affairs at Headquarters (thus fusing the function with that of Special Representative of the Secretary-General for Humanitarian Affairs in South-East Asia, already held by that Under-Secretary-General).

21. Most aspects of the work on maritime matters have been consolidated into the Office for Ocean Affairs and the Law of the Sea.

22. The resources implications of these changes are still being worked out at the time of writing this report, but preliminary estimates indicate that they should lead to a significant saving of posts, nearly half of them at the Professional level.

23. In the case of recommendation 20 - the proposed structuring of the Department for Disarmament Affairs so that it may better assist Member States in following disarmament negotiations and related disarmament questions - a review is underway, and the results will be implemented later this year.

24. These actions respond to recommendations 16, 17, 18, 19, 20 and 21 of the Group of High-level Intergovernmental Experts. Under the section entitled "Political affairs" in its report, the Group of High-level Intergovernmental Experts clustered some other recommendations that also have connotations for the economic and social spheres, namely, recommendations 22, 23 and 24. These accordingly form part of the overall review of the economic and social sectors to which I will turn next.

2. The economic and social sectors

25. The report of the Group of High-level Intergovernmental Experts points out the great importance of the economic and social sectors in the United Nations as reflected in the high percentage of resources allocated to them and their enormous complexity, variety and geographic dispersion. The problems identified by the Group relate not only to duplication, as in the political sector, but also on the perception that the work carried out in research, analysis and operational activities is not "sufficiently responsive to the changing realities at the global and regional levels".

26. My earlier observations about the sweeping transformations that have taken place in the world since the founding of the United Nations are even more apposite to the economic and social sphere. The United Nations has adopted a pragmatic approach in responding to these developments, in seeking a mutual accommodation to diverse interests and in balancing the innate contradictions between the inward-looking concerns of nationalism and the ever-more pressing demands for international co-operation. The resultant multiplicity of offices and range of effort reflect the constantly changing priorities of Member States as well as an increasing appreciation of the multi-disciplinary nature of economic and social development. The current review provides an opportunity to reassess both structure and functioning so as to ensure continuing relevance in our work.

27. I have in other contexts expressed my grave concern about the serious problems that afflict the international economy and, in particular, their negative impact on prospects for developing countries. In general terms then, the challenge to the international community is how to manage the growing interdependence of States. The plight of so many developing countries, mired in debt and forced to impose harsh adjustment policies that further reduce what are, in many cases, already pitifully meagre living conditions, is common headline news today. But the industrialized countries are themselves in the throes of difficult adjustment processes as a result of social and industrial

changes, brought about, *inter alia*, by the vertiginous advances in science and technology and the concurrent problems of unemployment and often widening income differentials. Nor can they remain immune or aloof from the troubles of the developing world, because the ultimate destinies and welfare of both are inexorably linked through commerce and, in the last analysis, by the finite nature of the world trading economy as a whole. Moreover, if the necessary resources for development are not made available, social deterioration can be expected to continue and become an increasingly serious source of political unrest and instability. There is, therefore, an immediate need to reverse current trends of stagnation and deterioration.

28. The requirement to see the world economy as a whole poses new and major demands on multilateral co-operation and offers a special role for the United Nations. In addition to carrying out many activities of direct benefit to peoples around the globe, the United Nations is uniquely qualified to be the forum for developing new working consensus for world economic and social development which integrates the various specializations within the Organization itself (e.g. environment, human settlements, etc.) and draws on the expertise of the system as a whole. First, the primary objectives of the United Nations, as set out in the Charter, coincide with the highest historical ideals of all of humanity. Second, its political base and universality make it a natural forum in which to pursue analytical approaches that differ from those of other organizations with special sectoral concerns and limited membership. Third, the United Nations is multi-disciplinary and should take greater advantage of this asset to adopt an innovative and more integrated approach to development and international economic co-operation issues. Fourth, its operational activities are neutral and have been effective, even in sensitive areas. They are, moreover, strongly slanted towards improving the quality of life and putting a human face on development. These special characteristics must shape any restructuring proposals made either by Member States in the context of the review of the intergovernmental machinery or, more generally, by myself.

29. These complexities, and the need to look at the problem from the perspective of making the economic and social structures and activities of the United Nations more attuned to the realities of today's world economy and social problems, call for an in-depth review, as recognized by the Group of High-level Intergovernmental Experts. Such a review was started in December 1986, in response to recommendation 25 (1), under the direction and responsibility of the Director-General for Development and International Economic Co-operation and is expected to be completed by the end of 1987.

30. This does not, of course, preclude immediate action and I have taken a number of important decisions in this regard, which are already being implemented:

(a)   With regard to enhancing the authority of the Director-General for Development and International Economic Co-operation in carrying out his responsibilities as set forth in General Assembly resolution 32/197 [recommendation 25 (3)], it is emphasized that the Director-General operates under the authority of the Secretary-General from whom his own derives; accordingly, no additional legislative authority is required. The Director-General will continue to assist the Secretary-General in arranging regular informal consultations among executive heads of the United Nations system, as well as to organize regular meetings of groups of managers within the United Nations to review and discuss activities in specific economic and social sectors, with the view to promoting greater co-operation and joint work in the implementation of work programmes;

(b)   As a practical measure to facilitate inter-agency co-ordination, the Assistant Secretary-General of the Office of the Director-General for Development and International Economic Co-operation has been designated to serve as well as Chairman and Secretary of the Organizational Committee and the Administrative Committee on Co-ordination, respectively;

(c)   General Assembly resolution 32/197 provides the basic framework for the clustering of activities in the economic and social sectors, in particular with regard to the Department of International Economic and Social Affairs, the Department of Technical Co-operation for Development, the United Nations Conference on Trade and Development (UNCTAD) and the regional commissions.   More recently, the Centre for Social Development and Humanitarian Affairs has been established as a separate entity as a part of a broader reorganization of social activities in Vienna. A review is underway with a view to defining more clearly the responsibilities and interrelationships of these basic units in the light of experience and current requirements in order to establish a basis for a more efficient, effective and coherent allocation of responsibilities in the economic and social sectors;

(d)   In response to recommendation 27, a Secretariat study on the regional commissions will be undertaken to consider further implementation of General Assembly resolution 32/197 as well as the desirability of concentrating areas of emphasis reflecting conditions in the respective regions and enhancing complementarities among the commissions and with other United Nations entities;

(e)   At Headquarters, the heads of the Centre for Transnational Corporations and the Centre for Science and Technology for Development will be reporting to me through the Under-Secretary-General for International Economic and Social Affairs. With regard to the Centre for Science and Technology for Development, I will recommend that the General Assembly resolution 34/218 ("United Nations Conference on Science and Technology for Development") be amended accordingly;

(f)   In Geneva, the Director-General of the United Nations Office at Geneva has assumed supervisory responsibility for human rights activities. This brings the double advantage of ascribing greater prominence to a key component of the Organization's activities that is vitally relevant to peoples all over the world, while at the same time contributing to the reduction of senior posts and the perceived "top-heaviness" and fragmentation of the present structures;

(g) In Vienna, in pursuance of the heightened focus on social issues predicated earlier, and in response to recommendation 25 (1), United Nations activities on social policy and development have been concentrated under the Director-General of the United Nations Office at Vienna, incorporating the Centre for Social Development and Humanitarian Affairs (which, for that purpose, has now been detached from the Department of International Economic and Social Affairs in New York) and, after the International Conference on Drug Abuse and Illicit Trafficking to be held in June 1987, the co-ordination of all United Nations drug-related programmes previously undertaken by the Under-Secretary-General for Political and General Assembly Affairs. This arrangement will have the substantive advantage of clustering together important interrelated activities in the social field that have previously been dealt with in a less unified manner and should enable the Organization to speak with a clearer and more coherent voice on major social issues, including many that are perceived worldwide as central to development in its most profound sense and to the attainment of political and social stability based on justice. The essential linkages with the economic activities of the Organization will be assured through close co-operation with the Department of International Economic and Social Affairs. A further advantage here too is the economizing of higher-echelon posts, as required in recommendation 15 of the Group of High-level Intergovernmental Experts;

(h) Globally, I have embarked on changes in the representation of the United Nations in the field. This is the level where the United Nations is best able to reach out and touch the lives of ordinary people. My objective is to obtain a rational pattern of United Nations representation that is both highly effective and efficient. The underlying principles I am applying in restructuring United Nations field offices are:

(i) The United Nations should have a presence that is able to reach every part of the world;

(ii) This presence should present a cohesive and focused image of the United Nations; but should not preclude the closing or merging of existing offices where this can be justified on grounds of cost-effectiveness without having a negative impact on programme delivery;

(iii) The creation of new field offices will be avoided and every opportunity taken to use common premises and share common facilities (recommendation 12). To implement this decision, a study will be conducted in the next three months under the aegis of the Joint Consultative Group of Programmes (UNDP, UNICEF, WFP and UNFPA) to provide a systematic assessment of field offices on a country-by-country basis to determine concrete steps on how the offices, including the use of common facilities, can be rationalized without diminishing the effectiveness of programme delivery. The Office of the United Nations High Commissioner for Refugees (UNHCR) will be associated with this exercise;

(iv) As a first practical step towards simplifying representation at the field level, I have decided, in agreement with the Administrator of the United Nations Development Programme, to consolidate United Nations Information Centres with the offices of the Resident Co-ordinators/Resident Representatives, wherever this is not already the case and it can be shown that a joint arrangement will be at once more cost-effective and efficient while at the same time respecting programme delivery requirements. An in-depth study is being undertaken, with the full participation of the Department for Public Information (DPI) and UNDP and on the basis of the principles enunciated above and on the understanding that such consolidation will not result in any additional cost to UNDP. This exercise will be co-ordinated with the review undertaken by the Joint Consultative Group of Programmes mentioned above. Any eventual expansion of the joint arrangement, which already exists in a number of countries, will have, among others, two major advantages: first, it could set an example for the rest of the United Nations system, and there is no doubt in my mind that a more frugal pattern of field representation would greatly improve both the image and the impact of the system as a whole; and second, it will release much-needed resources that can be used, *inter alia*, to improve and modernize DPI's operations overall. Thus, this action addresses both recommendations 12 and 37 (3);

(v) In order to clarify further the authority of the United Nations Resident Co-ordinator and thus enhance co-ordination at the field level, as required by recommendation 11, the Resident Co-ordinator will henceforth represent the Secretary-General in the country of assignment, except in those situations where other arrangements are more appropriate;

(vi) The administration of the special economic assistance programmes will henceforth be the responsibility of UNDP, except in cases of political sensitivity where other arrangements might be appropriate. This responds to recommendation 22.

31. In addition to the actions already taken in response to recommendation 25 (1), an in-depth programmatic review of activities in the economic and social sectors is in process. The clarification of responsibilities of the major entities will serve as a basis for the allocation of specific activities, including such adjustments as may be necessary to eliminate duplication and to enhance effectiveness and complementarity of action. The following broad areas have been identified as requiring detailed attention with a view to possible reform: global analysis and reporting, energy and natural resources, science and technology, economic and technical co-operation among developing countries (ECDC/TCDC), national development strategies, and the relationship between

operational and substantive activities. The review is to be completed by the end of 1987.

32. In order to eliminate overlapping of activities of the Department of Technical Co-operation for Development (DTCD) and other United Nations organs (recommendation 26), consultations are in process between the Department of International Economic and Social Affairs and DTCD and between UNDP and DTCD to ensure complementarity of activities between substantive and operational programmes in the first instance and between funding and executing roles in the second.

33. With regard to recommendation 24, the Office of the United Nations Disaster Relief Co-ordinator (UNDRO) is being retained as a separate entity located in Geneva, but measures will be taken to improve its performance. The comprehensive review and assessment of existing mechanisms and arrangements for emergency assistance and co-ordination called for in General Assembly resolution 41/201 will provide a basis for specific recommendations both in this regard as well as for the co-ordination and rationalization of emergency humanitarian and special economic assistance programmes called for in recommendation 23.

3. Public information

34. In recommendation 37, the Group of High-level Intergovernmental Experts called for a complete overhaul of the functions, working methods and policies of the Department of Public Information. There can be no doubt that the information capacity of the Organization must keep abreast of the revolutionary advances that have taken place in this field. Such an evolution should not only be technical but, even more important, consonant with the wider vision of the role and potential of the Organization. A conceptual framework, therefore, needs to be developed for specific reforms and improvements.

35. In my observations on the political role of the United Nations, I drew attention to the overwhelming importance of information and communication. It follows that the United Nations cannot afford to be a closed institution. To date, the Organization has concentrated mainly on communications with sovereign States, the first tier of the United Nations global constituency. This has to some extent ignored the tapping of the second-tier global constituency, the world's peoples. I am convinced that I must do everything in my power to assist Governments in expounding the principles of the United Nations, to the parliaments, the media and the universities of Member countries, and to ensure that they are aware of the measures being taken to translate them into practical actions of general benefit.

36. Ways and means must be found whereby the United Nations can offer a wider doorway through which non-governmental bodies and public movements

can express ideas and promote action programmes on matters of world concern and thus feel themselves to be a more integral part of international relationships and decision-making. Such a wider dimension would also enlarge the debate on political, economic and social issues and could help to break the stalemate on many problems now institutionalized within the Organization.

37. If the United Nations is to develop the capacity to undertake a tight, realistic and acceptable agenda for the 1990s, it must seek to enlarge the circle of active public opinion in support of the United Nations and develop a new awareness of its value and potential, especially among the younger generations, by helping people to discover and visualize tangible benefits that touch their lives directly.

38. The review of the activities of the Department of Public Information with these principles and objectives in view has begun on 1 March 1987 when the new Under-Secretary-General assumed the direction of the Department. Three phases are envisaged: the first, to be completed by the beginning of June 1987, will cover the Department's major fields of activities and the management system, including access to technology and funding policies; the second, to be completed before the forty-second session of the General Assembly, will examine the distribution of human, technical and financial resources, and ways and means of rendering policies and programmes more effective in reaching opinion-builders; while the third will consist of the implementation of a new structure, to be in place by the end of 1987.

4. Conference services

39. Most of the first seven recommendations of the Group of High-level Intergovernmental Experts, relating directly or indirectly to conference services, require action by Governments, acting individually or collectively: the strengthening of the Committee on Conferences; the significant reduction of the number of conferences and meetings; the streamlining of the procedures and methods of work under the General Assembly and its subsidiary organs, particularly its Main Committees; the enforcement of the principle that United Nations bodies should meet at their respective headquarters and, in any contrary case, that all additional expenses be covered by the host Government; and the curtailment of requests by Member States that their communications be distributed as official documents.

40. The Department of Conference Services can and should play an active, supportive role in bringing about these improvements. As a general practice it has co-operated closely with the Committee on Conferences in monitoring the use made by United Nations organs of conference services and in suggesting practical ways in which the resources placed at their disposal can be applied more effectively. The response has been encouraging and has contributed to a marked improvement in efficiency.

41. In the specific context of the implementation of General Assembly resolution 41/213, the Department has sent reminders on the need for reducing the frequency and cost of meetings to all relevant bodies, with a request for specific proposals. Furthermore, the Department has already submitted to the Committee on Conferences a number of draft recommendations concerning the strengthening of the Committee itself, the object of recommendation 1 of the Group of High-level Intergovernmental Experts as well as proposals for the servicing of other intergovernmental bodies. Action is also underway to ensure the harmonization of working procedures of conference services among all United Nations offices which provide them, thus meeting another of the Group's express concerns. It is also my hope that, as a result of the Special Commission's work, Member States will be able to effect an appreciable curtailment both in the flow of documents and in the frequency of meetings relating to the economic and social sector.

42. Recommendation 34 refers specifically to actions required within the Department of Conference Services itself, both as regards increasing its efficiency generally and improving the external printing arrangements and the publications programme. Within the limitations of the resources available to acquire new equipment and take advantage of the latest technological developments, the Department seeks, on a continuous basis, to minimize the resources needed to ensure the provision of effective services, in relation to the meetings, documents and publications required by member Governments. The technological innovations proposed in the programme budget for 1988-1989 aim to increase still further the efficiency and productivity of virtually all aspects of the conference-servicing operations. I am satisfied that these measures now in train will further strengthen the Department's ability to carry out all of its activities and servicing responsibilities.

5. *Administration and finance*

43. Probably the most important proposal of the Group of High-level Intergovernmental Experts under this heading was contained in recommendation 32, which called for all Secretariat activities relating to programming planning and budgeting to be brought together within a coherent structure. Its significance derives from the obvious correlation with parallel proposals to modify planning and budgeting mechanisms addressed later in the Group's report, as recognized by the Fifth Committee in its own report to the General Assembly (A/41/795).

44. After careful review, I have established an Office for Programme Planning, Budgeting, Monitoring and Evaluation in the Department of Administration and Management, which will consolidate appropriate functions heretofore performed by the Office of Programme Planning and Co-ordination (in the Department of International Economic and Social Affairs) and the Budget Division of the Office of Financial Services (in the Department of

Administration and Management). The functions of the new office, which came into being on 1 March, are described in the annex to the present report.

45. In keeping with the importance that I have always attached to improving the functioning of the Organization, I have taken prompt action on the other specific recommendations relating to administration in the report of the Group of High-level Intergovernmental Experts. They embrace the following aims: to simplify the structure of the administrative and support services; to reduce duplication of effort; to strengthen lines of authority and to suppress hierarchical layers, with the aim of achieving greater efficiency; and to contain costs in relation to posts, travel and consultants.

46. A preliminary review of the Department of Administration and Management has led already to a number of key changes. The post of Assistant Secretary-General in charge of General Services has not been filled.

47. Furthermore, the three executive offices that formerly serviced the Offices within the Department of Administration and Management (Finance, Personnel and General Services) have been consolidated into one office, as proposed in recommendation 40. This consolidation will facilitate the management of staff in the administrative sector, reduce risks of duplication and inconsistencies and ensure tighter budgetary and financial control. Staff savings will result.

48. Further changes can be anticipated over the coming months. I am convinced that particular attention must be paid not only to structures, but also to procedures and methods of work. This work will concentrate on further computerization and greater use of technological innovations. It will also address the simplification of procedures so as to shorten lines of communication, reduce processing delays, and delegate authority appropriately while, at the same time, pinpointing responsibility and ensuring adequate accountability and control.

49. In this connection, it is proposed to undertake a comprehensive improvement of the Department of Administration and Management, Executive Offices of the other Departments and the regional commissions. In the initial phase of such an exercise the overall effectiveness and efficiency of the Department, including its structure and major components, processes, roles and responsibilities, staffing levels and costs will be reviewed. An immediately subsequent phase will address the development of an overall framework for administrative and financial systems, which is greatly needed to ensure that accurate, timely information is available to decision-makers, that key operations and functions are properly supported and that available technology is used to the maximum.

D. *Matters pertaining to personnel and related to budgetary and administrative questions*

50. The whole thrust of the report of the Group of High-level Intergovernmental Experts has far-reaching implications for the personnel of the organization. There can be no doubt that the arduous task of reform and renewal of the United Nations will exact the highest quality of service from the Secretariat, particularly since the same - indeed, better - results will be expected from a staff significantly reduced in size. It is therefore of critical importance, as I have repeatedly stressed, to bring about the changes mandated by the General Assembly in ways that will avoid lowering morale already shaken by long months of financial uncertainty. Rather, the crisis should provide an opportunity to reorient personnel policies and practices, within the framework laid down by the Charter, so as to establish a sounder basis for the development of a highly-qualified and dedicated Secretariat rooted in recognition of merit, fair practices and conditions of service proper to the high professional and personal standards required and to the international character of the service, with due regard for geographical distribution and the representation of women. This is the spirit in which I have approached the implementation of General Assembly resolution 41/213.

51. Recommendation 15 is of key importance, since it recommends a substantial reduction in the number of staff members at all levels, but particularly in the higher echelons, and establishes certain principles about the quality and composition of the Secretariat, avoidance of any negative impact on programme activities and the need for new recruitment. Subsequently section IV spells out more detailed actions relating to personnel policy and management in recommendations 41 to 62.

52. I have already taken action towards the target of a 25 per cent reduction in the number of regular budget posts at the level of Under-Secretary-General and Assistant Secretary-General (recommendation 15 (2) (b)). Since such posts numbered 57 when the report of the Group of High-level Intergovernmental Experts was issued, a total of 14 would need to be eliminated in the stipulated period of three years. As a result of the restructurings already enacted and described in the previous section, I have to date decided not to fill nine such posts.

53. The same recommendation specifies a comparable reduction in posts at those levels funded from extrabudgetary resources. I have requested the heads of the organizations concerned to advise me how they propose to implement recommendation 15. In every case, the initial replies have outlined past efforts to limit the number of higher-level posts and concluded that, for various reasons, no reduction in the present level is possible without affecting programme delivery. Moreover, they have referred to the fact that the current number and level of posts has been approved by the respective governing

bodies. For my part, I am pursuing this matter further and I am bringing this part of recommendation 15 to the attention of the governing bodies concerned.

54. The target of a 15 per cent reduction in the overall number of posts within three years, propounded in recommendation 15 (2) (a), needs to be seen both within the context of the present and projected staffing of the Organization and of the structural reviews outlined in the previous section.

55. While I have at all times striven to separate the problems of the immediate financial shortfall, which demands expeditious short-term containment measures, from the process of reform, which needs carefully planned measures devised to have a long-term impact and shape the future of the Organization in the desired direction, it is difficult to maintain this distinction in the case of personnel, since 70 per cent of the regular budget is for staff costs. It was mainly for this reason, as I explained to the Fifth Committee during the forty-first session of the General Assembly, that I had no alternative, as a responsible administrator, but to extend the recruitment freeze imposed in April 1986 until such time as the finances of the United Nations are on an even keel once more and the present imponderables, which render efficient management of resources extremely difficult if not impossible, are dispelled. In one sense, a continued freeze and the resultant increase in the vacancy rate could expedite progress towards the 15 per cent target. This, however, would mean that I would not be able to respond to the injunction, in recommendation 15 (3) (d), and supported by many Member States, that recruitment should continue, especially at the junior Professional levels. I fully agree that it is essential and urgent for new blood to be injected into the Organization. I profoundly hope, therefore, that the contributions situation will soon be regularized so as to permit me to manage the Organization in a more rational manner.

56. A further drawback to the recruitment freeze is that it is a blunt instrument, which operates haphazardly and further distorts the geographical distribution of the Secretariat, whenever staff happen to leave the Organization, for whatever reason. It thus leads inexorably to an increasingly irrational distribution of resources in relation to programme needs, just at the time when those resources need to be husbanded more carefully because they are declining. In the present circumstances I remain convinced that, out of fairness to the staff, the reduction of posts must be achieved to the maximum extent through attrition. Furthermore, the Organization does not have the wherewithal to meet the considerable financial outlays required to offer early retirement which, I believe, can be desirable in some instances, or to offer agreed termination to staff in contractual status.

57. In order to counteract the adverse effects of a continuing recruitment freeze and the process of attrition, I introduced, in December 1986, a new system of vacancy management and staff redeployment. There are two main objectives: to identify existing current vacancies which it is essential to fill in order to fulfil key programme mandates; and to redeploy to those essential

posts staff occupying posts considered of less vital importance in the present contingency.

58. While this is essentially an emergency measure to alleviate the immediate impact of the financial crisis, it has been designed in such a way that it can logically lead into the phased retrenchment, linked to restructuring, required by the report of the Group of High-level Intergovernmental Experts. It will also pave the way for a more rational and equitable system of career development and of planned job rotation as posited in recommendation 49.

59. Simultaneously, preparations are underway for launching this more far-reaching process which will have a profound effect on the Organization for years to come. There is no time to be lost. As the chart on page 23˙ demonstrates, decisions on the future size and shape of the Organization must be in place by the end of this year if the timetable for completing the whole exercise by the end of 1989 is to be achieved.

60. The reduced and modified staffing table for the Secretariat will be fully reflected in my proposed programme budget for 1990-1991. I was obviously unable to include such changes in my programme budget for 1988-1989, which reflects the number and level of posts as approved in the programme budget for 1986-1987. In order to ease the transition towards an eventual post reduction of 15 per cent by the end of 1989, I have built into the 1988-1989 budget estimates a vacancy rate higher than usual.

61. As a conceptual framework for the exercise, a model staffing profile has been developed. Since a key objective is to achieve a more balanced and less top-heavy structure, it follows that reductions at the higher levels will have to be higher than 15 per cent while those at lower levels will be less.

62. Similarly, the 15 per cent reduction cannot be arbitrarily applied across the board to all departments and offices but has to take into account the current situation in each, the actual vacancy rate, the capacity to fulfil key mandated programmes, and so on. While any reduction lower than the norm in one part of the Organization has to be compensated by higher decreases elsewhere, the burden must also be seen to be shared on a reasonably equitable basis, hard as this is to demonstrate objectively. The structural reviews will also contribute significantly to the success of this operation, both quantitatively and qualitatively.

63. I have naturally taken careful note that recommendation 15 envisages that an initial 15 per cent reduction in posts [subparagraph (2)] within three years may be followed by additional reductions as a result of restructuring [subparagraph (4)]. In practice, the order of events is likely to be somewhat different. Because the current financial difficulties impose an abrupt decline

---

˙See *Chart on the implementation of reforms* following para. 67.

in the incumbency of posts that still figure in the budget, it becomes critically important - and indeed unavoidable - to effect the 15 per cent reduction of actual posts simultaneously with the structural reviews. This is necessary in order to limit the danger of extending the arbitrariness that is the unfortunate but inescapable accompaniment of the present financial stringency. Any other approach would perpetuate present anomalies and fail to endow the Organization with a sound framework and a staffing pattern that will allow it not only to meet the immediate objective of reducing costs, but also the even more crucial challenges of the 1990s and beyond. This cannot be a mere stop-gap operation.

64. In parallel with these fundamental changes, prompt action is also being taken on the numerous recommendations contained in section IV of the report of the Group of High-level Intergovernmental Experts. The Office of Personnel Services is being strengthened so that it can contend with the strenuous task that lies ahead and its name has been changed to the Office of Human Resources Management as required by recommendation 41. Since the actions listed in the remaining recommendations are mostly of a detailed nature, they are described in the annex to the present report.

65. I have also moved to reduce still further expenditure on travel (both of representatives travelling to the General Assembly and of staff) and on consultants, as required by recommendations 6, 38 and 35 and to study ways and means of reducing rental costs in accordance with recommendation 36. Details of these matters, as well as on actions to harmonize the format of programme budgets in general (recommendation 13) and of regional commissions in particular (recommendation 28) are given in the annex, which also describes the present arrangements for ensuring the autonomy of the internal audit function and concludes that they meet the requirements of independence posited in recommendation 39.

IV. CONCLUDING OBSERVATIONS

66. From the outline I have provided in this report of the reform measures that have been set in motion, two salient conclusions emerge:

(1) The present broad reforms must be undertaken not only to increase cost-effectiveness and rationalize utilization of resources - essential as these are - but also to strengthen the United Nations so that it will be capable of bringing the world forward towards the goals of the Charter in an environment of profound and continuing change.

(2) Despite the difficulties and the short time that has elapsed between the adoption of General Assembly resolution 41/213 and the presentation of this first progress report, considerable advances have been made both as regards actions already taken and those planned:

(a) Extensive restructuring and rationalization have already been effected in the political sector, a concomitant reduction in posts will result;

(b) Several important steps of like nature have been taken in the economic and social sectors and more will follow before the end of 1987;

(c) Key changes have also been introduced in the administrative section, most important (but not exclusively) through the merging of the programming and budgeting functions, and others will ensue during the rest of the year;

(d) Similar actions are underway in the areas of public information, where new structures reflecting a dynamic new approach to the key function of making the United Nations better understood by Governments and peoples alike should also be in place by the end of this year;

(e) Continuing reviews are underway in Conference Services with a view to achieving improved management, particularly through the application of new technologies;

(f) The "top-heaviness" of the staffing structure has been significantly alleviated by the reduction in the number of Under-Secretaries-General and Assistant Secretaries-General by some 15 per cent, as a first step towards the target of 25 per cent by the end of 1989;

(g) A vacancy management and staff redeployment plan has been introduced to ensure the optimum distribution of the reduced staffing resources available in relation to the requirements of the mandated programmes, and build the foundations of a more equitable and effective system of career development;

(h) Good progress has been made to identify posts for reduction over three years in accordance with the goal of 15 per cent; the longer-term retrenchment plan is expected to yield by the end of 1987 target staffing levels for each Department and office that will guide our actions in 1988 and 1989, which will then be reflected in the 1990-1991 budget.

67. I look forward to the comments, advice and support of Governments in this endeavour.

Note

1. *Official Records of the General Assembly, Forty-first Session, Supplement No. 49* (A/41/49).

Chart on the implementation of reforms

1987

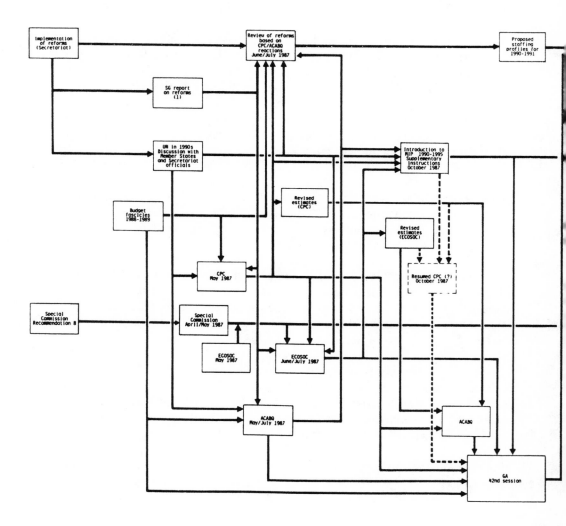

1988

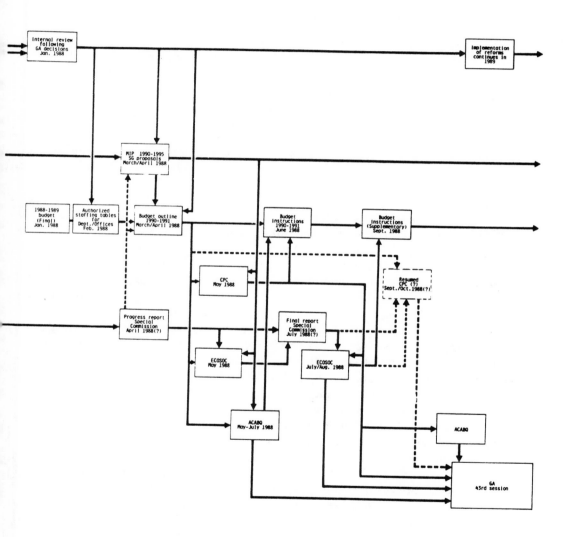

ANNEX

ADMINISTRATION AND MANAGEMENT

I. INTRODUCTION

1. The present annex contains details of the actions already taken in the area of general administration to implement General Assembly resolution 41/213 of 19 December 1986 and the recommendations presented by the Group of High-level Intergovernmental Experts, and of the plans in hand to carry out the remainder.

II. ADMINISTRATION, FINANCE AND PERSONNEL

A. Structure of the Department of Administration and Management

2. In his note to the General Assembly on the report of the Group of High-level Intergovernmental Experts (A/41/663) the Secretary-General indicated the importance he has consistently attached to improving the functioning of the Organization in order to be more responsive to the needs of the Member States and use the resources allocated in the most efficient and cost-effective manner.

3. To simplify the structure of the administrative and support services, the Secretary-General has established an Office within the Department for Administration and Management that brings together activities relating to programme planning and budgeting under a coherent structure.[1] In deciding upon this action, the Secretary-General has taken into consideration the General Assembly's decision regarding the programme planning and budgeting process and the views expressed by Member States in the Fifth Committee (A/41/795), as well as recommendation 32. The new Office of Programme Planning, Budgeting, Monitoring and Evaluation consolidates appropriate functions heretofore performed by the Office for Programme Planning and Co-ordination in the Department of International Economic and Social Affairs and the Budget Division in the Office of Financial Services. The main functions of this office will be to prepare the Secretary-General's medium-term plans based on submissions by departments and offices; to undertake cross-sectional and intersectoral analyses; to ensure co-ordination with specialized agencies in the preparation of medium-term plans; to prepare the Secretary-General's proposed programme budgets and assess the programmatic implications and estimated costs of new programmes considered by the General Assembly and its committees; to develop uniform planning, programming and budgeting techniques; to establish monitoring systems and prepare programme performance reports; to develop evaluation methods for programme managers and to conduct periodic in-depth evaluations of programmes; to assist in developing systems and data bases to facilitate the formulation of plans and programme budgets; to provide substantive support to intergovernmental and

experts bodies (Committee for Programme and Co-ordination (CPC), Advisory Committee on Administrative and Budgetary Questions, Fifth Committee of the General Assembly, etc.) and to clear documents prepared by other units for possible programme budget implications. The Office is headed by an Assistant Secretary-General who reports directly to the Under-Secretary-General for Administration and Management. The Secretary-General is convinced that this reorganization will enhance the Secretariat's contribution to the programme planning and budgeting process, including the substantive servicing of the Programme Planning and Budgeting Board (an internal advisory board), but most of all the servicing of CPC, the Advisory Committee and the Fifth Committee of the General Assembly.

4. Taking into consideration recommendation 31 and the need for a small internal management consultancy service to assist with the task of streamlining the Secretariat and enhancing its efficiency, the Management Advisory Service will now operate under the direct authority of the Under-Secretary-General for Administration and Management. This will shorten lines of communication and ensure maximum efficiency during this transitional period.

5. Furthermore, the administrative units servicing the offices within the Department of Administration and Management (Finance, Human Resources, General Services) have been consolidated into one office as proposed in recommendation 40. This consolidation will facilitate the management of staff in the administrative occupation and will ensure a tighter control of the budget and finances of these offices.

6. Recommendation 33 proposes the consolidation of the support activities of the permanent liaison offices in New York of various Secretariat entities in a single office. This matter is now under review in the light of the other structural reviews being carried out and in the context of the retrenchment plan required to implement recommendation 15.

7. It is essential to the maintenance of a proper and efficient control over the expenditures of the Organization that the internal audit function be conducted in compliance with the highest professional standards. This means, *inter alia*, its independence, and the non-subordination of the audit judgement as stated in recommendation 39. These standards are consolidated in present arrangements, whereby a separate division of the Department of Administration and Management, headed by a Director having the possibility of constant and direct access to the Under-Secretary-General, conducts audits of all Secretariat offices at Headquarters and other duty stations, and co-operates closely with the Panel of External Auditors. To ensure the autonomy of its functions, the Internal Audit Division reports directly to the head of the office being audited, and not through the Under-Secretary-General for Administration and Management. Thus, should the need arise, the Director of Internal Audit can report directly to the Secretary-General in the latter's

capacity as the Chief Administrative Officer of the Organization. These arrangements have proven satisfactory to all concerned.

B. Travel costs

8. In response to recommendation 6, the Secretary-General intends to include in the proposed programme budget for the biennium 1988-1989 a reduction in respect of travel of representatives to the General Assembly and make provision for one first class and four economy tickets for each of the 40 Member States included in the list of least developed countries.[2] The Rules Governing Payment of Travel Expenses and Subsistence Allowances in respect of Members of Organs or Subsidiary Organs of the United Nations[3] will be revised to reflect the above-mentioned recommendation. However, due to the financial crisis, reimbursement for travel of representatives to the forty-second session of the General Assembly will be further limited to one first class and two economy tickets for representatives of each of the least developed countries as proposed by the Secretary-General in his report on economy measures for 1987 and in accordance with General Assembly decision 41/466 of 11 December 1986.

9. Two measures have been taken to reduce the overall travel of staff as requested in recommendation 38. In January 1985, the Secretary-General established a procedure that requires staff to obtain prior authorization of the Executive Office of the Secretary-General for all official travel to conferences and meetings.[4] This procedure has been recently further strengthened as a result of a review of the experience in this respect and continues to play an important part in the efforts to reduce the travel of staff.

10. The second measure, introduced in January 1986, provides for a withholding of 20 per cent of the appropriations approved for travel of staff; it was taken in the context of the current financial crisis, and was extended to 1987. The proposed programme budget for the biennium 1988-1989 will also reflect reductions in resources for the travel of staff.

11. As set out in the relevant administrative instruction,[5] classes other than first class will continue to be the basic entitlement for both the United Nations Secretariat and those non-Secretariat officials covered by General Assembly resolution 37/240 of 21 December 1982.

C. Budgetary matters

12. Recommendation 13 states that efforts to harmonize the format of the programme budgets of the organizations of the United Nations system should be vigorously pursued. In 1985, the General Assembly adopted resolution 40/250 of 18 December 1985 on administrative and budgetary co-ordination of the United Nations with the specialized agencies and the International Atomic Energy Agency, in which, *inter alia*, it recommended "that further efforts be

made to achieve the maximum possible standardization and comparability in the budgetary and administrative practices of all organizations concerned".

13. In September 1986, owing to time constraints the General Assembly postponed consideration of item 113, "Administrative and budgetary co-ordination of the United Nations with the specialized agencies and the International Atomic Energy Agency", until its forty-second session.

14. In a document to the Fifth Committee (A/C.5/41/23), the Administrative Committee on Co-ordination (ACC) quoted from a statement by the Chairman of the Advisory Committee on Administrative and Budgetary Questions to that Committee at the thirty-ninth session of the General Assembly, as follows:

"... Many similarities existed in the ways the agencies prepared their budgets, as a result of the considerable efforts made over the years to promote standardization and harmonization. However, it was inevitable - but that should be no cause for concern - that differences would remain in technique and approach which were the result of a variety of factors, such as the structure and size of the agency, the procedures of its legislative body and the nature of its programme. The Advisory Committee therefore considered that, while further effort at standardization and harmonization should be encouraged, it should also be borne in mind that the prime objective in preparing a budget should be to set forth the estimates in a manner which was clear and understandable to the governing body concerned and which was responsive to the special requirements of that body."

15. Agreements have been worked out under ACC auspices over the years to harmonize budgeting practices and budget presentation among the organizations of the system. ACC stated at the forty-first session that these agreements constituted a solid basis for harmonization in budgeting practices and improved transparency and comparability of budget documents, to the extent that these aims are compatible with individual governing bodies' need for consistency in the presentation of successive budgets. As noted also by ACC, the Joint Inspection Unit work programme includes a comparative study, scheduled for completion in 1987, of the budgets of the organizations of the system. This matter will therefore be before the General Assembly at its forty-second session.

16. Recommendation 28 proposed that the format for the presentation of resources pertaining to the regional commissions should be harmonized in future programme budgets [to include costs of administration, conference and general services for the Economic Commission for Europe (ECE) budget section].

17. Under the present arrangement, resources for administration, conference and general services for different United Nations entities at Geneva, including ECE, are combined and administered by the United Nations Office at Geneva

(UNOG), whereas for the other regional commissions these resources are included in the regular budgets of these commissions, as noted in recommendation 28. The costs relating to administration, general services and conference services are included in the parts of sections 28 and 29 of the proposed programme budget, respectively, which deal with the budgets for UNOG. This integrated management system has proved to be effective and more efficient than having the resources administered by each of the entities concerned located in Geneva such as the United Nations Conference on Trade and Development, the Economic Commission for Europe, the Center for Human Rights and the Office of the United Nations Disaster Relief Co-ordinator.

18. In order to provide the required information without losing the advantages of the integrated management, the present system will be continued in the proposed programme budget for 1988-1989 but the resources provided in UNOG's budget relating to ECE will be indicated in the introduction of section 10 which pertains to ECE.

19. In accordance with recommendation 62, the Secretary-General has discouraged the practice of transferring extrabudgetary posts to the regular budget. Accordingly, no request for the transfer of such posts is included in his proposals for the 1988-1989 programme budget.

D. Rented space

20. A major consideration in the rental of outside premises has been the ability to consolidate offices and departments into rational units as regards utilization of space. While it is recognized that a logical consequence of the reduction in the overall size of the Secretariat will bring about a reduction in the requirement for office space, such space cannot be relinquished at the cost of sacrificing its rational use. Thus, the surrender of rental space (by whatever contractual means available to the Organization under the terms of existing leases), although in the long run reflecting the reduction in the number of staff members, cannot be strictly concurrent with this reduction.

21. In the latter part of 1986, a study of reciprocal rental arrangements between the United Nations, specialized agencies and other organizations within the system was initiated. In conjunction with this study, it is the intention to review the existing overall arrangements on rental premises, also including in that review a qualitative assessment to the Organization of renting out the premises.

E. Consultants

22. Recommendation 35 on the reduction of the amount spent on outside consultants by 30 per cent is being taken into account in the preparation of the proposed programme budget for 1988-1989. For 1987, expenditures for

consultants are being curtailed by approximately 35 per cent as part of the economy measures to deal with the current financial crisis in accordance with General Assembly decision 41/466 of 11 December 1986.

23. The last part of this recommendation calls for abolishing the practice of hiring retired staff members. The Secretary-General wishes to recall his view that an absolute prohibition against the hiring of retired staff members may not be in the interest of Member States, since such staff members often provide specific expertise on temporary assistance in a more effective and less costly manner than could otherwise be obtained; this is particularly true in the case of language services.

F. Meetings and conferences

24. In response to recommendation 4, the Secretariat has issued an administrative instruction that provides guidelines to Secretariat officials responsible for preparing and finalizing host Government agreements for meetings held away from Headquarters in order to ensure that additional costs to be borne by host Governments are determined in a consistent manner and that all additional costs are accounted for.

G. Conference facilities

25. Recommendation 5 will be implemented when the construction of new conference facilities is envisaged. The Secretary-General will present to the General Assembly at its forty-second session a progress report concerning the construction projects for the Economic Commission for Africa and for the Economic and Social Commission for Asia and the Pacific.

H. Management of human resources and delegation of authority

26. In response to recommendation 41, a review has been initiated of all delegations of authority in personnel matters and in other fields, such as financial matters, which may affect the management of human resources. This review will concentrate on delegations of authority given to departments and offices within the Secretariat, including those which serve particular organs, such as the regional commissions, the United Nations Conference on Trade and Development, the United Nations Environment Programme and the United Nations Centre for Human Settlements (Habitat). This review will result in the issuance of a comprehensive document on delegation of authority, which will include monitoring procedures.

27. Subsequently, consideration will also be given to the authority delegated to the heads of a number of subsidiary organs, which derives from General Assembly resolutions or decisions. If, as a consequence of this review, it is considered desirable to make revisions to the existing delegations of authority, the Secretary-General will take the necessary initiatives.

28. Also in response to recommendation 41, the name of the Office of Personnel Services has been changed to the Office of Human Resources Management.[6] The steps that have already been taken in this direction include recruitment planning, classification of posts, advertising of vacancies up to the D-1 level, competitive examinations (for external recruitment at the junior Professional levels and for promotion to these levels of staff from other categories) and, most recently, the development of career planning mechanisms on the basis of occupational groups. These mechanisms are already in place for staff in the General Service and related categories at Headquarters and will be set up in the near future for staff in the Professional category and above and for staff in the General Service and related categories at other duty stations. At the same time, more transparent methods of selection for appointment and promotion have been introduced. For instance, the system of vacancy management and redeployment of staff recently introduced to fill essential posts now vacant as a result of the recruitment freeze[7] ensures, in particular, that staff are selected for vacant posts through a process involving a review by the appointment and promotion machinery.

1. Staff regulations, staff rules and personnel manual

29. A review of the staff rules, as called for in recommendation 42, has been initiated to identify inconsistencies and ambiguities which would call for amendments to the provisions of the staff rules. Secondly, while the staff rules are amended regularly to implement General Assembly resolutions and consequential amendments to the staff regulations approved by the Assembly, the review will examine the degree to which other resolutions and decisions of the Assembly should be incorporated into the text of the staff rules. The review has begun with the disciplinary and appellate procedures governed by chapters X and XI of the staff rules. These rules are applicable to the Secretariat, including the staff of subsidiary organs of the Organization and the Registry of the International Court of Justice.

30. Recommendation 42 also calls for the establishment of a personnel manual. The preparation of a thematic personnel manual is a task that would require substantial human resources. At present, officials use a *Personnel Administrative Handbook* which is a compilation of all personnel related bulletins and instructions and is regularly updated and distributed to all offices. This *Handbook*, which has proved to be a very useful working guide for personnel administration, will be reproduced in a more handy and well-organized format together with a detailed subject-index on all personnel matters and with a comprehensive introduction. This initial project will be followed by the development of a manual, chapter by chapter, as resources become available.

31. This recommendation urges that the applicability of the rules and regulations to all entities of the United Nations system be considered; it has, therefore, been brought to the attention of the International Civil Service

Commission (ICSC) and the Consultative Committee on Administrative Questions (CCAQ). It should be borne in mind, however, that other organizations have no obligation to accept rules and regulations which do not emanate from their governing bodies. At the same time, there is agreement between the organizations to develop common personnel policies so as to ensure as much uniformity as is practicable concerning conditions of service. As a result of recommendations that may be expected from ICSC on common staff regulations, all organizations of the United Nations common system should in time have similar provisions in their staff regulations.

J. Principles and methods guiding the filling of posts

32. As mentioned previously (see paras. 67-68 of the report and para. 28 of the present annex), the recently initiated vacancy management system reviews vacant posts to determine which should be filled, in the light of programme priorities, work-load and classified job descriptions. As part of the review called for under recommendation 15 (see paras. 68-73 of the report), a post-by-post review is being undertaken in each department and office in light of programme priorities, legislative mandates and the restructuring of the Secretariat to achieve the desired staffing profile for the Secretariat in 1990.

33. Thereafter the Secretary-General will consider instituting permanent mechanisms to deal with vacancies in the light of programme orientation and changing mandates, as may be decided by the legislative bodies, to ensure efficient use of resources as proposed in recommendation 56. Candidates for the vacant posts deemed essential will be reviewed by the appointment and promotion bodies, which will establish a short list of candidates from which programme managers will select the staff member to be assigned to the vacancy in their area.

34. To fill Professional posts at the junior levels, competitive examinations are normally administered in a limited number of Member States each year. Until recently, these examinations were organized mainly in the Member States that were underrepresented or unrepresented. The scope of these examinations is being broadened, as requested in recommendation 43, to increase the participation of Member States currently adequately represented. In addition, the standards and criteria of the examinations are being reviewed to determine how to minimize the differences between internal and external examinations, while recognizing the differences deriving from the fact that one is a promotion exercise and the other a recruitment process.

35. Clear criteria for the selection of candidates for posts at other levels will also be established. It is intended to conduct tests to determine the drafting ability of external candidates who have not been selected through national examinations.

36. The basic thrust of recommendation 44 is to increase the proportion of appointments at the P-1 to P-3 levels. This objective has been taken into account in the overall retrenchment plan, which provides for a lower percentage of reduction in posts at the P-3 level while increasing the number of posts at the P-2 level. However, this recommendation will be implemented fully only when the financial situation allows it.

37. Recommendation 45 proposes that staff members be considered for permanent appointments after three years of service. The Secretary-General believes that this recommendation should be reviewed after the retrenchment and restructuring exercises have been completed. At the same time, the Secretary-General will need to retain necessary flexibility to take into account other factors besides performance such as the nature of the expertise required, the foreseen duration of functions, the source and expected duration of the funds. This will be an opportunity to review the proportion of staff on fixed-term or permanent appointments as requested in recommendation 57 and in accordance with General Assembly resolution 35/210 of 17 December 1980. This review will be done in conjunction with the planning of the Organization's human resources requirements.

38. As stated in recommendation 55, it is not desirable to have posts reserved for specific nationalities. The Secretary-General intends to maintain adequate representation for all Member States, while at the same time ensuring that no post is regarded as the exclusive preserve of any Member State.

K. Women

39. Recommendation 46 requests the Secretary-General to take additional measures to ensure a greater representation of women in the Professional category and above. The Secretary-General appointed a Co-ordinator for the Improvement of the Status of Women in the Secretariat and presented to the General Assembly at its fortieth session an action programme (A/C.5/40/30), which contained detailed work plans in the areas of recruitment, career development, training, conditions of service and administration of justice. The General Assembly, through resolution 40/258 of 18 December 1985, approved this programme and set the target of 30 per cent for the representation of women in posts subject to geographical distribution to be achieved by 1990.

40. The Secretary-General also established a high-level Steering Committee, with the Office of the Co-ordinator as its secretariat, to advise him on specific measures that could be taken to strengthen the participation of women in the work of the Organization. Thus far, the Steering Committee has submitted two reports containing some 40 recommendations covering a broad range of issues. These have been approved subject only to the present financial constraints; many of the proposed measures are already being implemented, and a timetable has been established for the remaining group of measures (related to training, career development, recruitment, conditions of service as they

affect family life, and the grievance redress system in the area of gender discrimination, which have been generally approved by the Secretary-General).

41. In this context, specific guidelines have been given to the departments and offices and to the appointment and promotion bodies to strengthen the promotion prospects for women by taking into account the length of their service at previous levels as well as at their current levels, in order to redress past inequalities. Moreover, the Secretary-General made a number of key appointments in the highest echelons early in 1987 (two at the level of Under-Secretary-General, two at the Director level).

42. As long as the recruitment freeze has to be maintained in view of the financial situation, it is not possible to make major improvements in the proportion of women in the Professional category, but in the few cases where exceptions are granted, efforts are made to select more women. While the Secretary-General is fully committed to increase the representation of women, full support from Member States will be required to achieve this goal. The Secretary-General intends to submit a detailed report on the progress made in this area to the Fifth Committee of the General Assembly at its forty-second session.

L. Nationals of developing countries

43. Recommendation 47 concerning the nomination of nationals of developing countries in senior level posts follows similar requests made by the General Assembly starting in 1975. The proportion of nationals of developing countries appointed to senior level posts has increased steadily and efforts will continue to be made. The indicative planning figures for appointments from each group of countries will be established and will be used as a basis for determining the progress made to achieve this objective taking into account the pattern of reduction of posts envisaged in the retrenchment plan.

M. Occupational groups

44. Staff members should be recruited and their careers developed on the basis of occupational groups according to recommendation 48. This view is shared by the Secretary-General. Since 1979, appointments and promotions to junior Professional posts have been made on the basis of examinations organized along occupational groups. Recruitment to Professional posts at other levels was reorganized along occupational lines in January 1985 with recruitment officers responsible for specific occupations. Vacancy announcements and publicity will similarly be reoriented along occupational lines.

45. In the area of career development, in order to ensure the effective and efficient placement of staff, a system has been designed that includes first the grouping of posts by occupation, and secondly, the mapping of clearly defined career paths within and between occupational groups. The assignment of posts

at the Professional level to the appropriate occupation is part of the process of job classification and has now covered over 60 per cent of all Professional and higher level posts. A computerized data base unit will show the occupation to which the staff member is assigned. Career paths have been developed for the statistical occupation and are being developed for the political affairs occupation. The emerging career development plan will cover all occupational groups for all categories of staff.

N. Rotation

46. Within the framework of the career development plan, a rotation and mobility system is being designed. The overall objective is to facilitate the assignment of staff to different duty stations and functions as well as to develop proposals on rotation and mobility schemes within and across duty stations, taking into account occupational groups and duty station classifications as established by the International Civil Service Commission. Mobility is being encouraged as part of the vacancy management and staff redeployment system referred to above (see para. 32 of the present annex).

O. Performance evaluation and promotions

47. Data on promotions of staff in the Professional category and at the Principal Officer (D-1) level in posts subject to geographical distribution have been reported to the General Assembly in the annual reports of the Secretary-General on the composition of the Secretariat from the thirty-eighth to the fortieth session, but not in the report to the forty-first session since the promotion review for that year had been postponed as part of the economy measures. Such data will be included in future reports with regard to staff in posts subject to geographical distribution and posts with special language requirements.

48. The system of performance evaluation is a major component of the career development plan and serves as a basis for the review of staff considered for promotion. A new improved and simplified performance evaluation system is being formulated which will take into account the element of comparability proposed in recommendation 50. A feasibility study on computerization of data on performance evaluation reports is in progress. It will address the reporting requirement contained in this recommendation.

49. The criteria for promotion have been developed over the years and take into account relevant General Assembly resolutions and decisions as well as the International Civil Service Commission recommendations. These criteria are brought each year to the attention of heads of departments and offices at the beginning of the yearly promotion exercise.

50. With regard to the functions and composition of the joint appointment and promotion bodies, care is taken to ensure the participation of staff from

various regions of the world and a proper balance between men and women. These bodies will be restructured along occupational lines as called for by the new career development system.

P. Training

51. Recognizing the necessity for effective training programmes geared to the needs of the Organization as called for in recommendation 58, a series of activities were conducted in 1985 and 1986, in co-operation with departments and offices, relating to training needs and impact analysis. Based on the results of these activities, which included pilot projects in key training areas, a number of changes were introduced in the 1987 training programme with the following objectives:

(a) Allocation of the existing limited resources to top training priorities;

(b) Reinforcement of co-ordination of training programmes Secretariat-wide;

(c) Definition and identification of target groups of participants in courses to optimize utilization of limited training resources in priority areas;

(d) Application of the training-the-trainer approach to multiply the impact of available resources;

(e) Evaluation of the effectiveness of training activities and their impact on the trainee and the organizational unit concerned.

52. The training activities included in the 1987 programme are far from satisfying the Organization's needs as, for instance, in the field of electronic data processing and other areas related to office automation and training in modern management skills. It is expected that training needs will increase as technological innovations are introduced and the Secretariat must deliver programmes with fewer human resources. Such needs, in order to be met, would require a greater allocation of resources than is now available.

53. There is no doubt that present allocations are too small for effective human resources development. In this regard, the ratio of training budgets to total staff costs can provide a useful indicator. The occupational training budget of the Secretariat represents approximately 0.06 per cent of total staff costs. Comparable ratios reported in a 1985 survey were 0.6 per cent in the United Nations Children's Fund, 0.8 per cent in the International Labour Organisation and 0.8 per cent in the World Bank - 10 to 13 times higher than in the United Nations. The training budget of national bureaucracies in some developed countries is 33 to 66 times higher than the United Nations training budget.

Q. *Staff union activities*

54. An overall review of the framework for staff-management relations will be undertaken as requested in recommendation 59. Such a review would include organizational arrangements. An administrative document consolidating texts regulating staff-management relations will be issued.

R. *Administration of justice*

55. At its forty-first session, the General Assembly decided to refer to the forty-second session reports presented to it by the Secretary-General relating to reform in the system of administration of justice. Having regard to this, and since such system requires a major overhaul to ensure both greater efficiency and lower cost, steps have been taken towards establishing a revised and simplified machinery by early 1988 as called for in recommendation 60, with related amendments to both chapters X and XI of the staff rules (see also para. 29 above). Meanwhile, emergency measures have been taken to eliminate the backlog of appeals before the Joint Appeals Board and to diminish the case-load of the United Nations Administrative Tribunal. Such interim measures are expected to effect perceptible improvement in the present situation.

III. OTHER MATTERS

Issues affecting the common system

56. Finally, issues that affect the United Nations common system, which are contained in recommendations 53 and 61, have been referred to the International Civil Service Commission as mandated in General Assembly resolution 41/213 of 19 December 1986.

57. The Secretariat also intends to avail itself of the expertise of the Commission on relevant issues.

Notes

1. ST/SGB/223 of 13 February 1987.
2. Afghanistan, Bangladesh, Benin, Bhutan, Botswana, Burkina Faso, Burundi, Cape Verde, Central African Republic, Chad, Comoros, Democratic Yemen, Djibouti, Equatorial Guinea, Ethiopia, Gambia, Guinea, Guinea-Bissau, Haiti, Kiribati, Lao People's Democratic Republic, Lesotho, Malawi, Maldives, Mali, Mauritania, Nepal, Niger, Rwanda, Samoa, Sao Tome and Principe, Sierra Leone, Somalia, Sudan, Togo, Tuvalu, Uganda, United Republic of Tanzania, Vanuatu and Yemen.
3. ST/SGB/107 of January 1971.
4. ST/SGB/207 of 5 December 1984.
5. ST/AI/249/Rev.2 of 15 August 1983.
6. ST/SGB/224 of 13 February 1987.
7. ST/SGB/221 and ST/AI/338, both of 22 December 1986.

APPENDIX

Index of recommendations by the Group of High-level Intergovernmental Experts

For the ease of reference, an index of the recommendations contained in the report of the Group of High-level Intergovernmental Experts relating to the work of the United Nations is provided below with an indication of the paragraphs of this report where they are mentioned.

Recommendation		Paras.	Recommendation		Paras.
1		39-42	33	Annex	6
2		39-42	34		42
3		39-40	35		65
3		39-40		Annex	20-21
	Annex	24	37		34
5	Annex	25	38		65
6		65		Annex	9-11
7		39-40	39		65
8		4		Annex	7
11		30	40		47
12		30		Annex	5
13		65	41		64
	Annex	12-15		Annex	26-28
14		12-13	42	Annex	29-31
15		30, 51-55, 58-63	43	Annex	34-35
	Annex	6, 32	44	Annex	36
16		24	45	Annex	37
17		20	46	Annex	39-42
18		18	47	Annex	43
19		20	48	Annex	44-45
20		23	49		58
21		20		Annex	46
22		30	50	Annex	47-48
23		33	51	Annex	49-50
24		33	53	Annex	56
25		29-31	55	Annex	38
26		32	56	Annex	33
27		30	57	Annex	37
28		65	58	Annex	51
	Annex	16-18	59	Annex	54
29		20	60	Annex	55
30		46-49	61	Annex	56
31	Annex	4	62	Annex	19
32		43-44			
	Annex	3			

2.9 Document A/42/7*

Progress Report of the Secretary-General on the Implementation of General Assembly Resolution 41/213 (A/42/234 and Corr.1)

Report of the Advisory Committee on Administrative and Budgetary Questions

1987

85. During its discussion of this report, the Advisory Committee met with the Secretary-General, the Director-General for Development and International Economic Co-operation and their senior colleagues; the Committee also discussed a number of extrabudgetary aspects of this report with the Administrator of UNDP. The Committee notes that the report is preliminary since it covers only the first few months of the reform and renewal effort. In order that the General Assembly may have the most up-to-date information at its forty-second session, the Committee has called for an updated progress report to be submitted to the General Assembly by 1 September 1987 (see para. 13 above**).

86. The Committee concurs with the statement in paragraph 4 (5) of the report that "renewal and reform must be a continuing and dynamic process following an orderly and sequential approach". This statement is in line with the Committee's views on the course of the reform process in the coming months (see para. 10 above**). In this connection, the question of revised estimates (referred to in para. 4 (5) of the report) is dealt with by the Committee in paragaraphs 12 and 14 above**.

87. In paragraphs 12 and 13 of his report, the Secretary-General states that reviews have been launched in virtually every aspect of the Secretariat's activities and that "some are virtually completed, others still in progress". The Committee trusts that the reviews and studies will have tangible results so that a new, more efficient organization of the Secretariat is achieved.

88. During its consideration of the budget sections for the regional commissions, the Committee noted considerable fragmentation in the programmes of activity. This situation will need to be examined in the context of the reforms now taking place pursuant to General Assembly resolution 41/213. The Advisory Committee notes that the work of the Special Commission of the Economic and Social Council (see para.14 above**) also affects the regional commissions. Furthermore, the Committee is of the view

---

*Official Records of the General Assembly, Forty-second Session, Supplement No. 7 (A/42/7), pp. 30-34.
**Not reprinted here.

that it is also essential to involve fully the regional commissions and their secretariats in the Secretariat study on the regional commissions (see recommendation 27 of the report of the Group of High-level Intergovernmental Experts[1] and para. 30(d) of the Secretary-General's report (A/42/234 and Corr.1)).

89. Public information is discussed in paragraphs 34 to 38 of the report of the Secretary-General. The Advisory Committee notes from paragraph 38 of the report that the review of the activities of DPI has already begun. As the Advisory Committee has pointed out, the resources requested under section 27 do not represent total resources devoted by the United Nations to public information activities (see chap. II, para. 27.8 below*). The Committee trusts that the review will encompass these activities as well. In this connection, the Committee notes that CPC has "recommended that the review should also include an examination of ways and means of consolidating the various information activities that were scattered through the Secretariat in the Department of Public Information, in accordance with the relevant provisions of General Assembly resolution 41/213".[2]

90. Paragraph 42 of the report of the Secretary-General refers to increasing the efficiency and productivity of conference services, particularly through the application of technological innovations. In this connection, the Advisory Committee recalls its consistent support of the introduction and use of technological innovations wherever gains in efficiency and productivity and staff savings were clearly identified. With regard to the programme of acquisitions for technological innovation in conference services contained in section 29 of the proposed programme budget for 1988-1989, the Committee has commented upon the fragmented presentation of the proposals under various programmes of activity. This fragmented approach hampered assessment of the overall merits of these innovations. Consideration of the proposals was further complicated, on this occasion, by the lack of information on potential expected economies,· particularly in staff savings. The detailed observations and recommendations of the Advisory Committee in this regard are contained in chapter II, paragraphs 29.15 to 29.17 below*.

91. A general discussion of administration and finance is contained in paragraphs 43 to 49 of the report of the Secretary-General. More specific information on administration and management is contained in the annex to the report.

92. The first part of the annex deals with the structure of the Department of Administration and Management. In paragraph 3 of the annex, an Office of Programme Planning, Budgeting, Monitoring and Evaluation is described. The Advisory Committee will return to this matter in the context of further developments.

---

*Not reprinted here.

93. Internal auditing procedures are discussed in paragraph 7 of the annex. The Advisory Committee sought a clarification of the arrangements described in that paragraph and was informed that, at the completion of each audit, the Internal Audit Division prepares a report containing findings and recommendations. To ensure the autonomy of its functions, the Internal Audit Division submits such reports directly to the head of department or office that has been audited and not through the Under-Secretary-General for Administration and Management. At the same time, in order to ensure that the Administration is aware of the problems that have been identified, copies are sent to the Under-Secretary-General for Administration and Management and other responsible officials, as appropriate.

94. The Committee notes developments with regard to travel costs, as described in paragraphs 8 to 11 of the annex to the report. In paragraph 8 it is stated:

> "In response to recommendation 6, the Secretary-General intends to include in the proposed programme budget for the biennium 1988-1989 a reduction in respect of travel of representatives to the General Assembly and make provision for one first class and four economy tickets for each of the 40 Member States included in the list of least developed countries. The Rules Governing Payment of Travel Expenses and Subsistence Allowances in respect of Members of Organs or Subsidiary Organs of the United Nations will be revised to reflect the above-mentioned recommendation."

In chapter II, paragraph 4.14 below*, the Advisory Committee recommends that consideration should be given to extending the application of that principle to subsidiary bodies of the Genberal Assembly and the Economic and Social Council. The Committee's recommendation with regard to travel of staff is contained in paragraph 41 above*.

95. A number of budgetary matters are discussed by the Secretary-General in paragraphs 12 to 19 of the annex. Harmonization of the format of the programme budgets of the organizations of the United Nations system is referred to in paragraphs 12 to 15. This matter has long been of concern to the Advisory Committee in the context of its activities concerning administrative and budgetary co-ordination with the specialized agencies and IAEA. In its report on this subject to the General Assembly at its thirty-ninth session, the Committee devoted considerable attention to the question of the budgeting practices of the agencies. The results of the Committee's consideration at that time are referred to in paragraph 14 of the annex. The Committee intends to return to this question in the near future.

96. The Committee notes the explanation offered in paragraph 17 of the annex with regard to the presentation of the costs for administration, conference, and

*Not reprinted here.

general services for ECE. The specific comments of the Committee are contained in section 10 of chapter II below*. In the relevant sections of chapter II below, the Committee has attempted to identify, to the extent possible, the costs of conference services at the other regional commissions.

97.   The Committee notes the following statement, in paragraph 19 of the annex:

> "In accordance with recommendation 62, the Secretary-General has discouraged the practice of transferring extrabudgetary posts to the regular budget. Accordingly, no request for the transfer of such posts is included in his proposals for the 1988-1989 programme budget."

98.   The Committee points out, however, that in the case of UNHCR, the Secretary-General has, in fact, decided to postpone consideration of the further transfer of posts to the regular budget until after the biennium 1988-1989 (see chap. II, para. 21.5 below*).

99.   The Committee's comments with regard to rented space (annex, paras. 20 and 21) are contained in chapter II, section 28D below*, where the Committee recommends a reduction in the estimates. As for consultants (annex, paras. 22 and 23), the Committee has made specific comments in paragraph 69 above*, where it also recommends a reduction.

100. The Advisory Committee notes the information on administration of justice provided in paragraph 55 of the annex. The Advisory Committee dealt with the appeals system for staff in chapter I of its first report on the proposed programme budget for 1986-1987, in which it recommended that a report should be submitted to the General Assembly at its forty-second session which would focus on the following:

> "(a) Simplifying rules and procedures so that the staff can more easily inform itself of its rights and obligations. In this way, misunderstandings and appeals as the result of confusion over the proper interpretation of complex texts can be minimized;

> "(b) Identifying those aspects of staff administration which give rise to an inordinate number of appeals, with a view to reform in those areas;

> "(c) Streamlining the appeals procedures so as to provide for (i) quick settlement of minor disputes prior to the appeals stage, (ii) a mechanism to reject applications for review that are frivolous, and (iii) a more efficient handling of cases that reach the Joint Appeals Board and Administrative Tribunal."[3]

---

*Not reprinted here.

101. The Committee stressed that in making this recommendation it was not intending to impose any specific set of solutions nor to interfere with the Secretary-General's authority and responsibility to administer the staff. The Committee stated its belief that the General Assembly should be given the necessary information to assure itself that the causes of the problem had been identified and that solutions had been formulated. The Committee also noted that the report should include information on what progress had been made as a result of measures already taken. The Committee's recommendation was endorsed by the General Assembly in its resolution 40/252 of 18 December 1985. In recommendation 60 of its report, the Group of High-level Intergovernmental Experts called for the Advisory Committee's recommendation to be "implemented without delay and the measures recommended taken as rapidly as possible".[4] Although the report submitted by the Secretary-General to the General Assembly at its forty-first session (A/C.5/41/14), upon which action was deferred (see General Assembly decision 41/462), attempted to address the concerns of the Committee, the Advisory Committee trusts that updated and more complete information will be available at the forty-second session of the General Assembly, either in the updated progress report called for in paragraph 13 above[*] or in a separate report.

102. In paragraphs 50 to 63 of his report (A/42/234 and Corr.1), the Secretary-General discusses the staff reductions that are now under way in response to recommendation 15 of the Group of High-level Intergovernmental Experts. In this connection, the Committee notes the following statement in paragraph 54:

> "The target of a 15 per cent reduction in the overall number of posts within three years, propounded in recommendation 15(2) (a), needs to be seen both within the context of the present and projected staffing of the Organization and of the structural reviews ...".

In paragraphs 57 and 58, the Secretary-General refers to the new system of vacancy management and staff redeployment, which was "designed in such a way that it can logically lead into the phased retrenchment, linked to restructuring, required by the report of the Group of High-level Intergovernmental Experts".

103. The Committee concurs in the view that application of a straight 15 per cent staffing reduction to each organizational unit would be counter-productive. The Committee trusts that the post reduction exercise now under way in the secretariat will take into account the relative requirements of the functional units of the Secretariat as they emerge from the results of the various structural reviews now going on. Consequently, there will be considerable redeployment of posts, and the Committee expects, therefore, that in certain

---

[*]Not reprinted here.

areas the reductions will exceed 15 per cent to compensate for other areas in which such a reduction may not be feasible. In paragraph 14 above, the Committee calls for the submission to the General Assembly at its forty-third session, of information on staffing (in tabular form) together with a set of revised estimates.

Notes

1. *Official Records of the General Assembly, Forty-first Session, Supplement No. 49* (A/41/49).
2. *Ibid., Forty-second Session, Supplement No. 16* (A/42/16), para. 211.
3. *Ibid., Fortieth Session, Supplement No. 7* (A/40/7), paras. 67-73.
4. *Ibid., Forty-first Session, Supplement No. 49* (A/41/49).

2.10 Document A/42/16*

Progress Report of the Secretary-General (A/43/234 and Corr.1)

Report of the Committee for Programme and Co-ordination

1988

295.   At its 12th, 14th, 15th and 18th meetings, on 4, 5 and 7 May, the Committee considered the progress report of the Secretary-General on the implementation of the recommendations of the Group of High-level Intergovernmental Experts to Review the Efficiency of the Administrative and Financial Functioning of the United Nations (A/42/234 and Corr.1).

296.   The Committee expressed its appreciation to the Secretary-General for having personally introduced his progress report. The Committee noted the conceptual framework of the report and appreciated the manner in which the Secretary-General's views were presented therein. The Committee also noted that the report reflected a sense of determination and vigour on the part of the Secretary-General and the Secretariat in the implementation of General Assembly resolution 41/213. The Committee noted in the Secretary-General's intention, and his reasons for its as expressed in his progress report, to pursue reforms in the Secretariat without waiting for the in-depth study of the United Nations intergovernmental structure and functions in the economic and social fields being undertaken by the Special Commission of the Economic and Social Council. At the same time, however, the Committee considered that, in accordance with Economic and Social Council decision 1987/112, the final shape of the Secretariat structure in the economic and social fields should be determined only after the Special Commission had completed its study. In noting that the reform exercise provided a unique opportunity to consider the United Nations agenda for the next decade and incorporate it into the medium-term plan for the period 1990-1995, the Committee stressed the importance of early and extensive consultations between the Secretary-General and Member States on the medium-term plan throughout this process of reform.

297.   The Committee agreed with the Secretary-General's view that it was essential for the successful undertaking of a rational process of reform and restructuring that there be an end to the present financial uncertainties. Member States should therefore fulfil their financial obligations as set out in the Charter of the United Nations.

298.   With respect to reform in the political area, the Committee generally supported the Secretary-General's initiatives in their overall aspects and his

---

Official Records of the General Assembly, Forty-second Session, Supplement No. 16 (A/42/16), pp. 52-54.

views on the role of the United Nations. The Committee noted that accurate figures on the resource distribution and savings achieved were not available at this time, since the reorganization was closely linked to other reorganizations being planned in the Secretariat. The outcome would be reflected in due course in revised budgetary proposals. Most delegations welcomed the creation of the new Office for Research and the Collection of Information, while a few delegations raised questions concerning the appropriate placement of this office within the Secretariat structure. It was noted that the functions of the new office would be as indicated in the Secretary-General's Bulletin of 1 March 1987 (ST/SGB/225) and in the Secretary-General's progress report (A/42/234, para. 19) and that duplication of research should be avoided.

299. The Committee agreed on the importance of the reform measures in the areas of administration, finance and personnel. However, it was pointed out that the recruitment freeze should not be an instrument for reducing posts. The Committee was informed by the Secretariat that the recruitment freeze was never intended to be a personnel management tool; it was imposed by the financial crisis, but its adverse effects have been partially offset by special measures, such as the vacancy management and staff redeployment scheme initiated at the end of 1986. The Committee was further informed by the Secretariat that the scheme had been designed in such a way as to lead logically into the longer-term retrenchment plan, which has already been set in motion.

300. The Committee agreed that the reduction of regular budget posts should proceed in accordance with General Assembly resolution 41/213, in particular paragraph 1 (b) of section I, whereby the Assembly decided that the percentages referred to in recommendation 15 of the report of the Group of High-level Intergovernmental Experts,[1] which were arrived at in a pragmatic manner, should be regarded as targets in the formulation of the Secretary-General's plans to be submitted to the General Assembly for implementation of the recommendation, and requested the Secretary-General to implement this recommendation with flexibility in order to avoid, *inter alia*, a negative impact on programmes and on the structure and composition of the Secretariat. The Committee stressed the need to bear in mind the necessity of securing the highest standards of efficiency, competence and integrity of the staff, with due regard to equitable geographical distribution, as stipulated in Article 101 of the Charter. In addition, questions were raised with regard to the reduction of posts at the Under-Secretary-General and Assistant-Secretary-General levels financed from extrabudgetary resources. It was considered that additional steps would be taken by the Secretary-General to reach the goal set by the General Assembly.

301. Some delegations questioned the proposed consolidation of United Nations information centres with the offices of the resident representatives of UNDP, since it appeared that the functions of those offices were quite different. Besides, those delegations believed that the proposal was a new concept of United Nations representation in member countries and as such

should be thoroughly discussed in an appropriate intergovernmental forum. Other delegations agreed with the proposed consolidation provided that no additional costs for UNDP would result from such consolidation. The Under-Secretary-General and Special Co-ordinator for the implementation of General Assembly resolution 41/213 confirmed there would be no additional costs for UNDP and also pointed out that the idea was not a new one since it had already been implemented successfully in several countries for a number of years; the extension to other countries would be done on a case-by-case basis while at the same time safeguarding the quality of information work and respecting programme delivery requirements.

Conclusions and recommendations

302.   The Committee endorsed the general approach of the Secretary-General in that improvements in the administrative and financial functioning of the United Nations should be designed to make the Organization more responsive to the increasingly complex global problems of today and better prepared to face the challenges of the coming decades. The Committee also agreed that the Secretary-General should continue in an effective and orderly manner with the reform process in accordance with General Assembly resolution 41/213. The Committee stressed the need to ensure that reforms do not have a negative impact on programmes.   The Committee also agreed that Member States should fulfil their financial obligations in accordance with relevant articles of the Charter. The Committee further agreed that there must be an end to the present financial uncertainties.

303.   The Committee recognized that adjustments in the structure of the Secretariat in the economic and social fields wold be required as a result of ongoing reviews and the in-depth study of the Special Commission of the Economic and Social Council established in accordance with Council decision 1987/112.

304.   The Committee requested the Secretary-General to submit appropriate information on further implementation of Assembly resolution 41/213, including pertinent programme budgetary proposals, to the forty-second session of the Assembly through this Committee, and looked forward in due course to reflection of the reforms in relevant official documents.

Note

1.   *Official Records of the General Assembly, Forty-first Session, Supplement No. 49* (A/41/49).

2.11 Document A/42/225/Add.1[*]

Questions Relating to the Programme Budget: Inflation and Currency Fluctuation, and the Level of the Contingency Fund

Report of the Secretary-General

Addendum

4 September 1987

1. The report of the Secretary-General on questions relating to inflation and currency fluctuation and the level of the contingency fund (A/42/225), submitted pursuant to General Assembly resolution 41/213 of 19 December 1986, was examined by the Committee for Programme and Co-ordination (CPC) at its twenty-seventh session and by the Advisory Committee on Administrative and Budgetary Questions at its spring 1987 session. Following consideration of that report, both CPC, in paragraph 320 of its report (A/42/16 (Part I)), and the Advisory Committee, in paragraph 107 of its first report[1] on the proposed programme budget for the biennium 1988-1989,[2] requested that a further report be prepared. The present report is submitted in response to these requests and focuses on issues relating to the contingency fund that, in the view of the two committees, require further clarifications. The question of inflation and currency fluctuation is not addressed in view of the intention of the Advisory Committee, as stated in paragraph 118 of its report, to look into this matter more closely with a view to formulating specific recommendations to be presented to the General Assembly at its forty-third session.

2. The contingency fund, as described in paragraph 8 of annex I of General Assembly resolution 41/213, is intended to accommodate additional expenditures relating to the biennium derived from legislative mandates not provided for in the proposed programme budget or, pending a decision by the Assembly on a question dealt with in paragraph 10 of the same annex, from revised estimates other than those relating to unforeseen and extraordinary expenses and to fluctuations in rates of exchange and inflation. It is understood that the expression "legislative mandates not provided for in the proposed programme budget", for which resources from the contingency fund may be utilized, is intended to cover those activities that would be dealt with in statements of programme budget implications of draft resolutions and decisions before the General Assembly. Thus, the "additional expenditures" relating to the biennium derived from such legislative mandates are understood to be those related to any activity envisaged in a draft resolution or decision the implementation of which would require resources additional to those included either (a) in the proposed programme budget (if the activity is being

[*]A/42/225/Add.1.

considered in the year preceding the biennium for implementation during the biennium, e.g., in 1989 for the biennium 1990-1991) or (b) in the appropriations for the biennium (if the activity is being considered during the first year of the biennium for implementation during the second year of the biennium, e.g., in 1990 for 1991).

3. The contingency fund should, thus, provide for:

(a)   The type of resources that have traditionally been added through consideration by the General Assembly of statements of programme budget implications of draft resolutions or decisions (excluding expenditures related to political activities of a "perennial" character whose mandates are renewed annually and their related conference costs, since such expenditures are to be included in the proposed programme budget);

(b)   Revised estimates, excluding those relating to unforeseen and extraordinary expenses and to fluctuations in rates of exchange and inflation.

4. As regards construction projects, the procedure followed up to the present for their consideration and approval could, with some modifications, be adapted to conform to the new budget process. Proposals for construction projects are not currently submitted to the General Assembly as part of the proposed programme budget.   After the Advisory Committee has been informed by the Secretary-General of the need for new construction or major alteration of existing premises, the Secretary-General submits to the Assembly proposals that include cost estimates for the preparation of preliminary designs as well as preliminary estimates of the cost of construction. If the decision of the Assembly is to proceed, the Secretary-General then submits to the Assembly a detailed report on the proposal, containing designs, a schedule for the completion of the work and the proposed appropriations that would be required in each budget period. Subsequently, annual progress reports are submitted to the Assembly and additional appropriations are sought, as required, in the context of such reports. In the future, the most appropriate way to make financial provision for such projects would appear to be in the context of the proposed programme budget, with upward adjustments, if required, being met through the contingency fund.   The procedure for consideration and approval of construction projects would remain unchanged; a preliminary estimate of the resources that would be required for a particular biennium would, however, be included in the outline to be submitted in the off-budget year and, subsequently, in the light of any decision taken on the outline by the Assembly, in the proposed programme budget. Annual progress reports would continue to be prepared and, on the basis of consideration of them by the Assembly, the amount of resources included in the proposed programme budget - or in the approved appropriations - would be adjusted as required.   To the extent that such adjustments would result in additional expenditures, they would be considered in the context of the contingency fund.

5. In the previous report (A/42/225, para. 28), it was suggested that the contingency fund in any biennium would cover only the first year of the biennium as it was thought unlikely that expenditures would arise in the course of the second year of the biennium for which resources from the contingency fund might be utilized. However, on further reflection, it is now suggested that the contingency fund be extended to the end of the biennium.

6. The budget process described in annex I to General Assembly resolution 41/213 does not provide any guidance as to whether the resources to be made available from the contingency fund should be divided between the two years of a biennium and, if so, in what proportion. In the absence of any guidance and of practical experience, it is considered preferable that no annual limit be placed at this stage on the proportion of resources to be utilized from the contingency fund but, rather, to let events take their course. The procedure could of course be adjusted if necessary at a later stage in the light of experience gained during its application.

7. In deciding on the establishment of a contingency fund and on the types of activities for which resources from that fund can be made available, the General Assembly also decided, in paragraph 9 of annex I of resolution 41/213, that "if additional expenditures [as defined in paragraph 8 of the annex] are proposed that exceed resources available within the contingency fund, such additional expenditures can only be included in the budget through redeployment of resources from low-priority areas or modifications of existing activities. Otherwise, such additional activities will have to be deferred until a later biennium". To give effect to this provision, a number of approaches are outlined in the following paragraphs, with their advantages and drawbacks highlighted in order to facilitate their consideration.

8. One approach would be for the General Assembly to take cognizance of all potential additions before taking a decision on the allocation of resources from the contingency fund. Such an approach would require that, at each session of the Assembly, both the adoption of any draft resolution whose implementation would require additional resources and the approval of revised estimates be held in abeyance until all such resolutions and revised estimates are identified and a decision taken as to whether additional funds would be provided. It would appear necessary to establish an earlier deadline than the traditional one of 1 December for submission to the Fifth Committee of all statements of programme budget implications and revised estimates. Once all such resolutions and revised estimates are identified, the Fifth Committee would establish a list containing the related estimated additional expenditures. To the extent that resources contained in the contingency fund are sufficient to cover all such additional expenditures, the Fifth Committee would so notify the Assembly in Plenary so that it might consider the draft resolutions. For its part, the Fifth Committee would proceed to appropriate the necessary resources in accordance with the established practice. It would also note the level of resources remaining in the contingency fund to be available in the next year of the biennium.

9.   The existing procedures for considering redeployment and the modification of existing activities would continue and at the same time be extended to revised estimates. Whenever a statement of programme budget implications or a report containing revised estimates is prepared, the statement or report would contain an indication as to whether the new activities proposed could be accommodated through redeployment and/or modification of existing activities. If it is determined that the new activities proposed cannot be accommodated through redeployment and/or modification of existing activities, the additional resources required would be deemed to be chargeable to the contingency fund.

10. To the extent that resources available in the contingency fund are not sufficient to cover all such additional expenditures, it is evident that it is the General Assembly in Plenary that would be required to make the final determination as to which of the proposed additional activities would have to be deferred until a later biennium. While on a purely theoretical basis it could be suggested that the Assembly in Plenary could, once all the competing proposals are listed, reach its determination, this would in practice be a burdensome process bound to affect adversely the orderly functioning of the General Assembly.   It appears therefore essential that the Assembly be provided with recommendations in this regard, a task that would appear to fall squarely within the mandate of the Fifth Committee as the administrative and budgetary committee of the General Assembly.   The question then is how should the Fifth Committee proceed in order to arrive at its recommendations regarding which activities would have to be deferred to a later biennium when resources in the contingency fund are not sufficient to cover all proposed additional expenditures.   That is of course a matter for the Fifth Committee itself to consider and decide upon, but the options would seem to be limited to establishing a negotiating working group or to drawing upon the advice of one or more of the established subsidiary bodies having a mandate for programme planning and advising on priorities (e.g., CPC, the Committee on Conferences and the Advisory Committee), depending on the type of activity involved. The Fifth Committee and the one or more subsidiary bodies would then undertake an exercise that would certainly include the consideration of possible redeployment (in fact, reprogramming if no further absorption is possible) or deferral.

11. Another approach would be to allow the contingency fund to operate on a "first come, first served" basis.   Under that approach, the Fifth Committee could consider statements of programme budget implications and revised estimates in a chronological order.   Each time the Fifth Committee considers a statement of programme budget implications of a draft resolution or a revised estimate, it would first ascertain whether resources are available in the fund.   If it concludes that additional resources are required but that such resources cannot be met through redeployment and/or modification of existing activities, the Committee would approve additional expenditures to be made available from the contingency fund.   If resources available in the fund are sufficient to cover all such additional expenditures, the Fifth Committee would proceed to appropriate the related funds in accordance with its established

practice. The level of resources remaining in the fund would thus be available in the next year of the biennium.

12. If, however, a point is reached during a session when the level of resources in the contingency fund is exhausted, any revised estimate not yet acted upon by the Fifth Committee would not be considered but would be taken into account in the proposed programme budget for the next biennium. As regards draft resolutions before the Assembly in Plenary requiring additional resources, the Fifth Committee would inform the Assembly that funds for the activities envisaged are not available and that, consequently and in accordance with the provisions of paragraph 9 of annex I of resolution 41/213, those activities would have to be deferred until a later biennium. In the case of draft resolutions being considered by the Main Committees, the related statement of programme budget implications would in each case indicate to the appropriate committee that resources are no longer available from the contingency fund and that, barring redeployment, should additional resources be required to implement the activities contained in the draft resolution, the Fifth Committee would inform the Assembly that those activities would have to be deferred until a later biennium, in accordance with paragraph 9 of annex I of resolution 41/213.

13. Since the use of the contingency fund is meant to cover additional expenditures arising from draft resolutions emanating from Main Committees or those considered directly by the Assembly without reference to a Main Committee, as well as revised estimates submitted by the Secretary-General, there would not appear to be any criteria that would help establish, in a satisfactory manner, an overall order of precedence. Since all statements of programme budget implications and revised estimates are issued as Fifth Committee documents (under the symbol A/C.5/xx/xxx), it could be argued that they should be considered in the sequential order in which they are issued. However, revised estimates submitted by the Secretariat, which are required to be available for consideration by 15 October, could all be issued for a given session of the General Assembly even before the opening of the session and would have thus a definite advantage over statements of programme budget implications. This would not seem to have been the intention of the General Assembly in its resolution 41/213.

14. Furthermore, some draft resolutions are relatively straightforward and the related statements of programme budget implications can be prepared in a relatively short time; others are complex and the preparation of the related statements of programme budget implications may require several days. Hence the possibility exists for statements of programme budget implications of two draft resolutions submitted at the same time to be issued days apart, as a result of which misunderstanding may arise and the impression given that the order in which such statements are issued is based on criteria not related to the time of submission of the draft resolutions.

15. One alternative would be to define "first come, first served" as the order in which the Fifth Committee decides to consider statements of programme budget implications and revised estimates. The drawback to this alternative is that if and when the point is reached where the level of the fund is about to be depleted and a number of proposals for additional expenditures are pending consideration or known to be in the process of preparation, the Fifth Committee may find itself in a situation where its attention would inevitably shift to considering and deciding - at a cost in time - the order in which the remaining proposals are to be taken.

16. As indicated above, none of the approaches is entirely satisfactory. The review of their advantages and drawbacks should, however, assist the General Assembly in determining the procedure to give effect to paragraph 9 of annex I to resolution 41/213.

17. If a "first come, first served" approach is retained, it is unlikely, as resources are drawn down from the contingency fund and the balance available diminishes, that the last statement of programme budget implications or revised estimates would require additional resources in an amount equal to the balance left in the fund. In such cases, consideration could be given to providing the balance of the fund for the activities described in that statement of programme budget implications or revised estimates, with the understanding that the activities would be undertaken only partially. Such an approach would appear feasible in those cases where the balance left in the fund would not be substantially inferior to the estimated additional requirements sought in the statement of programme budget implications or revised estimates. In those cases where the balance would be substantially inferior, for example if there were $20,000 remaining in the fund and the statement of programme budget implications indicated that the implementation of the draft resolution would require $500,000, it would not appear practical to proceed and provide the balance of the fund for the activities described in that statement. In such circumstances, it might be best to decide that the resources remaining in the contingency fund are not sufficient to fund the activities envisaged in the draft resolution and that consequently and in accordance with paragraph 9 of annex I of resolution 41/213, those activities would have to be deferred until a later biennium.

18. If it were agreed to follow the procedures outlined above, it would also seem necessary to establish some criteria to determine when to proceed with providing the balance of the contingency fund and when not to. The following guidelines could be considered: when the balance of the fund is not sufficient to meet the estimated additional requirements arising from a statement of programme budget implications or revised estimates, it would nevertheless be made available provided that the balance available in the fund is not less than 90 per cent of the additional requirements and the actual difference between the additional requirements and the balance available does not exceed $50,000. To the extent that these conditions are not met, the additional activity would be deferred until a later biennium.

19. Another issue to be clarified relates to the timing of the establishment of the level of the contingency fund. General Assembly resolution 41/213 provides that:

(a) The outline of the programme budget to be submitted by the Secretary-General in off-budget years shall contain an indication of the size of the contingency fund expressed as a percentage of the overall level of resources;

(b) On the basis of a decision by the Assembly, the Secretary-General shall prepare his proposed programme budget for the following biennium;

(c) The programme budget shall include a contingency fund expressed as a percentage of the overall budget level.

Since under any of the possible methods there would be a draw-down process from the contingency fund during the budget year, that is, before the initial budget appropriations are approved, it would seem necessary for the General Assembly, at the time it decides on the outline of the programme budget, to establish the level of the contingency fund not only in percentage but also in dollar terms.

Notes

1. *Official Records of the General Assembly, Forty-second Session, Supplement No. 7 (A/42/7).*
2. The programme budget as approved by the General Assembly was issued as *Official Records of the General Assembly, Forty-second Session, Supplement No. 6 (A/42/6/Rev.1).*

2.12 Document A/42/640[*]

Questions Relating to the Programme Budget: Inflation and Currency Fluctuation, and the Level of the Contingency Fund (A/42/225/Add.1)

Report of the Advisory Committee on Administrative and Budgetary Questions

12 October 1987

2.   The report of the Secretary-General was submitted pursuant to requests of both the Committee for Programme and Co-ordination (CPC) and the Advisory Committee for a further report on this matter following their consideration of the Secretary-General's earlier report on the same subjects (A/42/225).

3.   As a result of its consideration of both reports of the Secretary-General (A/42/225 and A/42/225/Add.1), the Advisory Committee submits to the General Assembly the following observations and recommendations.

Criteria for use of the contingency fund

4.   The Advisory Committee concurs with the Secretary-General that one of the uses of the contingency fund should be to provide for additional resources that may be required as a result of the consideration of statements of programme budget implications.   In paragraph 2 of his report (A/42/225/Add.l) the Secretary-General elaborates on what is meant by "legislative mandates not provided for in the proposed programme budget". In this connection, the Committee points out that such legislative mandates can refer either to strengthening or expansion of those activities which have already been programmed or to wholly new activities, as yet unprogrammed.   The Advisory Committee also points out that the level of additional expenditure resulting from statements of programme budget implications will in future be affected by the incorporation into the initial estimates of expenditures related to political activities of a "perennial" character, and of provision in the initial estimates for conference-servicing costs, hitherto considered in the context of the Secretary-General's consolidated statement of conference servicing costs.

5.   According to the provisions of annex I of General Assembly resolution 41/213 of 19 December 1986, the contingency fund should also cover additional expenditures relating to revised estimates except those specified in paragraph 11 of annex I (see para. 9 below).   It should be borne in mind, however, that there are several categories of revised estimates.   First, there are revised estimates dealing with those activities which had been included in the proposed

---

[*]A/42/640.

programme budget but which were not acted on at first reading, pending the submission of additional information. The Advisory Committee concurs with the view of the Secretary-General that only the amount requested over and above that included in the proposed programme budget, if any, should be reviewed in the context of the contingency fund (A/42/225, para. 28). However, the Advisory Committee recalls that in its first report on the proposed programme budget for the biennium 1986-1987, it noted that for a number of the sections

"revised estimates are being submitted to take into account studies or progress reports that were still pending at the time the initial estimates were being prepared. The Advisory Committee points out that the inclusion of provisional estimates in the proposed programme budget leaves the submission incomplete and makes general analysis and comparison with previous budgets more difficult. The Committee therefore requests the Secretary-General to ensure that in future special studies and progress reports will be completed in time to be taken into account in the proposed programme budget so that revised estimates will only be submitted in very exceptional circumstances".[1]

6. The question of revised estimates dealing with construction, although it can fall into the category mentioned in the preceding paragraph, warrants further explanation. As pointed out by the Advisory Committee in paragraph 109 of its first report on the proposed programme budget for 1988-1989, "the amounts involved as a result of the submission of additional information with regard to construction could be quite substantial and may fluctuate".[2] In paragraph 4 of his report (A/42/225/Add.l), the Secretary-General suggests the following:

"In the future, the most appropriate way to make a financial provision for such projects would appear to be in the context of the proposed programme budget, with upward adjustments, if required, being met through the contingency fund. The procedure for consideration and approval of construction projects would remain unchanged; a preliminary estimate of the resources that would be required for a particular biennium would, however, be included in the outline to be submitted in the off-budget year and, subsequently, in the light of any decision taken on the outline by the Assembly, in the proposed programme budget. Annual progress reports would continue to be prepared and, on the basis of consideration of them by the Assembly, the amount of resources included in the proposed programme budget - or in the approved appropriations - would be adjusted as required. To the extent that such adjustments would result in additional expenditures, they would be considered in the context of the contingency fund."

7. While the Advisory Committee concurs in general with the Secretary-General's approach as quoted above, it is of the opinion that the question of whether or not additional expenditures for construction should be considered in the context of the contingency fund should depend on the nature

of the upward adjustment that gave rise to the additional expenditures. Moreover, the Advisory Committee points out that each construction project budget makes separate provision for contingencies. Accordingly, most of the additional expenditures should be accommodated without requesting an additional appropriation. Should it be felt that in spite of this provision it is necessary to request an additional appropriation, the treatment of such a request should depend on its origin. Thus, a need for an additional appropriation that arises from increases, for example, in the costs of supplies and/or labour should be handled under provisions for dealing with increases due to currency fluctuation and inflation. Should, however, the request relate to a change in the scope of the project (such as a proposed addition of conference rooms or other facilities), the Advisory Committee believes that it should normally be considered in the context of the budget outline; however, if it is deemed to be an urgent matter it could be considered in the context of the contingency fund. A third cause of additional requirements relates to the effects of natural disaster (earthquake) or catastrophe (fire) or unforeseen obstacles (hitting an underground stream during excavation). The Advisory Committee believes that the potentially major costs associated with such calamities, in the event they should occur, should be handled by the General Assembly on an *ad hoc* basis and should not be covered by the contingency fund. Similar considerations could apply in cases of major maintenance and alteration.

8. Another major category of revised estimates is those related to legislative mandates, such as the revised estimates resulting from the decisions of the Economic and Social Council. The Advisory Committee believes that these should be dealt with in the context of the contingency fund. The Committee points out that this category of expenditure will, in future, be affected, for example, by the provision in the initial budget estimates for certain recurrent expenses related to human rights activities.

9. Another category of revised estimates is those that should not, at this point, be covered by a contingency fund. As indicated in paragraph 11 of annex I of General Assembly resolution 41/213, pending a decision by the Assembly on the question of a comprehensive solution to the problem of all additional expenditures, "the revised estimates arising from the impact of extraordinary expenses, including those relating to the maintenance of peace and security, as well as fluctuations in rates of exchange and inflation, shall not be covered by the contingency fund ...". The Advisory Committee believes that in the spirit of that directive it would also be advisable, at this point, to exclude from the contingency fund expenses related to actions that affect fixed costs, such as decisions and recommendations of the International Civil Service Commission and the United Nations Joint Staff Pension Board and proposals arising out of developments related to insurance. The additional expenses associated with such decisions, recommendations or proposals, while not strictly within the definition of inflation and currency fluctuation, are often closely related to developments thereto. Accordingly, the Advisory Committee believes that they

should be dealt with in that context; the Committee intends to take the matter up when it addresses the question of a "comprehensive solution" in its report to be submitted to the General Assembly at its forty-third session (see para. 14 below).

Period covered and pattern of use of the contingency fund

10. In paragraph 111 of its first report,[3] the Advisory Committee pointed out that in addition to providing for use of the contingency fund in the year preceding the biennium and in the first year of the biennium the possibility of additional requirements in the second year of the biennium, albeit slight, needed to be taken into account. The Advisory Committee notes that the Secretary-General, upon further reflection, concurs in this view (see A/42/225/Add.1, para. 5).

11. As for the pattern of use of the contingency fund, the Advisory Committee recommends that, at this point, no pre-determined proportion for a given year should be set. However, the Committee believes that prudent use of the fund requires that it should not be exhausted before the end of the period. The matter should be reviewed in the light of experience with the actual operation of the fund.

Operation of the contingency fund

12. The Advisory Committee firmly believes that procedures for the operation of the contingency fund should not be complicated or cumbersome or impede the work of the General Assembly. Taking into account the analysis provided by the Secretary-General in his reports (A/42/225 and Add.1), the Advisory Committee recommends the following:

(a) In the off-budget year, the Assembly would decide on the size of the contingency fund in accordance with the provisions of annex I of its resolution 41/213;

(b) Starting with the budget year (i.e., the year before the commencement of the biennium) and continuing throughout the biennium, the Assembly would decide on the actual amounts to be utilized from the fund on the basis of statements of programme budget implications and revised estimates;

(c) Each statement of programme budget implications and each proposal for revised estimates should contain a precise indication of how the provision of paragraph 9 of annex I of Assembly resolution 41/213 would be applied in case it is not possible to finance all or part of the additional requirements from the contingency fund. It would be understood that each draft resolution that would be accompanied by such a statement of programme budget implications would be adopted subject to the provisions of that statement;

(d)   The statement of programme budget implications and proposals for revised estimates, formulated as indicated in subparagraph (c) above, would be considered by the Assembly as in the past. The resolutions could be adopted by the Assembly subject to the understanding described in subparagraph (c) above; this would avoid the "logjam" that would result if the Assembly were to consider all such resolutions and revised estimates at the same time (i.e., after a certain date - see subparagraph (e) below);

(e)   A deadline could be set for the consideration of statements of programme budget implications and revised estimates. After that date, the Secretary-General would prepare and submit a consolidated statement of all programme budget implications and revised estimates considered at that session of the Assembly. The amounts in that statement would correspond to those previously recommended by the Fifth Committee upon its consideration of individual statements and revised estimates (see subparagraph (c) above). Should the consolidated amount be within the available balance in the contingency fund, the Assembly would proceed to appropriate the required amounts under the relevant sections of the programme budget;

(f)   Should the consolidated amount exceed the balance available in the contingency fund for that year, the Secretary-General would, in his consolidated statement, make proposals for revising the amount to within the balance remaining in the fund for that year. In so doing, the Secretary-General would be guided by the indications of alternatives appended to each statement of programme budget implications and included in each proposal for revised estimates. Such alternatives would have been before the respective legislative bodies concerned at the time they were adopting the decisions or resolutions in question (see subparagraph (c) above). The Secretary-General would also take into account such indications of relative urgency as each legislative body might wish to make as between the resolutions and decisions of that body. Upon consideration of this statement, the Assembly would proceed to appropriate the funds necessary under the relevant sections of the programme budget.

13. In annex I of its resolution 41/213 the General Assembly requires that in the off-budget year the Secretary-General submit an outline of the programme budget for the following biennium, which shall, *inter alia*, contain an indication of the size of the contingency fund expressed as a percentage of the overall level of resources. In this connection, the Advisory Committee notes that the first outline under the new budget process is to be submitted in 1988 and will relate to the proposed programme budget for the biennium 1990-1991. The Committee notes further that in paragraph 34 of his report (A/42/225) the Secretary-General indicates that "it would seem desirable to establish a contingency fund" for 1988-1989. The Advisory Committee repeats its position, as stated in paragraph 113 of its first report,[4] that a set of procedures for the fund should be in place when the operation of the fund starts.

14. In the paragraphs above the Advisory Committee has given its recommendations and observations on the establishment, scope and operation of a contingency fund. The Committee emphasizes that the establishment of the type of fund that it has discussed is only one step towards the comprehensive solution to the problem of all additional expenditures (referred to in General Assembly resolution 41/213) and relates primarily to contingencies of a programmatic nature. Still to be addressed, *inter alia*, is what appears to be the much larger question of how to deal with additional expenditures related to cost increases, such as those due to fluctuations in currency or inflation and to revisions in standard rates for salaries and common staff costs. As indicated in paragraph 118 of its first report,[5] the Advisory Committee intends to look into this matter closely with a view to formulating specific recommendations to be submitted to the Assembly at its forty-third session.

Notes

1. *Official Records of the General Assembly, Fortieth Session, Supplement No. 7* (A/40/7), para. 13.
2. *Ibid., Forty-second Session, Supplement No. 7* (A/42/7).
3. *Ibid.*
4. *Ibid.*
5. *Ibid.*

2.13 Document A/42/16[*]

Question of Accommodating all Additional Expenditures within the Overall Level of the Budget (A/42/225/Add.1)

Report of the Committee for Programme and Co-ordination

1988

57. At its 59th, 60th, 63rd and 65th meetings, on 22, 25 and 29 September, the Committee resumed its consideration of this question and had before it the addendum to the report of the Secretary-General entitled "Questions relating to the programme budget: inflation and currency fluctuation, and the level of the contingency fund" (A/42/225/Add.1).

Discussion

58. The Committee noted that the questions of inflation and currency fluctuation were not addressed in the report of the Secretary-General. In that connection, the Committee recalled that it had recommended at the first part of its twenty-seventh session, that the questions of inflation and currency fluctuations should be studied in depth (A/42/16 (Part I), para. 320).

59. The Committee recalled the relevant provisions concerning the contingency fund and additional expenditures, as contained in annex I of resolution 41/213. It agreed that the contingency fund should cover both years of a budget biennium.

60. Delegations commented on the relationship between the possible level of the contingency fund and the overall level of the programme budget. For some delegations, there was a clear linkage between the two concepts, which could and should be discussed together. Some delegations stressed the necessity to have agreement first on the definition of elements to be covered by the fund under "revised estimates". Other delegations, while recognizing the link between the two issues, were of the view that the overall level of the budget did not fall under the agenda item being discussed. Some other delegations also considered that, to some extent, the matter could have been addressed, in general terms, in accordance with regulation 4.8 of the regulations approved in General Assembly resolution 37/234 of 21 December 1982.

61. Several delegations were of the opinion that the Committee should advise the General Assembly on the appropriate level for the 1988-1989 programme budget, as the Committee had decided to do at its regular twenty-seventh

---

[*]*Official Records of the General Assembly, Forty-second Session, Supplement No. 16* (A/42/16), pp. 77-81.

session. Those delegations felt that the figure to be established should not exceed the current appropriations. Some delegations noted that the 1986-1987 programme budget was being implemented at a level substantially below the approved level of $1,711 million. They noted that revised estimates, reflecting the further implementation of resolution 41/213, would be submitted in the first part of 1988, and would have the effect of reducing the total resources required for the biennium 1988-1989, taking into account the recommendations of the Advisory Committee on Administrative and Budgetary Questions,[1] as approved by the General Assembly. Other delegations, while considering that additional economies would not be possible, thought that the comments and recommendations of the Advisory Committee, to a large extent, offer a useful basis for a decision on the level of expenditures for the next biennium. Other delegations were of the opinion that the initial estimates presented by the Secretary-General for 1988-1989 were adequate.

62. Some delegations considered that the contingency fund should be within the overall level of the programme budget, that is to say, the fund would be part of the total appropriation to be voted by the General Assembly for the following biennium. Some delegations, agreeing that the contingency fund should be within the overall level of the programme budget, felt that level was constituted by the figure approved during the off-budget year as a result of consideration of the Secretary-General's proposals on the outline budget. Other delegations were of the view that the contingency fund would be an addition to the overall level of the budget and would be subject to a separate appropriation by the Assembly, in accordance with paragraph 1 (d) of annex I to resolution 41/213.

63. Some delegations wondered about the possible different amounts of resources for the fund during the first and second years of the biennium, when the operation of the contingency fund should begin, what its level would be, on the basis of past experience, and what kind of additional expenditures would be accommodated under it and how that would be done, and what would be the modalities for its utilization.

64. As regards the distribution of the resources of the contingency fund over the biennium, some delegations were of the view that the resources should be divided equally between the two years, whereas others believed that the first year should have a slightly larger share than the second year. The Committee preferred to keep the division of resources flexible.

65. Several delegations proposed that the Committee recommend that the General Assembly establish, at its forty-second session, a contingency fund on an experimental basis to accomodate additional expenditure during the biennium 1988-1989, with the modalities for its operation to be approved by the General Assembly on the basis of recommendations that would be made by CPC and the Advisory Committee on Administrative and Budgetary Questions. They believed that the early establishment of the fund, albeit on an experimental basis, would be part of the early implementation of resolution

41/213 during 1988-1989, thus providing useful experience in dealing with the technical and procedural issues related to the management and operation of such a fund. Several delegations, bearing in mind, *inter alia*, the views of the Advisory Committee, as expressed in paragraph 15 of its report,[2] where it "does not believe that it is possible at this time to set an overall figure for the revised estimates for the 1988-1989 proposed programme budget" advocated adherence to paragraph 1 of annex I to Assembly resolution 41/213, which specified that the size of the contingency fund should be indicated by the Secretary-General in the outline of the programme budget to be submitted in off-budget years. Some delegations found it inadvisable to experiment with the introduction of such a fund during a transitional budget period, which would not constitute a solid basis for future budgets. Key issues would remain unresolved pending the completion of the Advisory Committee's study on a comprehensive solution to the problem of all additional expenditures, including those deriving from inflation and currency fluctuation, taking into account the desirability of accommodating those expenditures within the overall level of the budget, either as a reserve or as a separate part of the contingency fund, as well as the Secretary-General's report on the matter. Those delegations recalled that the General Assembly had, in paragraph 2 (a) of part II of resolution 41/212, reaffirmed the need to improve the planning, programming and budgeting process through full implementation of regulation 4.8 of the Regulations Governing Programme Planning, which governed co-ordination between CPC and the Advisory Committee on Administrative and Budgetary Questions. They agreed with the Advisory Committee that "it is absolutely necessary for the process of reform to proceed in an orderly, clear, coherent and timely manner". Other delegations were of the view that the observation of the Advisory Committee, as contained in paragraph 15 of its report, did not contradict the early introduction of a contingency fund since the Advisory Committee expressed the view that it would be difficult to set an overall figure for the revised estimates until the level of the contingency fund was determined and the treatment of inflation and currency fluctuations decided.

66. Some delegations warned against undue haste in establishing a contingency fund, even on an experimental basis, pointing out that the Secretary-General had yet to propose precise procedures for the operation of such a fund. Moreover, proposals were still to come from the Advisory Committee on Administrative and Budgetary Questions. They stated that such proposals would have both technical and political aspects. For instance, adopting the approach of a one-time overall determination by the General Assembly of the relative priorities among draft resolutions with programme budget implications and revised estimates might imply changes in the role, working procedures and mandate of CPC. Some delegations were of the view that a piecemeal approach to such an important matter as the operational modalities of a contingency fund could create precedents in such a way that difficulties could arise for the Organization in the future.

67. Some delegations stated that their agreement to starting the operation of a contingency fund, on either an *ad hoc* or an experimental basis, would be subject to a number of conditions: that it be without prejudice to the related provisions of resolution 41/213; that it be a 3 per cent of the expenditure level of the initial programme budget proposal of the Secretary-General for the biennium 1988-1989; that it be for the sole purpose of gaining operational experience before the establishment of the contingency fund called for in resolution 41/213; that the establishment of the experimental fund and its operation not constitute a precedent and that the General Assembly review the whole matter at its forty-fourth session based on the recommendations of CPC at its twenty-ninth session; that construction expenditures not be included in the experimental contingency fund; and that Member States work on the premise that additional expenditures derived from legislative mandates not provided for in the proposed programme budget would not exceed the level of the experimental contingency fund, except that during the biennium 1988-1989, but not in later biennium, if such excess were deemed necessary, the Assembly would take the necessary decisions to keep such additional expenditures to a minimum after the depletion of the fund.

68. A number of delegations favoured setting the size of the fund at a modest level, taking into account the inclusion in the proposed programme budget for 1988-1989 of activities under the "perennial" mandates and of requirements formerly covered by consolidated statements of conference-servicing requirements. They proposed adopting the level of 0.75 per cent of the initial programme budget proposal that was suggested by the Secretary-General (A/42/225, para. 34). Some delegations pointed out that the level of the contingency fund should be determined primarily by the assessment of anticipated additional requirements in future bienniums, which are likely to decline under the new budgetary procedure. Other delegations proposed higher levels for the fund, ranging from 2.5 to 3 per cent of the expenditure level of the initial programme budget proposal, basing their proposals on the levels of additional expenditures that had been incurred in the past three budget bienniums. They cautioned that a period of unknown levels and kinds of needs would necessarily follow wide-ranging reforms of both intergovernmental bodies and their supporting services and that past and present perceptions of requirements might not serve as an adequate guide in the future. Establishing a higher funding level to meet such unknown contingencies would therefore be a prudent course of action, without prejudice, in the present case, to the full application of United Nations financial regulations 4.2, 4.4 and 5.2 (d). Some delegations recalled that, according to resolution 41/213, in budget years, the proposed programme budget was to be considered in accordance with existing procedures.

69. In considering the kinds of additional expenditures that would be accommodated under a contingency fund, a number of delegations recalled that the General Assembly, in paragraph 11 of annex I to resolution 41/213, stipulated that pending a decision by it on the question of a comprehensive

solution to the problem of all additional expenditures, the revised estimates arising from the impact of extraordinary expenses, including those relating to the maintenance of peace and security, as well as fluctuations in rates of exchange and inflation, should not be covered by the contingency fund and should continue to be treated in accordance with established procedures and the relevant provisions of the Financial Regulations and Rules. Nevertheless, some delegations wanted the contingency fund to cover all expenditures that might be incurred beyond those provided for in the programme budget, while some others would exclude from the fund's coverage, pending the adoption by the Assembly of a decision on the aforementioned question of a comprehensive solution, expenditures arising from fluctuations in the rates of inflation and currency exchange and unforeseen and extraordinary expenditures. Still others would exclude from the fund's coverage all additional expenditures relating to major construction projects. Some delegations supported, in line with paragraph 4 of the Secretary-General's report (A/42/225/Add.1), the inclusion of the estimates for such projects in the Secretary-General's initial programme budget proposals and the accommodation under the contingency fund of any upward adjustment in costs that would result in additional expenditures during the biennium.

70. Delegations considered also whether the General Assembly should decide at a given point towards the end of its session on the allocation of the resources of the contingency fund among the additional expenditures proposed in revised estimates and draft resolutions and decisions, or whether the allocation should be made on a first-come, first-served basis. Several delegations advocated the former approach, believing that it would be the most equitable and rational way of allocating resources.

71. Another proposal was advanced by some delegations to avoid competition among the Main Committees for the resources of the contingency fund. They proposed that the Assembly establish a set of criteria according to which the resources available under the contingency fund would be allocated among the Main Committees.

Conclusions and recommendations

72. The Committee considered that the above discussion would constitute a useful input into the deliberations of the Fifth Committee of the General Assembly at its forty-second session and into the further consideration of those issues at the twenty-eighth session of CPC, without prejudice to any decision that the General Assembly might take at its forty-second session.

Notes

1. *Official Records of the General Assembly, Forty-second Session, Supplement No. 7* (A/42/7).
2. *Ibid.*

2.14 Document A/C.5/42/2/Rev.1*

Implementation of General Assembly Resolution 41/213: Programmatic and Budgetary Aspects - Update of the Progress Report of the Secretary-General (A/42/234)

Report of the Secretary-General

23 September 1987

Introduction

1. In presenting his proposed programme budget for the biennium 1988-1989, the Secretary-General made clear that his proposals were based upon and reflected the organizational structures of the Secretariat as they were at the end of 1986, despite changes that he had already initiated and others that were anticipated in response to General Assembly resolution 41/213 on the review of the efficiency of the administrative and financial functioning of the United Nations. This approach was necessitated by the need to adhere to the established process of budget preparation, including the need to meet the deadline for the presentation of the proposed programme budget to the Committee for Programme and Co-ordination (CPC) and the Advisory Committee for Administrative and Budgetary Questions (ACABQ). The preparation of the budget proposals was begun before the General Assembly had completed its consideration of the report of the Group of High-level Intergovernmental Experts to Review the Efficiency of the Administrative and Financial Functioning of the United Nations,[1] from which stem the various changes and reforms initiated and envisaged.

2. In his progress report on the implementation of General Assembly resolution 41/213 (A/42/234), the Secretary-General has outlined a number of reforms that he has already initiated in response to this resolution. During their consideration of the proposed programme budget, CPC and ACABQ were informed in broad terms of the implications of these reforms for organizational units, their functions and the resources assigned to them. CPC recommended that the Secretary-General provide the General Assembly, through the Committee's resumed session, with updated information on the implementation of its resolution 41/213, including both programmatic and budgetary aspects, and deferred full approval of certain budget sections to its resumed twenty-seventh session. ACABQ, in its first report on the proposed programme budget for 1988-1989,[2] recommended that Member States should be kept informed of the progress of reform through an update of the Secretary-General's progress report, to which might be annexed details of the budgetary implications of reforms already implemented on the initial estimates

---

*A/C.5/42/2/Rev.1.

for the biennium 1988-1989.[3] The present report gives fuller and more detailed programmatic and budgetary information on reforms already implemented, and outlined in the progress report of the Secretary-General, as they relate to the proposed programme budget for the biennium 1988-1989.

3. The budget proposals as currently presented reflect a virtually unchanged number, level and distribution of posts within the Secretariat, but take account of the goal of staff reductions set by the General Assembly through application of higher than usual turnover rates throughout the budget - 12.5 per cent for the Professional and higher categories and 7.5 per cent for General Service and related categories. It is the intention of the Secretary-General to achieve staff and other cost reductions in an orderly manner consistent with reforms being instituted, but the exact details of these reductions are difficult to quantify at a stage where the reform process has only just begun. Further changes are anticipated as a result of the work of the Special Commission of the Economic and Social Council studying the structure and functioning of the intergovernmental machinery in the economic and social fields and of internal reviews. These reviews, such as those in the Department of Administration and Management, the Department of Public Information and in the economic, humanitarian and social sectors, including human rights, will not all be completed in 1987. Their results in programmatic and budgetary terms will, however, be reflected appropriately in revised estimates to be submitted during 1988. Consequently, and in order to maintain the integrity and coherence of the budget presentation, the changes to the Secretary-General's proposals which are outlined below follow the same principles as the initial presentation and do not involve any net change in the overall level of the proposed budget. Information is given only for those sections of the proposed programme budget affected by reforms outlined in the progress report of the Secretary-General or included in the proposed agenda of the resumed session of CPC. Changes are cross-referenced between sections affected and summary tables are annexed, indicating the net proposed shift of resources between budget sections as well as the revised proposed programme budget on a section-by-section basis. To avoid repetitions, details of proposed redeployments of resources are given under the sections from which these resources are to be taken.

Section 1. Overall Policy-Making, Direction and Co-ordination

4. Reform measures undertaken by the Secretary-General in response to General Assembly resolution 41/213, as outlined in his progress report (A/42/234), affect subsections 2, 3, 6, 7, 8, 9 and 10 of section B (Executive direction and management) of section 1 and also involve the creation of a new Office for Research and the Collection of Information. The detailed resource implications of these changes for the proposed programme budget for the biennium 1988-1989 are outlined below.

Subsection 1.B.2.   *Executive Office of the Secretary-General*

[See also: subsection 1.B.12, para. 16]

5. Consolidation of research and information functions for the political area in the new Office for Research and the Collection of Information will entail redeployment of two Professional (one P-4 and one P-3) and one General Service (other level) post.

Subsection 1.B.3.   *Office of the Under-Secretary-General for Political and General Assembly Affairs and Secretariat Services (including the Division of General Assembly Affairs and the Division of Economic and Social Council Affairs and Secretariat Services)*

[See also: section 8, para. 40, and subsection 1.B.10, para. 12]

6. Responsibility for the technical secretariat servicing of the intergovernmental and related meetings and special conferences have been assigned to a new Division of Economic and Social Council Affairs and Secretariat Services in this Office from the Office of Secretariat Services for Economic and Social Matters, which has been discontinued. ...

7. Responsibility for co-ordination of all United Nations drug-related programmes has been transferred from the Under-Secretary-General to the Director-General of the United Nations Office at Vienna. This will not, however, involve any redeployment of resources.

Subsection 1.B.6.   *Office of the Under-Secretary-General for Special Political Questions*

[See also: section 3, para. 25]

8. The responsibilities of this Office have been consolidated into the new Department for Special Political Questions, Regional Co-operation, Decolonization and Trusteeship. Consequently, all resources related to this programme, namely, three Professional and higher level posts (one USG, one D-2 and one P-3) and three General Service (other level) posts, as well as $65,80C under other objects of expenditure, would then be redeployed to section 3 (Political affairs, trusteeship and decolonization). This subsection would then be deleted.

Subsection 1.B.7.   *Unit   for   Special   Economic   Assistance Programmes*

[See also: section 3, para. 25]

9.   Administration of these programmes will henceforth be the responsibility of the United Nations Development Programme (UNDP), except in cases of political sensitivity where other arrangements may be appropriate. Pending overall review of arrangements in this area, however, and to maintain a consistent approach to presentation of this transitional programme budget, it is proposed that resources related to this Unit, namely, six Professional and higher level posts (one established D-2, one temporary D-1, three temporary P-5 and one temporary P-4) and seven temporary General Service (other level) posts, as well as $444,400 under other objects of expenditure, would then be redeployed to section 3 (Political affairs, trusteeship and decolonization). This subsection would then be deleted.

Subsection 1.B.8.   *Office for Field Operational and External Support Activities*

[See also: subsection 1.B.12, para. 16, and section 28, para. 44]

10. The work of this Office relating to the dissemination of information is to be carried out by the new Office for Research and the Collection of Information, under subsection 1.B.12, and its other functions have been integrated into the Department of Administration and Management. As a result, it is proposed that four Professional and higher level posts (one ASG, one P-5, one P-4 and one P-2/1) and four General Service (other level) posts be redeployed to the new Office together with $45,400 under other objects of expenditure and nine Professional and higher level posts (one D-2, two P-5, two P-4, one P-3 and three P-2/1) and 12 General Service (other level) posts together with $13,000 under other objects of expenditure be redeployed to section 28D (Office of General Services, Headquarters). This subsection would then be deleted.

Subsection 1.B.9.   *Office of the Director-General, United Nations Office at Geneva*

[See also: section 23, para. 41]

11. The Director-General of the United Nations Office at Geneva has assumed supervisory responsibility for human rights activities. Provision of resources for these activities has been made under section 23 (Human Rights) of the proposed programme budget for the biennium 1988-1989. No revisions are proposed for this subsection.

Subsection 1.B.10. *Offi͜ce of the Director-General, United Nations Office at Vienna*

[See also: subsection 1.B.3, para. 7, and section 6, para. 37]

12. The Director-General of the United Nations Office at Vienna has assumed responsibility for United Nations activities on social policy and development. Provision for these activities will be made under a new section 6B in part IV (Economic, social and humanitarian activities) of the proposed programme budget for the biennium 1988-1989 to which resources will be redeployed from section 6 (Department of International Economic and Social Affairs). The Director-General has also assumed responsibility for co-ordination of all United Nations drug-related programmes for which provision is made in section 20 (International drug control). No revisions are proposed for this subsection.

Subsection 1.B.12. *Office for Research and the Collection of Information*

[See also: subsection 1.B.2, para. 5; section 1.B.8, para. 10; subsection 2A.B, para. 18; section 3, para. 26, and section 27, para. 42]

13. The Secretary-General is charged with responsibilities relating to the maintenance of international peace and security under Article 99 of the Charter of the United Nations as well as through specific political tasks mandated to him by the Security Council and the General Assembly. In carrying out these tasks, a key instrument is the regular and effective provision, analysis and dissemination of relevant information. Such information allows the Secretary-General to monitor actual and potential threats to peace and to provide the Security Council and the General Assembly with a sound and timely basis for their deliberations.

14. In order to improve the effectiveness of this work, the Secretary-General has established the Office for Research and the Collection of Information to rationalize and consolidate information activities in the political area as recommended in General Assembly resolution 41/213. The Office will be responsible for the collection and maintenance of current information, developing and co-ordinating research and assessment of global trends originating in different political departments and for undertaking *ad hoc* research, in co-ordination with other departments, for the immediate needs of the Secretary-General. It will also receive, consolidate and distribute political information from media sources and from United Nations information centres for use by the Secretary-General and his senior staff.

15. The Office brings together functions previously performed by the Executive Office of the Secretary-General and the Office for Field Operational and External Support Activities in section 1, as well as the Department of Political

Affairs, Trusteeship and Decolonization in section 3, the Department of Political and Security Council Affairs in section 2A and the Department of Public Information in section 27. This consolidation of functions brings together aspects of work covered by different programmes of the medium-term plan for the period 1984-1989 and will be reflected in an integrated manner in the proposed medium-term plan for the period 1990-1995. ...

16. The staffing required to carry out this programme of work has been the subject of internal review and the positions proposed have been duly classified. The resulting staffing table comprises 21 Professional and higher level posts and 21 General Service posts. When these requirements were set against the initial staffing proposals for the departments and offices affected by the transfer of functions to the Office for Research and the Collection of Information, a total of 15 Professional and higher level posts (one ASG, one D-2, one D-1, three P-5, five P-4, two P-3 and two P-2/1) and 21 General Service (other level) posts were identified for redeployment. The situation as regards the six Professional posts at the appropriate level not yet identified will be kept under close review and results will be reported at a later stage. In the mean time, the Office will begin the biennium with the reduced level of staffing indicated above.

Section 2A. Political and Security Council Affairs;
Peace-keeping Activities

17. Reform measures undertaken by the Secretary-General in response to General Assembly resolution 42/213, as outlined in his progress report (A/42/234), affect subsections B, C and D of section 2A. Programmatic and budgetary aspects of these changes are outlined below.

Subsection 2A.B.   *Department of Political and Security Council Affairs*

[See also: subsection 1.B.12, para. 15; subsection 2A.C, para. 22, and section 2B, para. 24]

18. As mentioned above, changes in the political sector include the establishment, under section 1 of the proposed programme budget for the biennium 1988-1989, of the Office for Research and the Collection of Information, which will rationalize and consolidate information activities in the political area as recommended in General Assembly resolution 41/213. As part of this consolidation, the functions relating to the provision of information by the Section for Co-ordination and Political Information of the Office of the Under-Secretary-General for Political and Security Council Affairs, as referred to in subparagraph 2A.11 (g) of the proposed programme budget, would be transferred to the new Office for Research and the Collection of Information (section 1), together with three Professional posts (one P-4, one P-3 and one P-2/1) and four General Service (other level) posts. In addition, the title of section 2A.B.1 would be revised to read "Executive direction and management:

Office of the Under-Secretary-General for Political and Security Council Affairs (including the Section for Co-ordination and Executive Management)".

19. In order to permit the consolidation of servicing for General Assembly agenda items related to zones and regions of peace and co-operation, the Secretary-General decided to assign the primary responsibility for servicing the *Ad Hoc* Committee on the Indian Ocean to the Department of Political and Security Council Affairs. This decision has programmatic implications for programme element 2.3 (Peace, security and co-operation in the sea and ocean areas) of subprogramme 2 (Service for Political and Security Affairs) of the proposed programme budget for the biennium 1988-1989. Outputs (iii) and (iv) will be deleted and a new programme element 2.4 will be added.

20. The Secretary-General has also indicated that most aspects of the work on maritime matters have been consolidated into the Office for Ocean Affairs and the Law of the Sea. The text of programme element 2.3 of section 2A.B should be amended in order to reflect this delineation of responsibility more clearly. ...

Subsection 2A.C. *Office for Ocean Affairs and the Law of the Sea*

[See also: subsection 2A.B, para. 20, and section 6, para. 33]

21. As mentioned above, the Secretary-General has decided to consolidate most of the activities related to maritime matters in the Office of the Special Representative of the Secretary-General for the Law of the Sea, now renamed the Office for Ocean Affairs and the Law of the Sea. The functions performed by the Ocean Economics and Technology Branch of the Department of International Economic and Social Affairs (section 6) would, therefore, be transferred to this section together with related resources, except for those related to maritime resources in development and maritime inputs to the World Economic Survey. Accordingly, activities to implement programme 1 (Law of the sea affairs) and most of programme 2 (Economic and technical aspect of marine affairs) of chapter 25 (Marine affairs) of the medium-term plan for 1984-1989 (A/37/6/Add.1) would be consolidated in this section. ...

22. In addition, responsibility for factual reporting on developments in the sea and ocean area will rest with the Office for Ocean Affairs and the Law of the Sea rather than the Department for Political and Security Council Affairs. This delineation of responsibility, which is also reflected in programmatic changes under section 2A.B, does not entail any redeployment of resources. ...

Subséction 2A.D. *Special Missions*

[See also: section 28, para. 44]

23. Among the reform measures implemented by the Secretary-General is the integration of the work of the Office for Field Operational and External Support Activities, other than dissemination of information, into the Department of Administration and Management under the Office of General Services. As programmes 3 (United Nations Supply Depot at Pisa) and 4 (Administrative and technical staff (communications personnel)) of section 2A.D have been administered by the Office for Field Operational and External Support Activities, it is also proposed that the functions and resources relating to them be transferred to section 28D (Office of General Services, Headquarters). This will involve redeployment of 1 Professional (1 P-5), 8 Local Level and 31 Field Service posts, together with $285,200 under other objects of expenditure from section 2A.D to section 28D of the proposed programme budget for the biennium 1988-1989.

Section 2B. Disarmament Affairs Activities

[See also: section 2A.B, paras. 19 and 20]

24. In order to permit the consolidation of servicing for General Assembly agenda items related to zones and regions of peace and co-operation, the Secretary-General has decided to assign the primary responsibility for servicing the *Ad Hoc* Committee on the Indian Ocean to the Department of Political and Security Council Affairs. This decision has programmatic implications both for that Department and for the Department for Disarmament Affairs. ...

Section 3. Political Affairs, Trusteeship and Decolonization

[See also: section 1.B.6, para. 8; section 1.B.7, para. 9;
and section 1.B.12, para. 15]

25. As indicated in his progress report (A/42/234), the Secretary-General has consolidated the responsibilities of the Office for Special Political Questions and the Department of Political Affairs, Trusteeship and Decolonization into the new Department for Special Political Questions, Regional Co-operation, *Decolonization and Trusteeship*, which also provides secretariat support for the Commissioner for Namibia and service for the United Nations Council for Namibia. This will also involve redeployment to this section of all resources currently provided for in subsection 1.B.6 (Office of the Under-Secretary-General for Special Political Questions). In addition, and as indicated above, resources provided under subsection 1.B.7 (Unit for Special Economic Assistance Programmes) should also be redeployed to this section pending the completion of the review of arrangements in this area.

26. The new Office for Research and the Collection of Information consolidates research and information functions in the political area, including some of those previously carried out by the Department of Political Affairs, Trusteeship and Decolonization. The continuing review of the work of the new Department for Special Political Questions, Regional Co-operation, Decolonization and Trusteeship has helped to identify certain posts that can be suitably redeployed to the new Office. Consequently, it is proposed that 6 Professional and higher level posts (one D-2, one D-1, two P-5 and two P-4) and 10 General Service (other level) posts be so redeployed.

Section 5A. Office of the Director-General for Development and International Economic Co-operation

[See also: section 8, para. 40]

27. Among the measures taken by the Secretary-General was the discontinuance of the Office of Secretariat Services for Economic and Social Matters and the transfer of its functions to the Office of the Under-Secretary-General for Political and General Assembly Affairs and Secretariat Services and the Office of the Director-General.

28. It is proposed that the functions and related resources concerned with technical secretariat services for intersecretariat meetings, other than editin g and reproduction of documentation, will be transferred to section 5A under the heading International co-operation for economic and social development, new part D, Intersecretariat co-ordination machinery as follows:

Subsection 5A.D. *Intersecretariat Co-ordination Machinery*

29. As a practical measure to facilitate inter-agency co-ordination, the Assistant Secretary-General of the Office of the Director-General for Devel opment and International Economic Co-operation has been designated to serve, as well, as Secretary and Chairman of ACC and its Organizational Committee, respectively.

30. With regard to the intersecretariat co-ordination machinery, the Assistant Secretary-General provides a central point of reference in the United Nations for matters relating to the technical servicing of inter-agency affairs. The Assistant Secretary-General establishes and follows up the programme of work of ACC and draft reports related to it and to its Organizational Committee and monitors their implementation. The Assistant Secretary-General will, through his Office, provide technical secretariat services, other than editing and reproduction of documentation, for ACC and the Organizational Committee as well as the two subsidiary bodies - the Consultative Committee on Substantive Questions (Programme Matters, CCSQ(PROG)), which deals with programming and related matters; and the Consultative Committee on Substantive Questions (Operational Activities, CCSQ(OPS)).

31. Specific tasks include preparatory work and technical secretariat services for approximately 20 intersecretariat meetings, excluding informal meetings and consultations that may far exceed the number of formal meetings; and the preparation of reports on monitoring of developments and decisions of intersecretariat bodies.

32. The Secretary-General has also decided that the heads of the Centre for Transnational Corporations and the Centre for Science and Technology for Development will report to him through the Under-Secretary-General for International Economic and Social Affairs, and that with regard to the Centre for Science and Technology for Development, he would recommend that General Assembly resolution 34/218 (United Nations Conference on Science and Technology for Development) be amended accordingly. Consequently, it is proposed that paragraph 5A.4(b)(iii) be deleted from section 5A.

Section 6. Department of International Economic and Social Affairs

[See also: subsection 1.B.10, para. 12; subsection 2A.C, para. 21, and section 28, para. 43]

33. The reform measures undertaken by the Secretary-General in response to General Assembly resolution 41/213 affect section 6 (Department of International Economic and Social Affairs) in a number of ways. Most aspects of the work on maritime matters have been consolidated into section 2A.C (Office for Ocean Affairs and the Law of the Sea), which has involved the transfer of most activities under subsection 6.B.3 (Economic and technical aspects of marine affairs) to that Office. Consequently, it is proposed that eight Professional and higher level posts (one D-1, one P-5, one P-4, three P-3 and two P-2/1) and three General Service (other level) posts, together with $109,200 under other objects of expenditure, be redeployed to section 2A.C of the proposed programme budget for the biennium 1988-1989. ...

35. Functions previously performed by the Office for Programme Planning and Co-ordination under subsection 6.C.1 relating to programme planning, monitoring and evaluation have been consolidated in the Department of Administration and Management under section 28. This will involve transfer to section 28 of all activities under programme 1 (Programme planning) of subsection 6.C.1, as well as output (iii) of programme element 1.1 (Cross-organizational review and programme analysis) of programme 2 (Co-ordination). As functions of the Office concerned with co-ordination have remained in the Department of International Economic and Social Affairs, the rest of programme 2 will remain in section 6.

36. This will also involve redeployment from section 6 to section 28 of 16 Professional and higher level posts (one ASG, one D-2, two D-1, four P-5, five P-4 and three P-3) and 10 General Service (other level) posts as well as $105,700 under other objects of expenditure.

37. Activities on global social development issues are now the responsibility of the Director-General of the United Nations Office at Vienna. Consequently, it is proposed that programme 5 (Global social development issues) of section 6 be transferred to a new section 6B (Activities on global social development issues) in part IV (Economic, social and humanitarian activities) of the proposed programme budget for the biennium 1988-1989. All resources related to this programme, namely, 52 Professional and higher level posts (1 ASG, 2 D-2, 4 D-1, 9 P-5, 18 P-4, 7 P-3 and 11 P-2/1) and 38 General Service posts (6 Principal level and 32 Other level), as well as $947,900 under other objects of expenditure, would then be redeployed to the new section. It should be noted that the review on the possible redeployment of other programme responsibilities and resources in this area has not yet been completed and will be reported on at a later stage.

38. The heads of the Centre for Transnational Corporations and the Centre for Science and Technology for Development will report to the Secretary-General through the Under-Secretary-General for International Economic and Social Affairs. This will have no budgetary implications.

39. Following the reallocation of various responsibilities to other budget sections, section 6, which presently contains the resources for the Department of International Economic and Social Affairs, will become section 6A.

Section 8. Office of Secretariat Services for Economic and Social Matters

[See also: subsection 1.B.3, para. 6, and section 5A, para. 28]

40. One of the reform measures outlined by the Secretary-General in his progress report (A/42/234) is the transfer of most of the functions of the Office of Secretariat Services for Economic and Social Matters to section 1, subsection 1.B.3 (Office of the Under-Secretary-General for Political and General Assembly Affairs and Secretariat Services, including the Division of General Assembly Affairs and the Division of Economic and Social Council Affairs and Secretariat Services). The remainder have been transferred to section 5A (Office of the Director-General for Development and International Economic Co-operation) under the heading International co-operation for economic and social development, new part D, Intersecretariat co-ordination machinery. This will involve redeployment of 20 Professional and higher level posts (one ASG, one D-2, one D-1, four P-5, six P-4, six P-3 and one P-2/1) and 17 General Service posts (2 principal level and 15 other level), as well as $367,900 under other objects of expenditure, to the new Division under section 1 and one Professional (one P-5) and one General Service (other level) post, as well as $54,000 for other official travel of staff, to section 5A. The Office of Secretariat Services for Economic and Social Matters has been discontinued and this section will be deleted.

Section 23. Human Rights

[See also: section 1.B.9, para. 11]

41. As indicated above, supervisory responsibility for human rights activities
has been assumed by the Director-General of the United Nations Office at
Geneva. A review of the staffing structure of the Centre for Human Rights
and of the allocation of relevant programme activities and related resources is
being undertaken and its results will be reported to the General Assembly in
due course. In the mean time, no functions or resources are proposed for
redeployment from this section.

Section 27. Public Information

[See also: section 1.B.12, para. 15]

42. The Office for Research and the Collection of Information under section
1 consolidates functions relating to political research and information,
including the briefing of United Nations information centres. The transfer of
this function will entail redeployment of two General Service (other level)
posts from section 27 to section 1.

Section 28. Administration and Management

[See also: subsection 1.B.8, para. 10, and section 6, paras. 35-36]

43. The Department has been kept under review with the aim of simplifying the
structure of administrative and support services; reducing the duplication of
effort and strengthening the line of authority and suppressing higher
hierarchical levels, with the aim of achieving greater efficiency. The results of
these reviews would be reflected in the context of revised estimates to be
submitted to the General Assembly during 1988. In the mean time, under the
measures announced by the Secretary-General in response to General
Assembly resolution 41/213, functions relating to programme planning,
budgeting, monitoring and evaluation have, as recommended, been brought
together under a coherent structure. This has involved transfer to the
Department of related functions from section 6 (Department of International
Economic and Social Affairs), together with the requisite resources.

44. Another measure has been the integration of the work of the Office for
Field Operational and External Support Activities, other than information
dissemination, into the Department of Administration and Management under
the Office of General Services. Resources should, therefore, be redeployed
from subsection 1.B.8 (Office for Field Operational and External Support
Activities) and from subsection 2A.D (Special Missions), namely the United
Nations Supply Depot at Pisa and administrative and technical staff
(communications personnel), since the staff and activities in the latter two
organizational units have been under the administration of the Office for Field

Operational and External Support Activities. A separate Division for Field Operational and External Support Activities will then be created under section 28D, adding a new programme which will be reflected in due course in the · medium-term plan proposals for 1990-1995.

45. The new Division would provide, in close co-operation and co-ordination with the Office of the Under-Secretaries-General for Special Political Affairs, administrative and logistic support to special missions, peace-keeping operations, relief operation missions and other such field missions as the Secretary-General may decide. The Division would be organized to discharge its responsibilities as follows:

(a) A Field Service Unit charged with administrative responsibility for staff members in the Field Service category;

(b) A Peace Forces Administrative Section responsible for providing administrative, budgetary, financial, personnel and logistics support to force-level peace-keeping missions such as the United Nations Interim Force in Lebanon (UNIFIL), the United Nations Disengagement Observer Force (UNDOF) and the United Nations Peace-keeping Force in Cyprus (UNFICYP);

(c) The Missions Administrative Section to provide the same type of support to established observer missions such as the United Nations Truce Supervision Organization in Palestine (UNTSO) and the United Nations Military Observer Group in India and Pakistan (UNMOGIP); in addition, the Missions Administrative Section would provide administrative support to visiting missions authorized by the Security Council and meetings organized by other bodies, including the Special Committee against *Apartheid*;

(d) The United Nations Supply Depot in Pisa as a central stocking area for equipment and supplies;

(e) Administrative and technical staff who are essentially Field Service communications staff (radio operators and radio technicians) assigned to the United Nations Office at Geneva, the United Nations Environment Programme at Nairobi, the United Nations station at Lusaka and the headquarters of the regional commissions.

Notes

1. *Official Records of the General Assembly, Forty-first Session, Supplement No. 49* (A/41/49).
2. *Ibid., Forty-second Session, Supplement No. 7* (A/42/7).
3. *Ibid., Supplement No. 6* (A/42/6).

ANNEX
Summary tables

Table 1.
Sections with budgetary implications of measures implemented
thus far in response to General Assembly resolution 41/213

(Thousands of United States dollars)

Section	Secretary-General's original proposed programme budget 1988-1989	Secretary-General's revised proposed programme budget 1988-1989	Total increase decrease
1. Overall policy-making, direction and co-ordination	41 947.5	43 749.9	1 802.4
2A.B. Department of Political and Security Council Affairs	10 942.7	10 391.0	(551.7)
2A.C. Office of the Special Representative of the Secretary-General for the Law of the Sea	5 889.4	7 067.8	1 178.4
2A.D. Special missions	52 827.6	48 777.6	(4 050.0)
3. Political affairs, trusteeship and decolonization	30 301.7	31 326.6	1 024.9
5A. Office of the Director-General for Development and International Economic Co-operation	3 627.9	3 886.1	258.2
6. Department of International Economic and Social Affairs	54 477.3	-	(54 477.3)

Section		Secretary-General's original proposed programme budget 1988-1989	Secretary-General's revised proposed programme budget 1988-1989	Total increase decrease
6A.	Department of International Economic and Social Affairs	-	40 651.8	40 651.8
6B.	Activities on global social development issues	-	9 772.1	9 772.1
8.	Office of Secretariat Services for Economic and Social Matters	4 209.3	-	(4 209.3)
27.	Public information	75 869.6	75 745.0	(124.6)
28.	Administration and management	344 108.2	352 833.3	8 725.1
	Total	624 201.2	624 201.2	-

Table 2.
Revised proposals for the biennium 1988-1989

(Thousands of United States dollars)

Section	Secretary-General's original 1988-1989 proposed programme budget estimates	Secretary-General's revised proposed programme budget 1988-1989
1. Overall policy-making, direction and co-ordination	41 947.5	43 749.9
2A. Department of Political and Security Council Affairs; peace-keeping activities	82 448.4	79 025.1
2B. Disarmament affairs activities	9 075.7	9 075.7
3. Political affairs, trusteeship and decolonization	30 301.7	31 326.6
4. Policy-making organs (economic and social activities)	1 188.0	1 188.0
5A. Director-General for Development and International Economic Co-operation	3 627.9	3 886.1
5B. Regional Commissions Liaison Office	653.9	653.9
6. Department of International Economic and Social Affairs	54 477.3	-
6A. Department of International Economic and Social Affairs	-	40 651.8
6B. Activities on global social development issues	-	9 772.1

Section	Secretary-General's original 1988-1989 proposed programme budget estimates	Secretary-General's revised proposed programme budget 1988-1989
7. Department of Technical Co-operation for Development	19 810.4	19 810.4
8. Office of Secretariat Services for Economic and Social Matters	4 209.3	-
9. Transnational corporations	9 599.5	9 599.5
10. Economic Commission for Europe	30 156.6	30 156.6
11. Economic and Social Commission for Asia and the Pacific	33 362.9	33 362.9
12. Economic Commission for Latin America and the Caribbean	40 486.8	40 486.8
13. Economic Commission for Africa	44 023.0	44 023.0
14. Economic and Social Commission for Western Asia	33 015.9	33 015.9
15. United Nations Conference on Trade and Development	65 805.8	65 805.8
16. International Trade Centre	12 274.8	12 274.8
17. Centre for Science and Technology for Development	4 037.7	4 037.7
18. United Nations Environment Programme	10 611.2	10 611.2
19. United Nations Centre for Human Settlements (HABITAT)	8 408.5	8 408.5
20. International drug control	6 977.8	6 977.8

Section	Secretary-General's original 1988-1989 proposed programme budget estimates	Secretary-General's revised proposed programme budget 1988-1989
21. Office of the United Nations High Commissioner for Refugees	36 672.6	36 672.6
22. Office of the United Nations Disaster Relief Co-ordinator	6 300.7	6 300.7
23. Human rights	14 242.8	14 242.8
24. Regular programme of technical co-operation	31 147.1	31 147.1
25. International Court of Justice	11 191.3	11 191.3
26. Legal activities	16 132.2	16 132.2
27. Public information	75 869.6	75 745.0
28. Administration and management	344 108.2	352 833.3
29. Conference and library services	309 201.9	309 201.9
30. United Nations bond issue	3 459.6	3 459.6
31. Staff assessment	268 504.0	268 504.0
32. Construction, alteration, improvement and major maintenance	18 041.8	18 041.8
Total	1 681 372.4	1 681 372.4

2.15 Document A/42/7/Add.1-10*

Implementation of General Assembly Resolution 41/213 - Programmatic and Budgetary Aspects: Update of the Progress Report of the Secretary-General (A/42/234 and Corr.1)

Report of the Advisory Committee on Administrative and Budgetary Questions

1988

1. In its first report on the proposed programme budget for the biennium 1988-1989,[1] the Advisory Committee on Administrative and Budgetary Questions discussed the progress report issued by the Secretary-General at the beginning of May (A/42/234 and Corr.1) on the implementation of General Assembly resolution 41/213 and called for an update to be submitted to the General Assembly at its forty-second session.[2] The Secretary-General states, in paragraph 2 of the update of the progress report (A/C.5/42/2/Rev.1), that "the present report gives fuller and more detailed programmatic and budgetary information on reforms already implemented, and outlined in the progress report of the Secretary-General, as they relate to the proposed programme budget for the biennium 1988-1989".

2. In paragraph 3 of the update of the progress report (*ibid.*), it is indicated that, "in order to maintain the integrity and coherence of the budget presentation, the changes to the Secretary-General's proposals ... follow the same principles as the initial presentation and do not involve any net change in the overall level of the proposed budget". The Advisory Committee notes the updated information provided in document A/C.5/42/2/Rev.1. Consistent with what is quoted immediately above, the various transfers and redeployments of posts referred to in that document do not affect the total number of posts in the staffing table.

3. The Advisory Committee points out that in the coming months the pace of reform should accelerate and that, in addition to such further organizational changes as the Secretary-General may deem necessary, work should be completed on the post reduction exercise.

4. In this connection, the Advisory Committee recalls that in paragraph 14 of its first report on the proposed programme budget for the biennium 1988-1989[3] it recommended that

---

Official Records of the General Assembly, Forty-second Session, Supplement No. 7A (A/42/7/Add.1-10), pp. 4-6.

"the Secretary-General should complete the review and studies now under way in time to prepare his proposals for revised estimates by 1 April 1988 for submission to CPC [the Committee for Programme and Co-ordination], ACABQ [the Advisory Committee] and the General Assembly at its forty-third session. The revised estimates should be accompanied by information on staffing (in tabular form) that would show the intended result of the application of recommendation 15 of the Group of High-level Intergovernmental Experts in comparison with the information included in the proposed programme budget. To the extent that these staffing tables would reflect redeployments among the sections of the budget (since some programmes will have lost more than 15 per cent of their posts, while others less), the estimates for each section should be adjusted accordingly".

5.   As requested by the Advisory Committee, the update of the progress report (A/C.5/42/2/Rev.1) contains an annex which indicates, for the purpose of the resolution on budget appropriations for the biennium 1988-1989, the budgetary implications of the measures taken by the Secretary-General. The Advisory Committee had pointed out in paragraph 12 of its report on the proposed programme budget, that "the preparation of such an annex, and action by the General Assembly upon it, would also allow the Secretary-General to implement, at the earliest time, changes that the General Assembly has already accepted, without having to request concurrence for transfers between sections prior to the forty-third session of the Assembly". The following table shows the effect of the proposals contained in table 2 of the annex to the update of the progress report on the recommendations of the Advisory Committee as originally contained in its first report on the proposed programme budget for the biennium 1988-1989. It should be noted that the total recommended by the Advisory Committee for the budget, as shown in the table below, is unchanged from that recommended in its first report.

Notes

1.   *Official Records of the General Assembly, Forty-second Session, Supplement No. 7 (A/42/7).*
2.   *Ibid.*, chap. I, paras. 12 and 13.
3.   *Official Records of the General Assembly, Forty-second Session, Supplement 7* (A.42/7).

Summary of the recommendations of the Advisory Committee on Administrative and Budgetary Questions compared with the Secretary-General's revised programme budget proposals for the biennium 1988-1989

Section	Secretary-General's revised programme budget proposal for the biennium 1988-1989 (see A/C.5/42/2/Rev.1)	Related recommendations of the Advisory Committee	Increase/(decrease)
	(Thousands of United States dollars)		
1	43 749.9	42 382.0	(1 367.9)
2A	79 025.1	75 731.8	(3 293.3)
2B	9 075.7	8 755.5	(320.2)
3	31 326.6	30 503.7	(822.9)
4	1 188.0	1 149.4	(38.6)
5A	3 886.1	3 783.0	(103.1)
5B	653.9	628.9	(25.0)
6	-	-	-
6A	40 651.8	39 083.0	(1 568.8)
6B	9 772.1	9 354.2	(417.9)
7	19 810.4	19 042.5	(767.9)
8	-	-	-
9	9 599.5	9 210.3	(389.2)
10	30 156.6	28 926.1	(1 230.5)
11	33 362.9	32 135.9	(1 227.0)
12	40 486.8	39 458.4	(1 028.4)
13	44 023.0	42 556.0	(1 467.0)
14	44 015.9	31 944.5	(1 071.4)
15	65 805.8	63 215.8	(2 590.0)
16	12 274.8	12 242.8	(32.0)
17	4 037.7	3 887.2	(150.5)
18	10 611.2	10 286.5	(324.7)
19	8 408.5	8 110.0	(308.5)
20	6 977.8	6 698.6	(279.2)
21	36 672.6	35 339.0	(1 333.6)
22	6 300.7	6 082.5	(218.2)
23	14 242.8	13 798.9	(443.9)
24	31 147.1	31 147.1	

Section	Secretary-General's revised programme budget proposal for the biennium 1988-1989 (see A/C.5/42/2/Rev.1)	Related recommendations of the Advisory Committee	Increase/ (decrease)
	(Thousands of United States dollars)		
25	11 191.3	11 012.1	(179.2)
26	16 132.2	15 390.4	(741.8)
27	75 745.0	73 426.8	(2 318.2)
28	352 833.3	344 426.7	(8 406.6)
29	309 201.9	296 564.4	(12 637.5)
30	3 459.6	3 520.8	61.2
31	268 504.0	262 282.0	(6 222.0)
32	18 041.8	17 874.8	(167.0)
33	-	-	-
Total	1 681 372.4	1 629 941.6	(51 430.8)

2.16 Document A/42/30[*]

Recommendations of the Group of High-level Intergovernmental Experts to Review the Efficiency of the Administrative and Financial Functioning of the United Nations

Report of the International Civil Service Commission

1987

13. The Commission had before it documentation prepared by its secretariat recalling, *inter alia*, that by its resolution 40/237 of 18 December 1985, the General Assembly decided to establish a group of high-level intergovernmental experts to review the efficiency of the administrative and financial functioning of the United Nations. By its resolution 41/213, section I, paragraph 1(c), the Assembly decided, *inter alia*, that the Secretary-General should transmit to ICSC those recommendations having direct impact on the United Nations common system (recommendations 53 and 61), with the request that it should report to the Assembly at its forty-second session, so as to enable the Assembly to make a final decision. The General Assembly also stated that the expertise of the Commission should be availed of in dealing with some other recommendations over which the Commission had a mandate to advise and make recommendations. In this regard, the Fifth Committee of the General Assembly identified recommendations 442, 43, 45, 48-50, 52, 55, 57, 58 and 60 as relating to issues over which the Commission had a mandate to make recommendations to organizations (articles 14 and 15 of the ICSC statute). In addition, the ICSC secretariat drew the attention of the Commission to five other recommendations of the Group of High-level Intergovernmental Experts (4, 9, 46, 51 and 59), which, although not specifically referred to the Commission by the Assembly, might be of interest to it. As requested by the Commission, the documents also contained a summary of all previous recommendations and decisions of the Commission on other matters dealt with by the Group, together with recommendations on those where further study was required.

Views of the organizations and the staff representatives

14. The Chairman of CCAQ stated that the organizations shared the Commission's view to the effect that there was no need to modify the mandate of the Commission since its responsibilities for establishing personnel standards and monitoring their implementation were clearly set out in the statute of the Commission. With regard to the issue of post-secondary education (recommendation 61), he recalled that it had been the subject of at

---

[*]*Official Records of the General Assembly, Forty-second Session, Supplement No. 30* (A/42/30), pp. 4-14.

least two reviews (ICSAB in 1968 and ICSC in 1978), both of which recommended that this entitlement should be maintained. He noted that the education grant had become a major factor in acceptance of employment and any tampering with it could only hamper further the organizations' efforts to recruit and retain high-calibre staff. He restated the position of ACC that the existing education grant status should remain unchanged. As to the issue of annual leave raised by recommendation 61, it had been the subject of review by four bodies (the Preparatory Committee (1946), the Flemming Committee (1949), the Salary Review Committee (1956) and the Special Committee for the Review of the United Nations Salary System (1971-1972), all of which recommended that the existing entitlements be kept unchanged. He referred to the clear trend towards an increase in leave entitlement sin national civil services. He restated the firm position of ACC that the current annual leave entitlements should remain unchanged. As to the other recommendations not explicitly referred to the Commission by the Assembly, CCAQ was of the opinion that they were not relevant to the common system, but more specifically to the United Nations. He recalled that all positions taken by CCAQ collectively or by individual organizations on each of the subject referred to remained valid. lastly, he expressed strong reservations about the recommendation that the Commission could specify issues on which there might be flexible *ad hoc* arrangements, if this were to imply that in the absence of such a recommendation no flexibility would be allowed.

15. The President of DICSA confined her statement to those recommendations that concerned the staff of the common system. FICSA could not accept recommendation 61 since it was based on totally unsubstantiated reasoning. With regard to the proposed reduction in annual leave from 30 to 20 days, FICSA supported the findings of the ICSC secretariat. Over 90 per cent of Professional staff being expatriate, the present entitlement to annual leave was by no means excessive in comparison with that of national civil services. Owing to their multilingual activities, the organizations had to rely on qualified General Service staff who, while locally recruited, were expatriate in many cases. In view of acquired rights of serving staff, a differentiated annual leave system would have to applied to staff working side-by-side, which would create great problems. FICSA underlined that the education grant for post-secondary studies was an important element in attracting and retaining expatriate staff. The proposed reductions in these two entitlements would lead to extremely serious tensions among staff. Concerning recommendations 45, 55 and 57, FICSA expressed regret that not all organizations had implemented the Commission's recommendation on the granting of permanent appointments. Recommendation 55, which aimed at limiting the proportion of staff on fixed-term appointments, was directed against the abuse of secondment of their nationals by some Member States and the practice of reserving posts for nationals of certain countries. FICSA fully subscribed to the application of this recommendation. In supporting recommendation 57, FICSA considered that the proportion of staff on permanent or fixed appointments should be left to each Organization to decide. FICSA approved recommendations 43, 48, 50 and

51 in so far as they would base career development and promotion on equitable and transparent criteria. FICSA had reservations with regard to the extension of the use of competitive examinations for promotion from the General Service to the Professional category to the organizations of the common system. In their present form, competitive examinations constituted additional barriers to the career development of General Service staff. Recommendation 46 on improving the status of women in the international organizations was fully supported by FICSA. It was essential to institute regular monitoring of progress made. Concerning recommendation 52, on the age of retirement, FICSA recalled that the extension of the mandatory age of separation from service was important in the international organizations, in view of the relatively short career of many staff who entered the system at age 40 or later. Recommendation 59 could not be endorsed by FICSA since the need for active participation of staff representatives was recognized in the staff rules and regulations of the organizations and the statute of ICSC. The release of staff representatives and support by organizations in providing secretarial assistance and office facilities was necessitated by the statutory involvement of staff representatives and support by organizations in providing secretarial assistance with international labour instruments and the practice of many national civil services. The administration of justice (recommendation 60) in the United Nations system left much to be desired, as demonstrated by recent judgements of the Administrative Tribunal of ILO on post adjustment and pensionable remuneration, which clearly showed that there was a legal vacuum for staff of the specialized agencies in respect of certain aspects of conditions of service.

16. The representative of CCISUA considered that many of the points of importance regarding the recommendations had already been brought to the attention of the Commission and it wished therefore to touch upon only two items, education grant and leave entitlements. The cost of education at all levels had been spiralling upward since the grant had last been considered. Therefore CCISUA not only strongly supported the retention of the education grant for post-secondary education, but also believed that there was ample evidence to warrant a considerable increase in the level of the grant. In addition, CCISUA felt that special consideration should be given to staff in duty stations where local educational facilities were inadequate or even non-existent, with a view to increasing the reimbursement of those who must send their children away to boarding schools, and to extending the grant to locally recruited staff on the basis of need. Regarding leave entitlements, CCISUA considered the leave currently afforded to staff was by no means excessive. On the contrary, the leave benefits of many national civil services were comparable, or in some cases superior, to those provide by the common system organizations. CCISUA wished to note once again that the vast majority of staff were expatriate throughout their careers.

17. The representative of the United Nations drew the attention of the Commission to the report of the Secretary-General entitled "Reform and renewal in the United Nations: progress report of the Secretary-General on the implementation of General Assembly resolution 41/213" (A/42/234 and

Corr.1), which outlined the position being taken by the Secretary-General with regard to the recommendations of the Group of High-level Intergovernmental Experts. He noted that the advice given by the Commission in the past had already been taken into account and assured the Commission that any further recommendations would also be taken into consideration.

18. The representative of IFAD said that his organization was conforming to the common system parameters. However, any further reductions in conditions of service would make it difficult for IFAD to compete with the regional development banks for the recruitment of staff. If reductions in highly visible conditions such as annual leave and the education grant were made, IFAD would have to consider discussing with its governing body the possibility of moving away from the common system. He pointed to the preliminary information provided by the ICSC secretariat and he supported the ICSC recommendation that "comparisons should be made on an overall basis, including expatriate elements".

19. The representative of UNIDO recalled that the Austrian federal legislation on annual leave provided favourable leave entitlements comparable to the length of leave provided by the United Nations. Furthermore, the Austrian federal legislation provided for 13 public holidays, plus one day for members of specified religious faiths, while the United Nations provided for 9 public holidays. Based on these facts, any reduction in the length of annual leave in the United Nations might result in an increase in salaries of the General Service and Manual Worker categories at Vienna. As for staff in the Professional and higher categories, 90 per cent of them in the common system were expatriates. It was therefore essential for them to maintain close touch with their home countries and cultures. Indeed, this was the reason why the staff regulation stipulated that minimum period of the annual had to be spent in the home country as a prerequisite for granting home leave. Furthermore, a great number of the Professional staff were serving on fixed-term contracts, which meant that most of them were expected to start a new career in their home countries and reintegrate their families in their respective societies. The representative of UNIDO agreed with ACC's position on the issues in question to the effect that no change should be made on either of the two entitlements.

Discussion by the Commission

20. The Commission considered that recommendations 53 and 61 were the crucial ones on which the Commission was required to report to the General Assembly. Some members proposed that the other recommendations should be discussed when they arose in the course of the work programme.

21. With regard to recommendation 53 dealing with monitoring the implementation of personnel management standards, the Commission considered that there was no need to modify the mandate of the Commission so that it could monitor implementation of personnel standards by the United Nations. Its responsibilities for establishing personnel standards and

monitoring the implementation of such standards by the United Nations as well as other organizations of the common system were clearly set out int its statute, in particular in articles 1, 9, 13, 14 and 17. The Commission did, nevertheless, express the hope that the Secretary-General would report annually to the General Assembly not only on action taken by the United Nations in response to recommendations and decisions of the Commission, but also in his capacity as Chairman of ACC on action taken through ACC to promote harmonized and co-ordinated action by all participating organizations in the common system regarding conditions of service pursuant to recent Assembly resolutions, including resolutions 36/233 of 18 December 1981, 40/244 of 18 December 1985 and 41/207.

22. Concerning recommendation 61 on the total entitlements of staff, the Commission considered three methods for dealing with the matter. These could be based, for example, on total compensation including expatriate elements, on salaries and pensions alone. One member said that there could be other methods of dealing with the issue. Two members of the Commission were of the view that the conclusion of the Group regarding a decrease in the level of staff entitlements was not without reason and pointed out that concern had been expressed not only by the Group but by many Member States as well. However, most members felt that the Group of High-level Intergovernmental Experts had not given a basis or rationale for its assertion in recommendation 61 that the total entitlements (salaries and other conditions of service) of staff members had reached a level that Gave reason for serious concern and should be reduced. The Group's specific recommendations concerning the elimination of a four-week annual leave system for all staff members could only be regarded as unsubstantiated and therefore subjective. Some members stated that they would have been able to understand such comments being made about the level of entitlements in the United Nations system before freeze of the level of remuneration through the post adjustment system in December 1984 pursuant to resolution 39/27 of 30 November 1984 and the Commission's recommendations at its twenty-fourth session to reduce the level of pensionable remuneration for staff in the Professional and higher categories. In the latter connection, they noted that the Assembly, in resolution 41/208, had, moreover, reduced the overall level of pensionable remuneration for such categories of staff with effect from 1 April 197. They wondered what would be achieved by further reductions in entitlements apart from causing further unease among staff as, in their view, the level of entitlements did not seem unduly high. In the circumstances, the claim by the Group of High-level Intergovernmental Experts that the total entitlements of staff members had reached a level that gave rise to serious concern and that the level should be reduced did not appear to be valid.

23. The Commission noted that since 1946 the education grant had been paid for the education of children, including post-secondary studies, up to age 21 in their home country. In 1955, this had been extended to attendance at local special national schools and international schools. In 1971-1972, the United Nations Special Committee for the Review of the United Nations Salary System

had recommended the extension of the age-limit; the Commission subsequently had made similar recommendations and in 1978 the General Assembly, in resolution 33/119 of 19 December 1978, approved use of the grant up to the end of the fourth year of post-secondary studies or the award of the first recognized degree, whichever was earlier, and its extension to the country or area of the duty station. In 1982, the Commission had recommended, and the General Assembly had approved, in resolution 37/126 of 17 December 1982, that national returning from another duty station to their home country could receive the grant for the balance of the school year. Other international organizations had similar provisions, while some countries provided free or nearly free university tuition to qualifying nationals or granted scholarships and tax relief or made other concessions that might not be available to expatriate United Nations system staff. The Commission further noted that the reasons for providing assistance to internationally recruited staff members in the post-secondary education of their children had not changed and that the need had rather grown, since on average United Nations system staff in the Professional and higher categories and experts were recruited in mid-career and about 90 per cent were expatriate, whereas at the inception of the United Nations system a lower percentage were expatriate. It also noted that over the years the number of Member States had increased from 51 to over 150 and the number of duty stations, particularly in the field, had increased from just a few to some 600 at the present time.

24. The Commission reiterated its conclusion drawn in 1978 that, if the General Assembly had decided subsequent to 1946 that post-secondary studies up to a certain age-limit should be eligible for reimbursement under the education grant, it would have to have very strong reasons for recommending now a change in that constant policy. No such reasons had been advanced; on the contrary, in the light of the general trend towards the expansion of post-secondary education, it would be anomalous to adopt a position more restrictive than that of 30 years ago. In reaching that conclusion, the Commission did not overlook the fact that many national Governments, including the one whose civil service was taken as the comparator for salary purposes, did not provide assistance (other than travel grants) for the post-secondary studies of children of their expatriate staff. However, the Commission was of the opinion that such comparisons must be made with caution, particularly where post-secondary studies were concerned, because the patterns of expatriation of such national officials and international civil servants were often significantly different. A diplomat was transferred from country to country more regularly than most international civil servants and, from time to time during his career, might serve for a period in his home country; his or her children were likely thereby to maintain closer ties with the home country than would children of international civil servants, who were often brought up entirely outside their parents' country; and the diplomat's children were thus also perhaps more likely as a matter of course to attend university in the home country.

25. In connection with annual leave, it was noted that the argument regarding the staff's expatriate status could be reasonably used only to justify the annual leave granted to staff in the Professional and higher categories. Information provided to the Commission showed that expatriate leave entitlements of other international organizations and of a number of national civil services, including home leave and local national public holidays, added up to more than 30 days of per annum. Regarding staff in the General Service category, their annual leave had to be justified on other grounds, namely, best prevailing conditions of service. In this connection the Commission noted that at a number of headquarters duty stations 30 days of annual leave and 9 public holidays were comparable to similar benefits provided by the best local employers, and in some cases even this package was less than what was provided locally.

26. In reviewing recommendation 42, on the issue of harmonization of staff regulations, the Commission noted that it had requested its secretariat to conduct a study on the harmonization of staff regulations of organizations of the common system and the continuation of this study was included in its proposed work programme for 1988-1989. While the Commission would therefore make recommendations on the development of common staff regulations to the organizations of the common system, including the United Nations, it understood that the United Nations would co-ordinate its effort in this area with those of the Commission and its secretariat.

27. While considering recommendation 43, dealing with competitive examinations, the Commission noted that its previous recommendations in this area[1] were certainly relevant to the United Nations. In addition, the Commission had made recommendations on interviewing techniques and the testing of the drafting abilities of candidates. It therefore considered that recommendation 43 was in line with the Commission's previous recommendations in this field.

28. Regarding recommendation 45, on the issue of eligibility of staff for permanent appointments, the Commission recalled that its earlier recommendation of five years[2] was made to cover the whole common system and was not intended as a minimum requirement for a career appointment. It considered the period of three years to be applied by the United Nations to be an improvement.

29. With reference to recommendation 48, on career development within occupational groups, the Commission recalled its earlier recommendations in this area.[3] On various occasions the Commission had emphasized the need for mobility of staff and noted that career development should certainly be implemented on as wide a basis as possible and should, in fact, not be limited to occupational groups. Careers should be developed by occupational and related groups in each organization and at each duty station to facilitate horizontal as well as vertical mobility.

30. In connection with recommendation 49, on the issue of mobility, the Commission observed that there was a general lack of mobility in the United Nations system. The Commission emphasized the necessity of encouraging mobility and linking it with career development. It was noted, however, that some organizations would always, due to the nature of their programmes and the fact that their location was confined to a single duty station, have limited possibilities for mobility.

31. Regarding recommendation 50, dealing with performance evaluation, the Commission recommended that the organizations should take into account the framework of performance appraisal principles and the guidelines developed by its secretariat and that they should regularly appraise the performance of all staff members up to the D-1 level. In addition, the Commission recommended that the organizations should make their performance appraisal systems consistent with the performance appraisal principles and guidelines no later than 1 July 1992. In this connection, the organizations were requested to send their performance appraisal systems and forms to the ICSC secretariat for appropriate consultations.

32. While reviewing recommendation 52, concerning the strict application of the mandatory age of separation from service, the Commission recalled that on two previous occasions it had not recommended a change in the mandatory age and that it had decided to keep the matter under study and to revert to the issue at a more appropriate time.[4] The Commission reiterated its views that the mandatory age of separation from service should meanwhile be applied as strictly as possible.

33. Concerning recommendation 55, on the issue of geographical distribution, the Commission reiterated its view that the ratio of permanent to fixed-term staff per Member State was an issue for the legislative bodies of organizations to decide upon based on the different needs of each organization.[5] It recalled its earlier conclusion that organizations had the flexibility to determine ratios of permanent and fixed-term staff according to the particular needs of their programmes.

34. With reference to recommendation 57, regarding the permanent to fixed-term staff, the Commission expressed the same view as for recommendation 55, to the effect that it was for the legislative bodies of the organizations to decide upon these matters and that organizations had the flexibility to establish such ratios on their own. In recalling its previous consideration of the issue[6] reflected in recommendations 55 and 57, the Commission had not deemed it appropriate to base its conclusions on national quotas.

35. In considering recommendation 58, on the subject of training, the Commission recalled its earlier recommendations in this area,[7] which should be used as guidelines for the implementation of that recommendation by the United Nations.

36. Regarding recommendation 60, dealing with the system of administration of justice, the Commission was informed that the working group set up by the United Nations to review the functioning of the organization's appellate and disciplinary processes had already completed its work. The Commission regretted that its role in this matter had been overtaken by events. It noted that, while the Secretary-General would no doubt be reporting on his findings in respect of the United Nations, the Commission had already decided to study this matter with regard to the common system and to report to the forty-fourth session of the General Assembly.

37. Regarding recommendation 4, on the issue of meetings of United Nations bodies at their respective headquarters or at the invitation of Governments, it was recalled that, according to article 1, paragraph 1, of the ICSC statute, the Commission was established for the regulations nd co-ordination of the conditions of serve of the whole United Nations common system and not only for the United Nations. As early as 1975, the Commission had established rule 4 of its rules of procedure, which the General Assembly had taken note of and which laid down the principle that the Commission meet away from United Nations Headquarters at the invitation of one of the participating organizations. Since 1975, the Commission had met regularly at other duty stations in order to maintain appropriate links with other organizations in the common system. The Commission noted the discrepancy between rule 4 of its rules of procedure, which made it possible for it to meet anywhere at the invitation of a participating agency, and resolution 20/243 of 18 December 1985, which limited it to meeting either at the Commission's headquarters, New York, or at the headquarters of a participating agency. The Commission had frequently expressed the view that it was useful to meet from time to time at a field duty station. The Commission felt that it had the flexibility to propose such a meeting, if appropriate, to the General Assembly.

38. Regarding recommendation 9, dealing with the subject of inter-agency co-ordination and *ad hoc* arrangements, the necessity of streamlining inter-agency co-ordination was an objective in line with the Commission's efforts to maintain and improve the common system in eliminating disparities in the conditions of service of common system staff. Every year, in considering the Commission's annual report the Assembly had recalled the co-ordinating role of the Commission and had taken decisions on individual recommendations of the Commission that had consequently affected actions of individual organizations and thereby promoted inter-agency co-ordination on these matters. Under article 17 of its statute, the Commission, moreover, reported annually to the General Assembly on the implementation of its decisions and recommendations by organizations, thereby facilitating the work of the Assembly and other legislating the work of the Assembly and other legislative bodies in co-ordinating the conditions of service of the staff of different organizations.

39. The Commission further noted that ACC, which consisted of executive heads of the United Nations and related agencies, was chaired by the Secretary-General, who, together with his representatives, participated actively in the deliberations of the General Assembly, which had primary legislative authority in the co-ordination of conditions of service among the United Nations and related agencies. The Secretary-General was therefore in a unique position to promote inter-agency co-ordination.   Not only did the Secretary-General communicate recommendations of the Commission and decisions of the Assembly to the executive heads of the other organizations pursuant to article 24 of the Commission's statute, but he also led the inter-agency consultations on conditions of service of staff, including problem areas, following which he informed the Commission and the Assembly of the collective views of ACC.

40. The Commission also observed that at the field level the differences in treatment of staff by different organizations could range from minor administrative details to major differences in the administration of benefits having significant financial implications. The important role of the United Nations resident co-ordinator in helping resolve such differences in consultation with the headquarters of all organizations was emphasized, and the active support of organizations in this regard was considered crucial. The ICSC Chairman and secretariat had from time to time drawn such discrepancies to the attention of the organizations in CCAQ, and improvements had been achieved through that body.

41. In reviewing recommendation 46, the Commission recalled that it had actively pursued efforts to increase the recruitment of women in the organizations. In 1985 it had adopted a number of recommendations aimed at improving the overall proportion of women in the Professional and higher categories, in particular at senior levels and in areas related to the mainstream, substantive work of the organizations.[8] Following these recommendations, the General Assembly had, at its fortieth session, adopted resolution 40/258 B of 18 December 1985, reiterating, *inter alia*, its request to Member States to support the efforts of the organizations of the common system to increase the proportion of women in the Professional and higher categories.   The Commission noted the limited progress in the organizations and decided therefore to reaffirm the validity of its previous recommendations and to continue to monitor progress on the status of women in the Professional and higher categories.   The Commission noted the limited progress in the organizations on the basis of biennial progress reports and in alternate years statistical data from the organizations.

42. Regarding recommendation 51, on promotion policy, the Commission concluded that recommendation 51 was in line with its previous recommendations on promotion policies.[9] However, reservations were expressed concerning the structuring of appointment and promotion bodies "on the basis of occupational groups". The Commission considered rather that a

single body composed of members from a number of occupational groups could ensure more consistency and fairness so that when considering the appointment and promotion of staff within any given occupational group they would, at the same time, ensure consistency with other occupational groups.

43. While considering recommendation 59, dealing with the role and functions of the Staff Union of the United Nations, the Commission noted that to date it had not specifically addressed the issue of staff-management relations. It had nevertheless done so implicitly through its recommendations in related areas such as promotion policy and performance evaluation. With respect to the modalities concerning the role, functions and financing of staff unions, it found that these feel more within the purview of the individual organizations.

Recommendations of the Commission

44. The Commission decided in regard to recommendations 53 and 61:

(a) To recommend that the mandate of the Commission should not be modified since its monitoring function was already clearly covered by articles 1, 9, 13, 14 and 17 of its statute;

(b) To reiterate its earlier recommendations regarding the education grant for post-secondary studies[10] and to recommend that the existing entitlement not be changed;

(c) To recommend that the current annual leave entitlement of 30 days per annum should not be changed.

45. In respect of recommendations 42, 43, 45 48-50, 52, 55, 57, 58 and 60, the Commission decided:

(a) To advise the Secretary-General that it would study the issue of the harmonization of staff regulations under the proposed work programme for 1988-1989 and that it understood that the United Nations would co-ordinate its efforts in this area with those of the Commission and its secretariat (recommendation 42);

(b) To reiterate its previous recommendations in the area of competitive examinations, interviewing techniques and testing of candidates[11] and to advise that recommendation 43 was in line with those recommendations;

(c) To welcome a minimum period of three years for permanent appointment in the United Nations (recommendation 45);

(d) To reiterate its previous recommendations on career development[12] and to recommend that this should not be limited to occupational groups, but should include related groups as well (recommendation 48);

(e)   To emphasize the necessity of encouraging mobility and linking it to career development (recommendation 49);

(f)   To recommend that the United Nations should take into account the framework of performance appraisal principles and guidelines adopted by the Commission at its twenty-sixth session (recommendation 50);

(g)   To reiterate its view that the mandatory age of separation from service should meanwhile be applied as strictly as possible pending its expected review of the subject (recommendation 52);

(h)   To reiterate its previous view that the issue of ratios of permanent to fixed-term staff was an issue for the legislative bodies of organizations to decide upon on the basis of the different needs of each organization[13] (recommendations 55 and 57);

(i)   To reiterate its previous recommendations regarding training,[14] which should be used as guidelines for the implementation of recommendation 58 by the United Nations;

(j)   To emphasize that it would study the question of the administration of justice in the common system as included in its proposed work programme for 1988-1989 and that the Commission would report on this matter to the General Assembly at its forty-fourth session (recommendation 60).

46. With regard to recommendations 4, 9, 46, 51 and 59, the Commission decided:

(a)   To note the discrepancy between rule 4 of its rules of procedure and resolution 40/243 and to express the view that it had the flexibility to propose holding a meeting at a non-headquarters duty station if appropriate (recommendation 4);

(b)   To emphasize that the enhancement of the common system should be actively pursued through ACC and CCAQ and, at the field level, with the assistance of the resident co-ordinator as well as through the Commission itself (recommendation 9);

(c)   To welcome recommendation 46, concerning the recruitment of women, which was in line with the Commission's previous recommendations in this area;

(d)   To note that recommendation 51, on promotion policy, was in line with the Commission's previous recommendations in this area,[15] but to advice that appointment and promotion bodies should be composed of members from a number of occupational groups;

(e) To note that the issue of the role, functions and financing of staff unions fell more within the purview of the individual organizations (recommendation 59).

Notes

1. *Ibid., Fortieth Session, Supplement No. 30* (A/40/30 and Corr.1), para. 263, and *ibid., Thirty-ninth Session, Supplement No. 30* (A/39/30 and Corr.1 and 2), paras. 219 and 220.

2. *Ibid., Thirty-seventh Session, Supplement No. 30* (A/37/30), annex I, appendix II, paras. 61-67.

3. *Ibid.*, para. 17, and *ibid., Fortieth Session, Supplement No. 30* (A/40/30 and Corr.1), paras. 239 and 240.

4. *Ibid., Forty-first Session, Supplement No. 30* (A/41/30 and Corr.1 and 2), paras. 150-152.

5. *Ibid., Thirty-seventh Session, Supplement No. 30* (A/37/30), annex I, appendix II, para. 67.

6. *Ibid.*

7. *Ibid.*, paras. 102-107, and *ibid., Thirty-ninth Session, Supplement No. 30* (A/39/30 and Corr.1 and 2), para. 226.

8. *Ibid., Fortieth Session, Supplement No. 30* (A/40/30 and Corr. 1), paras. 245-247.

9. *Ibid., Thirty-ninth Session, Supplement No. 30* (A/39/30 and Corr.1 and 2), paras. 222 and 223.

10. *Ibid., Thirty-first Session, Supplement No. 30* (A/31/30 and Add.1), paras. 279-293; *ibid., Thirty-third Session, Supplement No. 30* (A/33/30 and Add.1), paras 224-234; *ibid., Thirty-seventh Session, Supplement No. 30* (A/37/30), paras. 197 and 198; and *ibid., Fortieth Session, Supplement No. 30* (A/40/30 and Corr.1), para. 191.

11. *Ibid.*, para. 263, and *ibid., Thirty-ninth Session, Supplement No. 30* (A/39/30 and Corr.1 and 2), paras. 215 and 218.

12. *Ibid., Thirty-seventh Session, Supplement No. 30* (A/37/30), annex I, appendix II, para. 17, and *ibid., Fortieth Session, Supplement No. 30* (A/40/30 and Corr.1), paras. 239 and 240.

13. *Ibid., Thirty-seventh Session, Supplement 30* (A/37/30), annex I, appendix II, para. 67.

14. *Ibid.*, paras. 102-107, and *ibid., Thirty-ninth Session, Supplement No. 30* (A/39/30 and Corr.1 and 2), para. 226.

15. *Ibid.*, paras. 222 and 223.

2.17 Document A/43/286[*]

Reform and Renewal in the United Nations: Second Progress Report of the Secretary-General on the Implementation of General Assembly Resolution 41/213

8 April 1988

CONTENTS

		Para-graphs
I.	Introduction	1 - 7
II.	Planning and implementing the reforms	8 - 10
III.	The structure and functioning of the secretariat	11 - 91
	A. The political sector	11 - 17
	B. Co-ordination in the United Nations system and economic and social matters	18 - 35
	C. Public information activities	36 - 39
	D. Conference services and related issues	40 - 48
	E. Administration and finance	49 - 66
	F. Personnel matters	67 - 91
IV.	Concluding observations	92 - 94

---

[*]A/43/286.

I. INTRODUCTION

1. On 19 December 1986, the General Assembly, on the basis of the report of the Group of High-level Intergovernmental Experts to Review the Efficiency of the Administrative and Financial Functioning of the United Nations,[1] adopted by consensus resolution 41/213 entitled "Review of the efficiency of the administrative and financial functioning of the United Nations". The resolution sets for the Secretariat a difficult but vital task: the implementation of a process of reform and renewal. In it, the General Assembly requested the Secretary-General and the relevant organs and bodies of the United Nations to implement the recommendations contained in the report of the Group over a three-year period ending in 1989, and provided specific guidance on some of the recommendations. It also requested that a report be submitted to the General Assembly at its forty-second session.

2. In his first progress report (A/42/234 and Corr.1), the Secretary-General indicated what action had already been taken and his plans for implementing section I of resolution 41/213 dealing with the recommendations of the Group of High-level Intergovernmental Experts. Separate reports were submitted in response to section II of that resolution (A/42/214, A/42/225 and Add.1 and A/42/532), which deals with the planning, programming and budgeting process. Given the time-schedule for the preparation of the programme budget for the biennium 1988-1989, some of the reforms announced in the first progress report could not be reflected in the proposed budget. Therefore, updated information, including programmatic and budgetary aspects, was later presented to the Fifth Committee of the General Assembly through the Committee for Programme and Co-ordination and the Advisory Committee on Administrative and Budgetary Questions (A/C.5/42/2/Rev.1).

3. At its forty-second session, the General Assembly examined the two reports pertaining to section I of the resolution (A/42/234 and A/C.5/42/2/Rev.1) in conjunction with the proposed programme budget for the biennium 1988-1989. Following its consideration of the matter, the General Assembly adopted resolution 42/211 of 21 December 1987 on the implementation of resolution 41/213, which, *inter alia*, requested the Secretary-General to take into account the reviews, studies and decisions entrusted to the intergovernmental bodies and to co-operate with these bodies; to seek the approval of the General Assembly for a departure from the approved recommendations; and to reflect in the revised estimates the state of implementation of resolution 41/213. The General Assembly provided further guidance with respect to specific recommendations and requested another progress report on the state of implementation of that resolution to be submitted through the Committee for Programme and Co-ordination and the Advisory Committee on Administrative and Budgetary Questions.

4. In response to that request, the present report provides detailed information on action taken with respect to each recommendation of the Group

of High-level Intergovernmental Experts up to the first quarter of 1988 and plans for the remaining period (April 1988-December 1989). Specific data concerning most of the recommendations mentioned in paragraph 10 of resolution 42/211 will be provided in the revised estimates for the programme budget for the biennium 1988-1989 (A/C.5/43/1).

5.   Of the 71 recommendations contained in the report of the Group of High-level Intergovernmental Experts, a number were addressed either to Member States (recommendations 1, 2, 3, 4, 6, 7, 8, 64, 65 and 70) or to advisory bodies to the General Assembly such as the International Civil Service Commission (recommendations 53 and 61), the Joint Inspection Unit (recommendations 63 and 67) or the External Auditors (recommendation 67). The present report does not deal with these recommendations except to indicate actions taken by the Secretariat to facilitate their implementation upon the request of the competent bodies.

6.   The present second progress report, which covers slightly more than one third of the three-year period foreseen in General Assembly resolution 41/213, outlines the considerable progress that has been made in a number of areas. As indicated previously (A/42/234, para. 9), some of the recommendations approved by the General Assembly at its forty-first session are of a broad nature and are to be implemented over a much longer term than the first three years. It should also be mentioned that major studies and reviews on related items are being conducted concurrently by intergovernmental bodies and the Secretariat. The outcome of such studies is likely to have its full impact on the Organization after 1989.

7.   The Secretary-General has taken vigorous measures to reform the Secretariat with a view to making it more effective and efficient. Important as these measures are, they cannot by themselves fulfil the objective of resolution 41/213, which is to strengthen the effectiveness of the United Nations in dealing with political, economic and social issues. For the process of reform to reach fruition, Member States must, no less, provide their full support, politically and financially, to the Organization.

II. PLANNING AND IMPLEMENTING THE REFORMS

8.   At the beginning of the first progress report, the Secretary-General indicated that a number of common points of reference were needed as foundations for the future. One year later, he firmly believes that the nine points then presented remain valid. While not wishing to repeat them in this report, it is worth re-emphasizing that the reform process, in order to proceed in an orderly and planned way, needs to be undertaken in a climate free of financial uncertainties. The General Assembly agreed with the Secretary-General on this point and emphasized the importance of financial stability in its resolution 42/211. However, the Organization continues to face a financial crisis that is a source of grave concern, as reported at the end of the

forty-second session of the General Assembly (A/42/841). It is unfortunately in this environment that the reform process is being carried out.

9. In planning the reform programme, the Secretary-General has taken account not only of the findings of the Fifth Committee, as referred to in resolutions 41/213 and 42/211, with respect to the recommendations of the Group of High-level Intergovernmental Experts, but also of other relevant resolutions adopted during the last two sessions on activities or organizational units mentioned in the report of the Group. For instance, the General Assembly adopted resolution 42/162 A of 8 December 1987 on questions relating to information, which complements recommendation 37 on the same subject; likewise, resolution 42/170 of 11 December 1987 (referred to in resolution 42/211) provides guidance with regard to the economic and social fields and conference services.

10. For ease of reference, action taken on each recommendation is presented by major sector of activity as in the first progress report: political affairs, economic and social matters as well as co-ordination in the United Nations system, information, conference services, administration and finance, and personnel.

III. THE STRUCTURE AND FUNCTIONING OF THE SECRETARIAT

A. The political sector

11. The changes in this sector that the Secretary-General had first announced in March 1987 and developed in the first progress report are now in place and the reorganization is virtually completed (see recommendations 16, 18 and 22). There is now a clear delineation of responsibilities for each of the political offices. Through timely information and sound analysis, it will be possible to increase the Organization's preparedness to deal with emerging problems and, as the Secretary-General has stated before (A/42/234, paras. 14-19), to strengthen the institutional basis of preventive diplomacy to facilitate the work of the Security Council.

Recommendation 17

12. As reported previously (A/42/234 and Corr.1, para. 20), all of the work of the former Office for Field Operations and External Support Activities connected with the administrative support services for peace-keeping missions has been integrated into the Office of General Services, Department of Administration and Management, as the Field Operations Division. Its work relating to the dissemination of political information has been assigned to the new Office for Research and the Collection of Information, as also requested in recommendation 18.

13. Regarding the second sentence of recommendation 17, which proposed that most of the staff in the field missions be recruited locally and that the number of internationally recruited Field Service Officers be substantially reduced, the following points should be noted. A number of functions are already being performed by locally recruited staff whenever feasible. A field survey was undertaken in 1987 to determine the modalities for implementing this recommendation and for increasing further the proportion of locally recruited staff. The results of this survey and a careful analysis of political, technical and mobility factors confirmed that the possibilities for replacing internationally recruited Field Service Officers by local staff are limited. The reduction in the number of posts - both in the Field Service and at the local level - is being reported on separately, in the context of the implementation of recommendation 15 (A/C.5/43/1).

Recommendation 19

14. Proposals were made in the first progress report for the consolidation and strengthening of support services for activities relating to Namibia (A/42/234 and Corr.1, para. 20, and A/C.5/42/2/Rev.1, para. 25). These proposals were discussed in the Fifth Committee. The General Assembly, in its resolution 42/211, paragraph 10 (c), referred specifically to activities relating to Namibia, inviting the Secretary-General to consult with the United Nations Council for Namibia on the implementation of the recommendation. A number of meetings with the Bureau of the Council were held and clarifications concerning the reporting and administrative arrangements for the Commissioner for Namibia and his Office in the context of the consolidation of certain functions of that Office with the Department for Special Political Questions, Regional Co-operation, Decolonization and Trusteeship were provided and reflected in the records of the United Nations Council for Namibia (A/AC.131/SR.512 and 513). The organizational bulletin will outline the decisions taken in this respect. The pertinent budgetary aspects will be covered in the revised estimates for the programme budget for the biennium 1988-1989 (A/C.5/43/1). Activities flowing from the Council for Namibia will be undertaken by the Commissioner, who will report directly to the Council and will keep the Under-Secretary-General for Special Political Questions, Regional Co-operation, Decolonization and Trusteeship informed of developments in this area; the Commissioner will also have direct access to the Secretary-General and will have administrative responsibility for the Council's programme budget.

Recommendation 20

15. The review of the structure of the Department for Disarmament Affairs requested in this recommendation is under way. Once the results of the review have been fully assessed and decisions taken on implementation, it is expected that the outcome will be a reorganized department with streamlined activities and with due emphasis on activities referred to in recommendation 20.

Recommendation 21

16. In the course of implementation of this recommendation, the mandate of the Department of Political Affairs, Trusteeship and Decolonization has been substantially revised, as described in the first progress report (A/42/234 and Corr.1, para. 20 (b)) and in the update to that report (A/C.5/42/2/Rev.1, paras. 25 and 26). Functions in the area of research and information not directly related to the mandate of the Department have been transferred to the new Office for Research and the Collection of Information while the responsibilities of the former Office for Special Political Questions and the secretariat support for the Commissioner for Namibia have been integrated into this new department renamed the Department for Special Political Questions, Regional Co-operation, Decolonization and Trusteeship. Moreover, the Department has been assigned additional responsibilities in the area of regional co-operation, on matters dealing with African emergency-related questions of a complex nature and certain special economic assistance programmes of political sensitivity, as well as with responsibilities for monitoring the follow-up of the recommendations of the Second International Conference on Assistance to Refugees in Africa as described in the Secretary-General's report on implementation of the United Nations Programme of Action for African Economic Recovery and Development 1986-1990 (A/42/674, paras. 60-64). The new structure and staffing of the Department has been developed on the basis of a review of the status of continuing as well as new responsibilities assigned to it.

Recommendation 29

17. The General Assembly, in paragraph 10 (e) of resolution 42/211, invited the Secretary-General to review his decisions regarding implementation of this recommendation concerning the Office of Secretariat Services for Economic and Social Matters in the light of the debate of the Fifth Committee, and to reflect the results of his review in the revised estimates. As requested, the revised estimates for the programme budget for the biennium 1988-1989 provide detailed information regarding the implementation of this recommendation (A/C.5/43/1).

B. Co-ordination in the United Nations system and economic and social matters

Recommendation 9

18. The Administrative Committee on Co-ordination undertook a review of the functioning of its subsidiary machinery and adopted, in October 1986, a set of recommendations relating to its main subsidiary machinery, namely, the Organizational Committee and the four consultative committees (decision 1986/21). The outcome of this review was referred to in the Secretary-General's report on co-ordination in the United Nations and the

United Nations system, submitted through the Committee for Programme and Co-ordination to the Economic and Social Council and the General Assembly in 1987 (A/42/232-E/1987/68). In considering that report, the Committee for Programme and Co-ordination emphasized the need for more effective co-ordination at the inter-secretariat level and stressed the important role of the Administrative Committee on Co-ordination in this regard. The Committee noted that the machinery of the Administrative Committee on Co-ordination remained complex and recommended that the Administrative Committee should intensify the review of its functioning with a view to improving the form and substance of its considerations, streamlining its subsidiary machinery and reducing its costs substantially.

19. The General Assembly, in resolution 42/196 of 11 December 1987, invited the Secretary-General, as Chairman of the Administrative Committee on Co-ordination, to report to the General Assembly, through the Economic and Social Council, on the implementation by the Committee of its own recommendations adopted in October 1986.

20. The Organizational Committee, on behalf of the Administrative Committee on Co-ordination, has continued the review of the functioning of its machinery. A number of practical measures were adopted to strengthen the managerial role of the Organizational Committee and to rationalize meetings convened within the framework of the Administrative Committee. The number of meetings held under the auspices of the latter was reduced from 34 in 1986 to 29 in 1987; steps were taken to focus the discussion of the Administrative Committee on Co-ordination on a few selected and major issues on the basis of background papers prepared by relevant organizations in co-operation with others and/or inputs from the Committee's subsidiary machinery.

21. Efforts will continue to be made to streamline the machinery for inter-agency co-ordination while fully recognizing the increasing emphasis placed by Member States, particularly in the General Assembly and the Economic and Social Council, on the need to enhance co-ordination among organizations of the system as a means of improving their collective output, ensuring complementarity of activities and avoiding duplication of effort. The Organizational Committee, at its organizational session of 1988, identified a number of areas relating to the Administrative Committee on Co-ordination machinery and the corresponding secretariat support and the nature and format of inputs to the intergovernmental bodies, on which the review could focus and to which further consideration should be given in the light of the outcome of the work of the Special Commission of the Economic and Social Council on the In-depth Study of the United Nations Intergovernmental Structure and Functions in the Economic and Social Fields. It is expected that the Administrative Committee on Co-ordination will finalize the review of the functioning of its subsidiary machinery in October 1988 and will inform the Committee for Programme and Co-ordination and the Economic and Social Council of the outcome in its overview report for 1988.

Recommendation 10

22. The Administrative Committee on Co-ordination welcomed the emphasis on the need for discussion by the executive heads of major policy questions in the economic and social fields and for subsequent reporting to their respective intergovernmental bodies. The Committee has already undertaken such discussion in its regular biannual sessions and was of the view that the objective of this recommendation could be achieved by convening subject-oriented Committee sessions and/or by recourse to functional groups.

23. The Secretary-General believes that the objective of recommendation 10 could best be achieved through informal consultations among relevant executive heads on major policy questions. For that purpose, he has convened a number of informal meetings with relevant executive heads to consider issues relating to Africa, debt and development, and the functioning of the Economic and Social Council. In his report on the work of the Organization in 1987,[2] he also made a number of suggestions concerning the strengthening of the Council and, at the inter-secretariat level, arrangements to encourage an integrated approach to problems while taking advantage of the human resources of the system as a whole.

Recommendation 11 and 12

24. In his first progress report, the Secretary-General indicated that he had initiated efforts to achieve a pattern of United Nations field representation that is both effective and efficient (A/42/234, para. 30 (h)). The situation is now as follows:

(a) Various United Nations funds, the United Nations Development Programme (UNDP), the United Nations Children's Fund (UNICEF), the United Nations Population Fund (UNFPA) and the World Food Programme (WFP), in their Joint Consultative Group on Policy, have, during the past year, undertaken a systematic assessment of their field offices on a country-by-country basis. They have identified steps that should be taken to enhance co-operation and efficiency through the sharing of office premises and services in the field whenever this is feasible and cost-effective. The organizations in the Joint Consultative Group on Policy hope that the other organizations and agencies of the United Nations system will join in this development. The executive heads will report progress to the governing bodies of their respective organizations, which will in turn report to the Economic and Social Council. The Director-General will also report on progress to the General Assembly through the Council.

(b) An in-depth study has been undertaken by UNDP and the Department of Public Information of the Secretariat of the most cost-effective and efficient working relationships of United Nations information centres and the offices of the resident co-ordinators/resident representatives. A final agreement is expected to be reached shortly that will embody practical guidelines for co-operation in the field between these entities of the United Nations in countries where there are at present separate field offices, in countries where the Department of Public Information is represented by the resident co-ordinator/resident representative, and in countries where there is an information centre but no UNDP presence.

Recommendation 23 and 24

25. These recommendations deal with emergency assistance programmes and the Office of the United Nations Disaster Relief Co-ordinator (UNDRO). The General Assembly, at its forty-first session, adopted resolution 41/201 of 8 December 1986 on UNDRO, which, *inter alia*, reaffirmed the mandate of that Office and requested the Secretary-General to submit a report on the implementation of the resolution, including a comprehensive review and assessment of the existing mechanisms and arrangements within the system for disaster and emergency assistance and co-ordination.

26. In that report (A/42/657), the Secretary-General, *inter alia*, proposed the establishment of a central focal point in the Office of the Director-General for Development and International Economic Co-operation to ensure effective response by the United Nations system in the case of disasters and other emergency situations. The Secretary-General also recommended that UNDRO should focus its activities on sudden natural disasters and on preparation and prevention measures related thereto, and indicated that a study would be undertaken by the Management Advisory Service with a view to adjusting UNDRO's work programme and organization to reflect this basic orientation. With respect to complex emergency situations, the Secretary-General, in appropriate consultation with his colleagues, will make such arrangements as may be necessary. Further, the Secretary-General recommended that a joint UNDP/UNDRO task force be established to work out improved modalities for co-operation.

27. In its decision 42/433, the General Assembly welcomed the initiative of the Secretary-General to establish a central focal point in the Office of the Director-General. It also requested the Secretary-General to proceed with the implementation of the conclusions and recommendations contained in his report and to present a progress report to the General Assembly at its forty-third session.

28. The purpose of the Management Advisory Service study on UNDRO is to identify the organizational and other arrangements needed to permit UNDRO to focus its activities on sudden natural disasters and on preparation and prevention measures related thereto. Furthermore, a task force was established to review the modalities of co-operation between UNDP and UNDRO in the field. Other organizations of the system have been invited to participate in the work of the task force as appropriate. This exercise will lead to revised guidelines for co-operation and a memorandum of understanding

between the two organizations. As requested, the results of these activities will be reported upon to the General Assembly at its forty-third session in a progress report of the Secretary-General.

Recommendation 25 to 27

29. The reforms in the economic and social sectors are closely related to the work of the Special Commission established by Economic and Social Council decision 1987/112, in order to carry out the in-depth study of the United Nations intergovernmental structure and functions in the economic and social fields in implementation of recommendation 8. The Special Commission will submit its report to the Council at its regular session of 1988.

30. The in-depth programmatic review called for in recommendation 25 (1), which was initiated at the end of 1986, as indicated in the first progress report (A/42/234, para. 29), has been largely completed. The Office of the Director-General has assembled comprehensive information from programme managers - with particular emphasis on the broad areas identified in the first progress report (para. 31), i.e. global analysis and reporting, energy and natural resources, science and technology, economic and technical co-operation among developing countries, national development strategies and the relationship between operational and substantive activities.

31. The review of these areas has reached a stage where possibilities can be envisaged for changing the secretariat structure. None the less, it is necessary to have a clearer view of the changes that Governments intend to introduce in the intergovernmental machinery before reaching definitive conclusions on these changes. Accordingly, the specific decisions and/or proposals on the secretariat structure will be developed in the light of the outcome of the Special Commission of the Economic and Social Council on the In-depth Study of the United Nations Intergovernmental Structure and Functions in the Economic and Social Fields.

32. Without awaiting the results of the intergovernmental review, a number of conclusions may be reached based on the secretariat review. Firstly, a close examination of the analytical work being done on the world economy aspects indicated that there is less overlapping than was suggested, although there is room for streamlining certain activities such as the short- to medium-term analysis of the economic situation and prospects. More emphasis will be given to regular monitoring and the integrated study of major economic, social and environmental trends. Secondly, the review suggested the importance of integrating substantive and operational activities within the secretariat in some fields.

33. As far as the complementarity between subprogrammes is concerned, detailed consultations are taking place among the individual entities concerned with a view to streamlining their activities and strengthening co-operation between them. For example, the Department of International Economic and

Social Affairs and the United Nations Conference on Trade and Development (UNCTAD) have identified concrete possibilities for strengthening their co-operation in analytical work on the world economy and the development of data bases for this purpose. At the same time, the Department and UNCTAD are working on changes to their internal structure designed to give greater focus and coherence to their work in responding to intergovernmental mandates. The Centre for Social Development and Humanitarian Affairs of the United Nations Office at Vienna and the Department are fortifying their links with the Department of Technical Co-operation and Development with a view to undertaking joint activities. The Department of International Economic and Social Affairs has recently worked out new co-operative arrangements with the United Nations Environment Programme (UNEP).

34. In relation to recommendation 27, on the regional commissions, a study was carried out on their future role and activities. Based upon the findings of the study, consultations with the Executive Secretaries of the regional commissions and the heads of other entities concerned will shortly be completed and appropriate decisions and/or proposals finalized. Member States will be kept informed of developments.

35. Recommendation 25 (3) refers to enhancing the authority of the Director-General for Development and International Economic Co-operation so that he may fully exercise the functions envisaged in General Assembly resolution 32/197 of 20 December 1977. As the review has progressed, the importance of this recommendation with regard to both substantive and operational activities has become clear. There is a very close relationship between specific initiatives to strengthen the role of the Office of the Director-General, and the recommendations that will emerge from the work of the Special Commission of the Economic and Social Council concerning the strengthening of the Council's central role in policy-making and co-ordination.

C. Public information activities

Recommendation 37

36. In paragraphs 34-38 of his first progress report (A/42/234), the Secretary-General indicated his conceptual framework for the specific reforms and improvements of the Department of Public Information of the Secretariat, in response to the request contained in recommendation 37 of the Group of High-level Intergovernmental Experts. In essence, he pointed out that the previous information practice of the Organization, which concentrated on communications mainly with Member States, "ignored the tapping of the second-tier global constituency, the world's peoples". The report further indicated that "if the United Nations is to develop the capacity to undertake a tight, realistic and acceptable agenda for the 1990s, it must seek to enlarge the circle of active public opinion in support of the United Nations and develop a new awareness of its value and potential, especially among the younger

generations, by helping people to discover and visualize tangible benefits that touch their lives directly".

37. To that end, the Secretary-General indicated an approach for a three-phase review of the Department that he had initiated. These phases would be, firstly, a review of the Department's major fields of activities and the management system, including access to technology and funding policies; secondly, the examination of the distribution of human, technical and financial resources, and of ways and means of rendering policies and programmes more effective in reaching opinion-builders; and, thirdly, the implementation of a new structure.

38. The timetable envisaged for the implementation of the third phase had proved to be overly optimistic. It was hoped that the new structure would be in place by the end of 1987, but in fact it is at the present time only partially in place. The deliberate and meticulous exercise undertaken in connection with the implementation of recommendation 15 of the Group of High-level Intergovernmental Experts, that is, the post-reduction exercise, which affects the Secretariat as a whole, required a review that extended beyond the time originally planned, delaying a decision on the precise number of posts that would be requested for the Department. This having been established, the implementation will now proceed and should be completed prior to the opening of the forty-third session of the General Assembly.

39. Detailed information (programmatic, budgetary and structural) concerning the restructured DPI, will, of course, be included in the revised programme budget estimates that will be submitted to the General Assembly at its forty-third session, through the Committee for Programme and Co-ordination and the Advisory Committee on Administrative and Budgetary Questions (A/C.5/43/1).

D. *Conference services and related issues*

Recommendation 1

40. At its session in 1987, the Committee on Conferences discussed ways of strengthening its role and considered establishing the Committee as a permanent intergovernmental body. To assist the Committee in those deliberations, the Secretariat had prepared a detailed document containing both background information and suggestions on how the Committee might wish to approach the task of changing its mandate to reflect the role envisioned for it by the General Assembly in resolution 41/213 (A/AC.1/72/118). The Committee reviewed every aspect of the question of its status and future terms of reference and achieved a consensus on many important points. It will continue those deliberations during 1988 and is expected to submit its final recommendations on the matter to the General Assembly at its forty-third session.

Recommendation 2 and 3

41. Some success has been achieved in addressing recommendation 1 (e) on the planning and co-ordination of conferences and meetings, in particular, by staggering them throughout the year so as to utilize conference facilities and resources better. However, with regard to recommendation 2, on the reduction in the number and duration of meetings and conferences, and pending the completion of the work of the Special Commission of the Economic and Social Council on the In-depth Study of the United Nations Intergovernmental Structure and Functions in the Economic and Social Fields, the calendar of conferences for the biennium 1988-1989 does not reflect a diminished level of meeting activity.

42. On the other hand, in an effort to adapt the concept introduced in recommendation 1 (d), the Secretary-General, in formulating the programme budget submissions for the biennium 1988-1989, has for the first time incorporated into the resource base for temporary assistance the funding for servicing meetings other than the sessions of the General Assembly, which heretofore had been provided annually as non-recurrent funding through the consolidated statement of budgetary implications for conference servicing activities. Thus, at its forty-second session, the General Assembly approved as a part of the regular programme budget an overall level of resources for servicing the biennial calendar of conferences. The co-operation of all offices serving as substantive secretariats to intergovernmental bodies has been sought and they have been asked to exercise restraint and prudence in requesting and in their manner of using meeting and documentation services. In order to deploy the limited resources available as effectively and efficiently as possible, the importance of careful planning and the sharing of information has also been emphasized. As mandated by the General Assembly in its resolution 42/207 C of 11 December 1987 on the pattern of conferences, necessary measures will have to be taken to ensure the provision of conference services to the United Nations with adequate personnel, with due respect for the equal treatment of all official languages of the United Nations.

Recommendation 7

43. The impact of applying restraint in the utilization of conference resources and of measures aimed at controlling documentation has been monitored by the Committee on Conferences, which, during its 1987 sessions, had before it statistics provided by the Secretariat that reveal a trend towards a closer adherence to the 32-page limit for reports of subsidiary organs set by the General Assembly in its resolution 37/14 C of 16 November 1982. The Committee has also included in the agenda of its 1988 session the consideration of a report to be submitted by the Secretariat on communications from Member States circulated as documents of the United Nations. Furthermore, in an attempt to control and limit documentation, the Department of Conference Services, in co-operation with other offices at Headquarters, is

implementing measures aimed at reducing the overall quantity of documents that need to be distributed and printed.

Recommendation 34

44. The Department continues to identify those areas of document- and publication-processing activities where the introduction of new technologies or procedures has made it possible to increase efficiency and productivity further in order to update output indicators. A pilot project using optical disc technology as a partial solution for solving the problems of storage and retrieval of documentation will be launched in 1988 at the United Nations Office at Geneva, as recommended by the Joint Inspection Unit. This project is being supported by extrabudgetary funding. Small projects will also be implemented during the 1988-1989 period in order to test this new technology and to enable the Secretariat to make a close study of its possibilities and effectiveness as well as to evaluate its costs. To that effect, it is planned to examine further other technological innovations in conference services that could result in continued improvements in productivity.

45. The Department is also currently engaged in harmonizing terminology and statistical methodologies and presentations used in formulating the proposed programme budget for conference and library services.

46. Through the collaborative efforts of the author departments and the Department of Conference Services and under the auspices of the Publications Board, progress has been made in implementing the Organization's publications programme in a more cost-efficient manner. Believing that the quality of United Nations publications is measured more by the readership on the basis of content and timeliness of issuance than on expensive, glossy presentation, greater emphasis has been placed on printing as many publications as possible using the in-house printing and binding facilities. As a result, the external printing appropriations for the biennium 1988-1989 reflect a negative growth rate of 17.3 per cent over the total appropriations originally approved for the same purpose for the biennium 1986-1987. To enhance the quality of the Organization's publications, separate studies have been carried out by the Publications Board, resulting in a series of recommendations aimed at improving the timeliness of the publications and these have been passed on to author departments and processing services.

47. Pursuant to a recommendation of the Advisory Committee on Administrative and Budgetary Questions and as part of its efforts to rationalize the publications programme, the Publications Board, in consultation with the Office of Programme Planning, Budget and Finance, has recently developed a methodology for estimating the cost of producing recurrent publications. This methodology will be used in the preparation of the Secretary-General's proposed programme budget for the biennium 1990-1991 and in the planning and review of the consolidated publications programme for that period. Moreover, as requested by the Committee on Programme and Co-ordination

and with the assistance of the secretariats of the intergovernmental bodies that authorize the production of recurrent publications, the Publications Board is monitoring the reviews of the intergovernmental bodies concerned and will ensure the implementation of their decisions to discontinue or to reduce in volume or periodicity any publications that do not meet the criteria set forth in resolution 38/32 E of 25 November 1983. Guidelines are also being developed to help distinguish clearly between recurrent and non-recurrent publications. Moreover, efforts are being made for better co-ordination of the statistical publications programmes of the regional commissions and the Statistical Office at Headquarters.

48. To maximize the sale of successful publications, a marketing survey was conducted of North American acquisition librarians, who represent approximately 30 per cent of the overall sales market for United Nations publications. Specific recommendations to reach that targeted public more effectively were formulated and will be implemented. The reference publications most requested by libraries are the *World Economic Survey*, the *Yearbook of the United Nations* and the *Yearbook of the International Law Commission*. Some of the publications in greater demand in recent years are manuals and publications on standards such as the *Guidelines for Project Evaluation*, the *Manual for the Preparation of Industrial Feasibility Studies*, *System of National Accounts* and the *Standard International Trade Classification* (Rev.2). Based on a study, the list of magazines in which advertisements are placed has been revised. Currently, United Nations publications are advertised not only in the media but also at trade shows and exhibits and at book fairs. In 1987, a new video "On Common Ground", which provides a tour of the United Nations, has met with success, particularly in schools.

E. *Administration and finance*

49. Apart from those cases where the implementation of the recommendations is dependent upon the completion of reviews or studies in other areas (e.g. the reviews in the economic and social fields), most of the recommendations of the Group of High-level Intergovernmental Experts with regard to administration and finance have been implemented, as the information provided below indicates.

50. In addition, initiatives have been taken in the administrative area, particularly with respect to the information systems for budget, payroll, accounting and human resources. A major study is under way, as announced at the forty-second session (A/C.5/42/18), with a view to establishing an integrated management information system that will encompass not only the administrative area at Headquarters but also the administration of the other major offices. This integrated system will provide managers with up-to-date and comprehensive information that will facilitate decision-making.

51. During the rest of the reform period, it is intended to pay particular attention to the question of delegation of authority in administrative matters. Greater delegation of authority under clear rules and guidelines and with appropriate control mechanisms will result in increased efficiency. Such measures can only become possible with the introduction of a truly integrated information system covering not only Headquarters offices but also the other main duty stations.

Recommendation 5

52. At its forty-second session, the General Assembly adopted resolution 42/211, paragraph 10 (a) of which stated as follows:

"Regarding recommendation 5, the General Assembly takes note of the report of the Secretary-General (A/C.5/42/4) and invites him to proceed as necessary on both already approved projects in accordance with the provision of section I, paragraph 1 (a), of resolution 41/213, on the understanding that no additional appropriation will be required in that regard for the biennium 1988-1989".

Measures have already been taken on the implementation of the resolution and will be reported upon to the General Assembly at its forty-third session in the Secretary-General's annual report on the construction projects at Addis Ababa and Bangkok. The Committee for Programme and Co-ordination and the General Assembly will be advised through the Advisory Committee on Administrative and Budgetary Questions of the further financial requirements in this regard, in the context of the budget outline for the biennium 1990-1991.

Recommendation 6

53. The proposed programme budget for the biennium 1988-1989 (A/42/6, sect. 1, para. 1.5) reflected a negative growth of $2,748,400 of the resources requested for the travel of representatives of Member States attending the General Assembly. The General Assembly, at its forty-second session, adopted resolution 42/226 of 21 December 1987 approving the budgetary provisions for the reimbursement of travel costs for 5 representatives each of the 40 least developed countries.

Recommendation 13

54. The harmonization of budgets in the United Nations system requested in this recommendation has been included by the Joint Inspection Unit in its programme of work for 1988. Detailed information on the views of the Administrative Committee on Co-ordination and comments made by the Advisory Committee on Administrative and Budgetary Questions on the subject were already provided in the first progress report (A/42/234, annex, paras. 12-15).

Recommendation 28

55. In order to harmonize the presentation of resources pertaining to regional commissions, a concern expressed in this recommendation, the practice has been adopted, beginning with the proposed programme budget for the biennium 1988-1989, of identifying in the budget of the United Nations Office at Geneva those costs pertaining to the Economic Commission for Europe, as well as in the introduction to section 10 of the programme budget relating to ECE (A/42/234, annex, paras. 16-18).

Recommendation 30 and 32

56. Following detailed reviews conducted in each office and division in conjunction with the implementation of recommendation 15, measures were taken to streamline the Department of Administration and Management. The consolidation of programme planning and budget under one structure has also been completed as previously announced (A/42/234, annex, para. 3, and A/C.5/42/2/Rev.1, paras. 42-45). These changes resulted in a leaner department, particularly at the senior levels, with clearer lines of responsibility and with shorter reporting lines in several divisions.

Recommendation 31

57. The functions of the Management Advisory Service have been examined in the context of the reorganization of the department. During this past year, the staff formerly assigned to the Service have been conducting detailed management and administrative studies supporting the reviews being carried out in connection with the implementation of resolution 41/213. These functions are essential in that they provide the necessary framework for managerial decisions.

58. Recent experience has reconfirmed the assessment offered in the first progress report, where the continuing need for a small internal management consultancy service to assist in the task of streamlining the Secretariat and enhancing its efficiency was noted. This activity has now been placed with the Office for Programme Planning, Budgeting and Finance in order to permit it to be more closely supportive of the programme budget function and to ensure congruence with the programme evaluation function.

Recommendation 33

59. A review of the support activities for the liaison offices in New York of various secretariat entities will be carried out in the context of the implementation of recommendation 15. Further details on this matter are being provided in the revised estimates for the programme budget for the biennium 1988-1989 (A/C.5/43/1).

Recommendation 35

60. As requested, the appropriations for the programme budget for the biennium 1988-1989 included resources for consultants that reflect a negative growth of $1.6 million, representing a reduction of 19.1 per cent in real growth terms against the biennium 1986-1987.

Recommendation 36

61. This recommendation stated that "concurrent with the reduction in the overall size of the Secretariat, there should be a reduction in the requirements for rented premises". The Secretary-General has already reported on the administrative difficulties in reducing space concurrent with indicated staff reductions. While this recommendation refers to reductions in regular budget funded staff, space utilization in the organization includes meeting the requirements arising from activities funded from extrabudgetary resources.

62. A review of all outside bodies occupying space in the United Nations premises at Headquarters has been completed. A rent structure has been established for the various categories of tenants and the new rent structure, which is based on full commercial rates, is being implemented in a phased manner with full implementation scheduled for 1 January 1990.

Recommendation 38

63. Appropriations for official travel have been reduced by $4.3 million in the programme budget for the biennium 1988-1989, representing a reduction of 21 per cent in real growth terms against the biennium 1986-1987. A special procedure for the review of all requests for travel to meetings and conferences by the Office of the Secretary-General has been established and recently reinforced through the issue of a revised Bulletin. This procedure is believed to have contributed to a significant reduction in the number of officials attending meetings and conferences away from their duty stations, as indicated in the first progress report (A/42/234, annex, para. 9).

64. With regard to first class travel, which is also mentioned in this recommendation, the General Assembly has taken action at its last session by adopting resolution 42/214 of 21 December 1987 on standards of accommodation for air travel. The General Assembly decided that all individuals, with the exception of the Secretary-General and the heads of delegations of the least developed countries to the General Assembly who were previously entitled to first-class accommodations, would be required to travel at the class immediately below first class; it also authorized the Secretary-General to exercise his discretion in making exceptions on a case-by-case basis and requested him to report annually to the General Assembly on the implementation of the resolution.

Recommendation 39

65. This recommendation on the audit function has already been implemented, as explained in the first progress report (A/42/234, annex, para. 7).

Recommendation 40

66. The three former executive offices in the Department of Administration and Management have now been consolidated into one executive office for the whole department, as requested. This measure was taken also to implement recommendation 30 on the streamlining of the Department.

F. Personnel matters

67. The recommendations of the Group of High-level Intergovernmental Experts concerning personnel matters cover a wide range of issues that require careful consideration.   The Secretariat has embarked on an extensive programme of reforms in the area of human resources management. Given the work-load involved, priorities have been established and the implementation of these recommendations has been planned over the whole reform period. The need to plan staff retrenchment as a result of recommendation 15 has required that attention be given on a priority basis to policies and procedures to be introduced for facilitating the redeployment of staff, while strictly controlling appointments and with due regard being given to the principle of equitable geographical distribution and the situation of women in the Secretariat.   Such policies and procedures must be established after consultation with staff representatives, in accordance with chapter VIII of the Staff Regulations and Rules. Furthermore, the need to curtail the number of appointments during the retrenchment period has had an impact on the implementation of a number of recommendations, particularly those concerned with recruitment and permanent appointments.

68. Two recommendations were referred to the International Civil Service Commission (ICSC) for its consideration, as requested by the General Assembly, since they had system-wide implications and fall under the authority of the Commission.   These were recommendations 53, on monitoring the implementation of standards set by ICSC, and 61, on the level of total entitlements of staff.   The Commission has provided its views on these recommendations in its report to the General Assembly at its forty-second session.[3]

Recommendation 41

69. The question of strengthening the role and emphasizing the authority of the Office of Personnel Services in recruitment and other personnel matters throughout the Secretariat was discussed during the debates of the Fifth Committee at the forty-second session and information was provided at the

time by the Under-Secretary-General for Administration and Management. This can be summarized as follows: the Office has been renamed Office of Human Resources Management to reflect the fact that its role is not merely to service departments and offices, a vital function indeed, but also to provide policy guidelines that will help managers manage their staff and to ensure forward planning for the management of the most precious asset of the Organization, its staff; the responsibility for the security of staff world-wide has also been entrusted to the Assistant Secretary-General in charge of Human Resources Management; the central role of the Office has been further strengthened through its recent reorganization and the redeployment to that Office of responsibilities for salaries and allowances.

Recommendation 42

70. The Personnel Administrative Handbook referred to in paragraph 30 of the annex to the first progress report is being issued as a Personnel Manual to officers dealing with administrative and personnel matters in a revised format that will facilitate updating. It is foreseen that the development of the complete manual will take approximately 18 months, when sufficient resources become available. The manual will then contain an annotation of the Staff Regulations, Staff Rules and related issuances, including relevant policy decisions, and will thus promote their uniform understanding, interpretation and application.

Recommendation 43

71. The realignment of internal and external competitive examinations is being discussed and the matter will be reported to the General Assembly at its forty-third session.

72. The use of examinations for recruitment at the P-3 level and the implementation of drafting tests for recruitment at the P-4 and P-5 levels will have to await the end of the current financial difficulties. Meanwhile, despite the financial crisis, a recruitment examination for a small number of posts at the P-1/P-2 levels was held in 1987 and recruitment examinations at these levels will be held in 1988 in keeping with the spirit of recommendation 15.3 (d).

Recommendation 44

73. During the period 1 July 1985-30 June 1986, recruitments at the P-1, P-2 and P-3 levels accounted for 55.3 per cent of the 188 recruitments in the Professional and higher categories. The recruitment freeze was introduced in March 1986 as part of the economy measures necessitated by the financial crisis. During the following period, 1 July 1986-30 June 1987, when only 49 staff members were appointed, the percentage of recruitments at these levels was 51 per cent. During the last six months of 1987, 23 out of 30 staff

members appointed were at these levels (76.7 per cent). Some progress was thus achieved in the implementation of this recommendation.

Recommendation 45

74. As stated in the first progress report (A/42/234, annex, para. 37), the proposal to consider staff for permanent appointments after three years of service must await the completion of the retrenchment exercise.

Recommendation 46

75. Although, as explained above, appointments over the last two years have been very limited, efforts were made during that period to ensure that a higher percentage of women were appointed whenever exceptions to the recruitment freeze were granted. During the period 1 July 1985-30 June 1986, 34 women were appointed to posts subject to geographical distribution, representing 18.1 per cent of appointments; during the following period (1 July 1986-30 June 1987) 14 women were appointed, representing 28.6 per cent of appointments, and finally, during the last six months of 1987, 10 women were appointed, that is, 33.3 per cent of appointments. Likewise, a number of women have been appointed to senior-level posts; since the beginning of 1987, three women have been appointed to the Under-Secretary-General level and four women staff members promoted to the director level.

Recommendation 47

76. The nomination of nationals of developing countries to senior-level posts is being carefully monitored to ensure that this recommendation, as well as several directives given by the General Assembly over the years, are implemented as indicated in the progress report (A/42/234, annex, para. 43).

Recommendation 48

77. Competitive recruitment examinations at the P-1/P-2 levels are already organized along occupational lines. A pilot-project for recruitment at higher levels by occupational groups is being reviewed but implementation will have to await the end of the retrenchment period. Career paths are being developed but priority is now being given to staff redeployment and retrenchment plans as explained earlier. Work on the design of some of the components of a system of career development for all categories of staff, which was announced by the Secretary-General in his report of 16 October 1984 (A/C.5/39/11), was suspended owing to the more urgent need to devote the available resources to the redeployment of staff and the formulation and implementation of retrenchment plans. Consequently, the work described in the first progress report (A/42/234, annex, paras. 45-50) will be resumed when resources become available for this activity.

Recommendation 49

78. The staff redeployment programme is being refined and should form the basis for a future rotation system. By advertising secretariat-wide vacancies open to internal candidates only, the programme enables qualified staff members from all duty stations to be considered for posts in their area of expertise. They are then reviewed by a joint staff-administration advisory body, which guarantees an objective and fair review. Thus, a number of staff members have been reassigned to a different duty station. The experience of other agencies in the common system with rotation schemes is being studied with a view to developing an approach corresponding to the specific needs of the United Nations Secretariat.

Recommendation 50

79. Information on the promotions of staff, reported for women only in the last report on the composition of the Secretariat (A/42/636, table F), will be given for men as well as women in the next report. The performance evaluation system is still under review.

Recommendation 51

80. Specific criteria have been developed for the redeployment of staff to higher-level posts and for their promotion and have been communicated to the appointment and promotion bodies. Special criteria for the promotion of women have recently been extended to the vacancy management and staff redeployment programme. These criteria should together form the basis of a new promotion system based on open competition and clear requirements for each posted vacancy. The role and structure of the appointment and promotion bodies themselves are also under review.

Recommendation 52

81. Retirement age has been consistently adhered to except for cases falling under the terms of section VI of resolution 35/210 of 17 December 1980 and where it was imperative to retain the services of some staff members beyond the age of 60 in order to ensure the completion of essential or urgent work.

Recommendation 54

82. The Secretary-General is mindful of this recommendation concerning the renewal of the leadership of departments and offices and the length of service of Under-Secretaries-General and Assistant Secretaries-General. In contemplating new appointments or extensions of appointments at these levels, the Secretary-General is taking these concerns into account. He must also take into consideration other factors in the best interest of the Organization such as competence and the principle of equitable geographical distribution.

Recommendation 55 and 57

83. Recommendation 55 recalls resolution 35/210 and the principle that no post should be considered the exclusive preserve of any Member State. Recommendation 57 concerns the ratio between permanent staff members and staff on fixed-term appointments. The comments made in paragraphs 37 and 38 of the annex to A/42/234 are still valid. These issues will be reviewed further after the retrenchment period.

Recommendation 56

84. A stringent procedure, including a review by the Post Review Group and the Programme Planning and Budgeting Board, has been established. Authorization is given to proceed with redeployment or, in very exceptional cases, recruitment only when a post is deemed essential. Following the detailed review carried out to implement recommendation 15, such measures will no longer be needed. However, there will still be an ongoing need to examine the work-load of posts whenever they become vacant in order to implement this recommendation.

Recommendation 58

85. A number of changes were introduced in the 1987 training programme in order to ensure that United Nations training programmes are strictly geared to the needs of the Organization as outlined in the first progress report (A/42/234, annex, para. 51).

86. The implementation of recommendation 15 has prompted an increased emphasis on training since, in the context of the retrenchment exercise, training will support staff facing occupational adjustments stemming from organizational restructuring and staff redeployment. Training programmes in management development and supervision are being reoriented, providing managers and supervisors, secretariat-wide, with an opportunity to enhance their ability to manage effectively in the face of the ongoing process of retrenchment and post reduction. Furthermore, to maintain the necessary level of efficiency and effectiveness with a smaller number of staff requires, *inter alia*, greater reliance on office technology. This, in turn, creates a rapidly increasing demand in terms of the number of staff to be trained, number of areas requiring advanced skills and a more effective management training programme. In order to meet these needs, a training plan has been prepared that will guide the course and direction of programme activities in 1988 and 1989.

Recommendation 59

87. The Staff Regulations require the Secretary-General to establish and maintain continuous contact and communication with the staff in order to

ensure their effective participation in identifying, examining and resolving issues relating to their welfare, including conditions of work, general conditions of life and other personnel policies. They provide that related staff representative bodies shall be established. The Secretary-General is also required to create joint staff-management machinery at local and secretariat-wide levels to advise him on these matters. The consultation process enables staff views to be sought and considered before management decisions are taken on matters affecting staff interests and concerns, in accordance also with modern management practice. It has been of particular importance during the present difficult period characterized by acute financial constraints, rapid change, inevitable dislocation and increased work pressures for almost all staff members. Its breakdown at such a time could have serious consequences for the whole Organization, whose principal asset, as the Secretary-General has reiterated, consists of its staff. At almost all duty stations, the machinery is in place and the process is working reasonably well. However, the secretariat-wide Staff Management Co-ordination Committee meetings, held since the adoption of resolution 41/213, have paid particular attention to the need to improve the work effectiveness of that Committee, and to clarify certain questions of conflict of interest or role on the part of staff and management representatives.

Recommendation 60

88. The Secretary-General's first progress report indicated that steps had already been taken for the establishment of a revised and simplified machinery for the administration of justice in the Secretariat by early 1988. Further information was provided to the General Assembly during its forty-second session (A/C.5/42/28).

89. The Under-Secretary-General for Administration and Management assumed direct responsibility for the functioning of the appellate process on 1 February 1988 and, since that time, the Joint Appeals Boards have reported directly to him. There is already evidence that this streamlining may eradicate delays at the post-appellate stage. The composition, structure, functioning and procedures of the Boards are now being revised, and the process of consultation has begun regarding the continued existence of Boards away from Headquarters. The functioning of other specialized appeal bodies is also being examined. A timetable will in future be established for each appeal as it is registered to ensure its procedural progress and determination in a timely manner.

90. As regards disciplinary processes, a full-time secretary of the Headquarters Joint Disciplinary Committee was designated on 1 February 1988 to clear the backlog of cases. A study is being undertaken to examine the disciplinary process and to draw up, as appropriate, a system of rules, procedures and sanctions for misconduct; to propose, as necessary, revision of the Staff Regulations and/or Staff Rules, and to report thereon as soon as possible, with a view to having a new system in place by the end of 1988.

91. As regards the Discrimination and Grievance Panels, the review of their functioning indicated in the Secretary-General's report (A/C.5/42/28) has already begun. A number of other measures have also been instituted to facilitate a smoothly functioning system of administrative justice.

IV. CONCLUDING OBSERVATIONS

92. The Secretary-General has provided, in the present report as well as in the revised estimates for the programme budget for the biennium 1988-1989, detailed information concerning each recommendation that he was called upon to implement. These reports reflect action taken during the first 15 months of the 3-year period envisaged by the General Assembly. Extensive restructuring is now complete in the political and administrative areas, and is well under way in the Department of Public Information. Final restructuring in the economic and social fields must await the results of reviews undertaken by the intergovernmental bodies. Many recommendations aiming at streamlining the Secretariat and ensuring greater efficiency in its activities, whether in substantive or servicing functions, have already been fully implemented or will be put into effect during the remainder of the reform period. The co-operation of the staff during this most difficult period has been outstanding and should be fully acknowledged.

93. When the Secretary-General began the process of reform and renewal early in 1987, he indicated that improving the administrative and financial functioning of the United Nations without addressing the fundamental issue of "efficiency to do what?" would not achieve the desired results (A/42/234, para. 4). Delivering mandated programmes in the most efficient and cost-effective manner remains the most important task of the Secretariat and the Secretary-General will continue to take the necessary measures to ensure that this goal is met. By the same token, it is essential that Member States contribute their indispensable support to this joint endeavour towards strengthening the Organization and the services it renders to the international community in accordance with clearly stated priorities.

94. A final report will be submitted to the General Assembly at its forty-fourth session, as mandated by resolution 41/213, on the implementation of that resolution. In the mean time, the Secretary-General recommends that the General Assembly take note of the second progress report.

Notes

1. *Official Records of the General Assembly, Forty-first Session, Supplement No. 49* (A/41/49).
2. *Ibid., Forty-second Session, Supplement No. 1* (A/42/1).
3. *Ibid., Supplement No. 30* (A/42/30, chap. II, paras. 13-44).

2.18 Document A/43/651[*]

Reform and Renewal in the United Nations:
Second Progress report of the Secretary-General on the
implementation of General Assembly resolution 41/213 (A/43/286)

Report of the Advisory Committee on Administrative
and Budgetary Questions

3 October 1988

76. This report (A/43/286) has been submitted to the General Assembly through the Committee for Programme and Co-ordination and the Advisory Committee pursuant to the request in paragraph 11 of Assembly resolution 42/211. As stated in paragraph 4, the report provides detailed information on action taken with respect to each recommendation of the Group of High-level Intergovernmental Experts up to the first quarter of 1988 and plans for the remaining period (April 1988-December 1989). The Committee points out that this report should be read in conjunction with the Secretary-General's report on revised estimates (A/C.5/43/1/Rev.1), which contains the financial implications of a number of the developments described in the progress report.

77. The Committee notes that the report is general in nature, and it trusts that further progress in the months ahead will ensure that the final report on the implementation of General Assembly resolution 41/213 will be a comprehensive statement and will contain a complete description and justification for all that has taken place during the reform process.

78. As indicated in paragraph 39 of the report, detailed information concerning the restructured Department of Public Information is included in the revised programme budget estimates (A/C.5/43/1/Rev.1). The related comments of the Advisory Committee are to be found in paragraphs 40 to 60 above[**].

79. The Committee notes from paragraph 47 of the report that "pursuant to a recommendation of the Advisory Committee on Administrative and Budgetary Questions and as part of its efforts to rationalize the publications programme, the Publications Board, in consultation with the Office of Programme Planning, Budget and Finance, has recently developed a methodology for estimating the cost of producing recurrent publications. This methodology will be used in the preparation of the Secretary-General's proposed programme budget for the biennium 1990-1991 and
in the planning and review of the consolidated publications programme for the period". The Advisory Committee had discussed the publications programme

---

[*]A/43/651, pp. 18-19.
[**]Not reprinted here.

of the United Nations in paragraphs 70 to 78 of its first report on the proposed programme budget for the biennium 1988-1989.[1]

80. In paragraph 56 of the report the Secretary-General discusses measures taken to streamline the Department of Administration and Management and indicates that "the consolidation of programme planning and budget under one structure has also been completed as previously announced (A/42/234, annex, para. 3, and A/C.5/42/2/Rev.1, paras. 42-45)". In paragraph 92 of its first report on the proposed programme budget for 1988-1989,[2] the Advisory Committee had indicated that it would return to the matter of the structure of the Department of Administration and Management in the context of further developments. The Committee has received additional information on this matter and has no objection to the proposals of the Secretary-General in this regard as incorporated in his report on the revised estimates for 1988-1989 (A/C.5/43/1/Rev.1).

81. Information on steps taken to reform and streamline the system for the administration of justice in the secretariat is provided in paragraphs 88 to 91 of the report. The Advisory Committee understands that a separate report on this subject will be submitted to the General Assembly at its forty-third session.

Notes

1.   *Official Records of the General Assembly, Forty-second Session, Supplement No. 7 (A/42/7).*
2.   *Ibid.*

2.19 Document A/43/16˙

Reform and Renewal in the United Nations:
Second Progress Report of the Secretary-General on the
Implementation of General Assembly Resolution 41/213 (A/43/286)

Report of the Committee for Programme and Co-ordination

1989

66. At its 25th and 28th to 34th meetings, from 18 to 23 May, the Committee considered the report of the Secretary-General on reform and renewal in the United Nations: second progress report of the Secretary-General on the implementation of General Assembly resolution 41/213 (A/43/286).

Discussion

67. Several delegations pointed out that the imbalance in the proportional representation of nationals of developing countries at senior levels in the Secretariat *vis-à-vis* those of the developed countries was growing. It was stated that the report of the Secretary-General on the composition of the Secretariat (A/42/636, table C) indicated that the number of staff members from Member States that are developing countries in Africa, Asia, the Middle East, Latin America and the Caribbean in senior posts (D-1 and above) had decreased from 48.8 per cent in 1986 to 47.6 per cent in 1987 and that those from countries with developed market economies had increased from 41.5 per cent in 1986 to 42.9 per cent in 1987. In this connection, they recalled recommendation 47 of the Group of High-level Intergovernmental Experts, as approved by the Assembly in its resolution 41/213, which called for additional measures to be taken by the Secretariat to ensure that nationals of developing countries are duly represented at senior levels. They requested the Secretary-General to take the additional required measures without further delay and to report on his efforts in this regard to the General Assembly at its forty-third session .

68. Other delegations considered that in this connection,as in others, Assembly resolution 41/213 should be viewed as a whole.

Conclusions and recommendations

69. The Committee took note of the second progress report of the Secretary-General on the implementation of General Assembly resolution 41/213.

˙*Official Records of the General Assembly, Forty-third Session, Supplement No. 16* (A/43/16), pp. 13-15.

70. The Committee expressed its full support for the Secretary-General in his capacity as Chief Administrative Officer of the Organization in the fulfilment of mandates given to him by the General Assembly in resolutions 41/213 and 42/211.

71. The Committee endorsed the view of the Secretary-General that "for the process of reform to reach fruition, Member State must, no less, provide their full support, politically and financially, to the Organization" (A/43/286, para.7).

72. The Committee noted that action relating to reform in the economic and social fields would need to take action into full account the results of the in-depth study of the United Nations intergovernmental structure and functions in the economic and social fields.

73. The Committee reiterated the recommendation contained in paragraph 49 of part one of its report on its twenty-seventh session,[1] noted with satisfaction the appointment by the Secretary-General of the special representative and co-ordinator in the Office of the Co-ordinator of Assistance for the Reconstruction and Development of Lebanon and recommended that the remaining posts in the Co-ordinator's Office should be filled as soon as possible.

74. The Committee took note of the assurances given on behalf of the Secretary-General with regard to the financial aspects and the timetable for the construction projects that are proceeding in accordance with paragraph 10(a) of General Assembly resolution 42/211.

Note

1.   *Official Records of the General Assembly, Forty-second Session, Supplement No. 16 (A/42/16).*

2.20 Document A/43/324*

Questions Relating to the Programme Budget: Use and Operation of the Contingency Fund

Note by the Secretary-General

21 April 1988

1. In paragraphs 12 and 13 of its resolution 42/211 of 21 December 1987, the General Assembly concurred with the relevant observations and recommendations made by the Advisory Committee on Administrative and Budgetary Questions on the contingency fund as set out in the annex to that resolution. In paragraph 14 of the same resolution, the Assembly requested the Secretary-General to submit to it at its forty-third session, through the Committee for Programme and Co-ordination at its forty-third session, through the Committee for Programme and Co-ordination and the Advisory Committee, proposals for provisional procedures on the use and operation of the contingency fund based on the guidelines given in the resolution.

2. In section 1, paragraph 1, of its resolution 42/215 of 21 December 1987, the General Assembly endorsed the amendments to the Regulations and Rules Governing Programme Planning, the Programme Aspects of the Budget, the Monitoring of Implementation and the Methods of Evaluation, as recommended by the Committee for Programme and Co-ordination at its twenty-seventh session.[1] These amendments were designed, *inter alia,* to reflect changes in the budget process as indicated in sections A and B of annex I to Assembly resolution 41/213 of 19 December 1986. Included in the amendments recommended by the Committee for Programme and Co-ordination was a provision that once the Assembly had approved arrangements for the contingency fund and additional expenditures, a text reflecting those arrangements would be inserted in regulation 3.2 regarding the budget process.

3. Accordingly, it is proposed that the text of regulation 3.2 of the Regulations and Rules Governing Programme Planning, the Programme Aspects of the Budget, the Monitoring of Implementation and the Methods of Evaluation should be expanded, as indicated in the annex to the present note, to reflect the decisions on the contingency fund taken by the General Assembly in its resolution 42/211.

4. Should the General Assembly approve these changes to regulation 3.2, it might also be deemed appropriate, in due course, to modify the rules of procedure of the respective legislative bodies to reflect the consequential changes in their procedures.

---

*A/43/324.

Annex

Proposed supplementary article to the Regulations and Rules
Governing Programme Planning, Programme Aspects of the Budget,
the Monitoring of Implementation and the Methods of Evaluation

Regulation 3.2: Budget process

C. Contingency fund

1. Criteria for use of the contingency fund

8.   The following categories shall apply:

(a)   Additional resources that may be required as a result of the
consideration of statements of programme budget implications;

(b)   Revised estimates:

(i)   On the amounts required over and above the estimates of the
proposed programme budget for those activities which had been
included in the proposed programme budget but which were not
acted upon at firs reading pending the submission of additional
information;

(ii)   For construction, only additional requirements related to changes in
the scope of those projects which are so urgent that the matter
cannot wait to be considered in the context of the budget outline;
additional requirements related to cost increases shall be handled
under provisions for dealing with inflation and currency fluctuation;
similarly, additional requirements related to the effects of natural
disasters or unforeseen obstacles shall be handled on an *ad hoc* basis
and shall not be covered by the contingency fund;

(iii) Legislative mandates, such as those resulting from decisions of the
Economic and Social Council.

*2. Period covered and pattern of use of the
contingency fund*

9.   The contingency fund covers additional expenditures relating to the
biennium that are based on decisions taken in the year preceding the biennium
as well as during the biennium.

10. While prudent use of the fund requires that it should not be exhausted
before the end of the period of use, no pre-determined proportion for a given

year shall be set, pending review in the light of experience with the actual operation of the fund.

3. Operation of the contingency fund

11. In the off-budget year, the General Assembly shall decide on the size of the contingency fund in accordance with the provisions of annex I of its resolution 41/213.

12. Starting with the budget year (i.e., the year before the commencement of the biennium) and continuing throughout the biennium, the General Assembly shall decide on the actual amounts to be utilized from the fund on the basis of statements of programme budget implications and revised estimates.

13. Each statement of programme budget implications and each proposal for revised estimates shall contain a precise indication of how the alternatives mentioned in paragraph 9 of annex I to General Assembly resolution 41/213 would be applied in case it is not possible to finance all or part of the additional requirements from the fund. Each draft resolution accompanied by such a statement of programme budget implications shall be adopted subject to the provisions of that statement.

14. The statement of programme budget implications and proposals for revised estimates, formulated as indicated in paragraph 13 above, shall be considered by the General Assembly. Resolutions shall be adopted by the Assembly subject to the understanding described in paragraph 13 above.

15. A deadline shall be set for the consideration of statements of programme budget implications and revised estimates. After that date, the Secretary-General shall prepare and submit a consolidated statement of all programme budget implications and revised estimates considered at that session of the General Assembly. The amounts in that statement shall correspond to those previously recommended by the Fifth Committee upon its consideration of individual statements and revised estimates, as indicated in paragraph 13 above. Should the consolidated amount be within the available balance in the contingency fund, the Assembly shall proceed to appropriate the required amounts under the relevant section of the programme budget.

16. Should the consolidated amount exceed the balance available in the fund for that year, the Secretary-General shall, in his consolidated statement, make proposals for revising the amount within the balance of the fund remaining for the year. In so doing, the Secretary-General shall be guided by the indications of alternatives appended to each statement of programme budget implications and included in each proposal for revised estimates. The respective legislative bodies shall take action on such alternatives at the time they adopt the resolution or decision in question. The Secretary-General shall also take into account such indications of relative urgency as each legislative body may wish to make as between the resolutions and decisions of that body. Upon

consideration of this statement, the General Assembly shall proceed to appropriate the funds necessary under the relevant section of the programme budget.

Note

1. *Official Records of the General Assembly, Forty-second Session, Supplement No. 16* (A/42/16, part two, para. 74).

2.21 Document A/43/929*

Questions Relating to the Programme Budget: Use and Operation of the Contingency Fund (A/43/324)

Report of the Advisory Committee on Administrative and Budgetary Questions

9 December 1988

32. The size of the contingency fund is discussed in paragraphs 27 and 28 of the Secretary-General's report. A note by the Secretary-General on use and operation of the contingency fund has been submitted to the General Assembly (A/43/324).

33. In connection with procedures for the use and operation of the contingency fund, the Advisory Committee notes that the proposals of the Secretary-General in the annex to his note (A/43/324) follow the guidelines for the contingency fund contained in the annex to General Assembly resolution 42/211. The Advisory Committee therefore concurs in the proposals of the Secretary-General. The Committee also endorses paragraph 4 of the note, which concerns consequential changes to the rules of procedure of "the respective legislative bodies".

34. In paragraph 28 of the report on the proposed programme budget outline for the biennium 1990-1991 (A/43/524), the Secretary-General proposes that "the rate of 0.75 per cent should be adopted for the biennium 1990-1991 on the understanding that the Assembly should continue to keep under review the appropriateness and adequacy of this level". The Advisory Committee has no objection to the foregoing and accordingly recommends a contingency fund of 0.75 per cent of the preliminary estimate at 1990-1991 rates or $15 million, in round terms, for the budget outline for the biennium 1990-1991. At this stage, no advance appropriation should be made in respect of the contingency fund, but amounts, within its limit, should be appropriated as needed.

35. The Advisory Committee notes that the General Assembly, in paragraph 1 (d) of annex I to resolution 41/213, indicates that the size of the contingency fund shall be expressed as a "percentage of the overall level of resources", while in paragraph 8 of the same annex it is stated that the contingency fund shall be expressed as a "percentage of the overall budget level".

36. The Advisory Committee believes that it would be more consistent with the goal of setting a firm ceiling in the year the outline is considered if the size of the contingency fund did not fluctuate with the difference between the

---

*A/43/929, p. 9.

preliminary level of resources indicated in the outline and the level of the approved budget. In the opinion of the Committee the contingency fund should remain at the level set in the budget outline, with the understanding that the amount so approved is a ceiling, which need not be reached but cannot be exceeded. A similar approach could be taken with the reserve discussed above. Otherwise, every time the appropriations change (i.e., through recourse to the contingency or reserve) the size, in money terms, of the contingency fund and the reserve would change and predictability, which is at the core of the new budget process, would be eroded.

2.22 Document A/43/16*

Question Relating to the Programme Budget:
Use and Operation of the Contingency Fund (A/43/324)

Report of the Committee for Programme and Co-ordination

1989

75. At its 41st meeting, on 26 May, the Committee considered the note by the Secretary-General on questions relating to the programme budget: use and operation of the contingency fund (A/43/324).

Conclusions and recommendations

76. The Committee recommended acceptance of the proposal in the Secretary-General's note that the text of regulation 3.2 of the Regulations and Rules Governing Programme Planning, the Programme Aspects of the Budget, the Monitoring of Implementation and the Methods of Evaluation should be expanded, as indicated in the annex to the Secretary-General's note, to reflect the decisions on the contingency fund taken by the General Assembly in its resolution 42/211 of 21 December 1987.

77. The Committee noted that, should the General Assembly approve these changes to regulation 3.2, it might also be deemed appropriate, in due course, to modify the rules of procedure of the respective legislative bodies to reflect the consequential changes in their procedures.

Official Record of the General Assembly, Forty-third Session, Supplement No. 16 (A/43/16), p. 15.

2.23 Document E/1988/75*

Report of the Special Commission of the Economic and Social Council on the In-depth Study of the United Nations Intergovernmental Structure and Functions in the Economic and Social Fields

1 June 1988

CONTENTS

		Para-graphs
Introduction		1 - 7
I. Organizational matters		8 - 21
	A. Opening and duration of the Special Commission	8 - 9
	B. Attendance	10 - 15
	C. Election of officers	16
	D. Agenda and organization of work	17 - 18
	E. Documentation	19 - 21

Annexes

I.   Informal paper presented by the Group of 77 on 1 September 1987

II. Informal papers presented by delegations or groups of delegations

III. A.   Informal consolidated discussion paper presented by the Chairman on 21 April 1988

B.   Paper introduced by the Chairman on 23 May 1988 as a supplement to the informal consolidated discussion paper presented by the Chairman on 21 April 1988

IV. Chairman's text dated 4 May 1988 on the draft conclusions and recommendations of the Special Commission (E/SCN.1/CRP.1)

---

*E/1988/75, excluding section II and annexes V to X.

Introduction

1. At its organizational session for 1987, the Economic and Social Council, by decision 1987/112, established the Special Commission of the Economic and Social Council on the In-depth Study of the United Nations Intergovernmental Structure and Functions in the Economic and Social Fields, open to the full participation of all States Members of the United Nations on an equal basis, and invited Governments to participate at the highest possible level in the work of the Commission.

2. In accordance with the provisions of Council decision 1987/112, the Special Commission was to carry out the in-depth study of the United Nations intergovernmental structure and functions in the economic and social fields and its secretariat support structures, as called for in recommendation 8 of the Group of High-level Intergovernmental Experts to Review the Efficiency of the Administrative and Financial Functioning of the United Nations,[1] referred to in section I, paragraph 1 (e), of General Assembly resolution 41/213. Recommendation 8 of the Group of High-level Intergovernmental Experts reads as follows:

"Recommendation 8

"(1) A careful and in-depth study of the intergovernmental structure in the economic and social fields should be undertaken by an intergovernmental body to be designated by the General Assembly. This body should preferably have a limited membership, at the highest possible level of representation and based on the principle of equitable geographical distribution. In discharging its tasks, the body should seek the co-operation of the intergovernmental organs whose functions are being reviewed in the study and draw on the expertise of relevant United Nations bodies, such as the Joint Inspection Unit and the United Nations Institute for Training and Research.

"(2) In general terms, the study should include a comparative analysis of agenda, calendars and programmes of work of the General Assembly, the Economic and Social Council and related subsidiary bodies, in particular the United Nations Conference on Trade and Development, the United Nations Development Programme, the United Nations Fund for Population Activities, the United Nations Children's Fund, the United Nations Environment Programme, the United Nations Centre for Human Settlements (Habitat), the Office of the United Nations High Commissioner for Refugees and the World Food Council. The study should also include their support structures.

"(3)   The purpose of the study should be, *inter alia*, to:

"(a)   Identify   measures   to   rationalize   and   simplify   the
intergovernmental   structure,   avoid   duplication   and   consider
consolidating and co-ordinating overlapping activities and merging
existing bodies in order to improve their work and make the
structure more responsive to present needs;

"(b)   Develop criteria for the establishment and duration of
subsidiary bodies, including periodic reviews of their work and
mechanisms for implementing their decisions;

"(c)   Define in precise terms areas of responsibility for the various
bodies. Particular attention should be given to strengthening the
coherence   and   integrity   of   the   structure,   to   facilitating   the
formulation of a comprehensive approach to development issues
and to the necessity of putting more emphasis on regional and
subregional co-operation;

"(d)   Consider the establishment of a single governing body
responsible   for   the   management   and   control,   at   the
intergovernmental level, of United Nations operational activities for
development;

"(e)   Improve the system of reporting from subsidiary to principal
organs, thereby reducing the number of reports and avoiding
duplication of documentation;

"(f)   Strengthen on a continuous basis the co-ordination of
activities in the economic and social fields under the leadership of
the Secretary-General.

"(4)   The study should be undertaken as a matter of priority and its
findings and recommendations should be presented to the General
Assembly not later than at its forty-third session."

3.   In decision 1987/112, the Council requested the Special Commission to
consider, in the context of the in-depth study, the relevant provisions of
recommendation 2 of the Group of High-level Intergovernmental Experts. The
relevant   provisions   of   recommendation   2   of   the   Group   of   High-level
Intergovernmental Experts read as follows:

"*Recommendation 2*

"The number of conferences and meetings can be significantly reduced and
their duration shortened without affecting the substantive work of the
Organization. To this end:

"(a)   The Economic and Social Council should be invited to hold an annual session;

"(b)   The General Assembly and the Economic and Social Council should request their subsidiary bodies to review urgently their current agenda and schedules of meetings in order to reduce substantially their number, frequency and duration. In this context, the move towards biennialization of conferences and meetings, which has been initiated particularly in the economic and social fields, should be vigorously pursued;

"...

"(d)   Until 1978, a number of resolutions had requested that only one major conference be scheduled annually. The decision of the General Assembly that no more than five special conferences should take place in a given year and that no more than one special conference should be convened at the same time should be strictly implemented."

4.   In decision 1987/112, the Council requested all subsidiary bodies of the General Assembly in the economic and social sectors and all subsidiary bodies of the Economic and Social Council to submit to the Special Commission, within 30 days of the conclusion of their forthcoming sessions, their views and proposals on achieving the objectives envisaged in recommendation 8 of the Group of High-level Intergovernmental Experts regarding their functioning and that of their subsidiary machinery.

5.   The Council also requested the Secretary-General to submit to the Special Commission the following:

(a)   Information on the intergovernmental machinery of the United Nations in the economic and social fields and its secretariat support structures, including information concerning terms of reference, programmes of work, agenda, reporting procedures and periodicity of meetings, that information to be submitted to the Special Commission at its first session;

(b)   A list of available United Nations studies on the functioning and restructuring of the intergovernmental bodies in the economic and social sectors, as well as legislative decisions taken in that regard;

(c)   Other studies and analyses as required by the Special Commission.

6.   The Council also decided that the proceedings of the Special Commission would be governed in all other respects by the relevant rules of procedure of the Economic and Social Council (E/5715/Rev.1) and that, in undertaking its task, the Special Commission should establish, as appropriate, drafting or working groups.

7. In its decision 1987/112 the Council requested the Special Commission to make its final report available in time for consideration by the Council at its second regular session of 1988. In this connection, in the same decision and by resolution 1987/64, the Council requested the Secretary-General, to the extent possible within existing resources, to provide conference services, facilities and other necessary support on a preferential basis to the Special Commission to enable it to operate with sufficient frequency as from the first half of 1987 to fulfil its mandate in the limited time available.

I. Organizational matters

A. *Opening and duration of the Special Commission*

8. The Special Commission of the Economic and Social Council on the In-depth Study of the United Nations Intergovernmental Structure and Functions in the Economic and Social Fields held nine sessions at United Nations Headquarters from 2 March 1987 to 23 May 1988. The Special Commission held 36 meetings (1st to 36th) and a number of informal meetings.

9. The sessions were opened by the Chairman of the Special Commission, Abdel Halim Badawi (Egypt), appointed by the Economic and Social Council by decision 1987/112 of 6 February 1987.

B. *Attendance*

10. In accordance with the provisions of Economic and Social Council decision 1987/112, the Special Commission was open to the full participation of all States Members of the United Nations on an equal basis.

11. Representatives and observers of the following States attended the Special Commission:

> Algeria, Argentina, Australia, Austria, Bahamas, Bangladesh, Barbados, Belgium, Belize, Benin, Bolivia, Burundi, Byelorussian Soviet Socialist Republic, Cameroon, Canada, Cape Verde, Chile, China, Colombia, Costa Rica, Cuba, Cyprus, Czechoslovakia, Denmark, Dominican Republic, Ecuador, Egypt, Ethiopia, Finland, France, German Democratic Republic, Germany, Federal Republic of, Ghana, Greece, Grenada, Guatemala, Guinea, Guyana, Holy See, Hungary, Iceland, India, Indonesia, Iran (Islamic Republic of), Iraq, Ireland, Italy, Jamaica, Japan, Jordan, Kenya, Lesotho, Libyan Arab Jamahiriya, Madagascar, Malaysia, Malta, Mexico, Mongolia, Morocco, Mozambique, Nepal, Netherlands, New Zealand, Nicaragua, Nigeria, Norway, Oman, Pakistan, Panama, Peru, Philippines, Poland, Portugal, Republic of Korea, Romania, Rwanda, Saudi Arabia, Senegal, Sierra Leone, Somalia, Spain, Sri Lanka, Sudan, Suriname, Sweden, Tanzania, Togo, Trinidad and Tobago, Tunisia, Turkey, Uganda, Ukrainian Soviet Socialist Republic, Union of Soviet Socialist Republics,

United Kingdom of Great Britain and Northern Ireland, United Republic of Tanzania, United States of America, Uruguay, Venezuela, Viet Nam, Yugoslavia, Zambia.

12. The following specialized agencies were represented:

International Labour Organisation
Food and Agriculture Organization of the United Nations
United Nations Educational, Scientific and Cultural Organization
World Health Organization
World Bank
International Monetary Fund
International Fund for Agricultural Development
United Nations Industrial Development Organization

13. The International Atomic Energy Agency was also represented.

14. The following intergovernmental organizations was represented: European Community.

15. The following non-governmental organizations were represented:

International Chamber of Commerce
International Confederation of Free Trade Unions

C. Election of officers

16. At its 1st (organizational) meeting, on 13 February 1987, the Special Commission elected, pursuant to Council decision 1987/112 of 6 February 1987, the following four Vice-Chairmen by acclamation:

Chinmaya R. Gharekhan (India)
Adriaan Jacobovits de Szeged (Netherlands)
Lev I. Maksimov (Byelorussian Soviet Socialist Republic)
Mario Moya-Palencia (Mexico)

D. Agenda and organization of work

17. At its 2nd meeting, on 2 March 1987, the Special Commission adopted the agenda as contained in document E/SCN.1/1.

18. At its 25th meeting, on 18 January 1988, the Special Commission adopted its indicative programme of work as contained in document E/SCN.1/6.

E. Documentation

19. The Special Commission had before it the following documents:

(a)   Annotated provisional agenda (E/SCN.1/1);

(b)   Follow-up action to the recommendations contained in General Assembly resolution 32/197 relating to the functioning of the intergovernmental machinery of the United Nations: note by the Secretariat (E/SCN.1/2);

(c)   Secretariat support structures: note by the Secretariat (E/SCN.1/3);

(d)   Draft indicative programme of work: note by the Chairman (E/SCN.1/4);

(e)   Resolutions and decisions adopted by the Economic and Social Council at its second regular session of 1987 and the General Assembly at its forty-second session which are brought to the attention of the Special Commission of the Economic and Social Council on the In-depth Study of the United Nations Intergovernmental Structure and Functions in the Economic and Social Fields: note by the Secretariat (E/SCN.1/5);

(f)   Indicative programme of work (E/SCN.1/6).

20. In addition to the formal documentation listed above, the Special Commission also had before it informal working papers, including individual submissions made by all subsidiary bodies of the General Assembly in the economic and social sectors and all subsidiary bodies of the Economic and Social Council in response to the request made by the Council in decision 1987/112 (see annex VIII*).

21. In addition the Special Commission had before it synoptic summaries of its discussions on each of the subsidiary bodies, prepared by the Secretariat at the Special Commission's request (see annex IX*).

Note

1.   See *Official Records of the General Assembly, Forty-first Session, Supplement No. 49* (A/41/49).

---

*Not reprinted here.

ANNEX I

Informal paper presented by the Group of 77 on 1 September 1987

This paper is divided into three parts: section I describes the role and mandate of the Economic and Social Council; section II asks why the Council has not fulfilled its mandate; section III offers recommendations/proposals for reform.

I. Mandate of the Economic and Social Council

The functions and powers of the Council are spelt out in articles 60, 62 and 66 of the Charter of the United Nations. Its responsibilities were further clarified in section II of the annex to General Assembly resolution 32/197.

As articulated in the latter document the responsibilities of the Council are as follows:

(a) To serve as the central forum for the discussion of international economic and social issues of a global or interdisciplinary nature and the formulation of policy recommendations thereon addressed to member States and to the United Nations as a whole;

(b) To monitor and evaluate the implementation of overall strategies, policies and priorities established by the General Assembly in the economic, social and related fields, and to ensure the harmonization and coherent practical operation implementation on an integrated basis, of relevant policy decisions and recommendations emanating from United Nations conferences and other forums within the United Nations system after their approval by the Assembly and/or the Economic and Social Council;

(c) To ensure the overall co-ordination of the activities of the organizations of the United Nations system in the economic, social and related fields and, to that end, the implementation of the priorities established by the General Assembly for the system as a whole and in this task to engage itself in the budgetary process;

(d) To carry out comprehensive policy reviews of operation activities throughout the United Nations system, bearing in mind the need for balance, compatibility and conformity with the priorities established by the General Assembly for the system as a whole.

II. Has the Council fulfilled its mandate?

A plethora of reasons have been adduced to explain the failure of the Council to fulfil its mandate. Principal among these are:

(a) Restricted membership;

(b)   Expansion of its subsidiary machinery (necessitated, *inter alia* by the restrictive membership of the Council);

(c)   Short duration of meetings;

(d)   Inadequate secretariat support structure;

(e)   Lack of recognition of its authority by other (intergovernmental and inter-secretariat bodies) bodies of the United Nations system;

(f)   Dismal organization of work and reporting procedures.

III. Recommendations for reform

The following recommendations for the rationalization of the Council are proposed taking into account the close interrelationship between the Council and its subsidiary organs and the need to look at the reform of the Council bearing in mind that of its subsidiary machinery.

A. Universalization of its composition

This recommendation was mentioned in paragraph 13 of the annex to General Assembly resolution 32/197.

B. Relationship with its subsidiary machinery

The Council will assume to the maximum extent possible direct responsibility for performing the functions of its subsidiary bodies.

C. Integrated reporting structure by intergovernmental bodies in economic and social fields

The reporting procedure of the United Nations intergovernmental bodies in the economic and social fields should be modified to enable all bodies to report in the first instance to the Council and transmit to the General Assembly, it deemed appropriate, consolidated reports.

D. Increased duration of meetings and reorganization of working schedule

Reflective of its mandated responsibilities, the duration of its meetings should be increased. To better fulfil its functions of monitoring and evaluation, a reorganization of its schedule of meetings and methods of work should be achieved. Its working structure should also be reorganized in a manner that is consistent with and supportive of its role and functions.

E. *Relations with the work of the General Assembly*

The work and functions of the Council and the General Assembly should be co-ordinated and complementary, considering the pre-eminence of the General Assembly as the main and superior forum for policy-making in accordance with the Charter of the United Nations.

F. *Relations with specialized agencies*

Specialized agencies should participate actively in meetings of the Council. The specialized agencies should submit reports to the Council on how the latter's recommendations and policy guidelines are being fulfilled. This envisaged reporting arrangement would be different from that discarded in the 1970s, in that the reports emanating from the specialized agencies under the new arrangement will be more focused and specific, in particular regarding the implementation of the General Assembly guidelines.

G. *Relations with regional commissions*

The Council should increase its contribution to strengthening the co-operation and co-ordination of the activities of the regional commissions. The Council should devote more time to the consideration of substantive activities of the regional commissions (see para. 32 of A/42/232).

H. *Biennialization*

The Council should continue to biennialize, as appropriate, discussions/consideration of the items on its agenda and of the work of its subsidiary organs.

I. *Separate and identifiable secretariat support structure*

A separate and identifiable secretariat support structure, comparable to those of other chartered bodies, should be designed. The secretariat would among other things consolidate reports on related issues/themes that emanate from the United Nations system and make recommendations/summaries as appropriate (see para. 31 of A/42/232).

J. *Co-ordination of operational activities*

The Council should play its role of co-ordinating operational activities for development through an effective control and evaluation of management and implementation of these activities.

ANNEX II

Informal papers presented by delegations or groups of delegations

The following informal papers were presented by the delegations of
Australia, Canada, China, the Federal Republic of Germany (on behalf of the
member States of the European Community), Japan, Norway, Tunisia (on
behalf of the Group of 77), the Union of Soviet Socialist Republics (on behalf
of Bulgaria, the Byelorussian Soviet Socialist Republic, Czechoslovakia, the
German Democratic Republic, Hungary, Mongolia, Poland, the Ukrainian
Soviet Socialist Republic and the Union of Soviet Socialist Republics) and the
United States of America.

Delegation of Australia

Australia considers that the vital first step in the reform process is to agree on the principles or direction of reform, and then to settle on detailed arrangements.

Australia's views on the seven headings proposed by the Chairman of the informal meeting of the Special Commission on 14 April flow from our firm conviction that the aim of increasing the effectiveness and efficiency of the Economic and Social Council would be served by a net reduction in the resources required for the consideration of social and economic issues in the United Nations. The most commonsensical way of achieving this is to eliminate one level of debate at which issues are considered and to ensure that there are effective cross-organizational co-ordination mechanisms.

Therefore, under the heading: *"Role, responsibilities and relationships between the General Assembly, the Council and the Trade and Development Board"*, we seek to enhance and streamline the Council. In particular, we agree fully with proposals to reduce significantly the combined meeting time of the General Assembly and the Council, and to reduce substantially the unnecessary duplication of debate in these forums. Two general debates - perhaps at a spring session of the Trade and Development Board and at the General Assembly - could replace the current three at no loss to the United Nations system. The *World Economic Survey* and the *Trade and Development Report* could be combined in one useful, comprehensive study which would enjoy the prestige of being the report of the central United Nations organs on the state of the world's economy and its implications for developing countries.

Second, we believe that strong co-ordination is crucial to the successful operation of the intergovernmental machinery. Co-ordination between economic and social sectors, and within each of these sectors, is a difficult challenge which needs careful thought. What is needed is a mechanism for managing better the work-flow through the Council. In particular, we support proposals for an enhanced role for the Committee for Programme and Co-ordination (CPC). We also consider that the co-ordination function would be added by a modification of the secretariat procedures whereby the Secretary-General would be asked to present a report with recommendations on the Council's future work programme to the Council's annual organizational meeting. The Secretariat, in preparing its recommendations, would need to be directed to ensure that, to the greatest extent possible, the consideration of issues in the Council's subsidiary bodies was not repeated by the Council.

As regards the subsidiary bodies of the Council, we support with several other delegations, the elimination of as many subsidiary bodies as possible where the functions of those bodies are better carried out by another body or by the Council itself. For example, the Council could take over some of the functions from the Commission for Social Development, especially on broad social development issues and where economic factors are significant (for example, the World Social Situation). We also support the merger with the Council of some subsidiary bodies, such as the Committee on the Development and Utilization of New and Renewable Sources of Energy, and the Committee on Natural Resources.

Australia considers that operational activities for development issues should receive greater and more co-ordinated attention at the Council. We concur with delegations which propose that the Council should concentrate on the system-wide co-ordination aspects of operational activities, in particular exercising a cross-organization oversight or monitoring role to ensure that individual agencies' programmes are harmonized and consistent with one another.

Australia is of the view that there is a clear need for an examination of the macro-structure of the regional commissions and, in particular, the relationship between these regional commissions and the United Nations Development Programme (UNDP), but attention needs to be given to assigning priorities to programmes and activities within the regions.

It is again consonant with our objectives of increasing the United Nations efficiency and effectiveness that we would not want to see the universalization of membership of the Council, at least without the elimination of one entire level of debate in the economic and social fields. Such universalization without appropriate, durable reductions in other areas of the United Nations work would be unlikely to bring about greater efficiency, especially in relation to important functions such as co-ordination. Second, it would, in the economic field, duplicate the work already undertaken by the universal bodies with mandates in that field - the United Nations Conference on Trade and Development (UNCTAD), and the Second Committee of the General Assembly. Finally, it would make the Council's procedures more time-consuming. Such a change in the Council's composition would by itself not advance and may indeed run counter to the reform objective.

With regard to the last of the seven headings, we support the broad proposals of several other delegations for the streamlining and simplification of the secretariat structure so as to enhance, in particular, its ability to fulfil its important co-ordination function. In this regard, we would be interested in an elaboration of the proposal for a single integrated Council secretariat.

Delegation of Canada

Introduction: Reforms in the economic and social structure

As the Special Commission progresses to the final stage of its work, it is becoming increasingly apparent that some reforms are needed in order to make the United Nations economic and social sectors function more efficiently and effectively. In short, there is a need to make the present system less cumbersome and repetitive. There is also a need to enhance the ability of the Economic and Social Council in co-ordination and issue management, as envisaged by the Charter.

With this in mind, this paper offers suggestions for restructuring and reform on three fundamental levels:

(a)   The relationship between the General Assembly and the Council;

(b)   The relationship between the Council and its subsidiary bodies;

(c)   The secretariat support structure.

I. The relationship between the General Assembly and the Council

A major source of inefficiency and ineffectiveness in the economic and social sectors is the repetition and overlap between the work of the General Assembly and the Council. What is needed is a clearer division of labour between these two Charter bodies and a bolstering of the Council's role as an effective management "filter" and tool for the General Assembly. We are proposing:

For the General Assembly:

To shorten the duration and agenda of the Second (Economic) and Third (Social) Committees of the General Assembly:

(a)   Each would meet concurrently for three weeks from mid-November to December;

(b)   Each would concentrate on two annual agenda items:

Item 1. General Debate: World Economic/Social-Human Rights Situation;

Item 2. Executive Recommendations from the Council.

For the Council:

(a)   To convene an annual plenary session of the Council concurrently with the General Assembly session, but prior to the sessions of the Second and Third Committees of the General Assembly, in order to maximize the opportunity for high-level participation:

(i)   The plenary session of the Council would meet from end September to end October;

(ii)   The work plan of the plenary session of the Council would be organized in such a way as to complement the six-year medium-term plan cycle of the United Nations. It would ensure that over a period of six years, all sectors of the Council activity would be scrutinized by the Council at least once;

(iii)   The Council would act as a management "filter" for the General Assembly;

(iv)   For the first two weeks it would consider and, as much as possible, take decisions on recommendations emanating from economic/social subsidiary bodies;

(v)   For the third week it would consider and take decisions on the social and economic sections of the medium-term plan and of the biennial programme budget;

(vi)   A few days would be set aside to approve the Executive Report of the Council to the General Assembly. This single and brief document would highlight the key economic and social policy issues (with recommendations from the Council) which should be considered by the General Assembly;

(b)   To allow the Council to fulfil its Charter mandate and fully to play its co-ordinating role. The Council would therefore act as an executive board for those economic and social intergovernmental bodies that do not have their own board and as an overview and co-ordination organ for all other economic and social institutions in the United Nations system. The Council would have final legislative authority on most economic and social matters. In other words, the Second and Third Committees of the General Assembly would no longer reconsider and approve all Council work. Consequently the General Assembly would be "freed-up" to examine only key policy recommendations from the Council ("Executive Report"), and could more effectively consider emerging global issues and priorities each year;

(c)   In light of the aforementioned, to consider enlarging or universalizing the membership of the Council;

(d)   To convene an annual one week organizational session of the Council in late January for the purpose of incorporating new General Assembly mandates into the existing Council work programme and for holding Council elections and appointments.

II. The relationship between the Council and its subsidiary bodies

A major source of inefficiency and ineffectiveness in the economic and social sectors is due to the Council's inability to properly overview, analyse and co-ordinate its sectors of responsibility on a system-wide basis. What is needed primarily is a reorganization of the Council's Committee structure, better use/consolidation of expertise and resources within its sub-body structure, reporting tailored to the Council's needs, a biennial and triennial work programme and an improved interaction with the specialized agencies. We are proposing:

Committee structure:

(a)   To modify the Council's present Committee structure into shorter, more focused meetings taking place every two months, organized along sectoral lines as follows:

(i)   Operational activities/regional co-operation: in late March to review operational activities/regional economic commissions and economic/social programmes region by region;

(ii) Social co-operation/human rights: in late May to review social issues/human rights and intergovernmental bodies and institutions;

(iii) Economic co-operation/technical functional co-operation: meeting in mid-July to review economic issues/technical-functional co-operation and intergovernmental bodies and institutions;

Reporting:

(b)   To have the Council consider consolidated "management reports" on a given item or sector. In other words, the Council would no longer need to review individual technical reports from subsidiary bodies. "Management reports" to the Council would:

(i)   Provide a system-wide overview and analysis of latest developments in an item/sector and assess longer-term implications;

(ii) Give particular attention to co-ordination issues;

(iii) Monitor implementation of mandates and assess user-benefits (where applicable);

(iv)   Outline select policy recommendations for possible incorporation into the Council's final "Executive Report" to the General Assembly;

Subsidiary bodies:

(c)   To consolidate, to the greatest extent possible, the expertise and resources of related spheres of activities/sectors. In other words, rationalize, simplify and streamline the present subsidiary body structure of the Council, aimed at a clearer division of labour between the Council and its sub-structure:

Where possible, decentralize expertise and analytical capabilities to the technical expert level or the most established and capable United Nations research body in a given sector;

Work methods:

(d)   To adopt a biennial work programme for agenda items and a triennial system-wide review of Council sectors;

(e)   To adopt a thematic or priority issue approach during the system-wide review of each Council sector;

(f)   The Council and its subsidiary bodies would adopt improved working methods along the lines of those recommended by the Trade and Development Board and ECE in their submissions to the Special Commission;

Specialized agencies:

(g)   To encourage a more active and focused participation of specialized agencies (particularly the "Big Four": WHO, FAO, ILO, UNESCO) in the aforementioned work programme and Committee structure of the Council. This would be achieved through submission of brief thematic reports/statements, as well as through informal discussions or seminars;

(h)   To establish close administrative links between ACC and the secretariat of the Council;

Co-ordination:

(i)   To ensure that co-ordination becomes an integral aspect of the Council's work, through the improved reporting and Committee structure proposed above;

(j)   To ensure that the relationship of the Council and CPC is more complementary, particularly on system-wide co-ordination issues in the economic/social sectors:

The plenary session of the Council would devote one week for considering the economic and social sectors of the medium-term plan and the United Nations programme budget. The Council would also take on responsibilities for cross-organizational reviews of medium-term plans/cross-organizational programme analyses for areas of its responsibility.

III. The Secretariat support structure

The present secretariat support structure in the economic and social sectors would need to be modified in line with the structural and reporting changes outlined above. What is clearly needed is a substantive secretariat support structure to properly service a restructured Council, particularly with respect to quality control and preparation of "management reports" to the Council, as well as the Council's annual "Executive Report" to the General Assembly:

A separate secretariat unit for the Council drawn from expertise in the existing Secretariat structure (both substantive and support services).

We are proposing:

(a) To transfer, as much as possible, all project-oriented and programme-implementation secretariat units in the social field to Vienna;

(b) To transfer, as much as possible, all economic analysis secretariat units in the economic field to Geneva;

(c) To transfer, as much as possible, all secretariat units responsible for implementing operational activities to the regional economic commission;

(d) To consolidate all remaining economic or social policy secretariat units into a Council department based in New York;

(e) A Council department subdivided into two divisions:

(i) Operational activities;

(ii) Council support;

(f) The Council Support Division would be headed by an Under-Secretary-General, who would also be Head of the Department. The Under-Secretary-General for the Council would be a full member of ACC and would chair an "Economic and Social Sectors Committee" composed of the Heads of the Geneva and Vienna offices, the Director-General of UNCTAD, the Head of the Operational Activities Division and the Heads of all other economic and social sections of the Secretariat providing support to the intergovernmental bodies in sectors I, II, III, and VI of the Council (see appendix I);

(g)   The Operational Activities Division would be headed by a Director-General, who would chair an Operational Activities and Regional Co-operation Sectors Committee composed of the Administrator of UNDP, the Executive-Secretaries of the regional economic commissions, the Executive-Director of UNEP, and other intergovernmental bodies in sectors IV and V.

Appendix I: Sectoral structure of the Economic and Social Council

I.   Economic co-operation sector:

(a)   Commission on Transnational Corporations;
(b)   Committee for Development Planning;
(c)   Trade and Development Board;
(d)   World Food Council;
(e)   United Nations Environment Programme;
(f)   Committee on the Development and Utilization of New and Renewable Sources of Energy;
(g)   Committee on Natural Resources.

II.   Social co-operation sector:

(a)   Commission for Social Development;
(b)   Commission on the Status of Women;
(c)   Committee on Economic, Social and Cultural Rights;
(d)   Commission on Human Settlements;
(e)   Population Commission;
(f)   Commission on Narcotic Drugs;
(g)   Committee on Crime Prevention and Control.

III. Human rights sector:

Commission on Human Rights

IV.   Operational activities sector:

(a)   United Nations Development Programme;
(b)   United Nations Population Fund;
(c)   Department of Technical Co-operation for Development;
(d)   United Nations Capital Development Fund;
(e)   United Nations Children's Fund;
(f)   Office of the United Nations High Commissioner for Refugees;
(g)   Committee on Food Aid Policies and Programmes;
(h)   World Food Programme.

V.   Regional co-operation sector:

(a)   Economic Commission for Europe;

(b) Economic and Social Commission for Asia and the Pacific;
(c) Economic Commission for Latin America and the Caribbean;
(d) Economic Commission for Africa;
(e) Economic and Social Commission for Western Asia.

VI. Technical and functional co-operation sector:

(a) Intergovernmental Committee on Science and Technology for Development;
(b) Advisory Committee on Science and Technology for Development;
(c) Intergovernmental Working Group of Experts on International Standards of Accounting and Reporting;
(d) *Ad Hoc* Intergovernmental Working Group on the Problems of Corrupt Practices;
(e) United Nations Group of Experts on Geographical Names;
(f) Meeting of Experts on the United Nations Programme in Public Administration and Finance;
(g) *Ad Hoc* Group of Experts on International Co-operation in Tax Matters;
(h) Statistical Commission;
(i) Committee of Experts on the Transport of Dangerous Goods;
(j) Committee on Non-Governmental Organizations.

Appendix II: Committee structure of the Economic and Social Council

I. First Committee (Economic co-operation/technical-functional co-operation):

(a) Economic co-operation sector:
(i) Commission on Transnational Corporations;
(ii) Committee for Development Planning;
(iii) Trade and Development Board;
(iv) World Food Council;
(v) United Nations Environment Programme;
(vi) Committee on the Development and Utilization of New and Renewable Sources of Energy;
(vii) Committee on Natural Resources.
(b) Technical and functional co-operation sector:
(i) Intergovernmental Committee on Science and Technology for Development;
(ii) Advisory Committee on Science and Technology for Development;
(iii) Intergovernmental Working Group of Experts on International Standards of Accounting and Reporting;
(iv) *Ad Hoc* Intergovernmental Working Group on the Problems of Corrupt Practices;
(v) United Nations Group of Experts on Geographical Names;

(vi)   Meeting of Experts on the United Nations Programme in Public
         Administration and Finance;
(vii)   *Ad Hoc* Group of Experts on International Co-operation in Tax
         Matters;
(viii)   Statistical Commission;
(ix)   Committee of Experts on the Transport of Dangerous Goods;
(x)   Committee on Non-Governmental Organizations.

II. Second Committee (Social co-operation/human rights):

(a)   Social co-operation sector:
(i)   Commission on Social Development;
(ii)   Commission on the Status of Women;
(iii)   Committee on Economic, Social and Cultural Rights;
(iv)   Commission on Human Settlements;
(v)   Population Commission;
(vi)   Commission on Narcotic Drugs;
(vii)   Committee on Crime Prevention and Control.
(b)   Human rights sector:
         Commission on Human Rights

*III.   Third   Committee   (Operational   activities/regional   co-
operation):*

(a)   Operational activities sector:
(i)   United Nations Development Programme;
(ii)   United Nations Population Fund;
(iii)   Department of Technical Co-operation for Development;
(iv)   United Nations Capital Development Fund;
(v)   United Nations Children's Fund;
(vi)   Office of the United Nations High Commissioner for Refugees;
(vii)   Committee on Food Aid Policies and Programmes;
(viii)   World Food Programme;
(b)   Regional co-operation sector:
(i)   Economic Commission for Europe;
(ii)   Economic and Social Commission for Asia and the Pacific;
(iii)   Economic Commission for Latin America and the Caribbean;
(iv)   Economic Commission for Africa;
(v)   Economic and Social Commission for Western Asia

Appendix III: Scenario for sessions of the Economic and Social Council

Organizational Committee of the Council, one-week session - late January

The purpose of the Organizational Committee session of the Council would
be to:

(a)   Assess how the general or thematic debates held in the fall by the Second and Third Committees should impact on the Council's work-plan and on the United Nations system.   Specifically, to translate decisions and resolutions of the General Assembly into additional instructions for economic and social intergovernmental bodies funded under the regular budget or into statements of guidance for specialized agencies and for voluntary-funded organizations financing or conducting operational activities;

(b)   Call for specific studies and reports from secretariat units, intergovernmental bodies, specialized agencies and organizations;

(c)   Set the agenda and work-plans of the plenary session of the Council and other sectoral committees of the Council;

(d)   Hold Council elections and appointments.

Annual plenary session of the Council, end September to late October
New York

The purpose of the annual plenary session of the Council would be to:

(a)   Review the summary assessments and recommendations prepared by its sectoral committees;

(b)   Review the economic and social sections of the medium-term plan and biennial budget;

(c)   Consider and adopt the final "Executive Report" of select policy recommendations to the General Assembly (no resolutions or decisions).

The plenary session of the Council would be organized in such a way as to ensure that over a period of six years, corresponding to the operating cycle of the United Nations medium-term plan, all sectors, all regions, and a full set of economic and social issues have been scrutinized at least once.   The plenary session of the Council would convene primarily for the purpose of adopting a single "Executive Report" of key policy recommendations for consideration by the Second (Economic) and Third (Social) Committees of the General Assembly.

Appendix IV: Criteria for subsidiary intergovernmental bodies

Here are some preliminary thoughts on criteria that the Council might use to make decisions in regard to its subsidiary bodies. If this is of interest, we could further refine the ideas.

A. Criteria for establishment of new intergovernmental bodies

A recommendation for the creation of a new intergovernmental body (subsidiary to the Council) should not lead to the creation of a new body unless it has been subjected to the following "four-filter" mechanisms:

(a)   Filter one: Specialized agencies:

Would the proposed body deal with issues or questions that are within the mandate of an existing specialized agencies?   (E.g., UNESCO is already mandated and perfectly capable of taking on the activities of a science and technology body; there is therefore no reason to create one).

(b)   Filter two: Regional economic commissions:

Does the issue or question interest primarily the members of particular regions (e.g., because the expertise lies there)? Would the new body engage in activities or programmes that can have a direct impact on member States? Are the regional economic commissions able to provide support services?

(c)   Filter three: Structure of the Council and operating cycle:

(i)   Would it be possible to address the issue by amending or extending the mandate of an existing intergovernmental body?

(ii) Could the Council deal with the issue by integrating it in its operating cycle (i.e., looking at it as part of its regular overview of economic or social questions)?

(d)   Filter four: Expert group:

Can the issue be dealt with by an *ad hoc* group of experts that would meet as the need arises?

B. Mandating and monitoring

The first responsibility of the Council is to mandate properly the new intergovernmental body. The work of the Council would be simplified and made more rational if the three following criteria were adopted:

(a)   Complementarily criterion:

(i)   The Council would first assign the new body to a sector and adjust its mandate to ensure that there is no duplication with existing bodies;

(ii) The Council would then ensure that the rest of the sector is itself adjusted to take into account the new body.

(b) Practicality criterion:

The new body would be given (or asked to recommend to the Council) a formal definition of its objectives for its first two years (detailed plan of its work-programme) and a long-term outline for the first five years (only if the body is expected to be needed for that period of time).

(c) Monitoring criterion:

The Council would review the new intergovernmental body after it has completed its first 24 months. The purpose of the review being to make adjustments as required, in order for the body to function at peak effectiveness and efficiency.

C. Review, evaluation and reform

In the course of its regular six-year overview of all economic and social issues and intergovernmental bodies, and of all regions, the Council would review, evaluate and, if necessary, reform the new intergovernmental body. The work of the Council would be made simpler if the three following criteria were used:

(a) Effectiveness criterion:

(i) Does the intergovernmental body meet its stated objectives and is it fulfilling its work-programme?

(ii) Is the level of participation satisfactory?

(b) Efficiency criterion:

(i) How does the cost of running the intergovernmental body compare with the average?

(ii) How much secretariat service does it require to function?

(c) Overview criterion:

Every six years, the Council would review how well the current priorities of the member States are reflected in the structure and in the agenda of the intergovernmental bodies. The Council would also attempt to identify the lowest priorities.

D. *Merger, suspension or elimination*

Substantive review criterion:

> The intergovernmental bodies that are least effective or efficient (see
> above criteria) would be reviewed. Either their mandates and the
> work-programmes would be strengthened and updated or the bodies
> would be merged into others, temporarily suspended, or, ultimately,
> eliminated.

Structural review criterion:

> Intergovernmental bodies that are at the low end of the priority scale
> (whether or not they are effective and efficient) would be reviewed.
> Either their mandates and the work-programmes would be
> strengthened and updated or the bodies would be merged into others,
> temporarily suspended, or, ultimately, eliminated.

Delegation of China

The purpose of the structural reform of the United Nations system in the economic and social fields is to strengthen the role of the United Nations in enhancing economic co-operation and development and in promoting social progress. In other words, it is to enable the United Nations organs and bodies to better address the urgent problems confronted in the economic and social fields, to enhance their capabilities of coping with the challenges the future may present, and to revitalize them so that they can better fulfil their mandates under the Charter and serve the member States, particularly the developing countries, more effectively.

In order to achieve the above-mentioned objective, it is necessary to simplify and rationalize the existing system, raise the efficiency of the intergovernmental organs and the secretariat supporting structure.

In accordance with the relevant provisions of the Charter and General Assembly resolution 32/197, it is for the General Assembly to concentrate on the establishment of overall strategies, policies and priorities for the system as a whole while the Council should function in finding ways and means to monitor and evaluate the implementation of the strategies, policies and priorities, to serve as the central forum for the discussion of international economic and social problems and the formulation of policy recommendations and to co-ordinate the overall activities of its subsidiary bodies and specialized agencies.

There should be good co-ordination between the General Assembly and the Council with each having its respective focuses, and overlapping should be avoided. The strengthening of the role of the Council should be considered in conjunction with the strengthening of the role of the Second and Third Committees.

Practice has shown that the biannualized arrangement for the review of agenda items of the Council and for the meetings of the subsidiary bodies is effective and therefore should be continued.

The number and duration of meetings should be reduced as much as possible. Discussions should focus on important issues of common concern. The number of papers and documents should be cut down and the quality of meetings improved. The bureau should see to it that the secretariat prepares the papers and documents required for the meetings in good time. The meetings should start punctually and there should be a limitation on the length of statements to be made.

The Council convenes every year an organizational session to plan its work for the whole year and one regular session to consider the reports submitted by the subsidiary organs, specialized agencies and regional economic commissions, decide on the recommendations to be submitted to the General Assembly, and carry out policy planning and co-ordination within its mandate. *Ad hoc*, subject-oriented and high-level meetings may be convened when necessary. The regular sessions of the Council must not overlap with those of the General Assembly.

It is necessary to revise the reporting procedures for the intergovernmental organs in the economic and social fields. All these organs should first report to the Council, which should improve its filtering function so that its reports to the General Assembly are brief and to the point, with due emphasis on all major issues. The various organs should submit their respective reports in good time, and their chief executives should take an active part in the discussion. In addition, repetition in reports should be avoided and the number of similar reports should be cut down.

The Council should discharge its responsibility of co-ordinating and monitoring the functioning of its subsidiary organs in accordance with the relevant provisions of the Charter. It should turn the positive inputs from the subsidiary organs into concerted policies, provide those organs with policy guidelines, and follow their development to ensure the effective implementation of its policy decisions in day-to-day work and in all its activities. While strengthening the Council, measures should also be adopted to ensure the vitality of the subsidiary organs, increase the participation and input of professionals and improve the quality of meetings. With respect to the few subsidiary organs whose functions might be taken over directly by the Council, there should be clear-cut and strict standards, and the whole matter must be handled with great care.

In accordance with the relevant provisions of the Charter, the Council should co-ordinate the activities of the specialized agencies so as to avoid unnecessary overlapping. Of course, the Council should also consult the specialized agencies and respect the agreements signed with them. The specialized agencies should actively participate, as required by the functions of the Council, in the relevant Council meetings and submit to the latter implementation reports with proper focus, clear recommendations and inputs from experts so as to facilitate the work of relevant Council meetings.

While strengthening its role of co-ordination, the Council should pay attention to giving full play to the role of the existing co-ordinating organs, including CPC.

While strengthening the role of its Third Committee in co-ordinating development operational activities, the Council should also give full play to the role of existing organs of co-ordination, including the Joint Committee on Policy Co-ordination.

In accordance with the global development strategy and policies adopted by the General Assembly, the Council should put greater emphasis on considering the reports of the regional economic commissions concerning the implementation of their substantive activities, and should, in light of the need for co-operation among the regional commissions, co-ordinate the activities on a global basis and strengthen the role of the regional economic commissions.

It is essential to improve the quality of work of the supporting structure of the secretariat, strengthen the co-ordination among these units, reduce the structural layers within the secretariat, improve the quality of staff, and strictly abide by the principle of equitable geographical distribution in recruiting the staff so as to adapt to the new situation and new tasks of the Council after the reform.

*Delegation of the Federal Republic of Germany (on behalf
of the member States of the European Community)*

In accordance with General Assembly resolution 41/213 and Economic and Social Council decision 1987/112, it is the purpose of the in-depth study of the United Nations intergovernmental structure and functions in the economic and social fields to identify measures which would enable the United Nations - as an indispensable instrument for multilateral co-operation - to fulfil its functions better, as defined in the Charter (especially in Art. 1, paras. 3 and 4), to promote international economic and social co-operation and universal respect for human rights and fundamental freedoms. In line with recommendation 8 of the report of the Group of 18, which is based upon broad recognition of the need for the efficiency of the United Nations to be improved and for reform as a matter of priority, restructuring should aim at strengthening the effectiveness of the United Nations and improving its efficiency by simplifying and rationalizing the intergovernmental machinery and its secretariat support structure. In particular, in the economic field the areas of responsibility for the General Assembly, the Council and the Trade and Development Board of the United Nations Conference on Trade and Development must be defined more clearly, while in the social field the debate in the Council might be tailored more closely to its supervisory function and co-ordinating role *vis-à-vis* the functional commissions. Furthermore, any reform effort has to take into consideration the special and distinct emphasis given by the Charter to the issue of human rights as reflected also in the existing relevant institutional framework (Art. 68 of the Charter). This is why for the purposes of this paper a distinction is made between economic, social and human rights issues.

I. General Assembly

The General Assembly should play its role as the supreme United Nations organ in the economic and social fields (United Nations Charter, Art. 60), and as a forum for policy-making and harmonizing international action. The General Assembly should continue to give political guidance by formulating overall strategies and setting political priorities. The General Assembly, in its deliberative function in economic matters, should provide the forum for the general debate on macro-economic issues in the autumn, complemented by the general economic discussion of the Trade and Development Board (in the spring) with its emphasis on trade and development aspects, making redundant the traditional general debate on macro-economic issues in the Council. More generally, in order to fulfil these functions properly, the work of the General Assembly must be better prepared and more focused so that it becomes not only more effective, but also substantially shorter. This could be achieved by rationalizing its agenda, including by means of biennialization of agenda items. The Council should have the primary responsibility for establishing the agenda of the General Assembly in the social and economic areas.

II. Economic and Social Council

In order to facilitate better focused and shorter work of the General Assembly, the Council should submit to it reports on the work done by the Council and its subsidiary machinery in the economic field, with the current practice of technical reports in the social field to be continued. These reports in the economic field should - just as those submitted to the Council by the subsidiary bodies - highlight issues where political guidance by the General Assembly is needed, with the understanding that the General Assembly, in its concrete work, would concentrate on these issues, without prejudice to the comprehensive deliberative function of the plenary meeting of the General Assembly. The new reporting system would necessitate an appropriately focused input from the Secretariat.

In its co-ordinating role the Council is supported by the Committee for Programme and Co-ordination (CPC). The respective areas of responsibility for the Council and CPC must be defined more clearly, with the Council providing the necessary political authority, which CPC recommendations have been lacking so far:

(a) CPC, in accordance with its role as main subsidiary organ for planning, programming and co-ordination, and in view of its new responsibilities in the field of budgeting, should focus its co-ordinating efforts on the United Nations itself ("intra-co-ordination");

(b) The Council should, as envisaged in the Charter, co-ordinate programme activities effectively on a system-wide basis ("inter-co-ordination").

CPC co-ordination instruments such as cross-organizational programme analyses/cross-organizational review of medium-term plans, ACC/CPC meetings and ACC reports should be adapted to the role to be played by the Council. The Council should adopt a thematic/sectoral approach where applicable. It should establish its agenda on the basis of a flexible multibiennial work-programme. The cross-sectoral approach would necessitate the active participation of the agencies concerned. The working calendars of the subsidiary bodies would have to be adapted to the needs of the Council.

Concerning the regional commissions, the Council should ensure coherence between global and regional activities and facilitate interregional co-operation. Reports from the regional commissions should focus on questions which have actual or potential global implications or which have important implications for other regions. The Council and its subsidiary organs should be used as a framework for the preparation of, and the follow-up to international conferences and high-level meetings, which might themselves - as appropriate - take place within the Council context.

The Council's co-ordinating role should in particular be strengthened in the field of operational activities for development, with its role defined in more concrete terms.   The Council should concentrate on the system-wide co-ordination aspect of the implementation of policies and programme activities, defining - as necessary - specific areas of activity for the different United Nations agencies and organs in order to ensure coherent and effective programme delivery.   The primary responsibility for programme policy decisions and the review of programme implementation is to remain with the governing organs of the individual programmes and the agencies concerned. More specifically, for the years to come the co-ordination role of the Council should be defined along the lines of the provisions of General Assembly resolution 42/196, i.e. monitoring of the functioning of the inter-secretariat co-ordinating mechanisms and acting on policy proposals made by the Director-General to facilitate the solution of problems encountered in ACC, defining a more effective programming process overseeing the simplification and harmonization of delivery and the reporting procedures of the United Nations organs and agencies and re-examining the arrangements in the field in order to take action on the resident co-ordinator's role and on the co-location of field offices.   Every two years a special session of the Council should be devoted to operational activities, based on the report of the Director-General on operational activities, which will be biennialized.

In order to enable the General Assembly to focus on only a few major issues and to shorten its work substantially, a guiding principle for the structure of the Council's work must be a stringent delegation of authority, with most decisions to be taken by the Council itself and, preferably, at the level of the subsidiary bodies. Issues to be addressed by the Council should be highlighted in the reports and documents to be submitted to it.

In the context of a major effort to simplify drastically the subsidiary Council machinery, the following bodies deserve special attention: the Intergovernmental Committee on Science and Technology for Development, the Committee on the Development and Utilization of New and Renewable Sources of Energy, the Committee on Natural Resources, the High-level Committee for Technical Co-operation among Developing Countries and the Commission for Social Development.   These bodies should be merged as appropriate or their functions should be assumed by the Council or other United Nations bodies. For example, the natural resources questions could be transferred partly to UNCTAD/Committee on Commodities (minerals) and partly to UNEP (water) and partly taken up by the Council itself (energy). The co-ordination function of the High-level Committee for Technical Co-operation among Developing Countries could be absorbed by the Council and its more operational functions transferred to the UNDP Governing Council. In many cases, parts of the task which at present are undertaken by global bodies (e.g., in the field of technical co-operation among developing countries and natural resources) should be delegated to the regional commissions as the main development centres in their respective regions. One element of a streamlined Council machinery could be subject-oriented sessions on related clusters of issues, for which the Council has assumed direct responsibility or to which the Council has decided to give particular attention.

Such subject-oriented sessions could attract high-level participation. The subjects discussed in the subject-oriented session should not appear on the agenda of the regular session of the Council. WFC meetings should be biennialized.

In order to carry out these proposals, it will be necessary to make changes in the structure and timetable of Council meetings, taking into account the experiences of previous reform exercises. The thrust of our proposals is to restore the Council to the position envisaged for it in the Charter and to enable it to act effectively in the economic and social fields. At present, this task is impeded by the complex hierarchical structure which has tended over the years to weaken the functioning and authority of the Council. Leaving aside the question of membership, there are various adjustments to the structure which might be contemplated. These include consideration of the future of the organizational session and the subsequent regular sessions of the Council. One option might be to maintain broadly the present pattern, provided the proposals for the Council to act as a filter outlined in this paper can be effectively implemented. An alternate proposal would be for the Council to meet at the same time as the General Assembly. In that case, the present regular sessions of the Council should be consolidated in one session, meeting during the General Assembly and reporting to the Assembly direct or in a consolidated form through the Second and Third Committees of the General Assembly. The agenda and meeting time of the Second and Third Committees of the General Assembly might be adapted to make them compatible with the agenda and meeting time of the First and Second Committees of the Council. Co-ordination items would be taken up in the First and Second Sessional Committees of the Council, so that the Third Sessional Committee would then become redundant.

Consideration of structure and timetable has raised the question of the Council's membership. The proposals of restructuring described above in themselves would not, in our view, require universalization of the Council. Universalization of the Council in itself would not improve the effectiveness and efficiency of the United Nations. With four universal bodies in the economic field, the General Assembly/the Second Committee, the Council and UNCTAD, duplication and competition between these major United Nations bodies would become more apparent and even more difficult to avoid than under the present circumstances. For the Council itself universalization would make working procedures more cumbersome and time consuming. It goes without saying that on top of that universalization would require an amendment to the Charter, which in accordance with Article 108 has to be adopted and ratified by two thirds of the members of the United Nations, including all the permanent members of the Security Council. A change in the composition of the Council membership, like the proposed universalization, in itself would not bring about a profound and lasting improvement in achieving the purposes of the Charter in the economic and social fields. The question of a universal membership can only be discussed in the framework of a further-reaching, more radical reform package encompassing the General Assembly and its

Committees as well as the Trade and Development Board. The creation of a new universal body would undermine the credibility of the system even further, unless it proved feasible to organize a built-in constitutional mechanism to enable the General Assembly to focus in a disciplined manner on a few major policy issues, based upon the preparatory work of the Council. The Council would then become responsible for much of the present agenda of the General Assembly and its Committees and would have to hold its annual session during the General Assembly session. It could imply, for example, that the Council should take final action on most economic issues and that the General Assembly itself would focus on its deliberative functions through a general macro-economic debate.

III. Trade and Development Board of the United Nations Conference on Trade and Development

The Trade and Development Board (with only one session in the spring) would complement the overall macro-economic debate of the General Assembly, both debates constituting elements of one continuous dialogue (with no general debate in the Council). This must be reflected in the documents serving as the basis for these debates, i.e., the *Trade and Development Report* and the *World Economic Survey*. Part of a more effective division of labour could be the concentration of science and technology activities in New York, given the co-ordinating role of the Centre for Science and Technology for Development.

IV. Work methods

Suggestions made by the Trade and Development Board working group and ECE should be generalized. They concern work programmes, pre-sessional consultations, the calendar of meetings, the duration and conduct of meetings as well as documentation. In general terms the number of meetings of different organs should be reduced and the remaining meetings should be rescheduled in order to establish a logical sequence. The length of the different meetings would have to be decided upon after a close review, reordering and hopefully shortening of the respective agendas.

V. Secretariat structure

The outlined restructuring of the intergovernmental machinery would have to be reflected in a corresponding streamlining of the secretariat support structures reflecting the need for more rationalization and simplification on the one hand and better co-ordination on the other and the provision of adequate means for all agreed tasks. Particular attention should be given to the Department of International Economic and Social Affairs in the context of its relationship with the Office of the Director-General for Development and International Economic Co-operation, UNCTAD as the main subsidiary body of the General Assembly in the economic field and the United Nations Office in Vienna. The Office for Development and International Economic Co-operation must through redeployment be adequately equipped so that the Director-General would be in a position to carry out his central co-ordinating role, i.e., in the field of operational activities. Consequential changes for the secretariat support structures would have to be considered in the light of new arrangements for the intergovernmental structure in the different areas.

Delegation of Japan

I. Basic objectives

The basic objectives of the Special Commission are to strengthen the effectiveness of the United Nations in dealing with economic and social activities, by identifying measures to rationalize and simplify the intergovernmental structure, by avoiding duplication and overlapping activities and when needed merge existing bodies so as to improve their work and make the structure more responsive to their present needs as mentioned in recommendation 8 of the report of the Group of 18.

In the light of discussions and consultations so far made in the Special Commission, the following reforms should be undertaken to enhance the effective and efficient functioning of the United Nations system in the economic and social fields. However, these measures form only the first step towards attaining the above-mentioned objectives and should be reviewed constantly in the future.

II. Reform of the Economic and Social Council

A. Basic role

The basic role of the Council, as a chartered body, is to co-ordinate various activities of the United Nations organizations in the economic and social fields and consider basic policy guidelines, which are transmitted to the General Assembly in the form of recommendations or reports. It has been pointed out that the role of the Council in co-ordination and policy-making is not satisfactory, and basic reforms are strongly required. The Council needs to regain its authority as the central body of the United Nations in the economic and social fields. The duplications of discussion which are often noticed between the Council and the General Assembly are more or less the result from the facts that the Council takes up inappropriate topics in its discussion or that the General Assembly simply repeats the same discussions as the ones already made in the Council. These duplications should be eliminated by the joint efforts of member States both at the Council and the General Assembly.

B. Reforms to be considered

The items on the agenda of the Council are too many and should be substantially reduced. The Council meetings thereby should be subject-oriented, with in-depth discussions on a limited number of issues. These should be urgent or priority issues of the particular year or issues which require co-ordination. Its general debate should not deal with macro-economics and north-south problems in general, which should be discussed at the General Assembly. As to the other issues which are sent by the Council to the General Assembly, the member States should refrain from mere repetition of discussion simply because some of the members are not Council members and did not participate in the Council discussions.

There are at present too many reports submitted to and rubber-stamped by the Council. The reports which do not require substantive discussion by the Council should be sent directly to the General Assembly.

It should be considered that the Council should hold only one annual session. Its annual session could be held in New York and Geneva alternately.

The Council should absorb the functions of some subsidiary bodies.

C. Operational activities

The Council is not playing the expected role in co-ordination of the operational activities of the United Nations system. The co-ordination in the area of operational activities should be improved at two levels: policy-making level and operational level.

1. Policy-making level

The co-ordinating role should be drastically strengthened by the following measures:

(a)　A sessional committee on the Council should be developed to deal solely with the co-ordination of operational activities. This could be made by reforming the present Third Committee of the Council;

(b)　This sessional committee takes up at each year a limited number of priority issues which require co-ordination among agencies concerned. The executive heads of those agencies should be requested to participate in the in-depth discussion of this Committee;

(c)　The results of the discussion should be adopted in the form of recommendations to the General Assembly. The follow-up of the recommendations should be monitored closely and the agencies concerned should report back to the subsequent sessions of the Council about their follow-up for consideration of the Council.

2. Operational level

At the operational level, the role of resident co-ordinators should be strengthened by the following measures:

(a)　The authority and function of resident co-ordinators should be clearly defined;

(b)   The capacity of resident co-ordinators' authority should be secured from the recipient Governments and all United Nations agencies concerned, possibly in the form of a written agreement;

(c)   The resident co-ordinators should report regularly to the Council through the Director-General on actual constraints they face in pursuing co-ordination efforts in this field and the reports thus submitted should be thoroughly examined in the reformed Third Committee of the Council in the manner mentioned above.

III. Subsidiary bodies

There are a number of subsidiary bodies which need reforms and improvements in their functions. Considerations should particularly be given to the following bodies.

A. Commission on Transnational Corporations

Considering the nature of the issues taken up by the Commission, the Commission should work towards the biennialization of its session. The special session for the Code of Conduct should be held only when a clear perspective of progress on resolving pending substantive problems has emerged. As to the session of the Intergovernmental Working Group on Standards of Accounting and Reporting, biennialization of its work would be appropriate.

B. Committee for Development Planning

The activities of the Committee are satisfactory with higher quality of results. But those results are not sufficiently benefiting other United Nations bodies. Some measures should be considered so that a greater impact and interaction be assured between the works of the Committee and those of other United Nations bodies.

C. United Nations Group of Experts on Geographical Names

Considering the nature of the activities of the Group, triennialized meetings should be sufficient.

D. Ad Hoc Group of Expert on International Co-operation on Tax Matters

The Group should not necessarily meet on a biennial basis. The possibility of meeting on an *ad hoc* basis should be studied.

E. Committee for Programme and Co-ordination

The ACC/CPC joint meetings, currently held in Geneva just before the summer session of the Council, achieve very little. This is due to the number and levels of participants mainly from CPC members. There is a clear need to strengthen the joint meetings by changing the venue and timing of the meeting. Joint meetings should be held in New York in October when ACC holds its regular session so that the joint meetings may have a better participation, of member States at higher levels and assure substantial exchange of views between the representatives of ACC and CPC.

The role of CPC for programme co-ordination and budget outline should be strengthened as stipulated in General Assembly resolution 41/213.

F. Trade and Development Board of the United Nations Conference on Trade and Development

UNCTAD should improve its effectiveness especially in respect of adapting itself to the world economy which has undergone profound changes in the past quarter of a century of its existence. Realistic ways have to be sought to make UNCTAD responsive to the increasingly diversified needs of individual developing countries. Japan endorses the report of the *ad hoc* intergovernmental working group adopted at the resumed thirty-fourth session of the Trade and Development Board. The Trade and Development Board and its subsidiary organs should have a more focused agenda without duplication to discharge effectively their functions.

The possibility of merging the *Trade and Development Report* with the *World Economic Survey* should be explored since both reports sometimes deal with the same issues.

G. United Nations Environment Programme

Reform measures which were agreed on in the United Nations Environment Programme (UNEP) should duly be pursued and implemented. Steps should further be taken to streamline meetings and reduce documentation.

H. Population Commission

The distinction between the Commission and the United Nations Population Fund (UNFPA) in some activities are getting vague. There should be a clearer division of responsibility between the two bodies, taking due account of existing mandates.

I. Intergovernmental Committee for Science and Technology
for Development

Extremely low level of participation shows that member States are not interested in continuing the activities of the Committee. As a result, the Committee's achievements have been disappointing and the function of the Committee should be taken over by the Council. The Advisory Committee on Science and Technology for Development has achieved good results and therefore should be maintained. This Advisory Committee should report its activities to the Council.

J. Committee on Natural Resources

The Committee has not been able to exercise its mandate and has not had enough impact on other United Nations bodies. Its function therefore should be taken over by the Council.

K. Committee on Development and Utilization of New
and Renewable Sources of Energy

The Committee has not functioned satisfactorily although the area which is deals with remains important. The participation of member States in the meeting has been very poor. Considering the low interest of member States in the Committee's activities and yet the future possible change in energy situation, the following solution should be considered:

(a)   The Committee should be taken over by the Council and the Council should continue its deliberation on the area;

(b)   An *ad hoc* expert group may be formed and meet when necessary and the group, whose members are appointed in their individual capacity, may report its activities to the Council.

L. Committee for Social Development

Duplications are noticed in the activities of this Committee and other bodies and the items of its agenda are too many and not specific. Considering the nature of activities of the Committee, its function should be taken over by the Council.

IV. Secretariat support structure

In order to improve the co-ordination of the United Nations system in the economic and social fields, the role of the Director-General's office should be strengthened. The Director-General's office should make more use of the capacity of the Department of International Economic and Social Affairs in its co-ordinating activities.

The secretariat structure should be reformed in such a manner as corresponds to the reform measures to be taken at the level of intergovernmental bodies.

Delegation of Norway

Basic objectives

To strengthen the activities of the United Nations in the economic and social fields.

To simplify the present United Nations structure in these fields.

To ensure that substantive deliberations on economic and social issues are maintained in appropriate forums.

1. *Economic and Social Council*

(a)   Universal membership;

(b)   Will hold two regular annual sessions:

(i)   Organizational session in January/February. Bureau will play a more active management role. Its composition and size should be further explored;

(ii)   Substantive session in October/November;

(c)   Will hold *ad hoc* sessions - allocated as necessary throughout the year - on specific substantive or co-ordination issues;

(d)   Will base its activities on long-term agendas, in accordance with a biennial programme of work;

(e)   Will absorb most of the functions of a number of subsidiary bodies, including the Intergovernmental Committee on Science and Technology for Development, the Committee on the Development and Utilization of New and Renewable Sources of Energy, the Committee on Natural Resources, the World Food Council and the High-level Committee on Technical Co-operation among Developing Countries;

(f)   It should be considered to request the Commission on Human Rights to report directly to the General Assembly. This will ease the Council's work-load and prevent repetitious discussions;

(g)   To enhance the impact of overall macro-economic discussions they should be limited to one general debate in the spring (preferable in the Trade and Development Board) and one in the autumn (General Assembly).

2. *General Assembly*

(a)   The Second and Third Committees will meet for approximately two weeks in November/December;

(b)   Basic tasks should be:

(i)   Overall, general discussions on global economic and social issues, based on the reports, resolutions and recommendations from the Council;

(ii)   Formally adopt - and submit to the plenary - the reports, resolutions and recommendations from the Council.

3. *United Nations Conference on Trade and Development*

(a)   The economic sections of the Department of International Economic and Social Affairs should, to the largest extent possible, be merged with the UNCTAD secretariat;

(b)   The Trade and Development Board should hold one substantive annual session. It would take place in the spring and one major agenda item should be an overall, general debate on macro-economic issues;

(c)   The *World Economic Survey* and the *Trade and Development Report* should be consolidated into one annual report on macro-economic issues.

4. *Secretariat*

All reforms of the intergovernmental machinery - as outlined above - will necessitate corresponding streamlining, rationalization and simplification of the secretariat support structures.

Delegation of Tunisia (on behalf of the Group of 77)

I. General Assembly

The overall reform proposal aims at strengthening the role of the United Nations and of its supreme organ, the General Assembly, in the economic and social fields which are of the highest importance for achieving peace and international security through international co-operation and promote social progress and better standards of life in larger freedoms.

The General Assembly, as the supreme organ of the United Nations system, remains the principal forum for policy-making and for the harmonization of international action in respect of international economic, social and related problems, as established in the Charter and relevant General Assembly resolutions.

As a result of the overall reform proposal outlined in this paper, the Second and Third Committees should take the necessary steps to adjust their work to the changes deriving from it. These adjustments imply that the Second and Third Committees shall review their agendas, and the duration of their sessions.

Both Committees shall consider, *inter alia*, those matters brought to the attention of the General Assembly by the Council or directly by any Member State.

II. Economic and Social Council

In exercising its functions and power under the Charter and fulfilling its role as set out in the relevant General Assembly and Economic and Social Council resolutions, the Council, under the authority of the Assembly or in the performance of such functions as may be assigned to it by the Assembly, should concentrate on its responsibilities:

(a)   The Economic and Social Council shall serve as the central forum for the substantive co-ordination of international economic and social issues of a global or interdisciplinary nature and for the formulation of policy recommendations thereon addressed to Member States and to the United Nations system as a whole;

(b)   The Council shall monitor and evaluate the implementation of overall strategies, policies and priorities established by the General Assembly in the economic, social and related fields, and shall ensure the harmonization and coherent practical operational implementation, on an integrated basis, of relevant policy decisions and recommendations emanating from the United Nations conferences and other forums within the United Nations system after their approval by the General Assembly and/or the Economic and Social Council;

(c) The Council shall ensure the overall co-ordination of all activities of the United Nations system in the economic, social and related fields and, to that end, the implementation of priorities established by the General Assembly for the system as a whole;

(d) Such implementation shall include the elaboration of guidelines and priorities for the preparation of the introduction of the medium-term plan in the economic, social and related fields, as well as a thorough review of it for submission to the General Assembly;

(e) The Council shall recommend to the General Assembly the priorities for the programme budget of the organization in the economic and social fields;

(f) The Council shall recommend to the General Assembly the overall priorities and guidelines for operational activities throughout the United Nations system, and carry out comprehensive policy reviews.

Organization and programme of work

The Council continues to organize its programme of work on a biennial basis and provide for frequent subject-oriented sessions spread throughout the year.

In formulating its biennial programme of work, the Council shall decide on the schedule and agenda for its subject-oriented sessions which would, *inter alia*, deal with issues of the subsidiary bodies it has subsumed.

The Council shall meet in plenary as well as in sessional committees constituting:

(i)   The first (economic) committee;

(ii) The second (social) committee;

(iii) The third (operational activities and programming) committee, which will consider the reports of all funds, programmes, governing bodies and institutions of the United Nations system involved in operational activities and programming questions, with a view to co-ordinating, and recommending priorities and guidelines for those activities;

There shall be a high-level segment which will be part of the regular session of the Council.

The Council shall meet, in addition to the subject-oriented sessions as set out above, at an organizational and a regular session.

The Council shall set the periodicity of its sessions and shall organize its programme of work in the light of its new structure and responsibilities.

The Council shall not meet during the regular session of the General Assembly.

The agenda of the Council's session may be allocated as follows:

(a)   Organizational session:

(i)   Consideration of modalities for the implementation of the relevant decisions adopted by the General Assembly;

(ii)   Organization of work for its regular session;

(b)   Regular session:

(i)   Consideration of items on the biennial agenda and adoption of recommendations thereon;

(ii)   Consideration (transmission) of the report of the Trade and Development Board;

(iii) Consideration of the reports of the subsidiary bodies which report to or through the Council;

(c)   Subject-oriented sessions.

Consideration of specific issues including, *inter alia*, those that have been subsumed by the Council.

The Council shall propose the most appropriate dates for the meetings of the bodies reporting to it so that it could consider the reports of all those bodies in a timely and effective manner.

When considering the policy aspects of items on its agenda, the Council shall, at the same time, deal with all relevant reports of organs, bodies and agencies of the United Nations system, so as to ensure effective substantive co-ordination in economic and social fields. In this regard, the Council shall receive consolidated reports on the various social, economic and related issues submitted by relevant bodies and agencies of the United Nations system or prepared by the Council's secretariat, as appropriate. A world economic and social survey shall be issued annually and will be a basis for discussions at the Council.

The Council shall draw up its biennial programme of work, including the subject-oriented sessions, in good time to allow for the preparation of substantive analytical reports and their submission by all relevant organs and agencies of the United Nations system to the President of the Council for a given year in order to enable the Council's secretariat to integrate all inputs received, on a given issue, in a consolidated report for consideration at the respective session.

The Council should, to the maximum extent possible, refrain from establishing new subsidiary bodies, taking into account that subject-oriented sessions could undertake the task that may be assigned to a new body.

The Council shall assume direct responsibility for carrying out the preparatory work for *ad hoc* conferences convened by the Council or the General Assembly.

The Council shall prepare, for consideration at the forty-fifth regular session of the General Assembly, a thorough review of the relationship between the United Nations and the specialized agencies in order to enable it to fulfil its overall co-ordination functions under Articles 63, 64 and 66 of the Charter.

The Secretary-General and the executive heads of the organizations of the United Nations system should participate more actively in the deliberations of the Council and should provide all assistance to the Council in accordance with the general and specific directives.

The Council shall assume, to the maximum extent possible, direct responsibility for performing the functions of its subsidiary bodies in the economic and social fields; these bodies would accordingly be discontinued or their terms of reference redefined or regrouped. The regional commissions should continue in being.

The criteria for the possibility for the Council to perform the responsibility and the role of its subsidiary bodies are:

(i)   The need for application of the same general principles to the subsidiary bodies of the Council in both the economic and social fields;

(ii) The subsuming by the Council of its subsidiary bodies should not over-burden its agenda and should ensure appropriate attention and consideration by the Council of the respective issues;

(iii) Highly technical functions of some subsidiary bodies and expert groups may not be entrusted to the Council.

As a consequence of its new and enhanced role and responsibilities as set out above, the Economic and Social Council shall consist of all Members of the United Nations.

III. Secretariat support structure for the Economic and Social Council

(a)   A separate and identifiable secretariat for the Council shall be provided;

(b)   The new Council secretariat shall provide substantive as well as relevant conference services and facilities to the Council. Therefore, the secretariat shall be adequately staffed at both the Professional and General Service levels, in strict observance with the principle of equitable geographical representation; Professional staff should be of the highest quality in all the disciplines and issues dealt with by the Council, so as to provide the best possible assistance to the Council in accordance with its new functions;

(c)   The Council's secretariat shall, *inter alia*, collate, consolidate and produce, as appropriate, the reports requested to be submitted to the Council, with conclusions, as necessary;

The Council's secretariat shall be composed in such a way as to be capable of preparing requested substantive and analytical reports of a global or interdisciplinary nature covering both policy and co-ordination aspects for consideration by the Council, thereby enabling substantive co-ordination by the Council;

(d)   A periodic evaluation and appraisal of the quality and content of reports prepared for the Council shall be made;

(e)   Reports submitted to the Council shall be standard format to facilitate reading and consideration by all delegations.

IV. Trade and Development Board

The views and proposals of the Trade and Development Board on its functions and responsibilities as set out in informal paper TDB/1154 of 23 November 1987, will be incorporated in the final recommendations of the Special Commission.

It is also recommended that the substantive debate on the interrelated issues in the Trade and Development Board take place at its spring session with a corresponding change in the date of the autumn session of the Trade and Development Board.

V. Operational activities for development of the United Nations system

The implementation of operational activities by the United Nations system and its review should aim to promote the following:

(a)   The promotion of self-reliance of the developing countries in building up, *inter alia*, their productive capacity and their indigenous resources and by developing internalized and self-sustaining managerial, technical, institutional, administrative and research capabilities required in the development process and within the socio-cultural context of each recipient country;

(b)   Utilization of external technical co-operation and assistance should be for the benefit of the developing countries, at their request and in accordance with their own national plans, objectives and priorities;

(c)   The overall orientation of operational activities should reflect fully the overall strategies, policies and priorities of the General Assembly and the Council;

(d)   The achievement of optimum efficiency and the reduction of administrative costs in operational activities for development, with a consequent increase in the proportion of resources available to meet the assistance requirements of recipient countries;

(e)   A real increase in the flow of resources for such activities on a predictable, continued and assured basis.

The Council, as envisaged in General Assembly resolution 32/197, should reassert itself and carry out the co-ordination function of all operational activities of the United Nations system, setting priorities and giving policy guidance to all the funding and executive bodies.

The various intergovernmental governing bodies should primarily concentrate on implementing with effectiveness the policy guidance and priorities given by the Council and the General Assembly, as well as on programming, managing and efficiently utilizing the available resources to each body. Overall priorities and policy guidance should be established by the General Assembly based on the recommendations drawn by the Council.

Measures designed to enable the Council to assume its co-ordination functions would be included.

The Third Committee of the Council shall, *inter alia*, deal with both policy and co-ordination issues on an annual basis (substantive co-ordination).

The Third Committee of the Council shall, in addition, meet every three years to review at a global level the progress made in the operational activities field in fulfilling the objectives mentioned above and following the policy guidance of the General Assembly. The conclusions and recommendations of these triennial discussions will be reported to the General Assembly.

The other two years of each triennium, the Council shall monitor the implementation of the guidelines and policies established by the General Assembly and make recommendations in view of their full implementation. It shall also concentrate on providing clear guidelines on a thematic basis so as to avoid often conflicting priorities by agencies in the same sector. The Council Committee on Operational Activities should have before it on a thematic basis:

(a)   Conclusions from other Council Committees based on discussions of the consolidated reports;

(b)   Reports from the various governing bodies, funding and executing agencies;

(c)   Consolidated reports designed to facilitate sectorial integrated review;

(d)   Reports of the intergovernmental bodies relating to their specific areas of operational activities.

The Council's co-ordinating role in this field should concentrate on:

(a)   Reviewing and adjusting the programming process of operational activities so as to improve the efficient utilization of resources at a systematic level, simplify, harmonize and adapt this process to the needs of recipient countries and co-ordinate in a sectorial approach the activities of the various institutions involved;

(b)   Issues on improving the field co-ordination of operational activities by reviewing the procedure for appointing the resident co-ordinator and enhance its functioning on the basis of the needs of recipient countries and in accordance with relevant General Assembly resolutions.

The Council (Third Committee) should design tools for monitoring harmonization, evaluation and to ensure co-ordination of the entire system for operational activities.

The secretariat support structure should be strengthened so as to create capability to prepare reports and evaluations of different aspects of operational activities. UNCTAD would play a key role in the interrelated areas of money, finance and trade and other case programmes like economic co-operation among developing countries and the Substantial New Programme of Action.

Member States should endeavour to strengthen their level of participation in the Council Committee on Operational Activities.

The Council should clarify the role of and relationship between funding and executing agencies.

The role and function of the Bureau of the Second and Third Committee of the Council and other relevant bodies should be clearly defined.

Secretariat support structure

The secretariat functions and structures of the funding bodies in charge of operational activities for development shall be reviewed by the Economic and Social Council in 1989, taking into account, *inter alia*, the following:

(a)   The need for reducing substantially the administrative costs and maximizing the level of financial resources devoted to the projects;

(b)   The need for rationalizing and streamlining the secretariat support structures in view of achieving the highest possible level of decentralization and of transparency of its activities;

(c)   The need to comply with the principle of equitable geographical distribution;

(d)   The need to consolidate the secretariat functions for all aspects related to policy analysis, study and research in the field of operational activities for development in the Economic and Social Council secretariat structure.

Delegations of Bulgaria, Byelorussian Soviet Socialist Republic,
Czechoslovakia, German Democratic Republic, Hungary, Mongolia,
Poland, Ukrainian Soviet Socialist Republic and
Union of Soviet Socialist Republics

The basic objectives of reform should be:

(a)   To strengthen the activities of the United Nations and the United Nations system in economic and social fields, to bring those activities in line with the realities of interdependence of countries and issues in the world economy, as well as to make them more action-oriented and more responsive to practical interests of Member States;

(b)   To improve co-ordination of the activities of the United Nations and the United Nations system in those fields in order to allow for effective search for common and practical solutions to the economic and social problems on the basis of a coherent approach reflecting their interlinkages;

(c)   To rationalize the present United Nations structure in those fields accordingly.

In order to facilitate the achievement of those objectives it is suggested to consider, *inter alia*, the following:

1.   To strengthen the role and functions of the Council in:

(a)   Review and assessment of the world economic and social situation and identification of substantive areas which need multilateral consideration and action;

(b)   Strengthening the role of the Council in promotion of multilateral co-operation in solving international economic, social and related problems;

(c)   Promotion of an integrated approach to both economic and social development;

(d)   Substantive co-ordination of economic and social programmes of the United Nations and the specialized agencies;

(e)   Overall monitoring of the follow-up to relevant United Nations resolutions and decisions;

2.   To establish that all United Nations bodies in the social and economic fields should report to the Council as the final authority. This would help to avoid repetitive discussion of the same reports by the United Nations General Assembly. In this case, the work of the General Assembly on economic and social issues could be shortened and could concentrate on consideration of the

consolidated annual report of the Council and on examination of major economic and social problems of a global dimension in order to work out mutually acceptable ways and means of solving such problems.

3.   To improve co-ordination of general debates among the Council, the Second Committee of the General Assembly and the Trade and Development Board.   In principle, general debate in the Trade and Development Board should concentrate on the sectors of trade and development and the related issues of money, finance, debt, etc., the Council's general debate should be structured on the basis of sectoral inputs (from the Trade and Development Board and other key bodies) and should be aimed at developing a system-wide integrated approach to international economic and social policy with its intersectoral and regional dimensions.   The debates in the Second and Third Committees of the General Assembly should be centred on major global economic and social issues requiring priority attention of the international community, including those highlighted in the report of the Council.

4.   To restructure the sessional committees of the Council on the basis of organic merger and integration of substantive and co-ordination functions. Its sessional committees (economic, social and on operational activities) should not repeat the debates already held in the subsidiary bodies, but rather concentrate on working out coherent recommendations on the basis of a comprehensive analysis of specific proposals contained in the reports of those bodies.

5.   To ensure effective co-ordination by the Council of all United Nations operational activities through, *inter alia*, allocation of this function to one of its sessional committees which would be entrusted with working out policy recommendations on the principles and practical conduct of those activities.

6.   To ensure that the work of the Council provides for elaboration of action-oriented recommendations on an integrated approach to economic and social development and co-operation, as well as for an accountable follow-up and monitoring of the implementation of those recommendations. To facilitate this, it would be feasible, *inter alia*, to consider the following:

(a)   To ensure that the basic documentation annually submitted by the Secretariat to the Council facilitates an integrated discussion of economic and social issues, taking into account, *inter alia*, the title of the general debate item on the agenda of the Council, which is "General discussion of international economic and social policy, including regional and sectoral developments";

(b)   Whenever several draft resolutions are submitted by sessional committees on the same broad sectoral issue, they should be, as a rule, merged at the plenary level in order to provide the United Nations and its system with a coherent policy guidance on the issue;

(c)   Secretariat support structure should reflect the need for the Council to exercise more vigorously an integrated approach to economic and social issues, including an improved policy-planning and co-ordinating role of the Director-General's office.

7.   To strengthen the management role of the Bureau, in particular in such fields as elaboration of draft programme of work, allocation of items, monitoring the work of the Secretariat related to implementation of Council decisions, ensuring effective follow-up, timely preparation of documentation, etc.

8.   Consideration could also be given to holding, whenever feasible, informal meetings of members of the Council Bureau with members of the bureaux of other organs and specialized agencies. Such meetings could be arranged with no financial implications, when schedule and venue of various sessions so permit, or they could be financed from the funds allocated for intersecretariat co-ordination.

9.   Feasibility of participation of the Council bureau members in the work of ACC should also be explored in order to promote constructive system-wide dialogue.

10.   To take practical measures on the basis of the United Nations Charter in order to strengthen the role of the Council in co-ordination of social and economic activities of the United Nations system. In particular, as a matter of principle and in accordance with Article 64 of the Charter, United Nations resolutions on major economic and social issues should be brought by the Presidents of the General Assembly and the Council and/or by the Secretary-General to the attention of relevant organs of the specialized agencies with a view to obtaining regular reports from them, including reports on the steps taken to give effect to General Assembly and Council resolutions and recommendations.

11.   To strengthen the role of regional commissions as unique multidisciplinary forums responsible for development of multilateral co-operation within and among respective regions. To achieve a better integration of regional aspects in the Council's consideration of global economic and social problems.

12.   To oblige all United Nations subsidiary bodies in economic and social fields to reflect in their regular reports the measures taken in implementation of General Assembly and Council resolutions and decisions.

13.   To rationalize the reporting to the Council by subsidiary bodies through, *inter alia*, clustering major system-wide economic and social activities (medium-term plan structure could be used) and designating a lead body responsible for the preparation of a consolidated report of substantive work and level of co-ordination achieved in the respective field; such a report should also contain action-oriented recommendations. The Director-General's office might have a role in assisting in the preparation of such reports.

14.   To continue and improve the application of biennial approach to the work of the Council and its sectoral subsidiary machinery.

15.   To rationalize and synchronize the cycles of meetings of the Council and all subsidiary bodies so that to ensure timely submission of relevant reports to the Council and to allow for a meaningful in-depth consideration by the Council of their recommendations in a coherent and co-ordinated manner.

16.   When discussing measures to rationalize and simplify the United Nations subsidiary structure in economic and social fields to consider ways and means to increase the input of professional expertise into the United Nations work on sectoral issues.   Such professional input should not in any way substitute for decision-making functions at an intergovernmental level, but should rather help Governments and the Council to take fuller advantage from expert analysis and advice.

17.   The number and duration of annual sessions of the Council (recommendation 2 of the report of the Group of 18) as well as membership of the Council should be considered in the overall context of the final outcome of the study by the Special Commission, when it would be clear, whether a balanced approach has been ensured to all bodies under review - in economic, social and human rights fields.

18.   To ensure implementation of all United Nations decisions adopted in recent years concerning the organization and methods of work of the Council and its subsidiary bodies, including decisions on rationalization of documentation.

Delegation of the United States of America

The reform effort should aim at reducing the number of layers in the present United Nations system. This multi-tiered structure causes unneeded repetition of work (documentation, meeting time, debates, etc.) which produces no measurable increase in the output of the organization. A more streamlined system would include the following roles for the major bodies:

The General Assembly

As the highest body of the United Nations system, the General Assembly will inevitably continue to deal with economic and social issues. However, it should do so in a more focused, limited fashion, taking no more than two or three major issues each year. These issues would be developed at the Council:

(a)   Second and Third Committees would meet for two/three weeks at the end of each General Assembly;

(b)   Second Committee would hold a general debate and focus on one or two other key issues recommended to it by the Council;

(c)   Third Committee would discuss human rights (reported directly from the Human Rights Commission) and one or two other topics recommended by the Council.

Economic and Social Council

The Council will become the central United Nations organ for in-depth discussion of economic and social issues and for the co-ordination of United Nations activities in these areas. It will serve as the primary forum for policy-oriented debate and will be required to take final action on most issues. The Council will also select the limited number of issues to be referred to the General Assembly each year, refining these issues and preparing concise documentation for General Assembly use. To fulfil these functions, the following modifications would be recommended:

(a)   The Council would hold one substantive session each year. Deliberations would be held in New York from early September to mid-November each year;

(b)   The fall session would be issue oriented, with 5-8 day segments devoted to specific topics. The topics covered in these sessions would be determined in accordance with the need to biennialize the Council work programme. There would be no general debate;

(c)   These issue-oriented sessions would allow the Council to assume responsibility for many of its subsidiary bodies, such as:

(i)   Intergovernmental Committee on Science and Technology for Development;

(ii)   Committee on the Development and Utilization of New and Renewable Sources of Energy;

(iii) Committee on Natural Resources;

(iv)   Commission for Social Development;

(v)   Commission on Transnational Corporations;

(d)   Operational activities would also be discussed in the Council as a special segment on a biennial basis;

(e)   Macro-economic issues would be discussed first at the Trade and Development Board which would report its findings to the Council. The Trade and Development Board would meet annually in the spring. Its meetings would include a general debate and discussion on specific macro-economic issues. The *Trade and Development Report* would also be merged with the *World Economic Survey*;

(f)   The Council would be responsible for taking final action on all of the issues discussed at its fall session. A brief "executive summary" of its decisions would be compiled for submission to the General Assembly;

(g)   The Council would also select two or three key items for direct action by the General Assembly. These items would be determined at the organizational session of the Council to allow sufficient time for preparation of documents and for input from other bodies (e.g., the Committee for Development Planning);

(h)   The Council would also hold an organizational session in February in Geneva. This meeting would be used to determine the agenda for the fall Council session, to select the action items for the next General Assembly and to co-ordinate United Nations activity in the economic and social fields in light of the resolutions passed at the last General Assembly;

(i)   At the organizational session, much of the co-ordinating function should be done by a smaller group such as an expanded bureau.

ANNEX III. A

Informal consolidated discussion paper presented by the chairman on 21 APRIL 1988

Introduction

1.   The review of the functioning of the intergovernmental machinery in the economic and social sectors and its secretariat support should aim at achieving the following objectives:

(a)   To strengthen the role of the United Nations as an indispensable multilateral instrument for the promotion of international co-operation for economic and social development;

(b)   To ensure that the activities of the United Nations in the economic and social sectors will be more responsive to the needs of Member States;

(c)   To ensure that these activities will be more coherent and reflect better the realities of interdependence among countries and issues;

(d)   To enhance the effectiveness and efficiency of the functioning of the intergovernmental machinery and its secretariat support through appropriate rationalization and streamlining.

2.   It is recognized that in order to strengthen the United Nations in the economic and social sectors as a whole, it is important to strengthen the role of the General Assembly as the supreme body of the United Nations and the pivotal role of the Economic and Social Council as envisaged in the Charter. A more effective Council would complement and strengthen the respective roles of the General Assembly and the United Nations Conference on Trade and Development, as well as their subsidiary machinery.

3.   It is also recognized that the restructuring measures as outlined below cannot by themselves ensure the achievement of the above-mentioned objectives unless accompanied by the necessary political will on the part of Member States to make better use of the United Nations as a viable forum for international co-operation.

4.   Reform of the United Nations is a continuing process.   The present exercise should be seen in that context and should benefit from past experiences, including the implementation of decisions adopted. Restructuring measures should be devised in such a manner as to ensure their full translation into practice.   An appropriate monitoring device should also be envisaged.

I. The General Assembly

A. Functions

5.   The General Assembly, being the supreme body of the United Nations system, should carry out its political role in providing policy guidance for the activities in the economic and social sectors in accordance with the provisions of the Charter.

6.   The Assembly should establish the overall strategies, policies and priorities in the economic, social and related fields for the United Nations system as a whole.

7.   The Assembly should, while respecting the sovereign right of Member States to raise major economic and social problems of global dimension, focus on a limited number of policy issues each year.   The Economic and Social Council could assist in the identification of such issues.

B. Inputs

8.   The General Assembly should hold a general debate on macro-economic issues on the basis of the reports of the Council, the Trade and Development Board and the subsidiary bodies of the General Assembly.

9.   The General Assembly should receive a consolidated report on the work of the Council.   The consolidated report should highlight principal issues and draw the attention of the General Assembly to issues on which action is required.   The General Assembly would, where necessary, endorse the Council decisions in order to enhance their legislative impact, or formulate policy at the global level.

C. Agenda and programme of work

10. As a result of the overall reform which, *inter alia*, envisages the enhancement of the Council's ability to assist the Assembly in discharging effectively its responsibilities in the economic, social and related fields, the General Assembly would need to make adjustments in the agendas and programmes of work of its Second and Third Committees.

11. The process of biennialization of the programme of work of the Second Committee and improved synchronization with that of the Economic and Social Council should remain under review in order to bring about necessary improvements.

12. The question of the agenda and work programme for the Third Committee, which deals with social and humanitarian issues, needs to be similarly addressed.   There is considerable room for biennialization of its work

programme and greater synchronization of its activities *vis-à-vis* the Council with a view to avoiding apparent duplication.

13. In the context of the work of the Third Committee, the report of the Commission on Human Rights, which is presently received by the General Assembly after full consideration by the Council, should be transmitted directly for the consideration of the General Assembly, thus eliminating the existing duplication.

D. Output

14. The Secretary-General should be requested to prepare a consolidated report on the decisions adopted by the General Assembly in the economic, social and related fields, highlighting matters which require action by relevant organs, organizations and bodies of the United Nations system. This report should also indicate, in an integrated manner, the priorities laid down by the General Assembly as reflected in those decisions. Such reports should be made available to the organizations of the system and to the Council at its organizational sessions.

II. Economic and Social Council

A. Mandates and responsibilities

15. The Economic and Social Council should exercise fully and effectively the functions and power entrusted to it by the Charter and relevant resolutions of the General Assembly. For that purpose, its should concentrate on carrying out the following responsibilities:

(a)   To serve as the central forum for the substantive co-ordination of international economic and social issues of a global or interdisciplinary nature and for the formulation of policy recommendations thereof addressed to Member States and to the United Nations system as a whole;

(b)   To monitor and evaluate the implementation of overall strategies, policies and priorities established by the General Assembly in the economic, social and related fields, and to ensure the harmonization and coherent practical operational implementation, on an integrated basis, of relevant policy decisions and recommendations emanating from the United Nations conferences and other forums within the United Nations system after their approval by the Assembly and/or the Economic and Social Council;

(c)   To ensure the overall co-ordination of all activities of the United Nations system in the economic, social and related fields and, to that end, the implementation of priorities established by the Assembly for the system as a whole;

(d) To elaborate guidelines and priorities for the preparation of the introduction of the medium-term plan in the economic, social and related fields, as well as a thorough review of it for submission to the Assembly;

(e) To recommend to the Assembly the priorities for the programme budget of the United Nations in the economic and social fields;

(f) To recommend to the Assembly the overall priorities and guidelines for operational activities throughout the United Nations system, and carry out comprehensive policy reviews.

B. *Working relationship with the General Assembly*

16. There should be a co-ordinated and complementary working arrangement between the General Assembly and the Economic and Social Council, taking fully into account the pre-eminence of the Assembly as the supreme organ of the United Nations system in the economic and social fields and the desirability for the Assembly and the Council to have respective focuses. Overlapping could thus be avoided.

17. For that purpose, the Council should effectively carry out a managerial role in reviewing the work and the activities of the United Nations in the economic and social areas both at the intergovernmental and Secretariat levels.

18. The Council should be entrusted with the authority to take final decisions on reports of subsidiary machinery which hitherto reported to or through it to the Assembly, with the exception of the Trade and Development Board, which would continue to report through it to the General Assembly. The Council should also identify a limited number of policy issues for consideration by the Assembly each year. The Council should refine such issues and prepare concise documentation for the Assembly.

19. Henceforth, there should be two general debated each year on macro-economic issues, one of a more specialized nature, focusing on the interrelated issues of trade, money, finance and development, to take place in the Trade and Development Board in the spring, and the second with wider perspective to take place in the autumn in the General Assembly. The Economic and Social Council should address specific themes in its discussions during the high-level segment of its regular session,[1] focusing on issues which are multidisciplinary in nature, and paying particular attention to the co-ordination and operational aspects of such issues.[2] The discussion of the Council should aim at developing a system-wide integrated approach to international economic and social issues, taking fully into account their intersectoral and regional dimensions.

C. Relations with the subsidiary machinery

20. The Council should discharge more effectively its responsibility in reviewing, monitoring and co-ordinating the work of its subsidiary bodies. It should translate relevant inputs from these bodies into concrete policy decisions, provide policy guidelines, and monitor the effective implementation by those bodies of the Council's policy decisions. While strengthening the Council, measures should also be adopted to ensure the vitality of the subsidiary bodies through increasing· the participation and inputs of representatives and/or individuals with the relevant expertise and improving the quality of meetings.

21. The Council should assume, to the maximum extent possible, direct responsibility for performing the intergovernmental functions of some subsidiary bodies in the economic and social fields. These bodies will, accordingly, be discontinued or their terms of reference redefined or regrouped.[3]

22. The Council should convene subject-oriented sessions to deal with issues of the subsidiary bodies it has subsumed. Expert groups could be convened as necessary, to provide the Council with technical inputs.

23. The Council should, to the maximum extent possible, refrain from establishing new subsidiary bodies, taking into account that subject-oriented sessions could undertake the tasks that may be assigned to new bodies. For their part, subsidiary bodies of the Assembly and the Council should refrain from creating new subordinate sessional or intersessional groups without prior concurrence of the Council.

D. Work of the Council

1. Co-ordination

24. In order to enable the Council to carry out more effectively the above-mentioned responsibilities, the following considerations should be taken fully into account:

(a)   System-wide co-ordination should be an integral part of the work of the Economic and Social Council. The consideration of co-ordination issues should be integrated into the relevant substantive items of the Council's agenda;

(b)   When considering the policy aspects of issues/items on its agenda, the Council should also examine all relevant inputs from organizations of the system, so as to ensure substantive co-ordination. The Council should receive consolidated reports from its subsidiary bodies or as appropriate from the

Council secretariat. Such reports should highlight both the substantive and co-ordination issues in their respective fields of activities;

(c) Co-ordination instruments such as cross-organizational programmes of analyses for cross-organizational reviews of medium-term plans, CPC/ACC Joint Meetings and reports from ACC and its subsidiary machinery should be adapted to enable the Council to effectively carry out its co-ordination functions. Representatives of organizations of the system, including the regional commissions, should participate actively in the relevant deliberations of the Council, particularly in the high-level segment of the Council;

(d) The Council should continue to be supported by the Committee for Programme and Co-ordination in carrying out its co-ordination responsibilities. The respective areas of responsibilities of the Council and CPC should be defined more clearly, with the Council providing the necessary political and legislative authority which CPC recommendations lack.[4]

2. *Operational activities*

25. The role of the Council in operational activities for development should be strengthened. It should set priorities and provide policy guidance to all relevant governing bodies and executing organizations. It should also exercise a cross-organizational oversight role to ensure that individual organization's programmes are harmonized. The following guidelines could be envisaged for the future work of the Council and relevant governing bodies in the area of operational activities for development:

(a) Overall priorities and policy guidance should be established by the General Assembly based on the recommendations drawn up by the Council. Various governing bodies should focus on the effective implementation of these priorities and policies, in addition to their responsibilities in the management and programming of resources available to them;[5]

(b) The Council should, *inter alia*, deal with policy and co-ordination issues on an annual basis (substantive co-ordination). It should focus each year on a limited number of priority issues which require co-ordination or harmonization of action among relevant organizations of the system. The executive heads of those organizations should be invited to participate in the discussions;

(c) The Council should, in addition, undertake every three years[6] a comprehensive policy review. The conclusions and recommendations of these triennial reviews would be reported to the General Assembly;

(d) The Council, in the other two years of each triennium, should monitor the implementation of the priorities and policies established by the General Assembly and make recommendations for their full implementation. It should also concentrate on providing clear guidelines on a thematic basis so as to avoid conflicting priorities in the same sector.

(e)   Economic and Social Council's co-ordinating role in this field should concentrate on:

(i)   Reviewing and adjusting the programming process of operational activities so as to improve the efficient utilization of resources system-wide, simplify, harmonize and adapt this process to the needs of recipient countries and co-ordinate in a sectorial approach the activities of the various institutions;

(ii)   Improving the field co-ordination of operational activities by reviewing the procedure for appointing resident co-ordinators and enhancing their functioning on the basis of the needs of recipient countries and in accordance with relevant General Assembly resolutions;

(f)   The Economic and Social Council (Third Committee) should design tools for monitoring harmonization, evaluation and ensuring co-ordination of the entire system for operational activities.   The follow-up to the recommendations of the Council should be monitored closely and organizations concerned should be requested to report to subsequent sessions of the Council on their follow-up action;

(g)   The Secretariat support structure should be strengthened to prepare reports and evaluations of different aspects of operational activities.   The UNCTAD secretariat would play a role in the interrelated areas of money, finance and trade and other case programmes such as economic co-operation among developing countries and the Substantial New Programme of Action;

(h)   Member States should endeavour to strengthen their level of participation in the proposed Committee on Operational Activities for Development;

(i)   The Council should clarify the role of and relationship between funding and executing agencies;

(j)   At the operational level, the role of the resident co-ordinators should be strengthened.   The resident co-ordinators should report regularly to the Council through the Director-General on actual constraints which they face in pursuing co-ordination in the field.

3. Medium-term plan and programme budget

26. The Council should provide the appropriate policy guidance and priorities for the preparation of the medium-term plan in the economic and social

sectors, particularly its introduction. The Council should also review the outline of the proposed programme budget, together with the comments of the Committee for Programme and Co-ordination, with a view to ensuring the effective translation into the proposed programme budget of priorities laid down in the medium-term plan.

27. The Council could convene once every six years at an appropriate time a subject-oriented session for the preparation of the medium-term plan.

28. CPC could be requested to examine both the content and the manner in which the medium-term plan is prepared in order to make the plan and its introduction a more effective instrument for planning and co-ordination in the economic and social sectors.

4. Regional commissions

29. In accordance with the global development strategy and policies adopted by the General Assembly, the Council should put greater emphasis on the consideration of the reports of the regional commissions with a view to effectively integrating the regional inputs into the global discussion of substantive issues. The Council should also review and co-ordinate on a global basis interregional co-operation among the regional commissions. Regional commissions should draw the attention of the Council to questions with global implications or which are of relevance to other regions.

30. The Council should examine the structure and the work programmes of the regional commissions, including their relationships with UNDP and other relevant organizations of the system in the area of operational activities for development.

5. Ad hoc conferences

31. The Council should assume direct responsibility for carrying out the preparatory work of *ad hoc* conferences convened by the Council and the General Assembly.

6. Programme and organization of work, including schedule of meetings

32. The Council should adopt, to the extent possible, a six-year plan for its work. This work plan should, to the extent possible, harmonize with the cycle of the medium-term plan of the United Nations. Such a plan should ensure that the Council will review in depth all sectors of the activities of the United Nations in the economic and social fields at least once during this period.

33. Within that context, the Council should continue to draw up its programme of work on a biennial basis, with subject-oriented sessions to be convened at

appropriate times throughout each year. Such subject-oriented sessions should deal, *inter alia*, with issues of the subsidiary bodies whose functions it has assumed.

34. The Council should convene each year an organizational session in February in (New York/Geneva) and one regular session in (July/September)[7] in addition to subject-oriented sessions. The regular session should be held in (New York/alternately in New York and Geneva).

35. For its regular session, the Council should, in addition to its plenary meetings, convene the following sessional committees:

    (a)   First (Economic) Committee;

    (b)   Second (Social) Committee;

    (c)   Third (Operational Activities and Programming) Committee.[8]

The Council should devote a segment of its regular session to a high-level meeting on specific themes.

36. The work of the Council in a given year could be allocated in the following manner:

    (a)   *Organizational session:*

    (i)   Consider modalities for the implementation of relevant decisions adopted by the General Assembly and the Council;[9]

    (ii)   Review and approve a biennial programme of work, including the convening of subject-oriented sessions;

    (iii)   Organize the work of its regular session, including items to be considered during the high-level segment;

    (iv)   Identify two or three key items for direct consideration and action by the General Assembly;

    (v)   Review and approve the biennial calendar of meetings of the United Nations bodies in the economic and social sectors and the work programmes of its subsidiary bodies;

    (vi)   Elections and appointments.

(b) Regular session:[10]

(i) Consider items on the biennial agenda and adopt recommendations thereon, including reports of intergovernmental bodies reporting to or through it to the Assembly;

(ii) Consider and adopt an integrated "executive report" with executive summary for submission to the General Assembly.

(c) Subject-oriented sessions:

Consider specific issues including, *inter alia*, those subsumed by the Council.

37. The Economic and Social Council should draw up its biennial programme of work, including the subject-oriented sessions, in good time to allow for the preparation of substantive analytical reports and their submission by all relevant organizations of the United Nations system. This would allow the Council secretariat, in appropriate cases, to integrate all inputs received on a given issue in a consolidated report for consideration at the respective sessions.

38. The programme of work and schedule of meetings of intergovernmental bodies in the economic and social fields should be harmonized with those of the General Assembly and the Economic and Social Council. For that purpose, the Council should discharge more effectively its functions in setting up the overall calendar of meetings and in its review of the work programmes of bodies reporting to it to allow the Council to consider reports of all those bodies in a timely, coherent and co-ordinated manner. In principle, all intergovernmental bodies in the economic and social sectors should convene their meetings each year in the [first five months/January-July period]. Such meetings should be scheduled in co-ordination with the timing of the relevant subject-oriented sessions of the Council.

39. The practice of biennialization should continue to apply to the work of the Council and its subsidiary machinery and, as appropriate, to meetings of its subsidiary bodies.

E. *Reports and reporting procedures*

40. The Council should receive consolidated reports on the various social, economic and related issues submitted by relevant bodies and agencies of the United Nations system or prepared by the Council secretariat, as appropriate.[11]

41. The reports of the subsidiary bodies to the Council should be rationalized through, *inter alia*, clustering major system-wide economic and social activities and designating a lead body responsible for the preparation of a

consolidated report.   Such a report should contain action-oriented recommendations. The Secretariat should assist in the preparation of such reports.

42. All subsidiary bodies should reflect in their reports measures taken in the implementation of General Assembly and Council resolutions and decisions.

43. The Council should submit an executive report to the Assembly highlighting the key economic and social policy issues for its consideration, together with relevant recommendations of the Council. This consolidated report could be accompanied by a brief "executive summary" of its decisions, including those relating to the work of its subsidiary machinery.

F. Role of the Bureau of the Council

44. The role of the Bureau of the Council could be strengthened, in particular in such fields as elaboration of draft programmes of work, allocation of items, monitoring the work of the Secretariat related to implementation of Council decisions, ensuring effective follow-up, timely preparation of documentation, etc. The possibility of an enlarged Bureau could be considered. Consideration could also be given to holding, whenever feasible, informal meetings of members of the Council Bureau with members of the bureaux of other intergovernmental bodies, including the specialized agencies. Feasibility of participation of the Council Bureau members in the work of ACC should also be explored in order to promote a constructive system-wide dialogue.

G. Relationship with organizations of the system

45. Executive heads of the organizations of the United Nations system should participate more actively in the deliberations of the Council and should provide all assistance to the Council in accordance with the general and specific directives.

46. Executive heads of agencies of the system or their senior representatives should be encouraged to submit brief thematic reports/statements as well as to participate actively in informal discussions or thematic seminars to be convened by the Council.

47. In accordance with Article 64 of the Charter, the attention of relevant organizations of the system should be drawn to resolutions of the United Nations on major economic and social issues with a view to obtaining regular reports from them, including reports on the steps taken to give effect to those resolutions.

48. A close working relationship should be established between ACC and the Council secretariat.

49. The Council should prepare for consideration at the forty-fifth regular session of the General Assembly a thorough review of the relationship between the United Nations and the specialized agencies in order to enable it to fulfil its overall co-ordination functions under Articles 63, 64 and 66 of the Charter.

H. Membership

50. As a consequence of its new and enhanced role and responsibilities as set out above, the Economic and Social Council should consist of all States Members of the United Nations.[12]

I. Secretariat support

51. The present secretariat support structure in the economic and social sectors would need to be modified in line with the above-mentioned structural and reporting changes. There is need for a substantive secretariat support structure to properly service the restructured Economic and Social Council, particularly with respect to the preparation of reports to the Council as well as the preparation of the Council's own report to the General Assembly. For that purpose, the Secretary-General as chief administrator of the United Nations should be requested to make the necessary arrangements, taking into account the following considerations:

(a) A separate and identifiable secretariat for the Council should be provided;[13]

(b) The new Economic and Social Council secretariat should provide substantive as well as relevant conference services and facilities to the Council. Therefore, the secretariat should be adequately staffed at both the Professional and General Service levels, in strict observance with the principle of equitable geographical representation. Professional staff should be of the highest quality in all the disciplines and issues dealt with by the Economic and Social Council, so as to provide the best possible assistance to the Council in accordance with its new functions;

(c) The secretariat of the Council should, *inter alia*, collate, consolidate and prepare, as appropriate, the reports for submission to it, with conclusions as necessary. The Council's secretariat should be capable of preparing substantive and analytical reports of a global or interdisciplinary nature covering both policy and co-ordination aspects for consideration by the Council, thereby enabling substantive co-ordination by it;

(d) A periodic evaluation and appraisal of the quality and content of reports prepared for the Council should be made;

(e) Reports submitted to the Council should be of a standard format to facilitate reading and consideration by all delegations;

(f)   Efforts should be made to co-ordinate the work of the secretariats in Vienna, Geneva and New York more effectively;

(g)   The Office of the Director General for Development and International Economic Co-operation should be strengthened to enable the Director-General to effectively carry out his responsibility for co-ordination, particularly in the area of operational activities for development.

III. Trade and development board

52. The views and proposals of the Trade and Development Board on its functions and responsibilities, as set out in informal paper TDB/1154 of 23 November 1987, adopted at the resumed thirty-fourth session of the Board could be endorsed.

53. In this respect, it may be appropriate to underscore some of those recommendations which have a direct bearing on the work of the General Assembly and the Economic and Social Council.

(a)   In addition to serving as a main input for the debate of the Trade and Development Board on interdependence, the *Trade and Development Report* should be used as the main statement on overall policy issues covered by UNCTAD;

(b)   To ensure the best use of UNCTAD reviews of the interdependence of economic issues, the Council could draw on, *inter alia*, these reviews in its discussion of economic and social policies and in the promotion of a more integrated approach to the economic and social aspects of development, and in the exercise of co-ordination and monitoring responsibilities.

54. The Trade and Development Board substantive debate on the interrelated macro-economic issues shall take place at its spring session.[14] This debate shall concentrate on the sectors of trade and development and the related issues of money, finance, debt, etc.

ANNEX III. B

Paper introduced by the Chairman on 23 MAY 1988 as a supplement to
the informal consolidated discussion paper presented by the
Chairman on 21 APRIL 1988

IV. Subsidiary bodies in the economic, social and related areas

55. As appropriate, necessary steps should be taken by the General Assembly,
the Economic and Social Council and concerned subsidiary bodies in the
economic, social and related fields, to implement the following:

(a)   The Council should, at its organizational session each year, review the
programme of work and agenda of its subsidiary bodies with a view to
harmonizing the work programmes of the intergovernmental bodies in the
economic, social and related areas. The review should ensure that the General
Assembly and the Council are properly assisted in carrying out their Charter
responsibilities.   The Council should also in that context determine a
biennialized calendar of conferences and meetings.

(b)   The Council should review the membership of the subsidiary bodies
in order to ensure equitable geographical representation and more effective
participation.

(c)   Agenda of subsidiary bodies should be rationalized through
biennialization and the staggering of the consideration of some items, as well
as the adoption of thematic approach in the organization of work. To the
extent possible, the agenda for each session should be limited to no more than
five substantive items.

(d)   Arrangements should be made for subsidiary bodies to have, in
principle, a single consolidated document under each substantive item. The
Secretary-General should assist in achieving this objective.

(e)   Steps should be taken to implement measures envisaged in the
respective contributions and submissions to the Special Commission relating
to rationalization and streamlining of work including those relating to schedule
of meetings and the improvement in quality and reduction in volume of
documentation.

(f)   Timely submission of documents, particularly for meetings held away
from headquarters, should be ensured.

56. Specific recommendations in regard to the subsidiary bodies are given
below.

A. *Regional Commissions*[15]

57. Relevant provisions of General Assembly resolution 32/197 should be fully implemented in order to allow the regional commissions to exercise their roles fully and effectively under the authority of the Economic and Social Council, as the main economic and social development centres within the United Nations system for their respective regions.

58. The Secretary-General, in his review of the Secretariat support structure, should enhance the multidisciplinary research capabilities of the regional commissions in order to enable them to integrate better economic and social analysis at the regional level.

59. Subregional co-operation should be strengthened and should be integrated more effectively into the activities of each region, taking fully into account the priorities of Governments concerned. For that purpose, efforts should be made, *inter alia*, to strengthen subregional offices, bearing in mind the specific objectives for which these regional offices were established.

60. The Economic and Social Council should integrate better the work of the regional commissions into intergovernmental discussions and policy-making at the global level. For that purpose, the Council should consider discussing relevant inputs of the regional commissions under its substantive items and, as appropriate, draw the attention of other intergovernmental bodies to relevant parts of the reports of the regional commissions.

61. The Economic and Social Council should promote more effectively interregional co-operation among the regional commissions so as to enable them to take better advantage of each other's experiences.

62. In executing projects, the regional commissions should utilize to the maximum extent possible the existing technical and support capabilities of organizations of the system in their respective regions. The Economic and Social Council, in its policy review of operational activities for development, should examine and further clarify the role of the regional commissions as executing agencies for inter-sectoral, subregional, regional and interregional projects as well as sectoral, subregional, regional and interregional projects which do not fall within the purview of the sectoral responsibilities of specialized agencies and other United Nations bodies. For that purpose, the Council should ensure close co-operation between the regional commissions and the organizations of the United Nations system and avoid any overlaps which may exist. The relationship between the regional commissions and UNDP in particular should be further strengthened. The regional commissions should be actively involved in the preparation of UNDP's inter-country programming exercises.

63. Existing joint units between the regional commissions and other organizations of the system should continue and if necessary be further strengthened. Such a practice should also be extended to other appropriate organizations.

64. The possibility of integrating relevant United Nations regional offices into the regional commissions, particularly UNEP, should be further explored.

65. The working relationship between the regional commissions and the Committee for Programme and Co-ordination should be strengthened in order to allow the Committee, in carrying out its responsibilities as envisaged in General Assembly resolution 41/213, to take better into account the priorities and decisions of the regional commissions as reflected in their biennial work programmes and medium-term plans.

66. The Secretary-General should fully implement the decentralization of resources and administrative authority from headquarters to the regional commissions as envisaged in General Assembly resolution 32/197.

67. The regional commissions should continue to strengthen their working relationship with other regional bodies. For that purpose, joint meetings held between the regional commissions and such organizations should continue to be governed by the rules of procedure of the United Nations.

68. The Secretary-General should take urgent measures to reduce the high vacancy rates in the regional commissions in accordance with relevant General Assembly and the Economic and Social Council resolutions.

1. Economic Commission for Europe

69. The Economic Commission for Europe should implement all restructuring measures envisaged in its submission to the Special Commission (E/ECE/1150/Rev.1 - informal paper 14/Add.10).

70. While the ECE should continue to carry out its mandate in promoting economic co-operation among countries of the region, it should increase activities directed to supporting developing countries in other regions. Co-operation between the ECE and other regional commissions should be strengthened, particularly through appropriate joint projects.

71. The ECE should, with the assistance of the Secretary-General, examine the relevant parts of the United Nations regular budget, including conference services for its meetings, to determine whether certain activities and meetings of the Commission could henceforth be financed through extrabudgetary resources.

72. The participation of non-ECE member States in relevant meetings of the Commission should be encouraged.

2. *Economic and Social Commission for Asia and the Pacific*

73. ESCAP should implement its decision to reduce the number of its subsidiary bodies from nine to seven, which, on an experimental basis, should meet biennially for five working days.

74. In view of the size of the region, ESCAP should find practical arrangements to enhance subregional co-operation. As regards the Commission's activities in the Pacific, the ESCAP Pacific Operations Centre should have greater autonomy and receive more resources.

75. The Commission should refrain to the extent possible from resorting to outside consultants for the preparation of its documentation. Greater use should be made of existing Secretariat personnel.

76. ESCAP should utilize more effectively the increasing extrabudgetary resources available to it and should ensure that activities thus financed are consistent with the national and regional priorities of the developing countries concerned.

3. *Economic Commission for Africa*

77. The Conference of African Ministers for Economic Development and Planning should continue to be held on an annual basis given the continuing economic crisis in Africa and the necessity to monitor it continuously. Such a practice could be reviewed by the Commission in 1992. All other intergovernmental meetings of the Commission should henceforth be held on a biennial basis.

78. Multinational Programming and Operational Centres (MULPOCs) should be appropriately strengthened. Where the necessary subregional groupings do not exist, the Economic Commission for Africa should encourage the formation of such groupings and provide them with technical backstopping.

79. The General Assembly in its consideration of the United Nations programme budget should accord relative priorities for the activities of ECA, particularly in the light of its mandate for the implementation of the United Nations Programme of Action for African Economic Recovery and Development.

4. Economic Commission for Latin America and the Caribbean

80. The Economic Commission for Latin America and the Caribbean should further review its subsidiary machinery, bearing in mind the following:

(a)   The sessional committees on water and human settlements should be abolished;

(b)   The Committee on Trade should be reconvened;

(c)   A committee on debt and monetary issues should be established.

81. The report of the Commission to the Council should reflect more substantively its deliberations, focusing on major regional policy issues considered by the Commission.

82. The Commission should expedite the setting-up of a joint unit with the United Nations Conference on Trade and Development and enhance its co-ordination with the United Nations Development Programme.   UNDP should take better into account the macro-economic studies of ECLAC in preparing its country programmes in that region.

5. Economic and Social Commission for Western Asia

83. In accordance with the decision of the fourteenth session of ESCWA, the regular sessions of the Commission and the meetings of its Technical Committee should be held biennially.

84. ESCWA should make every effort to improve the implementation of its programme of work.

85. UNEP and UNIDO should resume and strengthen the arrangement of maintaining joint units with ESCWA.

B.   Operational activities for development[16]

86. Operational activities carried out by organizations of the United Nations system and their review should aim at promoting the achievement of the following objectives:

(a)   Promotion of the speedy economic and social progress of developing countries by enhancing their ability to buildup their productive capacity, better utilize their indigenous resources and develop the self-sustaining managerial, technical, institutional and research capabilities required in the development process within the socio-cultural context of each recipient country;

(b)   External technical co-operation and assistance should be provided at their request and should be for the benefit of the developing countries in conformity with their national plans, objectives and priorities;

(c)   The overall orientation of operational activities should reflect fully the overall strategies, policies and priorities established by the General Assembly and the Economic and Social Council;

(d)   The achievement of optimal efficiency and the reduction of administrative costs with a consequent increase in the proportion of resources available to meet the assistance requirements of recipient countries;

(e)   A real increase in the flow of resources for such activities on a predictable, continued and assured basis.

87. The Economic and Social Council should, as envisaged in General Assembly resolution 32/197, carry out effectively its responsibilities in ensuring greater policy cohesion and co-ordination of all operational activities of the system, at both the headquarters and field level.[17] It should also ensure that the priorities of the General Assembly and the Council are fully taken into account by the intergovernmental and governing bodies of the system involved in operational activities, bearing in mind the need to achieve optimal intergovernmental and intersecretariat co-operation and collaboration.

88. Coherence among operational activities for development, technical co-operation and disaster relief activities and the activities of funds administered by UNDP and other funds should be ensured, with a view to programme harmonization, rationalization of efforts at the field level and the effective integration of such activities in overall development efforts.

1. Governing Council of the United Nations Development Programme

89. In light of the role of the Economic and Social Council in operational activities, the Governing Council of the United Nations Development Programme (UNDP) should ensure the effective implementation of the policy guidance and priorities established by the Economic and Social Council and the General Assembly.   To that end, every effort should be made to avoid overlapping and duplication in the discussions held on operational activities by the General Assembly and the Economic and Social Council and in the high-level segment of the Governing Council, and among the issues on their agendas.

90. The work of the Governing Council should focus on ensuring the efficient and effective management, programming and utilization of the resources of UNDP and the funds administered by it, including the simplification and harmonization of programme and project procedures.

91. The UNDP country programming should be reviewed with a view to developing an appropriate and effective framework to ensure coherence in the programming of the operational activities of the United Nations system and their responsiveness to the priorities of the recipient countries.

92. The working methods, procedures, schedule, duration and membership of the Committee of the Whole and its Working Group should be reviewed and refined in order to support more effectively the work of the Governing Council, particularly in enhancing transparency in the UNDP management and in ensuring programme and project quality.[18]

93. The Governing Council should provide greater in-depth policy guidance and direction as well as administrative and management oversight to the Department of Technical Co-operation for Development and the funds administered by UNDP. Adequate time should be allocated for the discussion of these matters. The funds should be managed in an integrated manner, ensuring complementarily and mutual support with each other and with the regular indicative planning figures programme.

94. The sessions of the Governing Council should be held at a time that permits its timely reporting to the Economic and Social Council, and the number of its meetings reduced, bearing in mind the usefulness of developing a system of thematic reporting aimed at improved co-ordination of programmes and activities.

2. Executive Board of the United Nations Children's Fund

95. Stronger common policy guidance by the Economic and Social Council, in particular with a view to the effective co-ordinated execution of operational activities would permit the Executive Board of the United Nations Children's Fund (UNICEF) to direct its efforts towards the review of programme, financial and managerial activities.

96. The scheduling of the sessions of the Executive Board should be adjusted to avoid overlap with other major meetings; in this connection, the need for the timely review of the budget of UNICEF by the Advisory Committee on Administrative and Budgetary Questions should be taken into account.

97. The relationship between the administration of UNICEF and the Executive Board should be strengthened, especially with regard to financial and budgetary issues and with a view to ensuring optimal distribution of resources between operational and administrative costs.

3. *High-level Meeting on Technical Co-operation among Developing Countries*

98.   The High-level Committee, in view of its important mandate, was indispensable. As technical co-operation among developing countries was a system-wide issue, it could not be entrusted to any single governing body.[19]

99.   There is a need to improve system-wide co-ordination and enhancement of TCDC activities. In that context, the catalytic role of the Economic and Social Council and the Governing Council of the United Nations Development Programme should be strengthened.

100. Field offices of UNDP should have better information in regard to established technical co-operation programmes in developing countries in order to be able to promote the use of TCDC modalities at the project level. Resident representatives should play a more active role in assisting recipient Governments with information on possible sources of TCDC in their selection of inputs and executing agencies.

101. UNDP should adopt an appropriately high level of priority for TCDC. For that purpose, increased resources should be allocated within UNDP for the promotion of TCDC, including the strengthening of the TCDC secretariat.

4. *Committee on Food Aid Policies and Programmes*

102. There is a need to enhance co-ordination among the intergovernmental bodies of the system dealing with food, agriculture and development.

103. The Committee on Food Aid Policies and Programmes should address broad policy issues only once a year and improve its procedures for the consideration of projects.

104. The procedures for the election of members of the Committee should be reviewed.

105. The need to hold a separate pledging conference for the World Food Programme should also be reviewed.

5. *Executive Committee of the Programme of the United Nations High Commissioner for Refugees*

106. The Executive Committee of the Programme of the United Nations High Commissioner for Refugees should provide general guidelines to the Office of the High Commissioner on issues related to development activities, bearing in mind the humanitarian and non-political character of the work of the Office.

107. The Economic and Social Council should consider the activities of the UNHCR and the related activities of other organizations in an integrated manner. To this end, the format and scope of the annual report of the High Commissioner should be reviewed in order to facilitate its consideration by the Council.

108. Issues concerning refugees and returnees should be taken into account in the work of all development forums, especially the round-table meetings organized by UNDP, the consultative group meetings of the World Bank and other similar meetings, whenever the countries concerned host large numbers of refugees and returnees.

109. The duration of the meetings of the Executive Committee and its membership should be reviewed and measures should be taken to ensure the effective participation of observers in its work.

110. Steps should be taken to ensure the timely distribution of the documentation prepared for the sessions of the Executive Committee.

V. Other subsidiary bodies

A. Statistical Commission

111. The Commission should play a more active role in reviewing, evaluating and co-ordinating the work of the United Nations in this area including the enhancing of its advisory functions to other relevant intergovernmental bodies.

112. Co-ordination should be enhanced with respect to other United Nations bodies, such as the United Nations Children's Fund, the United Nations Population Fund and the United Nations Environment Programme; agencies such as the World Bank and the International Monetary Fund; other international organizations outside the United Nations system; and non-governmental organizations involved in statistical work on a global level.

113. The United Nations statistical data should be rationalized and standardized for enhancing its impact and usefulness for end-users. The Commission should review and undertake practical steps to enable better access by Governments to the United Nations statistical data. For that purpose, and where necessary, technical assistance to the developing countries should be enhanced.

114. The Working Group should be discontinued and its work assumed directly by the Commission.

B. Population Commission

115. There is a need for greater focus in its programme of work on issues relating to population policies, particularly concerning the co-ordination of the activities of the United Nations system.

116. The present arrangements, whereby reports of the Secretary-General on the activities of UNFPA for consideration by the UNDP Governing Council are available to the Population Commission and for the reports of the Commission itself to be available to the Governing Council, should continue. In this regard, the Governing Council, while considering the programme activities of UNFPA, should take into account in a more effective manner the deliberations of the Population Commission and its recommendations on population questions.[20]

117. The Secretary-General in his review of the Secretariat support structure in the area of population should take into account concerns regarding a better division of labour between the analytical, technical, funding and executing aspects of the various Secretariat units including the possibility of amalgamating technical units.[21]

C. Commission on Human Rights

118. The Commission should update its mandate by including references to economic, social and cultural rights and the Declaration on the Right to Development of the General Assembly.

119. The definition of discrimination embodied in the present terms of reference of the Commission should be rendered more comprehensive and in line with the definition contained in article 1 of the International Convention on the Elimination of All Forms of Racial Discrimination by adding colour, descent or national or ethnic origin.

120. One of the important elements requiring consideration is that of the procedures under Economic and Social Council resolution 1503 (XLVIII) dealing with communications relating to violation of human rights and fundamental freedoms. The mandate of the Working Group on Communications could be revised to allow for direct participation of representatives of the States concerned.[22]

121. Efforts should be made to ensure that the meetings of human rights treaty bodies do not coincide with those of the Commission.

122. The time allocated to each item should be reviewed periodically. Some items of the Commission's agenda could be discussed every two or three years.

123. The Commission should be the focal point in the drafting of international standards in the field of human rights and due account should be taken of

General Assembly resolution 41/120 on setting international standards in the field of human rights.

124. Efforts should be made to limit and improve the quality of the documentation of the Commission.

125. Limits should be set regarding the length of speeches at the Commission.

126. The role of the Bureau of the Commission should be strengthened. The Bureau should be more active in organizing the Commission's work.

127. The Sub-Commission on Prevention of Discrimination and Protection of Minorities should make efforts to rationalize its work and should be guided by the Commission. The Sub-Commission, when examining items extensively discussed elsewhere in the United Nations system, should concentrate on those issues to which it can make a distinct contribution. There should be a clearer division of labour to emphasize the expert advisory role of the Sub-Commission and the policy role of the Commission.

128. The Sub-Commission on Prevention of Discrimination and Protection of Minorities should assume the functions of its Working Group on Detention.

129. The work of the above-mentioned Sub-Commission should be open-ended.

130. The right to development should be a separate item of the Commission's agenda and should take into account developments in other forums.

131. Steps should be taken to achieve closer co-operation between the Centre, the Centre for Social Development and Humanitarian Affairs and the Department of International Economic and Social Affairs in the light of the complementarily of their respective research functions as well as other United Nations bodies, specialized agencies and regional human rights bodies.

132. There is need to increase the representation of underrepresented groups of States in senior and policy-formulating posts in the Centre for Human Rights, while safeguarding the principle of equitable geographical distribution in accordance with the relevant resolutions of the General Assembly.

133. Dissemination of public information on human rights questions should be strengthened in co-operation between the Centre for Human Rights and the Department of Public Information and through intensification of the Department of Public Information activities relating in particular to *apartheid* and the right to development.

D. Committee on Economic, Social and Cultural Rights

134. The reporting programme for States Parties to the International Covenant on Economic, Social and Cultural Rights previously adopted by the Economic and Social Council in resolution 1988 (LX) should be amended. States Parties should be requested to submit a single report within two years of the Covenant's entry into force for the State Party concerned and thereafter at five-year intervals.

135. There was agreement in principle with the holding of a week-long pre-sessional meeting of a working group prior to each session, as recommended by the Committee.

136. More attention should be paid to the implementation of the right to self-determination.

137. The amount of documentation produced for the Committee should be reduced.

138. Co-operation between the Centre for Human Rights and the Centre for Social Development and Humanitarian Affairs should be further enhanced in matters concerning the work of the Committee on Economic, Social and Cultural Rights.

139. The Economic and Social Council should discharge its function fully under article 21 of the International Covenant on Economic, Social and Cultural Rights.

140. Co-ordination between the Economic and Social Council and the Committee on the one hand and the other organs of the United Nations, the regional commissions and the specialized agencies in particular, should be intensified.

E. Commission for Social Development

141. The Commission should consider adopting a thematic approach in its programme of work in order to effectively discharge responsibilities entrusted to it by the Council. Major themes should be identified well in advance, taking into account and including emerging social problems, particularly those of concern to developing countries, such as rural integration and literacy.

142. Governments should, while nominating representatives to the Commission, take fully into account the need for expertise required.

143. The Secretary-General should ensure that the United Nations Office at Vienna is able to serve effectively as the centre for social policy and social development and that DIEC is enabled to ensure the effective integration of

social issues in the deliberations on development, both at the Secretariat and at the intergovernmental level.

144. The Secretary-General should utilize the work of the *ad hoc* expert group in such a manner that it would contribute more directly to the work of the Commission.

F. Commission on the Status of Women

145. The Commission should effectively carry out its role as the central co-ordinating body on issues relating to women and to ensure that these issues are examined in the context of economic and social development. The capacity of regional commissions should be better utilized through, *inter alia*, more effective regional input to the work of the Commission.

146. The global review of Forward-looking Strategies should be held in conjunction with the Economic and Social Council in-depth review once every six years.

147. In view of the multidisciplinary nature of issues relating to women, relevant organizations of the system are called upon to participate actively in the work of the Commission and to contribute to intersecretariat inputs.

G. Commission on Narcotic Drugs

148. The work programme of the Commission should be so adjusted to enable it to more effectively follow-up the results emanating from international drug conferences.

149. The Commission should adhere strictly to biennialization of its meetings and should refrain from requesting the convening of special sessions.

150. While recognizing the usefulness of the subsidiary bodies, the Commission should refrain from creating new bodies.

151. The Secretary-General, while reviewing the Secretariat support, should ensure the maximum complementarily of work between the Division and the International Narcotics Control Board secretariat.

H. Commission on Transnational Corporations

152. The Commission should serve as the main intergovernmental body, and the Centre on Transnational Corporations as the focal point in the system, responsible for co-ordinating all matters relating to transnational corporations, with a view to strengthening interrelationships in this area and avoiding overlaps and duplication.

153. To improve co-ordination, organizations of the system should be invited to provide information in regard to work undertaken by them relating to transnationals for inclusion in a report to the Commission and the Economic and Social Council. Such a report should be prepared every two years and should highlight priority issues.

154. The programme of work of the Commission should be rationalized with a view to biennializing a considerable portion of its agenda. Items such as the code of conduct and the activities of transnational corporations in South Africa and Namibia, should be reviewed annually. The duration of the Commission's sessions should be adjusted accordingly.

155. The Special Session of the Commission on the Code of Conduct should continue its work but its meetings should be scheduled as appropriate to enable it to proceed with finalization of the Code.

156. Efforts should also be made to improve the impact and effectiveness of the joint units with the regional commissions.

157. Co-ordination and exchange of information with other intergovernmental organs regarding work programmes should be improved, especially between the Commission and the regional commissions and with intergovernmental bodies such as the United Nations Conference on Trade and Development.

I. Commission on Human Settlements

158. The Commission should pay greater attention to operational activities undertaken by the Centre, particularly in regard to the promotion of low-cost housing, especially in the least developed countries of Africa.

159. Co-operation between the United Nations Development Programme and the Centre should be enhanced.

J. Committee on Non-Governmental Organizations

160. The Secretary-General in his review should ensure effective Secretariat support for the Committee, including the question of effective co-operation among units with responsibility in this area. The question of location of the NGO unit, which provides support to the Committee, should be further examined.

K. Committee on Natural Resources

161. Options whereby the mandate of the Committee, which continues to remain valid, could be carried out more effectively should be explored.

162. Programme of work and the function of the Committee should be rationally redefined in the broader context of that of other bodies. The possibility that the Committee would meet on an *ad hoc* basis should also be explored.

L. Committee on Negotiations with Intergovernmental Agencies

163. The Economic and Social Council should assume direct responsibility for the functions of this Committee.

M. Committee of Experts on the Transport of Dangerous Goods

164. Relevant subject-matters relating to the work of the Committee should be reviewed, as appropriate, by the Governing Council of the United Nations Environment Programme and the Committee on Transport of the United Nations Conference on Trade and Development.

165. The Secretary-General should continue his efforts to promote better participation of developing countries in the work of the Committee and to ensure adequate Secretariat support.

N. Committee on Crime Prevention and Control

166. While maintaining a biennial cycle of meetings, the Bureau of the Committee should convene if necessary an informal inter-sessional meeting to prepare for the work of the Committee.

167. The five-year cycle for the meetings of the Crime Congress should be maintained but the number of regional preparatory meetings should be kept to a minimum.

168. The agenda for such Congresses should be more focused and should concentrate, *inter alia*, on the implementation of international standards.

169. Steps should be taken to establish better working relations with other relevant intergovernmental bodies, particularly the Commission for Social Development and the Commission on Human Rights.

O. Committee for Development Planning

170. The programme of work of the Committee should take fully into account the issues before the Economic and Social Council and the General Assembly.

171. The Council could make specific suggestions in regard to the agenda of the Committee for Development Planning.

172. The Council should also benefit from the views of relevant organizations of the system on the recommendations of the Committee for Development Planning. The Secretary-General could explore the possibility of using existing inter-agency mechanism for such views to be provided to the Economic and Social Council.

173. The necessary expertise and independence of the members of the Committee for Development Planning should continue to be ensured.

174. On specific issues, the Committee should secure the active contribution of observers from relevant organizations.

175. The Economic and Social Council should make better use of the Committee report including its use as a background for the preparation of "agreed conclusions" of the President of the Council.

P. Ad Hoc Group of Experts on International Co-operation in Tax Matters

176. This *Ad Hoc* Group should meet only as and when requested by the Council.

177. Its programme of work should take into account the agenda of the Council. For that purpose the agenda could include consideration of the impact of tax treaties on trade and development.

178. The practice of using consultants for the preparation of inputs should be kept to a minimum.

179. The Secretary-General in his review should give consideration to the location of its Secretariat taking into account that the primary concern of the *Ad Hoc* Group is related to legal matters.

Q. Intergovernmental Working Group of Experts on International Standards of Accounting and Reporting

180. All options to ensure expert level participation from developing countries, including meeting travel costs, should be explored.

181. The Working Group should meet biennially and continue to report to the Commission on Transnational Corporations and the Economic and Social Council.

182. Emphasis should be placed on considering methods for bringing to the attention of Governments concerned, particularly developing countries, agreed approaches and results of the work of the Working Group. For that purpose, interested Governments should designate a national institution to act as a focal

point. The Centre should maintain an updated directory of such national institutions and provide them with information regarding the proceedings of the Working Group.

183. Efforts should continue to encourage the participation of other relevant intergovernmental and non-governmental organizations in the proceedings of the Working Group.

R. *Ad Hoc Intergovernmental Working Group on the Problem of Corrupt Practices*

184. The *Ad Hoc* Intergovernmental Working Group on the Problem of Corrupt Practices, which submitted its last report to the Commission on Transnational Corporations and the Economic and Social Council in 1978, should be abolished and an agenda item on the question of corrupt practices should be considered by the Commission on Transnational Corporations every two years.

S. *Committee for Programme and Co-ordination*

185. The Committee should improve implementation of its mandate, focusing on the essential programming and co-ordination role defined in its terms of reference contained in Council resolution 2008 (LX) of 14 May 1976, bearing in mind the implications of General Assembly resolution 41/213.[23]

186. The Committee for Programme and Co-ordination should harmonize its programme of work with that of the Council in order to assist the Council to fully carry out its co-ordination responsibility envisaged in the Charter.

187. The Committee should examine the process of preparation and content of the medium-term plan in order to ensure that the plan and its introduction constitute the most effective instrument for programme planning and co-ordination.

188. The Committee, in reviewing the draft medium-term plan and revisions thereto and in examining the proposed programme budget, should ensure implementation of the policy directives set by the Assembly and the Economic and Social Council.

189. The Committee for Programme and Co-ordination should, particularly within the context of its review of the medium-term plan and programme budget, continue to assist the Economic and Social Council in carrying out its system-wide co-ordination functions by, *inter alia*: (a) reviewing and appraising, with the assistance of the Administrative Committee on Co-ordination (ACC), the implementation of legislative decisions with a view to determining the degree of co-ordinated effort undertaken throughout the system in certain priority fields identified by the Council; (b) identifying the

areas in which co-ordination efforts should be strengthened; and (c) bringing to the attention of the Council decisions taken by the governing bodies of the United Nations system which might lead to duplication or divergent action with a view to their possible harmonization. To this end, the Committee should ensure the effective integration of the programming and co-ordination aspects of its work and adopt a thematic approach to its co-ordination responsibilities.

190. For the outcome of the Joint Meetings of the Committee for Programme and Co-ordination and the Administrative Committee on Co-ordination to be more beneficial to the Council, the agenda should be determined by the Council, reflecting its priorities and critical questions for the system in the economic, social and humanitarian fields. The duration of the joint meetings of the Committee for Programme and Co-ordination and the Administrative Committee on Co-ordination could be extended to two full days. In order to enhance the level of participation, the venue could be changed to New York, with the joint meetings scheduled close to those of the Committee for Programme and Co-ordination or the Administrative Committee on Co-ordination. The joint meetings of CPC and ACC should recommend concrete solutions to problems of inter-organizational co-ordination for the Council's consideration.[24]

191. In order to carry out its mandate in a more effective and efficient manner, the Committee for Programme and Co-ordination should strengthen its relationship and interaction with the Economic and Social Council, the Advisory Committee on Administrative and Budgetary Questions (ACABQ), ACC and the Joint Inspection Unit (JIU). In particular, active collaboration should be established between the Bureaux of the Committee and ACABQ. Arrangements should also be made for periodic joint consultations between the Committee and JIU.

192. Member States should be represented in the Committee for Programme and Co-ordination at a high level of expertise. Experts designated to serve on the Committee should have a high degree of experience and competence with regard to the programmes and activities of the United Nations system. Continuity of representation should also be ensured.

193. The Committee should continue reporting directly to the Council. Its report should highlight policy issues requiring action or decision by the Council.

194. The Committee for Programme and Co-ordination should meet in accordance with the pattern of meetings established for the Economic and Social Council, and at a time that permits its timely reporting to the Council and the Assembly and ensures its effective interaction with the Advisory Committee on Administrative and Budgetary Questions. As necessary, the Committee may meet twice each year up to maximum of seven weeks; the duration of sessions should be flexible and respond to requirements.

195. The Committee should systematically review follow-up and implementation of its conclusions and recommendations.

196. There should be improved complementarity of work programmes of the Economic and Social Council and the Committee for Programme and Co-ordination. While the Council should give guidance and set priorities in this regard, the Committee should use its instruments such as the medium-term plan, programme budget, cross-organizational programme analyses, ACC reports, and evaluation reviews to ensure consistency with directives set by the Council and the Assembly. On the other hand, the Committee for Programme and Co-ordination should recommend concrete measures that the Council could adopt to improve the interpretation of legislative mandates and harmonization of programmes on a system-wide basis.

197. Mechanisms and procedures exist for the results of the Committee's work to be brought to the attention of the relevant Main Committees of the Assembly and other intergovernmental bodies. To ensure that the committees' deliberations receive adequate attention, they should reflect a dynamic and rigorous approach to its responsibilities.

198. The Committee for Programme and Co-ordination should be supported by a substantive, identifiable and permanent secretariat.

T. *Intergovernmental Committee on Science and Technology for Development*

199. The mandate is important and relevant, but its execution by the Intergovernmental Committee is not satisfactory. While certain reforms would be necessary, it is too early to consider the transfer of its function to other bodies or terminating it. It should be operated in a more rationalized manner and reviewed at the end of the decade review in 1989.

200. The efforts of the Intergovernmental Committee to rationalize its work are appreciated, but these efforts should be continued. In this context, the present arrangements for documentation and a biennial two-week session is appropriate.

201. Co-ordination within the Secretariat support structure, especially its relations with the Office of the Director-General for Development and International Economic Co-operation and the Department of International Economic and Social Affairs, needs to be improved.

202. Co-ordination with other intergovernmental organs, including the Advisory Committee on Science and Technology for Development, should be rationalized and improved.

U. Advisory Committee for Science and Technology for Development

203. The number of *ad hoc* panels of the Advisory Committee should be rationalized.

V. Committee on the Development and Utilization of New and Renewable Sources of Energy

204. The mandate is valid, but there should be an improvement in the Committee's ability to discharge its functions especially with a view to carrying out the Nairobi Programme of Action.

205. The feasibility of establishing a small expert group to replace the Committee on the Development and Utilization of New and Renewable Sources of Energy should be examined.

206. The reporting procedure should be re-examined especially with regard to the role of the Economic and Social Council.

207. More efforts should be made to enhance public awareness of this issue. For that purpose, creation of appropriate projects or programmes such as an information centre, a data bank and an information network could be considered.

208. Selecting and concentrating a couple of themes and topics to be discussed in the Committee is welcomed, but in formulating the agenda, care should be taken to avoid repetition.

209. An appropriate and more visible secretariat is needed to reactivate and keep the momentum of the Nairobi Programme of Action.

210. Clearer focus and a greater degree of co-ordination should be necessary in the secretariat support structure; in this context the relationship between the Office of the Director-General for Development and International Economic Co-operation, the Department of International Economic and Social Affairs and the Department of Technical Co-operation for Development should be redefined.

211. The Office of the Director-General for Development and International Economic Co-operation and the offices of resident co-ordinators should play a more active role in ensuring a coherent and effective implementation of the Nairobi Plan of Action.

W. *Governing Council of the United Nations Environment Programme*

212. Its special mandate to work with non-governmental organizations and special interest groups should be further stressed.

213. The United Nations Environment Programme should prepare a consolidated report on system-wide environmental activities to be submitted directly to the Economic and Social Council.

214. Efforts to further streamline its work programme and meeting schedules as well as to reduce documentation should be encouraged.

215. UNEP's role as a co-ordinator of environment-related activities should be clearly defined. There is a need to develop simple methods to evaluate individual programmes and projects as well as to improve UNEP's information service.

216. UNEP's concern for transboundary problems such as the ozone layer and air pollution should be heightened. In addition, regional seas programme, a global view of marine affairs and the action on international rivers are among the issues to which UNEP should pay more attention.

217. Guidance and monitoring of implementation of environmental issues with relation to development should also be a focal point of UNEP's work in the years to come.

218. In order to enhance the fund raising capabilities, some measures should be considered in the context of current system-wide financial restraint.

219. Co-ordination with regional commissions is desirable, but regional offices of UNEP should be independently maintained.

220. The working relationship with other bodies such as Habitat, UNDP and regional commissions should be strengthened. However, UNEP's co-ordination function in environmental issues with relation to other bodies should also be enhanced in order to avoid overlapping with other bodies. For that purpose, establishing administrative units in charge of co-ordination within the offices of executing agencies would be desirable.

221. Also in this context, the Administrative Committee on Co-ordination should give increased focus to environmental issues.

X. *Group of Experts on Geographical Names*

222. In addition to a triennialization of its meetings, the Group of Experts could meet either concurrently with the conferences or every two and a half years between each conference.

223. The Group of Experts should implement procedures for the review and evaluation called for in resolution 4 of the Conference on the Standardization of Geographical Names and report to the Economic and Social Council.

224. Documentation for the conferences should not be excessive.

225. The Economic and Social Council should request the Group of Experts to identify bodies currently or potentially involved with geographical names and determine their ability to pursue geographical names standardization.

226. Measures should be taken toward a fuller integration of the Group of Experts within the United Nations system. Better relations should also be achieved with regional commissions.

Y. *World Food Council*

227. The World Food Council in its present form of a ministerial body should be preserved. The presence of ministers is useful in mobilizing support for issues in the area of food. The Food and Agriculture Organization of the United Nations and the World Food Programme should reflect in their agendas the recommendations of the World Food Council.

228. The World Food Council meets annually but is subject to the biennial programme of the Economic and Social Council. WFC may consider the idea of biennializing its ministerial sessions and holding regional ministerial consultations in the off-years.

229. The co-ordinating role of WFC should be strengthened within its mandate and with due consideration of the overall responsibility of the Council for policy guidance and co-ordination (see footnote 3 of document of 21 April 1988).

ANNEX IV

Chairman's text dated 4 May 1988 on the draft conclusions and
recommendations of the Special Commission (E/SCN.1/CRP.1)

Introduction

1.   There is agreement among all members of the Special Commission that the
main purpose of the exercise is to enhance the efficiency and effectiveness of
the United Nations intergovernmental structure in the economic and social
fields. There is also clear recognition of the need for reform and restructuring
of the intergovernmental machinery and its Secretariat support structure to
render them more effective and more responsive to the needs of Member
States.

2.   It is recognized that in order to strengthen the United Nations in the
economic and social sectors as a whole it is important to strengthen the role
of the General Assembly as the supreme body of the United Nations and the
pivotal role of the Economic and Social Council, as envisaged in the Charter.
A more effective Council would complement and strengthen the respective
roles of the General Assembly and the United Nations Conference on Trade
and Development (UNCTAD), as well as their subsidiary machinery.

3.   It is also recognized that the restructuring measures as outlined below
cannot by themselves ensure the achievement of the main objective of reform
unless accompanied by the necessary political will on the part of Member
States to make better use of the United Nations as a viable forum for
international co-operation.

4.   The Special Commission has undertaken the in-depth study of the United
Nations intergovernmental structure and functions in the economic and social
fields entrusted to it by the Economic and Social Council. There is general
agreement that the Council has so far been unable to carry out effectively the
functions and responsibilities entrusted to it by the Charter and relevant
General Assembly resolutions.

5.   Reform of the United Nations is a continuing process. The present
exercise should be seen in that context and should benefit from past
experiences, including the implementation of the decisions adopted.
Restructuring measures should be devised in such a manner as to ensure their
full translation into practice. The General Assembly and the Economic and
Social Council should establish a process of periodic review and evaluation of
the United Nations intergovernmental structure and functions in the economic
and social fields.

I. General Assembly

6.   The effectiveness of the General Assembly in fulfilling its responsibilities under the Charter in the economic and social fields should be enhanced by the following measures:

(a)   The Assembly, as the supreme organ of the United Nations system in the economic and social fields, should fully exercise its powers through the establishment of overall strategies, policies and priorities for the system as a whole in respect of international co-operation, including operational activities, in the economic, social and related fields;

(b)   The Assembly, as the principal forum for policy-making and for the harmonization of international action in respect of the economic, social and related fields, should provide policy guidance for the activities of the United Nations system in those fields.

7.   The General Assembly should rationalize its method of work in the economic and social fields. To that end:

(a)   The Assembly would focus each year on major policy issues to be identified by the Assembly in advance. The Economic and Social Council could appropriately assist in that process, as well as in its preparatory work;

(b)   The agenda of the General Assembly in the economic and social fields should consist of the following items:

(i)   General debate (in the Second Committee);

(ii)   Items inscribed on its agenda as set out in subparagraph 7 (a) above;

(iii)   Relevant chapters of the report of the Economic and Social Council;

(iv)   Reports of the relevant subsidiary bodies of the General Assembly.

(c)   Items considered and acted upon by the Economic and Social Council in a given year should not appear on the agenda of the General Assembly in the same year;

(d)   The duration of the meetings of the Second and Third Committees of the General Assembly would each be four weeks, on an experimental basis.

II. Economic and Social Council

8.   In exercising its functions and powers under the Charter of the United Nations and as set out in relevant General Assembly and Council resolutions, in an effective manner, the Council, under the authority of the Assembly, should concentrate on carrying out the following responsibilities:

(a)   To serve as the central forum for the substantive co-ordination of international economic and social issues of a global or interdisciplinary nature and for the formulation of policy recommendations thereon addressed to Member States and to the United Nations system as a whole;

(b)   To ensure the overall co-ordination of all activities of the United Nations system in the economic, social and related fields and, to that end, the implementation of priorities established by the General Assembly for the system as a whole;

(c)   To monitor and evaluate the implementation of overall strategies, policies and priorities established by the General Assembly in the economic, social and related fields and decisions adopted thereon, and to ensure the harmonization and coherent practical operational implementation, on an integrated basis, of relevant policy decisions and recommendations emanating from the United Nations conferences and other forums within the United Nations system after their approval by the General Assembly and/or the Economic and Social Council;

(d)   To make recommendations to the General Assembly for the preparation of the medium-term plan and its introduction, as well as the outline of the draft programme budget, particularly in regard to the priorities to be reflected therein;

(e)   To recommend to the General Assembly overall priorities and policy guidance on operational activities for development. For that purpose, the Third (Programme and Co-ordination) Committee of the Council would henceforth devote its deliberations to operational activities for development;

(f)   To consider and take action on issues emanating from its subsidiary bodies in the economic, social and related fields and, as appropriate, bring to the attention of the Assembly matters that require its policy guidance. In that way, the Council would be able to carry out its filtering role effectively.

9.   The Council should organize its programme of work along the following lines:

(a)   To achieve improved harmonization and rationalization of the work programme of the Assembly and the Council, as well as their subsidiary bodies in the economic, social and related sectors, the Council should henceforth hold one regular session each year in July/August for a period of four to five weeks to be convened in alternate years in New York and Geneva. A high-level segment of this regular session (in the plenary) could be convened for one week to undertake an in-depth review of selected programme areas. The Council, in considering its programme of work, would decide on the appropriate date for this high-level segment;

(b)   In the context of its biennial programme of work, the Council would convene an organizational session each year in February in New York. The Council would also convene subject-oriented sessions as appropriate. The Council would set the periodicity of its sessions and organize its programme of work in the light of its new structure and responsibilities;

(c)   The programme of work of the Council should reflect a more stringent biennialization of its agenda both in the economic and social sectors. In harmony with the cycle of the medium-term plan of the United Nations, the Council should carry out an in-depth review of each programme area once every six years. Such reviews should be an integral part of the biennial programme of work of the Council and should be undertaken in the context of relevant substantive items;

(d)   Meetings of the subsidiary bodies of the Council in the economic and social fields should be scheduled in the early months of the year in order to enable the Council to consider their reports in good time. Meetings of those bodies should be appropriately biennialized;

(e)   The Council should adopt an issue-oriented approach in its consideration and discussions of questions of a multidisciplinary nature, taking fully into account the need for an integrated approach to their economic and social dimensions.

10. The work of the Assembly and the Council would be facilitated by an improved system of reports. The Council should, as appropriate, have before it a consolidated report under each of its agenda items.

11. The Council should submit a substantive report to the Assembly highlighting actions taken by the Council, as well as the main issues and recommendations for appropriate action by the Assembly.

12. The report of the Council to the General Assembly would henceforth consist of the following chapters:

(a)   State of the world economic and social situation;

(b)   Decisions adopted by the Council on various substantive items as recommendations to the General Assembly (to be submitted to the plenary of the General Assembly for appropriate action);

(c)   Issues in the economic field requiring the attention of the General Assembly (Second Committee);

(d)   Issues in the social field requiring the attention of the General Assembly (Third Committee);

(e)   Issues in the area of operational activities for development requiring the attention of the General Assembly (Second Committee);

(f)   Issues that require consideration and action by the Fifth Committee of the General Assembly.

13. Some of the issues that are currently considered by a subsidiary body of the Council which would be subsumed might be considered at a subjected-oriented session of the Council. In such a case, the corresponding item would not appear on the agenda of the regular session of the Council in the same year.

14. The composition and role of the Bureau of the Council should be considered by the Council once the new arrangements enter into force.

15. Executive heads of the organizations of the United Nations system or their senior representatives should participate more actively in the deliberations and informal discussion of the Council and should provide all assistance to the Council in accordance with the general and specific directives.

16. In accordance with article 64 of the Charter of the United Nations, the Council should obtain regular reports from the specialized agencies on the steps taken by them to give effect to the relevant recommendations of the General Assembly and the Council in the economic and social fields.

17. The Council would consist of all States Members of the United Nations.

18. Concerning documentation:

(a)   Documents prepared by the secretariat of the Economic and Social Council should be substantive and analytical, of a global or interdisciplinary nature and should cover both policy and co-ordination aspects;

(b)   A world economic and social survey would henceforth be produced annually to serve as a background document for the relevant discussions of the Economic and Social Council and the General Assembly. The new survey would replace the present *World Economic Survey*;

(c)   Documentation for consideration by the General Assembly or the Economic and Social Council should be rationalized;

(d)   The Economic and Social Council should undertake a periodic evaluation and appraisal of the quality and content of reports prepared for it;

(e)   Reports submitted to the Economic and Social Council should be of a standard format to facilitate reading and consideration by all delegations.

III. Subsidiary bodies of the Economic and Social Council

19. The intergovernmental responsibilities of the following subsidiary bodies would be assumed directly by the Council:

(a) Intergovernmental Committee on Science and Technology for Development;

(b) Committee on Negotiations with Intergovernmental Agencies;

(c) High-level Committee on the Review of Technical Co-operation among Developing Countries;

(d) Committee on Natural Resources;

(e) Committee on the Development and Utilization of New and Renewable Sources of Energy.

20. The Council would convene, as and when required, meetings of experts to advise it on:

(a) New and renewable sources of energy;

(b) Energy;

(c) Mineral resources;

(d) Water;

(e) Public administration and finance;

(f) Geographical names.

21. The functions of the Working Group of the Committee of the Whole of the Governing Council of the United Nations Development Programme (UNDP) would be assumed by the Committee of the Whole.

22. The functions of the Intergovernmental Working Group on International Standards of Accounting and Reporting would be assumed by the Commission on Transnational Corporations.

23. Accordingly, the following intergovernmental/expert bodies would be discontinued:

(a) Intergovernmental Committee on Science and Technology for Development;

(b) Committee on Negotiations with Intergovernmental Agencies;

(c) High-level Committee on the Review of Technical Co-operation among Developing Countries;

(d) *Ad Hoc* Intergovernmental Working Group on the Problem of Corrupt Practices;

(e) Committee on Natural Resources;

(f) Committee on the Development and Utilization of New and Renewable Sources of Energy;

(g) Working Group of the Committee of the Whole of the Governing Council of the United Nations Development Programme;

(h) Meeting of Experts on the United Nations Programme in Public Administration and Finance;

(i) United Nations Group of Experts on Geographical Names;

(j) Intergovernmental Working Group of Experts on International Standards of Accounting and Reporting.

24. The Council should, in the future, carry out periodic reviews of the functions and functioning of subsidiary bodies in the economic and social sectors in conjunction with its in-depth review of related programme areas. Such reviews would be undertaken on the basis of an agreed set of criteria.

IV. Operational activities for development

25. Overall priorities and policy guidance should be established by the General Assembly based on the recommendations drawn up by the Economic and Social Council.

26. The Council should, *inter alia*, deal with policy and co-ordination issues on an annual basis. It should focus each year on a limited number of priority issues which require co-ordination or harmonization of action among relevant organizations of the system.

27. In addition, the Council should undertake every three years a comprehensive policy review. The conclusions and recommendations of those triennial reviews would be reported to the General Assembly.

28. The Council, in the other two years of each triennium, should monitor the implementation of the priorities and policies established by the General Assembly and make recommendations for their full implementation.

29. The governing bodies and agencies concerned would continue to exercise their responsibilities for programme policy decisions regarding the formulation, appraisal, approval, monitoring and evaluation of programmes and projects.

V. Regional commissions

30. In accordance with the global development strategy and policies adopted by the General Assembly, the Economic and Social Council should place greater emphasis on the consideration of the reports of the regional commissions with a view to effectively integrating the regional inputs into the global discussion of substantive issues. The Council should also review and co-ordinate on a global basis interregional co-operation among the regional commissions. Regional commissions should draw the attention of the Council to questions having global implications or of relevance to other regions.

31. The relevant provisions of General Assembly resolution 32/197 should be fully implemented in order to allow the regional commissions to exercise fully and effectively their role, under the authority of the Economic and Social Council, as the main economic and social development centres within the United Nations system for their respective regions.

32. Subregional co-operation should be strengthened and should be integrated more effectively into the activities of each region, taking fully into account the priorities of Governments concerned. For that purpose, efforts should be made, *inter alia*, to strengthen subregional offices, bearing in mind the specific objectives for which those regional offices were established.

33. The Secretary-General should take urgent measures to reduce the high vacancy rates in the regional commissions.

VI. Secretariat support

34. In the light of the above, the present secretariat support structure in the economic and social sectors would need to be modified. For that purpose, the Secretary-General should be requested to prepare proposals for the restructuring of the Secretariat in the economic and social fields for consideration by the General Assembly at its forty-third session, taking into account the following:

(a)   The need for a separate and identifiable secretariat for the Economic and Social Council;

(b)   The new Economic and Social Council secretariat should provide both substantive and technical support to the Council. Such secretariat should be adequately staffed at both the Professional and General Service levels, in strict observance of the principle of equitable geographical representation.   A multidisciplinary capability should be established in that secretariat in order to assist the Council in discharging its functions effectively;

(c) Efforts should be made to achieve greater complementarity between secretariats in Vienna, Geneva and New York, as well as the regional commissions;

(d) The Office of the Director-General for Development and International Economic Co-operation should be strengthened and adequately staffed in order to enable the Director-General to effectively carry out his responsibilities, particularly in the areas of co-ordination and operational activities for development.

VII. Trade and Development Board

35. The views and proposals of the Trade and Development Board on its functions and responsibilities, as set out in informal paper No. TDB/1154 of 23 November 1987 adopted at the resumed thirty-fourth session of the Trade and Development Board, should be endorsed.

36. The substantive debate in the Trade and Development Board on the interrelated issues would take place at the second part (spring) of its regular session with a corresponding change in the agenda of its first part (autumn) to focus on trade issues.

VIII. General

37. Ratification of the amendment to the Charter of the United Nations by the requisite majority, including all permanent members of the Security Council, would have to take place before all the above recommendations come into effect.

38. The Special Commission could recommend that the Economic and Social Council request the Secretary-General to submit a report to the General Assembly at its forty-third session on the modalities for the implementation of the above-mentioned recommendations, including suggestions regarding transitional arrangements, for the consideration of the Assembly.

Notes

1. See para. 33 below.
2. It was suggested that the following options could be considered for the Secretariat inputs:
    (a) The *Trade and Development Report* should continue to be available to the Trade and Development Board in the spring with the *World Economic Survey* to be broadened into a world economic and social survey which would serve as a background paper both for the Council and the Assembly.
    (b) The *Trade and Development Report* and the *World Economic Survey* should be merged. This new report will, in the first instance, be considered by the Trade

and Development Board in the spring. It will be upgraded and broadened for the general debate in the General Assembly in the autumn.

3. The following criteria have been identified for bodies whose functions would be assumed directly by the Council:

    (a) The need for application of the same general principles to the subsidiary bodies of the Council in both the economic and social fields;

    (b) The subsuming by the Council of its subsidiary bodies should not overburden its agenda and should ensure appropriate attention and consideration by the Council of the respective issues;

    (c) Highly technical functions of some subsidiary bodies and experts groups may not be entrusted to the Council;

    (d) The need to strengthen, where possible, expertise and analytical capabilities at the technical expert level, including better utilization of established United Nations capabilities.

    The following bodies have been identified as deserving special attention:

    (i)   Intergovernmental Committee on Science and Technology for Development (EEC, United States, Japan, Norway);

    (ii)   Intergovernmental Committee on the Development and Utilization of New and Renewable Sources of Energy (EEC, United States, Japan, Norway);

    (iii) Committee on Natural Resources (EEC, United States, Japan, Norway);

    (iv)   Commission for Social Development (EEC, United States, Japan);

    (v)   High-level Committee on the Review of Technical Co-operation among Developing Countries (EEC, Norway);

    (vi)   Commission on Transnational Corporations (United States);

    (vii) World Food Council (Norway);

    It was also suggested that some of the functions of the above-mentioned bodies could be assumed by other relevant United Nations bodies. For example, the natural resources questions of the Committee on Natural Resources could be transferred partly to UNCTAD/Committee on Commodities (minerals) and partly to UNEP (water) and partly taken up by the Economic and Social Council itself (energy). The co-ordination function of the High-level Committee on the Review of Technical Co-operation among Developing Countries could be absorbed by the Economic and Social Council and its more operational functions transferred to the UNDP Governing Council. In many cases, parts of the task which at present are undertaken by global bodies (e.g. in the field of TCDC and natural resources) should be delegated to the regional commissions as the main development centres in their respective regions.

4. It was suggested that the Committee for Programme and Co-ordination, in accordance with its role as the main subsidiary organ for planning, programming and co-ordination, and in view of its new responsibilities in the field of budgeting, could focus its co-ordinating efforts on the United Nations itself (intra-United Nations co-ordination). The Council on the other hand could focus, as envisaged in the Charter, on the co-ordination of programme activities on a system-wide basis (inter-organizational co-ordination).

5. It was suggested by a group of delegations that the primary responsibility for programme policy decisions and the review of programme implementation should remain with the governing organs of the individual programmes and agencies concerned. The role of the Council should be defined along the lines of the provisions of General Assembly resolution 42/196, i.e. monitoring of the functioning of the intersecretariat co-ordinating mechanisms and acting on policy proposals made by the Director-General to facilitate the solution of problems encountered in ACC, defining a more effective programming process overseeing the simplification and harmonization of delivery and the reporting procedures of the United Nations organs and agencies and re-examining the arrangements in the field in order to take action on the resident co-ordinator's role and on the co-location of field offices.

6. It was suggested by a group of delegations that this comprehensive policy review should take place henceforth on a biennial basis.

7.	While one group of delegations suggested that the Council should not meet during the regular session of the General Assembly, some other delegations maintained that the Council's regular session should take place concurrently with the General Assembly in September/October immediately preceding the Second and Third Committees, the duration of which would be correspondingly shortened. This would maximize the opportunity for high-level participation in the work of the Council.

8.	It was suggested that these committees either in a formal or an informal setting should meet in advance of the regular session of the Council in order to make the necessary substantive preparation.

9.	The Council should translate such decisions, as appropriate, into operational instructions for relevant United Nations intergovernmental and/or expert bodies in the economic and social sectors and statements of guidance for specialized agencies.

10.	The regular session of the Council would be organized in the following manner:

(a)	For the first two weeks it would consider and as much as possible take decisions on recommendations emanating from economic/social subsidiary bodies and those in the area of operational activities for development;

(b)	For the third week it would consider and take decisions on the social and economic sections of the medium-term plan and of the biennial programme budget and/or to convene a high-level segment of the plenary to consider selected issues to be identified at the organizational session;

(c)	A few days would be set aside to approve the executive report of the Economic and Social Council to the General Assembly. This single and brief document would highlight the key economic and social policy issues (with recommendations from the Council) for consideration by the Assembly.

11.	It was suggested that such reports should:

(a)	Provide a system-wide overview and analysis of the latest developments in an item/sector and assess longer-term implications;

(b)	Give particular attention to co-ordination issues;

(c)	Monitor implementation of mandates and assess user benefits (where applicable);

(d)	Outline select policy recommendations for possible incorporation into the Council's final "executive report" to the General Assembly.

12.	Some delegations were of the view that a change in the composition of the Council membership, like the proposed universalization, in itself would not bring about a profound and lasting improvement in achieving the purposes of the Charter in the economic and social fields. The question of a universal membership can only be discussed in the framework of a further-reaching, more radical reform package encompassing the General Assembly and its committees as well as UNCTAD/TDB. The creation of a new universal body would undermine the credibility of the system even further, unless it proved feasible to organize a built-in constitutional mechanism to enable the General Assembly to focus in a disciplined manner on a few major policy issues, based upon the preparatory work of the Council. The Council would then become responsible for much of the present agenda of the General Assembly and its committees and would have to hold its annual session during the Assembly session. It could imply, for example, that the Council should take final action on most economic issues and that the Assembly itself would focus on its deliberative functions through a general macro-economic debate.

13.	A suggestion was made that the following restructuring measures could be explored:

(a)	To consolidate as much as possible the capacity of the United Nations in the social field in Vienna, including relevant project-oriented and implementation units;

(b)	To consolidate as much as possible the basic macro-economic analytical capabilities of secretariat units in Geneva;

(c)	To decentralize to the extent possible responsibilities for the implementation of operational activities to the regional commissions;

(d)	To consolidate all economic and social policy units into an Economic and Social Council department in New York. This department could have two main branches:

(i)	Secretariat support for the Council;

(ii)	Operational activities for development.

14. It has also been suggested that the Board should hold one consolidated session each year in the spring.
15. See also paras. 29 and 30 of the informal consolidated discussion paper of 21 April 1988.
16. See also para. 25.
17. It was emphasized that the review process should enable the United Nations system to deliver its assistance in an integrated and cost-effective manner at the field level.
18. It was also suggested that the Working Group of the Committee of the Whole should be abolished and its functions assumed directly by the UNDP Governing Council.
19. The view was also expressed that the possibility of the UNDP Governing Council absorbing the operational aspects and the Council the co-ordinating aspects should be explored.
20. It was also suggested that the Commission should provide policy guidance for activities of the UNFPA.
21. It was also suggested that various population activities should be consolidated into a single identifiable Secretariat unit responsible for research, data collection, analysis, funding, technical assistance, and project guidance and monitoring.
22. Some other delegations stated that no change to the procedure envisaged in resolution 1503 (XLVIII) was necessary.
23. See also para. 24 of the informal consolidated paper presented by the Chairman on 21 April 1988.
24. It was also suggested that alternative arrangements to the CPC/ACC Joint Meetings should be explored, including the possibility of convening joint meetings between an enlarged bureau of the Economic and Social Council and the Administrative Committee on Co-ordination.

2.24 Document A/C.5/43/1/Rev.1[*]

Plans of the Secretary-General for the Implementation of Recommendation 15 on the Reduction of Personnel, as requested by the General Assembly in Resolutions 41/213 and 42/211

Report of the Secretary-General

27 July 1988

A. *Background*

8.   The Group of High-level Intergovernmental Experts to Review the Efficiency of the Administrative and Financial Functioning of the United Nations adopted recommendation 15 which reads as follows:

"(1)   A substantial reduction in the number of staff members at all levels, but particularly in the higher echelons, is desirable. It should be possible to undertake such a reduction in a relatively short period of time without causing any negative impact on the current level of programme activities of the United Nations, as determined by the General Assembly and other legislative organs.

"(2)   To this end:

"(a) The overall number of regular budget posts should be reduced by 15 per cent within a period of three years;

"(b) The number of regular budget posts at the level of Under-Secretary-General and Assistant Secretary-General should be reduced by 25 per cent within a period of three years or less, with a comparable reduction in posts at those levels funded from extrabudgetary sources.

"(3)   The Secretary-General should submit to the General Assembly his plans for implementing the recommendations in paragraphs (1) and (2) above. When drawing up such plans, the Secretary-General should, *inter alia*, be guided by:

"(a) The necessity of securing the highest standards of efficiency, competence and integrity of the staff, with due regard to equitable geographical distribution;

---

[*]A/C.5/43/1/Rev.1, pp. 6-21.

"(b) An analysis of work-loads in the various departments and offices taking into account the efficiency that can be gained through the consolidation of functions and the elimination of duplication;

"(c) The need to avoid any negative effects on the implementation of programmes;

"(d) The continuing need to recruit new staff members, especially at the junior Professional levels, to ensure a vigorous Secretariat structure. The number of staff members recruited at the P-1, P-2 and P-3 levels should not fall below the average number of those recruited during the years 1982, 1983 and 1984. Such new recruitment should, however, be balanced with an equivalent reduction in staff, so that the aim of a net reduction of 15 per cent is achieved within a three-year period.

"(4) A further reduction in the overall number of posts could be undertaken as a result of restructuring of the intergovernmental machinery and the Secretariat."

9. This recommendation was examined by the General Assembly at its forty-first session, in the context of its consideration of the report of the Group of High-level Intergovernmental Experts. The Fifth Committee of the General Assembly made extensive comments on recommendation 15, on the basis of information provided by the Secretariat.[1] The Assembly then decided, in resolution 41/213, section I, that the recommendations of the Group of High-level Intergovernmental Experts should be implemented, "in the light of the findings of the Fifth Committee" and, with regard to recommendation 15, subject to the following:

"The percentages referred to in recommendation 15, which were arrived at in a pragmatic manner, should be regarded as targets in the formulation of the Secretary-General's plans to be submitted to the General Assembly for implementation of the recommendation; further, the Secretary-General is requested to implement this recommendation with flexibility in order to avoid, *inter alia*, negative impact on programmes and on the structure and composition of the Secretariat, bearing in mind the necessity of securing the highest standards of efficiency, competence and integrity of the staff, with due regard to equitable geographical distribution."

10. At its forty-second session, the General Assembly, in its resolution 42/211 on the implementation of resolution 41/213, took the following decision:

"Regarding recommendation 15 on the reduction of posts in the United Nations, the Assembly stresses the importance that it attaches to the submission by the Secretary-General to the Assembly of his plans for the implementation of this recommendation in accordance with the provisions of resolution 41/213 and reiterates its conclusion that the Secretary-General should implement this recommendation with flexibility in order to avoid, *inter alia*, negative impact on programmes and on the structure and composition of the Secretariat, bearing in mind the necessity of securing the highest standards of efficiency, competence and integrity of the staff, with due regard to equitable geographical distribution."

11. Also in resolution 42/211, the General Assembly concurred with the relevant observations and recommendations made by ACABQ. These observations and recommendations are contained in the first report of the Advisory Committee on the proposed programme budget for the biennium 1988-1989. The Committee recommended that:

"The revised estimates should be accompanied by information on staffing (in tabular form) that would show the intended result of the application of recommendation 15 of the Group of High-level Intergovernmental Experts in comparison with the information included in the proposed programme budget. To the extent that these staffing tables would reflect redeployments among the sections of the budget (since some programmes will have lost more than 15 per cent of their posts, while others less), the estimates for each section should be adjusted accordingly."[2]

ACABQ also indicated that the possible budgetary implications of the results of the study on the intergovernmental machinery in the economic and social fields entrusted to the Economic and Social Council could be dealt with by the General Assembly in the context of its consideration of the revised estimates.

12. CPC, in considering the progress report of the Secretary-General on the implementation of resolution 41/213 at its twenty-seventh session, reiterated the provisions of this resolution regarding recommendation 15. The Committee *inter alia* "stressed the need to ensure that reforms do not have a negative impact on programmes".[3]

13. The Secretary-General established in mid-1987, through the Programme Planning and Budgeting Board, a Post Review Group. This Group had as its task to undertake, in consultation with the departments and offices, a detailed post-by-post review in all areas of the Secretariat for the implementation of recommendation 15. It reported to the Board in February 1988. The Board, after consultations with the programme managers, made recommendations to the Secretary-General who is presenting below to the General Assembly, through CPC and ACABQ, his plans for the implementation of recommendation 15.

14. In elaborating his plans, the Secretary-General took into account the following factors:

(a)   The notion of flexibility, stressed by the General Assembly for the implementation of recommendation 15, should first be applied to the overall reduction of posts. The Secretary-General was aware that the 15 per cent target was indicative and was not based on a scientific appraisal of the relationships between resources and activities of the United Nations of today or tomorrow. This was confirmed by the debate which led the Assembly to adopt resolution 41/213;

(b)   Flexibility was also applied to the reduction of posts in the various programmes, departments and offices of the Organization. A flat across-the-board reduction of posts among the various programmes would not have been in the spirit of resolution 41/213, nor of the ongoing reform of the Organization. In this connection, the Secretary-General sought to identify the larger reductions in the administrative, public information and common services entities;

(c)   Bearing in mind the parameters mentioned in recommendation 15, a profile of posts by grade for the Organization as a whole was developed in early 1987. This profile reflected the continuing need to recruit new staff members, especially at the junior Professional levels. Indicative reductions of posts by grade based on this profile were elaborated for each entity, but no uniform profile was imposed on all offices. Rather, an attempt was made to determine if the programmatic consequences of the targeted reduction merited in each particular case a departure from the indicative profile;

(d)   Certain programme managers were in a position to base their proposals on a clear assessment of their programmatic consequences. For most, however, a precise assessment was precluded by the nature of their activities. In addition, it is also a fact that in most cases the determination of the programmatic impact of staffing tables to be put in place for 1990-1991 was a somewhat theoretical exercise. While there is an important element of programme continuity in the Organization, the scope and content of programmes for the next biennium are yet to be determined;

(e)   The plans for post reduction took into account the results of reviews and decisions that affected in 1987 the staffing tables and programmes of certain departments and offices. Notably, posts had been redeployed from the Department for Special Political Questions, Regional Co-operation, Decolonization and Trusteeship and the Department of Political and Security Council Affairs to the new Office for Research and the Collection of Information, and from the Department of International Economic and Social Affairs to the United Nations Office at Vienna, Centre for Social Development and Humanitarian Affairs, to the Department of Administration and Management and to the Office for Ocean Affairs and the Law of the Sea. For the economic and social sector as a whole however, the Special Commission of the Economic and Social Council on the In-depth Study of the United Nations Intergovernmental Structure and Functions in the Economic and Social Fields requested that the Secretariat avoid pre-empting its conclusions. This request limited the possibility, at this point, to take into account the impact on staffing requirements of possible organizational and structural changes.

B. *Targets for post reduction by 31 December 1989*

15. The Secretary-General proposes a target of 1,465 regular budget-funded posts for possible abolition. Of these, 486 would be in the Professional category and above and 979 in the General Service and other levels category.

16. While the total number of posts approved under the regular budget for 1988-1989 is 11,422, this base should be adjusted downwards by 167 posts which were not considered during the post reduction exercise conducted by the Secretariat. These posts are the following: 52 in the secretariat of the International Civil Service Commission (ICSC); 19 in the secretariat of the Joint Inspection Unit (JIU); and 96 in the security service of the United Nations Office at Vienna. The reason why they were not considered in the exercise is that, while budgeted in the regular budget of the United Nations, they relate in fact to inter-agency joint services and are financed by all or several organizations of the United Nations system. The base to which the reduction should be applied is therefore 11,255 posts, and the target of 1,465 posts proposed for abolition by the Secretary-General represents 13.02 per cent of this adjusted base.

17. With such a reduction of 1,465 posts, the staffing of the Secretariat on 31 December 1989 would compare with the current establishment as follows:*

18. It may be noted that, besides a 25 per cent reduction of posts at the level of Under-Secretary-General and Assistant Secretary-General (excluding the post of Director-General), proportionately greater cuts are proposed for the levels P-5 to D-2 than for the P-1 to P-4 levels. The proportion of posts at the D-1, D-2, Assistant Secretary-General and Under-Secretary-General levels would decline from 10.7 per cent to 10.2 per cent of the total number of Professional and higher category posts. Only the proportion of posts at P-3 and P-2/1 levels would increase. It should also be noted that the proportion of General Service and other level posts would decrease slightly from 62.2 per cent to 61.6 per cent of the total number of posts.

19. Regarding posts at the level of Under-Secretary-General and Assistant Secretary-General, the Secretary-General had indicated in his first progress report on the implementation of resolution 41/213 that he intended to keep vacant nine of these posts falling under the regular budget, bearing in mind the recommended 25 per cent reduction over a period of three years (1987-1989).

---

*Shown on the following page.

	DG/ USG/ ASG	D-2	D-1	P-5	P-4	P-3	P-2/1	Sub- total	GS/ other	Total
Establishment										
Number	58	101	307	764	1 259	1 220	600	4 309	7 113	11 422
P&above %	1.3	2.3	7.1	17.7	29.3	28.3	14.0	100.0	-	-
Total staff %								37.8	62.2	100.0
Target for reduction	(14)	(18)	(42)	(112)	(149)	(131)	(20)	(486)	(979)	(1 465)
Resulting profile										
Number	44	83	265	652	1 110	1 089	580	3 823	6 134	9 957
P&above %	1.1	2.2	6.9	17.1	29.0	28.5	15.2	100.0	-	-
Total staff %								38.4	61.6	100.0

After a further review, the Secretary-General has decided to leave unfilled two more posts. During this past year, the Secretary-General received representations from various Member States regarding some of these decisions. It should be noted, in this respect, that the structure and the activities of the Secretariat in the economic and social fields are currently under review and cannot be completed until the Special Commission of the Economic and Social Council concludes its own work. Further possibilities for post reductions at these levels may then emerge. Besides an overall reduction of 14 regular budget posts at these levels before the end of 1989, detailed information on this question will be provided in the proposed programme budget for 1990-1991, to be submitted in 1989. The budget outline for these two years, to be submitted to the General Assembly at its forty-third session, will make provision for the reductions.

20. Recommendation 15 specifies that there should be a comparable reduction in posts at those levels which are funded from extrabudgetary resources. At the beginning of 1987, the Secretary-General brought this recommendation to the attention of the heads of organizations concerned and reported on their replies.[4] Heads of these organizations were subsequently requested to forward a note from the Secretary-General to their various governing bodies, highlighting the fact that the Member States which are represented on their boards had joined in the unanimous decisions of the General Assembly to adopt resolution 41/213, including recommendation 15. It since has been decided not to fill three posts at the Assistant Secretary-General level in the

United Nations Development Programme (UNDP), the United Nations Population Fund (UNFPA) and the United Nations Environment Programme (UNEP).

21. The distribution of the posts targeted for abolition among the parts of the 1988-1989 programme budget would be as follows:

Parts	Established and temporary posts No.	%	Target for reduction	Resulting distribution No.	%
I. Overall policy-making direction and co-ordination	273	2.4	(13)	260	2.6
II. Political and Security Council Affairs	821	7.2	(110)	711	7.1
III. Political affairs, trusteeship and decolonization	171	1.5	(17)	154	1.5
IV. Economic, social and humanitarian activities	4 274	37.4	(487)	3 787	38.1
V. International justice and law	167	1.5	(17)	150	1.5
VI. Public information	769	6.7	(108)	661	6.7
VII. Common support services	4 693[5]	41.1	(669)	4 024[6]	40.4
Undistributed USG/ASG posts	58	0.5	(14)	44	0.4
Total expenditure sections	11 226	-	(1 435)	9 791	-
Income sections	196	1.7	(30)	166	1.7
Grand total	11 422	100	(1 465)	9 957	100

This distribution shows that a larger percentage reduction is proposed for common services and public information. In percentages, the reductions range from 14.8 per cent in common support services - including conference services - to 4.6 per cent in overall policy-making, direction and co-ordination. The current allocation of posts between the parts of the programme budget would not, however, change drastically. Economic, social and humanitarian activities would represent 38.1 per cent, instead of 37.4 per cent of the posts in the regular budget, and common support services 40.4 instead of 41.1 per cent. It should be noted in this regard that 63 per cent of the established posts in common support services are in the General Service and other level category. In the economic, social and humanitarian part of the programme budget, the proportion is 56 per cent.

22. The proposed reduction by budget section for all posts in the Professional and General Service categories is given below. It should be noted that no reductions are proposed at this stage for liaison offices at Headquarters. This issue needs to be studied further and the results of the ongoing review will be brought to the attention of Member States as soon as they are available. The annex to chapter I contains a detailed breakdown of the proposed reduction, by budget section, category and grade of posts.

Proposed posts changes by section of the budget

	Budget section	Initial Jan. 1988 level	Adjust- ments	Target Dec.1989 level
01	Overall policy-making and co-ordination	273	(13)	260
2A	Political and Security Council affairs; peace-keeping activities	765	(104)	661
2B	Disarmament affairs activities	56	(6)	50
03	Political affairs, trusteeship and decolonization	171	(17)	154
5A	Office of the Director-General for Development and International Economic Co-operation	28	(4)	24
5B	Regional Commissions Liaison Office	6	0	6

	Budget section	Initial Jan. 1988 level	Adjust- ments	Target Dec.1989 level
6A	Department of International Economic and Social Affairs	392	(45)	347
6B	Activities on global social development issues	89	(20)	69
07	Department of Technical Co-operation for Development	205	(12)[7]	193
09	Transnational corporations	82	(12)	70
10	Economic Commission for Europe	232	(27)	205
11	Economic and Social Commission for Asia and the Pacific	562	(66)	496
12	Economic Commission for Latin America and the Caribbean	590	(70)	520
13	Economic Commission for Africa	629	(42)	587
14	Economic and Social Commission for Western Asia	313	(27)	286
15	United Nations Conference on Trade and Development	451	(47)	404
17	Centre for Science and Technology for Development	31	(6)	25
18	United Nations Environment Programme	103	(19)	84
19	United Nations Centre for Human Settlements (Habitat)	99	(19)	80
20	International drug control	59	(13)	46
21	Office of the United Nations High Commissioner for Refugees	288	(46)	242

Budget section	Initial Jan. 1988 level	Adjust-ments	Target Dec.1989 level
22 Office of the United Nations Disaster Relief Co-ordinator	35	(5)	30
23 Human rights	80	(7)	73
25 International Court of Justice	50	0	50
26 Legal activities	117	(17)	100
27 Public information	769	(108)	661
28 Administration and management	2 165	(312)	1 853
29 Conference and library services	2 528	(357)	2 171
Undistributed USG/ASG adjustments	58	(14)	44
Subtotal, expenditure sections	11 226	(1 435)	9 791
Income section 3	196	(30)	166
GRAND TOTAL	11 422	(1 465)	9 957

C. *Possible impact of the proposed reduction*

23. Globally, a reduction of slightly above 13 per cent of the posts in the Secretariat will have an impact on the activities of the Organization during the next biennium. It is clear that the same volume of programmed activities will not be possible. Programmes for 1990-1991 will have to be determined in the context of the preparation of the programme budget for the next biennium, and of its outline, in relation to a smaller Secretariat. Since there is in the United Nations a strong element of programme continuity, clearer priorities will have to be established. Programmes may have to be in some cases reduced, in other cases modified and still in other instances strengthened or expanded.

24. The Secretary-General wishes to stress, however, that there is not necessarily an automatic link, in all cases, between a smaller Secretariat and a reduced role of the Organization. Efficiency and productivity can be further improved in various parts of the United Nations through technological innovations, improvement in management procedures, as well as through consolidation of programmes and units. In addition, gains in quality should result from the application of rigorous standards for recruitment. These various measures will be successful only if they are fully and actively supported by Member States.

25. In this connection, special mention must be made of the Department of Conference Services. Conference and library services represent 23 per cent of the total establishment under the regular budget for 1988-1989. The Secretary-General came to the conclusion that, in order to achieve an overall target close to the reduction recommended by the General Assembly, post reductions at the two main conference centres - New York and Geneva - would have to be as close as possible to 15 per cent. The targeted reduction is 14.1 per cent for section 29 of the programme budget as a whole. Given the provisions of Assembly resolution 42/207 C, particularly regarding the principle of equality of languages, to effect staff cuts of that magnitude without causing a grave disruption in the provision of conference services to Member States would require a substantial reduction in the number of conferences and meetings. Such a reduction would have to be reflected in the calendar of conferences and meetings for the biennium 1990-1991 and onwards.

26. On the other hand, an overall 10 per cent post reduction in the staffing of Conference Services in New York and at Geneva could be achieved without an excessive reduction in the conference-servicing capacity of the Organization. This is based on two considerations: firstly, the overall impact on the substantive programmes of post reductions in other sectors of the Secretariat, if accompanied by adequate adjustments in the volume of demands from Member States, should bring about a reduction in the volume of documentation which the Organization will be required to produce in the next biennium. Secondly, a fresh outside look into further technological innovations in conference services should, like in other departments, result in continued improvements in productivity. Failing an agreement at the forty-third session of the General Assembly on the basic elements of a streamlined calendar of conferences and meetings for 1990-1991, an alternative such as a 10 per cent post reduction in the Department of Conference Services (New York and Geneva) would have to be actively considered by Member States. This would mean an overall post reduction of 12.1 per cent, instead of the 13.02 per cent mentioned in paragraph 16 above.

27. In the case of another service-providing Department - the Department of Administration and Management - the suggested reduction of 311 staff members (excluding the reduction in the income section), i.e. 14.3 per cent, will be possible without a negative impact on its capacity through the overall reduction in administrative requirements that would stem from the

implementation of these proposals and through the development of a management information system which will need additional funding over the next few years.

28. The question of the impact of staff reduction on the programmes and overall activities of the Organization cannot be separated from issues pertaining to personnel. The reduction proposed in the present document concerns posts and not staff members. The situation of staff will be dealt with in the context of the retrenchment exercise and enhanced mobility. The overall reduction of posts, however, cannot but have a most serious effect on the morale of the staff and hence on the functioning of the Organization. Their morale is already affected by the atmosphere surrounding the financial crisis including the impact of the 1986-1987 economy measures. The proposed post reductions are to be effected through a staff retrenchment plan to be implemented in the context of the current programme budget. Such a plan is being produced under the auspices of the Office of Human Resources Management, in consultation with heads of departments and offices and with staff representatives. Specific posts to be reduced are being identified and implementation procedures indicated to staff members. The plan is based upon the premise that retrenchment can be largely achieved for Professional staff through attrition. This will require carefully controlled recruitment to maintain vacancies close to the 15 per cent level which has been budgeted. It may however be necessary to recommend to the General Assembly the extension of the implementation period into the 1990-1991 biennium for the General Service category. Another main requirement of the plan is a stronger commitment to staff redeployment and staff mobility. However, effective implementation of these aspects would be greatly facilitated by a more innovative incentive programme which would require additional funding.

29. Programme managers have been asked to realize the new lower levels of staffing by the end of 1989 through a combination of attrition, redeployment and controlled recruitment. Programme managers, bearing in mind programmatic considerations, will be in a position to propose adjustments without altering the staffing profile recommended in this document by the Secretary-General, which, if approved by the General Assembly, will constitute a basic input to the forthcoming budget outline.

D. *Financial aspect for the biennium 1988-1989*

30. As noted in paragraph 11 above, ACABQ, in its first report on the proposed programme budget for the biennium 1988-1989, indicated that "to the extent that these staffing tables would reflect redeployments among the sections of the budget ..., the estimates for each section should be adjusted accordingly."[8] As the overall level of financial resources for posts in 1988-1989 has been based upon the assumption of a progressive transition from the existing staffing level to the target level, no change is proposed in total dollar provisions. Consequently, the existing budgeted provisions for salaries,

common staff costs and staff assessment are recommended for redistribution between sections to reflect redeployments among sections which would be occasioned by continued movement towards the targeted December 1989 staffing levels. The revised estimates entailed are shown below. These revised estimates are provisional pending the precise determination of which Under-Secretary-General and Assistant Secretary-General posts will be proposed for abolition. At that time, the section-by-section distribution of resources would change, but the total expenditure provisions will remain at their current level.

Proposed redistribution of resources by section

(In US dollars)

Budget section	Initial appropriation	Redistri- bution[9]	Revised estimates
01 Overall policy-making and co-ordination	44 932 900	2 588 000	47 520 900
2A Political and Security Council affairs; peace-keeping activities	80 462 100	768 800	81 230 900
2B Disarmament affairs activities	9 430 600	159 000	9 589 600
03 Political affairs, trusteeship and decolonization	31 824 500	884 000	32 708 500
04 Policy-making organs (economic and social activities)	2 040 600	-	2 040 600
5A Office of the Director-General for Development and International Economic Co-operation	3 840 100	110 100	3 950 200
5B Regional Commissions Liaison Office	641 000	89 300	730 300

Budget section	Initial appropriation	Redistri- bution	Revised estimates
6A Department of International Economic and Social Affairs	40 280 500	852 600	41 133 100
6B Activities on global social development issues	12 007 100	(1 023 300)	10 983 800
07 Department of Technical Co-operation for Development	19 922 900	1 478 200	21 401 100
09 Transnational corporations	9 529 200	(85 200)	9 444 000
10 Economic Commission for Europe	35 797 400	458 500	36 255 900
11 Economic and Social Commission for Asia and the Pacific	33 483 000	749 100	34 232 100
12 Economic Commission for Latin America and the Caribbean	43 069 900	18 400	43 088 300
13 Economic Commission for Africa	44 234 600	2 784 400	47 019 000
14 Economic and Social Commission for Western Asia	32 599 900	1 387 500	33 987 400
15 United Nations Conference on Trade and Development	78 936 000	1 717 900	80 653 900
16 International Trade Centre	12 242 800	-	12 242 800
17 Centre for Science and Technology for Development	3 971 300	(249 300)	3 722 000
18 United Nations Environment Programme	10 651 100	(200 200)	10 450 900
19 United Nations Centre for Human Settlements (Habitat)	8 356 100	(179 500)	8 176 600

	Budget section	Initial appropriation	Redistri- bution	Revised estimates
20	International drug control	8 750 200	(590 400)	8 159 800
21	Office of the United Nations High Commissioner for Refugees	39 444 400	(2 330 200)	37 114 200
22	Office of the United Nations Disaster Relief Co-ordinator	7 289 400	(37 100)	7 252 300
23	Human rights	17 008 800	773 000	17 781 800
24	Regular programme of technical co-operation	32 346 100	-	32 346 100
25	International Court of Justice	12 527 700	710 700	13 238 400
26	Legal activities	16 706 000	(29 200)	16 676 800
27	Public information	77 001 700	82 300	77 084 000
28	Administration and management	377 150 000[10]	(6 522 400)	370 627 600
29	Conference and library services	333 779 200	(4 365 000)	329 414 200
30	United Nations bond issue	3 520 800	-	3 520 800
31	Staff assessment	266 605 900	-	266 605 900
32	Construction, alteration, improvement and major maintenance of premises	19 202 500	-	19 202 500
	GRAND TOTAL	1 769 586 300	-	1 769 586 300

Notes

1. A/41/795.
2. *Official Records of the General Assembly, Forty-second Session, Supplement No. 7* (A/42/7), para. 14.
3. *Ibid., Supplement No. 16* (A/42/16), para. 302.
4. A/42/234, para.53.
5. Includes 19 posts in the secretariat of JIU, 52 in the secretariat of ICSC and 96 in the security services at the United Nations Office at Vienna. These 167 posts are not part of the base from which the 13.02 per cent reduction is derived.
6. *Ibid.*
7. To be offset by compensating adjustments in posts funded from the Special Account for programme support of extrabudgetary technical co-operation activities.
8. *Official Records of the General Assembly, Forty-second Session, Supplement No. 7* (A/42/7), para. 14.
9. Impact of redistribution of the resources pertaining to the targeted reduction of 14 USG/ASG posts is yet to be determined.
10. Includes $14,757,500 appropriated for the secretariats of JIU and ICSC.

2.25 Document A/43/651˙

Plans of the Secretary-General for the Implementation of Recommendation 15 on the Reduction of Personnel, as requested by the General Assembly in Resolutions 41/213 and 42/211 (A/C.5/43/1/Rev.1)

Report of the Advisory Committee on Administrative and Budgetary Questions

3 October 1988

4. Background on recommendation 15 of the Group of High-level Intergovernmental Experts is provided in paragraphs 8 to 13 of the report of the Secretary-General (A/C.5/43/1/Rev.1). In paragraph 14, the Secretary-General summarizes the factors that he took into account in elaborating his plans.

5. Information on targets for post reductions by 31 December 1989 is given in paragraphs 15 to 22 of the report. The Advisory Committee requested additional information on the process by which these targets were determined.

6. As indicted in paragraph 15 of the report, the Secretary-General proposes a target of 1,465 regular budget posts for possible abolition, of which 486 would be in the Professional category and above and 979 in the General Service and other levels category. The Advisory Committee was informed that this overall reduction of regular budget posts represented a firm offer by the Secretary-General based upon a thorough internal post-by-post review towards the implementation of recommendation 15.

7. The Advisory Committee notes that of the 11,422 posts approved under the regular programme budget for the biennium 1988-1989, a total of 167 posts were not considered during the post reduction exercise conducted by the Secretariat. These comprise 96 posts in the Security Service of the United Nations Office at Vienna, 52 posts in the secretariat of the International Civil Service Commission (ICSC) and 19 in the secretariat of the Joint Inspection Unit. As far as the Security Services posts at the United Nations Office at Vienna are concerned, the Committee was informed that, as a common service, 82 per cent of the cost is reimbursed to the United Nations by the International Atomic Energy Agency (IAEA), the United Nations Industrial Development Organization (UNIDO) and the United Nations Relief and Works Agency for Palestine Refugees in the Near East (UNRWA). Given this fact and the security requirements at Vienna, the Committee was informed that it was not

---

˙A/43/651, pp. 3-8.

considered feasible at this point (especially without detailed consultations with the agencies concerned) to recommend post reductions in this area.

8.   As for the jointly financed activities now appearing under section 28I of the programme budget, i.e., ICSC and the Joint Inspection Unit, the Committee was informed that the question of reductions for these two units would be addressed through the Administrative Committee on Co-ordination (ACC), as they involve inter-agency consultations. Any resulting reductions would be reported to the General Assembly in the context of the proposed programme budget for the biennium 1990-1991.

9.   According to the Secretary-General, the target of 1,465 posts proposed for abolition represents 13.02 per cent of the adjusted base of 11,255 posts.

10. Regarding posts at the Under-Secretary-General and Assistant Secretary-General levels, as discussed in paragraph 19 of the report, the Advisory Committee notes that detailed information on this question will be provided in the proposed programme budget for the biennium 1990-1991, and that the budget outline for the biennium 1990-1991, to be submitted to the General Assembly at its forty-third session, will make provision for the reductions.

11.   In paragraph 20 of his report the Secretary-General makes reference to the situation with regard to Under-Secretary-General and Assistant Secretary-General posts funded from extrabudgetary sources. For its part, the Advisory Committee has continued and will continue to follow up on this matter in the context of its consideration of the budgets of the relevant funds and programmes and its reports to the legislative bodies concerned.

12.   Tables showing the distribution of the posts targeted for abolition among the parts of the 1988-1989 programme budget and proposed changes in the number of posts by section of the budget are provided in paragraphs 21 and 22 of the report. In paragraphs 23 to 29, the possible impact of the proposed reductions is discussed. In paragraphs 28 and 29 the Secretary-General indicates:

"Specific posts to be reduced are being identified and implementation procedures indicated to staff members. The plan is based upon the premise that retrenchment can be largely achieved for Professional staff through attrition. This will require carefully controlled recruitment to maintain vacancies close to the 15 per cent level which has been budgeted. It may however be necessary to recommend to the General Assembly the extension of the implementation period into the 1990-1991 biennium for the General Service category. Another main requirement of the plan is a stronger commitment to staff redeployment and staff mobility. However, effective implementation of these aspects would be greatly facilitated by a more innovative incentive programme which would require additional funding.

"Programme managers have been asked to realize the new lower levels of staffing by the end of 1989 through a combination of attrition, redeployment and controlled recruitment. Programme managers, bearing in mind programmatic considerations, will be in a position to propose adjustments without altering the staffing profile recommended in this document by the Secretary-General, which, if approved by the General Assembly, will constitute a basic input to the forthcoming budget outline."

During the course of its consideration of this report, the Advisory Committee sought specific information from the Assistant Secretary-General of the Office of Human Resources Management on plans for carrying out the retrenchment programme.

13. In paragraph 28 of its first report on the proposed programme budget for the biennium 1988-1989,[1] the Advisory Committee recognized that the target reductions arrived at after the staffing reviews conducted by the Secretariat would and should not reflect the "straight-line" across-the-board reduction upon which the initial budget estimates for 1988-1989 were based. Since, as the result of the post reduction exercise carried out by the Secretariat, some programmes have lost a greater percentage of posts than others, it has been necessary to adjust the estimates for each section accordingly within the existing overall totals for salaries, common staff costs and staff assessment.

14. During its consideration of the revised estimates (A/C.5/43/1/Rev.1), the Advisory Committee paid special attention to the target reduction of 14.1 per cent proposed by the Secretary-General for section 29 of the programme budget (Conference and library services) in view of his statement that:

"to effect staff cuts of that magnitude without causing a grave disruption in the provision of conference services to Member States would require a substantial reduction in the number of conferences and meetings. Such a reduction would have to be reflected in the calendar of conferences and meetings for the biennium 1990-1991 and onwards" (*ibid.*, para. 25).

15. For the reasons given in paragraph 26 of his report the Secretary-General indicates that "an overall 10 per cent post reduction in the staffing of Conference Services in New York and at Geneva could be achieved without an excessive reduction in the conference-servicing capacity of the Organization". On the basis of information received by the Committee on the question of the most realistic target for reductions in the Department of Conference Services, and bearing in mind what has been stated in paragraphs 25 and 26 of the report, the Advisory Committee is of the opinion that the target for reductions in conference service posts under budget section 29 should be adjusted downward, with the "restoration" of 100 posts of the total of 357 posts originally proposed for elimination under section 29 (see A/C.5/43/1/Rev.1), table following para. 22). This recommendation is subject to the results of the study of the Special Commission of the Economic and Social Council on the

In-depth Study of the Unted Nations Intergovernmental Structure and Functions in the Economic and Social Fields and the decision by the General Assembly thereon. The restoration of 100 posts would bring the target for reductions under budget section 29 from 14.1 per cent to approximately 10.1 per cent. On the basis of information received, the Advisory Committee has concluded that the 100 posts should conform with the following profile:

Category	Headquarters	Geneva	Total
Professional and above			
USG			
ASG			
D-2			
D-1			
P-5	11	6	17
P-4	25	18	43
P-3	-13	-6	-19
P-2/1	-4	0	-4
Subtotal	19	18	37
General Service			
Principal	0	0	0
Other	41	22	63
Subtotal	41	22	63
Total	60	40	100

The 100 posts to be restored should be in the areas of translation, interpretation and meetings, publishing, editorial control and official records, with due regard being paid to the need for proportionate treatment of language services.

16. The Advisory Committee was informed that the full biennial costs of the 100 additional posts involved would amount, net of staff assessment, to $12,893,900 for the biennium 1988-1989. The restoration of 100 posts for conference services should make economies possible in other areas under section 29. Under the circumstances, the Committee recommends that at least $3 million of the amount required for additional posts be met from within existing resources under section 29.

17. In keeping with its belief that targets for reduction should not be formulated on a "straight-line" approach and that sections where the target reductions were below 15 per cent should be roughly compensated by greater reductions in other areas, the Advisory Committee recommends that the "restoration" of 100 conference service posts under section 29 should be partially offset by a reduction of 50 posts in areas of the Secretariat other than conference services. On this basis the total reduction for the Secretariat as a whole would become 12.57 per cent instead of 13.02 per cent (see para. 9 above).

18. The Advisory Committee requests the Secretary-General to present a report to the General Assembly at its forty-third session in which he indicates the post reductions by budget section and by grade level; this report should be submitted before 1 November 1988 (see also para. 21 below).

19. Taking into account the current overall vacancy situation as at 31 July 1988 of 16.6 per cent for Professional and higher categories and 10.7 per cent for General Service posts, the Advisory Committee believes that the remaining amount required to finance the net addition of 50 posts to the budget can be absorbed from the budget as a whole. The Committee therefore recommends that this amount be reduced "across the board", with the exception, in view of the special prevailing circumstances, of the regional commissions (other than the Economic Commission for Europe). The actual distribution of this reduction, on the basis of experience, will, of course, be shown in the second programme performance report for the biennium 1988-1989. The Committee does not expect, however, that there will be need at that time for any additional appropriation in this regard.

20. Since deciding to make that recommendation, the Advisory Committee has also considered the statement submitted by the Secretary-General on the programme budget implications arising from the report of the Committee for Programme and Co-ordination on the work of the first part of its twenty-eighth session (A/43/16 (Part I) Add.1). The related observations and recommendations of the Advisory Committee are contained in paragraphs 82 to 86 below. The recommendations made by the Advisory Committee in paragraphs 15 to 19 above are predicated on the assumption that, if the General Assembly wishes to maintain the overall level of the budget at that adopted at its forty-second session, it must offset increases in section 29 with corresponding reductions elsewhere.

21. The revised estimates by section are shown in the table following paragraph 30 of the Secretary-General's report (A/C.5/43/1/Rev.1). Under the circumstances, the Advisory Committee recommends that the General Assembly take no action on the revised estimates shown in that table pending submission by the Secretary-General of the report requested in paragraph 18 above; in that report the Secretary-General should also indicate the effect on each budget section of the further reduction of 50 posts in sections other than section 29, the restoration of 100 posts in section 29, the recommendation in

paragraph 16 above on economies under section 29, and the "across-the-board" recommendation in paragraph 19 above. It is only in this manner that a firm basis will be established for the approval and administration of the appropriations for the biennium 1988-1989 and the preparation of the proposed programme budget for the biennium 1990-1991.

Note

1.   *Official Records of the General Assembly, Forty-second Session, Supplement No. 7 (A/42/7).*

2.26 Document A/43/651/Add.1*

Plans of the Secretary-General for the Implementation of Recommendation 15 on the Reduction of Personnel, as requested by the General Asssembly in Resolutions 41/213 and 42/211 (A/C.5/43/1/Rev.1)

Addendum to the Report of the Advisory Committee on Administrative and Budgetary Questions

19 October 1988

1.   In paragraphs 15 to 21 of its report on the revised estimates for the programme budget for the biennium 1988-1989 (A/43/651), the Advisory Committee, *inter alia*, recommended that the target for reductions in conference service posts under budget section 29 should be adjusted downward, with the "restoration" of 100 posts at an estimated cost of $12,893,900 for the biennium 1988-1989. The Committee further recommended that this cost be offset by a series of compensatory measures and that the Secretary-General report to the General Assembly by 1 November 1988 on how these measures would be implemented.

2.   The Advisory Committee has since been informed that the Secretary-General is not in a position to submit proposals for post reductions over and above those reflected in his report on revised estimates (A/C.5/43/1/Rev.1), nor to comment on the other two elements of the offsetting mechanism. According to the Secretary-General, these estimates were the result of a detailed review aimed at achieving post reductions while attempting to minimize the impact on current programmes. Without the benefit of the results of all mandated intergovernmental and Secretariat reviews, any further reductions of resources would have an adverse effect on programmes.

3.   Upon receipt of this information, the Advisory Committee held further discussions with a representative of the Secretary-General. In this context the Committee was informed that it was not possible to quantify precisely the effect on programmes of the offsetting post reductions referred to by the Advisory Committee. In the opinion of the Advisory Committee, the effect on programmes of its recommendation should be considered in light of the following: the total base is 11,255 posts (see A/C.5/43/1/Rev.1, chap. I, para. 16); the offsetting reductions called for are likely to include posts in the General Service and related categories as well as Professional posts; and the Advisory Committee's recommendations will, in fact, result in a net increase of 50 posts for the budget as a whole.

---

*A/43/651/Add.1.

4.   The Advisory Committee reiterates its belief, first stated in paragraph 20 of its earlier report (A/43/651), that if the General Assembly wishes to maintain the overall level of the budget at that adopted at its forty-second session, the   increases in section 29 should be offset with corresponding reductions elsewhere.   Moreover, the fact that a fortuitous situation with regard to the vacancy rate allows a measure of absorption for 1988-1989 should not obscure the reality that the addition of 100 posts over and above the level used as the basis for the outline for the proposed programme budget for the biennium 1990-1991 (see A/43/524) will affect the level of resources required for future bienniums.

5.   Bearing in mind the above, the Advisory Committee maintains its previous recommendation (A/43/651, para. 17) that the "restoration" of 100 conference service posts under section 29 be partially offset by a reduction of 50 posts in areas of the Secretariat other than conference services.   In view of the difficulty pointed out by the Secretary-General to identify precisely these posts at this stage, the Committee recommends that the Secretary-General be requested to indicate in the context of the proposed programme budget for the biennium 1990-1991 how this recommendation has been implemented.   At this point, there should be no need to modify the revised estimates shown by budget section in the table following paragraph 30 of chapter I of the Secretary-General's report (A/C.5/43/1/Rev.1), on the understanding that the second performance report for the biennium 1988-1989 will reflect the savings related to the offsetting reduction of 50 posts and the necessary transfers between sections.   In this connection, it would be further understood that the amount to be transferred from other sections to section/29 in respect of the restoration of 100 posts would not exceed $9.9 million (see A/43/651, para. 16) and that, given prevailing vacancy rates and their effect on requirements for 1988-1989, there will be no request for any additional appropriation in this regard (see A/43/651, para. 19).

2.27 Document A/43/16*

Implementation of Recommendation 15 of the Group of High-level Intergovernmental Experts (A/C.5/43/1/Rev.1)

Report of the Committee for Programme and Co-ordination

1989

29. At its 28th to 39th meetings, from 19 to 25 May, the Committee considered the report of the Secretary-General on revised estimates, including plans of the Secretary-General for the implementation of recommendation 15 of the Group of High-level Intergovernmental Experts to Review the Efficiency of the Administrative and Financial Functioning of the United Nations[1] on the reduction of personnel, as requested by the General Assembly in its resolutions 41/213 and 42/211 (A/C.5/43/1 and Corr.1 and Add.1 and Corr.1, Add.2 and Corr.1, Add.3, 4, 5 and 7 (later reissued as A/C.5/43/1/Rev.1) and E/AC.51/1988/CRP.1).

Discussion

30. Some delegations reluctantly accepted the Secretary-General's proposals for an overall reduction of posts of 13.02 per cent on the understanding that the Secretary-General would proceed with the full implementation of recommendation 15 during the course of the next biennium. Some other delegations expressed agreement with the Secretary-General's proposals for an overall reduction of posts of 13.02 per cent with the understanding that the proposals of the Secretary-General should be accepted as a package, recognizing that the achievement of the full implementation of recommendation 15 of the Group of High-level Intergovernmental Experts is dependent upon the implementation of recommendations 1, 2, 3 and 8.

31. Some delegations recalled General Assembly resolution 41/213 and requested the full implementation of recommendation 15.

32. Some delegations were of the opinion that the implementation of recommendation 15 of the Group of High-level Intergovernmental Experts should be preceded by an in-depth review of Secretariat staffing requirements. They were also of the opinion that any formulation of a post reduction percentage, in pursuance of the above-mentioned recommendation, should be accompanied by precise indications as to the impact of any post reduction on United Nations activities anprogrammes.

Official Records of the General Assembly, Forty-third Session, Supplement No. 16 (A/43/16), pp. 6-8.

33. Some delegations expressed the view that the Secretary-General's proposal for a reduction of 14.1 per cent in the Department of Conference Services should be provisionally accepted, dependent upon the implementation by Member States of recommendations 1, 2, 3 and 8 of the Group of High-level Intergovernmental Experts as approved by the General Assembly in its resolution 41/213. Other delegations expressed the view tha progress on the implementation of these recommendations was dependent upon action by Member States and recommended a concerted effort in these areas.

34. Views were also expressed that the Committee should exercise its prerogative on priorities as provided in the Regulations and Rules Governing Programme Planning, the Programme Aspects of the Budget, the Monitoring of Implementation and the Methods of Evaluation, especially regulation 3.17 (now numbered 4.17 following the approval by the General Assembly in its resolution 42/215, part I, of a new article III).

Conclusions and recommendations

35. The Committee reiterated the need for the Secretary-General to implement recommendation 15 of the Group of High-level Intergovernmental Experts with flexibility, in order to avoid negative impact on programmes and on the structure and composition of the Secretariat, bearing in mind the necessity of securing the highest standards of efficiency, competence and integrity of the staff, with due regard to equitable geographical distribution.

36. The Committee recommended, without prejudice to the full implementation of recommendation 15 of the Group of High-level Intergovernmental Experts, as stipulated in General Assembly resolution 41/213, acceptance of the Secretary-General's proposal for post reductions, as adjusted by a 10 per cent reduction in the staffing of conference services in New York and Geneva, and considered that further reductions should be made, when possible, in the process of implementation of Assembly resolution 41/213 as a whole, with due regard to priorities and the principle of equal treatment of all official languages of the United Nations and the application of new technology.

37. The Committee recommended that the Secretary-General, in following the above-mentioned guidelines, keep in mind the concerns expressed by Member States regarding the proposed reductions in posts in smaller offices, especially in the areas of international peace and security, disarmament affairs, economic development and social programmes, including narcotic affairs, as well as in the regional commissions.

Note

1.   *Official Records of the General Assembly, Forty-first Session, Supplement No. 49* (A/41/49).

2.28 Document A/43/524[*]

Proposed Programme Budget Outline for the Biennium 1990-1991

Report of the Secretary-General

16 August 1988

CONTENTS

		Para- graphs
I.	Introduction	1 - 6
II.	Significant programmatic aspects	7 - 9
III.	Significant financial aspects	10 - 26
IV.	Size of the contingency fund	27 - 28

---

[*]A/43/524.

I. Introduction

A. *Mandate*

1. The present programme budget outline is proposed for the biennium 1990-1991 in accordance with the approved budget process as contained in annex I to General Assembly resolution 41/213 of 19 December 1986. By paragraph 1 of that annex, the Secretary-General is required to submit

> "an outline of the programme budget for the following biennium, which shall contain an indication of the following:

> "(a) Preliminary estimate of resources to accommodate the proposed programme of activities during the biennium;

> "(b) Priorities, reflecting general trends of a broad sectoral nature;

> "(c) Real growth, positive or negative, compared with the previous budget;

> "(d) Size of the contingency fund expressed as a percentage of the overall level of resources".

B. *Timing*

2. By paragraph 18 of General Assembly resolution 42/211 of 21 December 1987, the Assembly decided that the date of submission of the outline of the proposed programme budget should be 15 August of the off-budget year.

C. *Reform*

3. This outline is a significant component of the budget process mandated by resolution 41/213, and represents the fulfilment of many separate strands of the reform process. Thus, it is built on the premise that the approved programme contained in the revised medium-term plan will be carried out in 1990-1991 against a programme budget that will be fully financed once it has been approved and appropriated.

D. *Process, nature and scope*

4. The programme budget proposals of the Secretary-General heretofore were formulated by an iterative, Organization-wide process based upon approved pre-existing mandates and specific costing parameters. The proposed outline, conceived at a macro level, is prospective and hence contains an indication of resources preliminarily estimated, to which a contingency fund will be added. While the process of formulating the outline is necessarily centralized, it should be borne in mind that the core resource proposals relating to a retrenched

staffing table are the product of a long and very detailed review of staffing requirements against future programme activities, which involved each and every programme manager over a long period of time. The results of the review, which are before the General Assembly in document A/C.5/43/1/Rev.1, have been married with other planned changes in non-post resources and costed on a standardized basis to provide the required preliminary estimate. However, it should be clear that detailed programming down to output level has not been undertaken as a part of the outline process, but will be carried out at the time of developing the proposed programme budget for the biennium 1990-1991. Accordingly, the content of the proposed outline seeks to match aggregate resource requirements to the programme of activities for the biennium 1990-1991 that is expected to be derived from the revised medium-term plan. Furthermore, in terms of the evolving budgetary process, the Secretariat sees the outline proposal as the initial opening line in a dialogue with the Member States.

E. *Format*

5. The outline, while closely related to a future programme budget submission, differs from it in a number of important characteristics. Given the differences noted above with respect to process and nature, it has been conceived as a high-level overview of a future programme budget, which will facilitate policy choices. Consequently, the format reflects high levels of aggregation of resources and general trends that may be assessed in making decisions with regard to priorities. The tables are therefore presented at the level of parts of the programme budget.

F. *Proposals*

6. The target December 1989 staffing tables contained in document A/C.5/43/1/Rev.1 on revised estimates of the programme budget for the biennium 1988-1989 should form the basis of the staffing table for 1990-1991. The new 1990-1991 staffing table will allow a consolidation of the Secretariat around the new organizational structures resulting from the reform. The other proposals are in objects of expenditure other than staff posts; for example, they include the provision for non-recurrent costs for the implementation of recommendation 5 contained in the report of the Group of High-level Intergovernmental Experts to Review the Efficiency of the Administrative and Financial Functioning of the United Nations,[1] as approved by the General Assembly in resolution 41/213. Finally, a redeployment is proposed of other non-post resources away from expenditures that were complementary to staff to those that may substitute for staff.

---

*Not reprinted here.

II. Significant programmatic aspects

7.   The preliminary estimate of resources required for the biennium 1990-1991 is based upon the premise that the proposed programme of activities to be undertaken during the biennium 1990-1991 is defined by the scope and content of the revised medium-term plan for the period 1984-1991. Any additional programme activities based on decisions taken in the year preceding (1989) and during the biennium (1990-1991) would be chargeable to the contingency fund under the guidelines annexed to General Assembly resolution 42/211. Changes in programme activities to be undertaken in 1990-1991, but approved in 1988, would fall outside the scope of both the contingency fund and of the indicative estimate provided in section III below. Should such activities be approved by the General Assembly at its forty-third session, it is proposed that they should be considered as additional to the resource estimate provided in the present outline.   It is understood that charges for unforeseen and extraordinary expenditures would be outside the scope of both the preliminary estimate of resources and of the contingency fund.

8.   For historical reasons, intergovernmental decisions on priority setting in accordance with the Regulations and Rules Governing Programme Planning, the Programme Aspects of the Budget, the monitoring of implementation and the Methods of Evaluation have yet to be taken in regard to the subprogrammes of the medium-term plan (regulations 3.15, 3.16, 3.17 and 3.18).   Therefore the most practical approach at this time to indicating "priorities, reflecting general trends of a broad sectoral nature" in the outline, as recommended in resolution 41/213, is deemed to be at the level of the parts of the programme budget. It is considered that attempts, at the outline stage of budgeting, to set priorities at detailed levels of the programme elements in advance of detailed programming work, i.e., other than at the broad sectoral level, will be at variance with the purpose of outline budgeting. It should be kept in mind that in recent months a *de facto* process of setting priorities has taken place. On the one hand, as indicated in paragraph 4 above, an extensive review of future programme activities involving the programme managers was undertaken in the context of the implementation of recommendation 15 of the Group of High-level Intergovernmental Experts[2] up to and including the stage of the revisions to the medium-term plan. The proposed staff reductions contained in document A/C.5/43/1/Rev.1 reflect the priorities assigned by the Secretary-General to the various programmes of activities, inasmuch as the staff cuts have been modulated by departments and offices. This was done bearing in mind the views expressed by Member States at the forty-second session of the General Assembly.

9.   Table 1* reflects the relative priorities between the parts of the programme budget. The differentiation in proposed real growth rates is a function in very

---

*Not reprinted here.

large measure of the varying degrees of post retrenchment proposed in document A/C.5/43/1/Rev.1 and incorporated in this outline.

III. Significant financial aspects

A. *Methodology*

10. The methodology used in calculating the preliminary estimates of resource requirements is based upon the existing methodology for the preparation of the proposed programme budget, which was endorsed by the General Assembly at its thirty-third session in resolution 33/116 C, section II, of 29 January 1979. This methodology has been modified to take account of the different cycle associated with the outline, which must perforce take as its starting point the initial appropriations of the prior biennium rather than the revised appropriations, which is used as a starting point in preparation of proposed programme budgets as well as pending legislative action regarding the question of a comprehensive solution to the problem of all additional expenditures.

11. The point of departure is the initial appropriations (or, for income sections, the initial approved estimates) as approved by the General Assembly just prior to the commencement of a biennium; in this particular instance, the initial appropriations and estimates approved by the Assembly in resolutions 42/226 A and B of 21 December 1987.

12. The next steps consist of establishing the resource base. To do so, non-recurrent items of the current biennium, meaning those that concern activities that are not expected to be continued in the forthcoming biennium, are first discounted. The remainder, which represents budgetary provisions for continuing activities, is then costed at prices and rates of the base year - in this instance, at those for 1988. This is done by recosting the 1989 portion of the initial appropriations at 1988 prices and rates. Part of the process of establishing a base also involves the adjustment of turnover factors (or deduction for delayed recruitment) to the standard 5 per cent for existing posts in the Professional and higher categories. The standard 5 per cent turnover factor for Professionals has been replaced in this proposal by 3 per cent. In the case of General Service and other categories, the standard 0 per cent turnover factor has been utilized. As can be seen in the discussion of resource requirements throughout the present report, amounts referred to are at 1988 rates, i.e., before adding any inflation provisions for the years 1990 and 1991.

13. At this point, new non-recurrent items (i.e., activities that are deemed to be carried out in the biennium 1990-1991 but not retained thereafter) are added, also costed at 1988 rates.

14. The next step involves the indication of growth, either negative or positive, over the base. Real growth is expressed in dollars and percentages, both computed at 1988 rates.

15. Exchange rates used in the present estimates are those approved by the General Assembly in its resolution 42/226 A of 21 December 1987 on the basis of the recosting undertaken immediately prior to the adoption of the initial appropriation. However, the point at which these rates will need to be updated will need to be determined in the light of decisions to be taken by the Assembly on the most appropriate adjustment mechanism to handle currency fluctuations and inflation.

16. Following the establishment of the revalued base and of the proposed resource growth, both in terms of base year (1988) prices the preliminary estimate of resources at 1988 rates may be computed by addition of the two components. Should the General Assembly wish to continue to follow the principle of full-budgeting, the effect on the total of anticipated inflation for the years 1990 and 1991 may be added to the preliminary estimate of resources at 1988 prices to give the preliminary estimate of resources at current 1990-1991 prices.

B. *Components of the preliminary estimate*

17. The indicative estimates of recurrent resources for the biennium 1990-1991 at 1988 rates, excluding adjustments for currency fluctuations and inflation, are of $1,705.5 million, or 9.6 per cent lower than the revalued resource base for the biennium 1988-1989. Non-recurrent resources for the biennium 1990-1991, on the same basis, are estimated at $58.1 million, or 158 per cent higher than the similar provision in the biennium 1988-1989. This level of requirements, which represents a reduction of 9.6 per cent in real growth, may best be examined in terms of the components of the estimates as detailed in table 1* and summarized below:

	Millions of United States dollars
Initial appropriations, 1988-1989	1 769.6
1. Revaluation of the resource base	117.0
2. Recurrent resource growth, revised estimates (post reductions)	(177.5)
3. Recurrent resource growth (Bond issue)	(3.5)
4. Non-Recurrent resource growth	58.1
Preliminary estimate for the biennium 1990-1991 at 1988 rates	1 763.7

---

*Not reprinted here.

It may be noted that the two components of revaluation of the resource base and resource growth are substantially mutually offsetting, as the restoration of standard turnover factors in the base appears as a positive adjustment while the implementation of specific post reductions appears as negative resource growth.

C. *Revalued resource base*

18. One of the most significant aspects of the proposals for the forthcoming biennium results from the proposals contained in document A/C.5/43/1/Rev.1, and is contained in the revaluation of the resource base. The major factor affecting the level of the resource base is thus the adjustment of the turnover deduction. This factor is reflected as "special adjustments" in table 2*, which details the revaluation of the resource base by parts and by adjustment factors. These adjustment factors as components of the revaluation of the resource base may be summarized as follows:

	Millions of United States dollars
Initial appropriations, 1988-1989	1 769.6
1. Non-recurrent 1988-1989	(22.5)
2. Recosting to 1988 price levels	(29.0)
3. Special adjustments	168.5
Subtotal	117.0
Revalued resource base	1 886.6

19. It will be recalled that in appropriating the programme budget for the biennium 1988-1989, turnover rates were adjusted from a standard 5 per cent rate for Professional posts to 15 per cent. Similarly, turnover rates for General Service posts were adjusted from a standard zero rate to 10 per cent. In both cases the need for special rates arose as a transitional measure pending the identification of specific post reductions and the progressive reduction in actual numbers of staff. With the incorporation of such post reductions in staffing tables for 1990-1991 there is no further need for the device of transitional excess turnover rates. A reversion to more normal turnover levels is proposed in 1990-1991. The General Service posts would be budgeted at the standard 0 per cent rate, while the Professional and higher level posts would be set at a 3 per cent turnover rate. The position may be summarized as follows:

---

*Not reprinted here.

	1986-1987 and prior rates	1988-1989 initial appropriation rate	1990-1991 proposed rate
Professional	5 per cent	15 per cent	3 per cent
General Service	0 per cent	10 per cent	0 per cent

A turnover rate averaging 3 per cent for Professional and higher level posts for 1990-1991 as a whole is envisaged, bearing in mind proposed vacancy rates for December 1989 and the fact that the recruitment restraints that would have to be imposed to achieve the traditional 5 per cent level may impact severely upon programme delivery capacity. A 3 per cent average rate would accommodate a smooth adjustment to the traditional 5 per cent turnover rate by the end of 1991.

20. The reduction of turnover factors to give a turnover deduction rate of 3 per cent for Professional and higher level posts and 0 per cent for those in the General Service and related categories results in a positive adjustment of some $100.0 million at 1988 rates.

21. Other items in the revaluation of the base include: (a) the reduction of $22.5 million in respect of non-recurrent items in the biennium 1988-1989, which reflects the application of standard budgetary methodology; and (b) the downward adjustment of $29.0 million in respect of recostings to 1988 price levels, which differs from prior patterns observed in programme budget proposals.

D. *Resource growth*

22. Resource growth reductions of $122.9 million are reflected in table 1*. These are the net effect of proposed reductions of $181.0 million in recurrent resources and requirements of $58.1 million in non-recurrent resources. With respect to the negative recurrent resource growth, the largest single factor is a reduction in post numbers amounting to $177.5 million. A further $3.5 million in negative resource growth reflects the maturation of all United Nations bonds in the biennium 1988-1989.

23. The non-recurrent requirements as estimated at this time consist of $38.7 million for the implementation of recommendation 5 of the Group of High-level Intergovernmental Experts and a balance of $19.4 million distributed across other parts of the budget. They exclude any provision for items yet to be defined. The non-recurrent estimate of $19.4 million is derived from an examination of existing non-recurrent provisions. Those activities that are expected to be continued have been projected as non-recurrent for the

---

*Not reprinted here.

purposes of the present outline without prejudice to their categorization in the proposed programme budget estimates for the biennium 1990-1991. When detailed programming is undertaken, these activities will be carefully examined to determine whether they would most appropriately be classified as recurrent or non-recurrent. Should any of them appear to be more appropriately classified as recurrent activities, they would be so classified and incorporated within the programme budget proposals by an adjustment to the revalued resource base.

E. Treatment of 1990-1991 currency fluctuations and inflation rates

24. In accordance with established budget methodology, resource requirements at 1988 base rate could have been adjusted to projected 1990-1991 rates. With respect to the December 1987 exchange rates utilized, no adjustment is currently proposed to reflect subsequent realized or projected rates. Any adjustment in respect of these would need to be considered in the context of the proposals to be made by the Advisory Committee on Administrative and Budgetary Questions on the subject pursuant to paragraph 16 of General Assembly resolution 42/211.

25. As regards inflation adjustments, 1988 rates could have been projected forward to 1990 and 1991. These rates could have been applied directly to non-staff costs and salaries, and common staff costs could have been projected in the light of the need to bring post adjustments at certain duty stations into a correct relativity with the base of the post adjustment system at New York. Additionally, a review of the standard costs used for costing posts could have been undertaken to assess the adequacy of existing provisions for net base salaries and common staff costs in the light of observed trends and of proposals of the International Civil Service Commission (ICSC). Some cost increases in net base salaries have been observed in recent years arising in part as a side effect of the low rate of recruitment consequent upon retrenchment of posts. The average step in grade has risen, thereby increasing unit costs of staff. Provision for some future increase in net base salary would therefore be required. Similarly, ICSC proposals to increase education grant and dependency allowances as well as the expectation that the Organization's pension contribution rate will increase from 14.5 per cent of pensionable remuneration at the beginning of 1988 to 15.5 per cent in 1990-1991 means that common staff cost rates will need to be increased. Any adjustment in respect of these would need to be considered in the context of the proposals to be made by the Advisory Committee on the subject.

26. It should be clear, therefore, that the preliminary estimate of resources appearing in paragraph 17 is subject to adjustment by currency fluctuation and inflation. The present outline assumes that these adjustments will be made by the Assembly at its forty-third session following its consideration of the report of the Advisory Committee on the question of a comprehensive solution to the

problem of all additional expenditures, including inflation and currency fluctuation (see paras. 15 and 16 above). Were this not to be the case, the Secretariat may be requested to estimate these adjustments based upon the budgetary methodology applicable heretofore, utilizing the rates applicable at the point in time that the General Assembly so decides.

IV. Size of the contingency fund

27. The Secretary-General is required, by the terms of annex I to General Assembly resolution 41/213, to provide in the context of the outline an indication of the size of the contingency fund expressed as a percentage of the overall level of resources. The annex to Assembly resolution 42/211, in determining the criteria for use, the period and pattern of use and the operation of the contingency fund, further provides in section C, paragraph 1, that, "in the off-budget year, the General Assembly would decide on the size of the fund in accordance with the provisions of annex I to its resolution 41/213".

28. It is recalled that in the report of the Secretary-General concerning a contingency fund (A/42/225, para. 34), which was presented to the General Assembly at its forty-second session, it was observed that a contingency fund amounting to 0.75 per cent of the budget appeared reasonable to accommodate additional expenditures, excluding those arising from the impact of extraordinary expenses as well as fluctuations in rates of exchange and inflation. This level of contingency was neither approved nor rejected in principle by the Assembly at its forty-second session. Under the circumstances, it is proposed that the rate of 0.75 per cent should be adopted for the biennium 1990-1991 on the understanding that the Assembly should continue to keep under review the appropriateness and adequacy of this level.

Notes

1. *Official Records of the General Assembly, Forty-first Session, Supplement No. 49* (A/41/49).
2. *Ibid.*

2.29 Document A/43/929*

Proposed Programme Budget Outline for the Biennium 1990-1991

Report of the Advisory Committee on Administrative and Budgetary Questions

9 December 1988

2.   Introductory material is provided in paragraphs 1 to 6 of the report of the Secretary-General. The Advisory Committee notes from paragraph 6 that "a redeployment is proposed of other non-post resources away from expenditures that were complementary to staff to those that may substitute for staff". The Committee was informed that these non-post resources would be specifically identified in the context of the proposed programme budget for the biennium 1990-1991.

3.   Significant programmatic aspects are dealt with by the Secretary-General in paragraphs 7 to 9 of his report. With regard to paragraph 7, the Advisory Committee recalls that the submission date of 15 August was agreed upon to permit the incorporation in the 1990-1991 outline of the programme and funding implications of legislative decisions taken during the spring and summer. The Committee notes that this was not done for the outline in question. Under the circumstances, it believes that prior to final approval of the outline by the General Assembly, account should be taken of changes in programme activities to be undertaken in the 1990-1991 biennium but approved in 1988 (see para. 13 below). It is the view of the Advisory Committee that the Secretary-General, in submitting an outline of the proposed programme budget for the following biennium, should exercise the best possible discretion to anticipate changes in programme activities to be introduced during the year in which the outline is considered, taking into account intergovernmental discussions of the proposals which are likely to modify the existing mandates.

4.   The Advisory Committee concurs in the statement in paragraph 7 of the report that "it is understood that charges for unforeseen and extraordinary expenditures would be outside the scope of both the preliminary estimate of resources and of the contingency fund".

5.   Significant financial aspects are discussed in paragraphs 10 to 28 of the report. The Advisory Committee notes from paragraphs 10 and 11 of the report that the starting point for the preparation of the proposed programme budget outline for the biennium 1990-1991 was the initial appropriations for the biennium 1988-1989 rather than the revised appropriations for that biennium. The Committee agrees that this is necessary, but also believes that, before the

---

*A/43/929, pp. 1-9.

final approval of the outline by the General Assembly, account should be taken of updated forecasts for inflation during the next biennium and of the latest available rates of exchange (see para. 15 below).

6. In paragraph 17 of the report it is stated that "the indicative estimates of recurrent resources for the biennium 1990-1991 at 1988 rates, excluding adjustments for currency fluctuations and inflation, are of $1,705.5 million, or 9.6 per cent lower than the revalued resource base for the biennium 1988-1989". The Committee notes that the total estimates for the biennium 1990-1991 are $1,763.7 million at 1988 rates, compared with the initial appropriations of $1,769.6 million for the biennium 1988-1989.

7. Revaluation of the resource base, which accounts for an increase of $117 million, is analyzed in paragraphs 18 to 21 of the report. The Advisory Committee notes that this is a net figure, which includes an amount of $168.5 million for special adjustments. The Committee was informed that this amount represents the additional cost (at 1988 rates) involved in budgeting the original 1988 staffing table with the same vacancy rates (3 per cent for Professional and higher level posts and 0 per cent for General Service posts) used for the proposed reduced 1990-1991 staffing table. The amount of $168.5 million (at 1988 rates) added to the revalued resource base may be compared with a deduction of $177.5 million (at 1988 rates) from the preliminary estimate for 1990-1991 for post reductions, as shown in paragraph 17 of the report. The difference is attributable to variations in the level, grade and duty station composition of the proposed post reductions of 12.8 per cent for Professionals and higher level posts and 14.2 per cent for General Service posts from the "across-the-board" reduction represented by the adjustment in vacancy rates for the programme budget for the biennium 1988-1989.

8. Turnover rates are discussed in paragraphs 19 and 20 of the report. In paragraph 19 a turnover rate averaging 3 per cent for Professional and higher level posts is proposed instead of the traditional 5 per cent for this category of staff. In the opinion of the Advisory Committee, convincing evidence has not been presented to justify such a departure from the traditional rate. Indeed, as shown in the Advisory Committee's report on revised estimates (A/43/651, para. 19), the vacancy rate of 16.6 per cent for Professional and higher level posts as at 31 July 1988 is well ahead of the 15 per cent rate used for the initial appropriations for the biennium 1988-1989 to represent the average vacancy required in order to achieve implementation by 31 December 1989 of recommendation 15 of the Group of High-level Intergovernmental Experts to Review the Efficiency of the Administrative and Financial Functioning of the United Nations.[1] The Advisory Committee therefore recommends that a 5 per cent vacancy rate for Professional and higher level posts be used with a consequential reduction of $16,155,000 (at 1988 rates) from the revaluation of the resource base.

9. Resource growth is treated in paragraphs 22 and 23 of the report. As stated, the largest single factor is a reduction in post numbers, with a

consequential negative recurrent resource growth of $177.5 million. A further $3.5 million in negative resource growth results from the maturing of all United Nations bonds in the biennium 1988-1989.

10. With regard to the negative resource growth for the reduction in posts, this is based on the numbers of proposed posts shown in table 3 of the Secretary-General's report. As indicated in the heading to that table, it includes both recurrent and non-recurrent temporary posts. Therefore, the total of 11,248 shown for 1988-1989 includes 10,975 established posts, 251 recurrent temporary posts, and 22 non-recurrent temporary posts. This compares with a total of 11,422 posts shown in paragraph 16 of the Secretary-General's report on the revised estimates for the biennium 1988-1989 (A/C.5/43/1/Rev.1). The total shown in the tables of annex I to chapter I of that report includes 10,975 established posts under the expenditure sections, 194 posts under income section 3, 251 recurrent temporary posts under the expenditure sections and 2 recurrent temporary posts under income section 3. This total does not include non-recurrent temporary posts, as these were outside the scope of the post reduction exercise. The difference between the reduction of 1,438 posts shown in table 3 of A/43/524 and the target of 1,465 regular budget established and recurrent temporary posts proposed for abolition in A/C.5/43/Rev.1, paragraph 15, is explained by the fact that the reduction of 1,438 shown in table 3 of A/43/524 does not include a total reduction of 30 established posts under income section 3 but does include the reduction of 3 non-recurrent temporary posts under the expenditure sections.

11. In paragraph 17 of its report on the revised estimates (A/43/651), the Advisory Committee has, *inter alia*, recommended a net addition of 50 established posts to the programme budget for the biennium 1988-1989. The consequential effect of this recommendation on the preliminary estimate for the biennium 1990-1991 would be to add $5,308,000 (at 1988 rates, with a vacancy rate of 5 per cent).

12. Non-recurrent requirements are discussed in paragraph 23 of the Secretary-General's report (A/43/524). The Advisory Committee notes the statement that "when detailed programming is undertaken, these activities will be carefully examined to determine whether they would most appropriately be classified as recurrent or non-recurrent. Should any of them appear to be more appropriately classified as recurrent activities, they would be so classified and incorporated within the programme budget proposals by an adjustment to the revalued resource base."

13. In paragraph 7 of the Secretary-General's report, it is indicated that changes in programme activities to be undertaken in the biennium 1990-1991, but approved in 1988, would fall outside the scope of both the contingency fund and of the indicative estimate provided in paragraph 17 of that report. The report goes on to propose that, should such activities be approved by the General Assembly at its present session, they should be considered as

additional to the resource estimate provided in the outline. The Advisory Committee concurs in this approach. Of the statements of programme budget implications and revised estimates that have been considered or are awaiting consideration, several include activities that are to be undertaken in or are proposed for the biennium 1990-1991. The Advisory Committee has been informed that the related estimated costs in the biennium 1990-1991, at 1988 rates, are as follows:

A/C.5/43/No.	Title	1990-1991 $US
5	Economic and Social Council revised estimates	35 200
20	United Nations Institute for Disarmament Research	325 800 [2]
32	Least developed countries: Mozambique	37 400
39	Verification in all its aspects	151 000
48	Nuclear disarmament	67 000
49	International arms transfers	286 300
1/Rev.1	Revised estimates (Board of Auditors; ORCI)	544 600 [3]
24	Integrated Management Information System	12 817 500 [4]
	Total	14 264 800

14. Treatment of 1990-1991 currency fluctuations and inflation rates is dealt with in paragraphs 24 to 26 of the Secretary-General's report. As can be seen from those paragraphs, resource requirements have been based on the December 1987 exchange rates and 1988 inflation rates.

15. Bearing in mind what is stated in paragraph 5 above, the Advisory Committee requested information on the amount of the adjustment to the preliminary estimate for the biennium 1990-1991 of $1,763.7 million if it were recosted to 1989 rates and then recosted to 1990-1991 rates, taking into account the Advisory Committee's recommendation in paragraph 8 above to increase the vacancy rate for Professionals and higher level posts to 5 per cent, the net addition of 50 posts to the budget (see para. 11 above) and the additional requirements referred to in paragraph 13 above. The Advisory Committee was informed that the total adjustment to 1989 rates would be an addition of $84,921,200. The subsequent adjustment to 1990-1991 rates would require a further addition of $130,542,500.

16.   As shown in the table below, the total preliminary estimate recommended by the Advisory Committee for the biennium 1990-1991 at 1990-1991 rates is $1,982,523,700.

	Thousands of US dollars
1. Secretary-General's preliminary estimate at 1988 rates	1 763 642.2
2. Turn-over rates from 97 per cent to 95 per cent at 1988 rates	(16 155.0)
3. Net addition of 50 posts at 1988 rates	5 308.0
4. Additional requirements at 1988 rates	14 264.8
Sub-total at 1988 rates	1 767 060.0
5. Adjustment due to recosting at 1989 rates	84 921.2
6. Adjustment due to recosting at 1990-1991 rates	130 542.5
Total	1 982 523.7

17.   In keeping with General Assembly resolution 41/213, it is also necessary to address the problem of all additional expenditures, including those deriving from inflation and currency fluctuation. As stated in paragraph 10 of annex I to Assembly resolution 41/213, "it is desirable to accommodate these expenditures, within the overall level of the budget, either as a reserve or as a separate part of the contingency fund set up in paragraph 8 above".

18.   The question of how to deal with the effects of inflation and currency fluctuation is one of long standing in the United Nations system and has been studied extensively over the years. Indeed, in 1973 the Advisory Committee submitted a report to the General Assembly at its twenty-eighth session on the effects of continuing currency instability on the budgets of organizations in the United Nations system.[5] This report took into account a report on the same subject by the Administrative Committee on Co-ordination (ACC). The report of ACC was annexed to the Advisory Committee's report. In 1974, in connection with the programme budget for the biennium 1974-1975, a report of the Working Group on Currency Instability (A/9773) was submitted to the General Assembly at its twenty-ninth session. From 1975 to 1985 the effect of

continuing currency instability on the budgets of the organizations in the United Nations system regularly appeared as an item on the agenda of the Assembly.

19. The difficulties inherent in forecasting, for budgetary purposes, rates of currency exchange and of inflation have been described by the Advisory Committee in its report on Co-ordination to the General Assembly at its thirty-ninth session (A/39/592, paras. 5-17).

20. During its current consideration of this problem the Advisory Committee focused on how to deal with variations from the forecast rates and met extensively with officials of the United Nations Secretariat and of the specialized agencies and the International Atomic Energy Agency (IAEA). A summary of the practices of the specialized agencies and IAEA has been included in this year's report of the Advisory Committee on administrative and budgetary co-ordination between the United Nations, the specialized agencies and IAEA (A/43/760).

21. As can be seen in the report, a variety of methods are used by the agencies to deal with the effects of fluctuations in the rates of exchange and inflation. For example, a number of Swiss-based agencies, such as the Universal Postal Union (UPU), the International Telecommunication Union (ITU), the World Meteorological Organization (WMO) and the World Intellectual Property Organization (WIPO) express their budgets in Swiss francs (A/43/760, paras. 110, 172-173, 186 and 213); the International Maritime Organization (IMO), headquartered in London, expresses its budget in pounds sterling (*ibid.*, para. 193). Since the greatest portion of their expenditure is in the local currency, the attendant uncertainty of expressing their budgets in United States dollars is ameliorated.

22. "Split assessments", or collecting contributions in more than one currency, are utilized by the United Nations Educational, Scientific and Cultural Organization (UNESCO), the United Nations Industrial Development Organization (UNIDO) and IAEA (*ibid.*, paras. 66, 78, 247 and 263), while the International Labour Organisation (ILO) utilizes forward purchase of its currency needs (*ibid.*, paras. 35 (c)-37) and the Advisory Committee has been informed that the Food and Agriculture Organization (FAO) has also recently entered into such contracts for a portion of its currency needs. FAO also utilizes a reserve account, while the World Health Organization (WHO) has what it calls an exchange rate facility (A/43/760, paras. 54-55 and 143-148).

23. The operations of the United Nations are world wide. No way has yet been found to control inflation or currency movements on a global basis or to predict these factors with absolute certainty. The effects of inflation and currency fluctuation can be minimized but the ways and means to do so are not without their attendant costs. For example, requiring part of the assessments to be paid in currencies other than the United States dollar, while mitigating

losses in times of a falling United States dollar, would work the other way in times of a strengthening dollar. Moreover, it can be demonstrated that in times of a falling United States dollar, the total cost to a number of contributors of their final assessments for a particular financial period is lower, in terms of their own currency, than it would be had the dollar remained stable and the United Nations budget had not increased. There are also many practical difficulties associated with mixed currency or "split" assessments including, in the absence of large cash reserves, problems associated with cash flow (not receiving currencies in the right mix for current cash needs).

24. Another example concerns forward purchasing. This technique involves entering into contracts with banks for the delivery at a future date of a specific amount of one currency that will be paid for on the future date with another currency, the exchange rate having been fixed on the day the contract is made (see A/9773, para. 42). It should be pointed out that while "locking in" a fixed rate of exchange will save money in times of a falling dollar, it will lose money in times of a rising dollar. Moreover, the cost of forward purchase consists mainly of the differential between the prevailing interest rates for the currencies involved. Thus, forward purchase of a higher interest currency using a lower interest currency, such as the purchase by ILO of United States dollars with Swiss francs, generates a premium to the buyer. Conversely, the purchase of a lower interest currency using a higher interest currency, as would be the case with the United Nations, would result in a net cost to the purchaser. This cost rises with the degree of certainty required (i.e. how far in the future the contracts are for and the percentage of total foreign exchange requirements involved). The cost would, of course, be lower to the extent that the amount to be purchased would be less than the full requirement and if contracts were entered into closer to expected delivery dates. However, the degree of certainty for the total cost of the exchange requirement would decline proportionately.

25. The establishment of reserve accounts, to the extent they are funded, also has potential costs. For example, savings from currency transactions that are allowed to "sit" in a United Nations reserve account pending possible use in future are therefore not available for return to Member States, which could use them for their own account (including the earning of interest) pending some future further assessment.

26. Thus, there is an unavoidable cost to mitigating the effects of inflation and currency fluctuation. Faced with this situation, the General Assembly may wish to consider a continuation of the present system whereby the estimate of requirements is adjusted annually on the basis of the latest forecast by the Secretary-General of inflation and exchange rates. As stated by the Secretary-General in paragraph 41 of his report to the Assembly at its forty-second session on inflation and currency fluctuation and the level of the contingency fund (A/42/225):

"In the circumstances, it would appear that the current method of dealing with such adjustments, that is, increasing the appropriations and assessments whenever they give rise to additional expenditures and reducing the appropriations and assessments whenever they give rise to reductions, might still be the least inconvenient way of dealing with such changes."

27. However, if the General Assembly decides to proceed with seeking the comprehensive solution to the problem of all additional expenditures referred to in annex I, paragraph 10, of its resolution 41/213, a mechanism to achieve a greater degree of certainty than now exists could be explored. Such a mechanism could be the establishment of a reserve that would cover additional requirements due to:

(a)   Currency fluctuation;

(b)   Non-staff costs inflation;

(c)   Statutory cost increases for staff.

28. The reserve would have an overall total dollar amount that would be based on a projection of requirements for each of the components listed above. The projected requirements for each component would be expressed in terms of a percentage of the preliminary budget estimate contained in the outline to the proposed programme budget and would constitute a ceiling in each case.

29. The Secretary-General would not have automatic recourse to the reserve. The following safeguards would apply. To the extent the reserve is unfunded, the Secretary-General would seek additional appropriations, when necessary, through performance reports and revised estimates in much the same manner as is currently the case, thus assuring scrutiny and control by the General Assembly of these expenditures. Requests for additional appropriations in respect of each component could, if desired, be limited to the amounts approved for that component. If it were decided to fund all or a part of the reserve in advance, procedures could be established requiring prior concurrence or approval for recourse to the fund; procedures could also be established for replenishment of the fund. The limits for each component could continue to apply.

30. Based on the principles set forth in the paragraphs above, a complete set of procedures for the operation of the reserve and consequent changes to the United Nations Financial Regulations and Rules could be formulated by the Secretary-General and submitted for approval to the General Assembly at its forty-fourth session. At that time, the size of the reserve could also be considered in the context of the proposed programme budget for the biennium 1990-1991 and on the basis of the latest prevailing rates for currency and inflation.

31. In this connection the Advisory Committee emphasizes that no solution will really work until the current financial crisis of the United Nations is finally settled. Accurate forecasting of needs and requirements based upon full implementation of the approved work programme is at the heart of sound programme budgeting. This cannot be accomplished unless and until proper cash flow is assured through replenishment of existing reserves such as the Working Capital Fund and prompt payment of assessments by Member States.

Notes

1. See *Official Records of the General Assembly, Forty-first Session, Supplement No. 49* (A/41/49).
2. Projection based upon average subvention 1985-1988.
3. Consideration not yet completed by the Fifth Committee. Amount shown is based on recommendation by the Advisory Committee (A/43/651, paras. 70 and 72).
4. Consideration not yet completed by the Fifth Committee. Amount shown is based on recommendation by the Advisory Committee (A/43/7/Add.10).
5. *Official Records of the General Assembly, Twenty-eighth Session, Supplement No. 8A* (A/9008/Add.1-34), document A/9008/Add.16.

2.30 Document A/43/16*

Outline of the Proposed Programme Budget for the Biennium 1990-1991 (A/43/524)

Report of the Committee for Programme and Co-ordination

1989

13. At its 56th to 59th and 65th meeting, on 6, 7 and 13 September, the Committee, in accordance with its terms of reference, and in conformity with General Assembly resolutions 41/213 of 19 December 1986 and 42/211 of 21 December 1987, considered the report of the Secretary-General on the outline of the proposed programme budget for the biennium 1990-1991 (A/43/524).

Discussion

14. Some delegations stated their preference for a presentation of the budget outline according to the major programmes of the medium-term plan rather than by programme budget format.

15. Some delegations were of the view that the level of resources in the Secretary-General's proposals should have been all inclusive. They also felt that the preliminary estimates when adopted by the General Assembly should not be subject to modification. Other delegations were of the view that these estimates presented an indicative prelimimary figure that should be interpreted with flexibility.

16. In the calculation of the level of resources, some delegations would have preferred application of the standard 5 per cent turnover rate for Professional staff instead of 3 per cent; they would also have preferred staffing costs based on a 15 per cent post reduction reflecting recommendation 15 of the Group of High-level Intergovernmental Experts to Review the Efficiency of the Administrative and Financial Functioning of the United Nations,[1] rather than 13 per cent as proposed in the revised estimates. Other delegations thought that, in the circumstances, even the 3 per cent turnover rate was too high and that the staffing costs used should have been based on recommendations made by the Committee during its consideration at the first part of its twenty-eighth session of the revised estimates.

17. Some delegations considered that the contingency fund should have been included in an overall estimates. Other delegations agreed that it should be

---

Official Record of the General Assembly, Forty-third Session, Supplement No. 16 (A/43/16), pp. 68-72.

additional to the preliminary estimates and that it should be a part of the overall level of resources.

18. Some delegations felt tht the proposed level of the contingency fund was inadequate, while other delegations supported the recommendation of 0.75 per cent of the overall level of resources.

19. Some delegations were of the view that the process used to arrive at this figure should be reviewed, since it was based on the previous five years' experience, which may not be the most appropriate standard for the forthcoming biennium. Some delegations proposed that, meanwhile, a contingency fund at the level of 0.75 per cent could be considered experimental and subject to review during the initial biennium.

20. Some delegations accepted the figure of a negative 9.6 per cent real growth over the biennium 1990-1991 (see A/43/524, table 1) on the understanding tht it was calculated according to the methodology set out in the Secretary-General's report. Some other delegations were of the view that the figure of 9.6 per cent negative real growth was too high.

21. Some delegations, while recognizing the difficulty of setting priorities, emphasized that it was a *sine qua non* in the budgetary process, that the treatment of priorities in the report was disappointing, and that the Secretary-General's views on priorities, reflecting general trends of a broad sectoral nature, were required.

22. Some delegations were of the view that the serious socio-economic plight of the least developed countries should be given high priority, bearing in mind the implementation of the Substantial New Programme of Action for the Least Developed Countries for the 1980s and the Second United Nations Conference on the Least Developed Countries, to be held in 1990. Some delegations were also of the view that with regard to priorities on social matters, emphasis should be accorded to the welfare and development of children and the role of youth in the programmes of the Organization.

23. The Committee engaged in extensive consultations on the subject of priorities. Some delegations, however, considered that it was necessary to establish a list of priorities, in accordance with Assembly resolution 41/213. They considered that the following list of issues could serve as a framework for determining priorities reflecting general trends of a braod sectoral nature, the order of which does not imply any relative importance:

Priorities on political matters:

Apartheid and Namibia
Decolonization
Disarmament affairs

Exploration and peaceful uses of outer space
Maintenance of international peace and security
Nuclear-free zones and zones of peace
Peaceful settlement of international disputes
Question of Palestine

Priorities on economic matters:

Economic development of developing countries and international co-operation for development
Economic situation of Africa
Economic situation in the least developed countries
Environment questions
External debt, net transfer of resources and resource flows
Trade, money and finance
Transfer of technology, and science and technology for development

Priorities on social matters:

Condition of children, the disabled, the elderly and youth
Control of illicit drugs and drug abuse
Crime prevention
Human rights
Refugee assistance
Social development
Status of women

Priorities on legal matters:

Law of the sea
Progressive development and codification of international law

24. Some delegations among those favourable to the establishment of a list of priorities felt that the above list was too long to serve as a meaningful basis for determining priorities. Also, a number of delegations had reservations about some of the issues in the list.

25. Concerning the specific issues of maintenance of international peace and security, and peaceful settlement of disputes, some delegations noted these were crucial aspects of the object and purpose of the United Nations and thus their inclusion in the list would not be an endorsement of any propositions for comprehensive institutional modifications. Additionally, those delegations had reservations about the inclusion of nuclear-free zones and zones of peace and law of the sea as issues in such a list. Concerning the issue of external debt, net transfer of resources and resource flows, the view was expressed that United Nations activities in this area should not interfere with the work of the Bretton Woods institutions and it was urged that consideration of this issue be linked with considering the need for structural adjustment. Those delegations

believed that the issue of trade, money and finance was duplicative with other issues listed under priorities on economic matters.

26. One delegation expressed strong reservations about including the question of Palestine in such a list.

27. Some delegations stressed that priority setting in the next programme budget should be based on the medium-term plan as revised by the Committee, which is the programmatic framework for formulating the programme budget, and in accordance with General Assembly resolution 36/228 of 18 December 1981.

Conclusions and recommendations

28. The Committee considered the report of the Secretary-General on the outline of the proposed programme budget for the biennium 1990-1991 (A/43/524) in accordance with annex I of General Assembly resolution 41/213.

29. The Committee reiterated that the outline of the proposed programme budget, as with other aspects of the reforms mandated by the Assembly in resolution 41/213, is part of the process of improving the efficiency and effectiveness of the Organization in serving the international community.

30. The Committee recommended, in accordance with its mandate, that the Secretary-General's report constitute the basis for a decision by the General Assembly, taking into account the following:

　　(a)　Recommendations of the Advisory Committee on Administrative and Budgetary Questions on this subject, in accordance with its mandate as stated in Assembly resolution 41/213;

　　(b)　The level of resources given in the report of the Secretary-General does not include those types of expenditures mentioned in paragraphs 10 and 11 of annex I to Assembly resolution 41/213;

　　(c)　It does not inlcude expenditures resulting from decisions taken by intergovernmental organs in 1988, including those of the Committee at its twenty-eighth session (see A/43/16 (Part I)), particularly those on the revised estimates for the programme budget for the biennium 1988-1989 (*ibid.*, paras. 35-37);

　　(d)　The size of the contingency fund, expressed as a percentage of the overall level of resources, is to be in addition to the proposed preliminary estimates of the Secretary-General adjusted in light of subparagraph (b) and (c) above, and the size should be reviewed by the General Assembly in the light of the evolving situation, the report of the Advisory Committee and of all relevant decisions;

(e)   The outline of the proposed programme budget was built on the premise that General Assembly resolution 41/213 will be fully implemented and that the approved programmes contained in the revised medium-term plan will be carried out in 1990-1991 against a programme budget whose financing will be strictly observed once it has been approved and appropriated;

(f)   Further review by the Committee will be required to refine all aspects of the budget exercise, including the methodology for preparing future budget outlines so as to enhance their usefulness in providing greater predictability of resources and for comparison over time among successive budget outlines. This could include a clearer differentiation between teh preparation of the budget outline and that of the programme budget, as well as a better approach to the issue of the programmatic content of the outline;

(g)   The whole exercise is in a developmental period and during this period will be applied with flexibility in accordance with General Assembly resolutions 41/213 and 42/211;

(f)   Further review by the Committee will be required to refine all aspects of the budget exercise, including the methodology for preparing future budget outlines so as to enhance their usefulness in providing greater predictability of resources and for comparison over time among successive budget outlines. This could include a clearer differentiation between the preparation of the budget outline and that of the programme budget, as well as a better approach to the issue of the programmatic content of the outline;

(g)   The whole exercise is in a developmental period and during this period will be applied with flexibility in accordance with General Assembly resolutions 41/213 and 42/211;

(h)   It was understood by the Committee, on reassurances given to it by the representatives of the Secretary-General, that the proposals on the budget outline, including a reduced level of resources, would avoid negative impact on programmes mandated by the relevant bodies of the United Nations as stipulated by the Assembly in its resolution 41/213.

31. The Committee considered that the distribution of resources among parts of the budget outline was of an illustrative nature and decided not to consider this breakdown in detail. In this connection, the Committee pointed out that the distribution of staff resources among the various parts of the budget did not represent the establishment of priorities among the various activities of the Organization.

32. The Committee emphasized the need for the Secretary-General, in developing his detailed programme budget for the biennium 1990-1991, to reflect the priorities deriving from the current medium-term plan as revised. In the preparation of the programme budget for the biennium 1990-1991, priorities at the programme element level should be assigned in accordance

with regulation 4.6 of the Regulations and Rules Governing Programme Planning, the Programme Aspects of the Budget, the Monitoring of Implementation and the Methods of Evaluation.

33. The Committee further noted that future budget outlines would benefit from the full implementation of the provisions concerning priorities to be established in the medium-term plan in accordance with the Regulations and Rules Governing Programme Planning, the Programme Aspects of the Budget, the Monitoring of Implementation and the Methods of Evaluation. In this connection, the Committee emphasized the need to bring to the attention of intergovernmental subsidiary bodies the pertinent regulations and rules governing the setting of priorities and their responsibilities thereto.

34. The Committee requested the Secretary-General to present a report for consideration at its twenty-ninth session on the approach, particularly the methodological aspects to be adopted, for identifying "priorities reflecting general trends of a broad sectoral nature" in future programme budget outlines.

35. The Committee noted that the negative rate of 9.6 per cent in real growth over the biennium 1990-1991 proposed by the Secretary-General was mainly attaributable to the post reduction decided by the General Assembly in resolution 41/213 and reflected in the revised estimates. The Committee reiterated that the level of resources should be adequate for the fulfilment of the objectives of the Organization and that therefore a negative impact on the programmes to be included in proposed programme budget for the biennium 1990-1991 should be avoided.

Note

1. *Official Records of the General Assembly, Forty-first Session, Supplement No. 49* (A/41/49).

2.31 Document A/44/222 and Corr.1*

Final Report of the Secretary-General on the Implementation of Resolution 41/213

26 April 1989 and 11 July 1989

CONTENTS

		Para-graphs
I.	Introduction	1 - 11
II.	The intergovernmental machinery and its functioning	12 - 49
	A. Specific recommendations (recommendations 1 to 7)	12 - 29
	B. Comparative study of the intergovernmental machinery and its functioning (recommendation 8)	30 - 31
	C. Co-ordination (recommendations 9 to 13)	32 - 49
III.	Structure of the Secretariat	50 - 135
	A. General recommendations (recommendations 14 and 15)	50 - 57
	B. Political affairs (recommendations 16 to 24)	58 - 72
	C. Economic and social affairs (recommendations 25 to 29)	73 - 84
	D. Administration and other fields (recommendations 30 to 40)	85 - 135
IV.	Measures regarding personnel (recommendations 41 to 62)	136 - 178
V.	Monitoring, evaluation and inspection (recommendations 63 to 67)	179 - 188
VI.	Planning and budget procedure	189 - 194
VII.	Conclusion	195 - 197

---

*A/44/222 and Corr.1.

I. Introduction

1.   The General Assembly, in its resolution 40/237 of 18 December 1985, expressed its conviction that "an overall increase in efficiency would further enhance the capacity of the United Nations to attain the purposes and implement the principle of the Charter of the United Nations" and decided to establish a Group of High-level Intergovernmental Experts to identify measures for further improving the efficiency of the administrative and financial functioning of the United Nations, which would contribute to strengthening its effectiveness in dealing with political, economic and social issues. The Group met in 1986 to study the matter and presented its report to the General Assembly at its forty-first session.[1]

2.   At that session, the General Assembly reviewed the report of the Group of High-level Intergovernmental Experts, the related report of the Fifth Committee (A/41/795), the comments of the Secretary-General (A/41/663) and those of the Administrative Committee on Co-ordination (A/41/763, annex). The Secretary-General, at the time, welcomed the report and noted "the direct relationship between possible changes in the intergovernmental machinery and modifications in the size, composition and work of the Secretariat staff". While pledging to concentrate the efforts of the Secretariat on the improvement of the administrative and financial functioning of the United Nations, the Secretary-General highlighted the fact that these reforms were requested at a time when the Organization was facing its most serious financial crisis. He urged that ways be found to deal successfully with its root causes, which were primarily of a political nature (A/41/663).

3.   After lengthy deliberations, the General Assembly adopted what was then considered a landmark resolution on the review of the efficiency of the administrative and financial functioning of the United Nations, resolution 41/213 of 19 December 1986.

4.   In that resolution, the General Assembly endorsed the recommendations that the Group of High-Level Intergovernmental Experts had agreed upon and requested the Secretary-General to implement them in the light of the findings of the Fifth Committee and subject to a number of clarifications concerning recommendation 5, on construction projects; recommendation 15, on the reduction of posts; recommendations 53 and 61, which were to be examined by the International Civil Service Commission (ICSC); recommendations 55 and 57, on personnel matters, to the extent they were agreed upon, which were to be implemented taking into account Assembly resolution 35/210 of 17 December 1980; recommendation 8, on the intergovernmental review to be carried out by the Economic and Social Council; and recommendation 24, on the Office of the United Nations Disaster Relief Co-ordinator, which was to be implemented taking into account the related resolution 41/201 of 8 December 1986.

5.   The General Assembly, in section II of resolution 41/213, also adopted a number of important provisions concerning the planning, programming and budgeting process, although the Group of High-level Intergovernmental Experts had not reached full agreement on the subject.

6.   As mandated, the Secretary-General submitted two progress reports on the implementation of resolution 41/213 (A/42/234 and Corr.1 and A/43/286 and Corr.1) which were reviewed first by the Committee for Programme and Co-ordination and the Advisory Committee on Administrative and Budgetary Questions, and then by the Fifth Committee of the General Assembly. Separate reports were submitted to the General Assembly at its forty-second and forty-third sessions on various questions relating to section II of the resolution. Having considered these reports, the General Assembly adopted two resolutions, 42/211 of 21 December 1987 and 43/213 of 21 December 1988, by which it provided further guidance to Member States and to the Secretary-General for the implementation of resolution 41/213. In both these resolutions, the General Assembly emphasized that financial stability would "facilitate the orderly, balanced and well co-ordinated implementation of resolution 41/213 in all its parts" and renewed its appeal to Member States to meet their financial obligations in accordance with the Charter of the United Nations. The Assembly also stressed that the implementation of resolution 41/213 must not have a negative impact on mandated programmes and activities.

7.   At its forty-third session, the General Assembly, in resolution 43/213, requested the Secretary-General to present his final report on the implementation of resolution 41/213 to the Assembly at its forty-fourth session. The Secretary-General was also requested to submit to the Assembly at its forty-fifth session an analytical report assessing the effect of the implementation of resolution 41/213 on the Organization and its activities as a whole and how it had enhanced the efficiency of its administrative and financial functioning.

8.   The present report is therefore a factual review of all actions taken by the Secretary-General since 1 January 1987 to implement resolution 41/213, taking into consideration subsequent instructions from the General Assembly (resolutions 42/211 and 43/213, as well as other resolutions on related items). The report also presents actions taken by the General Assembly itself on a number of related issues. As indicated in previous reports, a number of the recommendations of the Group of High-level Intergovernmental Experts approved by the General Assembly were addressed to Member States or bodies reporting directly to the General Assembly (ICSC, the Joint Inspection Unit and the Board of Auditors). These bodies provided information for inclusion in the report so as to ensure that Member States would be able to review, in a comprehensive document, all actions taken regarding the implementation of resolution 41/213. Their reports are contained in sections IV and V under the relevant recommendations. Although a number of recommendations that were implemented during the first and second year of the reform period have

already been reported on in the two previous progress reports, they are none the less recalled here in order to provide comprehensive coverage.

9. While reviewing the present report, it should be kept in mind that it covers action taken over a period of two years and two months and not three years. There are several reasons for this. Firstly, given the calendar of meetings for the Committee for Programme and Co-ordination and the Advisory Committee on Administrative and Budgetary Questions, the report had to be finalized nine months before the end of the third year. Throughout the reform period, the Secretary-General has been requested to proceed on a number of proposed reforms only after the General Assembly expressed its opinion on such proposals. Some delays also occurred in areas where the General Assembly clearly indicated that the Secretary-General was to proceed with reforms only after taking into consideration the results of deliberations of intergovernmental bodies. This was the case, in particular, in the economic and social sectors, where it should be noted that the General Assembly took decisions in December 1988 (resolution 43/174 of 9 December 1988) on the basis of the results of discussions in the Special Commission established by the Economic and Social Council and in the Council itself at its second regular session of 1988.

10. Most of all, it should be recalled that, while embarking on an unprecedented reform programme, the Secretariat continued to face one of its most serious financial crises. Measures had to be taken in 1986 and 1987 that hampered the Secretary-General in his efforts to implement resolution 41/213 in all its aspects. Considerable effort had to be devoted to the management of this crisis rather than the implementation of structural reform. Reductions in staff were, at the time, less the result of a planned implementation of recommendation 15 on post reductions than of financial restrictions since posts were often left vacant that were never intended for abolition but could be filled neither through the redeployment of staff with the necessary skills nor through recruitment because of lack of funds.

11. At its forty-second and forty-third sessions, the General Assembly recognized the difficult conditions under which these actions were being taken (resolutions 42/211 and 43/213). In spite of these unfavourable circumstances, a substantial number of recommendations have been implemented. There is now a clearer distribution of responsibilities in a number of organizational entities, such as the political, social and common services areas. Several individual departments have substantially reviewed their structure in order to maintain and, where possible, to enhance their capacity to deliver mandated programmes while at the same time implementing recommendation 15 on post reductions. Some of the action taken, for instance, the establishment of an integrated information system in the administrative area, which was approved by the General Assembly at its forty-third session, will not yield results immediately, but will improve the functioning of the Organization in the long run. In other cases, the General Assembly has requested studies to be

submitted at its forty-fourth session or later (information, economic and social sectors).

II. THE INTERGOVERNMENTAL MACHINERY AND ITS FUNCTIONING

A. *Specific recommendations*

12. The Group of High-level Intergovernmental Experts, in its introduction to this section of its report, had noted that the expansion of the agenda of the United Nations had resulted in parallel growth in the intergovernmental machinery. It noted further that there was ample room for reduction in the number of meetings and the volume of documentation. However, as the present report will confirm, the expected reductions have not been achieved.

13. Most of the first seven recommendations of the Group of Experts, relating directly or indirectly to conference services, required action by Member States, acting individually or collectively: the strengthening of the Committee on Conferences; the significant reduction in the number of conferences and meetings; the streamlining of the procedures and methods of work of the General Assembly and its subsidiary organs, particularly its Main Committees; the application of the principle that United Nations bodies should meet at their respective headquarters and, should this not be the case, that all additional expenses should be covered by the host Government; and the curtailment of requests by Member States that their communications be distributed as official documents.

Recommendation 1

14. The Committee on Conferences submitted proposals to the General Assembly at its forty-third session to strengthen the Committee and to give it broader responsibilities. Those proposals, as amended during consultations in the Fifth Committee, were adopted as resolution 43/222 B of 21 December 1988, by which the General Assembly established the Committee on Conferences as a permanent subsidiary organ with 21 members, and set forth its revised terms of reference. In 1989, the Committee is expected to recommend to the General Assembly a draft calendar of conferences and meetings designed to meet the needs of the United Nations and to ensure the optimum utilization of conference-servicing resources. The Committee, which is also mandated to monitor the Organization's policy on publications, will in 1989 consider a report on recurrent publications as requested by General Assembly resolution 42/215 of 21 December 1987 based on the recommendation of the Committee for Programme Co-ordination.

Recommendation 2

15. The first paragraph of this recommendation invited the Economic and Social Council to hold only one session per year. The Secretary-General brought the recommendation to the attention of the Council through document E/1987/2 of 30 December 1986. In its decision 1987/112, on the in-depth study of the United Nations intergovernmental structure and functions in the Economic and Social Fields, the Council established a Special Commission to carry out the study called for in recommendation 8 (see below) and requested it to consider the relevant provisions of recommendation 2 in the context of this in-depth study. The Special Commission submitted its report to the Economic and Social Council at its second regular session of 1988 without having reached agreement on recommendations. At that session, the Council adopted resolution 1988/77 of 29 July 1988 by which it requested the Secretary-General to submit a report to the Council at its second regular session of 1989 "on the feasibility and comparative costs of holding at the United Nations, with the present in-sessional arrangements, one consolidated or two regular sessions of the Council". This was endorsed by the General Assembly in its resolution 43/174 and the study will be submitted as requested (see para. 31).

16. With respect to recommendation 2 (b) and (c), the Committee on Conferences is expected to discuss the utilization of conference services by a wide range of United Nations organs, on the basis of reports to be prepared by the Secretariat. While this recommendation has been under consideration by the Committee as well as other intergovernmental bodies during the preparation and review of the calendar of conferences for the bienniums 1986-1987 and 1988-1989, few bodies have decided to schedule sessions biennially instead of annually, or have significantly reduced the duration of their sessions since 1986. The calendar approved for 1989 does not seem markedly different from that approved for 1987.

Recommendation 3

17. In response to this recommendation and in accordance with the rules of procedure of the General Assembly, every effort is being made to streamline and thereby make more efficient the methods of work of the General Assembly and its Main Committees. The President of the General Assembly as well as the Chairman of the Main Committees continue to impress upon Member States the need for the timely commencement of meetings in order to utilize available services fully. A note verbale to that effect will be sent to delegations at the beginning of the forty-fourth session of the General Assembly. Every effort is being made to ensure that meetings of the Fourth Committee and of the Special Political Committee are held in sequential order with concurrent meetings being avoided as far as possible and with the flexibility necessary. It should be noted, however, that during the forty-third session, 8 of the 15 meetings held by the Fourth Committee overlapped with those of the Special Political Committee.

18. In his annual memorandum on the organization of work of the sessions of the General Assembly, adoption of the agenda and allocation of items, the Secretary-General has been recommending to the General Committee that related items be merged or phased in intervals; that agenda items be distributed among the Main Committees so as to ensure the best possible use of their expertise; and that no new subsidiary organs be created without discontinuing existing ones. Moreover, in his opening statement, the President of the General Assembly customarily urges Member States to reduce the number of resolutions and to exercise restraint in requesting reports of the Secretary-General.

19. A more effective use of the time and conference facilities by the General Assembly and its subsidiary organs is contingent primarily upon the co-operation of Member States.

Recommendation 4

20. In this recommendation, the Group of High-level Intergovernmental Experts addressed itself both to Member States and to the Secretary-General. To the General Assembly, it recommended that the principle that the United Nations bodies meet at their respective headquarters be strictly applied. Member States wishing to invite conferences or meetings should bear the additional costs involved in full. In this connection, the Secretary-General notes that, in accordance with paragraph 4 of General Assembly resolution 40/243 of 18 December 1985, the following bodies are authorized to meet away from their established headquarters:

> Governing Council of the United Nations Development Programme

> International Law Commission

> United Nations Commission on International Trade Law

> Economic and Social Council

> Functional commissions of the Economic and Social Council (subject to decision of the Council)

> Regular sessions of the Economic and Social Commission for Asia and the Pacific (ESCAP), the Economic Commission for Latin America and the Caribbean (ECLAC), the Economic Commission for Africa (ECA), the Economic and Social Commission for Western Asia (ESCWA), (subject to the approval of the Economic and Social Council and the General Assembly) and meetings of their subsidiary bodies

> International Civil Service Commission

Legal Sub-Committee of the Committee on the Peaceful Uses of Outer Space

Conference on Disarmament

21. Further, treaty bodies that have been created pursuant to a resolution or decision of the General Assembly and review conferences on the implementation of multilateral disarmament agreements, all of which are empowered to adopt their own rules of procedure, are not bound by the provisions of the established headquarters principle. Apart from the above exceptions to the rule, the General Assembly has on occasion authorized the convening of regional meetings at venues away from the established headquarters of a particular body as part of the work programmes of these bodies. This category includes the regional seminars and symposia organized by the United Nations Council for Namibia and the Committee on the Exercise of the Inalienable Rights of the Palestinian People.

22. Further, there are bodies of an administrative nature, such as the Advisory Committee on Administrative and Budgetary Questions, the Board of Auditors, the Investments Committee, the United Nations Joint Staff Pension Board, the Panel of External Auditors and the Administrative Tribunal, that sometimes meet away from their established headquarters as part of the implementation of their work programmes. These meetings, as well as those of organs referred to in paragraphs 20 and 21, are included in the official calendar of conferences and meetings and are approved by the General Assembly in adopting the calendar.

23. The Group of High-level Intergovernmental Experts also recommended that the methods of budgeting these additional costs be improved. In May 1987, Guidelines for preparing Host Country Agreements were issued by the Secretariat in the form of an administrative instruction (ST/AI/342) in order to ensure that additional costs to be borne by host Governments were determined in a consistent manner.

Recommendation 5

24. In approving this recommendation concerning the need to ensure that sufficient resources are available before undertaking new construction projects, the General Assembly clarified that the implementation of this recommendation should not prejudice the implementation of projects and programmes it had already approved. In its resolution 42/211, the General Assembly took note of a report on the subject submitted by the Secretary-General (A/C.5/42/4) and invited him to proceed as necessary on both already approved projects (at Addis Ababa for ECA and at Bangkok for ESCAP) on the understanding that no new appropriations would be required under the 1988-1989 programme budget. When approving this resolution, the General Assembly was informed that the Fifth Committee had sought a legal interpretation of the text it was proposing for adoption. Its understanding was

that the Secretary-General had received instructions to undertake the necessary work within the limits of funds available in the construction account, in order, in timely fashion, to give the Advisory Committee on Administrative and Budgetary Questions and the General Assembly the technical and financial information needed to justify any new allocation of resources under the two projects already approved by the General Assembly. The Secretary-General reported on the matter to the General Assembly at its forty-third session (A/C.5/43/16) and the Assembly, in its resolution 43/217 of 21 December 1988, took note of it.

25. The Secretary-General has therefore proceeded with these two construction projects as agreed by Member States. Tendering is completed for the project in Bangkok and a construction contract is expected to be signed in April 1989. The project in Addis Ababa is in the design phase and tendering is expected at the end of 1989 or at the beginning of 1990, with a construction contract to be signed shortly thereafter.

26. No new construction projects for conference facilities have been proposed since the adoption of resolution 41/213.

Recommendation 6

27. The reimbursement of travel costs was based on the principle that no Member State should be hindered by financial constraints from participating in the work of the General Assembly. Originally, Member States were eligible to claim reimbursement for up to five first-class round-trip air fares. In 1962, reimbursement was also authorized for one first-class round-trip air fare for each special and emergency session of the Assembly. In 1966, the Assembly decided that only one first-class air fare and four economy fares would be reimbursed. Pursuant to this recommendation by the Group of High-level Intergovernmental Experts and as approved by the General Assembly at its forty-second session in the context of the 1988-1989 programme budget, reimbursement for one first-class and four economy fares is provided only to the least developed countries, which now number 40. For the Assembly debate on the question of Palestine, which, during the last session, took place at Geneva, least developed countries were entitled to claim reimbursement for only one first-class round-trip fare from New York to Geneva.

28. In its resolution 42/225 (VI) of 21 December 1987, the General Assembly decided that consideration should be given to extending the application of recommendation 6 to subsidiary bodies of the General Assembly and the Economic and Social Council. A report containing a review of the entitlements accorded to members of these bodies and consideration for extending the application of recommendation 6 to them was presented to the General Assembly at its forty-third session (A/C.5/43/4 and Corr.1). The General Assembly decided to defer action on this issue (resolution 43/217 (IX)).

Recommendation 7

29. On the agenda of the Committee on Conferences at its 1990 session is an item concerning communications by Member States issued as official documents. In accordance with General Assembly resolution 41/177 D of 5 December 1986, this question was discussed by the Committee in 1987. At its 1988 session, the Committee considered a detailed report prepared by the Secretariat (A/AC.172/127) listing 1,126 documents, with a total of 4,165 pages, that had been submitted by Member States for circulation as documents of the United Nations between February 1987 and March 1988. The Committee "agreed to recommend that the General Assembly should renew its appeal to Member States to exercise restraint in their requests for the circulation of communications as United Nations documents, and that when they did make such requests they should endeavour to keep the length of the communication to a minimum". The Committee further "agreed to keep the matter under review and to discuss it again in 1990 on the basis of an updated report from the Secretariat".[2] In paragraphs 1-3 of its resolution 43/222 C, the General Assembly made such an appeal to Member States and requested the Committee on Conferences to keep the matter under review and report to the Assembly at its forty-fifth session.

B. *Comparative study of the intergovernmental machinery and its functioning*

Recommendation 8

30. For the implementation of this recommendation, the General Assembly in resolution 41/213 decided that the Economic and Social Council, assisted as and when required by relevant organs and bodies, in particular the Committee for Programme and Co-ordination, should carry out the study called for in that recommendation. For that purpose, the Council, by its decision 1987/112, established a Special Commission, which met from 2 March 1987 to 23 May 1988, to conduct an in-depth study of the United Nations intergovernmental structure and functions in the economic and social fields. At its second regular session of 1988, the Council noted that there were no agreed conclusions on recommendation 8 and decided to transmit the report of the Special Commission (E/1988/75) to the General Assembly at its forty-third session (resolution 1988/77).

31. In its resolution 43/174, the General Assembly took note of the report of the Special Commission and recognized that, although the Special Commission had conducted the in-depth study entrusted to it, it had been unable to reach agreed recommendations; stressed the common interest of all countries in the effective functioning of the United Nations in the economic and social fields so that it is more responsive not only to current issues, but also to emerging problems and issues, particularly those related to the development of developing countries; requested the Secretary-General to consult with all

Member States and seek their views on ways and means of achieving a balanced and effective implementation of recommendations 2 and 8 of the Group of High-level Intergovernmental Experts, taking into consideration all relevant reports, including the report of the Special Commission, as well as the outcome of the discussions in 1989 on the revitalization of the Economic and Social Council, and to submit to the General Assembly at its forty-fourth session a detailed report, in order to enable Member States to consider and take appropriate action with a view to enhancing the effectiveness of the intergovernmental structure and its secretariat support structures as well as programme delivery in the economic and social fields. At its forty-fourth session, the General Assembly will consider the report of the Secretary-General requested in resolution 43/174, together with the present final report on the implementation of resolution 41/213.

C. *Co-ordination*

Recommendation 9

32. As reported to the General Assembly at its forty-third session, the Administrative Committee on Co-ordination has since 1986 been undertaking a review of the functioning of its subsidiary machinery. The Committee reported on the progress made in this connection to the Committee on Programme and Co-ordination and to the General Assembly in 1987 and 1988. The comments and decisions of the Committee on Programme and Co-ordination and the Assembly were reflected in the second progress report of the Secretary-General (A/43/286 and Corr.1).

33. The Administrative Committee on Co-ordination continued the review of the functioning of its subsidiary machinery in 1988 and 1989 and will adopt additional measures. The deliberations and conclusions of the Committee will be provided in its annual report to the Committee on Programme and Co-ordination and to the Economic and Social Council.

34. The Administrative Committee on Co-ordination also reviewed the relevant provisions of Economic and Social Council resolution 1988/77 that have a bearing on the inputs of organizations of the system to the Council and on the functioning of the Administrative Committee on Co-ordination and its subsidiary machinery. The view of the Committee on these matters will be reflected in the report of the Secretary-General on the overall implementation of the resolution to be submitted to the Council at its second regular session of 1989.

Recommendation 10

35. In his first and second progress reports (A/42/234 and Corr.1 and A/43/286 and Corr.1), the Secretary-General informed the General Assembly that the Administrative Committee on Co-ordination welcomed the emphasis

on the need for discussion by the executive heads of the organizations concerned on major policy questions in the economic and social fields and for subsequent reporting to their respective intergovernmental bodies. He also stated that the objectives of the recommendation could best be achieved through informal consultations among relevant executive heads on major policy questions. Such informal meetings have been held in the past few years on issues relating to Africa, debt and development and the functioning of the Economic and Social Council. The Secretary-General will continue convening such informal meetings, including meetings in 1989 relating to debt and to the preparation of the special session of the General Assembly devoted to international economic co-operation, in particular to the revitalization of the economic growth and development of the developing countries.

Recommendation 11

36. The co-ordinating role of the United Nations Development Programme (UNDP) in the area of technical co-operation, which constitutes the central element in operational activities for development at the national level, has been reaffirmed in successive resolutions of the Economic and Social Council and the General Assembly. At the same time, there has been increasing concern over the erosion of certain aspects of this role, in particular those relating to the central funding of technical co-operation and to the utilization of the UNDP country programme as the frame of reference for operational activities organized in support of national development efforts.

37. In its resolution 42/196 of 11 December 1987, the General Assembly requested the Director-General for Development and International Economic Co-operation, in the context of the triennial comprehensive policy review of operational activities to be undertaken in 1989, to examine and report on these two issues, together with others relating to the overall organization and coherence of the activities of the United Nations system at the country level. These matters will be covered in technical annexes to the report of the Director-General to be submitted to the Economic and Social Council at its second regular session of 1989.

38. In resolution 42/196, the General Assembly also requested a review by the Administrative Committee on Co-ordination of the arrangements concerning the role and functions of the resident co-ordinators. This process was launched at the autumn session of the Consultative Committee on Substantive Questions (Operational Activities) (CCSQ (OPS)), a subsidiary committee of the Administrative Committee on Co-ordination, in 1988. It was the opinion of most participants that much could be achieved through the systematic application of existing arrangements and through the adoption of an interpretative statement that would provide an opportunity to confirm the mutual commitment of the organizations concerned to the concept of a resident co-ordinator and of the resident co-ordinator to the leadership and service functions exercised on behalf of the whole United Nations development system.

The Director-General therefore proposed that the review be undertaken in two phases.

39. The first, which should be completed by the Administrative Committee on Co-ordination in the course of 1989, would be based on the identification of specific measures by CCSQ (OPS) and would focus on the processes involved in identifying substantive goals for joint or collaborative action, the enhanced use of the advisory and other services of the resident co-ordinators, and the determination of the resources required to undertake these and other tasks. This phase might also include a new and more systematic review with individual recipient Governments of their interpretation of the mandate of the resident co-ordinators and the specific areas on which they would wish the United Nations development co-operation field teams to concentrate.

40. The second phase would provide for a more formal review of the existing arrangements of the Administrative Committee on Co-ordination with a view to making appropriate amendments to reflect significant developments in recent years, as well as specific actions related to the implementation of resolution 42/196. This review would be undertaken in 1990 and 1991.

41. The issue of the authority of the resident co-ordinators in relation to non-UNDP programmes is fully covered by existing arrangements. The annex to the Administrative Committee on Co-ordination arrangements adopted in 1979 stipulates that resident representatives should be fully informed, beginning with the request stage, of all comparable programmes of technical assistance carried out by a participating organization and their co-operation sought in ensuring full co-ordination between their respective programmes. In addition, participating organizations are expected to keep resident representatives fully informed as regional projects in which their countries might participate are being developed and carried out. These principles should continue to apply to the relations between the resident co-ordinator and relevant United Nations organizations.

Recommendation 12

42. The General Assembly, in its resolution 41/171 of 5 December 1986, on operational activities for development, addressed the issue of the field representation of the various programmes undertaken by the organizations of the United Nations system. In particular, in paragraph 17 of the annex to the resolution, the Assembly requests "the governing bodies of the organizations of the United Nations system to pay particular attention to the need to rationalize field representation of the organizations and, recognizing the necessity to consult with the recipient Government on such matters, to establish new field offices only if the required services cannot be shared with other organizations or provided in any other way".

43. In its resolution 42/196, the General Assembly again addressed the question of field representation of the United Nations system. In section IV,

paragraph 24, of that resolution, it invited "the governing bodies of the organizations of the United Nations system urgently to review and rationalize their field office structure to enhance co-operation, coherence and efficiency through, *inter alia*, increased sharing of facilities and services".

44. In paragraph 26 of the same resolution, the Assembly requested the Director-General "to report on the progress made in the review undertaken by the member organizations of the Joint Consultative Group on Policy and the Office of the United Nations High Commissioner for Refugees of the structure of their field offices, and [invited] other organizations of the United Nations system to participate in this review process".

45. In response to resolution 41/171, as explained in his first progress report (A/42/234 and Corr.1), the Secretary-General has initiated an exercise designed to develop a rational pattern of United Nations field representatives that is both effective and efficient. A study is being conducted on a country-by-country basis under the aegis of the Joint Consultative Group on Policy in order to provide a system-wide assessment of field offices for organizations under the Secretary-General's authority, and in turn to determine concrete steps on how the offices can be rationalized, including the use of common facilities, without diminishing the effectiveness of programme delivery. Along with the organizations of the Joint Consultative Group, UNDP, the United Nations Children's Fund (UNICEF), the United Nations Population Fund (UNFPA) and the World Food Programme (WFP), it was initially intended that the United Nations High Commissioner for Refugees (UNHCR) be associated with the exercise. However, UNHCR felt that, in view of its special mandate and the sensitive nature of much of its work and contacts at field level, it would not be in the best interests of the other partners, in the majority of cases, for it to join common premises.

46. On the basis of their country-by-country review in July 1988, the organizations of the Group addressed a joint statement to their field representatives entitled "Sharing common premises and services in the United Nations system". Essentially, the statement invites the field representatives to review together the possibility of sharing common premises. They are encouraged to include in their review any other organization of the United Nations system that is willing to be associated with the exercise. In future, each of the field offices of the Group will be required to indicate to their headquarters that they have explicitly considered the possibilities of sharing premises at the time they wish to renew an existing lease or to sign a new lease. If any organization wants to leave shared premises, the field office is requested to forward to its headquarters a written explanation. This explanation will have to be shared with the other field offices of the Group and at headquarters level will be circulated to a subgroup on common premises/services.

47. The Director-General invited the executive heads of the specialized agencies with field offices to ask their representatives to collaborate with the organizations of the Joint Consultative Group at the field level to implement this policy. In their responses, the executive heads concerned expressed general agreement with the principle of common premises and shared facilities wherever feasible and acceptable to the host Government concerned. However, several pointed out that their broader sectoral or normative responsibilities, as well as information-channelling and the provision of advisory services, required that they should maintain particularly close links with the relevant technical ministries of the host country administration. Consideration of proximity to such ministries would therefore be taken into account along with other factors in determining the benefits of co-location of offices.

48. With regard to the field operations of the Department of Public Information, the Secretary-General decided in 1987, in agreement with the Administrator of UNDP, to consolidate the United Nations information centres with the office of the resident co-ordinators/resident representatives wherever this was not already the case and it could be shown that a joint arrangement would be more cost-effective while at the same time respecting programme delivery requirements. To this end, a provisional Understanding was approved by the Department of Public Information of the United Nations and UNDP in October 1988. It confirmed that in countries where UNDP and the Department maintained separate offices, premises and facilities such as telecommunication links should be shared, although it was noted that many information centres received rent-free premises from host Governments and that they needed to be placed at centrally accessible and viable locations of the host city, close to the news media, universities, non-governmental organizations and other visitors. The Understanding has been forwarded to directors of United Nations information centres and to UNDP resident representatives for joint review and will be evaluated after one year in the light of operational experience. Recommendations concerning the feasibility of sharing premises in conditions acceptable to both parties are currently awaited.

Recommendation 13

49. Regarding the efforts to harmonize the format of the programme budgets of the organizations of the United Nations system, it was noted in the first progress report (A/42/234 and Corr.1) that agreements have been worked out over the years under the auspices of the Administrative Committee on Co-ordination to harmonize budgeting practices and budget presentation among the organizations of the system. It was the view of the Administrative Committee on Co-ordination that these agreements constituted a solid basis for harmonization in budgeting practices and improved transparency and comparability of budget documents, to the extent that these aims are compatible with the need of individual governing bodies for consistency in the presentation of successive budgets. At that time, the Committee noted that a comparative study on the budgets of the organizations of the system was

included in the work programme of the Joint Inspection Unit for 1987. That study was postponed and is now included in the 1989 work programme of the Unit (A/44/129), which states that the study will attempt to determine the most desirable budgeting techniques for the organizations. It will also examine the extent to which the differences in budgeting techniques should remain and consider measures needed to standardize them.

III. STRUCTURE OF THE SECRETARIAT

A. *General recommendations*

50. In its introduction to this section, the Group of High-level Intergovernmental Experts stated that some regrouping of organizational units in political affairs and the economic and social sectors could have a positive effect on the Secretariat. The restructuring in the political sector is now completed but that of the economic and social sectors is still pending. Delays in the reform process in this area can be attributed to a number of factors: the structure of the Secretariat and its work programme is closely linked to the structure of the intergovernmental machinery, as recognized by the Group of Experts; the General Assembly, in its resolution 43/174, noting the lack of agreement within the Special Commission, requested the Secretary-General to take a number of actions, which have been described in the preceding section of the present report; furthermore, he was instructed by resolutions 42/211 and 43/213 to proceed, taking into account the results of deliberations in the intergovernmental machinery. In the light of these developments, the Secretary-General believes that the reform period for the economic and social sectors should be extended to ensure that his proposals for reorganization are well conceived and planned, taking into account decisions at the intergovernmental level.

Recommendation 14

51. The simplification of the organizational structure called for in this recommendation is being carried out in stages, as explained earlier. Major reorganizations have occurred in the political, administrative and information areas. There are now clearer lines of authority here, more accountability and better communication. While the careful review of the Secretariat revealed that there was little real duplication, the Secretary-General welcomed this exercise as an opportunity to regroup similar activities, particularly in the political sector, thereby reducing the numbers of entities and of higher-level posts in accordance with recommendation 15. On the other hand, as noted in the section dealing with political affairs, it was found that important functions necessitated by the changed political environment were not being performed. During the reform process, efforts were made to address these issues, which are discussed in section B below.

52. The question of the consolidation of United Nations offices established at the same location has already been examined under recommendation 12. In many cases, the expected economies in personnel could not be achieved without negatively affecting one or other of the programmes concerned.

Recommendation 15

53. The plans of the Secretary-General for the implementation of recommendation 15 were presented in document A/C.5/43/1/Rev.1 to the General Assembly through the Committee for Programme and Co-ordination and the Advisory Committee on Administrative and Budgetary Questions. The Secretary-General proposed a target of 1,465 posts, or 13.02 per cent, for possible abolition by the end of 1989, and indicated that such a reduction would imply a change in the volume of programmed activities but not necessarily a reduced role for the Organization. Technological innovations, improved management procedures, consolidation of programmes and units, and rigorous standards for recruitment should, if actively supported by Member States, enhance the productivity and efficiency of a smaller Secretariat. The Secretary-General also indicated that the proposed reduction of 14 per cent for the Department of Conference Services would require a substantial reduction in the number of conferences and meetings, as envisaged in the report of the Group of High-level Intergovernmental Experts. In the absence of such a decision, only a 10 per cent reduction in the staffing of conference services in New York and Geneva would be possible without excessive disruption in the conference servicing capacity of the Organization.

54. The General Assembly, upon the recommendation of the Committee for Programme and Co-ordination and the Advisory Committee on Administrative and Budgetary Questions, decided in its resolution 43/213 that 12.1 per cent of posts funded by the regular budget should be abolished by the end of 1989, with a 10 per cent reduction to be made in the staffing of conference services in New York and Geneva, and that the Secretary-General should, in the context of his proposed programme budget for the biennium 1990-1991, present recommendations for absorbing costs related to the restoration of posts under section 29 of the programme budget. The Assembly reiterated that the post reduction and the overall implementation of its resolution 41/213 must not have a negative impact on mandated programmes and activities. It also requested the Secretary-General, in further implementing recommendation 15, to take into account a number of guidelines, including flexibility, work-load analyses where applicable and the necessity of securing the highest standards of efficiency, competence and integrity of staff with due regard to equitable geographical distribution.

55. In making its recommendation regarding post reductions, the Group of Experts also indicated that there should be a continued effort to recruit junior professional staff members (P-1 to P-3 levels). During the financial crisis and because of the post reduction exercise, the number of new appointments to the Secretariat in posts subject to geographical distribution has been severely

curtailed. However, in the light of this recommendation, efforts were made to ensure that at least the proportion of new appointments at these levels be maintained (see recommendation 44).

56. Regarding the 25 per cent reduction in posts at the Assistant Secretary-General and Under-Secretary-General levels, the Secretary-General had indicated in his report on revised estimates for the 1988-1989 programme budget (A/C.5/43/1/Rev.1) that, in addition to posts that were then vacant, further possibilities for post reductions might emerge from discussions in the Economic and Social Council on the economic and social sectors. In view of the results of these discussions and the need to maintain sufficient managerial control over the vast array of activities undertaken by the Organization, the Secretary-General is proposing the abolition of two posts at the Under-Secretary-General level and eight posts at the Assistant Secretary-General level that are currently on the 1988-1989 staffing tables; these abolitions will be reflected in the appropriate sections of the proposed programme budget for 1990-1991 (A/44/6). It should also be noted that one additional post at the Assistant Secretary-General level had been abolished in 1987 through the transfer of functions to another post on the staffing table as announced in the first progress report (A/42/234 and Corr.1, para. 20 (d)). Therefore, a total of 11 posts at these 2 levels on the regular budget will have been abolished since the adoption of resolution 41/213.

57. Recommendation 15 requested a comparable reduction in high-level posts funded from extrabudgetary resources. The Secretary-General drew this aspect of recommendation 15 and the General Assembly's mandate to the attention of the various governing bodies that approve the staffing tables of the subsidiary organizations of the United Nations funded from extrabudgetary resources. Three extrabudgetary posts at the Assistant Secretary-General level have remained unfilled, as indicated in the report of the Secretary-General on revised estimates to the 1988-1989 programme budget (A/C.5/43/1/Rev.1).

B. *Political affairs*

Recommendation 16

58. In 1986, when the Group of High-level Intergovernmental Experts examined the political departments and offices, it found that there were nine units dealing with these issues, namely, the Executive Office of the Secretary-General, the Office for Special Political Affairs, the Office for Special Political Questions, the Office for Political and General Assembly Affairs, the Department of Political and Security Council Affairs, the Department of Political Affairs, Trusteeship and Decolonization, the Office of the United Nations Commissioner for Namibia, the Office of the Special Representative of the Secretary-General to the Third United Nations Conference on the Law of the Sea, and the Office for Field Operations and External Support Activities. The Group recommended a consolidation and

streamlining in this sector in order to strengthen the capacity of the Organization to deal with these important issues. With these concerns in mind, the Secretary-General conducted a thorough review of the offices at Headquarters, and the process of reorganization has now been completed: the functions carried out in the Office for Special Political Questions and the Office for Field Operations and External Support Activities were redeployed to other existing departments (the Department of Political Affairs, Trusteeship and Decolonization, renamed Department for Special Political Questions, Regional Co-operation, Decolonization and Trusteeship, and the Department of Administration and Management respectively) and the Office of the United Nations Commissioner for Namibia was incorporated into the department already responsible for servicing the Council for Namibia, the Special Political Questions, Regional Co-operation, Decolonization and Trusteeship. Finally, the Office for Research and the Collection of Information was created to perform functions that were either not assigned to any existing office or were dispersed in various offices and required co-ordination. The establishment of the Office was part of the process of rationalizing and streamlining the political sector of the Organization, providing the Secretary-General with added capacity to carry out preventive diplomacy.

Recommendation 17

59. This recommendation addressed three issues. The first part recommended the transfer to the Department of Administration and Management of the administrative functions of the Office of Field Operations and External Support Activities. As explained under recommendation 16, this Office was abolished and the administrative functions relating to peace-keeping operations were therefore redeployed to the Department of Administration and Management.

60. The second issue concerned the political information function assigned to the Office of Field Operations and External Support Activities. Instead of merely reassigning such functions to one of the existing political departments, a careful assessment was made of the tools required to facilitate the task of the Secretary-General in a changed political environment. Further details are provided under recommendation 18 on the role of the newly created Office for Research and the Collection of Information in this respect.

61. Finally, this recommendation looked at the staffing of field missions. The overall situation with regard to such missions has changed dramatically and has become significantly more complicated since the Group of Experts presented its recommendations and resolution 41/213 was adopted. During 1988, three new missions were established, namely the United Nations Good Offices Mission to Afghanistan and Pakistan, the United Nations Iran-Iraq Military Observer Group and the United Nations Angola Verification Mission; in addition, the Organization is currently establishing its most complex and largest decolonization mission to date, the United Nations Transition Assistance Group. The establishment of these missions has placed an increasing burden

on the Organization, which must be able to establish new missions effectively and rapidly while at the same time maintaining adequate staffing levels at the existing field offices to provide the minimum operational requirements necessary for the proper functioning of the missions. Although, in accordance with the Group's recommendation, every effort is made to use local staff to the extent possible, the reservations expressed at the time the Group made its recommendations continue to be relevant, particularly in the context of some of the more recently established missions.

62. However, at established field offices, efforts have been made to replace internationally recruited staff with local staff. This was possible in a limited number of cases, for instance, where mobility requirements and available expertise so allowed. Furthermore, with the assignment of field service officers to the newly created missions on short notice, a heavier burden has had to be borne by locally recruited personnel at established missions pending recruitment of suitably qualified technical personnel.

Recommendation 18

63. The rationalization and co-ordination of the dissemination of news and political analysis activities in a number of United Nations departments and offices was called for in this recommendation. In his first progress report, the Secretary-General indicated that there was indeed a need for a more effective way of obtaining up-to-date, publicly available information so as to enable him to "institute expeditiously the most appropriate means of preventive diplomacy in particular situations of tension and potential conflict" (A/42/234 and Corr.1, para. 18).

64. The new Office for Research and the Collection of Information has developed an enhanced system for the daily collection of political information for the Secretary-General and other senior officials and daily produces three news information bulletins, a press review and a clipping service. It also prepares a weekly briefing book for the Secretary-General and special briefing files for the Secretary-General and other senior officials, and provides support for the peace-making efforts of the Secretary-General. The Office also carries out drafting assignments requested by the Secretary-General and other senior officials benefiting from its own research and that of other offices or departments; in so doing it seeks to assist the Secretary-General to identify emerging issues, demarcate their dimensions and identify options and strategies.

65. In the area of early warning systems, the Office has had consultations with other departments and agencies of the United Nations system, with research institutions world wide and non-governmental organizations in consultative status. These consultations have helped to lay the basis for developing an early warning system drawing upon publicly available sources of information. The Office is in the process of finalizing indicators for early warning and is computerizing the storage of information. Through this emerging system,

pertinent information is being provided to the Secretary-General, helping him in the exercise of his good offices. The Office is also co-ordinating its activities on early warning systems with other offices and United Nations agencies, particularly with respect to its function of monitoring indicators that cause massive outflows of refugees. With regard to the assessment of global trends, the Office is concentrating on emerging issues likely to affect the future political role of the United Nations in a world undergoing rapid transformation.

Recommendation 19

66. The consolidation of activities relating to Namibia has now been completed through the regrouping of the secretariat support for the Commissioner for Namibia and the support activities for the Council for Namibia provided by the Department for Special Political Questions, Regional Co-operation, Decolonization and Trusteeship. As requested by the General Assembly in its resolution 42/211, the Secretary-General consulted with the Council and subsequently reported to the General Assembly at its forty-third session in the context of the revised estimates to the proposed programme budget (A/C.5/43/1/Rev.1 and Add.1) on additional measures taken in this respect. In the context of this recommendation, the Assembly, in resolution 43/213, requested the Secretary-General to proceed with the reclassification of the post of Secretary of the Council to the D-2 level. This request has been complied with.

Recommendation 20

67. Since its establishment in 1983, the Department for Disarmament Affairs has consistently sought, within its resources, to fulfil its responsibilities and to implement all mandated programmes of the General Assembly to the best of its ability. In response to this recommendation, the Department has made further efforts to improve its assistance and services to Member States. To this end, it has been reorganized to include a Monitoring, Analysis and Studies Branch. This Branch is responsible, amongst other things, for monitoring and analysing developments concerning arms limitation and disarmament-related deliberations and negotiations and for the implementation of the action programme adopted by the International Conference on the Relationship between Disarmament and Development.

68. The Department of Disarmament Affairs will continue its efforts to implement this recommendation. In this connection, greater emphasis will be placed in future on developing the Department's capacity to acquire, store and disseminate information on disarmament issues for the benefit of Member States and other users.

Recommendation 21

69. The reduction of staff in the Department of Political Affairs, Trusteeship and Decolonization called for by the Group of Experts in this recommendation was examined in the context of the overall review of the staffing tables mandated by the General Assembly in connection with recommendation 15. The results of the review were described in document A/C.5/43/1/Rev.1 in the context of the revised estimates for the 1988-1989 programme budget. It should be recalled that, as noted in the two progress reports, new functions have been assigned to this Department. They consist of political activities formerly assigned to the Office for Special Political Questions as well as new responsibilities in the area of regional co-operation, African emergency-related questions and certain special economic assistance programmes of political sensitivity previously handled by it. Accordingly, the Department has been renamed Department for Special Political Questions, Regional Co-operation, Decolonization and Trusteeship, and the Office for Special Political Questions has been abolished. The proposed reductions, which took into consideration the views of the Group of Experts and the new responsibilities of the Department, were approved by the General Assembly at its forty-third session.

Recommendation 22

70. As part of the reorganization of the political sector and as indicated above, the political responsibilities of the Office for Special Political Questions were reassigned to the new Department for Special Political Questions, Regional Co-operation, Decolonization and Trusteeship. The administration of special economic assistance programmes previously entrusted to the Office for Special Political Questions have been transferred to UNDP, as requested in this recommendation, except for a small number of special programmes of political sensitivity that have been reassigned to the new Department as indicated in recommendation 21.

Recommendation 23

71. The report of the Secretary-General on the implementation of General Assembly resolution 41/201 on the Office of the United Nations Disaster Relief Co-ordinator (UNDRO) (A/42/657) included a comprehensive review and assessment of existing mechanisms and arrangements for emergency assistance and co-ordination. In its decision 42/433 of 11 December 1987, the General Assembly requested the Secretary-General to proceed with the implementation of the conclusions and recommendations contained in the report and welcomed the initiative of the Secretary-General to establish a central focal point in the Office of the Director-General for Development and International Economic Co-operation to ensure effective response by the United Nations system in the field of disaster and other emergency situations. The report of the Secretary-General on the implementation of this decision (A/43/731) outlines the specific measures that have been undertaken in this regard, including a review (completed in February 1989) by the Management

Advisory Service, Department of Administration and Management, to adjust the work programme and organization of UNDRO in order to focus its activities on sudden natural disasters, and the report of the joint UNDRO/UNDP task force, which contains specific proposals on strengthened co-operation, strengthened operations at the field level and the delineation of the responsibilities of the Director-General.

Recommendation 24

72. Pursuant to General Assembly resolution 41/201, which reaffirmed the mandate of UNDRO, the Secretary-General stated in his first progress report (A/42/234 and Corr.1) that the Office was being retained as a separate entity located at Geneva.

C. *Economic and social affairs*

Recommendation 25

73. The review of the economic and social sectors of the Secretariat envisaged in this recommendation is closely related to the in-depth study of the United Nations intergovernmental structure and functions in the economic and social fields pursuant to recommendation 8. As indicated in paragraphs 30 and 31, the review of the intergovernmental structure has not as yet resulted in agreed recommendations and will be considered again by the General Assembly at its forty-fourth session.

74. Previous progress reports of the Secretary-General have outlined some specific measures that have been taken, in particular the designation of the Assistant Secretary-General in the Office of the Director-General for Development and International Economic Co-operation as Chairman of the Organizational Committee and Secretary of the Administrative Committee on Co-ordination, respectively, the assignment of supervisory responsibility for human rights activities to the Director-General of the United Nations Office at Geneva, and the concentration of United Nations activities on social policy and development under the Director-General of the United Nations Office at Vienna, incorporating the Centre for Social Development and Humanitarian Affairs and the co-ordination of all United Nations drug-related programmes.

75. The in-depth programmatic review called for in recommendation 25 has focused on some broad areas as previously identified. This is an ongoing process and has already served as the basis for intensified consultations among the various secretariat entities involved with a view to eliminating duplication and enhancing responsiveness to the needs of Member States.

76. On the basis of the review thus far, the Secretary-General does not believe that a basic restructuring of the economic and social sectors of the Secretariat is necessary or appropriate at this time. Efforts will rather be directed at

enhancing the efficiency and effectiveness of the present structure. In this context, every effort will be made to ensure the capacity of the Director-General for Development and International Economic Co-operation, under the authority of the Secretary-General, to exercise fully the functions envisaged by the General Assembly in its resolution 32/197 of 20 December 1977.

77. It is not considered practical or feasible to establish at a single location all departments and offices of the United Nations dealing with economic and social affairs.

78. In its resolution 43/213, the General Assembly considered the question of the location of the functions related to liaison with non-governmental organizations in the context of this recommendation, based on the Secretary-General's proposal contained in his revised estimates to the 1988-1989 programme budget (A/C.5/43/1/Rev.1) and further explained in a report submitted to the Advisory Committee (A/CN.1/R.1089). The Assembly endorsed the recommendation of the Committee for Programme and Co-ordination to defer taking a decision on this question pending presentation of further relevant information, including the final outcome of the in-depth study of the United Nations intergovernmental structure and functions in the economic and social fields. It also endorsed the views of the Advisory Committee that, pending further information and the outcome of the work of the Special Commission, the Committee would refrain from submitting a definitive recommendation on the Secretary-General's proposal.[3] The Secretary-General will continue to consider this matter in the light of the decision of the General Assembly.

Recommendation 26

79. The recommendation should be seen in the context of the overall review of the economic and social sectors of the Secretariat in response to recommendation 25 (see above), which also makes specific reference to the Department of Technical Co-operation for Development. In addition, reference is made to the pattern of regular consultations between that Department and the Department of International Economic and Social Affairs on co-operation in substantive matters and with UNDP on operational activities.

Recommendation 27

80. Pursuant to this recommendation, a consultant was engaged and worked in close co-operation with the executive secretaries of the regional commissions and other senior officials of the United Nations system. The report of the consultant, "The Regional Commissions of the United Nations: Future Role and Activities", has been made available to Member States and has served as a basis for intensive consultations with the executive secretaries. The specific recommendations, as agreed, are to be reflected in the work programmes of the

respective commissions. As a general comment, every effort is being made to reflect the critical importance of the work of regional commissions both in procedural arrangements, as, for example, regular representation at meetings of the Administrative Committee on Co-ordination, as well as in substantive work, as, for example, secretariat support for the formulation of an international development strategy.

81. Pursuant to this recommendation and to recommendation 8 relating to the functioning of the intergovernmental machinery in the economic and social sectors, the Special Commission of the Economic and Social Council on the In-Depth Study of the United Nations Intergovernmental Structure and Functions in the Economic and Social Fields reviewed in-depth the role and activities of the regional commissions. Although the Special Commission, as mentioned above in the implementation of recommendation 8, did not arrive at a set of agreed recommendations, a number of suggestions were made concerning the regional commissions.[4] In addition, the Economic and Social Council, in resolution 1988/77, decided that, in considering the question of regional co-operation, it should concentrate on the policy review and co-ordination of activities, particularly with respect to issues of common interest to all regions and matters relating to interregional co-operation. This provision of the resolution, together with other aspects of it that have a bearing on the work of the regional commissions, were considered by the Secretariat in the context of meetings of the executive secretaries of the regional commissions. Observations and recommendations in this regard will be reflected in the report of the Secretary-General on the implementation of Council resolution 1988/77.

Recommendation 28

82. This recommendation proposed that the format for the presentation of resources pertaining to regional commissions should be harmonized to include costs of administration, conference and general services for the ECE budget section. As indicated in the first progress report (A/42/234 and Corr.1), the services for ECE mentioned above are administered by the United Nations Office at Geneva, which also administers these services for other substantive offices at Geneva (United Nations Conference on Trade and Development (UNCTAD), the Centre for Human Rights and UNDRO). To maintain this integrated management, which has proven more efficient and cost effective while answering the need for comparability among regional commissions, the proportion of resources provided by the United Nations Office at Geneva that pertain to ECE were indicated in the introduction to section 10 (ECE) of the 1988-1989 programme budget. The same presentation will be used for the 1990-1991 proposed programme budget.

Recommendation 29

83. Pursuant to General Assembly resolution 42/211 on the Secretary-General's action regarding the implementation of this recommendation, which

deals with the Office for Secretariat Services for Economic and Social Matters, a review was conducted and the results described in the report of the Secretary-General on the revised estimates for the 1988-1989 programme budget (A/C.5/43/1/Rev.1).

84. At its forty-third session, the General Assembly also adopted resolution 43/174 of 9 December 1988, which requests the Secretary-General to take into consideration the outcome of the Economic and Social Council discussions in 1989 on the revitalization of the Economic and Social Council when preparing the report called for in that resolution. Since the secretariat services for economic and social matters are an important component of this process of revitalization and the Economic and Social Council discussions are yet to take place, the Secretary-General will report further on the implementation of recommendation 29 and on other relevant findings in the context of the report he will submit to the General Assembly at its forty-fourth session through the Council.

D. *Administration and other fields*

85. The search for greater efficiency and cost-effectiveness has been a priority consideration in the administrative area throughout the reform period. Significant changes have occurred both in terms of organizational structure and in the procedures and methods of work. The basic structural changes are detailed below under recommendations 30 and 32. These modifications resulted in clearer lines of responsibility and better co-ordination. At the same time, a thorough re-examination of the information systems that support the decision-making process in the administrative area was conducted first in 1987 and completed in 1988 through an extensive study of all administrative processes in the Department of Administration and Management. The results of this examination led to the conclusion that, if a leaner Secretariat is to continue to administer the resources of the United Nations and provide the same level of services, a more efficient system for processing and recording transactions had to be developed. The Secretariat's information systems in the administrative area were built as separate applications on older technology with duplication of data and processing. Managers could not be provided with the most up-to-date information on the Organization's resources. These weaknesses became crucially apparent during the financial crisis and in the context of the post reduction exercise. A comprehensive proposal for an integrated information system was therefore submitted to the General Assembly at its forty-third session (A/C.5/43/24) and approved in the context of the revised estimates for the 1988-1989 programme budget. It should be noted that the significant post reductions proposed in the administrative area are predicated upon the streamlining resulting from such a system, although it should be emphasized that, given the magnitude of the task, the project is expected to spread over three and one half years.

Recommendation 30

86. The reorganization of the Department of Administration and Management is now completed. Through reassignment of functions, consolidation of responsibilities and streamlining, significant savings in posts, particularly at senior levels, were possible and have been reflected in the revised estimates for the 1988-1989 programme budget now approved; it should be noted, in this respect, that post reductions in that section of the budget (sect. 28) reached 14.3 per cent. Post reductions were, however, not the only goal in this exercise. For instance, the section dealing with salaries that was formerly in the Office of Programme Planning, Budget and Finance is now integrated into the Office of Human Resources Management, so that all aspects of staff entitlements - salaries, allowances and benefits - can be dealt with at the policy level in an integrated manner; procedures have been established to ensure that proper clearances from the Controller are obtained on these matters before final decisions having financial implications are taken. Likewise, the Office of Human Resources Management, two separate units dealing with the filling of vacancies (the former Career Development and Placement Section and the Recruitment Division) have now been merged so that vacancies in offices and departments can be filled more promptly and more efficiently. Duplication of tasks and the need for exchanging information have thereby been eliminated. A similar exercise was conducted in the Office of General Services, resulting in a more efficient structure with clearer lines of responsibilities.

Recommendation 31

87. Although the Group of High-level Intergovernmental Experts proposed the abolition of the Management Advisory Service, the Secretary-General reported in his second progress report (A/43/286 and Corr.1) that, upon careful examination of the question, he could not propose its abolition without seriously affecting the work of the Department of Administration and Management. The activities of the Office of Programme Planning, Budget and Finance would be especially affected by the abolition of the service. There is a need for a unit that can provide the necessary background information, through well-documented and well-researched studies, for the decision-making process. A careful analysis, from a management standpoint, of departmental proposals is most useful at the beginning of the programme budget process and as an integral part of that process. The integration of this unit into the Office of Programme Planning, Budget and Finance, which deals with such issues, has facilitated this process. The Service has performed particularly important functions during the present period of reform.

Recommendation 32

88. As has already been noted, the functions of programme planning, covering all aspects of United Nations activities and formerly carried out by the Department of International Economic and Social Affairs, have been redeployed to the office responsible for the budget in order to place these two

functions under a coherent structure, as requested in this recommendation. This reorganization has also proven valuable in the servicing of the Committee for Programme and Co-ordination and the Programme Planning and Budgeting Board, an internal body chaired by the Secretary-General or, in his absence, by the Director-General that was established in 1982 to assist the Secretary-General in the exercise of his responsibilities.

Recommendation 33

89. As reported in the second progress report (A/43/286 and Corr.1), a review of the liaison offices in New York of various secretariat activities was carried out in 1988 in connection with the implementation of recommendation 15. Its purpose was to study the feasibility of consolidating the 10 liaison offices at Headquarters that had a staffing table composed of regular budget posts or combined regular budget and extrabudgetary posts, namely the liaison offices of the World Food Council (WFC), the United Nations Environment Programme (UNEP), the United Nations Centre for Human Settlements (Habitat), the Centre for Human Rights, UNHCR, the United Nations Relief and Works Agency for Palestine Refugees in the Near East (UNRWA), UNCTAD, UNDRO, the Vienna-based units - the Centre for Social Development and Humanitarian Affairs, the Division of Narcotic Drugs and the secretariats of the International Narcotics Control Board and of the United Nations Fund for Drug Abuse Control - and the Regional Commissions Liaison Office.

90. The main finding of the review, based on replies to a questionnaire, on interviews and on desk surveys, was that the bulk of the activities of the liaison offices (between 53 and 85 per cent, depending on the office) was substantive in nature. Substantive work includes providing, gathering and exchanging specialized information on the work programme and the activities of the parent body and on developments of interest to them, providing inputs into statements and reports, participating in task forces, seminars, conferences and events, and having contacts and exchanges with Governments and permanent missions, with non-governmental organizations, with the academic, scientific, business and financial communities, and with the media. Given the diversity and complexity of the substantive mandates of the parent bodies, it was concluded that consolidating the substantive functions of the offices would have an adverse effect on programme implementation.

91. On the other hand, it was found that representation of the parent body at intergovernmental, inter-agency and inter-secretariat meetings at United Nations Headquarters, which was the original justification for establishing liaison offices in New York, accounted for less than half of total Professional staff time. Such representation was either in an observer capacity, or required replies to queries from representatives of Member States, particularly during informal negotiations leading to draft resolutions, in which case it became substantive work.

92. In view of the considerable overlap in attendance at intergovernmental and inter-agency meetings, liaison offices with similar work programmes have been asked to share attendance at meetings in an observer capacity to the extent possible, on an experimental basis. Consultations have taken place in that regard among the New York offices and the results of the experiment, which started in early 1989, will be monitored by the executive heads of the Secretariat entities. These arrangements will be evaluated after one year.

93. Regarding support services, it was concluded that there was no rationale for consolidating information and reference services, which were substantive in nature and did not overlap. Secretarial staff were fully occupied and pooling such staff would create problems in the allocation of priorities, especially during the visits of senior officials. Administrative work was the only area that offered some room for consolidation, but it accounted for a relatively small percentage of total General Service staff time and therefore consolidation of administrative support services would not lead to any post savings.

Recommendation 34

94. The Department of Conference Services has actively supported the implementation of recommendations on the calendar of conferences, as well as on documentation and publishing matters. The Department has co-operated closely with the Committee on Conferences in monitoring the use made by United Nations organs of conference services and in suggesting practical ways in which the resources placed at their disposal can be applied more effectively. The response has been encouraging and has contributed to a marked improvement in efficiency.

95. In the preparation of the draft biennial calendar of conferences for 1990-1991, the Department has stressed the need to comply with a series of General Assembly resolutions on the efficient and cost-effective management of the conference programme. These call for the scheduling of conferences and meetings throughout the year to avoid "peaks and valleys" of congestion and slackness in the meetings programme; avoiding overlapping meetings related to the same sector of activity; ensuring that requests for conference services correspond accurately to requirements; and considering a reduction in the number of meetings with interpretation services. The Department has also stressed the principles reaffirmed in General Assembly resolution 40/243, section 1, paragraph 4, and reiterated in recommendation 4 of the Group of Experts that United Nations bodies should meet at their respective established headquarters (see also paras. 20-23). Similarly, through repeated written communications, the Department has also impressed on departments responsible for the substantive servicing of intergovernmental bodies the need to observe the 24 single-spaced page limit on documentation originating in the Secretariat.

96. The Department continues to identify areas of its work where the introduction of new technologies or processes will make it possible to increase

efficiency and productivity. It has participated in the pilot project on optical-disc storage of documents, undertaken at the United Nations Office at Geneva in response to a recommendation made by the Joint Inspection Unit in its report on "Problems of storage and its costs in organizations of the United Nations system" (A/41/806 and Corr.1). The project, which began in 1988, is for the storage and long-distance high-speed transmission and retrieval of conference documents. One storage and two retrieval stations have been installed at the United Nations Office at Geneva. A terminal for the remote retrieval/display/printing of material was installed in September 1988 at Headquarters. The retrieval of Geneva-produced documents not yet available in New York has demonstrated the capabilities of the communications element of the system. It has also pointed to other potential uses of optical-disc technology, which provides a mass storage medium for full-text retrieval. This test project is being carefully monitored. Another pilot project using optical disk technology for a different application (personnel records) has been conducted in the Department of Administration and Management.

97. Alternatives to external typesetting, printing and binding have been under continuous review. Increasing use is being made of internal desktop publishing for the layout and typesetting of newsletters and for more complicated publications, such as *Transnational Corporations in World Development: Trends and Prospects*. A greater and more systematic use of this technique is being considered. At the same time, electronic typesetting using the IBM mainframe computer offers another possibility for increasing internal typesetting capacity and thus reducing reliance on external contractors; software applications have been developed that make it possible to use WANG word-processing diskettes as inputs for IBM typesetting in several official languages for certain categories of publications. This is but one of many examples of ways in which the application of computer and office automation technology is increasing the efficiency and effectiveness of conference servicing.

98. In 1989, the Chinese Typing Unit is the only remaining unit yet to be converted to word processing; the conversion is under way and is expected to be completed early in the next biennium; in addition, a computer-based document tracking system will have been established, providing more readily available information concerning the status of documents and publications in various stages of processing and facilitating the expediting of highest priority documents. The introduction of word processing for editors and translators is expected to facilitate their work and eventually reduce the work-load for the word-processing pools. In addition, linking editors' and translators' work-stations to a central reference and terminology data base should reduce the time and effort required for checking references and ensure a consistent use of standard terminology. Work is beginning on the establishment of a computer-based scheduling of meetings and of interpreter assignments to enable the Secretariat to respond quickly and flexibly to changing requirements for meetings servicing and to make the most efficient and effective use of

scarcè resources. Computer-based information systems to be installed in 1989 should also lead to a more efficient use of internal reproduction and distribution services. The Dag Hammarskjöld Library has begun work towards establishing an integrated system that will include various automated library functions and make possible a sharing of data within the integrated system to eliminate duplication of data entry.

99.   Much progress has also been achieved in the harmonization of the terminology and improved methodologies for the preparation of the programme budget for conference and library services. This will be reflected in the proposed programme budget submission for 1990-1991 under section 29.

100.   Through collaborative efforts within the Secretariat, the Organization is now relying less on external contractors to typeset, print or bind United Nations publications. In the belief that United Nations publications will be judged more on content and timeliness than on expensive glossy presentation, greater emphasis has been placed on producing as many publications as possible using the in-house printing and binding facilities. As a result, the external printing appropriations for the biennium 1988-1989 reflect a negative growth rate of 17.3 per cent over the total appropriations originally approved for the same purpose for the biennium 1986-1987. For the biennium 1990-1991, the goal is to produce the full publications programme, while remaining within the level of funding approved for the 1988-1989 biennium at revalued 1990-1991 rates.   To this end, each departmental publications programme proposal is carefully reviewed to determine that there is a clear mandate from an intergovernmental body; that the number of pages and copies are realistic; that parity is ensured as regards the treatment of official languages, in accordance with General Assembly resolution 42/207 C of 11 December 1987; and that the processing of the work is scheduled to make optimum use of internal facilities. Increasing use is being made of external publication arrangements with commercial publishers to permit a wider dissemination of United Nations publications at no cost to the Organization.

101.   Recommendations by the Publications Board in 1986 for improving the timeliness of publications were passed on to author departments and processing services.   In late 1988, the Board noted some improvements in the timeliness of publications and highlighted areas for further improvement.

102.   Moreover, as requested by the Committee for Programme and Co-ordination, the Publications Board has been monitoring the reviews of the intergovernmental bodies concerned and will ensure the implementation of their decisions to discontinue or to reduce the volume or periodicity of any publications that those bodies consider do not meet the criteria set forth in resolution 38/32 E of 25 November 1983.   In accordance with General Assembly resolution 42/215, the results of the review of recurrent publications, which should be completed by mid-1989, will be reported to the Committee on Conferences.   Efforts are also being made in the context of the review of recurrent publications and the formulation of the 1990-1991 consolidated

publications programme for a better co-ordination of the statistical publications of the regional commissions and Statistical Office at Headquarters. Guidelines to help distinguish clearly between recurrent and non-recurrent publications are also being developed. The Committee on Conferences will consider a report on these questions at its August 1989 session.

103. To maximize the sale of successful publications, a marketing survey was conducted of North American acquisition librarians, who represent approximately 30 per cent of the overall sales market for United Nations publications. Specific recommendations to reach that targeted public more effectively were formulated and are being implemented. The reference publications most requested by libraries are the *World Economic Survey*, the *Yearbook of the United Nations* and the *Yearbook of the International Law Commission*. Some of the publications in greater demand in recent years are manuals and publications on standards such as the *Guidelines for Project Evaluation*, the *Manual for the Preparation of Industrial Feasibility Studies*, the *System of National Accounts* and the *Standard International Trade Classification* (Rev.2). Based on a study, the list of magazines in which advertisements are placed has been revised. Currently, United Nations publications are advertised not only in media but also at trade shows and exhibits and at book fairs. In 1987, a new video "On Common Ground", which provides a tour of the United Nations, has met with success, particularly in schools; as have two new videos released in 1988, "Soldiers for Peace" and "Peacemaking".

104. Other measures taken include the computerization of the sales operation; as a result, orders can be processed more efficiently and promotional activities could be reorganized within existing resources. The Organization's policy on copyrighting its publications was also changed in late 1987, on an experimental basis through December 1989, in recognition of the need both to retain control over certain United Nations materials and to ensure that they were used in the best interests of the Organization, or to protect the revenues that might accrue from sales publications that would be adversely affected by unauthorized, competitive commercial publication. A revision to the methodology for the pricing of sales publications is also nearing completion. It is planned during the biennium 1990-1991 to invite a fresh outside look to determine whether the productivity and efficiency of the department could be further enhanced.

Recommendation 35

105. As requested, the appropriations for consultants for the biennium 1988-1989 represented a reduction of 19.1 per cent (negative growth of $1.6 million) against the 1986-1987 biennium. The proposals of the Secretary-General for the 1990-1991 programme budget reflect an analysis of the needs of each department or office, in the light of the post reductions and of the need to avoid a negative impact on mandated activities.

106.   The information concerning the use of consultants, including retired staff members, will be provided by the Secretary-General in his biennial report on the subject to the General Assembly at its forty-fifth session, in conformity with section I of resolution 43/217 of 21 December 1988 and paragraph 11 of A/43/7/Add.2.

Recommendation 36

107.   A comprehensive study of outside bodies occupying space in United Nations buildings was conducted in response to this recommendation. It was found that United Nations agencies constituted the largest single group of tenants.   In accordance with this recommendation, these agencies and other outside bodies have been requested to start paying rent based on commercial rates.   The rates to be charged in New York are based on the highest rates paid by the United Nations for rented space, that is, for the building of the United Nations Development Corporation at 2 United Nations Plaza.   Similar guidelines were applied to other duty stations.   It was further decided that the new policy should be implemented effective 1 January 1989 for Member States occupying space in United Nations buildings and 1 January 1990 for specialized agencies to permit them to make the necessary budgetary provisions through their own governing bodies.   All those affected by this new policy have been notified of the changes.

108.   Other groups that also use space in United Nations buildings have a special relationship to the United Nations, such as the Hospitality Committee for United Nations Delegations, staff recreation clubs, the Association of Former International Civil Servants and the World Association of Former Interns and Fellows.   For these groups, rent has either been waived or set at a lower concessionary rate in recognition of their special relationship or purpose.

109.   The new policy will, no doubt, have an impact on the amount of space rented in the United Nations. It is, however, too early to assess since most of the groups currently occupying space in United Nations buildings have opted to remain in spite of higher rents.   On the other hand, there are indications that, at Geneva, one or more agencies will seek space outside the United Nations complex because of the higher rents.

Recommendation 37

110.   Pursuant to paragraph (1) of recommendation 37, a thorough review of the functions, working methods and policies of the Department of Public Information was conducted.   A number of concrete measures have been implemented following this review, notably a revision of chapter 9 of the medium-term plan for the period 1984-1989 (extended till 1991) and revised programme budget proposals for the biennium 1988-1989, which reflected a major reorganization of the Department.

111.   The guiding principles for the review of the public information activities of the Organization were stated in the Secretary-General's first progress report (A/42/234 and Corr.1).   Reiterating the importance of information and communication, the Secretary-General noted that to date the Organization has concentrated mainly on communications with Member States, ignoring to some extent "the tapping of the second-tier global constituency, the world's peoples".

112.   The reforms should aim at assisting Governments in expounding the principles of the United Nations to parliaments, the media and the universities of Member States, and to ensure that they are aware of the measures being taken to translate them into practical actions of general benefit.   They should aim at finding ways and means to promote and facilitate the active participation of non-governmental bodies and public movements on matters of global concern.   They should also aim at enlarging "the circle of active public opinion in support of the United Nations and develop a new awareness of its value and potential, especially among the younger generations".

113.   The Secretary-General's proposed revisions to chapter 9 of the medium-term plan as modified by the recommendations of the Committee on Programme and Co-ordination were adopted by the General Assembly in its resolution 43/219 of 21 December 1988.

114.   The Secretary-General's conclusions relating to the review of the functions and working methods as well as of the policies of the Department of Public Information were reflected in the revised estimates for section 27 of the programme budget for the biennium 1988-1989 (A/C.5/43/1/Rev.1).

115.   The Executive Media Service was established so as to provide communication support to the activities of the Secretary-General and other senior staff and to strengthen links with the media.

116.   The approach to information activities will be based on two complementary concepts - promotion and coverage.   One will ensure that the planning and development of strategies as well as the production of public information materials will highlight the major themes and priority areas mandated by the General Assembly, through multimedia promotional campaigns, while the other will ensure adequate media coverage and public interest in the ongoing activities of the Organization.

117.   It was also concluded that greater effectiveness could be achieved by establishing a theme-oriented communications programming and planning unit (the Communications and Project Management Service), coupled with a reorganization of its production, distribution and servicing structures along functional lines (the Information Products Division and the Dissemination Division). It was proposed that the three units referred to above be integrated under the Bureau of Programme Operations and co-ordinated by the Director of that Bureau.

118.　The enhancement of the work of the information centres was another important element in the revitalization of the Department. To this end, an Information Centres Division was established at Headquarters, providing the centres with policy and operational guidance, monitoring their activities and providing them with general support, both substantive and administrative.

119.　Finally, the Division for Committee Liaison and Administrative Services was established to serve several important needs, particularly during the transitional phase of the implementation of the reforms and the achievement of the post reductions called for in recommendation 15. Its aim is to provide support to the executive direction and management function in the Department, including monitoring and evaluation functions, providing not only quantitative analyses but qualitative evaluations of information products and of their dissemination as well as data on public opinion trends about the United Nations. This Division is also responsible for servicing the Committee on Information and the Joint United Nations Information Committee, as well as for maintaining liaison with other intergovernmental and expert bodies; it thus ensures the co-ordination of the Department's policies established on the basis of mandates by the legislative organs with the agencies and programmes of the United Nations system.

120.　The Secretary-General's proposals were examined in detail by the Committee for Programme and Co-ordination, the Committee on Information, the Advisory Committee on Administrative and Budgetary Questions and the Fifth Committee. As a result of these meetings, further modifications, related in particular to the denomination and responsibilities of certain organizational units within the Communications and Project Management Service (Division) and the Information Products Division, are reflected in the proposed programme budget for the biennium 1990-1991.

121.　The Secretary-General's proposals also reflect the decision of the General Assembly based on the recommendation of the Fifth Committee to maintain intact the Anti-*apartheid* Radio Section in the Information Products Division (see A/43/901, and Corr.1, para. 5 (c)).

122.　An additional modification to the structure of the Department of Public Information was necessitated by the decision - as part of the implementation of recommendation 15 - to reduce by one the number of Director (D-2) posts in the Department and by the observations and recommendations of the Advisory Committee on Administrative and Budgetary Questions in its report (A/43/651 and Add.1), referred to in paragraph 17 of General Assembly resolution 43/213, regarding the Bureau of Programme Operations and a possible duplication with some of the activities of the Division for Committee Liaison and Administrative Services and other substantive units. Further observations in this regard were offered by the Joint Inspection Unit in the preparation of its study on United Nations public information networks, pointing to possible duplication and recalling recommendation 40 of the Group of High-level Intergovernmental Experts, which suggested that "the functions of the executive office in each department or office should be consolidated into the office of the head of department or office in a compact and streamlined unit".

123. In the light of these considerations, the Secretary-General's proposed programme budget for the biennium 1990-1991 reflects the abolition of the posts of Director, Bureau of Programme Operations and Director, Division for Committee Liaison and Administrative Services, and the establishment of a post of Director, Office of the Under-Secretary-General, in order to assist the Under-Secretary- General in co-ordinating the planning and implementation of the Department's activities and to provide secretariat services to the Committee on Information and to the Joint United Nations Information Committee (JUNIC). The Programme Evaluation and Communications Research Unit and the Executive Office would be consolidated into the Office of the Under-Secretary-General, reporting directly to the Under-Secretary-General.

124. The simplified structure resulting from the above actions would provide for a leaner and more efficient Department of Public Information as it moves to fully operational status after this transitional reform period. Efforts will be concentrated during the biennium on improving the Department's working methods, productivity and effectiveness.

125. Paragraph (2) of recommendation 37 called for the consolidation in the Department of Public Information of information activities conducted by several other departments and offices. The General Assembly, in paragraph 1 (12) of its resolution 42/162 A of 8 December 1987, requested the Secretary-General "to provide the Committee on Information with a feasibility study on the consolidation and co-ordination of all public information activities within the United Nations with specific reference to the financial implications as well as to the effectiveness of the Department of Public Information as the focal point for public information activities".

126. A study was therefore conducted to examine the feasibility of consolidating all existing public information activities within the Department of Public Information in the context of the reorganization of the Department and to study whether consolidation would improve the efficiency, effectiveness and coherence of public information activities in the Secretariat.

127. The study (A/AC.198/1989/8) is being submitted to the Committee on Information at its eleventh session (13-26 April 1989). Following a survey among some 25 departments and offices, covering a list of some 20 activities related to public information, the study indicated that offices other than the Department of Public Information devote staff time totalling about 432 work-months annually to activities considered strictly public information work. The survey also indicated that public information activities in the Secretariat outside the Department are dispersed among the regional commissions and

various departments located in different duty stations, with 42 per cent of the activities reported being undertaken at Headquarters and the remainder at offices outside Headquarters. The wide geographic separation between the overseas offices and the Department does not facilitate the close collaboration necessary to achieving timely and effective public information about the work of those offices. The survey also established the fact that, with a few exceptions, public information work is spread out among a number of staff members, forming a small part of the work-load of each. The study recommended that a further review of this area be made once the planned programmes and services of the Department of Public Information are fully operational and not earlier than 1992.

128. The study was made available to the Advisory Committee on Administrative and Budgetary Questions during the forty-third session of the General Assembly (A/43/651 and Add.1). The Committee indicated, *inter alia*, that it recognized the constraints involved in consolidating public information activities as enumerated by the Secretary-General. At the same time it believed that efforts to do so must continue and it therefore urged that the further review referred to by the Secretary-General be undertaken *no later* than 1992 (para. 60).

129. The General Assembly, in paragraph 17 of its resolution 43/213, invited the Secretary-General to implement recommendation 37 in accordance with, among other things, the above comments and observations of the Advisory Committee. The Secretary-General therefore intends to undertake the further review of public information activities of the Secretariat external to the Department of Public Information in 1992.

130. The implementation of paragraph (3) of recommendation 37 of the Group of Experts concerning the functions and activities of the United Nations information centres and the consolidation to the extent possible of such centres with other existing United Nations offices is mentioned under recommendation 12 above.

Recommendation 38

131. Regarding the level of official travel, appropriations were reduced by 21 per cent in real growth terms in the 1988-1989 programme budget in relation to the biennium 1986-1987. The proposals contained in the programme budget proposals for 1990-1991 will be comparable to those of 1988-1989. All requests for travel to meetings and conferences are reviewed by the Office of the Secretary-General in accordance with the procedure set out in a Bulletin (ST/SGB/207/Rev.1). This procedure has contributed to a significant reduction in the number of officials attending meetings and conferences away from their duty stations.

132. With regard to first-class travel, the General Assembly in resolution 42/214 of 21 December 1987 decided that such travel would be limited to the Secretary-General and to the heads of delegations of least developed countries and that others previously entitled to first-class would now travel on the class immediately below it. The Secretary-General was authorized to exercise his discretion in making exceptions on a case-by-case basis. He was also requested to report annually on the implementation of the resolution and on the exceptions and reasons for the exceptions made thereon. The provisions of this resolution have been in effect since 1 January 1988. The Secretary-General has, to date, submitted to the General Assembly two reports detailing the exceptions granted for first-class travel (A/C.5/42/9 and A/C.5/43/31) and will be submitting a similar report at the forty-fourth session.

Recommendation 39

133. As stated in the first progress report (A/42/234 and Corr.1), measures have been taken to ensure the independence of the internal audit function in the United Nations Secretariat, which is achieved, as required by professional internal auditing standards, through organizational status and objectivity. The organizational status of the Internal Audit Division is sufficient to assure a broad range of audit coverage and effective follow-up on audit findings and recommendations. The Director of the Internal Audit Division communicates directly with the head of the activity or the office being audited. The Director also has constant and direct access to the Under-Secretary-General for Administration and Management and can report directly to the Secretary-General if the need arises. The objectivity of the audit function is achieved through strict adherence to the professional internal auditing standards on the part of auditors.

134. These procedures and policies, which address the concerns expressed by the Group of High-level Intergovernmental Experts, have proven satisfactory to all concerned. An internal review conducted in 1988 by the Internal Audit Division confirmed that the present arrangements, as far as the independence of the audit function is concerned, were effective and should be maintained.

Recommendation 40

135. When the Group of Experts made its recommendation, there was in fact only one department, the Department of Administration and Management, where each office within the department had its own executive office; this apparent duplication had been found necessary in view of the size of the offices. In response to this recommendation, the three executive offices in the Department were consolidated into one single office, thus providing a tighter control over the use of its resources. Furthermore, through the integration of the Office of the Commissioner for Namibia into the Department for Special Political Questions, Regional Co-operation, Decolonization and Trusteeship, a consolidation of the two administrative offices was also achieved.

IV. Measures regarding personnel

136.   During the reform period, a number of issues had to be given priority that were not envisaged in the report of the Group of High-level Intergovernmental Experts. At the beginning, the financial crisis required special measures to deal with the need to fill vacancies through redeployment; more recently special efforts have been made not only for the staffing of the United Nations Transition Assistance Group but also to fill those vacancies left by staff assigned to that mission. At the same time, the implementation of recommendation 15 on post reductions required a number of studies to ensure an orderly and fair transition to new staffing levels in each office and procedures had to be developed for the redeployment of staff whose posts were being abolished. These activities had to be given priority in the allocation of resources. At the same time, the implementation of the proposed reforms has been pursued as time and resources permitted. Because of these constraints, some reforms will not be completed by the end of 1989, but efforts to implement them will nevertheless continue, as outlined below.

Recommendation 41

137.   As mentioned in the second progress report, the role of the Office of Personnel Services, renamed the Office of Human Resources Management, has been strengthened through a number of measures. The redeployment to this Office of key functions previously carried out by the Office of Programme Planning, Budget and Finance or the Office of General Services in the Department of Administration and Management (salaries and allowances, security of staff system-wide) has ensured a more co-ordinated approach in these areas and avoided the need for duplicative briefings and correspondence. Furthermore, similar functions have been consolidated in order to provide a better delivery of services. For this purpose, all activities leading to the filling of vacancies are now carried out by one unit, the Division of Recruitment and Placement, regardless of the source of candidates (internal or external). This was achieved through the merging of the Division of Recruitment and the Career Development and Placement Unit. A new Medical and Employee Assistance Division was created, regrouping the Medical Service, the staff counsellor's office and other social services.   The development of the integrated management information system approved recently by the General Assembly should also provide the Office of Human Resources Management with the tools necessary to enhance its role in the planning and delivery of services needed by offices and the staff.

Recommendation 42

138.   In this recommendation, the Group of Experts stressed the importance of clear, coherent and transparent rules in personnel management, which should be widely available. To this effect, a Personnel Manual has been issued to all officers dealing with administrative and personnel matters. It contains, at this stage, a compilation of documents arranged in the order of the chapters

of the Staff Rules with a detailed subject index, as well as an introductory chapter with thematic information and commentaries on the history, nature and applicability of the Staff Regulations and Staff Rules and on their administration. Information and commentaries on the articles of the Staff Regulations and the related chapters of the Staff Rules will be developed as resources become available.

139. A complete revision of chapter I of the Staff Rules, on the duties, obligations and privileges of staff, chapter V, on annual and special leave, and chapter VI, on social security, will soon be completed, taking into account, where applicable, recent decisions of legislative bodies. Chapter VII, on travel and removal expenses, is now being revised. As each chapter of the Staff Rules is revised, the relevant decisions of the General Assembly will be incorporated as requested in this recommendation. These rules apply to entities under the authority of the Secretary-General. With regard to the recommendation that these rules should also apply to other organizations in the common system, the question of common staff regulations has been under study by ICSC since 1987. Owing to other urgent agenda items (for example, a comprehensive review of conditions of service), the Commission has not yet completed its study. It is anticipated that it will deal with the item at its next session in 1989 or its first session in 1990.

Recommendation 43

140. The recommendation to fill entry-level posts at the P-1 and P-2 levels through competitive examinations, either internal or external, has been fully implemented. The national competitive examinations are now organized on as wide a geographical basis as possible. In 1988, for instance, national competitive examinations were held in 10 Member States and in 1989 examinations are also planned for 10 Member States. So far, 33 Member States have participated in these national examinations, which provide an opportunity not only to recruit from a wide geographical basis but, most of all, enable the Organization to select in an objective manner the best candidates in each country. The proportion of women successful in these examinations has increased each year, reaching 44 per cent in the 1987 examination. No examination was held in 1986, when the financial crisis forced the Organization to suspend its recruitment activities.

141. As a result of the lack of resources and other tasks related to retrenchment, work on the development of a methodology for holding P-3 examinations and of introducing them on an experimental basis has been postponed until the biennium 1990-1991. This matter will be reviewed on the basis of an assessment of the existing examination for recruitment at the P-2 level and following a study on the rationalization and distribution of P-1/P-2 level posts throughout the Secretariat.

142. The methodology to be used for testing the drafting ability of candidates for P-4/P-5 level posts as recommended by the Group of High-level

Intergovernmental Experts has also been postponed for the time being on account of other pressing priorities.

Recommendation 44

143.   As recommended, the proportion of appointments at the P-1 to P-3 levels is higher than at the other levels of the Professional category, since it is currently 55 per cent and has been above 50 per cent in the last five years, as the following data show:

Percentage of appointments in the Professional category

	P-1 to P-3	All other levels
1988	36 (55 per cent)	30 (45 per cent)
1987	125 (51 per cent)	24 (49 per cent)
1986	104 (55 per cent)	84 (45 per cent)
1985	140 (61 per cent)	89 (39 per cent)
1984	122 (54 per cent)	103 (46 per cent)

144.   Considering the turnover pattern of staff and the rate of vacancies at these levels, it is difficult to increase the proportion of appointments at the P-1/P-3 levels, but every effort will be made to maintain the current high percentage to the extent possible.

Recommendation 45

145.   As stated in the two previous progress reports, the recommendation that staff be considered for permanent appointments after three years of service must await the completion of the retrenchment exercise.

Recommendation 46

146.   The Secretary-General has thus far approved 51 special measures to improve the status of women in the Secretariat. These measures, which have been announced to all staff members through four Bulletins of the Secretary-General, are based on recommendations submitted by a high-level steering committee. This committee was established by the Secretary-General in accordance with the action programme approved by the General Assembly

at its fortieth session, a programme developed by the Co-ordinator for the Improvement of the Status of Women.

147. As a consequence of these measures, the proportion of women in posts subject to geographical distribution has risen from 23.1 per cent as at 30 June 1985 to 26.5 per cent as at 31 January 1989. The number of women promoted to decision- and policy-making levels has increased substantially; the number of women at the D-2 level, for instance, has risen from three to seven during the past four years and the proportion of women among staff promoted to the P-5 and D-1 levels has also increased, as illustrated below:

	1985	1988
P-5	27.8 per cent	47.6 per cent
D-1	10.7 per cent	13.3 per cent

148. A detailed account of the progress made may be found in the three most recent reports on the status of women presented to the General Assembly (A/C.5/41/18, A/C.5/42/24 and A/C.5/43/14).

Recommendation 47

149. The Secretary-General has always sought to maintain an equitable representation of developing countries at all levels, particularly at the senior levels. For instance, the average proportion of nationals of developing countries at levels D-1 and above during the five-year period 1984-1988 was 47.5 per cent. During the same period, the proportion of nationals of developing countries at the D-2 level and above was 47.4 per cent; and in the upper echelons (i.e. Assistant Secretary-General and Under-Secretary-General levels) it was 50 per cent. The overall average proportion of staff from these countries at all levels during this period was 42.9 per cent.

Recommendation 48

150. To facilitate the reassignment of staff to other functions, the Group of High-level Intergovernmental Experts recommended the recruitment of staff in the context of occupational groups. The Secretary-General endorses this approach. In fact, the recruitment of staff at P-1/P-2 levels through competitive examinations by occupational group rather than by post is now firmly established and has been found to be very beneficial both to the Organization and to staff. Furthermore, the introduction of the vacancy management and staff redeployment programme on 22 December 1986 has ensured that the selection of staff for vacant posts is guided by occupational considerations, in that candidates with relevant qualifications regardless of duty

station or departmental affiliation are considered, whereas under the promotion review conducted prior to the introduction of the vacancy management system, candidates were being compared to other staff members in the same organizational unit (department or office). The proposed career development plan is also based on occupational groups.

151.   The present recruitment practices and procedures are considered to be effective as they take into account the occupational group of all applicants and selections are made on this basis as well as on the requirements identified by departments and offices as essential for the delivery of mandated programmes. The roster of external candidates has also been designed to reflect occupational groups.

Recommendation 49

152.   Job rotation among duty stations for Professional staff has been recommended. The vacancy management and staff redeployment system, which was announced in December 1986 and implemented in 1987, is one of the measures taken to increase job rotation and staff mobility in general. Since the introduction of vacancy management, a total of 57 staff members in the Professional category (33 per cent of all internal placement cases) have moved from one duty station to another. As a further measure to facilitate staff mobility, the Secretary-General has approved enhanced entitlements upon assignment or transfer to hardship duty stations.

153.   The design and implementation of a planned rotation and mobility scheme as part of the career development plan is under study. The rotation plan linked to mobility is scheduled to be completed by the end of the biennium 1990-1991.

Recommendation 50

154.   As requested, information on the promotion of staff will be provided in the report of the Secretary-General on the composition of the Secretariat to be submitted to the General Assembly at its forty-fourth session.   The performance evaluation system is being reviewed with the assistance of outside experts, taking into account evaluation reports recently developed by other United Nations agencies. An improved system is expected to be implemented in the course of 1990.

Recommendation 51

155.   Criteria for the promotion of staff have been developed in the context of the vacancy management and staff redeployment system, which is now fully operational. Detailed guidelines were also established for the selection and placement of staff under this system.   The criteria are based on open competition and the matching of the candidate's qualifications with the requirements of the vacant post in the context of the relevant occupational

group. Under this system, a candidate who has been selected for a higher-level post is promoted after six months of satisfactory service. As at 1 March 1989, 53 staff members have already been promoted under this new system and 85 staff members who have been selected for higher-level posts will be promoted in the next six months subject to satisfactory performance.

156. The existing appointment and promotion machinery is used to process the selection and promotion of candidates under the new vacancy management system. The possibility of restructuring the appointment and promotion machinery along occupational lines was considered but it was found that it would be administratively very cumbersome and would not bring particular benefits. The members of the appointment and promotion bodies, with their diverse occupational backgrounds, are able to make sound and objective judgements as regards the professional and technical qualifications of the candidates under review, provided the requirements are clearly stated and the qualifications of the candidates are well documented.

Recommendation 52

157. The mandatory retirement age of 60 has been adhered to except for cases falling under the terms of resolution 35/210 of 17 December 1980 and when it was imperative to retain the services of some staff members beyond the age of 60 in order to ensure the completion of essential urgent work; this was particularly needed during the recruitment freeze and recently in order to ensure the staffing of the United Nations Transition Assistance Group.

Recommendations 53 and 61

158. In paragraph 44 of its thirteenth annual report,[5] ICSC recommended with regard to recommendation 53 that the mandate of the Commission should not be modified, since its monitoring function was already clearly covered by articles 1, 9, 13, 14 and 17 of its statute.

159. In respect of recommendation 61, the International Civil Service Commission reiterated its earlier recommendations regarding the education grant for post-secondary studies and recommended that the existing entitlement not be changed. It further recommended that the current annual leave entitlement of 30 days per annum should not be changed. The full consideration of these matters by the Commission were reported to the Assembly in paragraphs 20-25 of its thirteenth annual report.

160. The General Assembly, by its resolution 42/221 of 21 December 1987, took note of the views of the Commission expressed in paragraphs 44-46 of its report.

161. In addition, the International Civil Service Commission also provided advice to the Secretary-General on recommendations 42, 43, 45, 48-50, 52, 55, 57, 58 and 60, as requested by the General Assembly (para. 45). Furthermore,

it gave its views on recommendations 4, 9, 46, 51 and 59, which were also relevant to its work (para. 46).

Recommendation 54

162.   This recommendation concerning the length of service in the leadership of departments and offices in the Secretariat is taken into consideration when appointments or extensions of appointments are being considered at the Under-Secretary-General and Assistant Secretary-General levels.

163.   It should be noted that at present there are only nine senior officials who have served more than 10 years at the Assistant Secretary-General and Under-Secretary-General levels. Five among these nine officials have served in more than one department or office and four have served in the same department or office since their appointment.

Recommendations 55 and 57

164.   Recommendation 55 requests the Secretary-General to ensure that the principle set out in resolution 35/210 that "no post should be considered the exclusive preserve of any Member State or group of States" is faithfully observed. This recommendation is being duly taken into consideration in the selection of internal or external candidates for posts that become vacant.

165.   With regard to the question of the ratio between staff with permanent appointments and those with fixed-term appointments, this matter is constantly monitored and reported to the General Assembly in the Secretary-General's annual report on the composition of the Secretariat. As requested in General Assembly resolution 41/213, section I, paragraph 1 (d), recommendations 55 and 57, to the extent they were agreed upon, are being implemented taking into consideration resolution 35/210.

Recommendation 56

166.   The Group of High-level Intergovernmental Experts recommended that the work-load of an organizational unit be reviewed before a decision is taken as to whether a vacant post in that unit should be filled. As comprehensive a review as time and resources permitted has taken place in the context of the implementation of recommendation 15. This detailed review led to the establishment of revised staffing tables approved by the General Assembly at its forty-third session. These new staffing tables will serve as a basis for the recruitment and placement of staff during the biennium 1990-1991. Staffing tables will, of course, continue to be reviewed pursuant to this recommendation in the context of future proposed programme budgets.

Recommendation 58

167. In his first progress report, the Secretary-General outlined the changes he introduced in order to ensure that training programmes are geared to meet the changing needs of the Organization. In his second progress report (A/43/286 and Corr.1), he reviewed the major training programmes to be undertaken in the context of the retrenchment exercise and post reductions.

168. As the reform and retrenchment process has gained momentum, the need for training programmes to meet specific needs of departments has increased, particularly in the areas of office automation, management and supervisory training. Training in these areas will continue to be implemented on a priority basis for the balance of 1989 and well into the forthcoming biennium.

169. With the increasing involvement of the Organization in peace-keeping and field operations, training and orientation programmes for staff who are assigned to or being considered for field assignment are also being strengthened as resources permit. In January 1989, a special programme was launched to meet the immediate needs of the United Nations Transition Assistance Group mission.

170. In accordance with paragraph 12 of resolution 43/224 of 21 December 1988 and in order to facilitate redeployment of staff, training will focus increasingly on those staff members facing occupational adjustment. Retraining as well as systematic training to ensure continued professional competence of staff in their area of specialization will be initiated as soon as possible. At this stage, organizational analyses are planned to find out how best to meet the demand for such training.

171. Emphasis will also be placed on providing occupation-related language training courses for departments and staff members whose current or future functions require specific competence in one or more of the working languages of the Secretariat.

172. These training activities will be carried out in-house, through the external studies programme and, when possible, through a programme of exchange with universities and other educational and professional institutions. In view of the limited resources available, emphasis will be placed on increased co-operation and sharing of resources with other agencies of the common system.

Recommendation 59

173. This recommendation, which deals with the role, functions and financing of staff unions in the United Nations, has been carefully examined. During these last few years, a number of events required the full co-operation of staff unions working together with the administration to ensure that the reform process proceeded smoothly. At a time when the very survival of the

Organization was at stake, when staff members were asked to take on additional functions in order to compensate for vacancies in priority areas, when anxiety arose as a result of the post reduction exercise, the staff representatives carried out their activities in full respect of the managerial responsibilities of the Secretary-General. Chapter VIII of the Staff Rules and Regulations, on staff relations, which sets out the functions of staff representatives and their role, will be reviewed, pursuant to this recommendation, in the context of the overall revision of the Staff Rules and Regulations referred to under recommendation 42.

Recommendation 60

174. Considerable progress has been achieved in the area of administration of justice. The Secretary-General's second progress report outlined the steps taken to establish a streamlined and effective machinery in the administration of justice in the Secretariat by early 1988. Further information concerning the progress achieved was provided to the General Assembly at its forty-third session (A/C.5/43/25) and the Assembly endorsed such efforts in its resolution 43/224 on personnel questions.

175. The streamlining of the appellate process has resulted in the elimination of the backlog of cases before the New York Joint Appeals Board for the first time since at least 1970. For 1989, a tracking system has been established with a target of six months from the time a case is filed until a decision is taken by the Secretary-General on the Board's final report. The adoption by the Board, in December 1988, of internal guidelines on procedures and the strict enforcement of time limits at every stage in the appellate process has minimized delays and increased the productivity of the Board. The composition, structure, functioning and procedures of the Joint Appeals Boards away from Headquarters have also been reviewed.

176. As regards disciplinary processes, a revised system of rules, procedures and sanctions for misconduct is being considered and appropriate consultations of staff and management representatives are taking place. Finally, with regard to the Discrimination and Grievance Panels, emphasis has been placed on eliminating the backlog of cases and analysing whether and how these panels can be made more effective in the future.

Recommendation 61

177. Actions taken by the International Civil Service Commission on the question of total staff entitlements are indicated under recommendation 53 above.

Recommendation 62

178.   As reported in the first progress report (A/42/234 and Corr.1), the Secretary-General has discouraged the practice of transferring extrabudgetary posts to the regular budget. Accordingly, no request for the transfer of such posts is included in his proposals for the 1990-1991 programme budget.

V.   Monitoring, evaluation and inspection

Recommendation 63

179.   In the last two years, the Joint Inspection Unit has been providing a more detailed work programme than in previous years, with the intention of illustrating more clearly the Unit's agreement with this recommendation and its support for evaluation studies.   Thus, as the General Assembly was informed in the Unit's nineteenth annual report,[6] the Unit has introduced two new features into its work programme: specification of those studies which are evaluative and provision of advance notice of studies that the Unit plans to undertake in the coming two years.   This latter information is intended to encourage Member States to comment, *inter alia*, on the evaluation content of the work programme so that the Unit may make adjustments as necessary.

180.   The Unit believes that its recent work programmes respond positively to recommendation 63 and to the general concerns of Member States concerning evaluation.   Nevertheless, as the Unit has recognized in its twentieth annual report,[7] addressing the evaluation process is a long-term task.   Advising organizations on their methods for internal evaluation is an objective that will be reached over time through consultations with the participating organizations during the process of the annual development of the Unit's work programme.

181.   The General Assembly, in its resolution 43/221 of 21 December 1988, encouraged the Joint Inspection Unit "when drawing up future reports to limit where possible the narrative part and to expand the evaluative part therein".

Recommendation 64

182.   This recommendation was addressed to the General Assembly, suggesting that Member States give special emphasis to qualifications, particularly in the field of personnel management, public administration, inspection and evaluation.   It noted also that the selection should reflect different disciplines.   The General Assembly, in its resolution 43/221, underlined "the importance of the application of the highest standards ... and of the consultation process for reviewing the qualifications of the proposed candidates in accordance with article 3, paragraph 2, of the statute of the Joint Inspection Unit".

Recommendation 65

183.   This recommendation was also addressed to the General Assembly itself, suggesting that it give greater guidance on its programme of work with respect to the United Nations.

Recommendation 66

184.   The reports of the Joint Inspection Unit are made available to all Member States as requested in this recommendation. This practice has always been observed since these reports are circulated as General Assembly documents or, in a limited number of cases, at the request of the Unit, are submitted as Economic and Social Council documents.

Recommendation 67

185.   Actions have taken place in order to increase the co-operation between the Joint Inspection Unit and the Panel of External Auditors. At the Panel sessions in 1986 and 1987, the Unit and the Panel held joint meetings to discuss this recommendation. It was recognized that, in addition to a continuous liaison between the two bodies exercised through their Executive Secretaries, who keep in contact with each other throughout the year, inspectors and external auditors at the working level have always felt free to call on each other where a particular study on an organization, or area thereof, is to be carried out or is under way. In addition to this, there is an exchange of reports after they have been officially issued. Furthermore, the external auditors are provided with draft reports of the Joint Inspection Unit concerning areas that have been examined and/or reviewed by external auditors whose views and comments are requested.

186.   Others steps were adopted leading to increased co-operation. As external auditors extend their coverage into the area of value-for-money audit, they get closer to the evaluation work done by the Joint Inspection Unit; this presents an opportunity for establishing a sort of reciprocal watch programme, each body bringing to the attention of the other matters that are of interest to it. Through continuous contact between inspectors and external auditors at the working level unnecessary overlap may be avoided. Such contacts also provide opportunities for discussions and exchanges of specific information and work plans for individual studies.   These discussions take place when Joint Inspection Unit inspectors visit a particular organization, and relate to the studies or examinations that each group has under way.

187.   An exchange of work programmes on a regular basis between the Joint Inspection Unit and Panel of External Auditors was also agreed upon, not only to provide an opportunity for possible co-operation but also to help avoid duplication of work. It was also agreed that the findings and recommendations of one service would be reinforced by the other as a matter of principle whenever investigations by the latter lead to similar conclusions.   In this

connection, it was agreed that the recommendations that have been made in a particular year but are brought forward from prior years for lack of implementation should be reviewed by members of both bodies. Those recommendations are found in separate sections of the reports of the Joint Inspection Unit and the Panel of External Auditors.

188.   In connection with the second part of the recommendation requesting that the external auditors should put greater emphasis on management audits and other areas of importance as required by the legislative organs concerned, the external auditors have gradually increased their work in the area of value-for-money audits with the primary objective of providing governing bodies of United Nations organizations with independent information, advice and assurance about economy, efficiency and effectiveness in the administration of the organizations. The findings have been reported systematically and will continue to be reflected as appropriate in the external auditors' reports.

VI. Planning and budget procedure

189.   The recommendations contained in section II of resolution 41/213, in so far as they relate to the Secretariat, concern the improvement of the planning, programming and budgeting process in the United Nations, including the improvement of the consultative process for formulating the medium-term plan.

190.   Regarding the improvement in the planning, programming and budgeting process, the General Assembly recommended that regulation 4.8 of the Regulations and Rules Governing Programme Planning, the Programme Aspects of the Budget, the Monitoring of Implementation and the Methods of Evaluation, which governs co-ordination between the Committee for Programme and Co-ordination and the Advisory Committee on Administrative and Budgetary Questions, be fully implemented. This has been done in the context of the review by the two Committees of the programme budget for the biennium 1988-1989, including the revised estimates for that biennium submitted in 1988.

191.   The General Assembly further requested that the Secretariat ensure follow-up of implementation of the recommendations of the Committee for Programme and Co-ordination. The specific measures outlined for this follow-up were further described in paragraphs 43 and 44 of the note of the Secretary-General on the improvement of the work of the Committee for Programme and Co-ordination (E/AC.51/1986/13), and have been put into effect as recommended by the Committee.

192.   With a view to achieving improvements in the consultative process for the formulation of the medium-term plan, the General Assembly requested the full implementation of the Regulations and Rules Governing Programme Planning pertaining to the medium-term plan. It also requested that

consultations regarding the major programmes in the plan be undertaken in a systematic way with sectoral, technical, regional and central bodies in the United Nations and that a calendar for such consultations be drawn up by the Secretary-General, in consultation with the Committee for Programme and Co-ordination and the Advisory Committee on Administrative and Budgetary Questions. Such consultations are taking place for the preparation of the forthcoming medium-term plan, including its introduction.

193.   As requested by the General Assembly in its resolution 41/213, section II, the Secretary-General submitted to the General Assembly, through the Committee for Programme and Co-ordination, proposals on supplementary regulations and rules necessary for the improvement of the planning, programming and budgeting process in the United Nations. The General Assembly, in its resolutions 42/215 and 43/219, endorsed the Secretary-General's proposals as amended by the Committee for Programme and Co-ordination.

194.   One of the main aspects of the new budget process approved by the General Assembly as set forth in annex I to resolution 41/213, was that Member States should be involved in the budgetary process from its early stages and participate throughout the process. For this purpose, the Assembly requested the Secretary-General to submit, in off-budget years, an outline of the programme budget for the following biennium. Pursuant to that request, the Secretary-General, in 1988, submitted an outline of the programme budget for the biennium 1990-1991. The General Assembly, by its resolution 43/214 of 21 December 1988, which was adopted by consensus, established a preliminary estimate for the programme budget for the biennium 1990-1991 and a contingency fund of the programme budget for that biennium at a level of 0.75 per cent of the preliminary estimate. The Assembly also agreed to the concept of a reserve fund that would cover additional requirements arising from currency fluctuation, non-staff cost inflation and statutory cost increases for staff, and to address further at its forty-fourth session the procedure for the operation of the reserve fund.

VII. CONCLUSION

195.   In his first progress report on the implementation of resolution 41/213 (A/43/213 and Corr.1), the Secretary-General stated that the adoption by the General Assembly of the resolution to review the efficiency of the administrative and financial functioning of the United Nations and particularly the consensus reached on the budgetary process, could signify a historic turning point. The strong support by Member States for the Organization and its activities continued during the next two sessions of the General Assembly in spite of the unfavourable circumstances resulting from the financial crisis. In this connection, it is worth noting that the Secretary-General's proposed budget for 1988-1989 was adopted by the General Assembly at its forty-second session with three abstentions and no negative vote and that the revised estimates for

the same budget and the proposed outline for the 1990-1991 programme budget were adopted by consensus at the forty-third session.

196.   The Secretary-General, for his part, has endeavoured to do everything in his power to implement as rapidly and effectively as was possible, given the circumstances, the mandate given to him in resolution 41/213 and other relevant resolutions adopted since the forty-first session. The present report, which encompasses all actions taken since the beginning of the reporting period, illustrates the progress accomplished in a number of areas, whether through the establishment of new structures, the restructuring of existing entities, the consolidation of activities of a similar nature, the revision of policies and procedures, or the development of better management tools to enable managers to discharge their responsibilities more effectively in the context of a streamlined Secretariat.

197.   While resolution 41/213 envisaged the implementation of the approved recommendations by the Group of High-level Intergovernmental Experts over a three-year period, some recommendations cannot be implemented within a fixed period of time but are of an ongoing nature: this is particularly so in the area of human resources management.   Furthermore, actions by the Secretary-General must be based on decisions yet to be taken by Member States in the General Assembly or its subsidiary bodies, as is the case in the economic and social sectors and in the servicing of conferences and meetings. The Secretary-General therefore views the implementation of resolution 41/213 not as a finite process but as one that will continue to contribute to a more effective and efficient Secretariat.

Notes

1.   *Official Records of the General Assembly, Forty-first Session, Supplement No. 49 (A/41/49)*.
2.   *Ibid., Forty-third Session, Supplement No. 32* (A/43/32 and Corr.1 and 2), para./71.
3.   *Ibid., Supplement No. 7* (A/43/7).
4.   See relevant paragraphs of the Chairman's text dated 4 May on the draft conclusions and recommendations of the Special Commission contained in annex IV of the report of the Special Commission (E/1988/75) and the list of synoptic summaries of views expressed on the functioning of the intergovernmental machinery and subsidiary bodies of the Economic and Social Council and the General Assembly in the economic and social fields contained in annex IX of the same report.
5.   *Official Records of the General Assembly, Forty-second Session, Supplement No. 30 (A/42/30 and Corr.1)*.
6.   *Ibid., Supplement No. 34* (A/42/34), para. 9.
7.   *Ibid., Forty-third Session, Supplement No. 34* (A/43/34), para. 17.

2.32 Document A/44/7*

Final Report of the Secretary-General on the Implementation of General Assembly Resolution 41/213 (A/44/222 and Corr.1)

Report of the Advisory Committee on Administrative and Budgetary Questions

1989

90. The Advisory Committee found this report to be a useful factual summary of the events of the past few years. For its part, the Advisory Committee was able to refer to this report frequently as background during its consideration of the proposed programme budget for the biennium 1990-1991.

91. The Advisory Committee notes the difficulties faced by the Secretary-General in implementing the reform measures, referred to in paragraph 10 of his report. The Advisory Committee also notes the following statement in paragraph 197 of the report:

> "While resolution 41/213 envisaged the implementation of the approved recommendations by the Group of High-level Intergovernmental Experts over the three-year period, some recommendations cannot be implemented within a fixed period of time but are an ongoing nature: this is particularly so in the area of human resources management. Furthermore, actions by the Secretary-General must be based on decisions yet to be taken by Member States in the General Assembly or its subsidiary bodies, as is the case in the economic and social sectors and in the servicing of conferences and meetings. The Secretary-General therefore views the implementation of resolution 41/213 not as finite process but as one that will continue to contribute to a more effective and efficient Secretariat."

Official Records of the General Assembly, Forty-fourth Session, Supplement No. 7 (A/44/7), p. 30.

2.33 Document A/44/16*

Review of the Efficiency of the Administrative and Financial Functioning of the United Nations (A/44/222 and Corr. 1)

Report of the Committee for Programme and Co-ordination

1990

11. At its 14th, 15th and 16th meetings, on 16 and 17 May, the Committee considered the report of the Secretary-General on the implementation of General Assembly resolution 41/213 of 19 December 1986 (A/44/222 and Corr.1)

12. Many delegations noted that the report constituted an adequate basis for the debate of the Committee, but considered that it did not reflect in a global and integral way the process of implementation of the reforms. They expressed concern that the process of reform had taken place amidst a situation of financial crisis that still persisted, though admittedly some positive signs had been registered in recent periods. These delegations reiterated the provisions of General Assembly resolutions 42/211 of 21 December 1987 and 43/213 of 21 December 1988, which pointed to the need for overcoming the current financial crisis if the process of reform is to take place satisfactorily. Furthermore they noted that since the report did not cover the three-year period, it was necessary to provide updated information to the Fifth Committee at the forty-fourth session of the General Assembly.

Conclusions and recommendations

13. The Committee noted that the report was objective, factual and provided useful information on the implementation of General Assembly resolution 41/213. In general, significant progress had been achieved owing to the joint efforts of Member States, the Secretary-General and the staff of the Organization. The Committee observed, however, that the various recommendations contained in the report of the Group of High-level Intergovernmental Experts to Review the Efficiency of the Administrative and Financial Functioning of the United Nations,[1] approved by the Assembly in resolution 41/213, had not been implemented in a balanced manner. While concrete progress had been achieved in the areas of political affairs and administration and management, results were uneven in the implementation of recommendations addressed to intergovernmental bodies and Member States, particularly in the economic and social sectors. Nevertheless, an evaluation of

---

Official Records of the General Assembly, Forty-fourth Session, Supplement No. 16 (A/44/16), pp. 4-6.

results in those sectors should take into account the complexity of problems that had to be addressed in the context of an ever-changing world situation.

14. The Committee noted that the report did not cover the entire three-year period required by the General Assembly and therefore could not be considered as a final report. The Committee also underlined the fact that the reform process was a continuing undertaking that needed to be carefully monitored.

15. The Committee generally agreed that the purpose of the reforms was to enhance the efficiency and effectiveness of the United Nations, and not merely to achieve savings or staff reductions. The Committee therefore encouraged the Secretary-General to pursue his efforts in that respect.

16. The importance of the question of co-ordination within the United Nations system was underlined by the Committee, which reiterated the need to strengthen the role of the Secretary-General in that respect, as well as the role of Member States through intergovernmental bodies.

17. The implementation of recommendation 15 of the Group of High-level Intergovernmental Experts should take into consideration an analysis of work-loads, the effect of post reductions on staff and the need to apply the principles embodied in the Charter of the United Nations with regard to highest levels of competence and equitable geographical distribution. The Committee reaffirmed that this recommendation should be implemented with flexibility to avoid negative impact on programmes, especially those mandated by deliberative bodies, while ensuring an equitable geographical distribution of staff, particularly at senior levels. The Committee decided to pursue its discussions on the effects of the implementation of recommendation 15 in the context of the review of the Secretary-General's proposed programme budget for the biennium 1990-1991.

18. With respect to personnel questions, the Committee emphasized the need for greater transparency and coherence in personnel management, specifically in the United Nations Staff Rules and Regulations.

19. In the context of its review of action taken to implement recommendation 37 of the Group of High-level Intergovernmental Experts, the Committee stressed the need for the Secretary-General to reflect clearly in his reports decisions taken by Member States on the question of Palestine, particularly with respect to the structure of the Department of Public Information. The restructuring of that Department was being monitored carefully by Member States and should be implemented with flexibility and on the basis of mandates given by Member States. The Secretary-General should ensure, in particular, that United Nations information centres were given sufficient resources to enable them to function effectively.

20. The Committee believed that the secretariat services connected with peace-keeping operations should be given sufficient resources in order to enable them to fulfil their mandates.

21. With regard to conference services, the Committee emphasized the need to rationalize the work-load of staff within the Department of Conference Services, as well as the need to ensure that adequate services were provided for meetings and conferences. Further efforts should also be made to rationalize the calendar of conferences and meetings, in conformity with the provisions of General Assembly resolution 43/222 A of 21 December 1988. Furthermore, the Committee agreed that questions relating tot he Committee on Conferences should continue to be examined.

22. In the economic and social sectors, the reform process needed to be pursued more vigorously. Measures to be proposed by the Secretary-General in that area should be reviewed by the Committee to examine their effect on programmes. The Committee recommended that the General Assembly, in considering the report requested in paragraph 2 of its resolution 43/174 of 9 December 1988, should keep in mind the mandates of the Committee in accordance with resolution 41/213. The Committee stressed the need to adhere closely to rules and regulations relevant to that sector when considering future reforms.

23. The Committee noted with satisfaction that the budgetary procedures adopted by the General Assembly were being gradually implemented. Those procedures should be monitored carefully and reviewed when necessary, taking into account experience acquired. Flexibility should be exercised with respect to the contingency fund, which was still in a development phase.

24. While noting that the financial situation had improved somewhat recently, the Committee noted that it had not been conducive to a co-ordinated implementation of reforms. The Committee stressed the importance for Member States to monitor closely the financial situation and to fulfil strictly their financial obligations under the Charter.

25. The Committee stressed that, in order to carry out successfully the process of reform and restructuring, it was essential that the present financial uncertainties be dispelled.

26. With respect to the implementation of recommendation 5 concerning the two construction projects approved by the General Assembly, the Committee noted the progress made in that respect and emphasized the need to adhere closely to the schedule outlined by the Secretary-General in his report to the General Assembly at its forty-third session on the matter (A/C.5/43/16).

27. The Committee requested that the Secretariat provide the General Assembly at its forty-fourth session with up-to-date information on the

implementation of resolution 41/213 so as to facilitate its consideration of the implementation process as an integrated whole.

28. Finally, the Committee recommended that the Secretary-General should submit to the General Assembly at its forty-fifth session an update on the implementation of its resolution 41/213. The report of the Secretary-General should therefore contain an analytical and critical review of the process of reform, in the light of the objectives contained in resolution 41/213, and cover the three-year period, highlighting those issues which the Committee had noted in its discussions. The report should be structured along the following lines: (a) the first part should be an exhaustive presentation of recommendations fully implemented, partially implemented and not implemented, as well as those which, in the view of the Secretary-General, could not be implemented; (b) the second part of the report should provide explanations with regard to such implementation and an assessment of its impact on programmes, giving particular emphasis to those programmes which have been terminated or completed; and (c) the final part should provide a general critical assessment of the implementation of resolution 41/213 in the light of the objectives of that resolution, namely, the enhancement of the administrative and financial functioning of the Organization.

Note

1.   *Official Records of the General Assembly, Forty-first Session, Supplement No. 49* (A/41/49).

2.34 Document A/44/272*

**All Aspects of Priority-setting in Future Outlines
of the Proposed Programme Budget**

Report of the Secretary-General

26 July 1989

CONTENTS

		Para-graphs
I.	Legislative background	1 - 4
II.	Evolution of the legislative framework for priority-setting	5 - 16
III.	Practical application of the legislative framework for priority-setting	17 - 39
IV.	Need to reconsider priority-setting	40 - 54
V.	Conclusions and recommendations	55 - 57

---

*A/44/272.

I. Legislative background

1.   In its resolution 41/213 of 19 December 1986, the General Assembly approved a new programme budget process. One of the elements of the new process is the submission by the Secretary-General in off-budget years of an outline of the proposed programme budget for the following biennium, containing, as required in annex I, paragraph 1 (b), of that resolution, an indication of priorities, reflecting general trends of a broad sectoral nature.

2.   In compliance with this requirement, the Secretary-General submitted his proposed programme budget outline for the biennium 1990-1991 (A/43/524) to the General Assembly at its forty-third session, through the Committee for Programme and Co-ordination and the Advisory Committee on Administrative and Budgetary Questions. In paragraph 8 of the report, the Secretary-General indicated that, for historical reasons, intergovernmental decisions on priority-setting had yet to be taken in regard to the subprogrammes of the medium-term plan and, therefore, that the most practical approach to indicating priorities reflecting general trends of a broad sectoral nature in the outline was deemed to be at the level of the parts of the programme budget.

3.   At its resumed twenty-eighth session, the Committee for Programme and Co-ordination (CPC) held extensive discussions on the subject of priorities but could not arrive at an agreement on the issues to be accorded priority in the proposed programme budget outline for the biennium 1990-1991.[1] In view of these difficulties, the Committee[2] requested the Secretary-General to present a report for consideration at its twenty-ninth session on the approach, particularly the methodological aspects to be adopted, for identifying priorities reflecting general trends of a broad sectoral nature in future programme budget outlines. In paragraph 11 of its resolution 43/214 of 21 December 1988, the General Assembly stressed the importance of indicating in the outline of the proposed programme budget priorities reflecting general trends of a broad sectoral nature, endorsed the recommendations of CPC in that regard, and requested the Secretary-General to submit a report on all aspects of priority-setting in future outlines to the Assembly at its forty-fourth session through the Committee.

4.   The present report is submitted in response to that request.

II. Evolution of the legislative framework for priority-setting

5.   The legal framework for the current system of priority-setting in the United Nations emanates from Economic and Social Council resolution 2008 (LX) of 14 May 1978. In paragraph 2 (a) (ii) of the annex to that resolution, the Council entrusted CPC, as the main subsidiary organ of the Council and the General Assembly for planning, programming and co-ordination, with the task of recommending "an order of priorities among United Nations programmes as defined in the medium-term plan".

6. In the course of its review of the medium-term plan at its sixteenth, eighteenth and twentieth sessions (1976, 1978 and 1980), CPC assigned a specific rating, ranging from "well above average" to "well below average", for the growth of resources in real terms of each major programme in the plan. After their endorsement by the General Assembly, the ratings were incorporated in the budget instructions and they guided the allocation of regular budget resources to substantive programmes during the internal budgetary process of the Secretariat. However, as was noted in paragraph 19 of an earlier report of the Secretary-General on setting explicit priorities among United Nations programmes (A/C.5/36/1), the application of the system ran into several problems.

"The CPC growth ratings were formulated in a manner which necessarily excluded (a) common services and (b) extrabudgetary funds, and which created practical difficulties in their application to (a) policy-making organs, (b) political problems and (c) the programmes of the regional commissions. As a consequence, the system effectively covered programme activities representing, in the proposed programme budget for the biennium 1980-1981, approximately 30 per cent of the regular budget."

The General Assembly, in paragraph 6 of its resolution 35/9 of 3 November 1980, considered that CPC should not continue to set relative growth rates and requested the Committee, at its twenty-first session, to determine new criteria and methods to be employed in setting programme priorities.

7. At its twenty-first session, CPC devoted considerable attention to the whole question of priority setting.[3] Its overall conclusion stated:

"There is no necessary relationship between the priority of activities and the volume of resources required to conduct them. Many high priority activities may require fewer resources than lower priority activities. None the less, the practical purpose of establishing priorities is to indicate which activities should have first claim on resources and which activities could, with intergovernmental agreement, be curtailed or terminated in the event that high priority activities need more resources transferred to them. The setting of priorities should facilitate the rapid, rational and efficient execution of programmes and so maximize the impact of the United Nations on the problems at which its actions are aimed."[4]

8. The measures and guidelines for determining the order of priorities among programmes that the General Assembly subsequently laid down in resolution 36/228 A of 18 December 1981 were based on the conclusions and recommendations of CPC at its twenty-first session. Under the conception of the system, as stated in section II, paragraph 1, of that resolution, "the principal purpose of establishing priorities" was "to rationalize and order the activities and provide a guide for the preparation of the programme budget". Priorities were to be set at three levels:

(a)   At the highest level, the introduction to the medium-term plan should highlight objectives and policy orientations as well as indicate trends that reflect overall priorities, which would be derived from the overall objectives of the Organization as set out in the Charter of the United Nations and other authoritative international instruments;

(b)   At the subprogramme level in the draft medium-term plan or the proposed programme budget, the Assembly should establish the order of priorities by accepting, curtailing, reformulating or rejecting subprogrammes on the basis of the budget and programme performance reports, the detailed evaluation reports and the recommendations of the competent intergovernmental bodies. The priorities so established at the subprogramme level should contribute to the achievement of the overall priorities determined at the highest level;

(c)   At the third level, the text of the programme budget would continue to identify programme elements within each programme representing approximately 10 per cent of the resources requested to which the highest priority was to be assigned, and programme elements representing approximately 10 per cent of the resources requested to which the lowest priority was to be assigned.

9.   In section II, paragraphs 3 and 4, of resolution 36/228 A, the General Assembly also decided that the establishment of an order of priority should apply to all the substantive activities of the Organization and to the common services and serve as a guide for the allocation of all its budgetary and extrabudgetary resources. Further, it stipulated the following three principal criteria upon which the establishment of an order of priority should be based:

(a)   The importance of the objective to Member States;

(b)   The capacity of the Organization to achieve it;

(c)   The real effectiveness and usefulness of the results.

10. At its next session the General Assembly, by resolution 37/234 of 21 December 1982, adopted the Regulations Governing Programme Planning, the Programme Aspects of the Budget, the Monitoring of Implementation and the Methods of Evaluation,[5] which, together with the corresponding Rules, codified the recommendations of CPC and decisions of the Assembly, in particular resolution 36/228 A, on priority setting. Regulation 3.2 states that the medium-term plan:

"shall reflect Member States' priorities as set out in legislation adopted by functional and regional intergovernmental bodies within their spheres of competence and by the General Assembly, on advice from the Committee for Programme and Co-ordination.   In this context, subsidiary intergovernmental and expert bodies should, accordingly, refrain from making recommendations on the relative priorities of the major programmes as outlined in the medium-term plan and should instead propose, through the Committee, the relative priorities to be accorded to the various subprogrammes within their respective fields of competence."

11. Regulation 3.7 states that "the plan shall be preceded by an introduction, which will ... contain the Secretary-General's proposals on priorities". Regulations 3.15 to 3.18 further elaborate the General Assembly's decisions on the setting of priorities:

"Regulation 3.15: The establishment of priorities among both substantive programmes and common services shall form an integral part of the general planning and management process without prejudice to arrangements and procedures now in force or to the specific character of servicing activities. Such priorities shall be based on the importance of the objective to Member States, the Organization's capacity to achieve it and the real effectiveness and usefulness of the results.

"Regulation 3.16: Intergovernmental and expert bodies shall, when reviewing the relevant chapters of the proposed medium-term plan, recommend priorities among subprogrammes in their field of competence. They shall refrain from making recommendations on priority among major programmes. The Committee for Programme and Co-ordination, when making recommendations, and the Secretary-General, when making proposals on programme priorities, shall take into account the views of the above-mentioned bodies.

"Regulation 3.17: On the basis of the Secretary-General's proposals and of the recommendations of the Committee for Programme and Co-ordination, the General Assembly shall designate, among the subprogrammes it accepts, those which are of the highest and lowest priority.

"Regulation 3.18: Priorities, as determined by the General Assembly, in the medium-term plan shall guide the allocation of budgetary and extrabudgetary resources in the subsequent programme budgets. After the medium-term plan has been adopted by the Assembly, the Secretary-General shall bring the decisions on priorities to the attention of Member States and the governing boards of the voluntary funds."

12. As regards the programme aspects of the budget, regulation 4.3 states:

"The highest-priority subprogrammes, as decided by the General Assembly, shall have first claim on resources, if budgetary needs are demonstrated, and, if possible, through redeployment in the event that low-priority activities are curtailed or terminated by intergovernmental decision."

Regulation 4.6 provides:

> "Within the proposed programme budget the Secretary-General shall provide the General Assembly with ... an identification within each programme of programme elements of high and low priority, each category representing approximately 10 per cent of the resources requested."

13. The continuing difficulties encountered both by Member States and by the Secretariat to comply fully with these regulations occasioned another detailed review of the issue of priority-setting by CPC at its twenty-sixth session. In the context of the agenda item entitled "Improvement of the work of the Committee under its mandate with, *inter alia*, a view to its consideration of future programme budgets and medium-term plans", CPC recognized once more the importance of the setting of priorities in the plans and programmes of the United Nations, and recommended that:

> "the General Assembly, in its consideration of the proposed medium-term plan and proposed programme budget, should set priorities in accordance with the Rules and Regulations of the United Nations Governing Programme Planning, the Programming Aspects of the Budget, the Monitoring of Implementation and the Methods of Evaluation, as follows:
>
> "(a) In the medium-term plan:
>
> "(i)   At the programme level, on the basis of advice from CPC (regulations 3.2 and 3.15 and para. 2 (a) (ii) of the terms of reference of CPC);
>
> "(ii) At the subprogramme level, on the basis of the Secretary-General's proposals and of the recommendations of CPC (regulation 3.17); the Secretary-General should request intergovernmental and expert bodies to recommend priorities among subprogrammes in their field of competence and take their views into account (regulation 3.16);
>
> "(b) In the programme budget:
>
> "(i)   At the subprogramme level, in conformity with the decisions taken in the context of the review of the medium-term plan (regulation 4.3);
>
> "(ii) At the programme element level, on the basis of the proposal of the Secretary-General and advice from CPC (regulation 4.6)."[6]

14. In its resolution 41/203 of 11 December 1986, the General Assembly adopted these recommendations together with other conclusions and recommendations of the Committee at its twenty-sixth session.

15. Finally, the Group of High-level Intergovernmental Experts to Review the Efficiency of the Administrative and Financial Functioning of the United Nations also considered the question of priority-setting, noted that the problems experienced in that regard were primarily related to the lack of application by the intergovernmental machinery and the Secretariat of the criteria governing the setting of priorities and recommended:

> "In order to facilitate agreement among Member States on the content and level of the budget, the existing rules and regulations pertaining to the setting of priorities should be strictly applied by the intergovernmental bodies concerned and by the Secretariat. The Committee for Programme and Co-ordination should be requested to monitor this application and report thereon to the General Assembly."[7]

16. In its resolution 41/213, the General Assembly not only endorsed the recommendations of the Group but also reaffirmed the need to improve the planning, programming and budgeting process through, *inter alia*, the implementation of the recommendations of CPC cited in paragraph 13 above.

III. Practical application of the legislative framework for priority-setting

17. The preceding section outlines in some detail the evolution of the regulations and rules governing the setting of priorities among the activities of the United Nations. If nothing else, it indicates a continuous preoccupation with this issue over a long period of time. This preoccupation, in turn, reflects a situation in which Member States (a) attach considerable importance to the setting of priorities as an integral part of the planning, programming and budgeting process and (b) continue to be dissatisfied with the way the elaborate regulations and rules are implemented - or not implemented - both by intergovernmental bodies and by the Secretariat.

18. The Secretariat shares both these sentiments. In fact, over the years it has had numerous occasions to call to the attention of CPC and the General Assembly the difficulties encountered in this regard. Thus, the Director-General for Development and International Economic Co-operation, speaking before CPC at its twenty-second session of the introduction to the proposed medium-term plan for the period 1984-1989, noted that an important aspect of the planning process, in respect of which major difficulties persisted, related to priority setting. He stated that very few intergovernmental bodies had been able to formulate concrete recommendations on priorities in their review of the various draft sections of the plan, and the Secretariat, in preparing the introduction to the plan, had not been in a position to fully comply with the guidelines formulated by the General Assembly in its resolution 36/228 of 18 December 1981.[8]

19. Then, in the introduction to the proposed programme budget for the biennium 1984-1985, after an acknowledgement that some progress in the

setting of priorities, especially at the programme element level, had been recognized, it was noted that:

"The system of priority setting in the United Nations is not yet perfected and is experiencing a number of constraints. It is generally accepted that the scope of the activities of the Organization, ranging from the political, through the humanitarian, to a broad range of economic and social undertakings, renders difficult the establishment of a technical system of priority setting between programmes. As regards priorities within programmes, difficulties have been experienced both by Member States in establishing, and by the Secretariat in suggesting, priorities."[9]

20. Nevertheless, in paragraph 30 of a report entitled "Operation of the new system for setting priorities" (A/C.5/39/1), submitted to the General Assembly at its thirty-ninth session in 1984, the Secretary-General concluded that it was too early to draw any clear conclusions concerning the way the new system functioned and that it would be kept under review. Consequently, no changes were suggested in the conception of priority-setting established by the Assembly in its resolution 36/228 A or in the programme planning regulations and rules.

21. The difficulties repeatedly alluded to, but never spelled out in full, stem from a variety of sources, some definitional, some conceptual and others methodological.

A. *Definitional problems*

22. The first set of problems is related to the fact that the term "priority" has never been authoritatively defined by the United Nations. The Joint Inspection Unit some years ago made an attempt at a definition in a report on the setting of priorities and the identification of obsolete activities in the United Nations (A/36/171), but proved to be more successful in stating what priority is not than what it actually is. Thus in paragraph 9 of the report, the Inspector stated:

"The meaning of the word 'priority' is not as obvious as it seems. It can be defined as 'that to which most importance is attached' or 'that which is to receive most attention', but any such definition is very vague. To say that priority programmes are those which receive or ought to receive the largest amount of resources would lead to an inaccurate perception of the matter; the fact that some programmes may receive more resources than others because the mechanisms for implementing them are more costly in themselves does not mean that they are considered more important than others whose objectives can be achieved at less cost; the fact that a training subprogramme may cost more than a research subprogramme does not imply that the former has higher priority than the latter. Nor does the establishment of an order of priorities mean that, in the case of reduction of the existing resources, one would be prepared to eliminate entirely the programmes in the lowest category. However, it may mean that in such a situation the reductions in resources for the lowest-priority programmes would be larger than those for the highest-priority ones."

In paragraph 10, the Inspector concluded that "the concept of priority is therefore relative to a given situation".

23. The glossary of terms annexed to the programme planning regulations and rules contains the following definition:

"A priority is a preferential rating for the allocation of limited resources. Thus activities with highest priority are those that would be conducted even if total resources were significantly curtailed; activities with lowest priority are those that would be curtailed or terminated if all anticipated resources were not available or if activities with higher priority had to be commenced or expanded."

This definition may be useful as a practical guide but it should be noted that it is directed more to the application of priorities once they have been set than towards the criteria by which they should be established.

24. Another definitional problem is introduced by the requirement of General Assembly resolution 41/213, in which the Assembly requested the Secretary-General to indicate in the outline of his proposed programme budget "priorities, reflecting general trends of a broad sectoral nature". The term "sector" in United Nations usage is far from self-evident. It is used in the context of subsidiary organs of the Economic and Social Council but that is hardly applicable here. The modifying adjective "broad" contributes a further ambiguity.

B. *Conceptual problems*

25. A major source of the conceptual problems is the criteria for priority-setting. As noted above, these are identified as (a) the importance of the objective to Member States, (b) the Organization's capacity to achieve it and (c) the real effectiveness and usefulness of the results.

26. With respect to the first criterion, it can be regarded as almost axiomatic that while some objectives are important to some Member States, other objectives are important to other Member States, and that therefore there are no objectives identified in the medium-term plan which are not important, at least to some Member States. Inasmuch as all activities are based on legislative mandates, it can be assumed that the legislation would not have been introduced in the first place unless it was deemed important to its sponsor or sponsors. Consequently, satisfying the first criterion is a highly political act, which must be resolved in the negotiating process between Member States.

27. The second criterion gives rise to problems of a different kind. In fact it is an invitation to a "Catch-22" dilemma. If the Organization's capacity to achieve a certain objective is judged to be low, the activity is presumed to be assigned low priority. The designation of low priority, in turn, will assure that the Organization will not be able to improve its capacity to achieve the objective, which will lower even further the priority of the activity.

28. The third criterion, "the real effectiveness and usefulness of the results", is the one of the three which is best suited for objective determination, using all the available tools of the programme planning instruments developed over the past decade. The real problem here is the availability on time and the utilization by both intergovernmental bodies and the Secretariat of the findings of the reports on programme performance and evaluation. The Secretary-General, in a report to the General Assembly entitled "Application of evaluation findings in programme design, delivery and policy directives" (A/43/179), suggested some steps in that direction. How they might work in practice is illustrated by the report, currently before CPC, on the in-depth evaluation of the programme on development issues and policies in the Economic Commission for Africa (ECA) (E/AC.151/1989/4/Add.2).

29. Finally, it should be noted that while the regulations and rules on programme planning stipulate the three criteria, there is no guidance on a hierarchy between these criteria or how a conflict between them should be resolved (unless it is implicitly assumed that they are listed in a descending order of importance); nor is there guidance on whether all three criteria should be equally applicable at every level of the medium-term plan.

C. Methodological problems

30. An important element of the planning and programming process and, *pari passu*, of priority-setting is the process of consultation with sectoral, functional and regional intergovernmental bodies. Thus, the programme planning regulations and rules require consultations with these bodies every step of the way, which involves the draft introduction and individual chapters of the medium-term plan as well as sections of the proposed programme budget.[10]

31. As has been noted in two earlier reports of the Secretary-General on the question of consultations regarding the medium-term plan (A/C.5/35/4 and Corr.1 and A/43/329/Add.1 and Corr.1 and 2), the complexity of the calendar of meetings of regional, sectoral and functional intergovernmental bodies does not always accommodate the scheduling requirements of the preparation of the medium-term plan, revisions to it and the programme budget. By and large, sectoral and regional bodies are also averse to rescheduling their meetings for the purpose of considering draft chapters of the plan.

32. Two suggestions have, therefore, been made in case of a scheduling problem: (a) *ad hoc* planning committees could be set up to review the plan, or (b) since meetings of such bodies would have financial implications, the substantive secretariat units could circulate draft chapters of the plan to the members of the relevant programme-reviewing body for views and suggestions. While either of these methods could be considered as practical alternatives to full-scale intergovernmental reviews of plans and programme budgets, the question remains whether they would be equally suitable as a substitute for the direct give-and-take involved in the setting of priorities.

33. Another set of problems derives from the requirement of regulation 3.5, according to which "the plan shall cover all activities, substantive and servicing, including those to be financed partially or fully from extrabudgetary resources". The implications of this regulation for priority-setting are far-reaching. For units that are funded both from the regular budget and from extrabudgetary resources, it is extremely difficult - if not impossible - to foresee the nature and extent of the latter several years in advance, as it would be necessary by the exigencies of the preparation of the medium-term plan. In such circumstances, it is accepted that a certain degree of over-programming is inevitable, since it is preferable to have intergovernmental bodies review and approve a work programme that is clearly larger than the regular budget can finance and from which potential donors can choose activities, than to have donors unilaterally impose specific programmes or activities. The latter alternative can lead not only to a dilution of the programme content, but also to a process of priority-setting where choices must be made among programmed activities whose financing is essentially beyond the control of the Organization.

34. Finally, the requirement (regulation 4.6 (b) and rule 104.6 (b)) to identify within each programme those programme elements of high and low priority, each category representing approximately 10 per cent of the regular budget resources requested, creates its own set of problems. This practice was first recommended by CPC at its seventeenth session,[11] and endorsed by the General Assembly in section I, paragraph 4, of its resolution 32/206 of 21 December 1977. Subsequently, the Secretariat complied with this requirement by successively enlarging the number of sections in the proposed programme budgets in which the "10 per cent rule" was applied.

35. The practical application of the rule, however, has sometimes created more the appearance than the reality of compliance. The problem stems from the fact that priority activities - either high or low - frequently do not fall neatly into 10 per cent categories. This in turn confronted submitting units, and ultimately central reviewing units, with a dilemma and the need to resort to one of three possible solutions, none of them entirely satisfactory. When there was a discrepancy between what was considered to be an activity of high or low priority, on the one hand, and the resources required to carry out that activity, on the other, they could (a) assign high or low priority to that activity and

thereby designate perhaps 25 per cent of the resources as being of high priority and 3 per cent of the resources as low priority, thus violating regulation 4.6 (b), (b) assign high and low priority to those activities where the programme element happened to require 10 per cent of the programme's resources, regardless of whether the activity was deemed by Member States to be of high or low priority, thus negating the whole purpose of priority-setting, or (c) decide what activity deserved to be designated high or low priority and then arbitrarily assign to it 10 per cent of the resources requested, regardless of the actual relationship between the activity and its resource requirements. Of the three alternatives, the first perhaps violated the least the letter and spirit of what programme planning and priority-setting should be all about, but the choice of the lesser evil can at best mitigate but not exonerate.

36. The problem described in the preceding paragraph may account, at least to some extent, for the judgement rendered in the latest report of the Joint Inspection Unit entitled "Reporting on the performance and results of United Nations programmes: monitoring, evaluation and management review components" (A/43/124), namely, that priority designations at the programme element level "do not seem to make much difference" (*ibid.*, para. 78). This verdict derives, *inter alia*, from the observation that in the biennium 1982-1983, only 78 per cent of the "highest priority" outputs were implemented as compared to 72 per cent of those activities with no designation, and in some units the "highest priority" implementation rate was less than that for non-priority items. Examples were also cited from the biennium 1984-1985 where it was noted that in some departments the "highest priority" implementation rate was only 45 per cent.

37. The evidence from the report of the Secretary-General on the programme performance of the United Nations for the biennium 1986-1987 (A/43/326 and Corr.1 and Add.1 and Corr.1 and 2), issued since the appearance of the report of the Joint Inspection Unit, is far from clear-cut regarding the question of whether designation of priorities at the programme element level makes a difference. It seems that the situation improved in some respect and deteriorated slightly or remained unchanged in some others. It was concluded that the result was "modest yet significant when seen in the context of the financial crisis" (A/43/326 and Corr.1, para. 33).

38. Looking at the same problem from the angle of intergovernmental review, the report on the in-depth evaluation of the programme on development issues and policies in ECA (E/AC.51/1989/4 Add.2, para. 8), currently before CPC, notes:

"Programme performance reports submitted to the Conference of Ministers and the subsidiary bodies while including analysis of overall levels of implementation do not include separate analysis of the implementation of high and low priority activities."

39. In this context, it should be noted that while the evaluation report cited here deals specifically with ECA, the problem is a more generic one. Few sectoral, functional or regional intergovernmental bodies, or even central reviewing organs, make sufficient use of programme performance reports as guides to priority-setting in subsequent programme budgets, in spite of repeated calls from CPC and the General Assembly to do so. The timing of issuing these reports is probably one of the reasons, since programme performance reports are issued in off-budget years and there is, therefore, a time lag between the appearance of the report and the review of the next proposed programme budget. Nevertheless, as it is suggested in the next section, greater use of both programme performance reports and evaluation reports would contribute to the application of the proper criteria for priority-setting in medium-term plans and programme budgets.

IV. Need to reconsider priority-setting

40. The problems analysed in the preceding section notwithstanding, priority-setting is, as noted by the General Assembly in resolution 36/228 A, an integral part of the general planning and management process. There are several reasons for the need to improve the process:

(a) As shown above, it has not functioned in a satisfactory manner;

(b) The budget reforms instituted by the General Assembly in the past three years have introduced new elements in the process, including the presentation in off-budget years of a programme budget outline and the regulation regarding the contingency fund;

(c) The need to continue the dialogue, which commenced in 1988 in the context of the consideration of the draft introduction to the medium-term plan for the period 1992-1997 and the programme budget outline for the biennium 1990-1991, among Member States and between Member States and the Secretariat at all levels with a view to implementing the regulations and rules regarding priority-setting to the fullest extent possible.

41. Modification of the current system of priority-setting is proposed so as to take the requirements identified in the preceding paragraph into account. The purpose of proposing modifications at this stage is not so much to reach definitive conclusions but rather to start a dialogue between Member States and the Secretariat.

42. The modified system of priority-setting proposed here is based on the following assumptions:

(a) Acceptance of an additional criterion for priority-setting, initially proposed by the Secretary-General in the context of the preparation of the next medium-term plan (A/42/512, enclosure, p. 8), namely that the objective sought should be of a nature that multilateral action is demonstrably important to its achievement;

(b)   The primary focus of priority-setting would be the medium-term plan. Consequently, priorities identified in the programme budget (including the outline) should derive to the maximum extent possible from the priorities set in the medium-term plan;

(c)   As a corollary to paragraph (b), biennial revisions to the medium-term plan should include not only textual revisions but also - as and when needed - revisions of the priority designations of subprogrammes;

(d)   In order to make the process described in paragraph (c) fully effective, consultations with sectoral, functional and regional intergovernmental bodies should regularly be carried out on a biennial basis;

(e)   Under the modified system of priority-setting, CPC and the Advisory Committee on Administrative and Budgetary Questions would continue to fulfil their respective mandates and functions in accordance with their terms of reference.

43. Guided by these assumptions, the modified system of priority-setting at the various levels of the medium-term plan and programme budget is set out in paragraphs 44 to 54 below.

A. *Medium-term plan*

1. *Introduction*

44. Preparation of the introduction to the medium-term plan would continue to be guided by regulation 3.7. Concerning priority-setting, the only new element would be the addition of the new criterion proposed by the Secretary-General as mentioned in paragraph 42 (a) above.

2. *Major programme*

45. There has been no requirement to establish priorities among major programmes, and no change is proposed.

3. *Programme*

46. Although regulation 3.15 stipulates the establishment of priorities among both substantive programmes and common services, it has never been done. It is at this level that Member States would encounter the most difficulty in agreeing, and the Secretariat in proposing, priorities among broad and disparate categories of activities. The setting of priorities attempted and ultimately abandoned by CPC at its twenty-eighth session in the context of the

outline of the proposed programme budget for the biennium 1990-1991 vividly illustrated the problem.[12] It is, therefore, suggested that the establishment of priorities should not be attempted at this level.

4. *Subprogramme*

47. It is proposed that priority-setting should be primarily focused at this level. First, the subprogramme is at a level that is broad enough to allow assessment of its contribution to the overall objective of the programme, while narrow enough to allow choices to be made among activities that are essentially complementary in character. Second, it is the level at which sectoral, functional and regional bodies will most likely be able to come to an agreement on priorities that, in the first instance, should be proposed to them by the Secretariat. In this context, it should be noted that during the consultations with intergovernmental bodies on the preparation of the next medium-term plan, particular emphasis was put on the need to recommend priorities and so far the majority of these bodies have done so. Third and most important, the subprogramme is the principal link between the medium-term plan and the programme budget, and the setting of priorities at this level, therefore, has potential impact on the allocation of budgetary resources. As indicated in the table, it is also at this level that intergovernmental bodies could utilize - where available - the findings of evaluation reports as guides to the determination of the effectiveness and usefulness of the activities under review.

B. *Programme budget*

1. *Outline*

48. Regulation 3.2 A.1 (b), approved by the General Assembly in its resolution 42/215, requires the submission by the Secretary-General in off-budget years of a programme budget outline, containing, *inter alia*, priorities reflecting general trends of a broad sectoral nature. The outline for the biennium 1990-1991 (A/43/524) was submitted, through CPC, and the Advisory Committee, to the General Assembly at its forty-third session, and, having been the first of such an exercise, was somewhat of an experimental character in its developmental stage.

49. It is suggested that the point of departure for the establishment in the programme budget outline of priorities reflecting general trends of a broad sectoral nature should be the medium-term plan and its revisions. This would be in keeping with one of the assumptions of planning and programming, noted above, that is, that priorities in the programme budget would be derived to the greatest possible extent from the plan. Since the submission of both the medium-term plan or revisions to it and the programme budget outline is due in off-budget years, there is - or should be - a logical and practical connection between the two instruments. Furthermore, were the biennial revision of the medium-term plan to be carried out according to the assumptions contained in

paragraphs 42 (c) and (d) above, there is no reason why the medium-term plan should not serve as the base line for the programme budget outline. This would also be in keeping with one of the conclusions of CPC, namely:

> "Future budget outlines would benefit from the full implementation of the provisions concerning priorities to be established in the medium-term plan in accordance with the Regulations and Rules Governing Programme Planning, the Programme Aspects of the Budget, the Monitoring of Implementation and the Methods of Evaluation. In this connection, the Committee emphasized the need to bring to the attention of intergovernmental subsidiary bodies the pertinent regulations and rules governing the setting of priorities and their responsibilities thereto."[13]

50. It should, however, also be recognized that the relatively long lead-time needed for the preparation of a medium-term plan or even revisions to it does not always permit taking into account developments to which Member States attach great importance, in which the United Nations can - and should - play an indispensable role, and that therefore might become an activity of a higher priority than some others that have been so designated in the plan. For this reason, it is suggested that, subsequent to the determination of priorities in the programme budget outline, the original priority designation in the plan should be modified - if and when needed - to take into account these developments as reflected, e.g. in resolutions of the General Assembly, the Economic and Social Council, or a major international conference.

51. Beyond this, it is further recommended that the requirement that priorities in the outline should reflect "general trends of a broad sectoral nature" should be applied flexibly. Aside from the difficulties noted earlier in defining "sectors" in a precise way, it is entirely conceivable that some developments, which may engage the activities of the United Nations on a priority basis, are intersectoral in character, whereas others may be of the utmost significance but limited to a fairly narrow area. The Secretary-General would endeavour to present in each programme budget outline his proposals on priorities for the coming biennium based on the criteria specified in the table, regardless of the hypothetical confines of a "sectoral" character.

2. *Subprogramme*

52. According to rule 104.1 of the regulations and rules governing programme planning, the subprogramme structure of the programme budget should be identical to that of the medium-term plan. This applies also to priority designations at the subprogramme level, as noted in paragraph 42 (b) above, with the exception that departures from the priority designations of subprogrammes in the plan should be considered when the programme budget outline has shifted the focus of the broader priorities of the Organization.

3. *Output*

53. Although regulation 4.6 (b) requires designation of programme elements as being of high and low priority, each category representing approximately 10 per cent of the regular budget resources requested for the programme, it is recommended that this practice be discontinued. First, as discussed in paragraph 35 above, the actual application of this requirement in some instances has proved impractical or even impossible, thus creating the illusion rather than reality of compliance. Second, it tied too closely the designation of priorities to consideration of resources. Third, where programme elements had multiple outputs, the requirement automatically rendered all outputs of a programme element either of highest or of lowest priority, which may or may not have reflected the real scale of priorities. Finally, under the contemplated new structure of the medium-term plan, subprogrammes will almost take on the character of programmes in the current plan and, *ipso facto*, programme elements in the programme budget will virtually be broadened into subprogrammes. Under those circumstances, it is not even certain whether programme elements should be retained in future programme budgets or, if so, in what form. In any case, whether they are retained or not, it will continue to be extremely difficult to construct programme elements that would satisfy the "10 per cent rule", except in a highly artificial way.

54. It is therefore recommended that in future programme budgets priorities be designated at the output level. It is further recommended that these designations should be carried out according to the following principles:

(a) The number of outputs designated as being of highest and lowest priority within each programme should approximately balance each other (thereby assuming sufficient flexibility so that the balance will be required at the programme rather than the subprogramme level);

(b) In carrying out the designations in paragraph (a) above, care should be taken that the resources attached to the outputs designated highest priority are not disproportionate in relation to the resources attached to the outputs designated lowest priority;

(c) No programme should have less than 5 per cent nor more than 15 per cent of its programmed outputs designated highest priority, balanced with approximately an equal number of outputs designated lowest priority. (For illustrative purposes, in the biennium 1986-1987, 17.4 per cent of the programmed outputs of all budget sections reporting priority designations, but excluding section 27 (Public information), were designated highest priority and 6.7 per cent were designated lowest priority.);

(d) Outputs designated highest priority should have an implementation rate as close to 100 per cent as possible;

(e)   In case of unanticipated claims on allocated resources, those outputs designated lowest priority should be the first to be terminated, postponed or reformulated in order to accommodate higher priority activities so as to implement the provisions regarding the contingency fund;

(f)   The determination of priorities at the output level should be guided by priorities set at higher levels of the programme budget, but the findings of the latest programme performance report should also be taken into consideration;

(g)   This system of priority-setting at the output level should be reviewed after it has been in effect for two bienniums, and an interim report should be prepared after the completion of one biennium concerning compliance with principle (b) above.

V. Conclusions and recommendations

55. The modified system of priorities proposed in section IV above is unlikely to solve all the problems with the current system. For instance, no new definition for the concept of priority has been suggested, although an attempt has been made to divorce it in its practical application from resources by specifying the criteria to be applied and their basis for each level. Furthermore, practical solutions are proposed to alleviate the problems experienced in connection with the implementation of the "10 per cent rule" and those associated with changing the structure of the next medium-term plan.

56. Considerable emphasis has been placed on the necessity of strict compliance with the regulations and rules on programme planning, especially with those pertaining to priority-setting in the medium-term plan. Strict adherence to these regulations and rules, including assistance given by the Secretariat to intergovernmental bodies in their tasks and regular consultations with these bodies, will help the determination of priorities in the programme budget, including the outline.

57. In light of the above, it is suggested that CPC recommend to the General Assembly that:

(a)   The Secretary-General should implement the modified system of priorities for a trial period;

(b)   CPC and the Advisory Committee should review the results after the completion of the programme budget for the biennium 1992-1993.

Notes

1. See *Official Records of the General Assembly, Forty-third Session, Supplement No. 16* (A/43/16), part two, paras. 21-27 and 32-34.
2. *Ibid.*, para. 34.
3. *Ibid., Thirty-sixth Session, Supplement No. 38* (A/36/38). The records of this session of CPC contains perhaps the most exhaustive treatment ever accorded priorities by the Committee. For discussion, see paras. 72-102; for conclusions and recommendations, see paras. 453-472.
4. *Ibid.*, para. 453.
5. The Regulations and the corresponding Rules were subsequently issued, pursuant to General Assembly resolutions 37/234 and 38/227, first in ST/SGB/204 and later, in accordance with Assembly resolution 40/240, para. 8, in ST/SGB/PPBME/Rules/1 (1987).
6. *Official Records of the General Assembly, Forty-first Session, Supplement No. 38* (A/41/38), para. 37.
7. *Ibid., Supplement No. 49* (A/41/49), para. 64.
8. *Official Records of the General Assembly, Thirty-seventh Session, Supplement No. 38* (A/37/38), para. 54.
9. *Ibid., Thirty-eighth Session, Supplement No. 6* (A/38/6, vol. I), introduction, para. 6.
10. Regulations 3.12 and 4.3 of ST/SGB/PPBME/Rules/1 (1987), and new regulation 3.1.2 (c), contained in the report of CPC (A/42/16, part two, para. 74) and approved by the General Assembly in its resolution 42/215, sect. I, para. 1.
11. *Official Records of the General Assembly, Thirty-second Session, Supplement No. 38* (A/32/38), para. 2.
12. *Ibid., Forty-third Session, Supplement No. 16* (A/43/16), part two, paras. 23-26.
13. *Ibid.*, para. 33.

2.35 Document A/44/7[*]

All Aspects of Priority-setting in Future Outlines of the Proposed Programme Budget (A/44/272)

Report of the Advisory Committee on Administrative and Budgetary Questions

1989

92. The background of this report is given in paragraph 1 to 4 of the report. As stated in paragraph 3:

"In paragraph 11 of its resolution 43/213 of 21 December 1988, the General Assembly stressed the importance of indicating in the outline of the proposed programme budget priorities reflecting general trends of a broad sectoral nature, endorsed the recommendations of CPC in that regard, and requested the Secretary-General to submit a report on all aspects of priority-setting in future outlines to the Assembly at its forty-fourth session through the Committee."

93. The Advisory Committee notes that the Committee for Programme and Co-ordination, in its report, while having considered "that the report represented a first step in the direction of re-examining priority-setting in its broader contexts, taking into account the need for in-depth analysis of such related issues as mandates and sources of funding", also stated that "it did not have sufficient time to fully consider this very complex issue, and decided to transmit the report to the Economic and Social Council and to the General Assembly at its forty-fourth session, together with its views, for further consideration".[1]

94. The Advisory Committee took up the report in the context of its own mandate concerning consideration of the medium-term plan and the outline of the proposed programme budget.

95. The Advisory Committee takes note of the modifications proposed in paragraph 44 to 54 of the report for the system of priority-setting (A/44/272). The Committee agrees with the suggestion in paragraph 49 that the point of departure for the establishment in the programme budget outline of priorities reflecting general trends of a broad sectoral nature should be the medium-term plan and its revisions.

---

[*]*Official Records of the General Assembly, Forty-fourth Session, Supplement No. 7 (A/44/7), 1989, pp. 30-31.*

96. In this connection, the Advisory Committee recalls that in paragraph 4 of its report on proposed revisions to the medium-term plan for the period 1984-1989 (A/43/626) it stated its belief that "ideally, the medium-term plan should serve as the plan of work for the Organization, and that it should be set out in a manner that would permit Member States to review the work plan and the related priorities attached to different programmes in the plan and to give guidance as to what and how much can realistically be carried out during the plan period". For this to be possible, much has to be done to improve the form and content of the medium-term plan (see paras. 14 and 17 above*).

97. The Advisory Committee trusts that consideration of this report will form the basis for an agreement and consequential improvement in the presentation of priorities in both the medium-term plan and the programme budget outline. For its part, the Advisory Committee will be guided in its own consideration of the medium-term plan and the outline by such decisions as the General Assembly may take on the question of priority-setting.

Note

1.   *Official Record of the General Assembly, Forty-fourth Session, Supplement No. 16* (A/44/16), paras. 274 and 275.

---

*Not reprinted here.

2.36 Document A/44/16[*]

Priority-setting (A/44/272)

Report of the Committee for Programme and Co-ordination

1990

270. At its 44th meeting, on 2 June, the Committee considered the report of the Secretary-General on all aspects of priority-setting in future outlines of the proposed programme budget (A/44/272).

Conclusions and recommendations

271. The Committee expressed its satisfaction with the report of the Secretary-General and considered it very useful.

272. The Committee noted that the report highlighted the difficulties encountered in the setting of priorities and observed that it was a good basis for further consideration.

273. At the same time, the Committee was of the view that the problem of priority-setting had many parameters, and that the report had shed insufficient light on those problems.

274. In that context, the Committee considered that the report represented a first step in the direction of re-examining priority-setting in its broader contexts, taking into account the need for in-depth analysis of such related issues as mandates and sources of funding.

275. The Committee noted that it did not have sufficient time fully to consider this very complex issue, and decided to transmit the report, together with its views thereon, to the Economic and Social Council and to the General Assembly at its forty-fourth session for further consideration.

---

[*]*Official Records of the General Assembly, Forty-fourth Session, Supplement No. 16* (A/44/16), 1990, p. 38.

2.37 Document A/44/665[*]

Establishment and Operation of a Reserve Fund

Report of the Secretary-General

20 October 1989

1. The General Assembly, in paragraph 10 of its resolution 43/214 of 21 December 1988, agreed to the concept of a reserve to cover additional requirements due to currency fluctuation, inflation in non-staff costs and statutory cost increases for staff, requested the Secretary-General to formulate a set of procedures for the operation of the reserve fund to be submitted through the Advisory Committee on Administrative and Budgetary Questions to the Assembly at its forty-fourth session, and decided to address further at that time the question of setting up such a reserve for the biennium 1990-1991. In paragraph 9 of the resolution, the Assembly also noted the work undertaken by the Advisory Committee on the question of the effects of inflation and currency fluctuation on the budget of the United Nations. The Advisory Committee, in paragraphs 17 to 31 of its report (A/43/929), had addressed the request by the Assembly in resolution 41/213 of 19 December 1986, annex I, paragraph 10, for a comprehensive solution to the problem of all additional expenditures, including those deriving from inflation and currency fluctuation. This question had also been addressed by the Secretary-General in paragraphs 35 to 41 of his report to the General Assembly at its forty-second session (A/42/225 and Add.1). The present report provides a set of procedures for the operation of the reserve fund and deals with the nature of the reserve, its composition, arrangements for recourse to the fund and for its replenishment.

2. In expressing the need for a comprehensive solution to the problem of all additional expenditures, including those deriving from inflation and currency fluctuations, the General Assembly also indicated in resolution 41/213, annex I, paragraph 10, that it would be desirable to accommodate them within the overall level of the budget, either as a reserve or as a separate part of the contingency fund. The expenditures that the contingency fund was created to finance are different in nature from the additional expenditures that could be occasioned by variations in the forecast included in the programme budget in respect of currency fluctuation, inflation in non-staff costs and statutory cost increases for staff. Hence, the use of the same contingency fund as a mechanism to address two sets of separate issues was not felt to be practical or desirable.

3. In resolution 41/213, annex I, paragraph 11, the General Assembly urged the Secretary-General to make efforts to absorb additional expenditures arising

---

[*]A/44/665.

from inflation and currency fluctuation, to the extent possible, through savings from the programme budget, without causing in any way a negative effect on programme delivery and without prejudice to the utilization of the contingency fund. The practical impossibility of absorbing such additional expenditures, given their potential magnitude and the inability to foresee them with any degree of precision, was addressed in the earlier report of the Secretary-General (A/44/225 and Add.1).

4. The purpose of the reserve fund, therefore, would seem to be to minimize, during any given biennium and to the extent possible, changes in the level of the programme budget resulting from variations in the forecast included in the programme budget in respect of currency fluctuation, inflation in non-staff costs and statutory cost increases for staff or, as stated by the Advisory Committee in its report (A/43/929), to achieve a greater degree of certainty than now exists.

5. Seen in this context, the level of the reserve fund must be so established as to ensure that it is adequate to meet the additional requirements it may be required to deal with, namely, those arising from variations in the forecast included in the programme budget in respect of currency fluctuation, inflation in non-staff costs and statutory cost increases for staff. By definition, however, such requirements can only be projected but not accurately determined; hence the soundest way to arrive at what might constitute an adequate level would be from an analysis of past experience. In terms of amounts and expressed as a percentage of the programme budget, past experience reveals the following:

	Increase (decrease)							
Biennium	Currency fluctuation		Non-staff costs inflation		Statutory increases for staff		Total	
	(1)	(2)	(1)	(2)	(1)	(2)	(1)	(2)
1980-1981	(19.8)	(1.6%)	24.3	2.0%	47.2	3.9%	51.7	4.3%
1982-1983	(106.0)	(6.9%)	(3.9)	(0.2%)	(12.9)	(0.8%)	(122.8)	(7.9%)
1984-1985	(74.9)	(4.7%)	(2.0)	(0.1%)	29.2	1.8%	(47.7)	(3.0%)
1986-1987	147.6	8.4%	(10.2)	(0.6%)	(57.1)	(3.3%)	80.3	(4.8%)

(1): Millions of United States dollars.
(2): As a percentage of the proposed programme budget.

6. As regards the current biennium, the additional requirements arising from variations in the forecast included in the programme budget in respect of currency fluctuation, inflation in non-staff costs and statutory cost increases for staff approved in the context of the initial and revised appropriations amount to $133.9 million or 8 per cent of the proposed programme budget.

7. If, however, each component were to be considered separately and were to constitute in each case a ceiling, an adequate level would need to take into account the highest variation experienced in respect of each of them, namely, 8.4 per cent for currency fluctuation, 2 per cent for inflation in non-staff costs and 3.9 per cent for statutory increases for staff. These together add up to 14.3 per cent as opposed to the aggregate of 8 per cent mentioned above. This is due to the fact that the adjustments required in respect of the three categories do not always move simultaneously in the same direction.

8. Thus, a more reliable and realistic approach would be to treat the three categories within an overall framework and consider the establishment of the level of the reserve taking into account the combined net effect of the adjustments, the highest level having been experienced in this regard being 8 per cent.

9. If predictability and, hence, greater certainty, which is at the core of the new budget process, are to be assured by the determination at the outset of the level of resources to be available for a given biennium, such a reserve would need to be funded. Otherwise, the establishment of a reserve as a notional amount and the seeking of additional appropriations as and when variations in the forecast included in the programme budget in respect of currency fluctuation, inflation in non-staff costs and statutory cost increases for staff so warrant would be tantamount to the continuation of the present arrangements.

10. There appear to be two alternatives for the establishment and funding of a reserve: one as a separate fund outside the programme budget and the other as a section within the programme budget. In either case they would be funded through assessed contributions.

11. Under the first alternative, the General Assembly would establish a reserve as a separate fund and determine its level. The reserve would be funded from assessed contributions and replenished through savings due to variations in the forecast included in the programme budget in respect of currency fluctuation, inflation in non-staff costs and statutory cost increases for staff or through further assessed contributions, as necessary. At the relevant appropriations stages, the adjustments resulting from variations in the forecast included in the programme budget in respect of currency fluctuation, inflation in non-staff costs and statutory cost increases for staff would be submitted to the Assembly for approval. The amount approved by the Assembly would be included in the appropriations. When they represent additional requirements, they would be funded through the reserve. When they represent net reductions, they would be credited to the reserve up to the approved level of the reserve. Any surplus

beyond that level would be credited to Member States. At the beginning of each biennium, the reserve would be replenished to its approved level, such replenishment to be effected through assessed contributions if necessary. During the course of a biennium, should the amount in the reserve be insufficient to provide for the additional requirements resulting from variations in the forecast included in the programme budget in respect of currency fluctuation, inflation in non-staff costs and statutory cost increases for staff, the Secretary-General in presenting the additional requirements to the Assembly would make proposals regarding the manner in which the shortfall should be covered.

12. An indication of the manner in which the procedure outlined above would have operated is provided in annex I*, based on actual appropriations for the bienniums 1980-1981 to 1988-1989, excluding the role of miscellaneous income in the financing of assessments and assuming the establishment of a reserve of $150 million.

13. Under the second alternative, a reserve would be established for each biennial period within the programme budget. The level of the reserve would be established by the General Assembly at the time it takes a decision on the outline. Subsequently, the reserve would be included in the proposed programme budget as a separate identifiable section. At the relevant appropriations stages, the adjustments resulting from variations in the forecast included in the programme budget in respect of currency fluctuation, inflation in non-staff costs and statutory cost increases for staff would be submitted to the Assembly for approval. The adjustments approved by the Assembly would be reflected under the sections of the programme budget so affected, accompanied by a commensurate adjustment in the budget section relating to the reserve. During a biennium, the reserve would be drawn upon or replenished as need be except that once replenished to the approved level, any excess amount would be credited back to Member States. During the course of a biennium, should the amount in the budget section relating to the reserve be insufficient to provide for the additional requirements resulting from variations in the forecast included in the programme budget in respect of currency fluctuation, inflation in non-staff costs and statutory cost increases for staff, the Secretary-General in presenting the additional requirements to the General Assembly would make proposals regarding the manner in which the shortfall should be covered. At the end of the biennium, any amount left in the section relating to the reserve would be surrendered (in the subsequent proposed programme budget the reserve would again be included as a separate identifiable section). Annex II* provides an indication of the manner in which the procedure outlined above would have operated, using the same data as in annex I*.

---

*Not reprinted here.

14. The alternatives outlined above are both based on the premise that the reserve would be funded. They differ to the extent that, under the first alternative, the reserve is envisaged as a fund outside the appropriations, whereas in the second, the reserve would be an integral part of the appropriations and, hence, of the programme budget. In terms of impact on assessments, there would over time be no appreciable difference between the two alternatives - the individual variations that may be seen from annexes I* and II* are more apparent than real. Under the first alternative, the balance left in the reserve at the end of a biennium would not be surrendered and at the beginning of the subsequent biennium only the difference between the approved level and the balance would need to be assessed; under the second alternative, at the end of the biennium, any amount left in the section relating to the reserve would be surrendered and at the beginning of the next biennium a new reserve would need to be established and funded in full.

15. The return of any surplus in the reserve under either alternative would at this stage have to be seen in the context of the overall financial situation of the Organization. In this connection, it should be borne in mind that the provisions of regulations 4.3, 4.4 and 5.2 (d) of the Financial Regulations of the United Nations relating to surpluses at the end of financial periods have been suspended in respect of the past few biennia.

16. The table below summarizes the level of assessments per biennium under the two alternatives described above:

Biennium	Final appropriations	Reserve as separate fund	Reserve as part of budget
(In millions of United States dollars)			
1980-1981	1 341.7	1 440.0	1 341.7
1982-1983	1 469.6	1 521.3	1 469.6
1984-1985	1 609.0	1 608.3	1 609.0
1986-1987	1 711.8	1 632.1	1 711.8

17. At first view, it may be concluded that the second alternative is less onerous, the cumulative level of assessments over the four biennial periods being $69.6 million lower than the first alternative. However, at the beginning of the biennium 1988-1989, provision would have had to have been made, under the first alternative, for the replenishment of the reserve fund in the amount

*Not reprinted here.

of $80.4 million, whereas under the second alternative the proposed programme budget for the biennium 1988-1989 would have had to have included a reserve section in the amount of $150 million, or $69.6 million higher than under the first alternative.

18. In terms of practical application, the second alternative - a reserve as a separate section within the programme budget - would be administratively easier to operate than a reserve as a separate fund. The creation of a separate fund for the reserve would necessitate the addition of new financial regulations and the modification of existing ones. It would require a new procedure for the financing of appropriations, adding complexity to an already complex system. The establishment of a reserve as part of the programme budget, on the other hand, would require little more than a new section within the programme budget.

19. Under the circumstances, should the General Assembly decide to proceed with the establishment of a reserve fund to provide for adjustments resulting from variations in the forecast included in the programme budget in respect of currency fluctuation, inflation in non-staff costs and statutory cost increases for staff, it may wish to establish the following guidelines for its operation:

1.   The proposed programme budget shall contain a section that will include provisions for adjustments that may be required as a result of variations in the forecast included in the programme budget in respect of currency fluctuation, inflation in non-staff costs and statutory cost increases for staff. This section shall be entitled the "Reserve Fund".

2.   In off-budget years, the General Assembly shall decide on the level of the Reserve Fund, which will be included in the proposed programme budget for the next biennium.

3.   The Secretary-General shall, prior to each appropriation stage, submit to the General Assembly for its approval the adjustments required as a result of variations in the forecast included in the programme budget in respect of currency fluctuation, inflation in non-staff costs and statutory cost increases for staff.

4.   The adjustments approved by the General Assembly will be reflected in the appropriations. When such adjustments result in additional requirements, these will be reflected under the relevant sections of the programme budget concerned and will be accompanied by a commensurate reduction in the Reserve Fund section of the programme budget. When such adjustments result in reductions, these will be reflected under the relevant sections concerned and will be accompanied by a commensurate increase in the Reserve Fund section up to the level initially approved for the section. Any surplus would be classed as miscellaneous income.

5.   If the amount of funds in the Reserve Fund section of the programme budget is insufficient to provide for the additional requirements resulting from variations in the forecast included in the programme budget in respect of currency fluctuation, inflation in non-staff costs and statutory cost increases for staff, the Secretary-General, in submitting the proposed adjustments to the General Assembly, shall make proposals regarding the manner in which the shortfall should be covered.

6.   At the end of the biennium, any residual amount in the Reserve Fund section shall be surrendered in the context of the final appropriations for the biennium.

20. In accordance with its resolution 43/214, the General Assembly, in addition to considering a set of procedures for the operation of the Reserve Fund, is also to address further the question of setting up such a reserve for the biennium 1990-1991. While the procedures suggested above could not in their entirety be applied, the Assembly could nevertheless decide to set up a reserve fund for 1990-1991. In order to set up a reserve, however, it would be necessary for the Assembly to do so prior to completing consideration of the proposed programme budget for the biennium 1990-1991 in order that the adoption of the programme budget and the initial appropriations for the biennium 1990-1991 may include such a fund and the adjustments that will be required as a result of variations in the forecast included in the programme budget in respect of currency fluctuation, inflation in non-staff costs and statutory cost increases for staff may be properly reflected.

2.38 Document A/44/729*

Establishment and Operation of a Reserve Fund (A/44/665)

Report of the Advisory Committee on Administrative and Budgetary Questions

16 November 1989

1.   The Advisory Committee on Administrative and Budgetary Questions has considered the report of the Secretary-General on the establishment and operation of a reserve fund (A/44/665). The concept of a reserve had been agreed to by the General Assembly in paragraph 10 of resolution 43/214 of 21 December 1988, to cover additional requirements due to currency fluctuation, non-staff costs inflation and statutory cost increases for staff.   The Secretary-General was requested to formulate a set of procedures for the operation of the reserve.

2.   In his report, the Secretary-General, in response to that request, has proposed that a funded reserve be established as a section within the programme budget, to operate in accordance with the guidelines proposed in paragraph 19 of that report.

3.   The Advisory Committee has a number of difficulties with the concept put forward by the Secretary-General. For example, the idea of financing the fund from the outset through assessment, even before the need for recourse to it has been identified, would seem to present Member States with an unnecessary additional burden.

4.   The Advisory Committee notes in point 5 of paragraph 19 of the report of the Secretary-General the proposal that:

"5.   If the amount of funds in the Reserve Fund section of the programme budget is insufficient to provide for the additional requirements resulting from variations in the forecast included in the programme budget in respect of currency fluctuation, inflation in non-staff costs and statutory cost increases for staff, the Secretary-General, in submitting the proposed adjustments to the General Assembly, shall make proposals regarding the manner in which the shortfall should be covered".

5.   In the opinion of the Advisory Committee, the absence of a pre-determined procedure for dealing with an insufficiency in the reserve will lead to confusion. In response to inquiries, the Committee was informed that in fact the intention is to request appropriation of the additional necessary amounts.

---

*A/44/729.

6. On the basis of the Secretary-General's proposals, it appears to the Advisory Committee that Member States, early in the budget process, will not have a more precise idea of the final total amount to be paid than they have now and, in addition, will have to pay in advance for requirements that might or might not materialize (see para. 3 above).

7. The Advisory Committee notes the observations of the Secretary-General on certain aspects of the considerations set out by the Advisory Committee in its report of last year (A/43/929). In particular, the Secretary-General points out difficulties with respect to calculating a separate ceiling for each component of the reserve and to treating all or part of the reserve as a notional amount (paras. 7 to 9 of the report of the Secretary-General).

8. The Advisory Committee, however, does not see insurmountable difficulties in calculating amounts for each component, which for example could be adjusted proportionally to take into account the overall requirement. Nor does the Committee see the idea of a notional reserve as tantamount to a continuation of the present system.

9. Under the circumstances, the Advisory Committee is of the opinion that further thought has to be given to the question of the establishment and operation of the reserve. As has been stated many times, the new budget process is still in the formative stages and there is much to be learned, including the first experience with the operation of the contingency fund. Furthermore, the Committee notes from the table in paragraph 5 of the report of the Secretary-General that there have been net savings to the budget in two out of the last four bienniums.

10. The Advisory Committee therefore recommends that consideration of the question of a reserve should be deferred until the forty-sixth session of the General Assembly, at which time it should be taken up again on the basis of a further report of the Secretary-General. That report should re-examine the question in the light of experience; it should also contain a further analysis of the ideas contained in paragraphs 17 to 31 of the report of Advisory Committee (A/43/929). In the mean time, the present arrangement should continue in accordance with General Assembly resolution 41/213, annex I, paragraph 11.

2.39 Document A/45/226*

Analytical Report of the Secretary-General on the Implementation of General Assembly Resolution 41/213

27 April 1990

CONTENTS

		Para-graphs
I.	Introduction	1 - 8
II.	The intergovernmental machinery and its functioning	9 - 63
	A. Specific recommendations of the Group of High-level Intergovernmental Experts (recommendations 1 to 7)	9 - 37
	B. Comparative study of the intergovernmental machinery and its functioning (recommendation 8)	38 - 42
	C. Co-ordination (recommendations 9 to 13)	43 - 63
III.	Structure of the Secretariat	64 - 169
	A. General recommendations (recommendations 14 and 15)	64 - 83
	B. Political affairs (recommendations 16 to 24)	84 - 111
	C. Economic and social affairs (recommendations 25 to 29)	112 - 129
	D. Administration and other fields (recommendations 30 to 40)	130 - 169
IV.	Measures regarding personnel (recommendations 41 to 62)	170 - 219
V.	Monitoring, evaluation and inspection (recommendations 63 to 67)	220 - 228
VI.	Planning and budget procedure	229 - 241
VII.	Assessment	242 - 260

---

*A/45/226.

I. Introduction

1.   The General Assembly, by its resolution 41/213 of 19 December 1986 on the review of the efficiency of the administrative and financial functioning of the United Nations, set in train a process of restructuring and reform aimed at strengthening the effectiveness of the Organization in dealing with political, economic and social issues, on the basis of the report of the Group of High-level Intergovernmental Experts to Review the Efficiency of the Administrative and Financial Functioning of the United Nations[1] and the related findings of the Fifth Committee (A/41/795).   At that time the Secretary-General expressed his conviction that the report of the Group of Experts provided a basis for a process of change that could bring about the improvements in the administrative and financial functioning of the Organization needed for its long-term viability and on which Member States could come together, in accordance with their obligations under the Charter, to restore a sound and lasting financial foundation for the Organization (see A/41/663, paras. 2 and 11).

2.   As requested by the General Assembly in subsequent resolutions, the Secretary-General submitted two progress reports and a final report on the implementation of resolution 41/213 (A/42/234 and Corr.1, A/43/286 and Corr.1, and A/44/222 and Corr.1).   The present report must thus be seen as a supplement to those reports.   In addition, separate reports were submitted to the Assembly at its forty-second, forty-third and forty-fourth sessions on various questions relating to section II of resolution 41/213 concerning the planning, programming and budgetary process.   By its resolutions 42/211 of 21 December 1987, 43/213 of 21 December 1988 and 44/200 A to C of 21 December 1989, the Assembly provided further guidance to Member States and the Secretary-General.   Throughout, the Assembly emphasized that it was essential that the present financial difficulties be dispelled in order to carry out successfully the process of reform.   It also stressed that the implementation of resolution 41/213 should not have a negative impact on mandated programmes and activities.

3.   For his part, the Secretary-General stated in his first progress report (A/42/234 and Corr.1) that the process of renewal and reform must recapture the sense and purpose of the Charter of the United Nations in a world that is changing with a rapidity unprecedented in history, where one of the few constants is the ever-closer interweaving of the destinies of all countries and all peoples. He indicated a number of common points of reference that should be established as foundations for the future. At the end of the period under review, he believes that they remain valid. While not repeating them in full, he wishes to reaffirm them in order to place in its proper and full context the detailed information on specific recommendations which follows. In order to pursue the goal of reform in a manner that will increasingly witness the realization of the goals and objectives of the Charter, a genuine commitment to the revitalization of the Organization must be shared by all its Members; there must be an end to the present financial uncertainties; the responsibility

of the Secretary-General as Chief Administrative Officer of the Secretariat must not be eroded; renewal and reform must be a continuing and dynamic process following an orderly approach; and both Member States and the Secretariat must accept the practical consequences of the drive for rationalization and streamlining, namely, an unprecedented degree of restraint and a willingness to set aside national, sectoral or purely bureaucratic interests.

4.   In its resolution 43/213, the General Assembly requested the Secretary-General to present to it at its forty-fourth session his final report on the implementation of resolution 41/213 and to submit to it at its forty-fifth session an analytical report assessing the effect of implementation on the Organization and its activities as a whole and the way in which it had enhanced its administrative and financial functioning.

5.   In his final report (A/44/222 and Corr.1), the Secretary-General presented a factual review of all actions taken within his purview since 1 January 1987 to implement resolution 41/213, as well as actions taken by the General Assembly, the International Civil Service Commission, the Joint Inspection Unit and the Board of Auditors.

6.   In its resolution 44/200 A, the General Assembly encouraged the Secretary-General and Member States to intensify their efforts with respect to the implementation of the provisions of resolution 41/213 that fell within their respective purviews and renewed its request to the Secretary-General to submit an analytical report to it at its forty-fifth session. The Assembly also requested the Secretary-General to provide information in the following areas: an exhaustive   presentation   of   the   state   of   implementation   of   each recommendation; an explanation with regard to such implementation and an assessment of its impact on programmes, giving particular emphasis to those programmes which have been terminated or completed; and a general critical assessment of the implementation of resolution 41/213 in the light of the objectives   of   that   resolution.   The   Assembly   also   noted   that   the Secretary-General's final report was unable to cover the entire three-year period, as it was submitted to the Assembly through the Committee for Programme and Co-ordination (CPC) in April 1989, and requested the Secretary-General to include in the analytical report any further action taken to the end of 1989.

7.   In response to those requests, the present report provides detailed information concerning implementation of each recommendation of the Group of High-level Intergovernmental Experts through 31 December 1989 accompanied, where appropriate, by an explanation with regard to such implementation and an assessment of its impact on the relevant programmes. Detailed information concerning terminated, completed and postponed programme outputs appears in the report of the Secretary-General on programme performance for the biennium 1988-1989 (A/45/218 and Add.1). The present report also contains an overall assessment of the implementation of Assembly resolution 41/213 in the light of its objectives.

8. It is evident that the programme of administrative reforms initiated in 1986 has been largely implemented. The process of implementation has taken place - of necessity - during a period of continuing financial crisis and of additional major new responsibilities being entrusted to the Organization. The process has been an interactive one both in relation to the continuing dialogue between the Secretary-General and Member States since 1986 and in the context of the rapidly changing global situation. When the General Assembly adopted its resolution 41/213 in 1986, no one could have foreseen the events that have occurred since then and that have led, for instance, to the setting up of 4 new peace-keeping operations in 1988-1989, as against 13 over the previous 40 years, and the planning of several others. Similarly unexpected are the momentous developments in Eastern Europe and the new global concern emerging on environment and development and on drugs. As the Secretary-General has said in his report on the work of the Organization in 1989,[2] obstacles to stability, peace and balanced progress are many and the world's political, intellectual and moral imagination will need to be fully employed in overcoming them. Administrative reform is essentially a continuing process to aid in these efforts, but political and financial support is inevitably the key to capacity and performance.

II. The intergovernmental machinery and its functioning

A. *Specific recommendations of the Group of High-level Intergovernmental Experts*

9. Implementation of those recommendations relating to the need for more effective use of the intergovernmental machinery rests primarily with Member States. The Secretariat has played a supportive role, with a view to providing conference services world wide in as co-ordinated and cost-effective a manner possible.

Recommendation 1

10. The Committee on Conferences was strengthened and given broader responsibilities pursuant to resolution 43/222 B of 21 December 1988, in which the General Assembly decided to retain the Committee as a permanent subsidiary organ composed of 21 members with revised terms of reference covering the entire range of responsibilities recommended by the Group of High-level Intergovernmental Experts.

11. The calendar of conferences for the biennium 1990-1991,[3] as submitted by the Committee on Conferences to and approved by the General Assembly, in its resolution 44/196 A of 21 December 1989, was designed to ensure the optimum utilization of conference-servicing resources by the scheduling of conferences and meetings throughout the year to eliminate "peaks and valleys" in the meetings programme, avoiding overlapping meetings related to the same sector of activity, and ensuring that requests for conference services

correspond accurately to requirements. To this end the Department of Conference Services held extensive consultations with substantive secretariats.

12. In fulfilment of its mandate to monitor the Organization's policy on publications, the Committee at its 1989 session considered the results of reviews conducted by a number of intergovernmental bodies of their recurrent publications programme.[4] At its 1990 session, the Committee will undertake a further review of the recurrent publications programme, the level of resources devoted to the production thereof and the impact of such publishing activities on the overall programme of conference and documentation services.

13. At its 1989 session, the Committee on Conferences also discussed the distribution of conference activity among the various headquarters locations and requested updated information on available conference resources, services and facilities within the United Nations. With respect to its mandate "to make recommendations, as appropriate, to the General Assembly on means to ensure an improved co-ordination of conferences within the United Nations system, including conference services and facilities, and to conduct the appropriate consultations in that regard" (Assembly resolution 43/222 B, para. 4 (f), the Committee entrusted its secretariat with the task of examining the current status of co-ordination, identifying problems and suggesting possible solutions with a view to making the necessary improvements.[5] The Committee is expected to consider those issues further at its 1990 session.

Recommendation 2

14. The Secretary-General brought recommendation 2 (a), that the Economic and Social Council should hold only one session per year, to the attention of the Council (see E/1987/2). In its decision 1987/112 of 6 February 1987, the Council established a Special Commission of the Economic and Social Council on the In-depth Study of the United Nations Intergovernmental Structure and Functions in the Economic and Social Fields to carry out the study called for in recommendation 8 (see paras. 38-42 below) and requested it to consider the relevant provisions of recommendation 2 in that context. The Special Commission submitted its report (E/1988/75) to the Council at its second regular session of 1988 without having reached agreement. At that session, the Council adopted resolution 1988/77 of 29 July 1988, in paragraph 3 of which it requested the Secretary-General to submit a report to the Council at its second regular session of 1989 "on the feasibility and comparative costs of holding at the United Nations, with the present in-sessional arrangements, one consolidated or two regular sessions of the Council". The Secretary-General provided the requested information to the Council at its second regular session for 1989 in a report entitled "Revitalization of the Economic and Social Council" (E/1989/95). While the Council adopted resolution 1989/114, entitled "Further measures for the implementation of Council resolution 1988/77 on the revitalization of the Economic and Social Council" on 28 July 1989, it took no further action on the question of holding one session a year. In this connection, attention is drawn to Council decision 1990/205, adopted at its

organizational session for 1990, in which the Council decided to review its current sessional arrangements in the context of its consideration of major policy themes at high-level special meetings.

15. Recommendations 2 (b) and (c) have been partially implemented. The Economic and Social Council, in its resolution 1988/77, decided, *inter alia*, that it should further continue to consider the biennialization of the sessions of its subsidiary bodies and items on its own agenda and programme of work, taking into account the need for a balance between economic and social issues. Recommendation 2 (b) was brought to the attention of subsidiary bodies in the context of the in-depth study of the intergovernmental structures in the economic and social fields.

16. As was the case for the 1989 calendar of conferences and meetings, the calendar approved by the General Assembly for the biennium 1990-1991 is not markedly different from that approved for prior bienniums in terms of the number of meetings scheduled. While only a few bodies have decided to schedule sessions biennially instead of annually or have significantly reduced the duration of their sessions since 1986, some progress has been made during the period under review.

17. By its resolution 158 (XIV) of 5 April 1987, the Economic and Social Commission for Western Asia (ESCWA) decided to amend its rules of procedure to the effect that sessions of the Commission should normally be held every other year. The Economic Commission for Latin America and the Caribbean (ECLAC) also meets on a biennial basis. By its resolution 618 (XXII), the Economic Commission for Africa (ECA) decided that sectoral conferences of ministers and their technical, subsidiary bodies should meet on a biennial basis, with conferences limited to a duration of no more than six days with short and well-focused agendas and work programmes. The biennialization of sessions of the Intergovernmental Committee on Science and Technology for Development was introduced in 1987 and, after review, was reconfirmed in 1989.[6] The biennialization is intended to allow more time for preparation by the Secretariat of substantive themes in accordance with the decision of the Intergovernmental Committee at its tenth session in 1989.

18. On the other hand, however, a recommendation by the Commission on the Status of Women to change its cycle of meetings from biennial to annual was endorsed by the Economic and Social Council and the General Assembly, and the Commission has been meeting annually since its thirty-second session in 1988 as it considers that annual meetings best serve its functions of monitoring the implementation of the Nairobi Forward-looking Strategies for the Advancement of Women[7] and the system-wide medium-term plan on women and development.

19. The Committee on Conferences has discussed the utilization of conference services by a wide range of United Nations bodies, on the basis of reports

prepared by the Secretariat, and has expanded the statistical coverage of utilization data. The average utilization factor for United Nations bodies has shown improvement and has reached a level of over 70 per cent. In response to indications that time spent in informal consultations was not duly reflected in the statistical information studied, the Committee has agreed on a refined methodology to be put into effect, which would include information on the holding of informal meetings, together with information on time lost owing to late starting or early ending of meetings.

20. As recommended by the Committee on Conferences, the Assembly, in paragraph 3 of its resolution 42/207 B of 11 December 1987, requested United Nations organs to indicate with greater precision the actual number of meetings with conference services that they would require in their coming sessions; in paragraph 5 of resolution 43/222 A, it urged those United Nations organs which had failed to make adequate use of the conference-servicing resources provided to them to consider reducing the number of meetings they requested in future; and, in paragraph 5 of resolution 44/196 A, it urged all United Nations organs to intensify their efforts to improve their utilization of conference-servicing resources. In paragraph 4 of the same resolution, the Assembly also requested the Committee on Conferences to review the methodology on conference-servicing utilization rates in order to provide, if possible, a more accurate assessment of the overall use of conference resources with a view to enabling United Nations bodies to make the optimum use of conference services and to facilitate, where necessary, continued rationalization of their meeting requirements.

21. The Department of Conference Services, in close co-operation with the Committee on Conferences, is currently analysing past utilization patterns by United Nations bodies in order to suggest practical ways in which the conference-servicing resources placed at their disposal can be applied more effectively and used in the most cost-efficient manner.

Recommendation 3

22. As recognized by the Group of Experts, the responsibility for implementation of this recommendation rests with the presiding officers of the principal organs and with the representatives of Member States. The Secretary-General has been making every effort to assist Member States to achieve a more effective use of available conference-servicing facilities.

23. In his annual memorandum on the organization of the work of the General Assembly, the Secretary-General has recommended to the General Committee that related items be merged or phased in intervals, that agenda items be distributed among Main Committees so as to ensure the best possible use of the expertise and that no new subsidiary organ be created without discontinuing existing ones. The President of the General Assembly has continued to urge Member States to observe the need for the timely commencement of meetings,

to reduce the number of resolutions and to exercise restraint in requesting reports of the Secretary-General.

24. With respect to the scheduling of plenary meetings, efforts to reduce their overall number and to avoid night and weekend meetings have met with some success. The total number of plenary meetings decreased from 103 at the forty-first session to 88[8] at the forty-fourth session, while the number of meetings continuing into the evening decreased from 61 at the forty-first session to 27 at the forty-fourth session. This has been achieved partially through the scheduling of meetings only upon confirmation that the Assembly was ready to take action on the item to be discussed and through improved co-ordination between the secretariats of the General Assembly and its Main Committees. With particular emphasis on the need to reduce costs and enhance efficiency, it is encouraging to note that the number of meetings entailing additional costs has been cut significantly. Over the same period, however, the Second, Third and Fifth Committees have increased the number of meetings held.

25. With respect to biennialization of work programmes, the Second and Sixth Committees have well-established biennial programmes of work. Further attempts could be made to encourage all Main Committees to adopt a biennial programme. Although this would not significantly affect the number of meetings of each Committee, there would be a positive impact on the documentation to be submitted and the resolutions emanating therefrom.

26. Efforts are continuing to ensure that meetings of the Fourth Committee and the Special Political Committee are held in sequential order with concurrent meetings being avoided as far as possible. While 8 of the 15 meetings held by the Fourth Committee during the forty-third session overlapped with those of the Special Political Committee, only 4 of the 17 meetings of the Fourth Committee were held concurrently with the Special Political Committee during the forty-fourth session.

27. With respect to the agenda of the General Assembly, however, the number of agenda items has risen from 146 at the forty-first session of the Assembly to 161 at the forty-fourth session. The number of resolutions adopted has increased, yearly, from 311 at the forty-first session to 331 at the forty-fourth session (as at December 1989).

28. It is clear that the streamlining of procedures and careful planning can lead to savings in costs and enhanced efficiency. Co-operation of the respective Presiding Officers, a growing recognition by Member States of the need to conserve resources and improved scheduling by the Secretariat have contributed to the partial implementation of this recommendation.

Recommendation 4

29. The principle that United Nations bodies meet at their respective headquarters is being applied. In his report (A/44/222 and Corr.1, paras. 20-22), the Secretary-General provided information on those bodies authorized to meet away from their established headquarters in accordance with paragraph 4 of General Assembly resolution 40/243 of 18 December 1985, as well as other bodies which sometimes meet away from their established headquarters as part of the implementation of their work programmes. These meetings are included in the official calendar of conferences and meetings and are approved by the General Assembly when it adopts the calendar.

30. Furthermore, in accordance with established procedure, the Committee on Conferences meets during sessions of the Assembly to discuss and make recommendations, as appropriate, on the granting of departures from the rules and regulations governing conference planning, particularly as contained in resolution 40/243, in which the Assembly reaffirmed the established headquarters principle and exceptions to it.

31. As reported in the Secretary-General's final report (*ibid.*, para. 23), guidelines for preparing Host Country Agreements were issued in May 1987, in the form of an administrative instruction (ST/AI/342). In accordance with this instruction, the Department of Conference Services is responsible for ensuring that the conference-servicing staff assigned to the meeting or conference conforms to the standards approved by the General Assembly; that the conditions of employment of short-term conference staff conform to those agreed upon by all member organizations and the International Association for Conference Interpreters (AIIC) and Translators (AITC); and that they are reflected in the host Government agreement. The Department of Conference Services also determines the suitability of conference staff provided by the host Government. Those guidelines were established in order to ensure that costs to be borne by host Governments were determined in a consistent manner and properly accounted for and that all additional costs directly or indirectly involved when meetings are held away from their established headquarters, upon the invitation of a Government, would be defrayed by that Government and not accrue to the Organization.

Recommendation 5

32. The recommendation that construction of conference facilities should only be undertaken when sufficient resources are available has been implemented. In its resolution 41/213, the General Assembly stated that the implementation of that recommendation should not prejudice the implementation of projects and programmes it had already approved. The two projects approved were the construction of conference facilities at Addis Ababa for ECA and at Bangkok for the Economic and Social Commission for Asia and the Pacific (ESCAP).

These two construction projects are under way and a progress report will be submitted to the Assembly at its forty-fifth session.

33. The impact of the moratorium on construction of conference facilities has highlighted the need to renovate and modernize existing facilities for the Organization to meet the increasing requirements. This includes the upgrading and improvement of the mechanical and electrical systems and equipment, and the repair and refurbishing of the buildings' exteriors.

34. Owing to the advanced age of the structures and fabric of most of the older buildings world wide and the spotty major maintenance programme due to the financial crisis, certain facilities have fallen into disrepair. A major maintenance programme is required to prevent further deterioration of the physical plant, bring electrical and mechanical systems to optimum performance levels and introduce modern systems for conserving energy while adapting existing facilities as the Organization's needs change.

Recommendation 6

35. The recommendation was approved by the General Assembly in the context of the 1988-1989 programme budget and was implemented with effect from 1 January 1988. As a result, the claims for delegation travel decreased in the following manner. At the fortieth session of the Assembly, when each Member State was entitled to one first class and four economy class tickets, the total number of claims submitted was 588. At the forty-first session, owing to the 1986 economy measures, all Member States were entitled to one first class and two economy class tickets and 297 claims were submitted. Following the implementation of recommendation 6, which limited the entitlement to one first class and four economy class tickets for those Member States designated least developed countries, the number of claims at the forty-third session was only 126, without apparent decrease in attendance.

Recommendation 7

36. This recommendation has been partially implemented. This question was discussed by the Committee on Conferences in 1987 and 1988 and is on its agenda for review in 1990. Pursuant to its recommendation, the General Assembly in resolution 43/222 C renewed its appeal to Member States to exercise restraint in their requests for the circulation of communications as United Nations documents and to endeavour to keep the length of communications to a minimum. It further requested the Committee on Conferences to keep the matter under review and report to the Assembly at its forty-fifth session.

37. There was a reduction in the number of communications from Member States between 1988 and 1989 with 1,070 being received in 1988 and 742 in 1989 with a consequent decrease of 800 pages. It has proved difficult, however, to implement the recommendation further. Little progress has been made in

limiting the length of communications. There may be merit in considering the development of guidelines concerning communications from Member States, including the distinction between communications to be translated in their entirety into all official languages and those communications or parts thereof that may be issued in the language or languages of submission only, and a reconsideration of the timing permitted between submission and issuance of non-urgent communications to avoid undue pressure on translation and printing services. The practice of issuance of communications as joint documents of the Assembly and the Security Council or of the Assembly and the Economic and Social Council must be continued, and, to the extent possible, expanded. A reduction in the submission of communications from Member States for processing and distribution as official records will result in an overall decrease in the cost of processing documents. Co-operation from Member States in curtailing their requests, in accordance with this recommendation, is essential for further improvements in this area.

B. Comparative study of the intergovernmental machinery and its functioning

Recommendation 8

38. The careful and in-depth study of the intergovernmental structure in the economic and social fields to be undertaken by an intergovernmental body to be designated by the General Assembly, which was called for in this recommendation, was assigned to the Special Commission established by the Economic and Social Council in its decision 1987/112 (see para. 14 above). The Special Commission held nine sessions between March 1987 and May 1988. It was unable to reconcile the divergent views on a number of major questions and submitted its report (E/1989/75) to the Economic and Social Council at its second regular session in 1988 without any specific recommendations (see Council resolution 1988/77).

39. The Council, in that resolution, noted that there were no agreed conclusions on recommendation 8 and decided to transmit the report of the Special Commission to the General Assembly at its forty-third session. In its resolution 43/174, the Assembly, taking note of the in-depth study carried out by the Special Commission and recognizing that the Commission had been unable to reach agreed recommendations, requested the Secretary-General to consult with all Member States and seek their views on ways and means of achieving a balanced and effective implementation of recommendations 2 and 8 and to submit a detailed report to it at its forty-fourth session.

40. In the light of the report of the Secretary-General (A/44/747), the General Assembly, at its forty-fourth session, adopted resolution 44/103 of 11 December 1989, in which it decided to review the efficiency of the administrative and financial functioning of the United Nations in the economic, social and related fields, including the secretariat support structure, at its forty-fifth session, taking into account major international conferences

scheduled to take place in the beginning of the 1990s. The Assembly also requested the Secretary-General to present a report to the forty-fifth session of the General Assembly on the follow-up and implementation of its resolution 44/103.

41. It may be noted that the Economic and Social Council decided to address separately the question of its revitalization and, in this context, adopted resolution 1988/77 containing a set of interrelated measures to enhance its effectiveness and improve its working methods. Further measures to this end were embodied in its resolution 1989/114 and decision 1990/205. The Council will address the question of implementation of its resolutions on revitalization at its second regular session in 1990.

42. Within the framework of recommendation 8, a number of bodies of the Organization took action to streamline their structures. In the United Nations Conference on Trade and Development (UNCTAD), the Trade and Development Board reviewed the methods of work and structure of its intergovernmental machinery. Agendas were streamlined, the calendar of meetings was improved and three subsidiary bodies were abolished. In parallel, the secretariat of UNCTAD was reorganized. A comprehensive review of its functioning made by the Economic Commission for Europe (ECE) during a special session in 1987 led to a rationalization of its structure and methods of work, which resulted in a significant reduction in documentation and in the number of meetings. The Committee of the Whole of ECLAC made a careful study of its intergovernmental structure and recommended that the current institutional structure of ECLAC and its system be maintained, but decided to abolish two sessional committees with a view to rationalizing its mechanisms, procedures and meetings (resolution 489 of 14 August 1987). During its annual session in 1987, ECA also undertook a review of its intergovernmental machinery, taking a number of decisions with regard to the structure of the machinery, the periodicity and duration of meetings, agendas and programmes of work (resolution 618 (XXII)). These decisions have now been implemented and have led to a more coherent and integrated structure and improved functioning within the framework of the terms of reference of the Commission and the needs of member States. The ongoing review and evaluation of the Commission's Multinational Programming and Operational Centres (MULPOCs), the outcome of which will be submitted to the General Assembly at its forty-fifth session, represent another step towards the further rationalization of structures.

C. Co-ordination

Recommendation 9

43. In response to this recommendation and as part of its ongoing work, the Administrative Committee on Co-ordination (ACC) has reviewed the functioning of its subsidiary machinery during the period from 1986 to 1989. Practical measures adopted by ACC as a result of this review include the

strengthening of the managerial role of the Organizational Committee of ACC and the rationalization of the meetings of the subsidiary machinery of ACC. The number of meetings held under the auspices of ACC was reduced from 34 in 1986 to 22 in 1989. At the same time, a number of steps were taken to focus the discussion of ACC on selected major issues on the basis of background papers prepared by relevant organizations.

44. Provision has been made for more active participation by the regional commissions in the work of ACC and its subsidiary bodies. The Co-ordinator of the Executive Secretaries attends the meetings of ACC and standing arrangements exist for attendance at meetings of the Consultative Committee on Substantive Questions as appropriate.

45. In reviewing progress made in the implementation of this recommendation, CPC emphasized in 1987 the need for more effective co-ordination at the inter-secretariat level and stressed the important role of ACC in this regard. The Committee also noted that the machinery remained complex and recommended that ACC should intensify the review of its functioning with a view to improving the form and substance of its communications, streamlining its subsidiary machinery and reducing its cost substantially.[9] In 1989, CPC stressed the need to strengthen co-ordination in general through the improvement of co-ordination instruments and machinery with the United Nations system and in the United Nations itself. The Committee emphasized the need for greater co-ordination both in the policy-making process and in programmatic activities. With respect to the policy-making process, there was a perceived need to enhance the common response of the organizations of the United Nations system to emerging issues of importance to the international community and for an improved exchange of information and views between ACC and Member States.[10]

46. The General Assembly, in its resolution 44/194 of 21 December 1989, requested ACC to modify substantially the format and content of its annual overview report in accordance with the relevant conclusions and recommendations of CPC. In the same resolution, the Assembly invited the Economic and Social Council and CPC to improve their consideration of the annual overview report of ACC, in accordance with their respective mandates. The Secretary-General was requested to present the annual overview report of the ACC to CPC at its thirtieth session, to the Council and to the Assembly at its forty-fifth session, together with the relevant conclusions and recommendations of these bodies on that report in accordance with existing practice.

47. The question of the functioning of the subsidiary machinery will again be considered by ACC in the review of its own role in 1990. In so doing, ACC will take into account the main thrust of its work in the future, particularly requests that have been put to it by relevant intergovernmental bodies, in particular, the Council in its resolutions 1988/77 and 1989/114 and the Assembly in its resolution 44/194.

Recommendation 10

48. As reported previously, ACC welcomed the thrust of this recommendation, which underlines the need for discussion by executive heads of the organizations concerned of major policy questions in the economic and social fields. The Committee was of the view that such discussion was already being undertaken in its regular biannual sessions and that the objective of the recommendation could be achieved by convening subject-oriented Committee sessions and/or recourse to functional groups. The Secretary-General believes that the objective of this recommendation can best be achieved through informal consultations among various executive heads on major policy questions. To that end, the Secretary-General has in the past few years convened a number of informal meetings with relevant executive heads to consider specific issues. As and when required, the Secretary-General intends to continue resorting to such informal consultations to address selected major issues in the economic and social fields in the future, taking into account the emphasis placed by the Joint Meetings of CPC and ACC on the leading role of the Secretary-General, as Chairman of ACC, in the co-ordination of the activities of the system.

Recommendation 11

49. Implementation of this recommendation, which seeks to strengthen the co-ordination of operational activities at the national level, through reaffirmation of the central co-ordinating role of the United Nations Development Programme (UNDP), clarification of the authority of the resident co-ordinator, and confirmation of that authority with respect to non-UNDP programmes, is continuing.

50. In its resolution 42/196 of 11 December 1987, the General Assembly reaffirmed the central funding and co-ordinating role of UNDP and recommended to intergovernmental bodies that they take fully into account the need to preserve this role in considering new funding arrangements for technical co-operation. It also requested the Director-General for Development and International Economic Co-operation to provide at its forty-fifth session an analysis of the issues relating to the implementation of the central funding concept. The Director-General submitted the requested assessment as a technical paper annexed to his 1989 report on operational activities for development (A/44/324).

51. In its decision 89/20, the UNDP Governing Council noted that the full potential of the role of UNDP as the central funding mechanism for the United Nations system of technical co-operation had not yet been realized, and requested the Administrator to propose to the Council "elements for a funding strategy" based on the Director-General's report. The Governing Council will consider this proposed strategy at its thirty-seventh session in June 1990.

52. The question of successor arrangements for UNDP-agency support costs also bears on programme co-ordination and coherence in operational activities. It is the subject of another expert study to be considered at the June 1990 session of the UNDP Governing Council.

53. In its resolution 44/211 of 22 December 1989, the General Assembly stressed the value of the concept of central funding of technical co-operation through UNDP and urged all Governments to channel the maximum possible share of resources available for multilateral technical co-operation through UNDP. The Assembly further emphasized "the primary importance attached to funding through core resources in operational activities" and at the same time recognized "the value of special-purpose grant resources, provided they are designed as a means to ensure additional resource flows and their projects are coherently and effectively integrated in the programmes of the United Nations system" (resolution 44/211, para. 11).

54. In its resolution 42/196, the Assembly also requested the Director-General, in consultation with the Administrator of UNDP, to assess the constraints on the use of the UNDP country programme and programming process as a frame of reference for non-UNDP technical co-operation activities. The Assembly requested several other closely related studies and reports by the Director-General. The Director-General submitted the assessment regarding the "frame of reference" as a further technical paper with his 1989 policy review report and, in that report itself, provided comprehensive analyses of the country-level co-ordination question, with recommendations for synchronization of United Nations system allocation and programming cycles, cross-programming analyses and harmonization of procedures. The country-level programme co-ordination question was also addressed in depth in a report he commissioned by senior consultants who carried out integrated country reviews in 1989 and made extensive recommendations (A/44/324 Add.2).

55. Bearing in mind the Director-General's reports, the General Assembly, in its resolution 44/211, adopted a comprehensive programme of action with a view to more integrated and co-ordinated programming of United Nations system co-operation based on an overall national programme framework for such co-operation. It requested the Director-General, *inter alia*, to conduct an independent study aimed at developing ways to improve the United Nations system's co-ordination at the country level, including the concept of a document containing the integrated operational response of the system to the national framework for co-operation. This study should include an analysis of the impact of such an approach on the roles of both the resident co-ordinator and the leadership of UNDP. The Director-General will submit this study to the Economic and Social Council and the General Assembly in 1990. The Assembly also requested the Director-General to report in 1991 on possible ways of providing multidisciplinary technical advice from the United Nations system at the country level, including the concept of multidisciplinary teams.

56. With respect to the role of the resident co-ordinator, there have also been a number of developments. Pursuant to Assembly resolution 42/196, the Consultative Committee on Substantive Questions identified a number of areas to improve the functioning of the resident co-ordinator system, and examined them in detail in 1988-1989. In April 1989, ACC endorsed a set of principles (ACC/1989/DEC/1-20) that were reported to the General Assembly.

57. In paragraph 15 (b) of its resolution 44/211, the General Assembly decided to reinforce the team-leadership capacity of the resident co-ordinator within the United Nations system at the country level for the integration of the sectoral inputs of the system and for the effective and coherent co-ordination of the response of the United Nations system to the national programme framework, through, *inter alia*: (a) a clarified and strengthened mandate from ACC, in accordance with Assembly resolutions 32/197, 41/171 and 42/196; (b) the effective co-ordination of technical advice and input from the United Nations system; and (c) closer co-operation of the field representation of the United Nations system at the country level with the resident co-ordinator.

58. It is evident that the pace of implementation of recommendation 11 has markedly accelerated. The numerous provisions of resolution 44/211 are specific, integrated and cross-related. The Assembly explicitly called for a three-year schedule for implementation by all organs, organizations and bodies of the system.

Recommendation 12

59. Considerable progress has been made towards implementation of this recommendation. Following the system-wide review of field offices conducted pursuant to General Assembly resolution 42/196 and the joint statement addressed by organizations of the Joint Consultative Group on Policy (JCGP) (comprising UNDP, the United Nations Population Fund, the United Nations Children's Fund (UNICEF), the International Fund for Agricultural Development (IFAD) and the World Food Programme (WFP) in mid-1988 to their respective country-level staff on the question of sharing common premises and services, local-level JCGP groups in many countries have reviewed this question. Other organizations with country or subregional offices (the International Labour Organisation (ILO), the Food and Agriculture Organization of the United Nations (FAO), the World Health Organization (WHO), the International Civil Aviation Organization (ICAO), the United Nations Centre for Human Settlements (Habitat) and the Department of Public Information of the Secretariat in relation to United Nations information centres) have also endorsed the principle of common premises and shared facilities, subject to practical constraints which in some instances are considerable.

60. In its resolution 44/211, the General Assembly emphasized that the United Nations system at the country level should be structured and composed in such

a way that it corresponds to programmes rather than to its own institutional structure. To that end the Assembly requested, *inter alia*, all organs and bodies to make, without delay, the necessary arrangements, in co-operation with host Governments and without additional costs to developing countries, to establish common premises at the country level. The Director-General was requested to monitor and to report annually on progress made on this specific measure.

61. As the Director-General pointed out in his report to the General Assembly on this question (A/44/324), however, there are various constraints in terms of available space, the need to appropriate funds within the system for capital costs of building extensions, and other practical difficulties. Increased sharing of facilities at the country level can be expected to emerge over time.

Recommendation 13

62. It is the view of ACC that those agreements which have been elaborated over the years under its auspices to harmonize budgeting practices and budget presentation among organizations of the system constitute a solid basis for harmonization of budgeting practices and improved transparency and comparability of budget documents, to the extent that those views are compatible with the need of individual governing bodies for consistency in the presentation of successive budgets, as well as the specificity of organizations' mandates, structures and activities. In the opinion of ACC, the benefit to be derived from the search for greater harmonization of budgeting methods and techniques is primarily in the sharing of new ideas and the possibility of organizations building on the experience of others.

63. A study by the Joint Inspection Unit entitled "Budgeting in the Organizations of the United Nations System" (A/45/130), which will be before the General Assembly at its forty-fifth session, focuses on several aspects of budgeting in the organizations and attempts to examine the extent to which efforts by ACC have actually resulted in standardization and comparability in budgets of the United Nations system as well as the differences that have remained. It has been decided to reconvene in 1990 the Consultative Committee on Substantive Questions (Programme Matters) of ACC to consider, *inter alia*, approaches to the harmonization of programme budget and medium-term plan cycles in the United Nations system.

III. Structure of the Secretariat

A. General recommendations

Recommendation 14

64. This recommendation envisages a simplification of the organizational structure of the Secretariat, bearing in mind the need to develop clearer lines

of authority, responsibility, accountability and communication and to improve co-ordination in order to avoid duplication of work. As has been reported previously, with the further developments reported in paragraphs 84 to 111 below, major restructuring has been carried out in the political, administrative and information areas.

65. With respect to the secretariat structure in the economic and social sectors, General Assembly resolution 32/197 provides the basic framework for the current clustering of substantive activities, in particular with regard to the Department of International Economic and Social Affairs, the Department of Technical Co-operation for Development, UNCTAD and the regional commissions. In addition, in 1987 United Nations activities on social policy and development were concentrated under the Director-General of the United Nations Office at Vienna, incorporating the Centre for Social Development and Humanitarian Affairs (which for that purpose was detached from the Department of International Economic and Social Affairs) and the co-ordination of all United Nations drug-related programmes.

66. In line with recommendation 14, some entities of the Secretariat were reorganized. In UNCTAD, units were clustered around a few major related substantive programmes, the support for technical co-operation activities was strengthened and the production of data and statistical services was also rationalized. ECLAC decided on the merging of several organizational units with a view to simplification of its organizational structure. Following a review by ECA of its structure and organization with a view to implementing the tasks entrusted to it in a more co-ordinated and cost-effective manner, there was a substantial realignment of administrative structures and, while no programme was terminated, a consolidation and integration of programmes for enhanced programme delivery.

67. The Secretary-General recognizes that the restructuring of the economic and social sectors is still pending. Delays in the reform process in this area can be attributed to a number of factors, in particular, to the close linkage between the structure of the Secretariat and its work programme and the review of the structure of the intergovernmental bodies, which is still incomplete (see recommendation 8, paras. 38-42). Accordingly, the Secretary-General believes that the reform period for the economic and social sectors should be extended to ensure that proposals for such reorganization as may be appropriate are well conceived and planned, taking into account decisions at the intergovernmental level.

Recommendation 15

68. In section I, paragraph 1 (b), of its resolution 41/213, the General Assembly, with respect to recommendation 15, calling essentially for a reduction by 15 per cent of regular budget posts and by 25 per cent of high-level posts, noted that the percentages referred to therein were arrived at in a pragmatic manner and should be regarded as targets in the formulation of

the Secretary-General's plans for implementation. The Secretary-General was requested to implement them with flexibility in order to avoid, *inter alia*, negative impact on programmes and on the structure and composition of the Secretariat, bearing in mind the necessity of securing the highest standards of efficiency, competence and integrity of staff, with due regard to equitable geographical distribution.

69. The programme budget for the biennium 1990-1991,[11] as adopted by the General Assembly in its resolution 44/202, includes a staffing table of 10,057 regular budget-funded posts. As compared with a staffing table of 11,422 posts originally approved for the biennium 1988-1989, this represents a reduction of 1,365 posts, or 11.95 per cent, which has been achieved over the period of three years - 1987, 1988, 1989 - envisaged in recommendation 15.

70. It is worth recalling at this point the main steps of the process through which this post reduction of 12 per cent in rounded terms has been achieved. The Secretary-General presented his plans for the implementation of recommendation 15 to the General Assembly at its forty-third session, namely the abolition of 1,465 posts, or 13 per cent of the staffing table, including a reduction of 14 per cent in conference and library services (see A/C.5/43/1/Rev.1, chap. I). The General Assembly, in resolution 43/213, decided that only 10 per cent of the posts in conference and library services should be cut, thus reducing the staffing table of the Organization by 1,365 posts or 12.1 per cent. It also requested the Secretary-General to present recommendations for absorbing the costs of the posts "restored" in conference and library services, including, to the maximum extent possible, through the elimination of additional posts. It further requested the Secretary-General, in further implementing recommendation 15, to take into account a number of guidelines that had been formulated in resolution 41/213 and reaffirmed in resolution 42/211, as well as an additional guideline, and to implement recommendation 15 in a balanced manner, taking into account recommendations 41, 46, 47 and 54. In his programme budget for the biennium 1990-1991, the Secretary-General identified 1,368 posts for reduction - or 11.97 per cent - and stated that he was most definitely not in a position to propose further reductions to offset the cost of the posts "restored" by the General Assembly in its resolution 43/213. The Assembly modified slightly the proposal of the Secretary-General by restoring three posts at the Professional level - one in the secretariat of ECA and two in the secretariat of the Joint Inspection Unit - to arrive at an overall reduction of 1,365 posts, or 11.95 per cent, and a staffing table of 10,057 posts for the biennium 1990-1991.[12]

71. With respect to high-level posts, the staffing table of 10,057 regular budget-funded posts for the biennium 1990-1991 includes 47 high-level posts, that is, 1 post at the Director-General level, 26 posts of Under-Secretary-General and 20 posts of Assistant Secretary-General.[13] There were 57 such posts originally approved at the beginning of the biennium 1988-1989. The reduction has therefore been of 10 posts, or 17.5 per cent.

72. In his plans for the implementation of recommendation 15 presented to the General Assembly at its forty-third session (see A/C.5/43/1/Rev.1, chap. I), the Secretary-General had initially envisaged the suppression of 14 high-level posts. These 14 posts were, however, not identified. The Assembly accepted this proposal implicitly in its resolution 43/213 and adopted a programme budget outline for the biennium 1990-1991 with a total preliminary estimate reflecting, *inter alia*, that reduction of 14 high-level posts. In his proposed programme budget for the biennium 1990-1991, the Secretary-General proposed a reduction by 10 posts, instead of 14, which was endorsed by the Assembly through its resolution 44/202 A of 21 December 1989 on the programme budget for the biennium 1990-1991.

73. At the same time, the General Assembly, in its resolution 44/201 B, section I, reaffirmed its resolution 43/213, accepted the proposals of the Secretary-General (a reduction of 10 posts) and requested the Secretary-General to continue his efforts to identify, as soon as possible in the course of the biennium 1990-1991, four additional high-level posts for reduction.

74. In addition to regular budget-funded posts, the programme budget for the biennium 1990-1991 indicates that 2,549 posts will be funded by extrabudgetary resources. This represents an increase of 637 posts, or 33 per cent, from the beginning of the biennium 1988-1989. Most of these additional posts are in part IV - Economic, social and humanitarian activities - (512 additional posts) and in part VII - Common support services - (118 additional posts) of the programme budget. Among these 2,549 posts are 3 posts at the Assistant Secretary-General level, the same as in 1988-1989. These three high-level posts were and are in section 18, the United Nations Environment Programme, section 19, the United Nations Centre for Human Settlements (Habitat), and section 20, International drug control, of the programme budget.

75. There are currently the same number of high-level posts funded by programmes and funds which are not part of the programme budget, such as section 25 (International Court of Justice), UNDP, UNICEF and UNFPA, as at the time of the adoption of resolution 41/213. In his plans for the implementation of recommendation 15, the Secretary-General indicated that he had brought that recommendation to the attention of the heads of the organizations concerned and had requested them to highlight to their governing bodies the fact that the Member States represented in those bodies had joined in the unanimous decision of the General Assembly to adopt resolution 41/213. In the first progress report and the final report on the implementation of resolution 41/213 (A/42/234 and Corr.1 and A/44/222 and Corr.1), the Secretary-General informed the Assembly that he had made such requests to the various governing bodies concerned and that a few high-level posts funded from extrabudgetary resources had remained unfilled. The Assembly, in its various resolutions on the implementation of resolution 41/213, did not refer

specifically to the implementation of this particular target of recommendation 15.

76. In assessing the effects of the post reduction on programmes, it is necessary to make a distinction between the biennium 1988-1989 and the current biennium. During the first period, the process of post reduction took place. At present the Organization has a Secretariat with 12 per cent fewer posts funded from the regular budget.

77. The programme budget for 1988-1989 was adopted by the General Assembly with a 15 per cent turnover rate for Professional-level staff and a 10 per cent rate for General Service staff. This meant that budgetary financial resources were given for only 85 per cent of the Professional staffing table, on the grounds that the actual vacancy rate in the Secretariat was not less than 15 per cent and in order to implement the post reduction targeted also at 15 per cent by resolution 41/213. During the biennium, such a high vacancy rate was indeed maintained while posts were being first frozen and then suppressed - down to a level of 12 per cent - when the General Assembly adopted in December 1989 the programme budget for 1990-1991. In other words, the number and distribution of staff funded from the regular budget, actually on board, had to remain approximately the same in 1988-1989 as at the end of the biennium 1986-1987. A second factor is that the programmes for 1988-1989, presented by the Secretary-General and adopted by the Assembly, were, quantitatively and qualitatively, a continuation of those of the previous biennium. The programme budget for 1988-1989 (A/42/6) was presented as "transitional" and, in his introduction, the Secretary-General stated, explicitly, that this approach was imposed by the circumstances, including the request of the General Assembly that the reduction of the size of the Secretariat be implemented while avoiding a negative impact on programmes.

78. The combination of those two factors - continuity of staff levels and programme continuity - may explain to a certain extent why it was *a priori* conceivable for the General Assembly to assume, in adopting resolution 41/213, that the process of implementation of recommendation 15 would not, *per se*, affect negatively the delivery of the mandated activities of the Organization. A high vacancy rate was, however, not the only obstacle to overcome. The process of post reduction was in itself disruptive, by the attention it required from programme managers and by its obvious effects on the attitudes and morale of the staff. The Organization was also hampered by an acute financial crisis, coupled to some extent by an expressed lack of confidence from some Governments in its ability to perform its role. It had to devote a large amount of its energy to cope with a situation of daily financial uncertainty, while being criticized for its alleged uncontrolled growth, inefficiency, undue complexity, fragmentation and lack of effectiveness. At the same time, the Secretary-General received new mandates and took new initiatives, notably in the domain of peace and security, which required, *inter alia*, the mobilization of a significant part of the personnel of the Secretariat.

79. Yet, in this difficult context, mandated programmes were globally delivered, as confirmed by the report on programme performance for the biennium 1988-1989 (see A/45/218 and Add.1). Such programme performance, measured by the proportion of programmed outputs that were actually implemented during the biennium 1988-1989, was 74 per cent. This is a rough indicator, because a number of activities of the Organization, notably in peace-keeping matters, are not "programmed" and also because many services, including those provided by the Department of Conference Services, are not counted among the 8,954 programmed "outputs". It is, however, an indicator that can be compared with previous rates of implementation of 76 per cent for the biennium 1986-1987 and 82 per cent for the biennium 1984-1985. The outputs that were not implemented were either "postponed" or "terminated". Rates of postponement were 9 per cent in 1984-1985, 13 per cent in 1986-1987 and 11 per cent in 1988-1989, while rates of termination were, for the same three bienniums, 8 per cent, 11 per cent and 15 per cent. The lower number of postponements in 1988-1989 than in 1986-1987 is of course a positive sign. Furthermore, the increase in the number and proportion of outputs terminated suggests that more attention was given to redressing, during the implementation of the programme budget, the deficiencies of the programming process. Another indicator of programme performance is the number of outputs that were added during a biennium to those initially mandated, either through legislative decisions or at the initiative of the Secretariat. There were 441 such outputs in 1988-1989, as compared with 843 in 1986-1987 and 1,062 in 1984-1985. Thus, during the process of implementation of recommendation 15, the capacity of the Organization to expand its programmes and produce new outputs, while retained, was, nevertheless, reduced.

80. A negative impact on mandated programmes was, however, on the whole, avoided and this can be explained by the following factors:

(a) Parts of the organizational structure of the Secretariat were reorganized and improved, notably in the political and administrative sectors, and the technological modernization of the Organization was actively pursued;

(b) While the Organization increased dramatically its activities in peace-keeping and peace-making, programmes financed by the regular budget, representing most outputs and services and absorbing most of the budgeted resources, did not expand during the biennium 1988-1989. There was legislative restraint. As indicated above, the outputs added through revised estimates and statements of programme budget implications were below traditional levels;

(c) Programmes and added activities were implemented by stretching the capacity and improving the productivity of some parts of the Secretariat. Exceptional efforts responded to exceptional circumstances. There was no evidence of a decrease in the quality of the outputs and services provided by the Organization;

(d) The process of post reduction was undertaken, not through precise work-load analyses, for which neither was a scientific basis provided by the Group of High-level Intergovernmental Experts nor was time made available as a consequence of financial constraints, but through a pragmatic assessment of the capacity of the various departments and offices to manage their programmes while "absorbing" a cut. For some programmes, as noted above, the number of staff funded from extrabudgetary resources was increased. Some discretionary outputs were not produced. The structure and composition of the Secretariat were not significantly altered beyond those explicitly approved early in the process, as instructed by the General Assembly. The post reduction was not used as an instrument to redistribute resources among various activities in an attempt to establish priorities different from those determined by Member States in the programme budget.

81. The post reduction of 12 per cent became *de jure* effective with the adoption of the programme budget for the biennium 1990-1991. The programmatic content of this budget, which had been presented by the Secretary-General in the light, *inter alia*, of such a reduction, included mandated activities reflecting a strong element of continuity with previous bienniums. A number of programme elements and outputs were regrouped in order to enhance the capacity of the Secretariat to fulfil the objectives set by legislative mandate. Technological innovations and the modernization of the modes of operation of the Organization were embodied in the programme budget. The Secretary-General believes that the programmes that are part of the programme budget for the current biennium will not be negatively affected by the level of implementation of recommendation 15 at the end of 1989, and the General Assembly adopted the programme budget on such an understanding.

82. In its resolution 44/200 A, the General Assembly, recognizing the progress achieved to date on the implementation of the overall post reduction mandated by it in it resolution 43/213, acknowledged that the Secretary-General was not in a position at that stage to propose further post reductions and decided to consider, in the light of the present report, any further proposals that he might put forward.

83. At this juncture, it is important to consider the relationship between the level of staff resources and the volume of the programmes and activities that the Organization is mandated to implement. The Secretariat has to be in a position to respond effectively to new or enhanced mandates. Continuing efforts at more efficiency and greater effectiveness should not be perceived as a suggestion that all additional activities can be accommodated within existing resources. Redeployment of staff among programmes should be an integral part of the functioning of a dynamic organization, but there are technical as well as practical limits to this and other forms of redistribution of resources. A proper balance between the number of staff funded from the regular budget and the number of staff funded, in various ways, from contributions for

peace-keeping and voluntary contributions, has to be maintained in the Organization as a whole. Further structural reforms may be required, but their *raison d'être* must be to increase the capacity of the Organization to accomplish its role, not to reduce its staff. The Secretary-General sees the implementation of recommendation 15 in this context.

B. *Political affairs*

Recommendation 16

84. This recommendation has been implemented. Further to the extensive restructuring reported on in the Secretary-General's final report (A/44/222 and Corr.1), whereby the political sector was divided into seven entities with a view to a clear distribution of functions and elimination of duplication, the Secretary-General took additional measures to strengthen the Organization's capacity to deal with these primary responsibilities.

85. Owing to extensive and increasing demands for the good offices of the Secretary-General for the maintenance of international peace and security, and the heavy, additional responsibilities that this demand has placed on him, the Chef de Cabinet and the members of the Executive Office, the Secretary-General decided in 1988 to strengthen that Office and to make certain structural changes affecting that Office and the Office for Special Political Affairs. The responsibilities of the latter Office for supporting the Secretary-General in his peace-making activities in relation to Afghanistan, the Arab-Israeli conflict, Cyprus and certain other situations were transferred to the Executive Office, in accordance with the Secretary-General's intention that these activities should be handled under his direct, personal supervision. The Office of the Under-Secretary-General for Special Political Affairs retains responsibility for the conduct of the growing number of peace-keeping operations.

86. Furthermore, in January 1990, the Secretary-General established a Senior Planning and Monitoring Group for Peace-keeping Operations to assist and advise him in the planning and monitoring of peace-keeping operations. The Group is chaired by the Secretary-General or, in his absence, by the Under-Secretary-General for Special Political Affairs. The Group advises the Secretary-General on peace-keeping and related matters and, in particular, enhances inter-departmental co-ordination in this area by bringing together the senior officials with an overall responsibility for peace-keeping and related matters.

Recommendation 17

87. The recommendation that the administrative functions of the Office for Field Operational and External Support Activities should be transferred to the Department of Administration and Management has been implemented. The

Field Operations Division was established in the Office of General Services with responsibility for the administration of field missions established by the Security Council or by the Secretary-General. In addition, the recommendation that most of the staff in the field offices should be recruited locally has, to the extent possible, also been implemented.

88. In assessing the impact of implementation, it is clear that the situation with regard to field missions has acquired a totally different character since the adoption of resolution 41/213. The significant and unprecedented expansion of peace-keeping and related activities and the subsequent establishment of a number of new field missions during 1988 and 1989, coupled with the mandated retrenchments that have taken place during the same period, have had a serious impact on the ability of the Field Operations Division to carry on normal activities. The unpredictable timing of, and the particularly short lead-time normally allowed for, the establishment of new operations has created a range of difficulties.

89. As it is not possible to project accurately the level of peace-keeping operations and related activities which the Organization will embark on at a given time, it is particularly important for the Division to undertake all appropriate steps to enhance its ability to plan for and respond to new demands in a timely and effective manner. Procedures are also being developed to ensure the availability of a cadre of core personnel, skilled and trained in the required disciplines, who can be moved quickly to a new mission location, and to establish an appropriate reserve stock of commonly used equipment and stores items.

Recommendation 18

90. As indicated in the Secretary-General's final report (A/44/222 and Corr.1, paras. 63-65), most of the activities relating to the dissemination of news and political analysis to other departments have been consolidated in the new Office for Research and the Collection of Information and every effort has been made to eliminate duplication of effort by political departments and offices.

91. The former Department of Political Affairs, Trusteeship and Decolonization was not involved in any such activities except those specifically mandated to it by the General Assembly such as the dissemination of information on decolonization and political analysis on decolonization-related issues. The Department's role in the dissemination of information on decolonization has, since 1971, been mandated each year by a resolution of the Assembly, the latest being resolution 44/102 of 11 December 1989. The resolutions have been implemented each year by the issuing of bulletins on decolonization and through the Department of Public Information and by the publication of a number of pamphlets, booklets and other information material for which the Department provides the substantive input. The activities of the new Department for Special Political Questions, Regional Co-operation,

Decolonization and Trusteeship, formed by the consolidation of the former Department and the former Office of Special Political Questions, have been broadened by the additional responsibilities stemming from the programmes previously implemented by the Office of Special Political Questions. Those programmes include the monitoring and analysis of specific political situations in Africa in connection with the exercise of the good offices of the Secretary-General. In the fulfilment of its responsibilities the present Department has made extensive use of the information provided by the Office for Research and the Collection of Information and has co-operated closely with the Department of Public Information. Implementation of this recommendation has thus been beneficial to the cost-effectiveness of several subprogrammes of the Department for Special Political Questions, Regional Co-operation, Decolonization and Trusteeship.

92. With respect to the political analysis functions of the Department of Political and Security Council Affairs, those functions have been rationalized to avoid duplication with the work of other offices by focusing on three specific areas, namely, the analysis of political trends and developments with emphasis on their longer-range significance, the servicing of United Nations bodies dealing with issues specifically related to the strengthening of international security, and activities relating to the promotion of peace and follow-up to the purposes of the International Year of Peace. The transfer to the Office for Research and the Collection of Information of certain staff resources formerly engaged in the daily collection of political information has been achieved without adverse impact on programme delivery.

Recommendation 19

93. As indicated in the Secretary-General's report (A/44/222 and Corr.1, para. 66), this recommendation has been implemented. The Office of the United Nations Commissioner for Namibia now includes the secretariat of the Council for Namibia, which previously fell under the Under-Secretary-General for Special Political Questions, Regional Co-operation, Decolonization and Trusteeship. For the purpose of effective and efficient management of resources the entire Office of the Commissioner for Namibia has been brought under the overall umbrella of the Department for Special Political Questions, Regional Co-operation, Decolonization and Trusteeship. That measure, however, did not affect the reporting channels of communication between the Council and the Commissioner as established by the Assembly in its resolution 2248 (S-V) of 19 May 1967.

94. The administrative structure has been streamlined through the consolidation of the two administrative offices previously established within the Department and the Office of the Commissioner into one executive office in the Department for Special Political Questions, Regional Co-operation, Decolonization and Trusteeship. There is evidence that these organizational changes have not affected adversely programmes and services in this area.

95. As a result of Namibia's independence, a thorough review of the existing structure will be undertaken and the results will be reflected in the revised estimates to be submitted to the General Assembly at its forty-fifth session as mandated by the Assembly in section V of its resolution 44/201 B.

Recommendation 20

96. The recommendation has been implemented by the changes described below in the organizational structure of. the Department for Disarmament Affairs with a view to enhancing substantive output.

97. The establishment of a new Monitoring, Analysis and Studies Branch has combined under one organizational unit various interrelated activities previously carried out by a number of units of the Department. The primary tasks of the Branch are to follow up on developments concerning arms limitation and disarmament-related deliberations not only at the multilateral level but also at the bilateral and regional levels in order to implement the action programme of the International Conference on the Relationship between Disarmament and Development and to carry out various disarmament studies to be prepared by the Secretary-General with the assistance of experts, at the request of the General Assembly. The publication and information activities of the Department have also been consolidated as the Publications and World Disarmament Campaign Branch.

98. The Department's publication activities have been reviewed and improved in order to enhance their value to Member States, particularly those with limited resources for specialization and representation. The United Nations *Disarmament Yearbook* has been reorganized in order to improve its clarity and readability as a reference source and is now published well in advance of the session of the General Assembly following the one it covers. The Department's periodic review *Disarmament*, which is now being issued four times a year instead of three, covers a wider range of topics related to arms limitation, disarmament and security, and the range of contributors has also been broadened. In addition, the Department has begun a new reference publication, issued shortly after the adjournment of the General Assembly, containing a summary of relevant discussions and decisions taken during the session in order to facilitate preparation of assessments of the session by Member States themselves. This reference material is published in response to a request by the General Assembly to this effect and is a further concrete response to the intent of recommendation 20.

99. Within the framework of the World Disarmament Campaign, the Department is placing increasing emphasis on the implementation of those guidelines of the Campaign which call for the encouragement of bilateral and multilateral exchanges on the basis of reciprocity and mutual agreement among government officials and experts of different countries. Consequently, the Department now organizes high-level meetings of government representatives

and experts to discuss various topical issues on the agenda of deliberative and negotiating bodies with a view to facilitating their search for common ground. One such meeting held in 1988 dealt with the question of verification of disarmament agreements and the role of the United Nations. The other meeting, which took place in 1989, examined the question of disarmament and international security.

100. The Department's subprogramme relating to the Disarmament Fellowship Programme has been expanded to include the provision of training and advisory services to Member States upon their request. The activity includes the organization of workshops for junior governmental officials and the rendering of advisory assistance on various substantive matters of particular interest to a given Government and regional or subregional governmental organizations.

101. The Committee and Conference Services Branch and the Geneva Branch, whose work is most directly related to the needs of Member States, continue to carry out their functions as mandated.

102. It may be noted that while the implementation of recommendation 20 has not given rise to any adverse effects on the functioning of the Department, but rather to the contrary has enhanced its effectiveness, the addition of mandates entrusted to the Department by the General Assembly at its forty-third and forty-fourth sessions without additional resources has created heavy demands upon the existing structure.

Recommendation 21

103. Functions relating to decolonization and trusteeship are now the responsibility of the Division of Decolonization and Trusteeship within the Department for Special Political Questions, Regional Co-operation, Decolonization and Trusteeship. During the period 1980 to 1990, five territories became independent, which reduced the number of Non-Self-Governing Territories from 23 to 18 (Namibia excluded). The final result of the post reduction exercise as shown in the 1990-1991 programme budget indicates that only 13 Professional posts are now assigned to decolonization activities (excluding Namibia) compared to 23 at the beginning of 1987. Despite this reduced manpower, there has been no negative impact on programme delivery.

Recommendation 22

104. The administration of special economic assistance programmes has been transferred to UNDP except in cases of political sensitivity where the responsibility has been assigned to the Unit for Special Emergency Programmes in the Department for Special Political Questions, Regional Co-operation, Decolonization and Trusteeship. That Unit is, in particular, responsible for the implementation of special economic assistance programmes with regard to African emergency situations.

Recommendation 23

105. As indicated by the Secretary-General in his report (A/44/222 and Corr.1, para. 71), the report on the implementation of General Assembly resolution 41/201 entitled "Office of the United Nations Disaster Relief Co-ordinator" (UNDRO) (A/42/657) included a comprehensive review and assessment of existing mechanisms and arrangements for emergency assistance and co-ordination. In its decision 42/433 of 11 December 1987, the General Assembly requested the Secretary-General to proceed with the implementation of conclusions and recommendations contained in his report.

106. The report of the Secretary-General on the implementation of that decision (A/43/731) outlined the specific measures undertaken in this regard, including a review by the Management Advisory Service, Department of Administration and Management, to adjust the work programme and organization of UNDRO in order to focus its activities on sudden natural disasters. Subsequent organizational changes within UNDRO are reflected in the programme budget for the biennium 1990-1991. UNDRO has developed its information system, its assistance to Governments for disaster investigation programmes and its capacity to respond immediately and effectively to sudden emergencies. There has also been progress in the modalities of co-operation between UNDRO and UNDP following the report of the Joint UNDP-UNDRO Task Force, which contains specific proposals including the exchange of staff between the two organizations, a closer partnership in disaster investigation and in disaster response activities at the field level, a joint training programme and the delineation of the responsibilities of the Director-General.

107. In paragraph 6 of its resolution 43/116 of 8 December 1988, the General Assembly requested the Secretary-General to undertake studies and consultations in order to consider the need for the establishment, within the United Nations system, of a mechanism or arrangement to ensure the implementation and overall co-ordination of relief programmes to internally displaced persons. In his report (A/44/520), the Secretary-General concluded that he did not believe it necessary or appropriate to establish a new mechanism or arrangement for this purpose, but rather to strengthen existing arrangements in order to enhance accessibility and effectiveness.

108. Emergency and disaster situations are by definition extraordinary events whose nature and scope cannot be fully anticipated, nor is it possible to determine in advance the appropriate response mechanism. The variant nature of disaster and emergency situations requires a multifaceted response drawing on the capacities of various entities of the United Nations system. UNDRO was established to provide greater coherence and direction to these efforts. The measures outlined above have contributed to greater co-ordination and rationalization so as to minimize duplication and to ensure the most effective utilization of United Nations resources in the field. In this context, attention is called in particular to the recommendations of the Joint UNDP-UNDRO Task Force, which are being implemented. The primary focus of action is at

the field level where the UNDP resident representative/resident co-ordinator is called on to play a key role in emergency situations. There is a regular process of consultation with all relevant field representatives of the United Nations system, as well as with the donor community, both governmental and non-governmental, in co-operation with the host Government. Specific instructions have been prepared for UNDP resident representatives/resident co-ordinators advising them of their responsibilities in this regard.

109. The Special Emergency Programmes Unit within the Department for Special Political Questions, Regional Co-operation, Decolonization and Trusteeship deals with complex emergency situations that involve multiple factors and include politically sensitive issues requiring the Secretary-General to co-ordinate the work of a number of agencies in the United Nations system. Complex emergency situations are frequently characterized by civil strife, the presence of large numbers of displaced persons and varying degrees of famine. They can be distinguished, firstly, from those situations which fall within the mandate of a single United Nations agency, e.g. food shortages (WFP), epidemics (WHO), child health (UNICEF), locust depredations (FAO) and, secondly, from sudden natural disasters that require the intervention of UNDRO. With clear lines of demarcation for special emergency programmes, programme delivery has been enhanced.

Recommendation 24

110. As indicated in his first progress report on the implementation of General Assembly resolution 41/213 (A/42/234 and Corr.1, para. 33), UNDRO is being retained as a separate entity located at Geneva.

111. The General Assembly, in its resolution 41/201 of 8 December 1986, reaffirmed the mandate of UNDRO, while CPC at its twenty-ninth session noted recent decisions of the Assembly whereby the mandate, identity and location of UNDRO were to be maintained.[14]

C. Economic and social affairs

Recommendation 25

112. The review of the tasks performed by the various secretariat entities in the economic and social sectors envisaged in this recommendation is, as was recognized by the Group of Experts and indicated in previous reports of the Secretary-General, intimately linked to the review of the intergovernmental structure. As indicated above, there is still no agreement on the changes in the intergovernmental structure. During the secretariat review that was initiated in December 1986 under the direction and guidance of the Director-General for Development and International Economic Co-operation, particular emphasis was given to global analysis and reporting, energy and natural resources, science and technology, economic and technical co-operation among developing countries, national development strategies and the relationship

between operational and substantive activities. The review is an ongoing process and has already served as the basis for intensified consultations among the various secretariat entities involved with a view to eliminating duplication and enhancing responsiveness to the needs of Member States.

113. With respect to the evaluation of the activities of the Centre for Science and Technology for Development and consideration of the feasibility of integrating the Centre into the Department of International Economic and Social Affairs and the Department of Technical Co-operation for Development, it may be recalled that the Secretary-General proposed that the Executive Director of the Centre report through the Under-Secretary-General for International Economic and Social Affairs. This matter was considered by the General Assembly at its forty-third session and it was decided to take no action on the proposal.

114. A 10-year review of the Vienna Programme of Action on Science and Technology for Development,[15] which included the work of the Centre, was carried out by the Intergovernmental Committee on Science and Technology for Development,[16] at its tenth session.[17] On the basis of that review, the General Assembly, in its resolution 44/14 A of 26 October 1989, reaffirmed the validity of the Vienna Programme of Action and expressed support for the work of the Centre. In its resolution 44/14 C, the Assembly requested the Director-General for Development and International Economic Co-operation to ensure close monitoring and follow-up of the mandated programmes and activities of the United Nations system in the areas of science and technology for development. A further in-depth evaluation of the major programme on science and technology will be carried out in 1992, and a progress report will be submitted to CPC at its thirtieth session, in May 1990.

115. The question of the integration of the Centre for Science and Technology for Development into the Department of International Economic and Social Affairs and the Department of Technical Co-operation for Development was considered in the context of the implementation of recommendation 14 (see paras. 64-67 above). It is noted that the Intergovernmental Committee on Science and Technology for Development "was generally of the view that its existing secretariat support structure, in particular the organizational identity and autonomy of the Centre, should be maintained".[18]

116. With regard to enhancing the authority of the Director-General for Development and International Economic Co-operation to carry out his responsibilities as set forth in General Assembly resolution 32/197 and subsequent legislation, it is emphasized that the Director-General operates under the authority of the Secretary-General; accordingly, no additional legislative authority is required. The need to ensure the necessary capacity to the Director-General to carry out the responsibilities entrusted to him will be kept under constant review.

117. As a practical measure to facilitate inter-agency co-ordination, the Assistant Secretary-General of the Office of the Director-General for Development and International Economic Co-operation has been designated to serve as Chairman of the Organizational Committee and Secretary of the Administrative Committee on Co-ordination.

118. It has not been considered practical or feasible at this stage to establish at a single location all departments and offices of the United Nations dealing with economic and social affairs.

Recommendation 26

119. As indicated in relation to recommendation 25, the review of the economic and social sectors of the Secretariat has served as a basis for intensified consultations among the entities involved. In the case of the Department of Technical Co-operation for Development, General Assembly resolution 32/197 provides the basic terms of reference for field operational activities of technical co-operation and applied research and policy analysis. In this context, the Department has further strengthened and intensified its co-operation with other entities to further increase complementarity of work. Of particular importance in this regard is the enhanced co-operation between that Department and the Department of International Economic and Social Affairs, given the responsibility of the latter for research and global analysis.

120. In carrying out the tasks entrusted to it, the Department of Technical Co-operation for Development strives to be fully responsive to the actual needs of developing countries. The evaluation activities carried out at the programme level and at the project level, as well as the strengthened co-operative arrangements with other entities referred to above, are important elements in continuously enhancing the efficiency and effectiveness of the Department in responding to the needs of developing countries. The issue of possible overlapping and duplication with UNDP, which, when it occurs, is primarily due to the shifting of executing agency responsibilities and functions from the Department to entities like the UNDP Office for Project Services, is kept under careful monitoring; it has also been reviewed and commented on, *inter alia*, in the context of a recent report of the Joint Inspection Unit on the UNDP Office for Project Services.

Recommendation 27

121. Every effort continues to be made to reflect the importance of the work of the regional commissions in terms both of participation in consultative mechanisms and of substantive contributions to the work of intergovernmental bodies. In his report on the revitalization of the Economic and Social Council (E/1989/95), the Secretary-General noted that, in order to improve the interface between the regional commissions and the Council, the executive secretaries had proposed the holding of separate, informal meetings on selected

issues with members of the Council. Such meetings were held during the second regular session of the Council in 1989. Other measures have also been introduced to assist the Council in its consideration of issues relating to regional co-operation, including improvements in the format and content of the Secretary-General's annual report on regional co-operation to incorporate a section on interregional co-operation and to focus on issues requiring attention by the Council.

122. In response to that recommendation, the Director-General for Development and International Economic Co-operation commissioned a review of the functioning of the regional commissions. As a result, a report entitled "The Regional Commissions of the United Nations: Future role and activities" was discussed among executive secretaries, as well as between them and other concerned United Nations senior officials. The report was subsequently made available to Member States. Further action on the implementation of some of the recommendations in the report will be taken, as appropriate, following consultation between the Director-General and the executive secretaries.

Recommendation 28

123. Resources for administration, conference and general services for different bodies at Geneva, including ECE, are included under the budget of the United Nations Office at Geneva and managed in an integrated fashion, thus giving rise to economies of scale. To maintain this integrated management, which has proven to be both efficient and cost-effective while answering the need for comparability among the regional commissions, the proposed programme budget now includes, in the introduction to section 10 (ECE), the proportion of resources provided by the United Nations Office at Geneva to ECE. Further harmonization in the presentation of the programme budget proposals of the regional commissions is being contemplated, as suggested by the Advisory Committee on Administrative and Budgetary Questions in its first report on the proposed programme budget for the biennium 1990-1991.[19]

Recommendation 29

124. In his first report on the implementation of General Assembly resolution 41/213 (A/42/234 and Corr.1, para. 20 (c)), the Secretary-General stated that the functions of the Office of Secretariat Services for Economic and Social Matters relating to the technical servicing of meetings were being assumed by the Office for Political and General Assembly Affairs and Secretariat Services. The Assembly, in its resolution 42/211, requested the Secretary-General to review those arrangements. Pursuant to that resolution, the Secretary-General reviewed the matter and detailed information in this regard was subsequently provided in the revised estimates for the 1988-1989 programme budget (A/C.5/43/30 and Add.1 and Add.1/Corr.1).

125. In paragraph 2 (g) of its resolution 1988/77, the Economic and Social Council requested the Secretary-General, in the context of the implementation of General Assembly resolution 41/213, to submit proposals on the structure and composition of a separate and identifiable secretariat support structure for the Council which would undertake substantive functions and technical servicing. The Secretary-General, in his report on the subject (E/1989/95), advised that he was considering ways and means of providing effective and coherent secretariat support for the Council and of strengthening the Office of the Director-General for Development and International Economic Co-operation and would report further on the matter to the Assembly at its forty-fourth session. In paragraph 26 of its resolution 1989/114, the Council requested the Secretary-General to take the following points into consideration in providing secretariat support for the Council: (a) there should be an organizationally distinct and identifiable secretariat structure for providing substantive support in regard to the preparation of thematic analyses and consolidated reports; (b) the expertise of other organizations of the United Nations system should be drawn upon, as appropriate; and (c) such secretariat support should be provided, as appropriate, *inter alia*, within existing resources, through, *inter alia*, redeployment of staff and the use of extrabudgetary resources.

126. In his note to the General Assembly at its forty-fourth session on the United Nations intergovernmental structure and functions in the economic and social fields (A/44/747, para. 13), the Secretary-General conveyed his decision to assign to the Director-General for Development and International Economic Co-operation responsibility for providing the substantive support called for in Economic and Social Council resolution 1989/114.

127. In paragraph 4 of its resolution 44/103 on restructuring and revitalization of the United Nations in the economic and social fields, the General Assembly stressed the need for the full implementation of Economic and Social Council resolutions 1988/77 and 1988/44, including the provisions related to the secretariat support structure of the Council, and requested the Secretary-General to present a report on the implementation of these resolutions to the Council in order to enable it to review this matter at its second regular session of 1990.

128. The Secretary-General has also noted that several major international deliberations that were expected to develop new approaches and identify priority concerns of the international community would have critical implications for the United Nations intergovernmental structure and functions in the economic and social sphere. Accordingly, the Secretary-General believes that it would be appropriate to await the results of those deliberations and to integrate them into his recommendations concerning secretariat services for economic and social matters.

129. With respect to the aspect of the recommendation dealing with editing, a thorough review has confirmed that there is no duplication of editing efforts, but rather a rational division of labour between editors in the Editorial and Official Records Division of the Department of Conference Services and editors in the Office for Political and General Assembly Affairs and Secretariat Services who work in a well co-ordinated and co-operative manner, following the same editorial guidelines and practices.

D. Administration and other fields

130. The search for greater efficiency and cost-effectiveness has been a priority consideration in the administrative area throughout the reform period. Significant changes have occurred both in terms of organizational structure and in procedures and methods of work. The basic structural changes are detailed below under recommendations 30 and 32. These modifications resulted in clearer lines of responsibility and better co-ordination. At the same time, a thorough re-examination of the information systems that support the decision-making process in the administrative area was conducted first in 1987 and completed in 1988 through an extensive study of all administrative processes in the Department of Administration and Management. The results of that examination led to the conclusion that a more efficient system for processing and recording transactions had to be developed. A comprehensive proposal for an integrated management information system was therefore submitted to the General Assembly at its forty-third session (A/C.5/43/24) and approved in the context of the revised estimates for the 1988-1989 programme budget. At its forty-fourth session, the Assembly approved an amount of $8.5 million for the biennium 1990-1991 under the regular budget.

Recommendation 30

131. The reorganization of the Department of Administration and Management is now completed. Through reassignment of functions, consolidation of responsibilities and streamlining, significant savings in posts were possible and have been reflected in the 1990-1991 programme budget now approved.

Recommendation 31

132. Although the Group of High-level Intergovernmental Experts recommended the abolition of the Management Advisory Service, the Secretary-General reported in his second progress report (A/43/286 and Corr.1, paras. 57-58), that, upon careful examination of the question, he could not propose such abolition without seriously affecting the work of the Department of Administration and Management. The integration of this unit into the Office of Programme Planning, Budget and Finance has facilitated the work of the Service, which has performed particularly important functions during the period under review and continues to do so.

Recommendation 32

133. The functions of programme planning, covering United Nations activities in the economic and social sectors and formerly carried out by the Department of International Economic and Social Affairs, have been redeployed to the Office responsible for the programme budget within the Department of Administration and Management. The functions of planning, programming, budgeting and monitoring are now placed under a single organizational unit.

Recommendation 33

134. As reported in the second progress report (*ibid.*, para. 59), a review of the liaison offices in New York of various Secretariat activities was carried out in 1988 in connection with the implementation of recommendation 15 (see A/C.5/43/1/Rev.1, chap. I).

135. The main finding of the review, based on replies to a questionnaire, on interviews and on desk surveys, was that the bulk of the activities of the liaison offices was substantive in nature. Substantive work includes providing, gathering and exchanging specialized information on the work programme and the activities of the parent body and on developments of interest to them, providing inputs into statements and reports, participating in task forces, seminars, conferences and events, and having contacts and exchanges with Governments and permanent missions, with non-governmental organizations, with the academic, scientific, business and financial communities, and with the media. Given the diversity and complexity of the substantive mandates of the parent bodies, it was concluded that consolidating the substantive functions of the offices would have adverse effect on programme implementation. Regarding support services, it was concluded that there was no rationale for consolidating information and reference services, which were substantive in nature and did not overlap.

Recommendation 34

136. The Department of Conference Services, in close co-operation with the Committee on Conferences, has undertaken various measures designed to better plan and service the calendar of conferences, improve the cost-effective delivery and utilization of conference and documentation resources, and introduce and closely monitor the application of quality and quantity controls on documentation and publications. The Department also continues to identify areas of its work where the introduction of new technologies or processes will make it possible to increase efficiency and productivity. For the most part, it can be stated that the efforts of the past three years form part of the normal work programme of the Department.

137. Progress has been achieved in harmonizing the terminology and improving methodologies used for the preparation of the programme budget

for conference and library services, at Headquarters and Geneva, and continuing efforts will be made to achieve further improvement.

138. New applications of technological innovations have been particularly important during the years 1987 through 1989. Word-processing technology had been applied to all official languages by the end of 1989. The introduction of word-processing has resulted in an estimated improvement of 25 per cent in the productivity of word-processing services and has greatly facilitated the processing of documents at every stage. Work has advanced on the development of a computer-based system for scheduling meetings and interpreter assignments to enable the Secretariat to respond quickly and flexibly to changing requirements for meetings servicing and to make the most efficient use of scarce resources.

139. The Department has also participated in the pilot project on the optical disc storage of conference documents, undertaken by the United Nations Office at Geneva in response to a recommendation made by the Joint Inspection Unit in its report entitled "Problems of storage and its costs to organizations of the United Nations system" (A/41/806 and Corr.1). In section XVI of its resolution 44/201 B, the General Assembly requested the Secretary-General to implement the optical disc project. In addition, progress has been made in the design and installation of a computer-based documents recording, information and tracking system, which is expected to become operational during the biennium 1990-1991.

140. Monitoring of the calendar of conferences has made it possible to make fuller use of permanent staffing capacity, thereby reducing reliance on costly temporary staff at Headquarters. The average utilization factor for United Nations bodies has shown improvement over the past few years, reaching a level of over 70 per cent. On the other hand, the late submission of documents for processing has continued to cause additional expenditures.

141. With respect to external printing arrangements, progress has been achieved in reducing the reliance on external contractors in the processing of United Nations publications and making optimum use of available internal typesetting, printing and binding facilities. Local conditions at some duty stations require that the Organization produce externally the publication programmes of some author departments. In such cases, efforts are made to ensure that such services are purchased under the most favourable conditions.

142. The introduction of desk-top publishing technology for the layout and typesetting of newsletters and for more complicated publications has already begun. It is expected to alleviate some of the burden of purchasing external typesetting services by permitting author departments to prepare camera-ready materials at the time of drafting publications. At the same time, electronic typesetting using the IBM mainframe computer offers another possibility for increasing internal typesetting capacity and thereby reducing the need to incur external processing costs. Software applications have also been developed that

make it possible to use WANG word-processing diskettes as inputs for IBM typesetting in several official languages for certain categories of publications.

143. Those processes demand greater support from graphic presentation and printing technicians in terms of providing guidance and advice on the design of desk-top published materials in line with the Organization's general visual image and established editorial standards. To standardize procedures in this fast-developing field, the Under-Secretary-General for Conference Services and Special Assignments, at the request and with the approval of the Publications Board, has issued an administrative instruction (ST/AI/189/Add.26 of 25 September 1989) governing the use of electronic publishing equipment in the production of United Nations documents and publications, and the Under-Secretary-General for Administration and Management has issued an administrative instruction (ST/AI/359 of 12 December 1989) that sets standards for desk-top publishing software and hardware.

144. The computer-based systems installed in the printing, cartographic, reproduction and distribution areas have already led to a more efficient use of internal reproduction and distribution services, a reduction in the wastage of paper and supplies, an improvement in the quality of the output, and an improvement in the timeliness of issuance of publications and documentation.

145. The recent introduction of a computer system in the printing services has permitted a higher degree of analysis and, therefore, of managerial control in the evaluation and selection of vendors. The system has made it possible to study in more detail the product lines and cost structures available on the market and to conduct an educated cost-benefit analysis when purchasing services. Whenever possible, printing services are purchased in bulk. For example, given their regular schedules of delivery of manuscripts, it has been possible to enter into a yearly contract for the production of the *Monthly Bulletin on Statistics* and the *Development Forum* periodical. Such "bulk" purchasing at lower cost is also applied to the printing of envelopes and stationery. Careful attention is also given to contracting on as wide a geographical basis as possible, taking into account pressure of deadline and responsiveness to the needs of the Organization. Success in this regard has been achieved in the production of the *UN Chronicle*, which beginning in 1990 will be produced in its six language versions using services in Moscow, Beijing, Egypt and Mexico. Efforts have also been undertaken to improve co-ordination between the printing facilities at Headquarters and the United Nations Office at Geneva so that work may be moved between the duty stations, as technically feasible, and enable a balanced use of available capacities. This effort has been particularly helpful in respect of the processing of some volumes of the United Nations *Treaty Series*.

146. The Department of Conference Services has also installed equipment that has increased the in-house capacity to print and bind documents and produce higher quality publications. For example, the Goss Unit installed in the

Publishing Division makes it possible to print 32 pages on both of the printing presses, increasing production from 126,436,264 page impressions in 1985 to 303,057,220 yearly page impressions at present. The Unit also is capable of printing an eight-page document and an eight-page saddle, making it possible to meet the early morning deadlines for delivery of parliamentary documentation and the daily *Journal* of meetings. The installation of a computerized projection system and new controls on the printing presses have minimized human error and reduced the correction time for lateral and circumferential registers, resulting in a reduction of the make-ready waste that inevitably occurs in the preparation of materials. Similarly, a computer-based stock inventory system has resulted in better stock control management and replenishment, while a computer-based system for generating and storing cartographic materials has improved the quality of the materials produced and made them more readily available.

147. In addition, the decision to relinquish in 1987 the external storage space for publications, taken at the recommendation of the Joint Inspection Unit in its report entitled "Problems of storage and its costs to organizations of the United Nations system" (A/41/806 and Corr.1), resulted in a yearly savings of approximately $400,000 in rental costs. Balancing the objective of a wide dissemination of information about the Organization and its work with the need to cut costs and manage within existing storage space, distribution lists have been pruned to streamline initial print runs by making every attempt to better identify and reach the target audience, attain a reasonable proportion between free and sales distribution, and minimize stock.

148. The Publications Board has continued its regular programme of reviewing and revising, as necessary, the Organization's publishing policies. In accordance with the terms of reference of the Committee on Conferences established in General Assembly resolution 44/196 B, that Committee considered at its 1989 session a report on a review of recurrent publications against the criteria set forth in Assembly resolution 38/32 E with a view to identifying publications that could be discontinued or reduced in volume or periodicity of issuance (see A/AC.172/131). The reviews, which had been undertaken at the request of the Assembly on the recommendation of CPC were conducted during the years 1986 through 1989 by the intergovernmental bodies that authorize the issuance of recurrent publications. The exercise resulted in a net increase by 22 in the number of requests for recurrent publications: from 233 in the biennium 1986-1987 to 255 in the biennium 1990-1991. The Committee on Conferences will continue its consideration of this matter at its 1990 session.

149. As recognized by the Member States, the Joint Inspection Unit and the readership, delays in the issuance of United Nations publications detract from their quality and sales potential. In 1986, the Publications Board conducted an in-depth study of the factors causing the delays in issuance, and approved and circulated to author departments and processing services recommendations

aimed at redressing the problems and bottle-necks encountered. In late 1988, the Board noted that in some areas progress had been achieved, although there was still ample room for improvement. To illustrate, while electronic publishing technology made it possible to cut down on production time, staffing shortages in a number of areas, particularly in the drafting and editing phases, and conflicting demands placed on processing services by parliamentary documentation in fact were creating new delays. Author departments and the Department of Conference Services, under the auspices of the Publications Board, are continuing to address these problems.

150. Studies have revealed that the reference publications most requested by libraries are the *World Economic Survey*, the *Yearbook of the United Nations* and the *Yearbook of the International Law Commission*. Some of the other publications in greater demand in recent years are manuals and publications on standards in the fields of project evaluation, national accounting, international trade classification and industrial feasibility studies. Such computer-generated information on the publications of interest to different sectors of the market was used as a basis for analysing how best to attempt to reach them. Based on the study, the list of magazines in which advertisements are placed has been revised and every effort is being made to continue to advertise United Nations publications not only in the media but also at trade shows and exhibits and at book fairs. Increasing use has been made of external or co-publishing arrangements with commercial publishers to permit a wider dissemination of United Nations publications at no cost to the Organization.

151. With reference to the proposed fresh outside look envisaged in the Secretary-General's previous report (A/44/222 and Corr.1, para. 104), the General Assembly, in paragraph 10 of its resolution 44/196 A took note of the intention of the Committee on Conferences to play a role in the review of the Department of Conference Services on the understanding that the role to be determined by the Committee at its 1990 session would be in full accordance with its mandate and in conformity with resolution 43/222 B.

Recommendation 35

152. The appropriations for consultants were, in rounded terms, $8.5 million in the biennium 1986-1987, $6.4 million in the biennium 1988-1989 and $7.1 million in the biennium 1990-1991. A reduction of 25 per cent was, therefore, achieved in 1988-1989, while recommendation 35 called for a reduction by 30 per cent. The slight increase of 10 per cent for the current biennium over the biennium 1988-1989 was made necessary by the need to implement mandated programmes and expanded activities with a smaller secretariat financed by the regular budget of the Organization. Regarding the second part of recommendation 35, the hiring of retired staff members as consultants is not a common practice. It cannot, however, be systematically excluded. The experience gained by retired staff members is one of the assets of the

Organization, as the experience of the United Nations Transition Assistance Group has once again confirmed.

Recommendation 36

153. The recommendation that the Organization should pursue optimum utilization of space and should charge current commercial rates to Member States and other users occupying space in United Nations premises has been implemented. The rent structure for tenants on United Nations premises has been changed to reflect commercial rates as recommended. These rates are now in effect and are the basis of rental income projections for the biennium 1990-1991.

154. As a result of the implementation of this recommendation, the estimates of rental income in the programme budget for the biennium 1990-1991 reflect an increase of approximately $4 million over the corresponding 1988-1989 income. The increase results basically from the application of a policy whereby in New York specialized agencies, Member States and other users occupying space at United Nations premises are now charged commercial rates based on the highest rates paid by the United Nations for rented premises, that is, at 2 United Nations Plaza. In Geneva the rates charged to organizations and offices occupying space at United Nations premises at locations other than the Palais have been increased to 70 per cent of the higher rate charged for office space at the Palais itself.

155. In the course of the current biennium, a global review of United Nations office space will be undertaken. In the context of this review, a determination of revised rental charges that may be charged to occupants not financed by the regular budget at Addis Ababa, Bangkok and Nairobi will be made. The possibility of obtaining additional reimbursement from extrabudgetary programmes for office accommodation will also be explored.

Recommendation 37

156. Paragraph (1) of recommendation 37, which called for a thorough review of the functions and working methods as well as of the policies of the Department of Public Information, can be considered implemented. The specific steps taken by the Secretary-General in implementation of this recommendation, which have been described in detail in his final report (A/44/222 and Corr.1, paras. 110-130), included the submission to the General Assembly of proposed revisions to chapter 9 of the medium-term plan for the period 1984-1989, extended through 1991,[20] which were adopted by the General Assembly, as modified by the recommendations of CPC,[21] in its resolution 43/219 of 21 December 1988.

157. Following a thorough review of the functions and working methods as well as of the policies of the Department of Public Information, the Secretary-General submitted his conclusions thereon to the General Assembly

in the context of revised estimates for section 27 of the programme budget for the biennium 1988-1989 (A/C.5/43/1/Rev.1, chap. IV, sect. D).

158. As a result of reviews of those proposals by CPC, the Committee on Information, the Advisory Committee on Administrative and Budgetary Questions and the Fifth Committee, and in the light of the recommendations of the Joint Inspection Unit, the Secretary-General submitted further modifications to the structure of the Department in his proposed programme budget for the biennium 1990-1991.[22] Those modifications related in particular to the denomination and responsibilities of certain organizational units within the Communications and Project Management Division and the Information Products Division, as well as to the need to provide a simplified management structure for the Department, as called for in, among others, recommendation 40. The further modifications included in the proposed programme budget for the biennium 1990-1991, in particular the elimination of the Bureau of Programme Operations and the Division for Committee Liaison and Administrative Services, and the subsequent transfer of part of their functions to the Office of the Under-Secretary-General, were also necessitated by the decision - as part of the implementation of recommendation 15 - to reduce by one the number of Director (D-2) posts in the Department. The proposals of the Secretary-General in this regard were approved by the General Assembly in its resolution 44/202 A and have now been put into effect.

159. During this process of restructuring, the Department has discharged its mandate without any major negative impact on programme delivery. With the revised organizational structure now in place, it is expected that the full benefit of the reforms will be felt in the course of the current biennium, in the sense of improved efficiency, productivity and effectiveness.

160. Paragraph (2) of recommendation 37, which called for the consolidation in the Department of Public Information, to the extent possible, of information activities currently conducted by several departments and offices in the Secretariat, is still under consideration by the Secretary-General.

161. In a related report to the General Assembly (A/43/651), the Advisory Committee on Administrative and Budgetary Questions, while recognizing the constraints involved in consolidating public information activities, stated that efforts to do so must continue and urged that the further review referred to by the Secretary-General be undertaken no later than 1992. The General Assembly, in paragraph 17 of its resolution 43/213, invited the Secretary-General to implement recommendation 37 in accordance with, *inter alia*, the comments and observations of the Advisory Committee (*ibid.*, paras. 40-60).

162. A preliminary study was conducted to examine the feasibility of consolidating all existing public information activities within the Department

of Public Information and the extent to which such consolidation would contribute to improving the efficiency, effectiveness and coherence of public information activities in the Secretariat. The results of the study were submitted to the Committee on Information at its eleventh session in 1989 (A/AC.198/1989/8). The study indicated that offices other than the Department devoted some 432 work-months annually to activities considered strictly public information work. It also noted that such activities are dispersed among the regional commissions and various departments located at different duty stations, a factor which did not facilitate the close collaboration necessary to achieving timely and effective public information about the work of those offices. In the light of those and other constraints, the study recommended that a further review be made once the then planned reforms of the Department were fully in place in 1992.

163. Paragraph (3) of recommendation 37 called for a review of the functions and activities of the United Nations information centres and, to the extent that the quality of public information activities would not be hampered, the consolidation of such centres with other existing United Nations offices. The Secretary-General, in agreement with the Administrator of UNDP, decided to consolidate the United Nations information centres with the offices of the resident co-ordinators/resident representatives, wherever that was not already the case and it could be shown that a joint arrangement would be more cost-effective while at the same time respecting programme delivery requirements. To this end, a provisional Understanding was approved by the Department of Public Information and UNDP in October 1989. It confirmed that, in countries where UNDP and the Department maintained separate offices, premises and facilities such as telecommunication links should be shared, although it was noted that many information centres received rent-free premises from host Governments and that they needed to be placed at centrally accessible and viable locations of the host city, close to the news media, universities, non-governmental organizations and other visitors. The Understanding was to be evaluated after one year in the light of operational experience. The evaluation is in process and, while some modifications may be expected in regard to certain administrative arrangements, the basic elements related to the consolidation of premises remain valid. The Department and UNDP intend to pursue and, wherever possible, intensify their collaboration including, in particular, in duty stations where UNDP has offices but where no information centre exists. The close co-operation described above will no doubt contribute towards the objective of enhancing the administrative and financial functioning of the Organization at duty stations away from Headquarters.

Recommendation 38

164. This recommendation has been implemented. Appropriations for official travel were reduced by 21 per cent in real growth terms in the 1988-1989 programme budget, compared to the 1986-1987. A further reduction of 4.1 per cent from the 1988-1989 resource base was included in the Secretary-General's

budget proposals for 1990-1991. The reductions were aimed principally at reducing the number of staff attending meetings and conferences. With respect to first-class travel, the Secretary-General continues to exercise his discretion in making exceptions on a case-by-base basis. Details of such exceptions are contained in annual reports to the General Assembly, most recently A/C.5/44/12.

Recommendation 39

165. The intent of recommendation 39, to ensure the independence of the internal audit function, was already achieved in the existing administrative arrangement whereby the Internal Audit Division was and continues to be a separate entity of the Department of Administration and Management conducting audits of Secretariat offices, activities and projects at Headquarters and other duty stations. Its audits are planned and carried out independently, and the resulting findings and recommendations are communicated directly by the Director of Internal Audit to the heads of the audited entities. As reported (A/42/234 and Corr.1, para. 7), should the need arise, the Director of Internal Audit can report directly to the Secretary-General in the latter's capacity as the Chief Administrative Officer of the Organization.

166. In accordance with generally accepted internal auditing standards, the independence of the audit function is achieved through its organizational status and the objectivity of its audits. It is the consistent policy of the Secretary-General to maintain the Internal Audit Division as an autonomous entity in the Department of Administration and Management to examine and appraise activities for which he has administrative responsibility. Its main goal is to assist programme managers achieve the economical, efficient and effective implementation of their programmes. The present organizational status of the Division ensures that the internal auditors are independent of the activities they audit. That allows them to carry out their work freely and objectively and permits them to render impartial and unbiased judgements. In carrying out their duties, the United Nations internal auditors have full, free and unrestricted access to all such activities and related records, property and personnel.

167. A self-evaluation exercise by the Division in 1989 reaffirmed that the present administrative arrangement ensured its independent and effective functioning. The review found also that the findings of an independent assessment in 1985 by an established accounting firm, acting as outside consultants, continued to be valid. The Division's staffing would have to be brought up to the strength demanded by the audit work-load generated by the growing volume of activities financed from extrabudgetary resources as well as under the regular budget. These activities include peace-making and peace-keeping operations, assisting and protecting refugees, implementing technical co-operation projects, protecting and preserving the environment and combating drug abuse.

168. The General Assembly, on the advice of the Advisory Committee on Administrative and Budgetary Questions, has once again expressed its concern that the Division be equal to its task to give effective audit coverage of the extrabudgetary expenditures, which are currently above the annual level of the regular budget. Accordingly, efforts are under way to secure the extrabudgetary funds required to bring the staffing and associated resources of the Internal Audit Division to a level that would ensure effective audit coverage of all the extrabudgetary activities, particularly those that are carried out at duty stations outside Headquarters and at the country level.

Recommendation 40

169. Executive offices are, in a number of cases, directly attached to the offices of the head of department under the heading "Executive direction and management". In recent years, however, some executive offices have been consolidated in order to put several departments or offices under a common administration. The search for efficiency and the need for a close relationship between programmes and administration are two basic requirements that, at present, call for a variety of organizational arrangements.

IV. Measures regarding personnel

170. As indicated in the Secretary-General's final report (A/44/222 and Corr.1, paras. 136-178) and in the present report in the context of recommendation 15 (see paras. 38-42 above), during the period under review, priority in the area of human resources management had to be accorded to a number of activities, some of which were not envisaged at the time that the Intergovernmental Group of High-level Experts submitted its report. In particular, the continuing financial crisis necessitated special measures to deal with the need to fill vacancies through redeployment. The implementation of the post reductions pursuant to recommendation 15 required significant time and staff resources in order to ensure an orderly and fair transition to new staffing levels in each office, as well as the development of procedures to redeploy staff whose posts were abolished. The staffing of the United Nations Transition Assistance Group and a number of other missions, as well as the filling of vacancies left by hundreds of staff assigned to those missions, stretched the resources of the Department of Administration and Management. Owing to these constraints, the implementation of the proposed reforms has thus been pursued as time and resources permitted. In those cases where implementation was not completed by the end of 1989, efforts will continue as outlined below.

Recommendation 41

171. The general result of the administrative streamlining of the Office of Human Resources Management, which was reported in detail in the Secretary-General's final report (*ibid.*, para. 137), has been a marked

improvement in co-ordination and efficiency. There is, however, an increasing need to strengthen the long-term policy formulation and human resources planning function. The project of centralizing information and planning activities under the direct supervision of the Assistant Secretary-General for Human Resources Management needs to be revived and implemented.

Recommendation 42

172. The Secretary-General has made every effort to implement this recommendation as of the end of 1989. Chapters I, V, VI and X (and correlated provisions in other chapters) of the Staff Rules have been revised as recommended. The revisions were submitted to and approved by the General Assembly at its forty-fourth session. Work on other chapters is continuing.

173. A priority task for 1990 will be the incorporation of amendments required by the General Assembly's decisions on the comprehensive review of the conditions of service of the Professional category (see resolution 44/198, sect. I).

174. A personnel manual compiling instructions and directives for the application of the Staff Rules and Regulations has been produced and distributed to users world-wide and is being regularly updated. Work is progressing on the addition of sample rulings on interpretation of rules to serve as jurisprudence for decisions. Plans for a simplified, more easily usable manual have had to be deferred until staff resources for this project become available.

Recommendation 43

175. The recommendation to fill entry-level posts at the P-1 and P-2 levels through national competitive examinations has been implemented. The recommendation to fill posts at the P-3 level through competitive examinations has not been implemented owing to lack of resources and other exigencies related to retrenchment. The matter will be reviewed during the current biennium.

176. The recommendation that internal and external examinations be governed by the same standards and criteria has been implemented. The examination format is the same in both the external and internal examination, except that outside candidates are subject to a structured interview related to personal working experience. This interview is necessary because external candidates are not known to the Organization, whereas internal candidates have their records on file with the Organization. Admission criteria are the same, but factors that are specific to internal candidates such as length of service and performance records are taken into account. Implementation of the recommendation that a drafting test be used for filling posts at the P-4/P-5 levels has been postponed.

177. The result of the implementation has been positive. The national examinations are now organized on as wide a geographical basis as possible. In 1988, for example, 10 Member States, including 7 under-represented Member States, participated in national competitive examinations. In 1989, 10 Member States participated, including 4 under-represented Member States. Examinations are also planned for at least 10 Member States in 1990, possibly including 2 unrepresented and 5 under-represented Member States. As a result, geographical distribution was improved. In addition to enhanced geographical representation, the proportion of women successful in these examinations has increased each year.

Recommendation 44

178. The recommendation calling for an increase in the proportion of appointments at junior Professional levels (P-1 to P-3) has been implemented. The figures of appointments by levels since 1986 are as follows:

Appointments in the Professional category

	P-1 to P-3		All other levels	
1989	111	(66.5 per cent)	6	(33.5 per cent)
1988	36	(55.0 per cent)	30	(45.0 per cent)
1987	25	(51.0 per cent)	24	(49.0 per cent)
1986	104	(55.0 per cent)	84	(45.0 per cent)

179. As the average age range of appointments at the P-1 to P-3 levels is 25 to 40, a higher percentage of appointments at these levels would bring down the age average of Professional staff and thus contribute to the rejuvenation of the Secretariat.

Recommendation 45

180. In his final report (A/44/222 and Corr.1, para. 145), the Secretary-General reported that the recommendation that staff be considered for permanent appointment after three years of service must await the completion of the retrenchment exercise.

181. By section IV, paragraph 5 of its resolution 37/126, the General Assembly decided that staff members on fixed-term appointments should be given every reasonable consideration for a career appointment upon completion of five years of continuing good service. By section VI, paragraph 5 of its resolution 38/232, the Assembly recommended that organizations normally dispense with the requirement for a probationary appointment as a prerequisite

for a career appointment following a period of five years of satisfactory service on fixed-term appointments.

182. In the context of recommendation 45, the Secretary-General would propose to dispense in appropriate cases with the requirement for a probationary appointment as a prerequisite for permanent appointment following a period of three years of entirely satisfactory service.

Recommendation 46

183. The recommendation to appoint more women, particularly at the higher levels, requires continued implementation. In addition to the 51 special measures to improve the status of women in the Secretariat referred to in the Secretary-General's final report (*ibid.*, para. 146), the Office of Human Resources Management has adopted further measures to be implemented in 1990 with a view to achieving the goal of 30 per cent representation of women in the Professional category by the end of 1990. A rigorous monitoring system of efforts to attain this goal is in place. Special attention will be paid to appointments of women at the senior level. Successful implementation of these measures requires collaboration of the Member States.

184. While the continued implementation of this recommendation leads to the improvement in morale of the Secretariat, more effort is still needed to achieve a better balance at the higher levels. The need to recruit more women will have an effect on the number of projected vacancies available for the upward mobility of internal staff.

Recommendation 47

185. The Secretary-General has been making every effort to ensure that nationals of developing countries are duly represented at the senior levels. In 1989, 25 per cent of appointments at the D-1 level and above were of nationals from developing countries. The representation of developing countries at senior levels has evolved as follows:

Level	31 Dec.1986 No.	31 Dec.1986 %	31 Dec.1987 No.	31 Dec.1987 %	31 Dec.1988 No.	31 Dec.1988 %	31 Dec.1989 No.	31 Dec.1989 %
D-1 and above	177	49.2	172	47.4	165	48.0	178	48.1
D-2 and above	64	47.4	63	47.7	61	46.2	58	45.0
ASG and above	28	50.9	23	50.0	21	47.7	21	48.8

Recommendation 48

186. The recommendation to recruit staff members on the basis of occupational groups is being implemented. By introducing the concept of occupational groups for both the Professional and General Service categories, career development prospects of staff members have been broadened. Movement between departments and duty stations has been facilitated. As a whole, careers in which staff members broaden their knowledge and experience and acquire additional skills by changing jobs are more rewarding for both the individual and the Organization than careers in which staff members remain in only one job and in one occupation. A career development handbook for the General Service staff at Headquarters has been prepared by the Office of Human Resources and Management and is expected to be published shortly. This handbook introduces the concept of career paths which is based on the concept of occupational groups. A handbook for Professional staff, which is in a conceptual stage, will also be based on these concepts.

Recommendation 49

187. The Vacancy Management and Staff Redeployment Programme is working as a mechanism for rotation by encouraging staff to move between duty stations. Special rotation schemes for specific occupational areas (language services, administration and personnel) are being considered. The mobility incentive scheme that will come into effect on 1 July 1990 pursuant to General Assembly resolution 44/198 is likely to further encourage movement of staff away from Headquarters duty stations. It is envisaged that the recommendation to develop a job rotation system among the various duty stations for staff members in the Professional category will be implemented during the current biennium.

Recommendation 50

188. This recommendation is being implemented through the development of a new system of performance evaluation that will be pilot-tested in 1990 and, after appropriate staff-management consultations, introduced in 1991. It includes an overall numerical rating that will permit direct comparison in the rating of staff.

Recommendation 51

189. Promotion procedures are an integral part of the vacancy management system, and they are being further developed and refined through appropriate staff-management consultations. The structure, functions and composition of the appointment and promotion bodies were reviewed in early 1990 in consultation with staff associations with the intention of securing impartiality and objectivity in the management of appointments and promotions, and at the same time ensuring a balance between a healthy turnover in the memberships and a degree of continuity in the criteria and practices of those bodies. It was

agreed, *inter alia*, that a number of nominees sufficiently greater than those required would be sought to facilitate consultations on the composition of the appointment and promotion bodies; that the maximum tenure of their members would be between three and five years and that whenever possible one third of the membership would be retained from year to year; and that standardized rules of procedure would be established to be adopted with flexibility by each body.

Recommendation 52

190. The mandatory age of retirement is normally applied through the strict observance of the guidelines emanating from General Assembly resolutions. An exception was instituted in 1989 to facilitate the extension of female staff members beyond retirement age in cases where the prospective retiree's office is understaffed. By its resolution 44/185 D of 19 December 1989, the Assembly raised the mandatory age of separation for staff members appointed on or after 1 January 1990 to 62.

Recommendations 53 and 61

191. The International Civil Service Commission noted in its annual report for the year 1987[23] that it did not accept the premises on which recommendations 53 and 61 were based. With respect to recommendation 53, the Commission considered that there was no need to modify the mandate of the Commission since responsibilities for establishing personnel standards and monitoring their implementation were clearly set out in its statute, in particular articles 1, 9, 13, 14 and 17.

192. With regard to recommendation 61, the Commission was of the view that the Intergovernmental Group of High-level Experts had not given a basis or rationale for its assertion and that its claim did not appear to be valid.[24] As a result of the comprehensive review of the conditions of service of the Professional and higher categories, carried out in 1989, at the request of the General Assembly, the Commission reached the opposite conclusion, namely, that the remuneration had fallen to the point that recruitment and retention were becoming a problem for the Organization.[25] The outcome of the Commission's recommendations on the comprehensive review and its endorsement by the General Assembly are reflected in resolution 44/198, section I.

193. With respect to the more specific part of recommendation 61 concerning the education grant for post-secondary studies and the annual leave system, the Commission recommended that entitlements should remain unchanged.[26]

Recommendation 54

194.   The situation with respect to this recommendation concerning the length of service in the leadership of departments and offices in the Secretariat remains as reported in the Secretary-General's final report (A/44/222 and Corr.1, paras. 162-163). It is taken into account by the Secretary-General when appointments or extensions of appointments are being considered at the Assistant Secretary-General and Under-Secretary-General levels.

Recommendation 55

195.   This recommendation, requesting the Secretary-General to ensure the faithful observance of the principle set out in Assembly resolution 35/210 that "no post should be considered the exclusive preserve of any Member State or group of States" is being duly taken into consideration in appointments of new staff members.

Recommendation 56

196.   In the context of the implementation of recommendation 15, revised staffing tables, effective 1990, were approved by the General Assembly at its forty-third session in the context of its resolution 43/218 A (see also A/C.5/43/1/Rev.1, chap. I). These new staffing tables will serve as a basis for the recruitment and placement of staff during the biennium 1990-1991. Staffing tables will of course continue to be reviewed in the context of future proposed programme budgets.

197.   Furthermore, under the provisions of the vacancy management system, all posts that become vacant must be reviewed by the substantive department and by the Office of Human Resources Management before a decision is taken as to whether a vacant post should be filled, either by internal movement or external recruitment, as appropriate.

Recommendation 57

198.   The ratio between staff with permanent appointments and those with fixed-term appointments is constantly monitored and reported on annually to the General Assembly by the Secretary-General.

199.   In compliance with section IV, paragraph 5, of General Assembly resolution 37/126, upon completion of five years of continuing good service on fixed-term appointment all staff members are being given every reasonable consideration for a career appointment.

200.   With effect from 1988, the Secretary-General decided that all candidates who successfully passed the national competitive examinations would, upon recruitment, be granted probationary appointments, a first step towards career

status. Additionally, some ccuntries have given notice that their nationals are henceforth free to apply for employment directly to the United Nations and seek career appointments from the United Nations. These developments will ensure a more adequate range between permanent staff members and staff members on fixed-term appointments, and will reflect more faithfully the principle of equitable geographical distribution among both categories of staff.

Recommendation 58

201.   As indicated in his previous reports, the Secretary-General attaches high priority to training programmes geared to meet the changing needs of the Organization. Given the rapidly changing environment and the new demands being made and likely to be made in the future on the United Nations by its Member States, the Organization is not able to subscribe to a narrow definition of training programmes. The General Assembly itself has recognized the broader meaning of training in its annual and systematic support for language training, which aims at increasing the linguistic balance in the Secretariat and to which two thirds of all training funds are dedicated.

202.   In a broad sense, a paramount need of the Organization is to have a staff equipped with the skills and knowledge required to carry out effectively the Organization's current as well as foreseeable mandates. The concept of an international civil service implies that a significant number of staff will spend a large portion of their careers in the Organization. Although at the time of recruitment staff are expected to meet the highest standards of competence, it can and should not be assumed that the knowledge and skills they possess when entering will adequately equip them for years of service in an Organization. This is particularly true in today's world where rapid changes in the political, social and economic environment constantly present the Organization with new challenges. Other organizations have recognized this fact from their inception. In recent years, certain organizations within the United Nations system have been addressing this problem, with, indicatively, UNICEF contributing 2.4 per cent of its regular budget to its training programmes. By comparison, the United Nations in its 1990-1991 budget devotes 0.46 per cent to its training budgets. As indicated above, two thirds of this sum is in support of the language programme.

203.   Beyond language training, by necessity, because of the limited availability of funds, programmes have been concentrated on meeting urgent needs of the Organization as defined by departments. A needs analysis was completed in 1988 and systematic training in the three top priorities thus identified, office automation, basic supervision, and drafting for specific occupational applications, have absorbed the majority of training resources.

204.   However, the Organization fully supports the need to evaluate the impact and usefulness of its training programmes and is developing, as part of workshops sponsored by the Consultative Committee on Administrative

Questions, evaluation tools that will enable it to monitor the optimum utilization of allocated resources.

Recommendation 59

205.   As stated in previous reports, staff-management machinery is in place at all duty stations and the consultation process has, as a whole, been working reasonably well.   As the Secretary-General has repeatedly stated, the staff is the Organization's principal asset.   During the past three years, a period of rapid change, retrenchment and restructuring, staff-management consultations have been especially important.

206.   Regulation   8.1   of   the   Staff   Regulations   requires   that   "the Secretary-General   shall   establish   and   maintain   continuous   contact   and communication with the staff in order to ensure the effective participation of the staff in identifying, examining and resolving issues relating to staff welfare, including conditions of work, general conditions of life and other personnel policies".   The same regulation provides that related staff representative bodies shall be established.   The Secretary-General is also required to create joint staff-management machinery at local and Secretariat-wide levels to advise him on these matters.   The consultation process enables staff views to be sought and considered before management decisions are taken on matters affecting staff interests and concerns.

207.   Within the framework of the Staff Regulations, the requirements for the staff management consultative process have evolved over the years, but have not always been explicitly defined and/or budgeted.   Furthermore, some developments in this area have not been reflected in the relevant staff rules. With a view to redressing this situation, a number of steps were initiated and partially implemented during the period under review.

208.   As part of the reform process, a review of chapter VIII of the Staff Rules was initiated.   This review will take into account the administrative instructions that provide additional guidelines on staff-management issues and attempt to consolidate texts regulating staff-management relations.

209.   The Secretary-General has always been of the view that the cost of staff representation activities is to be included in his proposed programme budget and that, once the budget is approved, the provisions of the Administrative Instruction ST/AI/293 of 15 May 1982 outlining facilities to be provided to staff representatives in the performance of their functions must be made effective.   In order to define the level of current requirements and to endeavour to fulfil them appropriately, a review of the requirements for staff-management activities was initiated in 1989 in consultation with the staff and   discussed   by   the   Secretariat-wide   Staff-Management   Co-ordination Committee at its fourteenth session (8-14 March 1990).   It is envisaged that this review, which is expected to be completed in 1991 after further discussions

in the Committee, will result in a more coherent, transparent and cost-effective framework for staff-management activities.

Recommendation 60

210.   This recommendation concerning the need to render the internal justice system more efficient and less costly has been implemented.   In his comprehensive report on the revised internal justice system submitted to the General Assembly at its forty-fourth session (A/C.5/44/9), the Secretary-General outlined improvements made in the appellate machinery, the disciplinary area and the informal settlement of grievances.   The General Assembly welcomed the progress made in its resolution 44/185 B of 19 December 1989.

211.   The internal appeals procedures have been streamlined and a newly established Joint Appeals Board at Headquarters, fully representative of the Secretariat, has adopted internal rules of procedure, enforcing the strict observance of time-limits and ensuring the expeditious consideration of appeals.   Reports of the Board are now submitted directly to the Under-Secretary-General for Administration and Management who, since 1988, has assumed direct responsibility for the administration of justice.   The application of the Secretary-General's policy of accepting unanimous recommendations of the Board, provided they do not impinge on major questions of law or principle, results in a prompt final decision on appeals.

212.   The consistent application of streamlined procedures has led to the elimination of a long-standing backlog of appeals. The caseload of pending cases before the Headquarters Board has been reduced from 95 in 1985 to 30 in December 1989, the lowest number of cases pending before the Board in 18 years.   Such improvement is especially significant in view of the fact that during the 1980s the number of new appeals filed annually is virtually double the number filed in the previous decade. The average time of cases pending before the Board has been reduced from over two years to four months. The Boards at Nairobi and Vienna have disposed of all pending cases and the Board at Geneva is expected to complete consideration of the majority of cases in 1990.   The improved procedures should contribute to a restoration of confidence by the staff in an effective redress system.

213.   In respect of disciplinary matters, the Secretary-General has, after extensive consultations with staff representative bodies at the major duty stations, promulgated a fully revised set of disciplinary rules which replaced chapter X of the Staff Rules, effective 1 January 1990. The revised rules, *inter alia*, strengthen due process safeguards, including the entitlement of staff charged with misconduct, both in the field and at Headquarters, to consideration of their cases by a Joint Disciplinary Committee, introduce greater flexibility regarding the range of disciplinary measures, thereby permitting closer proportionality between the gravity of the misconduct and the

sanction imposed, and expedite consideration and disciplinary action in cases of fraud.

214. A new Joint Disciplinary Committee has been established at Headquarters with an extended membership, fully representative of the Secretariat, to deal with the increased number of disciplinary cases.

215. An assessment of the impact of the revised substantive and procedural aspects of the disciplinary process, effective 1 January 1990, will be submitted to the General Assembly at its forty-fifth session, as requested in resolution 44/185 B.

216. As indicated by the Secretary-General in his report (A/C.5/44/9), it is his intention to follow up reforms in the appellate and disciplinary areas with improvements in the informal procedures for the amicable resolution of staff grievances. Cost-effective informal settlement of disputes has been achieved through the intervention of grievance panels at Headquarters and other duty stations as well as through the assistance of members of the Panel of Counsel who assist staff members in preparing appeals and provide counselling with a view to obviating the need for formal litigation. In accordance with resolution 44/18 B, the Secretary-General will also report to the Assembly at its forty-fifth session on improvements in such informal procedures.

217. In order to assess closely the effectiveness in the light of practical experience, it will be necessary to monitor closely the implementation of the revised rules and procedures. To this end, consultations will continue with staff representatives. At the fourteenth session of the Staff-Management Co-ordination Committee (8-14 March 1990), the administration agreed to a proposal from the staff to establish a working group within the context of the New York Joint Advisory Committee to address problems related to the administration of justice.

Recommendation 61

218. This recommendation has been treated with recommendation 53 (see paras. 191-193).

Recommendation 62

219. The practice of transferring extrabudgetary posts to the regular budget continues to be discouraged. No such transfers were proposed in the proposed programme budget for the bienniums 1988-1989 and 1990-1991. In respect of the latter, an exchange of posts between the regular budget and the voluntary funds of UNHCR was proposed by the Secretary-General and approved by the General Assembly. This resulted in no net additional posts to the regular budget.

V. Monitoring, evaluation and inspection

Recommendation 63

220. Recent work programmes of the Joint Inspection Unit have been redesigned in form and substance to give Member States a clear sense of the overall thrust of those programmes and a better initial understanding of the individual studies contained therein. By extending the time frame of the work programmes from one to three years the Unit gives advance notice of forthcoming studies, thereby providing an opportunity for early comment on the evaluation content of the work programme. The General Assembly, in paragraph 2 of its resolution 44/184 of 19 December 1989, requested the Unit to give even greater attention to management, budgetary and administrative issues.

221. The General Assembly has not yet found it convenient to deal with the name change of the Unit.

222. The Joint Inspection Unit is in full accord with recommendation 63 and its enhanced emphasis on the evaluation aspects of its work. As the General Assembly was informed in the Unit's nineteenth annual report,[27] the Unit has introduced two new features into its work programme, namely, to identify those studies which are evaluative and to provide advance notice of studies that the Unit plans to undertake in the coming two years. This latter information is meant to encourage Member States to comment, *inter alia*, on the evaluation content of the work programme so that the Unit may make adjustments as necessary. The Unit believes that its recent work programmes respond positively to recommendation 63 and to the general concerns of Member States concerning evaluation. Nevertheless, as the Unit has recognized in its twentieth annual report,[28] addressing the evaluation process is a long-term task. Advising organizations on their methods for internal evaluation is an objective whose fulfilment will be achieved over time through consultations with the participating organizations during the process of the annual development of the Unit's work programme.

Recommendation 64

223. This recommendation was addressed to Member States. In paragraph 13 of its resolution 43/221 of 21 December 1988, the General Assembly underlined the importance of applying the highest standards in selecting candidates for appointment as inspectors, as stipulated in chapter 2 of the statute of the Unit, and of giving special emphasis to experience in national or international administrative and financial matters, including management questions, and, where possible, knowledge of the United Nations or other international organizations. In paragraph 14 of the resolution, the Assembly also underlined the importance of the consultation process for reviewing the

qualifications of the proposed candidates in accordance with article 3, paragraph 2, of the statute of the Unit.

Recommendation 65

224. This recommendation was also addressed to the General Assembly. In paragraph 2 of its resolution 44/184, the General Assembly requested the Joint Inspection Unit, in the development of its work programme, to give even greater attention to management, budgeting and administrative issues relevant to the agendas of the governing bodies of its participating organizations and to their main and common concerns.

Recommendation 66

225. The reports of the Unit have always been made available to Member States. They are circulated as General Assembly documents or, in a limited number of cases, at the request of the Unit, as Economic and Social Council documents. Comments of the Secretary-General and/or ACC on the reports are also submitted, where appropriate, to those bodies. Furthermore, the Secretary-General in his annual report to the General Assembly on the implementation of recommendations of the Unit outlines the action taken by the Organization pursuant to the Unit's report.

Recommendation 67

226. The Panel of External Auditors and the Joint Inspection Unit have continued to give great importance to an increased co-operation between the two bodies. The measures that were adopted at their joint meetings in 1986 and 1987 have proved to work towards this end. As a result, inspectors and external auditors maintain contact at the working level when particular studies are to be carried out or are under way. Reports issued by both bodies are mutually exchanged and in cases where reports of the Unit cover areas that have been examined and/or reviewed by external auditors, they are requested to provide their views before the reports are finalized. The Executive Secretaries of the Panel and of the Unit maintain contact with each other throughout the year and discuss matters of mutual interest on behalf of the two bodies. Other measures adopted by the Panel and the Unit include the exchange of work programmes on a regular basis and the reinforcement of recommendations of one service by the other whenever investigations lead to similar conclusions.

227. At its regular session in November 1989, the Panel of External Auditors decided to start issuing good practice guides for use by its members in their examinations of specific areas of management. It was felt that the Panel had already recognized the need to develop a common approach by the issuance of audit guidelines that provide statements of best practice for the conduct of audits, and that there might be considerable additional benefit obtained if audits of management topics could also be conducted on a broadly common

basis. The Panel considered that an area where joint efforts and co-operation between the Unit and the Panel is of mutual benefit. Steps are being taken by the Panel to co-ordinate with the Unit the preparation and issuance of good practice guides.

228. The request that external auditors should put greater emphasis on management audits and other areas of importance, as required by the legislative organs, concerned, has been given special attention by the external auditors who have substantially increased their work in the area of value-for-money audits, as requested by the General Assembly and legislative bodies of the different organizations of the United Nations system. The findings in the areas of economy, efficiency and effectiveness in the administration of those organizations have been regularly reported and will continue to be included in the external auditors' reports.

VI. Planning and budget procedure

229. In section VI of its report, the Group of High-level Intergovernmental Experts made a critical assessment of the planning and budget procedures of the United Nations. It stated that the medium-term plan, the programme budget, the monitoring and the evaluation systems were meant to constitute an integrated process through which wide agreement should evolve on activities that should be financed by the regular budget of the Organization.[29] The introduction to the medium-term plan did not actually permit a constructive dialogue among Member States on the policy orientations of the plan. The plan itself did not properly reflect goals, objectives and policies that could be transformed into action through resource allocation and the setting of priorities in the programme budget.[30] Priority setting, in both the plan and the programme budget, was not done in conformity with the existing regulations and rules. The programme budget was nothing more than "the financial compilation of a number of decisions and recommendations taken by a large number of intergovernmental bodies and interpreted in the various departments and divisions of the Secretariat".[31] Furthermore, throughout the planning and budgeting process, Member States were not in a position to intervene early enough and to make significant changes in the activities of the Organization. The Group of Experts added that the medium-term plan and the programme budget should and did not currently have "the necessary flexibility so that priorities and resources could be adjusted to the changing international circumstances and the new challenges and problems that might arise".[32] These deficiencies should be rectified and planning and budget procedures should be developed to "facilitate agreement among Member States on the content and level of the budget of the Organization".[33]

230. The programming and budgeting procedures thus analysed by the Group had been progressively developed since the beginning of the 1970s. The General Assembly, in resolution 3043 (XXVII) of 19 December 1972, approved on an experimental basis the introduction of a biennial budget cycle. In resolution 3195 (XXVIII) A to C of 18 December 1973, the Assembly adopted

the first programme budget of the Organization, which was for the biennium 1974-1975. That same year, the Assembly considered the first medium-term plan, covering the period 1974-1977. Subsequently, regulations and rules on programme planning, the programme aspects of the budget, the monitoring of implementation and the methods of evaluation were progressively developed and codified by the Assembly in its resolution 37/234 of 21 December 1982.

231.   The Group of Experts did not question the validity of those instruments nor their evolutive character. Rather, it asserted that they were not properly used and that the regulations and rules were often ignored or insufficiently applied. Hence it adopted recommendation 68 on priority setting, in which the Group stressed that the pertinent rules and regulations should be strictly applied by the intergovernmental bodies concerned and by the Secretariat. The same recommendation 68 stipulates that CPC should monitor this question of priority setting and report thereon to the General Assembly. Besides this, the Group of Experts did not formulate other recommendations on the planning and budget procedure. It indicated three different groups of proposals that were focused on the respective roles of CPC and the Advisory Committee on Administrative and Budgetary Questions, and in which views were expressed on an outline, a contingency fund and the need for consensus on budgetary matters.

232.   The Fifth Committee considered these questions in 1986 and, in its report to the General Assembly (A/41/795), endorsed recommendation 68 on full application of regulations and rules for priority setting and also the basic aspects of a reform of the planning, programming and budgeting process, that is, a greater, earlier and more structured involvement of Member States in this process, an outline containing, *inter alia*, an indication of the overall level of resources to accommodate the activities of the Organization during the following biennium, and a contingency fund. The Fifth Committee, however, listed a number of points to be resolved, namely, the decision-making process, the intergovernmental machinery, the definition of "add-ons", and the basis for determining the level of resources in the outline. Subsequently, the General Assembly adopted resolution 41/213, section II of which provides the main elements for improving the planning, programming and budgeting process. Its annex I contains the new elements that should govern budget preparation.

233.   The implementation of recommendation 68 and of the relevant provisions of resolution 41/213 can be briefly described under the following headings: consultative process, priority-setting, outline and contingency fund.

A. Consultative process

234.   With regard to the medium-term plan, Member States considered in the fall of 1987 some perspectives of the Secretary-General on the work of the United Nations in the next decade, intended to provide a framework for the preparation of the medium-term plan for the period 1992-1997 (A/42/512).

They were invited, through a note verbale, to provide written comments on these perspectives. Member States then considered in 1988 a draft introduction of the same plan, together with proposals on its structure (A/43/329). A calendar of consultations of functional, regional and sectoral intergovernmental bodies on the various chapters of the plan was also submitted to CPC and to the General Assembly in 1988 (A/43/626). Such consultations occurred during the course of 1989, within the constraints of the schedule of the meetings of intergovernmental bodies. Thus, the medium-term plan for the period 1992-1997 and its introduction (A/45/6), to be adopted by the General Assembly at its forty-fifth session, upon recommendations of the Advisory Committee on Administrative and Budgetary Questions, CPC and the Economic and Social Council, will have been the subject of extensive consultations.

235. Intergovernmental bodies had the opportunity in 1988 and 1989 to give comments to the Secretariat on the programmes of work upon which the proposed programme budget for the biennium 1990-1991 was built. The first report of the Advisory Committee on this programme budget provided a summary of these consultations and suggested that they were of uneven intensity and quality.[34] CPC made similar observations and the General Assembly, in section I of its resolution 44/194 on programme planning, underlined the need for a more effective role of functional, regional and sectoral intergovernmental bodies in the planning, programming and budgeting process. The Secretary-General indeed believes that the preparation of both the medium-term plan and the programme budget would benefit from a greater involvement of specialized intergovernmental bodies. Obstacles to overcome are, however, extremely severe. They pertain to the complexity of scheduling meetings in relation with several constraints and objectives, as well as to the difficulty, for Member States and within the Secretariat, to develop and share a common language on matters of programming and budgeting.

B. *Priority setting*

236. According to the current legislation, the introduction to the medium-term plan should have priorities proposed by the Secretary-General; the medium-term plan itself should include priorities among subprogrammes; the outline should contain priorities reflecting trends of a broad sectoral nature; and the programme budget should have, within each programme, priorities among programme elements. In addition, the use of the contingency fund and the deferral or suppression of activities that could not be financed from it are linked to priority setting. The practical and political difficulties of setting priorities are commensurate with the neatness of this theoretical framework. A report of the Secretary-General (A/44/272) outlining all aspects of priority setting in future outlines of the proposed programme budget was presented to the General Assembly at its forty-fourth session and is still under discussion this year. The question of the impact of extrabudgetary resources on activities with a high or low priority designation will receive increased attention. The proposed medium-term plan for the period 1992-1997 (see

A/45/6) demonstrates some improvement in the capacity of the Organization to identify subprogrammes with high priority. In the coming years, efforts to implement more strictly the pertinent regulations and mandates should be accompanied by further reflection on the notion of priority and of its practical application.

C. Outline of the programme budget

237. In accordance with resolution 41/213 an outline of the programme budget for the biennium 1990-1991 was presented by the Secretary-General in August 1988 (A/43/524). Upon recommendations from CPC and the Advisory Committee, the General Assembly adopted resolution 43/214 of 21 December 1988, in which it reaffirmed the basic rationale for this new feature of the budgetary process and recognized that its methodology required further improvement and that the whole exercise should be applied with flexibility. It also decided on a preliminary estimate to be used by the Secretary-General as a basis for preparing his proposed programme budget for the biennium 1990-1991.

238. The need for improvement in the format and methodology of both the programme budget and the outline was stressed again by the Assembly by its resolution 44/200 on the implementation of resolution 41/213. A proposed outline for the programme budget for the biennium 1992-1993 will be considered by the Assembly at its forty-fifth session, on the basis of the recommendations of CPC and the Advisory Committee.

D. Contingency fund

239. Also in accordance with the relevant provisions of resolution 41/213 a report of the Secretary-General (A/42/225 and Add.1), entitled "Questions relating to the programme budget: inflation and currency fluctuation, and the level of contingency fund", was presented to the General Assembly at its forty-second session in 1987. In its resolution 42/211, on the implementation of resolution 41/213, the Assembly approved guidelines for the contingency fund, with respect to criteria for use, period covered and pattern of use, and operation of the fund. Several reports were subsequently presented, and in December 1988, in paragraph 6 of its resolution 43/214, the Assembly decided that the contingency fund of the programme budget for the biennium 1990-1991 should be established at a level of 0.75 per cent of the preliminary estimate (given by the outline) i.e., $15 million, should be appropriated as needed and should be used according to the purpose and procedures set out in the annexes to its resolutions 41/213 and 42/211 and relevant regulations and rules. When considering and adopting one year later the programme budget for the biennium 1990-1991, the General Assembly decided on the use of a portion of this contingency fund on the basis of statements of programme budget implications for activities which were not programmed in the budget. The use and operation of the contingency fund will be reviewed by the General Assembly in 1991.

240. It should be noted that, apart from the contingency fund, the request of the General Assembly to find a comprehensive solution to the problem of all additional expenditures, including those deriving from inflation and currency fluctuation, has yet to be met. The established procedures, that is, the annual recosting of estimates, have been maintained and the search for a different solution remains on the agenda of the Assembly.

241. Since the adoption by the Assembly of resolution 41/213, the trend towards the adoption of decisions on budgetary matters by consensus has been very evident, culminating in the adoption by consensus of the programme budget of the Organization for the biennium 1990-1991. Thus, the fundamental objective of the reform in this domain, that is, to facilitate agreement among Member States on the content and level of the budget of the Organization, has been achieved. The new instruments put into place will evolve with experience. Continuous efforts on the part of Member States and of the Secretariat will be needed to ensure that the new planning, programming and budgeting process responds appropriately to the ever-changing role and mandates of the Organization.

VII. Assessment

242. In order to provide a general critical assessment of the implementation of General Assembly resolution 41/213 in the light of the objectives of that resolution, namely, the enhancement of the efficiency of the administrative and financial functioning of the Organization, it is necessary to recall the circumstances leading to the adoption by the Assembly of resolution 40/237 of 18 December 1985 establishing the Group of High-level Intergovernmental Experts. In 1985, two seemingly contradictory situations co-existed. On the one hand, the commemoration of the fortieth anniversary of the foundation of the Organization gave Member States an opportunity to reaffirm faith in its fundamental principles and objectives. On the other hand, the United Nations was facing one of the most difficult phases in its history. A severe financial crisis posed an immediate threat not only to its financial solvency, but to its very integrity. Not unconnected with this menacing financial situation, and no less detrimental to the future of the Organization, was a widespread feeling of malaise regarding its effectiveness and efficiency, resulting, not least, from sharp differences among the membership, in particular, among the major Powers. This perception was especially pronounced on the part of some of the major contributors to the United Nations budget and, in particular, in the Government of the major contributor. The majority of Member States, however, while in agreement to some extent with the need to improve the efficiency and effectiveness of the Organization, were of the view that the activities of the Organization were suffering from a lack of political will on the part of the major contributors.

243. The withholding of financial contributions and the linkage of this withholding to, *inter alia*, the demand for financial and administrative reforms

heightened the atmosphere of suspicion surrounding the consultations prior to the adoption of resolution 40/237. The final text reflected a balance between the diverging views and objectives of the Member States. In the resolution the Assembly reiterated the principle of the sovereign equality of all States and emphasized that the improvement of the efficiency of the administrative and financial functioning of the United Nations was not an end in itself, but a means to attain the purposes and implement the principles of the Charter in the maintenance of international peace and security and in the promotion of development and international co-operation.

244.   This central interaction between diverse and sometimes fundamentally diverging objectives of Member States was carried into the Group of High-level Intergovernmental Experts and was present throughout its deliberations. The protracted debate on the recommendations emanating from the Group of Experts during the forty-first session of the General Assembly also reflected sharp divergence of views. The prolonged consultations on the report culminated in marathon sessions chaired by the President of the General Assembly himself, which went well beyond the target date for the adjournment of the forty-first session and which were crowned with agreement by consensus on what became resolution 41/213. The adoption of this resolution was in itself an important factor in setting the stage for a revival of confidence in the United Nations.

245.   The recommendations of the Group of High-level Intergovernmental Experts ranged from very broad, general proposals to detailed specific administrative instructions. All reflected, to some extent, a set of political compromises. In view of the charged background, the underlying tensions during the work of the Group, and the short period given to it to complete its task, it was hardly surprising that the recommendations did not necessarily rest, in all cases, upon documented facts or scientific appraisals. Owing to their magnitude and complexity, economic and social activities of the Organization were identified as an area of particular importance requiring reform. In addition to the specific and general prescriptions concerning secretariat arrangements addressed to the Secretary-General, a Special Commission was set up by the Economic and Social Council to deal with the rationalization of the intergovernmental machinery. These two exercises are closely interrelated. After two years of negotiations, the Special Commission failed to reach agreement. Thus insufficient reform has taken place in the overall structure at either the intergovernmental or the secretariat level. Some progress has been made, however, in improving the efficiency and effectiveness of individual entities and in revitalizing the Economic and Social Council.

246.   During the period under review, a solid consensus has emerged among Member States to the effect that the enhancement of the administrative and financial functioning of the United Nations, important as it is, is not an end in itself but an essential means of enabling the Organization to carry out its varied tasks more efficiently. This consensus is a welcome departure from the previous atmosphere of sharp confrontation that dominated the initial debates

on the subject of reform. It augurs well for the development of the United Nations and its continuing evolution in an ever-changing world.

247.   Parallel with this development, the world has witnessed a remarkable improvement in the political climate at the global level. The state of East-West confrontation and tension that dominated international relations and adversely affected the work of the United Nations is coming to an end at a breathtaking pace. While it is difficult to predict with any certainty where these historic developments may lead, and certainly there will be challenges and pitfalls ahead, it is already clear that Member States are manifesting renewed confidence in the Organization and the increasing desire to enable it to deal effectively with the whole range of problems that confront the international community. There is evidence of a marked change for the better in the political climate at the United Nations. During the past session of the Assembly 215 resolutions (65 per cent of all resolutions) were adopted without a vote.

248.   More directly relevant and significant in relation to the administrative and financial efficiency of the Organization is the fact that Governments of Member States are increasingly turning to the United Nations and entrusting the Secretary-General with functions that are extending the limits of past experience. Namibia, Central America, Afghanistan, Iran-Iraq, Western Sahara and Cambodia are cases in point. Indeed, mediation, good offices and the assistance of the United Nations are being sought as never before in its history. The achievements of United Nations peace-keeping forces have been recognized by the award of the Nobel Peace Prize.

249.   Experience has shown that close working co-operation and mutual support between the Secretary-General and Member States is the corner-stone of success in all facets of United Nations activities. The Organization has witnessed in recent years a steady improvement in that direction and this trend needs to be carefully nurtured, deepened and widened. This development is clearly evident in the area of maintenance of international peace and security falling within the responsibility of the Security Council. The increasing number of new peace-keeping operations entrusted to the Secretary-General since 1988 is clear evidence of this growing and harmonious partnership. The decision-making process on political matters has, as the Secretary-General had occasion to state in his annual report to the Assembly at its forty-fourth session,[35] vastly improved, with daily co-operation between the Security Council and the Secretary-General.

250.   In the administrative and financial areas, a satisfactory process of confidence building between Member States and the Secretariat is also emerging following the implementation of the new procedures adopted by the General Assembly in resolution 41/213. The greater convergence of views on questions related to administration, budget and management was reflected in the adoption without a vote of all resolutions in the Fifth Committee during the forty-fourth session of the Assembly. The consensus votes on the revised

estimates at the forty-third session and on the programme budget for 1990-1991 at the forty-fourth session of the Assembly are especially encouraging indications. The reforms in the budgetary process have thus gone through their first full cycle and, by and large, achieved their purposes. They have resulted in an increased consciousness among Member States and within the Secretariat about the way in which the United Nations spends its resources and encouraged a more effective use of available resources. They have also largely allayed the concerns of the major contributors.

251. In the area of human resources management, some of the recommendations are of an ongoing nature and their full effect will be felt in the future. In several areas, the capacity of the Secretariat to fulfil its tasks has been stretched to its maximum limits by the staff reductions. The mounting of four new peace-keeping operations (UNIIMOG, UNAVEM, UNTAG and ONUCA) in 1988-1989, as against 13 operations over the previous 40 years, and the planning of several others have stretched to the limit the human and financial resources of the Organization. In addition, under the regular budget, there was an increase in the number of special missions from two to four with the addition of the United Nations Good Offices Mission in Afghanistan and Pakistan (now renamed the Office of the Secretary-General in Afghanistan and Pakistan) and the United Nations Mission to verify the electoral process in Nicaragua. Thus, including the United Nations Peace-keeping Force in Cyprus, there were, at the end of 1989, a total of 11 peace-keeping missions in the field, compared with only 5 at the beginning of the biennium on 1 January 1988. The staff as a whole has responded to those challenges with extraordinary devotion to the Organization. During the entire reform period staff members have coped with the uncertainties and, in many cases, increased workloads in a spirit fully in conformity with the expressed aims of the reform process.

252. In this context, it must be recognized that the employment of the staff so as to secure the highest standards of efficiency, competence and integrity is an obligation under the Charter. It is essential that the Organization provide staff with appropriate conditions of employment and guarantee their security. The Secretary-General attaches the highest priority to these objectives.

253. A practicable consensus on action required in the economic and social sectors has not yet emerged, in contrast to the progress achieved in the political, administrative and financial areas. The Secretary-General has been requested once again to submit proposals to the Assembly at its forty-fifth session, including recommendations for reforms in the intergovernmental sector. He intends to do so taking into account the results of a number of important meetings and deliberations taking place this year.

254. The difficulties inherent in achieving more adequate programming and co-ordination of the many agencies and programmes operating in the economic and social field are well known. The problem of maintaining a proper balance between growing operational activities of the various entities funded through

extrabudgetary resources and their mandated programmes under the regular budget still remains to be addressed in full. At the Secretariat level the interrelationships between research and policy analysis and operational activities require further study.

255. With respect to intergovernmental machinery, experience has shown how difficult it is to overcome certain obstacles whenever reforms have been attempted. These stem from the persistent basic political divergence of views among Member States over priorities, over the role and decision-making powers of the various United Nations organs and over their functions in relation to other forums within the system, as well as the strong vested and often legitimate interests of influential constituencies. The subject of reform in the economic and social sector cannot be dealt with piecemeal or in a fragmented manner. What is needed, above all, is a fresh and courageous re-examination of positions and attitudes, particularly in the light of the momentous changes that are taking place in different parts of the world.

256. The Secretary-General believes that opportunity exists to extend to the economic and social spheres the same spirit of co-operation that has recently been harnessed to achieve positive results in the political field. It should be possible for Member States and the Secretary-General to forge the same level of mutual co-operation that has evolved in the political and administrative areas. The improved political climate and renewed confidence in multilateralism should enable Governments to use the United Nations as a more effective instrument for collective action to address areas of critical importance in the economic and social fields as well as to meet new challenges. The seriousness and urgency of the economic and social problems confronting the international community, and the developing countries in particular, render the role of the Secretariat in assisting Member States to consider economic and social issues in an integrated manner, in programme formulation, in setting of priorities and in enhancing co-ordination and coherence in the United Nations system, even more important. Decisions taken at the forty-fourth session of the General Assembly reflect an increasing awareness by Member States of the need for the United Nations to play an increasingly dynamic role in the economic and social field and a willingness to use the United Nations as an instrument for collective action to meet new challenges.

257. During the current year the Assembly has already held a special session to consider the question of international co-operation against illicit production, supply, demand, trafficking and distribution of narcotic drugs (seventeenth special session) and adopted a comprehensive programme aimed at combatting the international scourge of drug abuse (resolution S-17/2 of 23 February 1990). The special session of the Assembly devoted to international economic co-operation, in particular to the revitalization of economic growth and development of the developing countries (eighteenth special session) has provided an opportunity to develop a new framework for international economic co-operation. Among the significant issues discussed were the implications of recent developments in countries of Eastern Europe, both in

terms of the integration of their economies into the international economy and their potential enhanced contribution to the world-wide development process. The special session was an opportunity for focusing the North-South dialogue on new realities. The elaboration of the international development strategy for the fourth United Nations development decade is under way. The Second United Nations Conference on the Least Developed Countries is expected to address the problem of the widening economic gap between the developed and developing countries, in particular the least developed. The preparatory work for the United Nations Conference on Environment and Development has begun, setting in motion important negotiations among Member States that are essential for the success of the Conference in 1992. These multifaceted development issues engaging the attention of Member States are a clear manifestation of the fact that the United Nations is seen by many Member States, particularly the developing countries, as an important forum in which to develop a comprehensive and integrated approach to the growing number of interconnected global issues. The United Nations is not only a universal organization but must also be concerned with the totality of the human condition on earth. Nowhere else can national policies, priorities and concerns come together, interact and forge a global consciousness as a foundation for comprehensive collective action, for the betterment of that condition.

258. In concluding, the Secretary-General is of the view that the lengthy political process that culminated in the adoption by the General Assembly of resolution 41/213 and subsequent resolutions has largely achieved its purpose. The Organization received a mandate for reform to be implemented over a three-year period, which it has fulfilled to the best of its abilities. The mandate has been carried out without serious negative effects on programmes, but not without pain. Retrenchment has put considerable strain on several parts of the Secretariat, particularly in view of the fact that implementation of the reforms has had to be carried out during a period of continuing financial crisis and rising demands on the Organization. In a climate of renewed confidence in the capacity of the Organization, the reforms may be seen as a contributing factor in changing attitudes towards the United Nations and its ability to respond to new challenges. Today there is a greater and more effective use of the Organization's capabilities and the assistance of the United Nations is being sought by Member States in an unprecedented manner. There is a noticeable improvement in public perceptions of the Organization as an institution for the resolution of conflict. On the basis of these objective criteria, it may be concluded that the ultimate purposes in the mind of the legislators, namely the enhancement of the overall effectiveness of the Organization, have been achieved.

259. While there may be different perceptions concerning details of the implementation of the reform process initiated by the report of the Group of High-level Intergovernmental Experts, the Secretary-General is of the view that the time has come for the Organization to consolidate itself and to move forward into the last decade of the twentieth century on the basis of the medium-term plan for the period 1992-1997 (see A/45/6), which aims to

ensure that the Organization will be capable of attaining the objectives of the Charter in relation to peace, security and sound development.

260. This is not to argue that the task is over. The financial viability of the Organization has yet to be restored. The revitalization of the economic and social sector has still to be addressed, taking into account decisions to be taken at the intergovernmental level. Further changes may be required to enable the Organization to adapt itself to respond fully and effectively to new and emerging issues. The goals and objectives of the Organization will be achieved only through recognition of the interdependence of Member States, the continuation of a partnership of confidence and trust between Member States and the Secretariat, and by the restoration of the financial viability of the Organization. The effectiveness of the United Nations system as a whole depends on timely and full payment by all Member States. The plans, programmes and budgets developed to meet the mandates and priorities of Member States can be translated into action only if they have solid financial support. As the Secretary-General has said frequently, reform is not a finite process, nor an end itself, but implies a constant review of the functioning of the Organization in relation to its objectives. The Secretary-General's commitment to administrative and financial effectiveness and efficiency will be maintained.

Notes

1. *Official Records of the General Assembly, Forty-first Session, Supplement No. 49 (A/41/49).*
2. *Ibid., Forty-fourth Session, Supplement No. 1 (A/44/1).*
3. *Ibid., Supplement No. 32 and corrigenda (A/44/32 and Corr. 1-3), annex III.*
4. See *Official Records of the General Assembly, Forty-fourth Session, Supplement No. 32 and corrigenda (A/44/32 and Corr. 1-3), sect. IV.*
5. *Ibid.*, para. 117.
6. See *Official Records of the General Assembly, Forty-fourth Session, Supplement No. 37 (A/44/37), sect. II, decision 1 (X).*
7. *Report of the World Conference to Review and Appraise the Achievements of the United Nations Decade for Women: Equality, Development and Peace, Nairobi, 15-26 July 1985* (United Nations publication, Sales No. E.85.IV.10), chap. I, sect. A.
8. Figures reflect meetings between September and the end of December.
9. *Official Records of the General Assembly, Forty-second Session, Supplement No. 16 (A/42/16), part one, para. 260.*
10. *Ibid., Forty-fourth Session, Supplement No. 16 (A.44/16), para. 329.*
11. *Ibid., Supplement No. 6 (A/44/6).*
12. Of these 10,057 regular budget-funded posts, 9,959 are established and 98 are temporary. Th's staffing table of 10,057 posts does not include 24 posts which, although funded from the regular budget, are non-recurrent.
13. A temporary post at the Assistant Secretary-General level, attached to the Conference on Disarmament, is not included in this staffing table. On the other hand, a post of Assistant Secretary-General was suppressed after the adoption of resolution 41/213 but before the adoption of the programme budget for the biennium 1988-1989.
14. *Official Records of the General Assembly, Forty-fourth Session, Supplement No. 16 (A/44/16), para. 223.*

15. *Report of the United Nations Conference on Science and Technology for Development, Vienna, 20-31 August 1979* (United Nations publication, Sales No. E.79.I.21 and Corr. 1 and 2), chap. VII.
16. *Ibid.*
17. See *Official Records of the General Assembly, Forty-fourth Session, Supplement No. 37* (A/44/37).
18. *Ibid., Forty-second Session, Supplement No. 37* (A/42/37), para. 142.
19. *Ibid., Forty-fourth Session, Supplement No. 7* (A/44/7 and Corr. 1 and 2), para. 10.5.
20. *Ibid., Forty-third Session, Supplement No. 6* (A/43/6).
21. *Ibid., Supplement No. 16* (A/43/16), part one, paras. 100-141.
22. *Ibid., Forty-fourth Session, Supplement No. 6* (A/44/6/Rev. 1), sect. 27.
23. *Ibid., Forty-second Session, Supplement No. 30* (A/42/30 and Corr. 1), para. 21.
24. *Ibid.*, para. 22.
25. *Ibid., Forty-second Session, Supplement No. 30* (A/42/30 and Corr. 1), para. 44 (b).
26. *Ibid., Forty-second Session, Supplement No. 30* (A/42/30 and Corr.1), para. 44 (b).
27. *Ibid., Supplement No. 34* (A/42/34), para. 9.

29. *Ibid., Forty-first Session, Supplement No. 49* (A/41/49), para. 59.
30. *Ibid.*, para. 66.
31. *Ibid.*, para. 61.
32. *Ibid.*, para. 57.
33. *Ibid.*, para. 61.
34. *Ibid., Forty-fourth Session, Supplement No. 7* (A/44/7), para. 71.
35. *Ibid., Supplement No. 1* (A/44/1).

2.40 Document A/45/617*

Analytical Report of the Secretary-General on the Implementation of General Assembly Resolution 41/213 (A/45/226)

Report of the Advisory Committee on Administrative and Budgetary Questions

12 October 1990

20. As stated in paragraphs 6 and 7, this report has been submitted pursuant to General Assembly resolution 44/200 A and "provides detailed information concerning implementation of each recommendation of the Group of High-level Intergovernmental Experts through 31 December 1989 ...". In this connection, the Advisory Committee notes the Secretary-General's statements that "it is evident that the programme of administrative reforms initiated in 1986 has been largely implemented," (para. 8) and that "the lengthy political process that culminated in the adoption by the General Assembly of resolution 41/213 and subsequent resolutions has largely achieved its purpose" (para. 258). Accordingly, "the time has come for the Organization to consolidate itself and to move forward ... on the basis of the medium-term plan for the period 1992-1997 ..." (para. 259). At the same time, the Secretary-General acknowledges that the task is not over and that "further changes may be required to enable the Organization to adapt itself to respond fully and effectively to new and emerging issues". In this connection, he notes that "reform is not a finite process, or an end itself, but implies a constant review of the functioning of the Organization in relation to its objectives" (para. 260).

21. In the view of the Advisory Committee, enhanced efficiency and effectiveness will be compromised if efforts to streamline cumbersome administrative, personnel and budgetary procedures are not redoubled. The Board of Auditors has discussed a number of these procedures in its report A/45/5, which are mentioned in the Committee"s related report A/45/570 and Corr. 1. In the preceding paragraphs, the Committee has also drawn attention to the need to further improve the consultative process as well as the evaluation process; these issues are discussed in parts V and VI of the Secretary-General's analytical report. The Committee's observations in respect of the outline, and contingency fund, also discussed in the analytical report, will be submitted in the context of its consideration of the Secretary-General's reports on these subjects.

---

*A/45/617, p. 6.

2.41 Document A/45/16 (Part I)*

Review of the Efficiency of the Administrative and Financial Functioning of the United Nations (A/45/226)

Report of the Committee for Programme and Co-ordination

20 June 1990

12. At its 15th, 17th, 18th, 20th and 21st meetings, on 16 to 18 and 21 and 22 May, the Committee considered the analytical report of the Secretary-General on the implementation of General Assembly resolution 41/213 (A/45/226).

Conclusions and recommendations

13. With respect to the methodology followed by the Secretary-General in preparing the analytical report, the Committee noted that the report did not adhere strictly to the provisions of paragraph 28 of the Committee's report on its twenty-ninth session. The Committee concluded, however, that by following the structure of the report of the Group of High-level Intergovernmental Experts to Review the Efficiency of the Administrative and Financial Functioning of the United Nations,[1] it provided updated information on the status of implementation of the specific recommendations of the Group.

The Committee noted that the Secretary-General's report, in general, provided a useful account of action taken to implement General Assembly resolution 41/213 of 19 December 1986 and of the areas in which further action was required.

The Committee expressed appreciation for the progress achieved in many areas where reform was called for in resolution 41/213, as a result of the joint efforts of Member States, the Secretary-General and the staff of the Organization.

While noting areas in which progress had been limited or not possible, *inter alia*, in the economic and social sectors, the Committee concurred with the Secretary-General that the Organization had, in a number of areas, fulfilled the mandate for reform to the best of its abilities. The Committee also concurred that the improvement of the efficiency and effectiveness of the administrative and financial functioning of the Organization was a continuing process and that the Organization should enter a stage of consolidation in order to strengthen its capacity to meet the challenges of the 1990s.

---

*A/45/16(Part I), pp. 9-11.

The Committee noted that, as indicated during its discussion of the programme performance report, the indices contained therein did not lend themselves easily to an overall assessment of the real impact of the implementation of recommendation 15 on programmes.

The Committee agreed that the relationship between posts and programmes funded from the regular budget and those funded from extrabudgetary resources required further analysis and consideration.

The Committee emphasized the need for continuing action in certain areas, as follows:

(a)   Political sector: the Committee requested the Secretary-General to consolidate the results achieved in the restructuring of the political sector.

(b)   Personnel questions and posts: the Committee, while recalling the recommendations concerning questions of personnel and posts of the Group of High-level Intergovernmental Experts, as approved by the General Assembly, stressed the need for further efforts to achieve the relevant objectives of resolutions 41/213 and all subsequent relevant resolutions.

(c)   Conference services: while noting many positive improvements in the area of conference services, the Committee expressed the view that further progress required full co-operation on the part of Member States and the Secretariat and recognize the important role of the Committee on Conferences in that regard, which should be exercised in accordance with resolution 43/222 of 21 December 1988.   The Committee recommended that the General Assembly should request the Committee on Conference to develop further guidelines for its consideration with a view to reducing the volume of documentation, including that circulated by Member States.

(d)   Economic and social sectors: the Committee expressed the hope that the improvement in the global political climate might extend into co-operation in the economic and social spheres, thereby contributing to the necessary restructuring and revitalization of the United Nations in the economic and social sectors, in accordance with the provisions of resolutions 44/103 of 11 December 1989 and 44/200, and as indicated in paragraph 67 of the analytical report of the Secretary-General. The Committee reiterated its view that any measures to be proposed by the Secretary-General in that area should be reviewed by the Committee in order to examine their effect on programmes.

(e)   Construction: the Committee reiterated its view that the Secretary-General should adhere closely to the schedule outlined in his report on the matter to the General Assembly at its forty-third session (A/C.5/43/16).

(f)   Co-ordination: while reiterating the views expressed at its twenty-ninth session, the Committee emphasized the importance of co-ordination as a policy instrument in improving the performance of the organizations of the system, ensuring complementarity of effort and increasing cost-effectiveness.

The Committee recommended that the General Assembly request the Secretary-General to highlight systematically, in the existing reporting mechanisms pertaining to the above areas, or, as necessary, through a specific report, the progress achieved.

The Committee noted that, despite the many difficulties encountered, the role of the Organization as a centre for harmonizing the actions of nations had been enhanced during the period under review. The Committee concurred with the view expressed by the Secretary-General that Governments of Member States were increasingly seeking the assistance of the United Nations.

The Committee noted that, despite the additional tasks entrusted to the United Nations, financial uncertainty had continued. In that regard, the Committee stressed the essential need for all Member States to respect their legal obligations concerning full and timely payments of assessed contributions.

The Committee observed that in order to achieve the objectives of Member States, as reflected in the programmes of the United Nations, the financial viability of the Organization was required. To that end, not only timely and full payment of assessed contributions, but also proportionality between resources and programmes, an appropriate relationship between regular budget and extrabudgetary resources, careful determination of priorities and constant vigilance in securing the highest possible standards of effectiveness were also required.

The Committee recognized that the operation of the new budgetary process had resulted in the adoption by consensus of the outline and the programme budget for the biennium 1990-1991. The Committee recalled, also, that the new budgetary process was still in a developmental stage and that several methodological issues were still pending. The Committee likewise recalled that the decision-making process was governed by the provisions of the Charter and the rules of procedure of the General Assembly.

The Committee recognized that the Organization had entered a new era in which, as never before, both member States and the Secretariat would be challenged to develop new visions and attitudes.

Note

1.   *Official Records of the General Assembly, Thirty-ninth Session, Supplement No. 38* (A/39/38), para. 388.